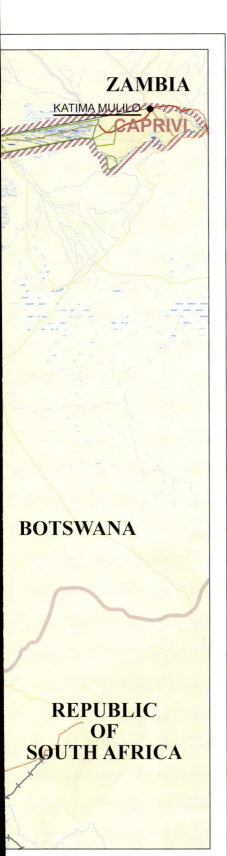

REPUBLIC OF NAMIBIA

Land mass:	824 269 km²
Average rainfall:	270 mm
Commercial agriculture (1996):	36,2 million ha.
Communal areas (1996):	33,5 million ha.

Population

Total population (2001):	1 826 854
Female:	936 718
Male:	890 136
Annual growth:	2,6%
Rural to urban (1998):	61% to 39%
Density (2001):	2,2 per km²

Economy

Annual per capita income (2000):	N$3 608
Potential labour force (2000):	56%
Economically active (1991):	34% of total population
Unemployment (1997):	35%
GDP composition (1999):	agriculture 12% industry 25% (mining 20%) services 63%
Inflation rate (2000):	9,1%
Foreign aid as % of GDP (1999):	6,6%
Government expenditure as % of GDP (1999):	29,3%

Health (2000)

Life expectancy (excl. HIV/AIDS):	55,8 years
(incl. HIV/AIDS):	43 years
Namibia's global rating:	7th most infected country
Living with HIV/AIDS (2001):	219 000
AIDS as percentage of all deaths:	26% (1999)

Education

Adult literacy (2000):	81%
Primary school enrolment (2000):	91,5%
Secondary school enrolment:	45,5%
Public expenditure on education:	8,3% of GDP

Publication of this book was made possible by the generous financial support of the Carl Schlettwein Foundation, Basel (CH) and of the University of Namibia Foundation, Windhoek. Renunciation of remuneration on the part of editors and authors makes this a non-profit project.

Department of Sociology Faculty of Humanities and Social Sciences University of Namibia Private Bag 13301 Windhoek, Namibia	Carl Schlettwein Stiftung Klosterberg 21 CH–4051 Basel Switzerland
Contact: V. Winterfeldt – Tel (++264-61) 206 3415 e-mail: vwinterfeldt@mweb.com.na T. Fox – Tel (++264-61) 206 3808 e-mail: tom@iway.na	University of Namibia Foundation

The publication of this book has been prepared for the occasion of the celebrations of the 10th anniversary of the University of Namibia, Faculty of Humanities and Social Sciences, Windhoek, 2 to 7 September 2002.

© Editors and individual authors

All rights reserved. No reproduction, copy or transmission of this publication, or parts thereof, may be made without written permission. Any person carrying out any unauthorised act in relation to this publication, may be liable to criminal prosecution and civil claims for damages.

© Map of Namibia: all rights reserved, property of Fachhochschule Dresden (HTW). Reproduction by courtesy of Fachhochschule Dresden, for educational purposes only.

© Photographs: all rights reserved, individual authors or collections, as indicated.

First published 2002

Cover: etching and design by Roland Graf, Windhoek
Language editing: Sally Wood, Windhoek
Formatting: Peter Bateman, Windhoek

ISBN 99916–59–41–2

Printed by typoprint, Windhoek

Namibia · Society · Sociology

Edited by

Volker Winterfeldt · Tom Fox · Pempelani Mufune

University of Namibia Press
Faculty of Humanities and Social Sciences
Windhoek 2002

CONTENTS

1 ECONOMY, LABOUR AND ENVIRONMENT 1

A social assessment of Namibia's economic achievements
since independence – a round-table debate
Johan de Waal / Herbert Jauch / Henning Melber / John Steytler 3

From liberation struggle to social partnership? The challenge
of change for the Namibian labour movement
Herbert Jauch 27

Labour migration in Namibia – gender aspects
Volker Winterfeldt 39

Land distribution and sustainable development
Mary Seely / Juliane Zeidler 75

2 SOCIAL INEQUALITIES AND SOCIAL INSTITUTIONS 85

Religion and its impact on Namibian Society
John Paul Isaak / Christo Lombard 87

Difference, domination and 'underdevelopment' – notes on the
marginalisation of Namibia's San population
James Suzman 125

Women's advancement in Namibia – the concept of
empowerment revisited
Saskia Wieringa / Immaculate Mogotsi 137

Understanding the family sociologically in contemporary Namibia
Volker Winterfeldt / Tom Fox 147

Small town élites in northern Namibia – the complexity
of class formation in practice
Mattia Fumanti 169

Youth in Namibia – social exclusion and poverty
Pempelani Mufune 179

Two societies in one – institutions and social reality of traditional
and general law and order
Manfred O Hinz 197

3 TRADITIONALISM, CULTURE AND ART 225

Traditionalism – social reality of a myth
Volker Winterfeldt 227

'Education for all' in independent Namibia – reality or political ideal?
Elisabeth Magano Amukugo 239

Constructing cultural identities in contemporary musical traditions – strategies of survival and change
Minette Mans 253

(Con)fronting the mask – some (con)texts of protest in Namibian drama
Terence Zeeman 271

Entertainment through violence? The social impact of the visual media in Namibia
Tom Fox 281

Namibian society in fiction – the Namibian novel
Chrisna Beuke-Muir / Helen Vale / Marianne Zappen-Thomson 295

4 SEXUALITY AND HEALTH 315

The culture(s) of AIDS – cultural analysis and new policy approaches for Namibia
Tom Fox 317

Sexual cultures in transition in the northern Kunene – is there a need for a sexual revolution in Namibia?
Philippe Talavera 333

How to make sense of lover relationships – Kwanyama culture and reproductive health
Britt Pinkowsky Tersbøl 347

Traditional and Western medical knowledge systems in Namibia – is collaboration in diversity possible?
Debie LeBeau 361

5 EPILOGUE 373

Sociological perspectives?
Volker Winterfeldt / Tom Fox 375

6 ABOUT THE AUTHORS / E-MAIL ADDRESSES ...... 393 / 397

LIST OF ACRONYMS

BCCSA	Broadcasting Complaints Commission of South Africa
CCN	Council of Churches in Namibia
CDM	Consolidated Diamond Mines
CoD	Congress of Democrats
COSATU	Congress of South African Trade Unions
CSO	Central Statistical Organisation
DRSW	Directorate of Rural Water Supply
DSTV	Digital Satellite Television
DWA	Department of Women's Affairs
ELCIN	Evangelical Lutheran Church in Namibia
EPZ	Economic Processing Zone
FDI	Foreign Direct Investment
GDP	Gross Domestic Product
GDR	German Democratic Republic
GRN	Government of the Republic of Namibia
(H)IGCSE	(Higher) International General Certificate of Secondary Education
IBA	Independent Broadcasting Authority (SA)
ILO	International Labour Organisation
IMF	International Monetary Fund
LAC	Legal Assistance Centre
LaRRI	Labour Resource and Research Institute
LMS	London Missionary Society
MANWU	Metal and Allied Workers Union
MBEC	Ministry of Basic Education and Culture
MLRR	Ministry of Lands, Resettlement and Rehabilitation
MoHSS	Ministry of Health and Social Services
MUN	Mineworkers Union of Namibia
NAFAU	Namibia Food and Allied Workers Union
NAFINU	Namibia Financial Institutions Union
NAFTU	Namibian Federation of Trade Unions
NAFWU	Namibia Farmworkers Union
NANGOF	Namibia Non-Governmental Organisations Forum
NANSO	Namibia National Students Organisation
NANTU	Namibia National Teachers Union
NAPCOD	Namibian Programme to Combat Desertification
NAPWU	Namibia Public Workers Union
NATAU	Namibia Transport and Allied Workers Union
NBC	Namibian Broadcasting Corporation
NDAWU	Namibia Domestic and Allied Workers Union
NDC	Namibian Development Corporation
NDP	National Development Plan
NEPRU	Namibian Economic Policy Research Unit
NGO	Non-Governmental Organisation
NISER	Namibian Institute for Social and Economic Research
NLO	Northern Labour Organisation (SWA)

NNFU	Namibia National Farmers Union
NPC	National Planning Commission
NPSM	Namibian People's Social Movement
NSX	Namibian Stock Exchange (Windhoek)
NUM	National Union of Mineworkers (SA)
NUNW	National Union of Namibian Workers
OATSU	Organisation for African Trade Union Unity
OMEG	Otavi Minen- und Eisenbahngesellschaft (SWA)
PLAN	People's Liberation Army of Namibia
PHC	Primary Health Care
SABC	South African Broadcasting Corporation
SADC	Southern African Development Community
SAFPB	South African Films and Publication Board
SIDA	Swedish International Development Agency
SLO	Southern Labour Organisation (SWA)
SSD	Social Sciences Division, University of Namibia
STD	Sexually Transmitted Disease
SWA	South West Africa
SWANLA	South West Africa Native Labour Association
SWAPO	South West Africa People's Organisation
UN	United Nations
UNAM	University of Namibia
UNDP	United Nations Development Programme
UNIN	United Nations Institute for Namibia (Lusaka, Zambia)
UNTAG	United Nations Transition Assistance Group
WTO	World Trade Organisation

INTRODUCTION

Why a book on Namibian society and sociology? Why write on Namibian society from a sociological perspective? What can sociology offer that disciplines such as economics and history cannot?

To answer these questions we can at least attempt to state what sociology is and does. A 'science of society': that is what Comte famously called it, the French father of sociology. From its early 19th century European origins right to the present, it has built a rich foundation of social knowledge that continues to be added to by professional practitioners across the globe.

Sociology attempts to establish an understanding of what makes a society work; or rather, how a society is even possible. It looks at social structures and central regulating institutions such as the family, the educational system and the state. It also studies the cementing force of culture, revealing belief systems and core shared values. While history can in part tell us where some of these elements originated, it is not concerned with explaining *how* they function and *why* in contemporary conditions. Equally, economics can offer advice on how economic growth might be achieved, but provide little information on the causes of persisting social inequality and hardship even in periods of high growth. Sociology is good at showing us how societies are constituted: how they function and what the basis for their social regulation might be. It is also the discipline for revealing the underlying social structural causes of poverty, crime and social unrest, the social blocks to economic development, and of racial discrimination. It explains how sexuality is socially constructed (particularly in relation to the spread of HIV) – how it is 'culture', and not just 'nature'; it distinguishes between sexuality (in terms of the physical differences between male and female) and gender as spelling out the sociocultural valuation of these differences. It both asks and answers questions that other disciplines are less equipped to address.

Why a 'Namibian Sociology'? Simply, because it is time for it. Namibia needs to understand itself – not just economically or politically, but in terms of what constitutes a distinct 'Namibian Society'. There are profound practical reasons for establishing such an understanding. An array of pressing social problems requires not simply statistical measurement of their extent, but the laying open of the structural *social* factors generating them. A systematic causal, sociological application is the basis for extending our knowledge of modern Namibia, and contributory to its social development.

Also, there are well-known historical reasons. Sociology was not encouraged to develop in South West Africa/Namibia (nor for a long time with any serious degree of academic independence, in South Africa) during most of the apartheid era; moreover, until the Academy was established in Windhoek in 1980, Namibia did not have any institution providing tertiary education at university level. Anthropology reigned as the favoured study of society, or more accurately, of social ethnicity in a time that was obsessed with racial division, separation and containment. Any sociological examination of Namibian society and key social issues took place in an atmosphere of political distrust or, at best, indifference. The result has been the underdevelopment of a Namibian sociology.

Academically, sociology in Namibia was first established in 1983 at the Academy as part of the Social Work programme. In 1984, the Department of Sociology came into being, integrated into the Faculty of Humanities and Social Sciences of the newly established University of Namibia (UNAM) in 1993. In the independence era, only a small number of people in Non Gvernmental Organisations (NGOs), government and education institutions lay claim to the label 'sociologist'. This contrasts markedly with the secure institutional place sociology holds in many other nations.

The editors of this book are all based in the country's only Department of Sociology at UNAM. Since its inception, and increasingly for the last couple of years, the Department has been committed to the expansion of sociological practice in the country, as well as to the establishment of an identifiably Namibian sociology – a task we addressed in a slogan as the *namibianisation* of the discipline. Much international material – including theoretical and empirical studies – is available for other societies. Namibia has yet to create work of comparable quantity and quality, a situation probably quite unique in the world, and all the more challenging. Even if sociology here can utilise pre-existing frameworks from this international resource base, analysing the unique Namibian characteristics of the social and cultural landscape remains a task in its own right. The southern African context, owing to the evident historical and contemporary commonalities, presents the closest frame of reference. In combining international debate and national research, Namibian sociology can contribute to the verification and progress of the international body of sociological theory. It is in this broader sense that we conceive the term *namibianisation*. This is admittedly no easy task.

Our book is a first step in this process. We, editors and authors, attempt here to offer examples of what a Namibian sociology might look like. Not all the authors are sociologists – the lack of available local specialists (itself a product of an unsympathetic intellectual past) required us to find authors who were familiar with or attracted by such a philosophical and social scientific approach. We trust that this does not weaken our central task. On the contrary, through the stages of the production of this book, the long process of exchange and interdisciplinary debate has taught us to learn from the other disciplinary approaches, and we feel it has enriched our sociological knowledge. All contributions provide examples either from their direct fieldwork, or from their interrogation of the Namibian social terrain. All attempt to intellectually illuminate elements of Namibian social structure from within cultural, political and economic contexts. Many more subject areas could have been discussed, if money and time had allowed. We hope this may later be possible. In the last instance, we hope that something that distinctly displays both the methods and imagination of sociology is both recognisable and understandable here.

1 ECONOMY, LABOUR AND ENVIRONMENT

A social assessment of Namibia's economic achievements since independence – a round-table debate
Johan de Waal / Herbert Jauch / Henning Melber / John Steytler

From liberation struggle to social partnership? The challenge of change for the Namibian labour movement
Herbert Jauch

Labour migration in Namibia – gender aspects
Volker Winterfeldt

Land distribution and sustainable development
Mary Seely / Juliane Zeidler

A SOCIAL ASSESSMENT OF NAMIBIA'S ECONOMIC ACHIEVEMENTS SINCE INDEPENDENCE – A ROUND-TABLE DEBATE

Johan de Waal / Herbert Jauch / Henning Melber / John Steytler

Introduction

Namibian independence from South African rule in 1990 was followed by a commitment on the part of the new government to engage in a total restructuring of the economy. The achievement of improved living standards for the entire population based on wealth and income distribution, as well as the promise of redistribution of productive wealth (including land), and improved economic and social opportunities stood as the primary goals of economic policy. To what extent have these goals toward social improvement been achieved, eleven years on, into the new millennium? To find informed, academic answers to this question, a discussion group was agreed upon as the best way forward. The editors presented the participants with detailed questions which are provided in the text below.

The present article is thus based on a round-table debate held at the University of Namibia on 9th July 2001. The following experts agreed to attend the panel discussion: Tsudao Gurirab, MP CoD; Nangolo Mbumba, Minister of Finance; Herbert Jauch, Labour Resource and Research Institute; Henning Melber, Nordic Africa Institute, Uppsala; John Steytler, Bank of Namibia, Research Department; Johan de Waal, MP DTA. Two speakers were at the last minute unable to attend, as will be clear from the text. Their views would have been welcomed and useful, but it is hoped that the overall debate is not unbalanced because of their absence. Those who contributed have provided a thoughtful assessment of Namibian socio-economic transformation. The discussion was recorded, transcribed, and later presented to the panellists for further reflection and revision.

Offered in this contribution is a range of informed assessments and opinions highlighting the panellists' views of the successes and failures of Namibian economic policy, and providing clear views on the extent and reasons for the failures of key socio-economic goals.

Socio-economic questions presented to the panellists

Question 1: Namibia inherited a distorted economy from the South West African colonial regimes, with little room for manoeuvre left in terms of social equity.
- To what extent were the strategies and policies adopted to rebuild the Namibian economy and society after independence successful?
- In which fields were they successful?
- Where did they fail?

Question 2: Beyond its strictly economic goals, Namibia's first five-year development strategy, NDP 1, considered social progress a crucial precondition for economic development. By investing in people, the national strategy emphasises meeting people's basic needs and providing economic opportunities for all Namibians. On the other hand, the redistribution of wealth and income has shown little change in real terms since 1990. Average per capita income has even fallen slightly to around N$3 800 per annum.
- Scrutinising the budget allocations since independence, would you maintain that economic policies in practice were consistently guided by the desire for social progress?
- With an eye to the nation's social structure, who are the winners and who are the losers of the past decade?
- Have economic policies induced social structural change?
- Do you see a contradiction between economic success and social equity when analysing economic policies since independence?
- What are your predictions for the future?

Question 3: The policy of national reconciliation drawn up in 1989/90, guaranteed the continuance of the existing relations of production and property. Within the framework set by the United Nations (UN) and the Western Contact Group, and adopted to prevent a detrimental drain of capital and human resources, it was designed to assure the economically powerful of their future in post-apartheid Namibia.
In your opinion, is such a policy – in principle – compatible with the objective of equitable social progress?

Question 4: The majority of the black Namibian population is confined to unskilled economic activities. It is only a minority that meets the requirements to access skilled, professional opportunities in the formal sector.
- Against this backdrop, can affirmative action and black empowerment be more than a developmental tool for privileging a socio-economic élite of the black African population groups?

Question 5: In the early 1970s, Gerhard Tötemeyer's research in the Ovambo region had already identified a strong desire in the rural communities for the privatisation of agricultural land in the communal areas. Surprising as the findings of that time may seem, they reflect current practices of fencing off communal land as well as individualised patterns of ownership in the Herero and Rehoboth economy. The right of leasehold grants provided for by the recent Communal Land Reform Bill for a period of 99 years (ch.4, sec.II, §30, 34) has a similar focus. Such an imperative for the economic future of rural society has not been publicly reflected in the discussion of the land issue, as yet.

- Should land be privatised, whether redistributed or communal land, and should agricultural policies be aimed at commercialisation?

Additional questions

Question 6: Around 200 000 individual and corporate taxpayers – as opposed to two million Namibians – contribute to the monetary wealth annually available for the state's budget and its economic development policies. Such a narrow basis reflects the heterogeneous character of the Namibian economic structure in which capitalist market relations and the subsistence mode of production are forced to coexist.
- Where does Namibia's economic and social future lie? Which of the two sides do Namibian economic policies favour?
- Which of the two – or any other alternative – should they favour?
- What are the social structural implications?

Question 7: In your view, has Namibia's participation in the war in the Congo and the Angolan conflict affecting northern Namibia, had detrimental effects on the Namibian economy?

Question 8: Is the Namibian economy hampered by or inflicted with corruption in any sense? If yes, what form does it take and what are its implications for the future?

Question 9: Despite the major changes in the political structure and character of the country due to successful de-colonisation, socio-economic research has repeatedly argued that little real change has occurred in terms of control of the commanding heights of the economy. The ethnic background of capital owners and business leaders remains overwhelmingly white, whether Namibian or South African.
- Does this have a negative effect on the country's efforts to overhaul the underdevelopment and dual nature of the economy, as President Nujoma formulated it in his foreword to the First National Development Plan (NDP1)?
- Did the three Namibian governments since independence fail in this respect?

Question 10: What exactly is smart partnership? How is it designed to address unemployment (currently over 30%) and poverty (affecting over half of the population)?

Question 11: Linked to the previous question, what is the economic and social value of Economic Processing Zones (EPZs) currently in operation at Walvis Bay and some other parts of the North?

The debate – a social assessment of Namibia's economic achievements since independence

Winterfeldt: Good afternoon. Let me welcome all of you and thank you for your willingness to share your expertise. This debate will assess Namibia's economic achievements strictly within a sociological framework. It is not so much a discussion about economic achievements per se, but rather about economic development and progress for whom? Who has benefited? Sociologically, we want to identify how much the advantaged groups and classes have gained, and how much the other strata and classes have been disadvantaged. This is the background against which we will try to formulate our questions.

To start the debate, we want to assess the first decade of the Namibian economy: how did governments after 1990 deal with structural colonial legacies and pursue economic restructuring? What were the achievements and what were the setbacks?

de Waal: Well, I'll be very short, my answer is very simple. The policies adopted were the right policies but they never got implemented, and that is where the problem lies as far as I'm concerned. We can look at the education policies and also the Labour Reform Conference. The conference should have been followed up with a proper policy implementing and speeding up that process (of reform). The national reconciliation policy, also investment policy have been good. The First National Development Plan was a fantastic document. The problem lies not in the formulation of policies, but with the implementation.

Melber: I would go a step further and state that the policy was drafted on an ad hoc basis. Maybe I'm too polemical. I agree with Johan de Waal to that extent, that if you look at the single documents they seem to be rather impressive, but as a matter of fact they were not coordinated in such a way that it would merit the label of an overall policy. Even the First National Development Plan lacked conceptualisation or at least commitment to the implementation of its overall defined targets. Among its declared priorities, was next to poverty alleviation, the reduction of unemployment, but we have an increase of unemployment, if not even poverty. It further wanted to have the budget deficit limited to a maximum of 3% per annual budget. The annual budgets tell a different story, with one or two exceptions. Between 3,5 and 4,5% deficit per year are the order of the day. We have a borrowing strategy for consumptive purposes and not for productive investment. So, taking stock ten years down the road, I'm afraid my basic thesis reads: it's neither fish nor meat. Neither can I see a policy in the sense of a clear-cut neo-liberal approach emphasising market forces. Neither is it a clear-cut approach for deliberate redistribution of income and productive wealth in a society in transition and transformation. It's something in between and, depending on what you look at, the answer to our first question for this debate differs. I would even go a step further and refer to empirical evidence. Sometimes budgetary policies look like a very enlightened redistributive policy, but at the end it is redistributive only for the benefit of a very small privileged new élite and not for society as a whole.

Thus, relating to the guiding question for our discussion – who are the beneficiaries? – I'm tempted to answer: it is not the majority of the Namibian people, but it is a new élite, to some extent based on the political positions acquired at independence. Its members gained access to economic privileges through their positions obtained within the state apparatus. I think the role assigned to the state is the real issue. Analysing post-independence policies, for me the most striking element appears to be how the state was used over the first eleven years to compensate for policy failures elsewhere in terms of lack of delivery to the people. We started off with a public service of 42 000. For political reasons I find it totally understandable that there was a rapid expansion during the first and second year, simply because the public service had to be reformed. I understand that a new government recruits what they see as politically reliable new personnel into the structure. But now we are at almost double the original size. We are rapidly approaching 80 000, despite the fact that since 1995 downsizing became the magic catchword. Ever since downsizing was introduced we have had an increase. Hamza Alavi (a political sociologist) in the early 1970s discussed the idea of the overdeveloped post-colonial state with reference to Pakistan and Bangladesh. Some thirty years later we seem to be confronted with a very similar situation where policy-issues that might have been met with different strategies were sidestepped by bloating the civil service. Some of it may have been done for understandable reasons: a type of social policy, for example, to employ the ex-combatants. It still is disputable, but you could maintain it's a social policy. But I think other decisions will backfire in the long term, because it's not what you can see as sustainable development. In the long run, we cannot afford that. From the annual budget, more than 50% of current expenditure is paid on wages and salaries, while the capital budget has never exceeded 20%. Real expenditure in terms of the capital budget for almost all of the eleven years amounted to less than 15%. So where is the productive investment? Coming back to the question, I don't see clear-cut policies. I just see a sequence of ad hoc oriented issues.

The land issue might serve as another example, a very good example in the sense that the land issue was raised at a very early stage (of independence). But if you compare the findings of the Land Conference in 1991 with what happened in the next ten years, there has been no legislation. Where were the policies to compensate emotionally for the desire for land? Maybe this is too polemical, but what has happened since then that really counts? There was not even a land tax introduced.

de Waal: Well, we did introduce it recently. The law was passed at the end of last year I think. But up till today we do not have the regulations, so we don't know exactly what it will look like once it gets implemented. It's the same with the anti-corruption policy. We spent millions of dollars two or three years ago on a number of conferences. I was on a working group and many other people were on a working group. Nevertheless, until today no law was tabled in Parliament. I tend to agree with Henning Melber. When you look at job creation, in other words getting investment into the country, there are several different policies. The Ministry of Finance follows a certain policy, Trade and Industry has got a certain policy. Now Trade and Industry for instance must certify somebody as being an investor, and while this is done that person must go to the Ministry of Finance, and Finance must clear the tax part of his application. Between those two ministries there were inconsistencies to such an extent that people just dropped it and said: it's not worthwhile, we can't get progress. We encounter all sorts of different policies at different levels but they are not coordinated.

Mufune: What prevents this coordination? I'm sure both the executive and the legislature know that things are not coordinated.

Jauch: With regard to (government) coordination, three years ago the unions asked the National Planning Commission to report back on the achievements of the first National Development Plan. Their assessment was that the targets were not achieved, but that this was not the Commission's problem since they only wrote the plan and it was the individual ministries that were in charge of implementation. I assume we have to take it that if a gap arises between planning and implementation it is the responsibility of neither. The ministries are not the planners and the Planning Commission is not the implementing agency. It was a ridiculous scenario, but it goes even further. Between ministries you find hardly any coordination of policies. Take basic labour rights as an example: they were entrenched in our Labour Act of 1992 as basic human rights. Three years later Parliament passed the EPZ (Export Processing Zone) Act that stated initially that the Labour Act would not apply in EPZs. This represents a fundamental violation of the Declaration of the International Labour Organisation (ILO) that Namibia had already ratified at the time. But not only that, there are even contradictions in interpretation between ministries. Trade and Industry believes that the right to strike must be withheld from EPZ workers to attract foreign investors, while the Ministry of Labour supports the labour movement's demands that the right to strike is a fundamental right and should not be denied anywhere in Namibia. So you have this disjuncture at all levels. There seems to be no authority vested anywhere, except personally in the President, to hold individual ministries together. All ministries seem to have the freedom to decide on programmes almost independently of each other. That might be one of the reasons why we have such disjuncture between the task of economic planning and its practical implementation.

Steytler: There are also duplications in terms of coordination. First of all, there's the National Planning Commission which is supposed to coordinate. But you also have other agencies, for example, the Economic Advisory Council of the President. Though, in my opinion, it does not really function. Then Commission 2030 was set up, another coordinating body. In the end there is a lot of confusion as to who is coordinating. On top of that, there is another aspect contributing to this problem. We notice a lack of capacity, in particular in the National Planning Commission. There are many projects that are being supported by personnel from the European Commission. Some of these projects run over one year, two years or sometimes even three years, but as soon as these consultancies are handed over to the National Planning Commission there is no continuity. Transfers of skills didn't take place and there is often no one who can carry the job forward.

I agree with Henning Melber on policy implementation, that there are no clear policies. However there is a tendency for government to be neo-liberal. The reason for that may be historical. When we attained independence we were caught in a sort of 'catch 22' situation. Independence came at a very inappropriate time when communism had collapsed and there was only one way forward. At that point, our planners did not really plan. Some of them had more of a social bias in their ideas, but suddenly there was a vacuum. External experts who came in to advise did so according to the then dominant ideology. They advised to open up, to look at our investment policy. We did not consider alternative development plans. I think we just believed there was just one development pathway and we did not question whether it was appropriate. Globalisation is taken as a fact. But is it really a given, or are there alternatives? Globalisation gives no scope for the state to intervene. On the one hand, our state machinery is ballooning; but on the other hand, the state does not intervene in the economy. Given the private sector that we have, the state has an obligation to intervene, but selectively and in a smart way. Here we failed, and this explains why we still don't have a vibrant private sector, why unemployment is still high, poverty worse than before and people migrating from rural areas to Windhoek.

Fox: I see an interesting contradiction there. You were arguing that the state should intervene more, yet we have been saying that there seems to be a lack of coordination in government, a managerial crisis. So the idea of going down a more socialist (interventionist) road seems to conflict with the fact that the mechanisms and structures aren't able to cope with the task. There seems to be a structural crisis in this respect.

Winterfeldt: There is a tendency to answer this question about 'achievements and setbacks', concentrating on aspects of efficiency or dysfunction. Is this really the main point to focus on?

Melber: I would say not exclusively. But it is part of the story and I think the Namibian state we witnessed throughout the 1990s is almost a classic case of post-colonial states that are neither strong nor weak. Or actually they are both – it just depends on what you look at. They are extremely strong when they choose to intervene. In Namibia, the Re-Insurance Bill, the intervention into the fisheries sector, the EPZ case and the Labour Act are some examples of a strong state defending its manoeuvring space and pursuing interventionist or regulatory practices. It is at the same time an extremely weak state in terms of meaningful control over the basic structures of the economy. The property relations inherited at independence were not changed. With reference to the Constitution, to the policy of national reconciliation, the state has developed very little ambition so far to interfere with the principal matters of the mode of production.

As John Steytler has pointed out, Namibia became independent at a time when a perceived natural ally had been lost. The political leadership was left disoriented because socialist Germany, the German Democratic Republic, all of a sudden was no longer the Germany they had always dealt with. A newly reunited Germany now became the imperialist enemy, a situation the leadership was hardly able to cope with. The other 'natural' ally, the Soviet Union, virtually collapsed around the same time. I remember very vividly that some Soviet experts visited Namibia in 1990 and advised us to embark on a market-oriented approach. Now what must have been going on in the minds of those who had always believed that nationalisation and socialisation were the key to success? Their allies strongly advised opting for the market economy, for the neo-liberal capitalist development path. At that historical point in time the policy-makers omitted to pause for a conceptual break, analysing the situation of the Republic of Namibia in 1990/1991 and asking themselves: what do we want to achieve, what are our realistic goals? Looking back, our policy-makers wrongly felt that they could not afford to put aside the necessary time to reflect on the future of Namibian society. They resorted to a more pragmatic muddling through, not sufficiently defining priorities. Although the Constituent Assembly had given the National Planning Commission an extremely prominent place in the Constitution, no one seemed to accept the implications. In practice, no institution was prepared to acknowledge that from now on it would be accountable to the National Planning Commission Secretariat for the planning. On the contrary, the Secretariat was made to understand that it should mind its own business. So, Trade and Industry went its own way, the Ministry of Works, Transport and Communication went its own way, and Agriculture went its own way. Ministries even established their own research departments. What actually was created was a toothless planning tiger. Just recruited, the poor staff of the National Planning Commission (NPC) was expected to deliver. The result was what Herbert Jauch described, though even this is not a true reflection because the First National Development Plan was mainly drafted by external, foreign advisors. Afterwards, the NPC refused responsibility since it could not claim authority over the line ministries.

de Waal: I just want to say that one must give credit where credit is due also. For instance, if I look at what government achieved in the field of telecommunications we should be proud of that. It is working and it is functional. We have the Internet. NamPower is working, if you do not worry too much about the financial statements but look at the fact that we have electricity twenty-four hours a day. One must be reasonable and fair enough to say that some of the policies, like the privatisation or commercialisation, were successful in a certain sense. I'd now like to comment on the view that we don't have a vibrant private sector. I tend to differ. We do have a vibrant private sector, but the problem is that it is a vibrant sector of traders. Look at the new Trade Centre. We've got the Trade Centre now, we've got Game, we've got Pick 'n Pay, we've got everybody trading. Even the Chinese are trading now in Namibia on a large scale. We are a nation of traders. I thought after independence this would be one of the first things that a new government would backtrack on, stopping this nation of traders and starting instead to produce. However, once you start producing you don't get the support from government, from Trade and Industry, from Finance.

Coming to the other side of the coin: one of the biggest hindrances in getting the economy growing, one of the biggest mistakes of this government, is that they have increased the gap between rich and poor. Can you imagine a civil servant earning a million dollars a year? Can you imagine that? This is happening in Windhoek today, while the guy working in my garden earns N$30 per day. Now why did this government, once they took over, increase the salary scale of everybody to a point where it is totally out of control? 77 000 civil servants at a reasonable salary might be sustainable for a while, but at the current salaries it's not sustainable at all. The budget will not balance. I fail to understand why this government has built this very rich black élite group which is now going past the white élite group.

Jauch: I think this is the crux of the question of social equity. To give you an example: the unions' experience was that at independence the Prime Minister promised a review of the whole salary structure of the public service because of its colonial-shaped, top-heavy structure. What happened to this promise? The structure became even more top-heavy. In terms of self-enrichment, the managers in parastatals went a step further, and this presented a classic example where the state power that Henning Melber talked about was used for individual gain. As far as the majority of the population was concerned, there were definite improvements in the provision of education and health care services after independence. These services were made available on a broader scale, but there was no clear policy of systematic redistribution. The government has, for example, never granted larger amounts to schools in disadvantaged areas that have no facilities, compared to schools in privileged areas, despite calls from unions like the Namibia National Teachers Union (NANTU). What happened after independence was a policy of gradual equalisation by spending the same amount of money for each Namibian student, no matter what the historical legacy in a particular area may be. In terms of redistribution policies there was no attempt to systematically redress inequalities. When government introduced new salary and benefit structures after independence, they were favouring top earners in the management positions. Currently, we have this absurd situation that (in relative terms) the NamPower Managing Director earns more than his counterpart in Norway, an oil producing country with a Gross Domestic Product (GDP) several times higher than Namibia's.

Overall, Namibia's economic policy is following the neo-liberal line of thought and the government actively intervenes in only a few sectors. Fishing is a case in point, where an attempt is made to utilise the resources to the benefit of an increasing number of Namibians. By contrast, the mining sector has remained under the firm control of foreign mining companies. The government is not getting what it should out of negotiations with these companies. Otherwise, how could it give the AngloAmerican Corporation EPZ status for the Skorpion Zinc Mine? You exempt one of the richest companies in the world from paying taxes to a country like Namibia, where mining taxes historically have formed a significant part of government revenue. Secondly, when it comes to negotiations with investors,

Namibia took a slavish stance in granting them whatever they demanded. This, however, did not result in Namibia becoming a major investment destination. Comparing the investment inflow to outflow, last year alone (2000) we had an inflow of N$795 million as opposed to an outflow of over N$2 billion. We are exporting capital from this country on a huge scale year after year. At the same time, we call for foreign investments, regarding them as a panacea to development. That's unlikely to work out. The past five EPZ years – where we hoped to attract investors by offering immense concessions – have shown the defects of such an economic policy. The EPZ policy did not work and is unlikely to achieve the expected results in the years to come. When it comes to economic resources and policies government seems to rely totally on foreign investors. We seem to have no belief in our strength and no strategy to tap into our own resources like the Asian countries did. This 'Asian Tigers' economic 'miracle' was built on substantive investment from domestic sources and investments were also channelled by government into specific sectors. This was not part of a socialist programme but the state understood the need to intervene in the economic development process and did not leave it to market forces. Namibia is a very weak state in this respect, we do not intervene at all: we let the money find its own way, even out of the country. We sign more and more deals for market liberalisation, allow for financial deregulation as part of the World Trade Organisation (WTO) agreements. Thus we allow the outflow of billions of dollars – N$1,2 billion in 2000 alone. This indicates that in the economic arena we have a very weak state. We have a much stronger state in some other respects but economically speaking, I agree with John Steytler that we are following the neo-liberal line of government, withdrawing from the economy and indiscriminately allowing market forces to shape development.

Steytler: There is another aspect, the availability of financial credit. Eleven years after independence, we still have a situation where people have no access to credit. When I speak of people then I'm speaking of mainly small and medium-sized, in many cases micro-enterprises which consist of one person, both in rural and in urban areas. These people would benefit from funds. Here the state has to intervene.

On ownership matters, if you look at the ownership structure in the private sector, if you look at the Trade Centres and the Games, these stores are always South African entities. If you look at our financial sector, it is South African-owned, and companies have an interest in taking capital out of Namibia. As long as this pattern prevails, then capital will continue to flow out. Johan de Waal mentioned the lack of investment opportunities. But when government introduced Commission 28, financial institutions were compelled to invest at least 35% domestically. It was then that we started to realise the lack of domestic investment opportunities. Still, a substantial amount of money is being drawn out, but at least we see some structures coming up. The financial structure has started to diversify. We have financial auxiliaries, we have more asset managers, stockbrokers, etc. and that was achieved by legislation. This indicates that it is time to go further. In terms of the banking sector, why is it that we do not find bank branches in rural areas? Is there a way that government can put pressure on banks to entice them, to induce them to open branches in rural areas? I think more can be done and I think the solution is partly linked to the ownership question.

Winterfeldt: I suggest that we come to the second question. We have touched on it already. It addresses the economic realities of social progress, the social realities of economic progress. It is between these two poles that we should discuss the issue. May I also mention an angle that the discussion has ignored so far, from my point of view? We have focused exclusively on the formal sector. We are all aware that the Namibian economy, and with it Namibian society, consists of much more than this formal component. Could this be brought into the picture as well? I think it's quite an important aspect.

Melber: Yes, but just to go back to John Steytler's last question: why is government not trying to put pressure on private financial institutions to establish rural branches? It is not a purely legislative matter. Pragmatically, it requires government to identify rural development as a top priority and to develop rural infrastructure that creates (economic) networks in the regions. This would be attractive for the financial sector, which would then open branches. Isn't the tragedy that prior to independence there were more bank branches in the rural areas than there are today? Does this not tell a story? It points to a missing development strategy concerned with rural areas and the more remote places.

Now coming to the second question. You want to identify the beneficiaries of economic policies. I think it is mainly the urban-based minority that has gained. I do not see where there were meaningful trickle-down effects for the majority still dependent on land. Looking at the contribution of agriculture to GDP, you notice a very striking feature. Commercial agriculture is anything between 6 or 7% these days and it is declining. This contrasts with the fact that more than half of Namibia's population is directly or indirectly dependent on land. One would assume that this contradiction had to be be reflected in some kind of socio-economic strategy, but I don't see a strategy. If now the land issue comes to the fore as an effect of what is going on in Zimbabwe, then this is a revealing story. Because one would assume that one of the first things after the Land Reform Conference in 1991 would have been to implement certain policies, to test certain measures, even without claiming to have found the recipe for a final solution. There we come back to the role of the state. If you wanted to use the state apparatus as an interventionist tool to achieve social redistribution, then even under the constraints of the status quo-oriented Constitution there is a very simple instrument: tax policy. All enlightened capitalist states employ it. It is the most basic instrument you use if you want to achieve social redistribution. It may not necessarily always be successful or very impressive in the beginning, but I fail to understand why the Namibian government did not decide on a land tax in the early 1990s. It would have been a very simple and possibly efficient tool to skim off profit where it is created. Such a tax system must certainly not punish those commercial farmers who are not well off. It is an ideological blunder to say that commercial farmers are all filthy rich persons. But there are some of them, even in Johan de Waal's party, who are filthy rich, and I don't see any reason why they should not be thoroughly taxed, but only to the point where it is still worthwhile for them to continue in business.

de Waal: I agree with you about the land tax. But we must be very careful. I think one of the problems is that government does not have the answer to the land issue. You come with a new argument to me. You say, when you implement land tax you must tax those people that make a profit and not the one's that don't make a profit. I always thought that land tax should be introduced on the size of the land, but it should be a very low percentage, 1%, 2%, 3% or whatever the case may be; low taxation, but based on the size of the land. Normal income tax already caters for the filthy rich, who in any case pay 36% tax on income already.

Melber: But 36% or even 42% is far too little. I remember when the government increased personal income tax up to 42%, everyone cried 'foul'. When the media asked me, I said I don't mind paying 42% because I have a bloody high income compared with the majority of our population. If this is my individual contribution to redistribution and maintenance of social peace, I'm prepared to give away 50 or 60% of income bracket because...

de Waal: I don't agree with that.

Melber: Then Johan, you have never been to countries like Sweden.

de Waal: I don't want to go there... (laughter)

Melber: If you believe it or not, they pay their taxes without complaining.

de Waal: You must also see the other side of the coin. They pay their taxes, but they get a hell of a lot for free.

Melber: But this is what I'm trying to argue. If the state then delivers, yes, redistributes and contributes to meaningful social stability, where the rich ones know they will earn their high salary in another ten years time, we have a chance to overcome this widespread lack of confidence which lies behind the drain of capital out of this country.

de Waal: Referring to the N$1,2 billion drain of capital – who is exporting this sum? It is not the rich farmers, it is not the white business people. The money comes from the banks, from the insurance companies. That is why you can't call it 'white' money because the insurance companies get their money from black people. The financial institutions take out insurance policies. The problem lies in the investment opportunities. I'm investing a N$100 000 now in soil, not buying a farm, but putting up a bloody factory. But I'm the only clod that is doing it, and unless we can find more clods that are prepared to take their little spare money and invest it back in this country – because they are confident in the future of this country – that money will continue to leave Namibia. This is where the State President should not make statements like the ones of the last six months. You must satisfy your citizens, your citizens must feel secure enough to take that 100 000 and put it in the local economy. However, certainly we must look into the 1,2 billion dollars flowing out of the country and note where they come from.

Jauch: John Steytler has already partly answered that question. It is the foreign-owned companies in Namibia that make most of the profits that are exported. But you're right. The insurance companies and banking institutions constitute a huge part of the outflow. And that is the area where government has been very reluctant to intervene. Net export of capital was the case even six years ago when the President did not make any controversial statements, when Namibia was in fact hailed as 'the' success story in Africa. Looking at the figures for 1996, we find an inflow of 780 million, an outflow of 1,6 billion – more than double the inflow was leaving the country at that time already. I really doubt that investors are really preoccupied that much with stability. The biggest investment flows in southern Africa are directed to, believe it or not, Angola – because foreign investors are basically just extracting wealth, in that case oil. If foreign investors were primarily considering political stability in their investment decisions, how could Angola receive the most Foreign Direct Investment (FDI) in Africa? Therefore, the question rather is: how do we stop the leakage of capital invested by the local people into the financial institutions we just mentioned? Here government is required to intervene. Also, we must channel part of the budget to infrastructural development in order to move away from an urban-based development strategy. Not so much infrastructure investment for capital (like the infrastructure set up with public funds for EPZ companies), but rather infrastructure for an overall development agenda. This would have a spin-off effect, for example better schools, health care and other facilities in rural areas so that qualified teachers, doctors and businesses are prepared to go there.

de Waal: Can I test another idea? What if you partly privatise NamPower, selling 45% or 49% of the shares to some of these insurance companies? You take the money that you would get out of that deal and you invest it in the rural areas. You build the infrastructure and then businesses will go there; the small businesses first, and then eventually the bigger ones and then the banks will open up a branch there once such a scheme is successful.

Steytler: I agree on the necessity of generating more revenue for government. Still, the question to what extent government has used budgetary mechanisms as a tool for redistribution since independence is unclear. Over the years, a lot of money has been channelled into social services, welfare and education. But if you look at regional government, then one finds that the biggest budget portions were spent in Windhoek. There was no redistribution. Certain regions have been neglected, some for political reasons, and this I find unfair. Government must represent more than a political party or a certain political constituency.

Melber: I mainly agree, but we must equally consider where and also on what the revenue is actually spent. Nevertheless, without revenue you cannot spend on redistribution. Therefore, we do have to ask how the state might use its authority to increase its income. Since independence Namibia has been a net exporter of capital. There's not a single year that this was not the case. One of the ironies of the Namibianisation policy was the opening of the Windhoek Stock Exchange. The NSX was a loophole to export capital because the shares traded there are shares from (South African) companies listed at the JSX, the Johannesburg Stock Exchange. The handful of Namibian companies on the NSX are a meagre excuse for further net export, legal net export of capital, because people are not inclined to buy the Namibian shares. They are transferring their money into the South African multi-national companies. So we also have to look beyond the declared aim (that NSX represents Namibianisation).

For me, the fishing quota and levies on fishing are another classical example. Looking at the recent January 2001 NEPRU report by Peter Manning on the fishing industry, he comes up with a very interesting calculation. Ever since 1994 the levy on the quota declined. Manning calculated that if the levy on the quota of 1994 would had remained at the same level, up to 2001 we would have accrued an additional revenue income for the Namibian state of N$3,5 billion. That is one-third of the annual budget. Of course, if it is spent for a war in Angola or the Congo, it is questionable whether this would make any difference. But if you spend it on material infrastructure in rural areas or similar, then it could make a very big difference. However, the levies on fishing companies were decreased. This policy was meant to foster Namibian participation in the fishing industry. Formally speaking, a new network was established allowing locals to gain ownership of companies. There are even joint ventures – and more recently what has been labelled *shotgun weddings* – with foreign companies. Behind the façade you realise that this is a much more complicated network where you have some formal Namibian ownership but even more de facto ownership by international companies since the mid-1990s. Formal Namibianisation allows for an even higher transfer of money abroad through international companies. This would seem to suggest that the N$3,5 billion of lost revenue has not been reinvested into Namibia through private ownership policies or private investment. International companies instead paid less tax over the last seven years. So their profit margins increased. I'm not so sure that the policy-makers know that this is the effect. But one should make them aware of it, although there is the ugly suspicion that they know very well, because if you look at the ownership patterns of the Namibian companies, these are the main beneficiaries. Namibia's government policy seems to be guided by very narrow-minded individual interests. This is a very sad part of post-colonial reality. Answering the editors' question from this evidence, the cogent conclusion would be that the new élite – which is mainly politically defined – is the real beneficiary of the economic policies of the past decade. This is at the expense of the majority of the population. Namibian society today faces the situation that we are the world record holder, so to speak, in income discrepancies (income inequality patterns) according to official data calculating the GINI-coefficient. Namibia is a so-called lower middle-income country with an average per capita income of roughly US$1 600 to 2 000. This income level has been declining on average since 1990. But nobody in Namibia earns such an average income. Half of the population lives in absolute poverty but on the other side, 6% or 8% of the population controls two-thirds of the national wealth. And in analysing this I think we need to be careful. To some extent, we rightly still refer to the racial patterns of wealth, to white and black. We continue to relate to the imbalance inherited from the colonial past, while almost clandestinely the class structure changes, turning away from this exclusive racial aspect. Of course, you still have the Werner Lists, but now you have the Mathew Shikongos and the Frans Indongos. You have others from the north, some of them not even paying taxes to this day. You have those with 2 000 or 3 000 head of cattle in so-called communal areas, not paying tax on a single head of cattle. So we are getting into a system where the access to privilege is not confined to the colour of one's skin any longer. Or it appears even the other way round – that you need to be black to get access to resources and privileges. Genuine capitalism, though, is colour blind. We see it nowadays in South Africa, with the comrades in business. They still play the colour card to cash in, but in the long run the idea is to have a colour-blind capitalist system.

In the Namibian context, this is at the expense of the rural people. I hope Herbert Jauch agrees, when in reviewing the past eleven years I draw the conclusion that such a development is also at the expense of the workers in the classical (Marxist) sense of the term. Their number is smaller today than in 1990 and they are not better off. The trade unions were to some degree co-opted as an emerging labour aristocracy. Some trade unions participate in the new set-up, while those who withstood co-optation are now not influential. Given this co-optation, a shift in government policy towards serious redistribution of the available social wealth in this country is not likely.

Steytler: I think we must also mention the gender aspect within this budget analysis. We looked at class, at black and white. To some extent, government has tried to address the plight of women. But also to a large extent, I think, it has failed in that regard. In rural areas, the people who are really suffering, doing all the work, yet while living in poverty, it's mainly women.

Winterfeldt: We already jumped right into the middle of our third question regarding the structural conditions of a policy of social equity. May we approach this question from a more specific angle by trying to look into 'reconciliation'. It is a policy paradigm, and since 1990 a structural condition of future policies. To what extent is there a chance for a policy of social equity under the structural conditions of reconciliation – reconciliation being understood not only in terms of black and white, but also in terms of laying down distinct relations of property and production based on the capitalist model?

de Waal: Now my feeling there is that you can do both. May I explain it in very simple terms by saying that I don't believe in trying to cut the cake, the existing cake of national wealth, into a million pieces. Then you are going to have a million poor people. What we need to do is to increase the cake and make sure that the increase goes to the poor people...

Winterfeldt: The question is: who cuts the cake? Who, by virtue of his social and political privileges, should be in charge of cutting the cake? Who is entitled to define the size of the slices?

de Waal: The government should try and cut it.

Winterfeldt: Under the existing conditions?

de Waal: The government should try and cut it, that's its function. If you compare the budgets of 1990 and 2000, budgetary means increased tremendously. The question is, what happened to that money, where did it go and what portion of it was spent on the poor people? If you ask the question: who benefited between 1990 and 2000, it is the white people. There is no doubt about it, it is the white people and it is also the new black élite. The people that did not benefit were the poor 50% of the population. I'm worried when people maintain that you can't have both national reconciliation and upliftment of the poor. I say you can. In fact, the only way you can uplift the people is to have national reconciliation. But then government must develop a specific policy to achieve that upliftment, even if it does not have all the answers. This is where we need institutions like NEPRU and other professionals that can assist us. National reconciliation is essential in order to solve the problem of poverty.

Jauch: The actual crux of the matter lies in the interpretation of reconciliation. Reconciliation, as defined in all the policy debates during the transition period, was limited to the question of racial reconciliation. Of course, that was necessary and affirmative action played a part in redressing some of the racial imbalances in our society. It is being implemented in the formal employment sector, amongst management in the civil service, in parastatals, increasing the numbers of black employees especially in the management cadre. However, this process was not gender-neutral as black women were often overlooked. This can be seen for example in the civil service where black men were the main beneficiaries when it comes to promotions and appointments into key decision-making positions after independence. By comparison, what happened in the private sector workplaces? There too, women remain concentrated in the lower-paid, long-hour jobs. So you have a double discrimination, because reconciliation – and even affirmative action – was never really concerned with this. We introduced reconciliation saying let's forget the past, let's not look at human rights abuses, let's from now on appoint more black employees to decision-making positions – but otherwise let things stay as they are. This is going to haunt us, now and in future. Social peace cannot be maintained on an élite basis. Of course, you now have formerly white schools whose pupils are today perfectly integrated on a colour basis. But you also have to look at who the parents of the children at those schools are. They are mostly middle class parents, while the children of the poor are still at the same disadvantaged school in the townships like before independence. So, of course, in the middle class areas, reconciliation works well to some extent. Then you go to Ombalantu or to Tseiblaagte and you look at the schools there. Working class people still battle with economic problems to an extent that shows the social limits of reconciliation.

No doubt, although socio-economic conditions have not improved, the end of war has nevertheless meant a dramatic change in peoples' lives in the north. If it were not so, SWAPO would not have won the elections so overwhelmingly. The mere end of the war period has allowed the population to return to some kind of normality. The bit of infrastructure that later came including water and electricity supply has made a change in the rural peoples' lives. That is why you have a 95% SWAPO vote which is a reflection of the people's conviction that their lives have improved.

de Waal: People say, we can cope with what we've got.

Jauch: Yes, from the perspective of an affluent urban-based population, the living conditions in the North look very much like ten years ago. But it seems that people there feel that their lives have changed in those ten years, and this influences the (political) dynamics in Namibia. This is why the government gets away with an absence of distinct redistribution policies. It might take another ten years before issues of redistribution and socio-economic equality enter the political debate more forcefully. However, at the moment these issues are largely absent from our political debates.

Melber: I think it's important what Herbert Jauch says, but the government did deliver in certain areas with a policy strategy. It delivered to its main (political) base in the four 'O' regions in terms of infrastructure. In the previous war-damaged Ovamboland, SWAPO strengthened its social base to gain acceptance both as a national liberation movement, but also in the country itself, and there its success story began. This is true also of Katutura. If you go to Katutura today and compare it with the Katutura I knew before I was banned in the mid-1970s, it's a different world. New schools and health centres were built, roads were tarred in high-density areas, electricity and water are provided. But also the perception changes. Now comes the stage where if you don't have money for the tikkie box you can't use the public telephone, which Telecom installs also in Ondangwa or Oshakati. The interesting question is: how much longer is it going to take until the post-colonial government will be confronted by its problems of delivery? Are we not reproducing a socio-economic structure that has striking similarities with the previous apartheid system? It is just a matter of time. The liberation effect that is still a very strong one will meet an expiry date, as we can see with ZANU-PF in Zimbabwe. Politics for quite a while have turned to a populist rhetoric which resorts to strategies similar to those in Zimbabwe, bringing the land issue into play and implying that you just have to address injustices inherited from the apartheid era. Will that in the long run be successful in diverting the public from the burning issue of redistribution and social equity?

Summarising with regard to national reconciliation and social equity: I think in principle they are contradictory but they are not antagonistic. In our current analysis, one should not abandon the notion of class struggle. Certainly in 1990, class struggle was not the conceptual priority on the (independence) agenda. Clearly, controlled constitutional change now contradicted the concept and abandoned it lock, stock and barrel. All social forces within Namibia agreed on the principles imposed by the Western Contact Group as the bottom line of the Constitution. Dirk Mudge and Theo-Ben Gurirab were the ones who recalled that in 1992 at a meeting in Freiburg, which is well documented in a conference volume. Still, there would be room for manoeuvring if national reconciliation is re-defined and if the redistribution of wealth became the main focus of a socially conscious policy of national reconciliation. No doubt, such a policy would have to differ markedly from the current one. Under the given framework there are still options and I refuse to accept the argument that the Constitution defined once and for all what will happen in Namibia.

Mufune: There's a lot of pressure, I think, coming from those who have not benefited or who say that redistribution has not yet really occurred and I'm just wondering how was the government able to deal with this kind of pressure from the unions, from their members.

Jauch: You're quite right. I remember this started already back in 1989. You are familiar with the link of the major trade union federation National Union of Namibian Workers (NUNW) to the (SWAPO) party. The first outcry came as a reaction to the way the Parliamentary List was compiled. The unions felt that the political activists inside the country were marginalised to accommodate certain people, mainly those who had been (in exile) outside the country in leadership positions. Then, in 1992 when the new Labour Law was tabled, the unions expected a law that would clearly be biased towards workers. Traditionally, SWAPO had played the card of being the workers' party very strongly and very loudly as the party had its roots in the workers' movement. Key leaders like Nujoma and ya Toivo had been migrant workers themselves. However, when the first draft of the Labour Bill became public, the trade unions criticised it saying that some of the fundamental rights of workers were not taken into consideration. The Act was based on a notion of 'social partnership', which may be suitable in a situation where there is a balance of social power between business and labour, as is the case in some of the industrialised countries in Western Europe. But in the Namibian scenario, the Labour Bill did not address the huge power imbalances in favour of the employers. The unions then met with SWAPO and government to demand certain changes. The result was still not what the unions had expected, but it was kind of an agreement that they could live with. All parties had agreed to a compromise. But that experience gave rise to doubts in the trade union movement. Was this a government that was willing to run the country in favour of workers, beyond this notion of social partnership? Later in the mid-1990s, parliamentarians requested an increase in their allowances for domestic services and all kinds of other benefits. The unions protested loudly against such blatant self-enrichment, and threatened to take action. SWAPO reacted very effectively to these emerging tensions by co-opting key people from the unions into party positions or into Parliament and the civil service. This started in 1990 when Ben Ulenga as the general secretary of the mineworkers union spearheaded a move to review the role of the NUNW in independent Namibia. The terms of co-operation between party and unions had visibly changed since the 1980s and Ulenga was spearheading the move to redefine the role of the labour movement after independence. A few weeks before the congress, Ulenga was called to State House and without any prior consultation was appointed Deputy Minister of Environment and Tourism, thus depriving the NUNW of one of its most prominent leaders. We had since then a whole string of people moving into Parliament without them articulating workers' interests in the legislative. Peter Ilonga is perhaps the only exception to the rule, but generally the co-optation into Parliament and the civil service has helped the SWAPO party to absorb some of the pressure from labour.

Around the NUNW's 1993 Congress, there were signs that part of the labour movement wanted to review its affiliation to the SWAPO party, questioning whether it still could be regarded as beneficial for workers. Some unionists expressed fears that the NUNW may become a tool for the party to control labour. Others in the labour movement thought the link to the ruling party could be used to labour's future advantage. The debate is still raging. SWAPO has also very cleverly applied a process of consultation (of labour and other social partners), rather than participation in decision making. This strategy may work for a time. But unless tangible benefits come – and that includes solving the problem of high unemployment – it will fail to appease the demand for socio-economic redistribution.

Winterfeldt: I suggest that we approach question four: affirmative action and black empowerment. We formulated the question provocatively to bring the social structural elements to the fore. Can these developmental tools go further than just privileging a small portion of the black African population? Are they more, can they be more?

Steytler: It's a tough one. I think they can, if reassessed. We have to observe different criteria. The issue of nepotism comes up, then the issue of skills. The imperatives of affirmative action are the one thing to follow, but it is not always the best person who gets the job. Sometimes it is people who lack the skills, but are appointed just because they're classified as part of a designated group with the necessary connections. But definitely, affirmative action can contribute to black empowerment provided that it reaches the target groups and it is not used just as a tool to promote a few, or as a tool of window dressing as happens particularly in the private sector.

Jauch: It is disappointing and surprising to see, in the approach to affirmative action, that its scope is limited to formal employment. The labour movement and NGOs have always conceived affirmative action as a central element of policy. Looking at employment patterns, a typical structure prevails: white management, black workers. Restructuring based on affirmative action is a must. But it is limited if you construct it that way. It can be more: it can be applied as a general policy of redressing imbalances in various socio-economic fields. For example, in agricultural development, the affirmative loan scheme was used to give black communal farmers preferential access to loans to buy commercial farms. In the fishing industry, affirmative action policy initially was formulated so that fishing quotas were beneficial to the Namibian community instead of yielding a profit only for foreign fishing companies. However, the challenge still is to ensure that affirmative action benefits communities instead of individuals only as is currently the case. Legally, this is possible, but it requires a much broader conceptualisation of affirmative action.

Winterfeldt: You mention the term 'community'. From a sociological perspective, we would interject that every community is a structured one. If someone or something serves a community, who then is served within the community? Can we really assume that the community in its entirety benefits from affirmative action? Or does affirmative action rather tend to privilege the upper layers of a community?

de Waal: I doubt the affirmative action proposed by Herbert Jauch. What I would rather see is workers getting a percentage of the ownership of the company. It's much more beneficial to everybody instead of trying to serve a community. To confer a quota on the condition that the company distributes some 40% or 30% of its shares to the workers, I think that's a viable and equitable solution. Coupled with the extended family, it will also help in the rural areas. I have doubts that affirmative action at the moment is working. Black employees are often appointed just to fulfil the quota. What I would much rather see is the know-how of the established businessperson and the skills and the enthusiasm of the black employee combined to establish a new style of company. That's where I think we should go. You should combine the two to get rid of the traders' nation.

Melber: Yes, Johan, affirmative action and black empowerment do work very well. It is a bit ironic, the way I mean it. The policy works very well. Conceived as an ideological tool to modify the class structure, it perfectly fulfils the purpose. Affirmative action and black empowerment have in part modified the class structures since independence. The new political élite uses its power of definition, also co-opting representatives of other social forces, to create and put into place a new group of people that directly participates and benefits from the existing social structures without basically changing them. In this respect I think the notion of affirmative action is an ideological blunder because it pretends to transform society. The mistake is that what we are talking of, again, is colour, as if it made any difference in terms of social structures if the new minority élite is black or pink or yellow. In terms of social structure, it does not make a decisive difference. If social transformation is on the agenda, you don't need to call it affirmative action because it's sufficient to call it social transformation. Conceptually, then you start in a different way. You don't start by fiddling around with management positions only. You critically inquire where government expenditure is going. You investigate the social effects, you explore capacity building to empower the marginalised, the underprivileged. The tricky issue, though, is that of time. How long does it take to get meaningful, measurable achievements under given structural constraints? Social transformation that is not based on revolutionary transformation takes a bloody long time and requires a lot of patience. To what extent can government claim credibility in the medium-to-long run if the social effects of their policies a decade after independence display clear contradictory traits? Credibility as a non-material aspect of consciously transforming, developing a society is very important. Those in power today are expected to display a certain degree of modesty – self-restraint does not mean that they have to live in shacks. But there is a certain limit where legitimacy is not just vested in formal political legitimacy, the 76% of the votes won in an election. There is also moral legitimacy, the way you exercise power. Beyond these limits, the pressure of those excluded from the benefits of affirmative action arises in the long run. The examples of Zambia and Zimbabwe show this. Those who are the main beneficiaries of affirmative action might then become the targets of the frustration and disappointment of those who begin to understand that affirmative action is a very selective tool, modifying the existing class structure without modifying its fundamental antagonisms.

Jauch: You questioned the term community. You have both, disadvantaged groups and communities in their entirety, and you have a few individuals that represent those communities, often benefiting on their behalf. I envisage equitable affirmative action policies prescribing, for example, a certain percentage of profit-yields from fishing quotas to be invested into schools, healthcare centres, housing projects, eradicating squalid conditions in areas where fishing communities live. Look how people are forced to live in Walvis Bay today, in Kuisebmund. Compare that with the profits that the fishing companies make. The solution cannot be to have a few individuals co-opted on management boards and then call it affirmative action. Summarising my answer to your question: affirmative action can be formulated very differently. It is necessary in Namibia. The economic structures ten years after independence have not changed, the majority is still excluded from tangible economic benefits and there is a need for a systematic redistribution of resources and the benefits associated with them. In my view, the scope for affirmative action has been too limited.

You asked whether affirmative action can be more than what it is right now. It has been shown in other places that it can achieve a lot more. We are following the American model of affirmative action, which is focused on the individual, designed merely to make institutions representative, and that misses the point of a broader programme of redistribution. That's the tragedy, to have the wrong philosophical model for affirmative action that, ironically, was introduced here by the ILO. I differ with some of the comments made, in that I think the policy has the potential to bring about a lot more than what it does right now. It is a pity that we allow it to be so narrow that the benefits accrue to only a few.

Winterfeldt: With the right philosophical model, could you implement such a policy of social reform? Do we have the right social model to implement the right philosophical model? Does the social structural background allow this?

Melber: This would be my counter argument. I think Herbert Jauch is too enthusiastic, the positive reference to affirmative action within the context of Namibia's social structure of today is misleading. We are not talking about affirmative action. We are talking about a co-option strategy within a particular social structure. Salary discrepancies are just a function of this structure. The affirmative action we have is, as I've said before, affirmative of the class structure. It's not transformative action.

Steytler: We must pay more attention to empowerment. Empowerment is taking place and empowerment entails many things. Some of them Herbert Jauch already alluded to, like education. We can empower people if we force a big company to invest in education facilities. It's a way of empowering people if we invest in their physical health. Speaking out, being able to articulate yourself, being able to take decisions whether it's in an NGO or for a multi-national company – these are all facets of empowerment.

Winterfeldt: Coming to question number five, a very short introduction. Recently, I was struck by a statement I found in Tötemeyer's PhD. Referring to the early 80s, the author claimed that the majority of his 250 interviewees in the former Ovamboland favoured a privatisation or commercialisation of land. To me, this runs counter to public perceptions of the land issue. The question: should land be privatised and redistributed? Should communal land be privatised and should agricultural policies aim at commercialisation? Such a perspective is not voiced in the debate on the land issue.

Melber: We have witnessed a process of commercialisation ever since the apartheid days. For whatever reasons, the policy makers never publicly address the issue – maybe because some of them were directly involved in this process. Their individual interests again explain why the land issue in the past ten years was never seriously raised as a practical policy issue. For a long time, the so-called communal areas revealed a predominantly commercial approach to land. It varies from region to region, but people have very clear concepts of individual titles, land utilisation, changing land use. Power structures at a local level play a role in this commercially motivated access to land, this combination of a centralised authority vested in the state and of the local and regional power structures vested in the so-called traditional communities.

I think the land issue currently plays a much more prominent role than would be the case if the other aspects of social transformation were given priority. I cannot believe that Namibia's future rests in land. That's unrealistic compared with any other country considering the climatic, economic and political constraints when it comes to Namibia and the land issue. First of all, the land issue is presented in disguise – as if it were an issue of or for the rural majority. Now in historical terms more than half of the population has never been exposed to the process of the colonial expropriation of land. They have at best been denied competition with the white colonisers within the Police Zone. The target group of populist rhetoric, in historical fact, is not identical with those who were deprived of their land and livelihood. Is Ponhele ya France really the advocate of the Bushmen, Nama, Damara and Herero? I doubt it. But those are the main groups to redress if you discuss restitution of land rights and redistribution of land. But even if these groups' claims could be satisfied, I doubt that this could present the solution to the socio-economic plight of Namibians. I do not see that in land there is a meaningful social transformation to be expected. Sure, the land issue has its cultural, psychological and political connotations, reflecting the longing for the restitution of identity. But if all the other more burning economic demands were met, the land issue would not be of such central importance. The land is, so to speak, the place for the projection of general social frustration. Therefore symbolically, it stands for much more than just land. Land stands for participation in the social benefits of the society. If the country is able to share social benefits with the majority, it eases the pressure in terms of the land issue.

de Waal: A short answer, I think land should be tradable somehow in communal areas. What the exact format should be I'm not quite sure, at this stage. Moreover, the question of inheritance must be approached. If a family has been apportioned land in the communal area and the father dies, the family should not be kicked off. I tend to agree with Henning Melber that communal land is anyway going the way of commercialisation.

Jauch: A huge number of people live in a kind of a subsistence economy. It's imperative not to attempt to commercialise the land they live on. The majority in the north are living from hand to mouth from the land. If they are deprived of their omahangu fields they will literally starve. In the absence of clarity on communal lands, the richer communal farmers seize the opportunity to fence off big tracts of land. The NNFU has taken up this issue. Fencing off communal land is a de facto privatisation effectively reserving certain areas of land for private use only, excluding neighbouring communal farmers. The excluded homesteads are faced with ever-smaller plots of land available for subsistence agriculture. If we go ahead and privatise the communal areas, especially in the north, it means that some peasants would have significant commercial farms at their disposal in fairly good rainfall areas. But the many that are hit by unemployment, that are just living from hand to mouth, are going to face starvation. In the 1991 Land Conference document, the Namibian government has already admitted that the solution to the land question is to get people employment in other sectors. But in the absence of it, what do you do? If you cannot create employment and then turn the communal areas into commercial, privatised land then you create famine in Namibia. The solution to long-term needs lies in extra-agricultural economic development. But right now the communal northern lands are a vital survival base.

de Waal: I agree with you entirely.

Melber: I also think it's very important to re-emphasise what Herbert Jauch has just said. The 1991 document warned that the fencing-off of land should be stopped; though interestingly, this process of fencing later actually gained momentum. Of course we are talking about the basic means of survival of a large proportion of the people. You are absolutely right, and the solution cannot be just to accept growing commercialisation. But irrespective of this land reform question, we have first and foremost to envisage a land reform in the so-called communal areas. It is not the commercial areas that should be at the core of meaningful land reform, as is tacitly implied by policy makers. Large-scale commercial agriculture is not where the majority of the rural population lives. Even if you redistributed the existing private agricultural property, it would contribute far less to reducing the social pressure than restructuring in the so-called communal areas. The key to transformation is not in the commercial farming sector.

Winterfeldt: Thank you very much.

FROM LIBERATION STRUGGLE TO SOCIAL PARTNERSHIP? THE CHALLENGE OF CHANGE FOR THE NAMIBIAN LABOUR MOVEMENT

Herbert Jauch

Introduction

Despite the prominent role played by Namibian trade unions in the final years of the country's liberation struggle, and despite the fact that the labour movement is still the strongest organised force among Namibia's 'civil society' organisations, it has attracted very little interest from academics. Due to the large rural population and the underdeveloped manufacturing sector, trade unions might seem to represent only a small minority of the population and consequently be an insignificant player in the country's economic and political life. Some economists went as far as describing Namibian workers as a privileged 'labour aristocracy' (Hansohm and Presland 1997:11). This notion was first used by Arrighi and Saul in 1973 who argued that urbanised, unionised wage earners secured a privileged position in society at the expense of subsistence farmers, the unemployed and the casually employed (Klerck/Murray/Sycholt 1997:5). Although it can be argued that Namibia's formal sector workers are in a better financial position than informal sector workers and subsistence farmers, they do not constitute a labour aristocracy. Mbuende (1986:177-179) has pointed out the close links between the Namibian peasantry and the industrial working class as a result of the contract labour system. Even today, workers' wages contribute significantly to the survival of family members in the rural areas and Namibia's industrial workers bear a substantial burden caused by widespread unemployment of about 35% (Namibia Labour Force Survey 1997:xiii). Despite the emergence of a permanent urban working class over the past decade, the vast majority of workers in formal sector employment share their income by way of remittances with members of their extended families in urban and rural areas. The labour force survey of 1997 revealed that about 45% of Namibia's national household incomes are derived from wages (Ministry of Labour 1998). Describing Namibian workers as a 'labour aristocracy' is thus a misconception, which ignores their social reality.

A brief look at the Namibian labour market reveals that 225 000 workers (41% of the economically active population) are employed in the formal sector. This is a much higher proportion than in most other sub-Saharan African countries and indicates that Namibia's formal sector has a much greater significance than the informal sector. Although reliable data are scarce, indications are that an average of 5-8 dependants rely on each worker's wage for their survival. The dominant sectors in terms of employment are the public sector accounting for about 70 000 workers, the farming sector (35 000 workers), the retail sector (19 000 workers), the domestic workers' sector (18 000 workers), as well as the manufacturing and construction sectors with about 12 000 workers each. The mining industry which employed about 14 000 workers at independence, accounts for only about 7 000 workers today (Ministry of Labour 1998).

Namibian trade unions organise in all sectors including domestic and farm workers. The overall unionisation rate achieved (according to the figures supplied by trade unions) stands at about 50% – which is high by international standards. However, unionisation rates vary greatly between the well-organised public and mining sectors (60-80% unionisation) and the difficult farming and domestic workers sectors (5-20% unionisation).

The Namibian labour movement consists of over 20 trade unions, most of which belong to one of the country's three trade union federations: the 70 000 member-strong National Union of Namibian Workers (NUNW), the 45 000 member Namibia Federation of Trade Unions (NAFTU), or the Namibia People's Social Movement (NPSM) whose affiliates have a combined membership of about 14 000 (LaRRI 1999:11).

This article focuses mainly on the NUNW, which is not only Namibia's largest trade union federation, but also played the most prominent role during the liberation struggle and in the public policy debates after independence. Its history is in many ways similar to that of the Congress of South African Trade Unions (COSATU), as both played a critical role in terms of mass mobilisation during the liberation struggle. After decades of intense repression, the NUNW unions emerged from the mid-1980s onwards as key players in the economic and political arena. They linked the struggle at the workplace with the broader struggle for political independence, and formed links with other social and political organisations such as the Namibia National Students Organisation (NANSO) and SWAPO. The NUNW understood its role as that of a social movement, which could not address workers' issues separately from those affecting the broader community. Exploitation at the workplace was thus linked to the broader struggle against racial and political oppression.

The achievement of independence in 1990 had a tremendous impact on the labour movement and required a re-definition of the role that trade unions wanted (and were able) to play. The function of political mobilisation, which had taken centre stage before independence, was taken over by SWAPO whose leadership returned to Namibia in 1989 and became the government with independence. Given the close structural links between the NUNW unions and SWAPO as well as the fact that most union leaders played a prominent role in the party, there was a widespread expectation among workers that the SWAPO government would be a workers government. A few years before independence, even leading SWAPO intellectuals such as Kaire Mbuende had still argued that the interests of workers and peasants constituted the dominant position in SWAPO (Mbuende 1986:199). However, once in power, SWAPO did not pursue revolutionary working class politics and instead maintained the predominantly capitalist structure of the economy while introducing the notion of social partnership in labour relations. Trade unions were expected to define a new role within this framework, and although the NUNW had previously called for radical change, it accepted the new framework with little resistance.

This article aims to briefly sketch the history of the NUNW and to outline the social forces shaping its development as well as some of the challenges and choices facing trade unions today. Emphasis will be placed on the challenges arising from social, economic and political factors that have shaped the labour movement's developments after independence. These include the issue of political affiliation, the introduction of tri-partism and conservative economic policies.

A brief history of the NUNW

The NUNW's history is closely linked to that of SWAPO, and its origins can be traced back to SWAPO's consultative congress in Tanga, Tanzania in 1969-70, at which several new departments were established, including a Department of Labour. Although the congress documents did not mention the formation of trade unions, a decision to establish the NUNW in exile was taken on 24 April 1970. Solomon Mifima was SWAPO's first secretary of labour from 1972 to 1976. In 1976, he was accused of being a South African spy, arrested and replaced by John ya Otto who then represented Namibian workers at international forums like the International Labour Organisation (ILO) and the Organisation for African Trade union Unity (OATUU). The work in exile focused on education as SWAPO started to train trade unionists under the name of NUNW (Peltola 1995:114, 132).

In 1979 the NUNW set up its headquarters in Luanda, Angola, under the leadership of ya Otto who was serving as SWAPO Secretary for Labour and NUNW Secretary General at the same time. Ya Otto prepared an NUNW constitution for adoption by SWAPO's National Executive Committee, though it was never approved. Some party leaders even responded negatively to the union initiative fearing a strong and independent labour movement after independence (Peltola 1995:14, 133, 142).

At that time, the NUNW did not have its own social base inside the country and merely operated as the workers' wing of SWAPO. For Namibian workers inside the country, the workers' struggle was intertwined with the struggle against racial discrimination and colonial occupation. The struggle against the contract labour system that culminated in the general strike of 1971-72, for example, highlighted the link between economics and politics. It was as much a struggle against the contract labour system as it was against colonialism (Mbuende 1986:184). Peltola noted that the class struggle waged by workers was seen as one and the same as the liberation struggle of SWAPO (1995:93). However, as Mbuende pointed out, "the level of political consciousness of the African working class is determined, among other things, by the type of industry in which they are employed and by the nature of the wider urban environment in which they live" (Mbuende 1986:184). Political and class consciousness thus was highest in places where workers were concentrated in hostels which extended their interdependence beyond the point of production (ibid.:185). This explains why the first and strongest unions emerged in the mining and fishing industries.

Most of Namibia's trade unions were established inside the country from the mid-1980s. Although several attempts to form unions had been made before, they were suppressed by the colonial regime time and again. However, the earlier efforts laid the foundations for the later emergence of the National Union of Namibian Workers (NUNW) and its affiliates (see Peltola 1995:167-197; Bauer 1997:69). Community organising surged inside Namibia from 1984 onwards, focusing on the crises in housing, employment, health, education and social welfare. In the absence of trade unions, workers began to take their workplace problems to social workers at the Roman Catholic Church and the Council of Churches in Namibia (CCN). At that time, the umbrella of the churches provided political activists with a shield under which they could start organising workers. Unlike trade unions, which had been crushed by the colonial state, churches were able to operate across the country. By 1985, workers and community activists had formed a Workers' Action Committee in Katutura which became the forerunner of trade unions (Bauer 1997:70).

At the same time, South Africa's National Union of Mineworkers (NUM) began to organise workers at Namibia's CDM and Rössing mines in Oranjemund and Arandis. They linked up with the Workers' Action Committee and formed the Rössing Mineworkers Union by April 1986. This union later became the Mineworkers Union of Namibia (MUN) (Bauer 1997:70). The MUN and other NUNW-affiliated unions provided workers with an organisational vehicle through which they could take up workplace grievances as well as broader political issues, which were always seen as linked to the economic struggle.

Another factor which contributed to the emergence of trade unions inside Namibia, was the release of Namibian political prisoners from 1984 onwards. Some returned to Windhoek and began working for the SWAPO structures again. A decision was taken to reactivate the NUNW inside Namibia and by April 1986 a Workers Steering Committee had been formed. It incorporated the Workers Action Committee and all other efforts to organise workers around the country. Fieldworkers began organising workers at several workplaces and in September 1986, the NUNW's first industrial union was launched: the Namibia Food and Allied Workers Union (NAFAU), led by John Pandeni, a former Robben Island prisoner (Bauer 1997:70). Shortly afterwards, the Mineworkers Union of Namibia (MUN) was launched, led by another former Robben Island prisoner, Ben Ulenga. In 1987, the Metal and Allied Workers Union (MANWU) and the Namibia Public Workers Union (NAPWU) were launched, followed by the Namibia Transport and Allied Workers Union (NATAU) in June 1988, the Namibia National Teachers Union (NANTU) in March 1989, the Namibia Domestic and Allied Workers Union (NDAWU) in April 1990 and the Namibia Farmworkers Union (NAFWU) in May 1994. In 2000, the Namibia Financial Institutions Union (NAFINU) was launched as the first NUNW union catering for white-collar workers. These unions constitute the affiliates of the NUNW today.

The exiled and internal wings of the NUNW were merged during a consolidation congress held in Windhoek in 1989. At that time the NUNW unions inside Namibia had already established themselves and were a formidable force among grassroots organisations. They enjoyed huge support even beyond their membership and played a critical role in ensuring SWAPO's victory in the elections of 1989.

Continued political affiliation

The NUNW maintained its links with SWAPO after independence through its affiliation to the ruling party. This link has led to heated debates both within and outside the federation. While the majority of NUNW affiliates argued that a continued affiliation would help the federation to influence policies, critics have pointed out that the affiliation would undermine the independence of the labour movement and that it would wipe out prospects for trade union unity in Namibia.

The NUNW's rival trade union federations, particularly NAFTU, have repeatedly stated that they differ fundamentally from the NUNW on the question of political affiliation. They have charged that the NUNW could not act independently and play the role of a watchdog over government as long as it was linked to the ruling party. There is also a growing public perception that the NUNW is merely a workers' wing of the ruling party, although the NUNW and its affiliates have on several occasions been the most vocal critics of government policies. They took issue with government over Namibia's huge income inequalities, the slow process of land redistribution, education reform and the self-enrichment by politicians. How can this contradiction be explained?

There are two contradictory trends at work within the NUNW. On the one hand, there is a high level of loyalty and emotional attachment to SWAPO as a liberation movement and 'mother of independence'. This applies to the union membership and leadership alike who understood the liberation struggle as primarily geared towards national liberation. Although there were attempts in the 1980s to link the struggle against colonialism with the struggle against capitalist exploitation, the predominant ideology was that of national liberation. As a result, there was a limited class-consciousness among Namibian workers and even union leaders, which allowed SWAPO to introduce a non-racial but still capitalist social order after independence with little resistance from the labour movement.

On the other hand, the NUNW and its affiliates still experience high levels of socio-economic inequality and are confronted by dissatisfaction (at shop floor level) with the slow pace of social change in Namibia since independence. The continued inequalities are reflected not only in the skewed salary structures favouring management in the public service, parastatals and private companies, but also in the highly uneven distribution of national resources. As a result, trade unions have demanded policies that will eradicate these inequalities, such as an effective land reform policy and the introduction of minimum wages for vulnerable workers in the farm and domestic workers' sectors. Trade unions are thus caught in a dilemma of loyalty to the ruling party (which is common among union leaders and workers alike) and dissatisfaction with the slow process of social change. Although few of the unions' demands for redistributive measures have been met, the majority of NUNW affiliates still believe that a continued affiliation to SWAPO will be the best vehicle for influencing broader socio-economic policies in favour of workers.

The question of defining the labour movement's political role and an appropriate strategy to influence socio-economic policies will certainly be a key challenge for the years to come. There is no doubt that a progressive labour movement has to be political by nature and deal with socio-economic issues beyond the workplace. However, the NUNW will have to show how its present affiliation helps the federation to advance the interests of its constituency. The labour movement will have to develop an understanding of its particular class base and define its role in terms of serving the specific interests of that social class. The NUNW will also have to consider that trade union unity will be an impossible goal for as long as it maintains its party political affiliation.

With every election since independence, several trade unionists from the NUNW and its affiliates have entered Parliament though there is little evidence that their presence has influenced policies in favour of workers. Once in Parliament (or Cabinet), they are accountable to the party and bound by government policy. SWAPO's overall direction has long departed from the socialist agenda it proclaimed in the late 1970s and 1980s. Few of the trade unionists who entered Parliament have dared to publicly oppose government plans – one exception being the former general secretary of the Namibia Public Workers Union (NAPWU), Peter Iilonga, who recently opposed the government's privatisation initiatives in Parliament. Overall, the former labour leaders have had to adapt to government policies and trade unions have had little success in shaping economic policies as will be demonstrated below.

Introducing social partnership

A major challenge confronting the NUNW after independence was to adapt to a new role within the framework of a tripartite dialogue as set out by government. Once in office, the SWAPO government embarked upon a path of reforming Namibia's colonial labour relations' system. The overall aim was to move towards a new system of 'social partnership', governed by the Labour Act which was passed in 1992. Tripartite consultations and collective bargaining were seen as critical for the implementation of this new labour dispensation. The government envisaged an improvement in the living and working conditions of Namibian workers brought about by a combination of effective economic policies and successful trade union engagement with the private sector. The government defined its own role merely as that of 'referee', trying to create a level (and enabling) playing field for collective bargaining between business and labour.

However, the consultative process leading to the formulation of the Labour Act was driven by government as the dominant partner, who decided upon the scope of the consultations. Unlike in a corporatist, institutionalised arrangement wherein capital, labour and state are jointly formulating socio-economic policies (Sycholt and Klerck 1997:88), social partnership in Namibia does not usually take the form of a joint decision-making process. In the process of drafting the Labour Act of 1992, government consulted with labour and capital but reserved the right to take the final decision without trying to achieve consensus with the social partners.

The Labour Act constituted a significant improvement compared with the previous colonial labour legislation. It extended its coverage to all workers, including domestic workers, farm workers and the public services. The new law encouraged collective bargaining, entrenched basic workers' and trade union rights, set out the procedures for legal strikes and provided protection against unfair labour practices (Bauer 1993:11). However, the Act fell short of some of the expectations of trade unions who felt that employers had unduly influenced the law through 'behind the scenes' lobbying. The Act did not make provision for minimum wages (as SWAPO had promised in its 1989 election manifesto) and it did not guarantee paid maternity leave. Payment during maternity leave was only introduced with the Social Security Act of 1996. Other key demands of the NUNW that were not accommodated in the Labour Act were the 40-hour working week, and 21 working days annual leave for all workers (Jauch 1996:91).

Overall the new act constituted a significant improvement for labour, but it also served to reduce worker militancy by shifting the emphasis away from workplace struggles to negotiations between union leaders and management. Bargaining issues in Namibia were (and still are) narrowly defined and usually deal with conditions of employment only (Klerck and Murray 1997:247). The trade unions' main function was thus narrowed to being the representative of workers in a tripartite arrangement. While this enabled trade unions to win improved working conditions in well-organised sectors like mining, fishing and the public service, collective bargaining remained meaningless for farm and domestic workers. The ongoing adversarial nature of labour relations, coupled with racial polarisation at many workplaces and huge wage gaps, are further obstacles to the notion of social partnership.

Against the background of huge imbalances in terms of economic power between capital and labour, the state's chosen role as 'neutral referee' and creator of an enabling environment for collective bargaining, effectively benefited business interests. Business representatives went as far as describing worker militancy as an obstacle to job creation and economic development. Such sentiments were even echoed by some government officials and politicians, which was just one indication that the close political ties between labour and SWAPO did not prevent the entrenchment of a pro-capitalist state after independence. This process was also assisted by the lack of political clarity on the side of trade unions regarding the development of a different social order after independence. Notions of worker democracy, worker control and social transformation had just emerged in the late 1980s but had not been developed into a coherent concept within the labour movement at the time of independence.

Despite the broad acceptance of social partnership by the government, labour and business, there are limitations to what this concept can achieve under the current conditions. Collective bargaining and tripartite consultations alone will not be able to address the question of Namibia's socio-economic inequalities that are among the highest in the world. Trade unions are thus faced with the task of promoting worker participation in economic and social decision-making as well as developing broader policy proposals to bring about socio-economic transformation. Increased 'goodwill' and a change of attitude on the side of business towards labour will be a necessary but, on its own, insufficient precondition for Namibian workers to become partners in a tripartite arrangement. Effective measures of redistribution to reduce income gaps and to spread resources more evenly will be preconditions for long-term social partnership arrangements. At present, the prospects for such partnerships are bleak as redistributive policies were abandoned in favour of 'market-related' wage and economic policies.

Conservative economic policies

The biggest challenge facing labour after independence was to define an effective strategy of influencing broader socio-economic policies in favour of its working class base. This task proved extremely difficult in the face of an onslaught by the neo-liberal ideology that was usually portrayed as the only practical policy option for Namibia and other countries in the region. Klerck accurately described governments' response to globalisation as: "an open-ended encouragement of foreign investment; the marital stance towards the International Monetary Fund (IMF) and World Bank; the confinement of social transformation to an extension of representative institutions; a tendency to reduce black empowerment to increasing the black entrepreneurial classes; and a failure to conceive of an economic policy that departs in substance from that of the colonial powers" (1997:364).

IMF and World Bank advisors have become regular visitors to Namibia and 'assisted' with the country's public expenditure review and with 'training' of high ranking staff members of economic government institutions. Local economists by and large seem to be trapped in the neo-liberal dogma and continue promoting the very policies (e.g. structural adjustment programmes) that have caused severe social hardship in other (SADC) countries. The Namibian government increasingly slides towards neo-liberal policies as manifested, for example, by the introduction of Export Processing Zones (EPZs) and privatisation programmes. Opposition to such policies by the labour movement is often countered by accusations that trade unions are still living in the (ideological) past and are obstacles to economic growth and job creation. In the absence of a comprehensive alternative development strategy by labour, trade unions were forced on the defensive on several occasions and found themselves sidelined from economic policy formulation.

The developments surrounding the establishment of Export Processing Zones (EPZs) in Namibia are a case in point. The NUNW opposed the initial EPZ Act of 1995, which was passed by Parliament without any consultation of trade unions and went as far as 'freeing' investors from the provisions of the Labour Act. The NUNW saw this as a violation of both the ILO convention and Namibia's constitution, and instructed its lawyers to challenge the constitutionality of the EPZ Act in court. However, during a high level meeting between the government, SWAPO and the NUNW in August 1995, a compromise was reached. It stipulated that the Labour Act would apply in the EPZs, but that strikes and lockouts would be outlawed for a period of five years.

Five years on, the no-strike clause is now being reviewed. The NUNW still insists that EPZ workers must have the right to strike, but does not systematically challenge the broader negative implications of the EPZ policy. A recent study carried out by the Labour Resource and Research Institute (LaRRI) – found that the EPZ programme has fallen far short of government's expectations and that the programme's costs by far outweigh its benefits. This study received significant public and media attention but neither the NUNW nor the other trade union federations have taken up the issue and challenged the policy as a whole. They confined themselves narrowly to the debate over the right to strike.

This exemplifies the current weakness of labour to systematically challenge conservative policies and to develop coherent policy alternatives. The same can also be observed in the debate surrounding privatisation and commercialisation, which is being implemented by government despite opposition by the trade union federations NUNW and NAFTU.

Defining a new role

The government's vision of trade unions becoming a social partner within a tripartite arrangement is just one of the options open to the Namibian labour movement. Unions could concentrate on their core functions of representing members at the workplace, of collective bargaining and of playing a role at tripartite fora such as the Labour Advisory Council, the Vocational Training Board and others. However, trade unions will have to expand their activities if they wish to influence broader policies, to promote the specific class interests of their constituency and to contribute towards building a more egalitarian society. Playing such a role will require a strengthening of unions' capacity to carry out research on socio-economic policy issues from a labour perspective. Union will also have to develop education programmes for workers, shop stewards, and union leaders at various levels on social, economic, and political issues, including the effects of globalisation and how this process can be confronted. Such programmes are essential to ensure worker participation in policy debates with a view of building labour's positions based on the interests of its members. Broadening policy debates is also critical to ensure that union leaders operate on the basis of mandates from their constituency and that union policies enjoy the full backing of the membership.

At the beginning of 1998, the labour movement established the Labour Resource and Research Institute (LaRRI) to meet this challenge. With LaRRIs assistance, trade unions have now incorporated issues such as globalisation and labour's responses into their education programmes. For the first time in Namibia, such topics were taken out of the realm of (mostly neo-liberal) 'experts' who have so far dominated Namibia's economic policy debates. Although such programmes constitute merely a starting point, they will be critical in preparing the ground for a new discourse on policy alternatives and development strategies. It will be equally important for Namibian unions to work closely with other progressive unions and NGOs in the region and beyond on the question of building alternatives to the neo-liberal agenda.

Conclusion

The Namibian labour movement underwent significant changes during the first decade of Namibia's independence. The NUNW and its affiliates, in particular, had to shift from political mobilisation that dominated the unions' activities in the run-up to the independence elections in 1989, to a process of engagement with government and business under a new tripartite arrangement. In the absence of sufficient internal capacity to develop an alternative development framework that would benefit labour's working class constituency, trade unions by and large accepted a more confined role within tripartite arrangements. They now serve on fora like the Labour Advisory Council, the Vocational Training Board and the President's Economic Advisory Council with the aim of influencing policy decisions in favour of workers. Such participation is however, narrowly confined in terms of its scope and offers no possibility of promoting a broader agenda for fundamental change in the socio-economic decision-making process.

Although it can be argued that tripartite participation as a strategic option does not necessarily conflict with the larger goal of bringing about social transformation, collective bargaining and tripartite consultations alone are certainly insufficient to address Namibia's huge socio-economic inequalities. In order to become an engine of social change, trade unions will have to deepen their roots in Namibia's working class constituencies and become the genuine workers' voice on issues beyond the workplace. Secondly, the labour movement will need to develop effective strategies for influencing policies, particularly in the economic arena which is dominated by the neo-liberal line of thought.

Despite its current weaknesses, the Namibian labour movement still has the potential to become (once again) a key organisation in the quest for socio-economic justice. The labour relation survey of 1995/96 revealed "the deeply held belief of NUNW members in the principles of rank-and-file democracy and their willingness to engage in struggle if their needs are not met" (Klerck 1997:363). Trade unions have structures (albeit sometimes weak) all over the country and a significant membership base unmatched by any other organisation in Namibia. Provided they can strengthen their internal capacity and achieve the level of rootedness in their working class constituency that they had in the late 1980s, the labour movement can become the driving force for more fundamental socio-economic social change. This will also require that trade unions intensify and concretise their links with other progressive organisations that represent socially disadvantaged groups. An example of such a link was the alliance formed between the NUNW, the Namibia NGO Forum (NANGOF) and the (communal) Namibia National Farmers Union (NNFU) around the slow process of land reform. The three organisations presented a joint petition to government on May Day 1999 demanding a faster and more effective programme of land redistribution.

Namibia's trade unions face two possible scenarios today. Provided they can meet the challenges outlined above and redefine their role as 'struggle organisations' with a specific class base and a strategic agenda, they are likely to play a central role in the fight for the interests of Namibia's disadvantaged majority. Failure to seize this opportunity could result in Namibian unions gradually losing their mass base while union leaders are being absorbed with bargaining issues, union investments and tripartite participation without addressing (or challenging) the fundamental socio-economic structures that uphold the continued skewed distribution of wealth and income.

Bibliography

Bauer, GM 1993. Defining a role: trade unions in Namibia. In: Southern Africa Report vol.8, no.5, pp.8-11

Bauer, GM 1994. The labour movement and prospects for democracy in Namibia. PhD thesis. University of Wisconsin: Madison

Bauer, GM 1997. Labour relations in occupied Namibia. In: Klerck, G et al. (eds.). Continuity and change: labour relations in independent Namibia. Windhoek: Gamsberg Macmillan

Hansohm, D / Presland, C 1997. Poverty and policy in Namibia. Paper presented at a workshop on the role of the state in poverty alleviation. Gaborone, Botswana, October 1997

Jauch, H 1996. Tension grows: labour relations in Namibia. In: South African Labour Bulletin vol.20, no.4, pp.90-93

Klerck, G / Murray, A / Sycholt, M 1997. Continuity and change: labour relations in independent Namibia. Windhoek: Gamsberg Macmillan

Klerck, G 1997. The prospects for radical social transformation. In: Klerck, G et al. (eds.) 1997

Klerck, G / Sycholt, M 1997. The state and labour relations: walking the tightrope between corporatism and neo-liberalism. In: Klerck, G et al. (eds.) 1997

Labour Resource and Research Institute (LaRRI) 1999. Understanding the past and present – mapping the future: the National Union of Namibian Workers (NUNW) facing the 21st century. Windhoek: LaRRI

Mbuende, K 1986. Namibia, the broken shield: anatomy of imperialism and revolution. Malmoe, Sweden: Liber

Ministry of Labour 1998. The Namibian labour force survey 1997: an interim report of analysis. Windhoek: Ministry of Labour and National Planning Commission

Murray, A / Wood, G 1997. The Namibian trade union movement: trends, practices and shop floor perception. In: Klerck, G et al. (eds.) 1997

Peltola, P 1995. The lost May Day: Namibian workers struggle for independence. Helsinki: The Finnish Anthropological Society in association with the Nordic Africa Institute

LABOUR MIGRATION IN NAMIBIA – GENDER ASPECTS

Volker Winterfeldt

To start with a statement which introduces the broader sociological setting for the topic: labour migration in Namibia reflects a distinct gender pattern in the social division of labour.

Or, to formulate a slogan: men migrate, women don't.

However, such a statement is in fact inaccurate, when we focus mainly on the last decade. A superficial look at Windhoek's central and north-western Katutura districts already explains why. These suburbs of the capital are the main arrival points of Namibia's current migrants. Women's share in this migration is considerable. They account for nearly half of the total residents of these areas[1]. It is evident that such locations cannot be compared with the places of residence of earlier contract workers. Thirty years ago, labourers within the Contract Labour System were accommodated in male compounds[2].

So, from a historical angle, the slogan has to be reformulated: men migrated, women didn't.

In the colonial past, women were prevented from leaving the rural economy by the rules governing the recruitment of migrant labourers. Today, with freedom of movement, women increasingly migrate in search of a wage income. The major barriers to female migration were removed in 1972. At that time the institutionalised labour recruitment system was dissolved. The Bantustan governments, mainly the Ovamboland government, were to take over recruitment by setting up and running Labour Bureaux[3]. Also, the pass laws were repealed[4]. However, women still migrate to a lesser extent. Statistically, labour migration remains largely a male domain.

With that, the difference between the historical forms of labour migration in South West Africa and its current features in Namibia is marked. The historical background will be discussed here, given its importance as a reference point for contemporary migration. To briefly outline the contents of the article:

labour migration
- its historical background
  - contracting labour as a basic trait of German colonisation
  - later, under South African rule, the formation of the institutionalised Contract Labour System based on the migration of male workers,

---

[1] 1995 figures – for Central Katutura (northern enumeration areas of the 1995 survey): females 47,6% of the population; for the north-western areas – 42,2%. Municipality of Windhoek; 1995 Residents Survey Report ,vol.1: p.27

[2] This only applies to the workers recruited from outside the Police Zone comprising the central and southern regions accessible through main roads or the railway trunk lines, excluding the northern regions of the Kavango, Caprivi, Kaokoland and the Ovambo regions. Within the area formerly under formal jurisdiction and police administration of the German colonial regime, Nama, Herero, Damara and Rehobother inhabitants had (conditional) access to the urban areas where they could live with their families. Peltola 1995:73.

[3] Cronje 1979:87

[4] Introduced by Native Administration Proclamation No.11 of 1922, repealed by Proclamation No.83 of 1972. Gebhardt 1980:33, 41

- segregated from female population outside the Police Zone
- the current situation, empirically illustrating the following aspects closely linked to urbanisation:
  - who migrates (sex and age distribution)?
  - where from, where to (ethnic origin, destination)?
  - for how long do people migrate?
  - why do people migrate?
  - how extensive are migratory movements amongst Namibian populations?
- cultural effects (migration situating men and women, at times of their biography at least, in different lifeworlds: the westernised, urban environment and the indigenous rural setting, the consumer-oriented world of 'modern' wage labour and the subsistence-oriented, 'traditional' peasant world; contradictory structural change resulting from this)
- economic effects (labour migration, at times, places men and women in two different economic worlds; it attracts the one to the capitalist mode of production and confines the other to the subsistence economy; this creates a framework of transition which, from a sociological perspective, reveals traits typical of an economic structure of underdevelopment)
- social effects (particularly looking at the impact on family structures in Namibia)
- exacerbation of gender inequalities due to labour migration (a new gender division of labour, instigated by modern migration, transferring to women, and children, the tasks formerly attributed to the male peasant; forcing women also to take over the duties and responsibilities of husbands and fathers, but without vesting them with independence and supremacy over the household, since they usually remain subject to other male relatives within the multigenerational family)
- the spread of the AIDS epidemic in Namibia as an effect also of labour migration
- class structural background of labour migration, touching on two aspects:
  - which men/women are affected by labour migration?
  - does labour migration irrevocably create a modern wage labouring class?

Labour migration in the colonial eras

Contract labour: the decades under German rule

Whenever it comes to the processes of migration and urbanisation, both push and pull factors are part of the pattern of analysis. This applies also to the Namibian case. However, in this particular instance, a simple question has to be asked at the outset: why did both the German and the South African colonial regimes resort specifically to the limited-period, contract form of wage labour?

Tentatively, an answer: the German protectorate, always confronted with a shortage of labour, introduced the contract form as a coercive means of extending the periods of service of indigenous labourers. Furthermore, the contract served the purpose of policing the movements of migrants from the 'reserves' where they were forced to live. The South African mandate, on the other hand, used the contract as a format for limiting employment periods, in its endeavour to control the structural development of an indigenous labouring class which in the long run may have presented a political threat to the stability of the colonial regime.

Responding to the needs of the colonial accumulation process, labour migration reflected the political determination of an economy displaying a hybrid structure. The colonial economy combined the newly introduced Western, capitalist mode of production, based on wage labour, and the customary African subsistence activities, based on family labour. From the very beginning, the labour market was intensely governed by political means. Economic mechanisms alone did not generate the instruments to cope with a situation characterised by the confrontation of utterly different economic cultures and lifeworlds, and, of greatest importance, by utter power differentials. Over long periods, the capitalist demand for labour exceeded supply from the subsistence sector. Therefore, the colonial administration undertook it to ensure, organise and regulate the flow of labour power.

But we have to distinguish between different forms of migration corresponding to the two colonial epochs. The German administration, over three decades, never really managed to solve to its satisfaction what became the colonial labour question. It relied mainly on the Nama, Damara, Herero and Rehobother labour force recruited from the populations within the Police Zone. The Ovambo reservoir of labour in practice remained of marginal numerical significance, though German policies from 1905 onwards attached great importance to it. Until the middle of the 1920s, the Ovambo peasants got their way, preferring to leave their homesteads for short periods only, following the seasonal rhythms of their agriculture[5]. It was mainly from the 1940s that labour migration became a dominating feature in every male Ovambo peasant's life.

Moreover, the difference in the structure of migration also shows in the gender patterns. As a rule, German settler farmers relied on female personnel recruited mainly from the Herero community, but not excluding Nama and Damara workers, attending to domestic chores and milking, the latter being an assignment culturally despised by Herero men. Thus, until the end of German rule, women represented a relatively significant portion of wage labour. After World War I, complaints about their alleged unreliability and their "strong contamination with sexual diseases" led to their gradual replacement with Ovambo picaninnies, young men under the age

---

[5] In the beginning, the Ovambo labourers as well as their kings imposed their will limiting contracts to a six-month-term. Only under South African rule, with Master and Servants Act, Proclamation No.34 of 1920, was the duration of a single contract extended to a sojourn in the south of 12 to 18 months at a time. After a three months interval spent in Ovamboland, a new contract could ensue, up to a maximum of five years. Peltola 1995:64. Tötemeyer mentions that the traditional authorities were anxious to see these limitations enforced, because "too long a sojourn outside the country is apt to (...) disrupt the traditional values." Tötemeyer 1978:156

of sixteen[6]. Both elements – administrative restrictions and the cultural reluctance of Ovambo women to leave their homesteads – changed the gender picture of migration under South African rule. Labour migration became an exclusively male domain.

As far as the pull factors are concerned, historical research points out influences connected with the capitalist patterns of production emerging in the Southern Zone. Patricia Hayes identifies merchant and mining capital as the two initial economic agents of change attracting labour[7]. Dierks and Banghart mention that large-scale employment had already started in the 1840s with the discovery of offshore guano deposits on some small northern coast islands[8]. Rädel and Peltola refer to the early, short-lived copper mining ventures of the late 1850s in the central region, employing mainly Herero labourers[9].

As far as the push factors are concerned, the internal reasons accounting for the willingness to migrate vary according to the origin of the migrant groups. During German rule, the ethnic groups within the Police Zone had by conquest been deprived of land and livestock as their principal means of subsistence. Had this not sufficed, colonial taxation was intended to do the rest. The German colonial administration had introduced grazing and dog taxes. Moreover, its fiscal policy demanded considerable charges from the indigenous mining and metal work industries. The colonial regime had expropriated and displaced most of the indigenous Nama, Herero and Damara people[10]. It had even forced those who had survived the earlier wars of resistance into concentration camps and, from there, the prisoners of war went straight into dependent labour.

There was no alternative to wage labour. The deliberate destruction of their customary subsistence mode of production forced the peasants from the Police Zone into dependence on the emerging capitalist mode of production. Their situation did not change under South African domination. The creation of new reserves and the policy of strict ethnic segregation only aggravated the conditions of survival[11].

On the other hand, the picture within Ovambo societies differs somewhat. The Ovambo kingdoms and chieftaincies were never directly subjected to German colonial rule. Nevertheless, the Ovambo population also migrated on its own initiative. A whole set of internal socio-economic constraints and cultural reasons played a role. Taxation, to anticipate the argument, was not one of them. The Ovambo regions south of the Portuguese-Angolan border had only been administratively incorporated into South West Africa in 1915, when the South African

---

[6] Rädel 1947:262-266
[7] Hayes 1992:i
[8] Dierks 1999:9, 11; Banghart 1969:19
[9] In the Rehoboth, Kuiseb and Khomas areas. Rädel 1947:11-12. Matchless Mine, belonging to the Cape-English Walfish Bay Mining Company, exploiting copper deposits west of Windhoek, and also Bethany. Peltola 1995:56
[10] By Imperial Regulations of the years 1905 to 1907. Cf. Amoo's account (2001):90 and footnotes 8, 9, 10
[11] Rädel, in his meticulous economic analysis of South West Africa, dedicates an interesting section to the statistical examination of the question whether the reserves were suitable for subsistence. He comes to the conclusion that the reserves were designed in line with the 'labour question', resulting in an "indirect constraint to wage labour". Rädel:219

military took over the territory previously under German rule. Previously, the area had not generally been subjected to Portuguese domination. Thus, in contrast with the Southern (or Police) Zone of colonial rule, the historical Ovambo polities did not experience any colonial taxation or expropriation policies forcing peasants to migrate in search of alternative means of survival. However, an increasing amount of payments of tributes in kind had been exacted by their own Ovambo chiefs and nobility.

Later, when the South African administration introduced grazing taxes in the newly created reserves, this provision only applied to the Police Zone[12]. Whatever dramatic impact these policies had had on those concerned, they did not directly affect the large Ovambo population. Only under the South African regime were they to form the bulk of migrant wage labourers. As a result, the hypothesis that labour migration in general had been forced upon the Ovambo population by colonial taxation turns out to be a widespread simplification[13].

Research indicates that socio-economic change and environmental impacts historically combined to a process of ongoing pauperisation of the Ovambo peasantry. Moorsom depicts the internal realignment of the tributary Ovambo polity. Consequently, we observe the exacerbation of class divisions between chief/king, nobility (lenga) and the peasantry. This was revealed in an increasing taxation in cattle, starting with the 1870s[14]. Very likely, the new greed of the élites, costly as it was, was made possible by the availability of sophisticated arms imported into the region by European traders. We view an internal class polarisation, based on the erosion of peasant subsistence levels. This becomes one of several factors driving peasants to migrate and look for paid labour. Historically, this process seems to have reached a significant stage before the Ovambo economies were hit in

---

[12] Rädel 1947:197

[13] See Kauluma, Hishongwa and others. The actual evidence: the German colonial administration had introduced a dog tax in SWA (Police Zone only) by Ordinance on the 23.2.1907. The South African military administration repealed the ordinance by Dog Tax Proclamation No.1 of 1917. The repeal, in turn, was repealed in 1921 by Proclamation No.16 ordering dog taxation; the latter was withdrawn in 1927 by Ordinance No.14, after having already in 1922 (by Dog Tax Reduction Proclamation No.6) been reduced to half of the rates stipulated the previous year. Moreover, if one follows Gottschalk's assertion, the dog tax aimed at reducing the number of hunting dogs of hunter – pastoralist ethnic groups mainly, in order to affect their livelihood and force them into migrant labour (Gottschalk 1978:79).The only effective legal prescription could have been in 1929 Ovamboland Affairs Proclamation No.27. After constituting Ovamboland as a reserve (previously a magisterial district), it provided in principle for the imposition of levies on the (male) population, understood as an instrument motivating workers to migrate. But at that time the demand for labour dropped sharply since the mining sector in southern Africa was heavily affected by the global depression. Therefore, this Proclamation was never really enforced. Actually, recruitment from Ovamboland was stopped at the end of the year 1931 and prohibited in July 1932, to be resumed only in June 1934 (Rädel 1947:310-311). Peltola states that, similarly, "in 1935 a bill establishing a tax payable in grain could not be put in practice." Peltola 1995:67-68. As a matter of fact, taxation did play a role as an incentive to migration. But this was in the early period of colonialism, when the Ovambo kingdoms were still independent. Taxation then originated from the internal demand, from the Ovambo rulers themselves. Siiskonen 1990:233. On the critique of the assertion of taxation as a motive force also see Banghart 1969:91.

[14] The tributary state shows a growing need for additional sources of income, due to the increasing power of the lenga, asking a larger share in the appropriation of peasant surplus, once the nobility had been conferred the task of taxation of the peasantry. Moorsom 1989:84. Also, the impact of colonial trade began to be felt. Both kings and élites demanded cattle from the peasant in order to buy arms form the colonial traders, partly to back their raiding activities, partly to satisfy the increasing luxurious propensity for game hunting which, in fact, lead almost to the extinction of game in the northern expanses. Peltola 1995:69-70. Siiskonen adds that, historically, the dwindling of raids into neighbouring Ovambo communities, due to the declining productivity of subsistence economy, deprived the Ovambo kings of a traditional source of income. Taxation of migrants provided them with an alternative source of income. Siiskonen 1990:233-234

1897 by the devastating rinderpest, followed by four years of drought from 1900 to 1903, the locust and caterpillar plagues of 1907 and 1914, the famines of the years 1908 and 1911, and the flood of 1909. These adverse natural phenomena, obviously, added to the already severe economic deterioration[15]. They became the other factors behind migratory movements.

Hayes also brings the expectations of lineage into play. Young Ovambo men were expected to contribute to the homestead's cattle resources. Such a social demand, too, was instrumental in creating a cultural 'climate' conducive to migration[16]. In fact, asking the question, Who migrated from Ovamboland? contemporary travel diaries show that migrants mostly were unmarried younger men, 'sons of poor people'[17]. These "men without cattle"[18] usually migrated in comparatively large groups. Pre-colonial customs of gender division of labour within the family shaped such migratory patterns. Due to intensified tributary demands, peasants were increasingly stripped of cattle. This exclusively concerned the males, whereas the millet production organised by the female members of the community was largely left untouched[19] by the described processes of economic deterioration. Thus, labour migration remained a male preserve, since men fell short of their contribution to the household's livelihood. In addition, as Peltola points out, the matrilineal kinship structure contributed towards men's readiness to leave the intimacy of the family behind.

In such a way, the historical forms of gender division of labour provided not only the material, but also the cultural background for men's propensity to migrate. The loss of prestige connected with the diminution of cattle stock could be counteracted by wage labour, a fact becoming of utmost importance after the rinderpest of 1897. Also, young men by social custom possessed a migrational experience which was not open to women. Raiding and transhumance stand for this gender culture in terms of an existing male group solidarity which allowed men to tackle the considerable hardships of migration[20]. Moreover, the traditional salt-fetching journey to the Etosha Pan that had always been considered an initiation rite, began to be replaced by the journey to the south for labour purposes. Enduring the hardships of migration initiated an Ovambo youth into manhood[21]. But the "idea of manliness"[22] was also fed by the attractions of a radically new cultural (and consumerist) world.

Both these elements also influenced women's attitudes with respect to marriage. A migrant worker was seen as a more suitable candidate, not only having proven his ability to earn his living in a foreign world[23], but also superior in his

---

[15] Moorsom 1989:65 et passim
[16] Hayes 1992:150
[17] Hayes 1992:149-150, 275
[18] Clarence-Smith / Moorsom 1975:376
[19] Clarence-Smith / Moorsom 1975:376. Siiskonen 1990:234-235
[20] Moorsom 1989:90-91
[21] Peltola 1995:72
[22] Tötemeyer 1978:154. See also: Voipio 1972:xv-xvi
[23] Tötemeyer 1978:167

cultural horizon. Culture also accounted for women's disinterest in engaging in migration. Besides this, and perhaps even more significant, the migration of Ovambo women was actively prevented. Ironically, colonial and traditional authorities found themselves in rare unanimity in their recourse to patriarchal morals. The Regional Commissioner for Ovamboland suggested alleged 'immoral effects' in 1918, when Ovamboland already was under South African domination. On the Ovambo side, the male leaders and family heads combined in what Hayes terms "a discourse of responsible patriarchy (...) in concern over social disintegration"[24].

During the German period, the cultural values and economic interests of the northern migrants coming from and returning to the agricultural subsistence economy seem to have prevailed. Unlike the migrants from the reserves within the Police Zone, Ovambo migration maintained a certain level of independence. Notwithstanding all legislative and executive efforts, colonial policies fell short of effectively enforcing a strict regulation of the circulation of labour adequately serving the interests of the capitalist accumulation process. Neither in the number of workers, nor the duration of contracts, nor in the direction of workers to specific employers did they fully control the northern labour supply. But they did dispose of the labour reservoir of the other ethnic groups of the protectorate.

Inherently, these statements indicate the initial dual geographical roots of migrant labour. Until the replacement of the German administration in the course of World War I, the absolute majority of the labour force was recruited from the Herero, Damara and Nama reserves and, to a lesser extent, from the Rehoboth Basters, the Coloureds and the San populations. The other significant source of migrant labourers is found in the northern expanses of Namibia, mainly in the flood-plain areas of the southern chieftaincies/kingdoms of the historical Ovambo territories. Their proportion was destined to rise sharply during the following 75 years.

German demand for labour constantly exceeded supply from the colonial core territory[25]. Moreover, inside the Police Zone, farming interests and the demand for domestic labour traditionally took priority in terms of supply of local labour from the Southern Zone. Thus the German administration had to look for new sources and, as a policy, directed mining and construction labour demand to Ovamboland[26].

Only the last five years of German rule saw the proportion of Ovambo migrants rising. Statistical evidence for the years 1911 and 1913 indicates the dominance of the Southern Zone ethnic groups. Of a registered non-European male work force of 20 033 in 1911 in the Police Zone, 30,2% were Herero men, 24,2% Damara, 21,5% Nama, 4,7% San, and 2,4% Baster and Coloureds. They made up for 83% of the whole male work force, whereas the proportion of Ovambo workers amounted to 17%. For the year 1913, the whole male work force was

---

[24] Hayes 1992:288-289
[25] Hayes 1992:ii. Moorsom sees labour shortage as a "chronic" or "endemic" feature of South West African economy (1977:55)
[26] Clarence-Smith / Moorsom 1975:378

22 082: 31% Herero, 22,4% Damara, 15,4% Nama, 4,5% San, 1,7% Basters and Coloureds, amounting to 75% of the whole African labour force within the Police Zone. The proportion of Ovambo workers had by then risen to 25%[27].

It is interesting to note the sectoral distribution of the different ethnic groups. German employers, including the colonial state, evidently followed a kind of 'tribal' pattern separating Ovambo workers from labourers of other ethnic origin. They employed the 'internal' migrants mainly on farms and for domestic service, as well as in inferior positions of public works and services. Ovambo migrants were concentrated mainly in the secondary sector, i.e. mining. In fact, an ordinance of the year 1913 'reserved' Ovambo labourers exclusively for railways and mines – the discovery of the first diamonds in 1908 made itself felt[28]. In 1913, of 12 540 farm and domestic workers, 89,8% were 'internal' migrants, 4,8% Ovambo migrants, and the remaining 5,8% were of non-Namibian African origin (from the Cape and from other German 'territories' on the continent). Of the 2 259 transport, construction, etc. workers in public service, 90,8% were 'internal' migrants, 6,1% Ovambos and 3,1% non-Namibian Africans. On the other hand, of the 9 532 indigenous workers of the secondary sector, the Ovambo migrant formed the majority, amounting to 48,1%, as compared with 31,3% 'internal' and 20,6% of non-Namibian African migrants[29].

The first Ovambo contract workers were signed on in the Police Zone as early as 1891[30]. In January 1905, a representative of the German administration negotiated terms of recruitment of labour with the Ovambo kings, backed by the Finnish missionary Rautanen[31]. But for as long as the military operations of the extermination war lasted, recruitment agents were not allowed into the Ovambo regions without the permission of the governor, in order not to risk the spark of revolt within the Police Zone spreading to the populous Ovambo territories. Recruitment was limited to the Okaukuejo Fort station. Only in 1908, when official treaties were concluded subjecting the Ovambo chiefs/kings administratively to the Schutzgebiet, colonial authorities in exchange for the 'protection' offered by the German Reich were granted labour recruiting rights[32] – though by then the end of their colonial era was imminent.

The provision of labour opened a new source of income to the traditional authorities in the northern kingdoms. Historical evidence shows that the kings exacted 'gifts' from the contract returnee, often demanding a cow[33] – presumably on the basis of strong cultural obligations which the peasant felt. The Ovambo kings as well as the peasants insisted on short-term contracts not exceeding six

---

[27] Rädel 1947:93-94. No figures available for female labour force
[28] Rädel 1947:80-81. Banghart 1969:27-28, 31
[29] Rädel 1947:97-98
[30] Tötemeyer 1978:154. Relying on official annual reports, Rädel mentions a first contingent of 42 Ovambo workers employed by the Swakopmund railway administration only in 1899. But with reference to oral information he adds that in all probability Ovambo workers had already been employed by the South West Africa Company in the Otavi copper mining works (1947:52).
[31] Rädel 1947:84. Clarence-Smith / Moorsom 1975:376. Tötemeyer 1978:41
[32] Rädel 1947:35-36
[33] Moorsom 1989:84, 90

months. Ovambo migrant labour under German rule succeeded in imposing contractual terms allowing the temporary wage workers to return home in due time for the agricultural season. The cycles of peasant production, at this stage, dictated the terms of contract. The German economy never managed to subordinate Ovambo migrants to the longer-term exigencies of capitalist production[34]. Systematic recruitment on a larger scale in the Ovambo regions only started at the end of the extermination wars against the Nama and Herero populations.

From the outset, the recruitment of labourers was heavily regulated, and the 'labour question' (as demand for labour was judged from the colonial masters' perspective) became linked with the 'land question'. The latter arose from the contradictions within the early colonial policy. The Kaiserreich – principally its chancellor Bismarck – had long remained undecided on the dilemma as to whether to take the colonial initiative and dare to become an imperial power, or to adopt a wait-and-see policy, supporting the activities of a number of private entrepreneurs and soldiers of fortune like Lüderitz. Once the decision had been taken, in order to generate at least some public income, the colonial authorities started ceding large areas of the territory to concessionary companies. Hoping particularly for mining riches, the concessionaires at the turn of the 19th century already owned some 295 000 km^2 to which the indigenous population was denied legitimate access. Initially, an imperial ordinance of 1 October 1888 had tried to put a stop to further expropriation of 'tribal' land through seizure and fraud from individual farmers and the concessionary companies[35].

Ten years later, on 10 April 1898, the administration laid the essential foundation stone for the expropriation of the indigenous societies within the Police Zone. It issued a law creating 'unalienable reserves' for the African populations. On the one hand, the concessionaires' expansion was thereby cut down to size; on the other hand, the various ethnic groups – the Namas in the south and the Rehobother Basters and Hereros in the centre – were once and for all confined to those small areas to which they had been driven as a result of colonisation. Until then, only the Ovambo societies had not yet suffered any serious territorial interference. Thus, in 1903, of the Namibian territory of 834 000 km^2, only 336 000 km^2 were declared 'native land'. The concessionary territory, plus another 204 000 km^2 defined as crown land together with a minor portion of private 'white' farm land made up for 60% of the whole country[36].

The Herero and Nama revolts further aggravated this state of affairs. According to the martial law of the victorious power, these ethnic groups had forfeited their rights to land altogether. Their territories were transformed into colonial crown land[37]. As a solution to the 'labour question', the German authorities of

---

[34] Moorsom 1976:109,113-114
[35] The special land and mining rights of the Concessions Companies were only cancelled by Proclamation No.59 of 1920 under South African rule. Banghart 1969:34
[36] Rädel 1947:30-31, 38-40
[37] By ordinances of 26.12.1905, 23.3.1906 and 8.5.1907. Together with the land bought in the following years from the concessionary companies, in 1910 crown land amounted to 452 000, 'native' areas to 80 000, concessionary land to 189 000 and commercial farm land to 108 000 square kilometres. Rädel 1947:55, 58

South West Africa (SWA) in 1906 distributed some 15 000 prisoners of war in forced labour amongst all sorts of employers[38]. A colonial ordinance dated 25 January 1906 for the first time outlined the framework for the recruitment and the modalities of indentured labour within the Police Zone. In 1909, the German magistrate of Grootfontein entered into negotiations with the traditional authorities of the Kavango region to explore recruitment possibilities, resulting in the first small contingent of labourers in 1910[39]. In 1911, a new ordinance provided for the replacement of the (until then) still private recruiting agents by ordering the centralisation of recruitment through a public agency[40].

The most momentous three decrees were issued on 18 August 1907. These ordinances, proclaimed by the new governor Friedrich von Lindequist were at that time judged the "Magna Charta of native administration". The first, "Massregeln zur Kontrolle der Eingeborenen" (Rules for the control of natives), introduced the registration of 'natives' of the Police Zone with the German colonial authorities; the restriction of large stock of indigenous farmers, and the restriction of the mobility of the population accused of vagrancy, if sufficient living was not verifiable. Of greatest significance: 'natives' were banned from acquiring usufruct titles or property rights to land without permission from the German administration. The second, "Passpflicht der Eingeborenen" compelled all non-whites above the age of seven to carry passes when leaving their districts. Such documents were to be issued by the German authorities. The third, "Dienst- und Arbeitsverträge mit Eingeborenen des südwestafrikanischen Schutzgebietes", introduced an individual work logbook or work register which every non-white worker (except Coloureds) was supposed to carry at all times and to produce in order to legitimise his status. This document was made a condition for any employment contract; the contract had to be registered on it; without a work pass and a valid contract no employment was allowed.

Looking systematically at labour migration under German rule, we find a sectoral distribution and a demand for labour constantly changing and reflecting the stages of early colonial capital formation:

- early mining and guano works (since the 1840s and after 1892)
- trade (1880s and 1890s)
- Swakopmund harbour construction (1893 to 1903)
- railway construction (Swakopmund – Windhoek, 1897 to 1902), Windhoek – Otavi (1903 to 1906)

---

[38] Already in 1891, by ordinance of 17 May, the authorities had prevented a further exodus of Damara and Nama workers recruited from the Cape authorities in the late 80s. This was followed by two additional ordinances of 26.10.1898 and 30.11.1901. Rädel 1947:49

[39] Rädel 1947:89

[40] "Verordnung betreffend die Anwerbung und Arbeitsverhältnisse der eingeborenen Arbeiter", dated 16.12.1911. The outbreak of the war hindered the enforcement of the ordinance. However, the appointment of a resident Native Commissioner in Ovamboland put an end to any private recruitment initiative. In the Kavango, a Native Commissioner was appointed only in 1921. Rädel 1947:283

- mining (Otavi copper mines and Lüderitz diamond fields opening in 1906 and 1907, respectively)[41].

The number of Ovambo labourers working in these sectors, in the decade until 1908, more or less stagnated, never exceeding 2 000. During the remaining German period it rose sharply to an average of 10 000[42]. Workers of Ovambo origin numbered roughly 9 000 in 1911, 6 000 in 1912, 12 000 in 1913 and 11 500 in 1914[43].

Concluding this section with a provisional balance, we take a critical look at the identity of the migrant: Who is to be defined as a migrant, which ethnic group(s)? As illustrated, within the scope of the colonial economy under German rule, all ethnic groups of the Police Zone were expropriated of land and livestock, displaced and confined to reserves with an uncertain chance of survival. They were segregated, racially discriminated against, socially degraded, economically deprived and reduced to a subservient status, restricted in their mobility and, consequently, forced into wage labour by a set of political measures and economic constraints. Wage labour, given the restrictive imbalance of power and its legislative reflections, over a long period emerged as migrant labour only.

But German policies did not really solve the contradiction they had themselves brought about: the labouring class they wanted never satisfied the needs of the colonial economy. On the one hand, policies were expressly aimed at alienating the indigenous population from their customary subsistence-based economy, in order to form a labour reservoir, and to create a stable working class. The creation of reserves is clearly to be seen in this line. On the other hand, the instruments deployed to attain such a goal also had a counterproductive effect. They reduced the African population to an economic function, to merely a labour force. Segregation in reserves involved the refusal of the coloniser to establish a responsible social relationship, and it defined their cultural inferiority. Confining the labour force to reserves and to an existence as a migrant labour force, in the long run limited its availability on the labour market, a somewhat fictitious market. This market was administratively regulated and populated by individuals compelled to live in two different economic, social and cultural worlds, never in a position to leave behind their customary subsistence-oriented origins for good, and conse-

---

[41] Moorsom 1989:79; Hayes 1992:149; Clarence-Smith / Moorsom 1975:378

[42] Clarence-Smith / Moorsom 1975:153, 273-274

[43] Banghart 1969:28. These are the widely accepted and commonly quoted figures picturing the extent of early indentured labour. Interestingly, these figures do not correspond to the numbers of Ovambo migrants actually registered in the Police Zone. Official population statistics of the Police Zone for the years 1911 and 1912 produce some 2 800 and 5 100 labourers, respectively, of Ovambo origin. One possible assumption is that migrants signed short-term contracts only. This explanation is suggested by Rädel (1947:87). The population statistics based their data on the cut-off date principle, therefore showing only the number of present residents, whereas the annual labour reports listed the overall number of workers on contractual agreement in the respective categories. However, the above explanation does not sufficiently account for the noticeable discrepancies in the figures. To reach the number of workers indicated, the number of residents would have to be quadruplicated, resulting in three-months contract period only for the year 1911 – which is unlikely. On the other hand, for the year 1912 such a calculation would lead to a number of labourers roughly three times as high as actually indicated. Possibly, the data basis commonly found in the literature is defective; possibly, the population statistics as quoted by Rädel are not reliable.

quently reluctant to rely on wage relations only, particularly as this meant submitting oneself to the white coloniser. So, while proletarianisation was initiated, it was at the same time hindered.

Historically, all the actors involved solved the contradiction pragmatically. Many of the 'internal' migrants of Herero, Damara and Nama origin and, as we have seen, farm workers in their majority, settled in their new rural destinations, though still retaining some of their social ties with their extended families in the reserves. As permanent[44] farm workers, or settling in urban areas serving on successive contracts, they forfeited their existence as migrant labourers. This permanent labour force suited the white settler farmer as well since it marked an economic constant. Also, because of the paternalistic design of the new relationship, it cemented the worker's extreme dependence on the employer, and therefore his vulnerability. As far as the labour demand of the rapidly growing mining sector was concerned, the solution was found by concentrating on those migrants coming from outside the Police Zone, the Ovambo labourers. To counter their reluctance to engage in longer-term work relationships, economically and culturally motivated, the German administration resorted to the instrument of contractual obligation.

Thus, defining the migrant at the close of the German era – and with a view to his future identity – we refer to those (male) workers originating from the northern regions outside the Police Zone whose presence as wage labourers is tied to a contract, limited in time, periodically rejected, restricted in mobility by by-laws, socially regulated and administratively controlled. In historical terms, the migrant worker is no longer the 'internal' migrant from the Herero, Damara, Nama and Baster reserves or of San origin, now settled, but usually the Ovambo on contract in the Police Zone.

The institutionalised system of labour migration under South African rule
The South African Union inherited this situation – defective as it was, judged from a colonial perspective – when she conquered the South West African colony at the beginning of World War I. The League of Nations conferred the territory as a so-called 'C '- mandate "upon His Britannic Majesty" in 1920, "to be exercised on his behalf by the Union of South Africa", judging the people of Namibia "not yet able to stand by themselves under the strenuous conditions of the modern world"[45]. The new rulers extended the previous German policies of dispossession. During the segregation era (1915-1948) South African land settlement policies

---

[44] Permanent in the sense that their employment terms contained no explicit time limit, not in the sense of a lifelong permanence with one and the same employer.
[45] This judgement is formulated by Article 22 of the League Covenant. United Nations Office of Public Information 1974:3. A 'C'- mandate allowed the mandatory power to govern a region under its tutelage as an integral part of its own territory.

were instrumental in implementing a strictly centralised labour policy[46]. It served to establish the predominance of British colonial capital in the mining sector[47].

The close link between the expropriation, displacement, racial segregation and regulation of black labour supply and its distribution is evident. The Treaty of Peace and South West Africa Mandate Act No.49 of 1919 under section 4 declared all land in the Southern Zone (except for land held in private ownership by white settlers or mining companies) to be South African Crown land[48] disposable for settlement purposes. The indigenous population was effectively made landless with a stroke of the pen. The Union continued with the restrictive administrative treatment of the Ovambo region, preventing any uncontrolled white settlement in the area by issuing Prohibited Area Proclamation No.15 of 1919. Following a new land settlement scheme introduced in 1920, South Africa allotted land generously to white settlers, creating commercial farm estates. At the same time, "whilst desirous of retaining for local labour requirements (...) the native population within the vicinity of employing centres", the colonial government decided to "affirm the general principle of segregation". This is how an official report put it in 1920. Its findings resulted in the 'reform' of the colonial state apparatus in 1922[49]. Segregation, in this reading paradigmatic of the first phase of South African rule, aimed at spatial isolation. It had not yet envisaged the idea of separate economic development that became the central theme of the apartheid era.

The Suppression of Vagrancy and Idleness Proclamation No.25 of 1920[50] took a first step in realising segregation. It confined Africans to reserves, threatening them with hard labour. It prevented them from making free use of their bargaining power as a labour force. This perfidious enactment, reading between the lines, imposed a restricted mobility on the African labour force and legislated for the restriction of the freedom of African citizenship in general. Once more in colonial history, it regulated access to the labour market politically and administratively. Seen in the context of segregation policies, mobility was reduced to labour purposes exclusively[51]. The Native Administration Proclamation No.11 of 1922 then provided for the final creation[52] of reserves, to which the population already made landless was then moved, based on the proclamation of reserves in the years 1923 to 1925.

---

[46] According to Gottschalk, the Administrator-General Gijsbert Hofmeyr in 1920-21 made the equation labour question = native question = land question. Gottschalk 1978:78

[47] Mbuende 1986:77

[48] In concurrence with Crown Land Disposal Proclamation No.13 of 1920. Amoo 2001:91. During the period of military occupation after the cease-fire agreement of Khorab with the German military command, no settlement legislation appeared. However, "grazing licences" were issued to Union farmers who migrated to South West Africa. At the end of the war, these Afrikaner farmers started to claim greater security, setting legislation in train. Crown Land Disposal Proclamation apportioned land to new Afrikaner farmers with a relatively small capital background. Moreover, credits were freely given and interest terms and rates extremely favourable. Rädel 1947:105

[49] Quoted in Rädel 1947:194

[50] Vagrancy or idleness was defined as a visible lack of means of support, visibility, in its turn, meant the ownership of at least ten large stock or forty small stock or a certificate of employment. Gottschalk 1978:80

[51] Therefore, migration cannot be looked at only as an element of labour policies. From the very beginning it is revealed as a component of a complex social and economic system of colonial domination.

[52] The creation of reserves had been declared lawful in principle already with Treaty of Peace and South West Africa Mandate Act 49 of 1919.

Except for the Ovambo and Kavango regions[53], these reserves were mostly located in desert or semi-desert areas. Lack of subsistence opportunities and of employment forced people into migration for labour purposes. In addition, the introduction of commodities, though a slow process, served to create a new dependence on a monetarised economy[54]. The compulsion to sell one's labour, in this manner, became a permanent structural feature of South West African society; a compulsion forced on the population not only economically, but also by legislative means. Ten head of large or 40 of small stock were defined as the minimum required for subsistence, below which an African peasant within the Police Zone could be administratively forced to take up wage labour[55]. Thus, the reserves were despicably referred to as the 'parking places of native labour'[56]. The patterns of segregation did not change fundamentally until the end of colonial rule. Nevertheless, demand for African cheap labour always exceeded the supply from the reserves within the territories known as the Police Zone. Therefore, recruitment efforts were increasingly directed to the northern regions.

In order to control the migratory movements thus started, a set of pass laws was promulgated and adapted through various enactments throughout the colonial period of domination. They complemented the creation of reserves and the vagrancy provisions. A first step was taken with the Control and Treatment of Natives on Mines Proclamation No.3 of 1917. It vested colonial officers with administrative rights of control, investigation and punishment of work-related offences. It stated the duties of workers and imposed written contracts on employers and workers, marking the unofficial beginning of the (not yet fully institutionalised) Contract System. Crown Lands (Trespass) Proclamation No.7 of 1919 defined the general restrictions of mobility on crown land, preventing especially natives from entering and settling.

The Masters and Servants Proclamation No.34 of 1920 regulated the rights and duties of employers and employees. It repealed the previous Masters and Servants Proclamation No.1 of 1918. Both proclamations resumed the paternalistic tradition initiated by the German administration hierarchising labour relations on a racial basis, pitting the white master against the black servant. The Native Administration Proclamation No.11 of 1922, sections 4 and 5, stated that no non-white above the age of 14 be entitled to enter the non-reserve areas of the Police Zone without official permission. This document was normally issued for work purposes only, and solely to men[57]. Within this area, 'natives' were allowed to leave their location, reserve, farm, place of residence or employment only with an

---

[53] Ovamboland remained a magisterial district until 1929 when it was made a reserve.
[54] During German colonial rule, plans to establish trading posts in the Ondonga kingdom failed because of the king's resistance. The first factory was set up in December 1924 by the Ondonga Trading Co. to explicitly serve the purpose of "awakening needs and so to increase the readiness for work". Five years later, a branch was opened in Omafe; in 1939 another company settled in Ukwanyama. Rädel 1947:241. Also cf. Banghart 1969:91. Later SWANLA set up several stores in Ovamboland. Banghart's research indicates that the majority of his interviewees "left to work in the Police Zone to purchase non-essential items (luxury items)".
[55] Banghart 1969:41
[56] Rädel 1947:225
[57] Kane-Berman 1972:12

additional permit. Travelling, buying a railway ticket, visiting a 'foreign' reserve or 'foreign' urban area also required a permit. Documents had to be produced to prove the existence of a contract of employment or to identify oneself as a casual labourer, to seek work, or to be a legal visitor[58]. Moreover, with a view to implementing segregation, Proclamation No.11 aimed to administratively prevent the settlement of Africans on white farms in larger numbers, by defining illegal 'squatting' as the settlement of more than five families[59].

In 1925, the renewed Native Labour Control and Treatment Proclamation No.6 redefined the provisions of 1917, broadening the range of sectors beyond mining to which the limitations were to apply. In addition, section 3(d) now vested the Administrator-General expressly with legislative powers in labour matters, again enforcing the contractual relationship between employers and black workers whose minimum age was set at 18 years. Together with the subsequent Government Notice of Native Labour Regulations No.26 of 1925, it aimed to narrowly control the migrants' influx and mobility, as well as stating the conditions of service and living down to the last detail. These two legislative steps, in close temporal and functional connection with the consultations between colonial entrepreneurs and state administration on a new recruitment procedure, anticipated the institutionalisation of labour recruitment in 1926.

The Native Administration Proclamation No.15 of 1928, ch.5, legislating for the control of 'native living' and terms of residence, provided for the segregation of black Africans to 'locations' to be established in urban areas. The Extra-territorial and Northern Natives Control Proclamation No.29 of 1935 issued instructions for male (only!) northern migrants to carry identification passes and produce them at all times on request, as a prerequisite to take up employment within the Police Zone (sections 3, 6, 9)[60]. No employer was to demand services from a migrant not in possession of such a document. The Natives (Urban Areas) Proclamation No.56 of 1951 updated the directions concerning the control of contracts and residence of migrants, once again confirming their confinement to urban locations on the basis of racial segregation of habitat. South Africa's Native Laws Amendment Act No.54 of 1952, extended to South West Africa by the Amendment Ordinance No.25 of 1954, further specified the restrictions of residence and mobility of non-whites in the Police Zone, limiting any lawful stay in an urban area to a maximum of 72 hours. The Aliens Control Act No.30 of 1963 brought the identification rules as formulated in the Aliens Control Act No.1 of 1937 into line with the territorial revisions envisaged by the Bantustan policies.

It is interesting to note that neither the Native Administration Proclamation No.11 of 1922 nor the Extra-territorial and Northern Natives Control Proclamation No.29 of 1935 apply the request for identification and permits to women. Women were thus responsible to a large extent for the temporary expansions of urban

---

[58] United Nations Office of Public Information 1974:11
[59] Larger farms had to apply for special permission. Rädel 1947:203
[60] Exceptions were made only for chiefs and headmen, teachers, clerical personnel, and administrative personnel. Kooy 1973:90

populations within the Police Zone[61]. Male migration seems to have been accompanied by a trend of female urbanisation not directly linked with wage labour but rather with the need to escape the harsh economic conditions within the subsistence sector created by the waves of economic depression in the late 1920s and 1930s.

The colonial administration had stepped up the pace in 1925 creating the legal framework for the establishment of a new instrument of labour recruitment. Launching the Southern and Northern Labour Organisations (SLO and NLO) in 1926, owned on a private capitalist basis but run on a non-profit principle, the colonial state committed itself to withdrawing from recruitment[62]. Between 1923 and 1925 the diamond industry had suffered a serious labour crisis[63] resulting from the independent attitudes of the Ovambo peasant migrants. In addition, the global depression had made itself felt mid-decade in affecting mining activities in the mandate. As a result, migrant labour had been redirected to the commercial farming sector. This clashed with the Ovambo workers' traditional reluctance and resistance to be employed on farms, ill-famed for their extremely personalised, unjust and above all, badly paid working conditions. As a result, the number of available migrants had decreased considerably.

From the very beginning, the SLO in Ondangwa and the NLO in Grootfontein enforced standard contracts of a one-year duration. The bureaucratisation of the procedures prevented the indigenous applicants from choosing their employers, by allocating them according to employers' requests in hand. Now the contractual conditions forcibly alienated the male migrant from the agricultural production cycle. Moorsom points out the "long-term effects of social disruption"[64] diminishing agricultural productivity.

The contract form shows the narrow limits set on the free commercialisation of the labour force. The tenor of the contract designs the relationship between employee and employer bluntly as a hierarchical dependence of the 'servant' on the 'master', clearly along the lines of a racially biased paternalism. The employers are not even signatories, since the contract defined the relationship between the recruitment agency and the worker. Wage labour, in this case, is not yet founded on the direct exchange between capital and labour. Moreover, a conspicuous portion of the remuneration for the worker is given in services and kind. Such services (medical care and transport to/from the place of work) are financed by the recruitment agency; the employer is bound to supply the worker with a specified weekly amount of food, with housing, clothes and blankets[65].

The two bodies were at work from 1926 to 1943, when they merged in one exclusive, monopolistic recruitment agency for non-white wage labour north of the

---

[61] For example, during the years 1927 to 1930 and 1934 to 1937. Rädel 1847:220-221
[62] Rädel 1947:286
[63] Moorsom 1989:100-101. In 1923, a conference of representatives of mining capital estimated their demand for labour as high as 14 000. Rädel 1947:283
[64] Moorsom 1977:68
[65] Kane-Berman 1972, Appendix:iii

Police Zone, SWANLA, the South West African Native Labour Association (Pty.) Ltd. It is no secret that SLO and NLO were mainly owned on a capital share basis by the major colonial enterprises in SWA[66]. NLOs main shareholders were the Otavi Minen- und Eisenbahngesellschaft (OMEG), the S.W.A Company and SWA Mines[67]. The SLO, which almost exclusively catered for the needs of the diamond mining industry south of the Red (Veterinary) Line (and in South Africa[68]) was under the influence of the De Beers group. Thus, first of all, it recruited for the diamond mines, allocating workers on the basis of a rough classification according to physical ability and previous professional experience within the migrant labour system. It functioned as the appropriate agency for Ovambo workers. The NLO was designed for the labour market of the Kavango and Caprivi regions; it also took over those applicants from the SLO which had not been classified as first category hands for the mines. Recruits from NLO considered unfit for labour in the (non-diamond) mines were to be passed on to the commercial farming sector[69]. Again, SWANLA's shareholders mainly represented mining capital interests, explicitly excluding farmers' representatives, though it had to cater for the labour demand of commercial agriculture[70].

SWANLA and its predecessors, apart from mining, catered for the labour demand in farming, in fishing and fishing industries, railway, construction, commerce and public and private services[71]. Their recruiting efforts counted on the support of traditional authorities[72], as well as from Christian missions and churches. Headmen and chiefs received perquisites for their assistance; they themselves were exempt from going on contract. The Anglican and Roman Catholic missions were required by the Administrator-General of SWA to submit a written promise that they would work on the indigenous dignitaries to persuade peasants to apply for wage labour. SWANLA had its head office in Grootfontein. The agency was given the exclusive right to attract workers from the northern regions of the country, from Ovambo (including Angola) and Kavango. The monopoly included the distribution of the labour force to employers, who were charged for the placement[73].

In 1948, the introduction of the racist apartheid concept of 'separate development' of the white and non-white populations ended the 'segregation era'. It guided South African policies officially until 1977. It certainly didn't replace the ideology of white supremacy of the Afrikaner and German settler class. Neither did it annul the harsh property policies of the preceding four decades of colonial

---

[66] "The Northern Labour Organisation had the Otavi Minen- und Eisenbahngesellschaft, the South West Africa Company, and the South West Africa Mines Ltd. as members. Provision was also made for other major employers (...) to join. The Southern Labour Organisation was meant for the Diamond Mines and had the Chamber of Mines as a member. Mbuende 1986:83

[67] Banghart 1969:45

[68] Lovisa Ndaoya vividly pictures the fate of those workers recruited from the Namibian north for the South African farms and mines. Ndaoya 2000 (mimeo)

[69] Mbuende 1986:83. NLO had to reimburse SLO of its recruiting costs. Rädel 1947:285-286

[70] Banghart 1969:46

[71] Moorsom 1977:74-76

[72] First 1963:324

[73] Tötemeyer 1978:23, 155, 170. The charge included the recruiting fee, return fare for the worker, food for the journey, basic clothing and blankets. Kooy 1973:91

alienation which had seen approximately six million hectares transferred to immigrants from South Africa[74]. However it did apply changes to the reserve system of segregation, replacing it, in the 60s, with the bantustans. Within the scope of the Odendaal Plan, and in flagrant contravention of the decision of the United Nations to terminate South Africa's mandate[75], six regions initially were declared homelands of Africans[76], whereas the 'white homeland' (in accordance with the South West Africa Affairs Act No.25 of 1969) was to be incorporated into South Africa. This policy aimed to strip the rest of the South West African economy of its independence. The pressure applied by international public on the apartheid republic increasingly obstructed the implementation of the Odendaal policy. The intended incorporation of the core Southern Zone territories into the South African economy as a fifth province ultimately proved a failure[77]. It would have completed the process of provincialisation of the South West African economy.

Despite its failure to fully implement 'separate development', the labour regulation policy remained an essential pillar of the political framework of the South African accumulation process. The Native (Urban Areas) Proclamation of 1951 prevented migrants from looking for labour in urban centres[78]. Mbuende presumes that in formulating this policy, the SA administration was reacting to the decline in agricultural productivity in the reserves in the early 1950s[79]. The 1968 Bantu Labour Regulations preceded the Bantustan laws, already preventing Africans from entering the prescribed areas of the Police Zone other than as contracted labourers[80].

Working and living conditions under contract in many respects came close to forced labour. Of those endured indentured labour and left written records of their hardships, Vinnia Ndadi's autobiographical notes in 'Breaking Contract' is without doubt one of the most impressive records. James Kauluma also presents some biographical notes in his study of 'The migrant contract labour situation in Namibia and the response to it'. Helmut Angula condenses some of the migrants' experiences to a fictitious biographical account in 'The two thousand days of Haimbodi ya Haufiku'. Ruth First, assassinated in 1982 in Maputo for her resistance to the apartheid system, in her study of 'South West Africa' vividly portrays the assault on the dignity of labour the migrants had to bear. Ndeutala Hishongwa in her recent monograph on the social effects of the Namibian Contract Labour System, too, has collected much material showing the inhuman conditions of daily life and work imposed on the migrants[81]. Susan Hurlich illustrates the different facets of

---

[74] Gebhard 1980:26
[75] Decision of the General Assembly on 27 October 1966. United Nations Office of Public Information 1974:26-28
[76] By Development of Self-Government for Native Nations in South West Africa Act No.54 of 1968. These were Damaraland, Hereroland, Kaokoland, Okavangoland, Eastern Caprivi, Ovamboland. Amoo 2001:93. Later, further four bantustans were added.
[77] Mbuende 1986:93
[78] "No African work-seeker was allowed to remain in any urban area for longer than 72 hours without official permission." Cronje 1979:30
[79] Mbuende 1986:86
[80] Kane-Berman 1972:4
[81] Hishongwa 1992

the unbearable misery of migrant labour on the farms, in the factories and in the mines, in her documentary drama 'One day in the life of a migrant worker'[82]. Gillian and Suzanne Cronje, in their classical study on Namibian labour presented to the UN Sub-Commission on Prevention of Discrimination and Protection on Minorities, report in minute detail the economic exploitation and individual plight of contract workers. The Finnish missionary Rauha Voipio in 1970 started an empirical research project focusing on the 'responsibility of the church to look after the family life of immigrant workers' which resulted in her well-known booklet 'Contract work through Ovambo eyes'. Kane-Berman's report on the strike and the state of affairs of contract labour after the dissolution of SWANLA in 1972, both sympathetic and objective, presents an overview of the changes in the legal status and material conditions within the scope of the revised contract[83]. Last, but not least, Robert Gordon's participatory picture of migrant labourers in 'Mines, masters and migrants' provides an extremely informative insight into their everyday living and working conditions as well as their life stories. Gordon collected his evidence during his employment as a personnel officer at the mine.

As a concomitant social effect of labour migration, one central feature emerges from all these documents. Workers were not allowed to migrate with their families, whom they had to leave behind in the reserves/homelands. That this inevitably contributed to social disruption on a large scale, can easily be imagined. The customary family and kinship systems came under pressure, as well as the customary sexual morals. Hishongwa states, as an underlying motive, the radical policy of preventing Africans from settling in 'white areas'[84].

In addition to this racial motivation, economic intentions undoubtedly played a key role. The whole range of legal limitations imposed on the African labour force indicates that colonial entrepreneurs (given the modest, peripheral character of the capitalist accumulation process of the time) were not interested in the formation of a stable, self-recruiting working class. As long as wage labour is available as migrant labour, its costs of reproduction are mainly borne in the subsistence sector[85]. This allows for moderate labour costs. Thus far, colonial labour regulation policy goes beyond mere economic regulation. It reveals an element of control of social structural development, too, clearly for political reasons of systemic stability.

Assessing labour migration in the South African era in terms of figures, one realises its extent. Disclosing the real dimensions of industrial relations in colonial Namibia is a difficult task, due to the reluctance of the South African authorities to release any reliable data on the situation in its mandate. Nevertheless, several studies have produced significant evidence. According to Moorsom's estimates, the proportion of Ovambo men on contract (as a percentage of all Ovambo men)

---

[82] Hurlich 1884
[83] Kane-Berman's appendices to the report contain facsimiles of the old and the revised contract forms.
[84] Hishongwa 1992:87
[85] Peltola 1995:64. In a broader theoretical perspective, Claude Meillassoux makes this economic aspect of overexploitation of labour force a subject of his discussion of the conditional framework of the process of capital accumulation in peripheral, underdeveloped economies. Meillassoux 1979

varies between one fifth and one third in the period between 1910 and 1971[86]. However, Rädel in his economic analysis of South West Africa published in 1947, emphasises the considerable variations in the recruitment figures. According to official reports, it took a dozen years after the establishment of SLO / NLO to raise the number of Ovambo workers again to pre-depression levels (around 7 000). Thus, approximately one fifth of the male Ovambo population migrated during the last pre-war years in the search for monetary income[87]. Green, in his manpower estimates prepared in 1977 for the Lusaka (Zambia) United Nations Institute for Namibia (UNIN) in view of the implementation of the policy of transition to independence, even calculates a rate of 50% of non-European Namibian households in 1977 sending a male member to distant employment. In absolute figures, this amounts to some 110 000 Namibians, of whom 75 000 originated from the northern Bantustans[88].

The Cronjes, in their labour force analysis published in 1979, list a range of contradicting statistical data based on official manpower figures and on independent research. The extremely low calculations of the South African administration state a figure for black workers in the cash economy ranging between approximately 50 000 in 1969 and 70 000 in 1975. Excluding domestic workers in private service and agricultural workers in the subsistence and the commercial sector, these figures fail to account for the majority of the working population. Non-official research, however, assumes that contract workers constitute between half and three quarters of the totality of non-European labour force in Namibia in the 1970s. Tötemeyer compiles a table listing approximately 8 000 migrant labourers in 1942, a figure more than doubling during the following decade and reaching around 43 000 in 1971, at the time of the abolition of the official contract labour system[89]. Official SWANLA recruitment figures stated by Banghart for the years 1960/61 to 1967/68 vary between approximately 25 000 and 38 000 workers[90]. Hishongwa indicates for the first half of the 1960s that the bulk of contract workers were distributed amongst mining (30%) and farming (25%)[91]. It is interesting to note the shift in the sectoral distribution of the migrant labour force. While the share of domestic services over the three decades of SWANLA remained more or less the same (between 4% and 5%), agriculture's share dropped to a quarter of the initial 80%. The mining industry's share doubled to more than 30% and the secondary sector's share increased by more than twenty times[92]. Similarly, Kooy reports official figures for 1966 showing an even higher share of mining, commerce and industry where nearly 53% of all Ovambo migrants were concentrated, 95% of them in the category of unskilled or semi-skilled labour[93].

---

[86] Moorsom 1975:67
[87] Rädel 1947:326, 330
[88] Green 1978:9
[89] Tötemeyer 1978:156
[90] Banghart 1969:49
[91] Hishongwa 1992:58-59
[92] Tötemeyer 1978:156
[93] Kooy 1973:92

Looking at the phenomenon of contract labour from the perspective of the individual, the extent is even more notable. Ovambo men spent more than a quarter of their adult life on contract[94], in this manner forming an extremely unstable working class fraction of part-lifetime unskilled labourers originating from a peasant existence. Migration became an almost inevitable stage in the lives of most Ovambo men, mainly in the age period between 25 and 44 years, wage labour becoming a prerequisite for marriage and acquisition of usufruct rights to land and of cattle[95]. At the beginning of the 1970s, the majority, i.e. 60% of male manpower of employable age was compelled to work outside the home region, 80% of whom were married and had to leave their families behind[96].

Data analysing the age structure of migrant labourers during apartheid clearly indicate migration as a prerequisite for marriage. As for the effects of male migration on women, labour migration became part of family planning. It obviously changed the established patterns of courtship, since it preceded (and postponed) the usual date of marriage. Migratory wage earnings were used for acquiring land access and cattle as a basis for the establishment of an independent homestead. As before, women were not part of the migration picture. Moorsom cites 1 500 women categorised as wage-earners in the 1960s[97]. Hayes refers to the so-called 'free Ovambo' women who at the beginning of the South African mandate, with some men, formed a small group of workers residing outside Ovamboland[98].

Post-apartheid labour migration

Dissolution of the indentured system of labour migration
SWANLA was dissolved following the 'Grootfontein-Agreement' in February 1972. On the 13th of December 1971, several thousand contract workers had engaged in a strike against the contract system, advocating its complete abolition. Their number rose to tens of thousands of strikers at 23 different venues by mid-January[99]. The strike was suppressed violently, and workers were deported in huge numbers to Ovamboland – some 13 000 by the second week of January[100]. In January/February 1972, as a reaction to peasants rising in political protest in Ovamboland[101], the SA administration declared a state of emergency[102]. Frantic attempts to recruit labourers from other parts of the southern African region failed[103].

---

[94] Figures for 1968, workers above the age of 15; according to Banghart, as quoted in Moorsom 1975:70
[95] Banghart 1969:63-76
[96] Tötemeyer 1978:165-166; Banghart 1969:65
[97] Moorsom 1977:72. Though, these women are rather to be classified as petty-bourgeois self-employers.
[98] They had left Ovamboland at the very end of German rule, mainly trying to escape the famine of 1915. Hayes 1992:289
[99] According to official figures. Kane-Berman 1972:6, 27. For a detailed report on the strike also see Kooy 1973:96-102 and Moorsom 1978:125-139.
[100] Kooy 1973:99
[101] Helmut Angula recounts the days of protest in his prose The two thousand days of Haimbodi ya Haufiku.
[102] Proclamation No.17 of 1972. Dierks:137-138
[103] Kauluma 1977:47

The dissolution of SWANLA, however, did not put an end to labour migration as such. In March 1972, the South African government proclaimed the Regulations for the Establishment of Employment Bureaux in the Territory of South West Africa No.83. Applicable within[104] the Police Zone, the regulations excluded the "Native Nations" as defined by the 1968 Act. Separately in 1972, as part of the new dispensation, the Bantustan governments of Ovambo and Kavango were vested with the authority to administer the new recruiting institutions[105]. Proclamation No.83 implemented the labour agreements signed at Grootfontein between the two conflicting parties. Section 2 of the Schedule contained in the new law allowed for the establishment of employment offices in every Native Commissioner's area of jurisdiction[106]. It defined 'employees' or 'work seekers' going back to the Native Administration Proclamation No.15 of 1928 which did not distinguish between male and female employees. But since the pass laws, namely the 1935 Extra-territorial and Northern Natives Control Proclamation, had always reserved the issuing of identification and travel documents to men, the gender bias characteristic of labour migration remained untouched.

The new legal framework did not yet establish a free labour market. Though introducing the category of 'work seekers', it referred to previous legislation (and therefore practice) in circumscribing it. Thus, it forced all people of working age (aged 16 and above) to make themselves available to the labour market. It was still not the individual's choice whether he applied for wage work or not, according to his own needs. Moreover, registration with the labour bureaux in actual practice remained restricted to male 'work seekers'. The new labour law did not allow the work seeker to approach an employer directly without placement through the local employment agency, since the employer was not allowed to employ him without a referral from the labour bureau. Employees were only allowed to deviate from the contractual terms of their employment if so authorised by the labour bureau's mediation, otherwise termination of contract became a matter of civil action.

Above all, the contract form as such remained, albeit a revised version, but still a contract entered into with the labour administration on behalf of the employers. The agreement could not be signed on a legally independent basis between employer and employee. The most perfidious modification is found in a seemingly harmless administrative measure: the individual work seeker, compelled to register with the labour bureaux, is listed in one of eight sectoral categories (agriculture, mining, manufacturing, etc.) at the discretion of the employment officer. Since this bureaucratic decision may not be revised throughout the mi-

---

[104] Official Gazette no.3244:242; Kane-Berman 1972:33. Under this regulation, labour recruitment was placed under the responsibility of the colonial state administration. Local employment bureaux were to be set up and run by employment officers. All employers would be compelled to register and to present their requests for employees to them. On their side, male individuals were defined as 'work seekers' and as such were required to contact the labour bureau when unemployed, reaching the age of 16 or having completed formal education. This forced all potential labour force to declare themselves available for employment. The labour bureaux also acted as arbitrators in labour related disputes (op.cit.:33-35).

[105] Kane-Berman 1972:6, 11. The Bantustan governments opened seven labour offices in Ovamboland and five in Kavango.

[106] Mutwa 1978:7

grant's life, it may be nothing short of an occupational life sentence[107] restricting the power of negotiation for better wages and freedom of wage labour in general.

However, some of the most degrading recruitment procedures were abolished, such as the medical classification of workers and the fixed-term contract[108]. Also, the regulations revised some of the relevant apartheid by-laws limiting the personal and professional mobility and freedom of the non-white population. Those migrants who could prove continuous employment with the same employer over a period of at least ten years, and those who had resided for at least fifteen years in a specific area of jurisdiction, were accorded further rights of residence[109]. Most of the restrictive decrees however were only repealed between 1975 and 1978, when the apartheid system as a whole was effectively replaced with the veiled, but still vibrantly racist policies of the Internal Settlement Scheme. Proclamation No.15 of 1975 repealed the Master and Servant decrees of the 1920s as well as the Extra-territorial and Northern Natives Proclamation of 1935, relaxing labour control and the restrictions on internal mobility[110].

Even then, the system of a regulated and controlled labour supply for the capitalist sector of the economy could not be expected to dissolve by legislative means. It had after all been in force for more than three quarters of a century, and formed an integral part of the colonial economy. However, whereas migration under the rigid apartheid system was inevitably defined as labour migration only, under the Internal Settlement Scheme potentially it became 'free' migration, shaping the process of urbanisation. The attractions of urban life, be they real or supposed, came into the picture as a pull factor.

The elimination of obstacles to personal mobility laid the foundations for transforming a labour force now free from formal hindrances into a commodity, though the economic framework and residential patterns of colonial segregation remained effective. They continued to shape migration largely as mobility for work purposes, predominantly for males. Women now were at least not prevented by regulations from joining the migratory trend. Although a 'free' capitalist labour market, it remained based on segregation, separating the white from the non-white and the female from the male labour force.

Some other changes also transpired. The rigidity of the Contract Labour System had left migrants with no legal choice but to alternate periods of wage labour with an agricultural subsistence existence. Post-apartheid migration, on the other hand, left it to the migrant to decide whether s/he returns to the former subsistence existence or rather cling to the developing urban working class world.

Of course, statistical evidence shows that labour migrants even today travel on a return ticket, so to speak. Labour migration may now become linked with the other major indication of mobility, that is urbanisation. But they are not at all the same. Migration is still largely limited to those periods of a Namibian lifetime which

---

[107] Gottschalk 1978:95-96
[108] Kane-Berman 1972:8-11
[109] Kane-Berman 1972:35. Those who did not qualify were ordered to leave for their place of origin.
[110] Gottschalk 1978:95

are characterised by wage labour (or rather, by the often futile attempt to sell one's labour on a markedly restricted urban market). When labour is terminated, for whatever reason, be it age, illness, market crises or other, the urban economy expels the migrant. For a time, he may manage to survive, turning to the informal sector or family support. Eventually, he will return to his rural roots. It is not only economic factors playing a role: the social ties of kinship and the social security therein, as well as cultural practice, guide him in his choice.

This, at any rate, is what statistical evidence suggests. Thus, urbanisation is a trend, fed by labour migration, but its subject, the migrant 'personnel', is in a constant state of change. One could say that it remains forever young. This is a reflection of the age structure of urbanisation, which is mainly comprised of the age groups between 25 and 45.

Empirical patterns of current labour migration

Turning to the current trends of migration and its gender structures in detail: in a study investigating the reasons and patterns of urbanisation and internal migration in post-independence Namibia, Henning Melber introduces an interesting cultural aspect. Migration due to wars (the extermination war of 1904-1907, the anti-colonial liberation war in the 1970s and 1980s) and the long experience of labour migration create a cultural experience of migration[111]. In my opinion, one would have to add the habitual mobility historically connected with the cattle-based economies of the Nama and Herero populations until they were forcibly resettled in reserves. Moreover, uprooting, displacement and spatial segregation as practised by the colonial authorities implementing the Odendaal Plan, certainly did not foster identification with the bantustan areas of 'origin'. Such a 'collective experience' facilitates a migrational propensity and becomes a strong motive power of its own in favouring mobility. Moreover, regional imbalances, mainly in the shape of the north-south divide and of urban-rural differentials[112], provide the geo-economic push factors. It is this complex background which might explain the extraordinary extent to which the Namibian population seems to have been 'on the move' for the past decade.

Research on internal migration in Namibia currently lacks in-depth studies focusing on the increasing significance of regional population movements within the northern periphery. Intra-regional migration to regional metropolises such as Oshakati/Ondangwa or Rundu became a conspicuous phenomenon after independence. However, there are a number of studies analysing the extent and circumstances of migration mainly to the capital Windhoek. North-to-north migration is mainly a post-independence occurrence, north-to-south migration, as we have seen, reflects the conditions of both colonial and post-independence economy and society.

---

[111] Melber 1995:3
[112] In incomes, educational and other services, in infrastructure and, obviously, in employment opportunities

According to the figures provided by the 1991 census, migration reflects a normal state of affairs, rather than an exception – if one can call a state of affairs motivated by extreme poverty 'normal'. In most of the census districts north of the Windhoek – Swakop line and south of the 'red' veterinary line, the proportion of in-migrants in districts to the native population amounts to between one half and three quarters of the residents[113] – an astounding figure! The question is: can we assume that all these migratory movements are to be classified as labour migration? The answer can be hypothetically given from two different angles:

- The historical experience of the institutionalised Contract Labour System clearly indicates the link between the economic policy of capitalisation and commodification and the creation of a migrant labour force;
- The current situation also reflects the efforts of a deprived population compelled to migrate in seeking more sustainable economic opportunities.

Already a first glance at the field of research reveals that post-independence migration must be assessed as 'labour migration'. When asked, the migrants themselves indicate that their reasons for leaving their home districts were mainly the desire for employment and/or the satisfaction of basic needs based on income from employment/self-employment[114]. The cultural attraction of 'modern', urban life also plays a role when young migrants try to extricate themselves from the atmosphere of social control typical of rural society. Empirical evidence indicates however that this is of minor importance.

The destination of all migrants' hopes: Katutura and Windhoek's north-western districts

Drawing a demographic profile of migration proper, the situation of the informal settlements in the north-western districts of Windhoek appears typical. In 1995 (according to an extensive Residents Survey conducted by the Municipality of Windhoek), the informal areas represented nearly a sixth of the total population of the city of Windhoek. As the settler phenomenon only started in 1990, it indicates the extent of migration (though not in its entirety, since some migrants also join the formal Katutura settlements). The residential status of the Greater Katutura population as a whole (Katutura Central, its extensions and the north-western areas of informal settlement) has not changed significantly since independence. According to Pendleton's study, three quarters of the residents were migrants[115]. Thronging to the capital to find work and earn a living, their hopes remain just that – hopes. The Windhoek survey of the informal areas paints a sad picture. House-

---

[113] Melber 1995:19, table 7

[114] In Wade Pendleton's study of the year 1996 on migration to and within Katutura two thirds of all respondents indicated economic reasons (lack of money, lack of job); however, there are hints that there is an increasing portion of the population also migrating in search for better schooling opportunities (their number nearly doubled, from 7% in 1991 to 12% in 1996. Pendleton 1996:19

[115] 74% compared to 80% in 1991; the on-going migrational trend is reflected by the slightly rising proportions of the population residing in Katutura for less than five years – 1991 : 41%, 1996: 47%. Pendleton 1996:19

hold income on average falls short of half the amount indicated as the official 'Primary Household Subsistence Level' for that year, with north-western area households averaging a monthly expenditure of N$427 (as compared to N$860)[116].

The migratory trend persists. Though data from the 2001 national census are not yet available, figures recently announced by the Municipality of Windhoek confirm the trend. Since 1991, the capital has experienced a 5,4% population growth. Currently, some 60 000 people, in their overwhelming majority migrants, populate the informal settlements. Every month, the town has to accommodate 600 newcomers, 85% of whom have migrated to the metropolis from northern Namibia[117].

Who are the migrants? Looking at the distribution by sex: nearly three fifths of the informal settlers are males (57,8% male, 42,2% female population). This is a higher proportion of men to women than the overall urban average of Windhoek, where out of every 100, 52 are male. The ratio exactly reverses the all-Namibia figures, in which women number 52 out of every hundred people[118]. Two hypotheses arise from these indications. First of all, migration is still primarily a male domain. But secondly, female migration is rapidly catching up. Pendleton's study confirms this trend, stating that, in fact, there is a "substantial increase in urban migration by women"[119]. Looking at the distribution by age: nearly three quarters of the population fall within the 20 – 44 years age group – the core group of labour force. Only a small number of older people still reside in town. The average age of the informal settlers amounts to a mere 23,78 years[120].

To better assess these figures, one must compare them to the other Namibian population pyramids. The population distribution by age and sex for Namibia as a whole indicates the absolute dominance of the age groups under 20 years of age as well as a slight dominance of the female population. The urban situation (population of all urban centres in Namibia by age and sex) shows a different picture. The age groups between 15 and 34 years of age are in the majority, and this refers to women as well as men. There is only a small percentage of people over the age of 45 living in urban areas. Children's age groups, on the other hand, would appear to indicate that urban migrants settle in towns without their children, but start to raise a new generation once in town. Focusing on the rural population, on the other hand, the figures clearly indicate the rural drain of males between 20 and 35 migrating to the urban areas. The dominance of the very young population is evident[121].

Compared to Windhoek's urban population as a whole: there is a slight preponderance of those aged 20 – 40, with a slight prevalence of males. Once again, there are few people over the age of 50, a new generation born in town and a

---

[116] Windhoek Residents Survey 1995, vol.1:3
[117] Aloe 2001:1
[118] Windhoek Residents Survey 1995, vol.1:3
[119] Pendleton 1996:5: "Of the adult female migrants who have moved to North-West Katutura, almost half moved in the last two years".
[120] Windhoek Residents Survey 1995, vol.1:3
[121] Windhoek Residents Survey 1995, vol.1:30, table 2.5

smaller number of children and teenagers. Comparing Windhoek's population pyramids for the years 1985, 1991 and 1995, we detect distinct signs of rapid urbanisation based on the settlement of a new migrant labour force. One has to keep in mind that the influx to the capital gained momentum with the abolition of the apartheid laws restricting mobility at the end of the 1970s. Since then, Windhoek has attracted migrants. Back in 1985, the majority of the population was composed of the working age groups between 15 and 40. However the young population and, to a lesser extent, the elderly were also part of the picture. Moreover, in the age group 5 – 30, the female population formed the majority. Only six years later, by 1991, the picture had changed considerably. The younger age groups – except for the new generation of residents up to five years of age – became relatively smaller. Male residents of the core labour force age groups between 20 and 40 won the majority over the female population, reversing the situation of 1985. Independence made itself felt.

This trend is even reinforced in 1995. The 25 – 35 age group has grown in size – at least this can be said of the male population. The share of the younger people has decreased – again with the exception of the new generation born in town. Female migration seems to have gained strength with independence. In 1995 the proportion of the female population of the working ages between 25 and 45 had increased, whereas in the 5 – 20 age group it stagnated or even decreased slightly[122].

This demographic analysis shows that Windhoek remains a reservoir for migrant labourers. The figures reveal that the change is mainly fed and shaped externally, by the continuous inflow of new residents. The picture of the centres of migration in Windhoek itself – the northern and north-western areas within the municipal boundaries – confirms this. Where do the migrants come from, and what is their destination within the urban area? The most predicative portrait is given by the north-western areas[123], which received nearly a third of all migrants[124] coming to the capital. Nearly all the migrants (85,22%) settling in this area came from the four-'O'-regions[125]. Figures relating to language distribution by Windhoek areas indicate that almost 80% of the informal settlers are Oshivambo speakers, with an additional 10% Damara/Nama speakers[126]. The population is a very new one. Fewer than 1% of the residents[127] had been living in this part of the town for more than ten years. The bulk (about three quarters) had only been residing there for a period of between 6 months and 4 years[128].

---

[122] Windhoek Residents Survey 1995, vol.1:32, table 2.6
[123] Including Goreangab, Big Bend and all the other suburbs of informal settlement
[124] Windhoek Residents Survey 1995, vol.1:62
[125] Omusati, Oshana, Ohangwena, Oshikoto. Windhoek Residents Survey 1995, vol.2:6. However, we have to note that these regions dominate the migrational picture in absolute figures only due to their high population, accounting for their high population density (Omusati: 15,1 persons per square kilometre, Oshana: 26,0, Ohangwena: 17,9; data from 1991 census) and pressure resulting from it. In percentages of migrants to the total regional population, other regions range far ahead of the Oshivambo speaking regions. Cf. Melber 1995:21
[126] Windhoek Residents Survey 1995, vol.1:42
[127] Windhoek Residents Survey 1995, vol.1:59
[128] As compared to 43% for the same period, which is the figure given for all areas of Windhoek. Windhoek Residents

However, one must consider that there are also internal movements within the Windhoek destinations of migration. With independence definitively bringing freedom of movement, such internal resettlements are facilitated. All the same, more than half of the informal settlers has resided in Windhoek for less than ten years[129]. The northern areas serve as an initial reservoir for migrants from the north of Namibia. The north-western areas receive nearly all their 'internal' migrants (94,44%[130]) from there (that is, Katutura, Wanaheda and their extensions, Hakahana and Okuryangawa). The Windhoek Residents Survey of 1995 points out a typical pattern of linking external and internal migration by saying that "any migrants move to the northern areas first to live with family and friends and then later establish their own households, mainly in the north-western informal areas."[131]

The population pyramid of the north-western areas, the core area of post-independence migration, reveals one important aspect of change. The proportion of the entire female population is, on the one hand, considerably smaller than that of its male counterpart (42,2% versus 57,8%)[132], confirming the well known trend. It concentrates on specific age groups, on the other hand, indicating that female participation is possibly becoming one of the salient features of future migration. There is a considerable preponderance of women in the youngest working age group (14 – 20 years). Above this age, the female proportion decreases markedly, leaving a clear majority of male labourers of the 25 to 45 age group.

In general, the marked presence of working age groups represents the main characteristic of Windhoek's informal settlements areas. About 60% of the population is between 20 and 40 years[133]. There is only an insignificant proportion of residents older than 50 years, only a very small number of children and juveniles between 5 and 20, and, compared to all the other districts, a considerable number of children under five. This demographic picture of the informal settlements combines to form a kind of emphasis of all the dominant features of the socio-economic condition typical of migrant labour settled in Windhoek. This is even highlighted by the fact that average household sizes for the north-western areas lie below the all-Windhoek average (3,75 as compared to 4,07 persons per household)[134].

Some further details: the absolute majority of all household heads among the informal settlers are males[135]. The household composition indicates that in only three fifths of the households is there a spouse to be found, whereas the number

---

Survey 1995, Annexures, table 3.8
[129] 57,97%. Windhoek Residents Survey 1995, vol.2:10, table 2.2
[130] Windhoek Residents Survey 1995, vol.2:9
[131] Windhoek Residents Survey 1995, vol.2:10
[132] Windhoek Residents Survey 1995, vol.1:28
[133] Windhoek Residents Survey 1995, vol.1:33, graph.2.7
[134] Windhoek Residents Survey 1995, vol.1:34
[135] 91,5% compared to 18,5% female-headed households; the all-Windhoek figures are 74,4% and 26,4% respectively. Windhoek Residents Survey 1995, vol.1:38

of relatives of the same generation even exceeds (statistically speaking) the number of household heads; and nearly two thirds of these relatives belong to the typical age groups between 20 and 29 years[136]. Notwithstanding this volume of a potential labour force, the occupational status of the members suggests how precarious and vulnerable the socio-economic status of the households is. Although more than half state they work or have a business of some sort[137], a quarter of them are unqualified workers, and another third, unemployed[138]. Most of them are classified as 'general workers', as the survey puts it[139].

Concluding from this evidence: looking at labour migration not from the individual's point of view, but from the perspective of the development of Namibia's market economy, migration does not generally add to the accumulation of capital. It rather adds to the spending of private revenues of the affluent population. In other words, labour migration in independent Namibia reflects the well-known, distinct inequalities in the distribution of resources and wealth as regularly reported in the annual United Nations Development Programme (UNDP) country reports. Migrant labour is to a large degree channelled into unproductive labour, and does not contribute to the productive expansion (in terms of capital) of the economy. Labour migration, still today, rather reproduces the structural imbalances of a dependent economy as created in colonial times. And this economy, in turn, relies heavily on migrant labour. To quote the 1993 report of Namibia's Population Planning Unit of the National Planning Commission[140]:

> "Although migrant labour laws were scrapped more than a decade ago, the structure of the Namibian economy still serves to reinforce the pattern of migrant labour."

This statement can be further qualified. Since the databases only refer to rural-urban migration and exclusively to the flow of labour into the capital, they leave out the movements to smaller industrial centres (such as the coastal towns) as well as the rural-rural migration (commercial farm workers). Consequently, migrant labour producing capital (speaking in the analytic terms of Marx's political economy) does not form part of the statistics, distorting the picture.

So far, the phenomenon of rural-to-urban migration has been examined from the angle of the pull factors. A look at the factors driving peasants from the communal areas throughout Namibia to migrate to Windhoek is also necessary, and the picture is unambiguous. Nearly two thirds of the informal settlers of Windhoek indicated unemployment as the main reason for giving up the comparative security of their areas of origin[141]. It seems evident that current land distribution patterns

---

[136] Windhoek Residents Survey 1995, vol.1:44-.45
[137] Windhoek Residents Survey 1995, vol.1:48
[138] Windhoek Residents Survey 1995, vol.1:50
[139] The majority of the residents of the north-western areas work in non-industrial areas of the capital (about 56%%) like the Central Business District or the well-off residential suburbs; and only a minority in Northern, Southern and Lafrenz Industries. Windhoek Residents Survey 1995, vol.1:52
[140] Quoted in Melber 1996:8
[141] Windhoek Residents Survey 1995, vol.2:11

in subsistence agriculture do not sufficiently cater for the basic needs of the rural population. Poverty thus exaggerates the attraction by the market economy and its alleged employment opportunities. In addition, urban life inevitably seems to attract the younger generation which takes in its Western consumerist cultural flair. This, too, accounts for their readiness to leave the traditional social environment and to turn a deaf ear to all the negative experiences of their predecessors. After all, nearly five sixths of all informal settlers admit that none or only some of their expectations which motivated them to migrate, were met[142].

Cultural and economic effects

Migration sees men as wage labourers as opposed to women as subsistence peasants – at least, at certain times of their lifetime. The gender traditions in the division of labour are thus enforced rather than transformed in a changing socio-economic environment. Moreover, migrants returning to their rural existence dispose of the scarcest resource in the agricultural subsistence economy: cash. With this, patriarchal patterns of dominance are also enforced.

Basically, men and women live in two distinct worlds created by migration[143]:
- they differ in the modes of production: migrants, as paid workers, become (a very vulnerable) part of the capitalist commodity economy; women, as peasants, remain at the mercy of subsistence economy;
- they differ in orientation, opposing subsistence and market orientation; opposing the immediate, direct satisfaction of basic needs and the strive for money where the satisfaction of needs is mediated through commodities; therefore, they follow different patterns of consumption;
- their lifeworlds oppose each other not only economically; men and women occupy different spaces and places of living, opposing countryside and town, natural and artificial, technological worlds;
- they develop different values and live by different cultural ranges[144], the urban world feeling much more the Western, metropolitan influence;
- they become part of different social environments, in particular, of different and changing family environments.

This last issue represents one of the most momentous effects of labour migration in Namibia[145]. In addition to such structural changes, Rauha Voipio, discussing the "detrimental effects of the contract system" on Ovambo workers, portrays the spread of adultery and promiscuity, notwithstanding the traditionally severe moral directions of both the Ovambo and the Christian cultures She also states the

---

[142] Windhoek Residents Survey 1995, vol.2:14

[143] Minette Mans in her contribution to this book ("Constructing cultural identities in contemporary musical traditions") analyses some of the cultural changes originating from the spread of migrant labour in terms of a new definition of gender roles.

[144] Peltola mentions even the change in moral standards in the migrants' urban world, labourers entering new sexual relationships in town, in addition to those at their places of origin. Peltola 1995:73

[145] Cf. Winterfeldt/Fox in this book: "Understanding the family sociologically in Namibia"

emotional shortfalls between the spatially divided partners in marriage and describes the estrangement between the absent father and his children[146]. The aspect of social alienation, in conjunction with the aspect of exploitation, became a matter of serious complaint on the part of the Lutheran Church in 1971, lodged against the South African authorities publicly and labelling migrant labour as forced slavery[147].

Spread of HIV/AIDS as an effect of labour migration

In a research report published in 1993, Webb/Simon emphasise that as a consequence of migrant labour movements "complex sexual networks"[148] develop. The rapid spread of HIV/AIDS, since the detection of the first statistical case in 1986, is linked, with several other factors, with the influx of the 43 000 exiles into Namibia at the end of the liberation war and independence[149]. But apart from repatriation, labour migration as a structural factor is to be attributed as major responsibility for the HIV/AIDS epidemic[150]. Repatriation, moreover, is very soon turned into labour migration, with returnees belonging to the most mobile population group.

Statistical evidence from case histories of HIV patients in the Onanjokwe and the Okatana Mission Hospitals, both in the Ovambo region, seem to support this hypothesis. Two main variables point to labour migration as an important cause for the introduction of sexually transmitted diseases into the local communities. Firstly, the sexual networking of HIV-positive patients shows that more than two thirds had had sexual relationships outside the Ovambo region within the three months previous to diagnosis. Secondly, STD cases rise sharply in coincidence with the seasonal returns of migrants, at Christmas and in March/May, during millet harvesting[151].

Another aspect relates to the effect of migration on women, as far as HIV/AIDS is concerned: Webb/Simon's research shows that the drought of 1991-1992 heavily affected rural women's food security. Some women tried to overcome this material predicament by generating income through sexual favours[152]. Being left behind without cash resources in a depressed subsistence economy, women's economic vulnerability is considerable. Against the backdrop of men's requests and in concomitance with unequal sexual power relations, attitudes of commodifi-

---

[146] Voipio 1972:xvii -xxxii
[147] Kauluma 177:66-67
[148] Webb / Simon 1993:1
[149] The majority of the returnees came from Angola (85,7%) and from Zambia (9,2%), which were epidemiologically highly critical areas. Webb / Simon estimate that near to 4 000 HIV-carrying exiled contributed to a sudden spread of infection. Webb / Simon 1993:3
[150] Pendleton / Frayne discuss the influence migration and its rural-urban-rural links have on the spread of the epidemic in Namibia. Pendleton / Frayne (probably: 1998):5
[151] Webb / Simon 1993:4, 6
[152] Webb / Simon 1993:6

cation towards their own body enter sexual relationships. Empirical research indicates that this happens to a significant extent[153].

Labour migration can be identified in terms of a social epidemiology. Therefore, it has to be added to the 'classical' factors of spread in sub-Saharan Africa: trading networks (itinerant traders and location of trading centres), transport networks (mainly focusing on truck drivers as a high risk group) and location of military bases often bear evidence of the vicinity of prostitution. To summarise: marginalisation through gender, showing in sexual subordination, and marginalisation through economic status, reflecting the contradiction between subsistence agriculture and wage labour migration, both explain in terms of a social epidemiology of HIV/AIDS, the specific vulnerability of women.

The class structural context of labour migration

Taking a sociological perspective, one of the most obvious effects of labour migration is the social structural one. In its institutionalised form, labour migration delays and limits the transformation of peasants into workers. In this way it delays and limits the formation of a class of colonial wage labourers. Pre-capitalist subsistence agriculture is not replaced by capitalist industry as a driving force towards socio-economic development. The emergence of the capitalist mode of production created the typical dual structure of interdependence between subsistence economy and market oriented capitalist sectors – the structural condition for the phenomenon for which sociology coined the term 'development of underdevelopment'. To dissolve the 'traditional', pre-colonial ways of subsistence and social life, but at the same time, to prevent the formation of an alternative 'modern' economy, society and culture – these two opposed and complementary actions characterise the pivotal effect of labour migration.

Moorsom, in terms of class analysis, takes a divergent stand. He regards migrant labourers as "members of a social stratum in transition from small-scale agrarian production to wage-labour"[154]. More likely, the proposed conceptualisation of social transformation as characterised by plain structural restrictions suggests that migrant labour should be defined as a hybrid social category[155]. It is a hybrid class, rather than a social layer in transition. The latter assumes that – a priori – the direction of change is certain: proletarianisation. This can be questioned[156]. The last three decades, particularly the first decade of independence, prove that the structures of underdevelopment that intertwine the subsistence and capitalist market sectors are stable and persistent ones. Labour migration is boosted and

---

[153] Webb / Simon 1993:28. Also, and picturing this aspect more in detail: Britt Pinkowsky Tersbøl's paper "How to make sense of lover relationships" in this book

[154] Moorsom 1975:54

[155] Relating to Basil Davidson's analysis, Magubane speaks of a "dual character of migrant labourers" in Africa. Magubane 1976:183

[156] As Magubane puts it on a more general and historical basis: "The historical specificity of imperialism in Africa lay in the fact that, although it integrates Africa within the world capitalist economy, it did not create in Africa a wholly capitalist social milieu." Magubane 1976:177

does not (yet?) lead to the emergence of a self-recruiting labour class of urban roots. The signs for a self-evident transformation overcoming the basic contradictions are not sufficiently consistent. Even Namibia's current bowing to the global economy does not fundamentally reverse the picture. On the contrary, globalisation generates new forms of restricting the freedom of labour, as the establishment of labour hire companies catering for the Namibian EPZs shows. As for the rest of the formal economy, the commodification of labour there remains limited in size and (life)time. It is not the supposed future status of the labour force, but its current contradictory character that defines its social structural place.

Turning to another social structural aspect of underdevelopment connected with internal labour migration: in referring to current problems of the country's economy, explanations often concentrate on the continuous drain of natural resources during the colonial era – and even today. There is no doubt whatsoever that both German and South African colonial regimes appropriated huge riches. Profits were either transferred and reinvested abroad or redistributed as revenues within the country on a highly unequal racial/ethnic basis. The latter did not entail any notable developmental progress for the majority of the indigenous population. Even investive redistribution, if it took place at all, did not involve the non-white population, and therefore the often advocated trickle-down effects remained minimal.

This drain of wealth is a historical reality, and as such is not to be refuted. It is continuing, for all one can gather from Namibia's regional dependency on the dominant South African economy and on the world economy. But in terms of long-lasting effects, colonial exploitation rather appears in the structuration of the Namibian labour force. In the main instance, colonial exploitation affected humans, affected the labour force. It limited the mobility of migrant workers, restricted their powers of negotiation and their purchasing power. It effectively confined them to a passing existence in the market oriented sector. It forced them to live a double-faced existence as subsistence peasants as well as wage labourers. This structural effect of institutionalised, colonial labour migration in hindering the formation of an indigenous working class and, therefore, in slowing down the expansion of the internal market is perhaps the major drawback in terms of self-sustaining growth and social progress.

Colonial profit-seeking, moreover, shaped an economic system relying on separate development for white and non-white populations. The racial bias of apartheid may not be exclusive any more, but the discrepancies between affluent and exploited populations remain. The structural contradiction between the mining economy, finance, commercial agriculture, modern infrastructure, communication, services and a few industries on the one hand, and subsistence agriculture and informal sector activities on the other – is it not still active today? It is legitimate to ask this question, since the agent of this contradiction is Namibia's still vast migrant labour force. The major current social structural effect of the historical institutionalisation of migrant labour lies in the creation of a hybrid class. Its members, in their personal life stories, are continuously forced to bridge the gap between the peasant and worker existence, between subsistence economy and capitalist relations of production, between 'tradition' and 'modernity', between a rural and an urban world. And it is this hybrid existence which, in turn, consolidates an economic system based on the exploitation of migrant labour.

However, there is one aspect where this class loses its hybrid character, and this points to the second main social structural effect of labour migration: it basically appears as a male class. The gender component of Namibia's social structure still continues to divide women not participating in migration from male migrants. It divides women struggling for survival as subsistence peasants in the communal areas from men struggling for a poor living as wage workers in the urban areas.

Recommendations?

Undoubtedly, it is a very pleasant Namibian custom to end an analysis suggesting practical steps to be taken. But, in this case, it seems quite impossible to formulate any recommendations.

The analysis has tried to identify the historical and structural groundwork of migration along class and gender lines. It argued in terms of the basic structures of exploitation (of male as well as of female labour). It shows the structural constraints as given by the economic system and by cultural setting. The economic system is built on the dominance (not exclusivity) of capitalist market relations of commodity production; it subjects and exploits subsistence labour in a very specific way – and this is mainly composed of female labour. The cultural environment represents an explosive mixture of patriarchal elements of Western, Christian culture and the no less patriarchal ones of many Namibian, ethnically based cultures. It provides the subjective patterns of dominance and of its justification and acceptance.

Now, one can hardly 'recommend' how to change these structures of crass social inequality. Sociologically speaking, by their nature they are not changeable in response to mere recommendations. Only a concerted economic and social policy directed at replacing a colonially-instigated migrant labour system and its underlying class structure could contribute to labour development and a transformation of gender relations.

Bibliography

Amoo SK 2001. Towards comprehensive land tenure systems and land reform in Namibia. In: South African Journal on Human Rights vol.17, part 1. Witwatersrand

Amutenya, Peter / *Andima,* Jochbeth / *Melber,* Henning 1993. Population distribution and migration (NEPRU Working paper no.22). Windhoek

Andima, Jochbeth / *Kahuika,* Saul / *Melber,* Henning 1994. Population issues in Namibia (NEPRU Working paper no.32). Windhoek

Angula, Helmut Pau Kanguloh 1990. The two thousand days of Haimbodi ya Haufiku. Windhoek

Banghart, Peter D 1969. Migrant labour in South West Africa and its effects on Ovambo tribal life (unpublished MA thesis, mimeo). University of Stellenbosch

City of Windhoek 1996. 1995 Residents survey report (vols. 1, 2 and Annexures). Windhoek

City of Windhoek 2001. Aloe – monthly newsletter for the residents of Windhoek. Issue 2, March. Windhoek

Cronje, Gillian and Suzanne 1979. The workers of Namibia. London

Dierks, Klaus 1999. Chronology of Namibian history – from pre-historical times to independent Namibia. Windhoek

First, Ruth 1984. The dignity of labour. In: Namibia Support Committee/ United Nations Institute for Namibia. Namibia 1884-1984: readings on Namibia's history and society, pp.324-329. London

Gebhardt, Bettina 1978. Namibian rural proletariat – the socio-economic status of the rural Namibian proletariat. In: Namibia Today, vol.4, no.5/6 1980, pp.26-47. Windhoek. (Reprint; original in: South African Labour Bulletin, vol.4, no.1-2, January-February 1978, pp.145-173. Durban

Gordon, Robert 1978. Mines, masters and migrants – life in a Namibian compound. Johannesburg

Gottschalk, Keith 1978. South African labour policy in Namibia 1915-1975. In: South African Labour Bulletin, vol.4, no.1-2, January-February 1978, pp.75-106. Durban

Green, RH 1978. Manpower estimates and development implications for Namibia (UNIN's Namibia Studies Series no.1). Lusaka

Hayes, Patricia 1992. A history of the Ovambo of Namibia, 1880-1935 (doctoral dissertation, mimeo). University of Cambridge, St. John's College

Hishongwa, Ndeutala 1992. The contract labour system and its effects on family and social life in Namibia – a historical perspective. Windhoek

Hurlich, Susan 1984. One day in the life of a migrant worker: a docu-drama in three parts. In: Namibia Support Committee/ United Nations Institute for Namibia; Namibia 1884-1984: readings on Namibia's history and society, pp.335-346. London

Kane-Berman, John 1972. Contract labour in South West Africa (paper of the South African Institute of Race Relations, Johannesburg). Johannesburg

Kauluma, James (no date, probably 1977). The migrant contract labour situation in Namibia and the response to it (mimeo). Windhoek

Kooy, Marcelle 1973. The contract labour system and the Ovambo crisis of 1971 in South West Africa. In: African Studies Review, vol.16 (1), pp.83-105

Magubane, Bernard 1976. The evolution of the class structure in Africa. In: Gutkind, Peter CW / Wallerstein, Immanuel (eds.). The political economy of contemporary Africa, pp.169-197. Beverly Hills, London

Meillassoux, Claude 1979. Overexploitation and overpopulation: the proletarianisation of rural workers. In: Social Scientist – Monthly Journal of the Indian School of Sciences, vol.7, no.6, January 1979. Trivandrum

Melber, Henning 1996. Urbanisation and internal migration: regional dimensions in post-colonial Namibia (NEPRU Working paper no.48). Windhoek

Moorsom, Richard JB / Clarence-Smith, WG 1975. Underdevelopment and class formation in Ovamboland, 1845-1915. In: Journal of African History, XVI, 3 (1975), pp.365-381

Moorsom, Richard, JB 1977. Underdevelopment, contract labour and worker consciousness in Namibia, 1915-1972. In: Journal of Southern African Studies, vol.4 (1) 1977, pp.52-87

Moorsom, Richard, JB 1978. Migrant workers and the formation of SWANLA, 1900-1926. In: South African Labour Bulletin, vol.4, no.1-2, January-February 1978, pp.107-115. Durban

Moorsom, Richard, JB 1978. Worker consciousness and the 1971-1972 contract workers' strike. In: South African Labour Bulletin, vol.4, no.1-2, January-February 1978, pp.124-139. Durban

Moorsom, Richard JB 1989. The formation of the contract labour system in Namibia, 1900-1926. In: Zegeye, Abebe / Ishemo, Shubi (eds.). Forced labour and migration: patterns of movement within Africa, pp.55-108. London

Mutwa, Gilbert 1978. Migrant labour in Namibia (paper presented at the conference on Migratory labour in southern Africa, Lusaka / Zambia, 4-8 April 1978, organised by the UN Economic Commission for Africa, Multinational Programming and Operational Centre for Eastern and Southern Africa (MULPOC)). Lusaka

Ndaoya, *Lovisa* 2000. Oshiwambo-speaking migrant workers on the Witwatersrand Gold Mines from 1940 to 1969 (mimeo). Paper presented at the conference on Public history: forgotten history, organised by the Dept. of History at the University of Namibia, 22-25 August 2000. Windhoek
Peltola, *Pekka* 1995. The lost May Day – Namibian workers struggle for independence. Jyvöskylö
Pendleton, *Wade* 1996. Katutura: migration and change in the 1990s (mimeo, draft). Windhoek
Pendleton, *Wade* **/ Frayne,** *Bruce* (no date, probably 1998). Migration as a population dynamic in Namibia (paper for the IIASA project evaluating alternative paths for sustainable development in Botswana, Mozambique and Namibia). Multi-Disciplinary Research Centre – Social Sciences Division, University of Namibia. Windhoek
Rädel, *Fritz Emil* 1947. Die Wirtschaft und die Arbeiterfrage Südwestafrikas (von der Früuhzeit bis zum Ausbruch des Zweiten Weltkrieges) (unpublished dissertation, mimeo). University of Stellenbosch
Republic of Namibia 1991. Housing and population census 1991. Government of Namibia, Central Statistical Office. Windhoek
Siiskonen, *Harri* 1990. Trade and socio-economic change in Ovamboland, 1850-1906. Helsinki
Tötemeyer, *Gerhard* 1978. Namibia old and new – traditional and modern leaders in Ovamboland. London
United Nations Office of Public Information *1974.* A trust betrayed: Namibia. New York
University of London 1993. Migrants, money and the military: the social epidemiology of HIV/AIDS in Owambo, northern Namibia. Centre of Developing Areas Research (CEDAR), Dept. of Geography (CEDAR research papers no.8). London
Voipio, *Rauha* 1972. Kontrak – soos die Owambo dit sien. In: Kane-Berman. Contract labour in South West Africa, pp.xv-xxxii (two chapters extracted and translated from the original Afrikaans version). Johannesburg. Another English version: Contract work through Ovambo eyes reprinted in: Green, RH / Kiljunen, K / Kiljunen, ML (eds.) 1981. Namibia – the last colony, pp.112-131. Harlow (Essex)

LAND DISTRIBUTION AND SUSTAINABLE DEVELOPMENT

Mary Seely / Juliane Zeidler

Sustainable development encompasses economic, social, political, cultural and environmental sustainability. What can the role of land redistribution be in attaining this overall goal? Or, if approached from another direction, what is it about current patterns of land use and distribution that mitigates against sustainable development?

Aridity and climate variability – the template for land redistribution?

Namibia is the most arid country south of the Sahel. It is within this unpropitious context, either with or without land redistribution, that environmental sustainability must be sought. Aridity increases from the north-east, where in the semi-arid climate over 500 mm of rain occurs, to the west coast with less than 20 mm rainfall per annum. This spatial variation in climate means that livelihoods based on natural resources, and potential for land distribution, vary greatly throughout the 834 000 km^2 of Namibia's surface area. How important is physical environment as a template for land redistribution and improved livelihoods? The climate of Namibia experiences great temporal variability, with annual rainfall totals ranging from less than a quarter of the long-term mean to more than twice this value. Moreover, the potential evaporation is more than five times the annual rainfall. It is estimated that of the total rainfall in an area, 83% evaporates almost immediately, 3% is available for runoff and groundwater recharge, while the remaining 14% is taken up by the soil and used for plant growth, returning to the atmosphere by evapo-transpiration. These basic characteristics of the Namibian environment (Dealie et al. 1993, Heyns et al. 1998, Jacobson, et al. 1995, Seely and Jacobson 1994, Seely et al. 1995) would appear to have wide ranging implications for the sustainability of livelihoods, land management and hence for land redistribution.

The implications of environment and climate variability for land redistribution and sustainable development are manifold and contradictory. Land redistribution could relieve pressure in over-populated communal areas reducing land degradation. In the north and north-east, however, communal lands have the highest, least variable rainfall and highest vegetation growth, although surface water may be limited because of the sandy soils. If quality of climate is the template for land redistribution, the resettlement of people from areas experiencing relatively good rainfall should not be considered. While climate variability could and does serve as a part of the template for land redistribution, it is clear that this is not the only or even the main factor.

Although not often clearly stated, the demand for land redistribution in Namibia usually refers not to land per se but to availability of and access to soil, water and vegetation, with a view to the improved livelihoods of people resettled. While basic availability reflects rainfall and landscape, access to soil, water and vegetation is determined by a number of political, economic, institutional, cultural and social factors. As a consequence, the current pattern of access to natural resources and hence of livelihoods, land use and natural resource management only partially reflects the prevailing aridity and climatic variability. It also strongly reflects past and present political, economic and social influences (SDP7 1999).

Land tenure variations as a template for land redistribution? – A case study

The inequality of the land tenure system in Namibia is usually cited as one of the components preventing sustainable development that could be rectified by land redistribution. This question was recently re-examined in north-western Namibia.

Land and natural resource management strategies and opportunities determine the ability of farmers to react to variable climatic conditions that prevail in north-western Namibia. In arid environments it is necessary for farmers to maintain flexibility and respond quickly in order to cope with extreme situations. Farmers need established social safety nets and to be prepared for 'extreme' years, e.g. years of drought, through foresight in planning and the accumulation of resources.

A case study was conducted in the southern Kunene region within the boundaries of the Huab catchment. Land and natural resource management practices and habitat condition were studied at three farms of differing land tenure history to establish whether land tenure and management practices affect or are affected by habitat condition. The main constraints to farming in such marginalised areas under differing management systems were also investigated. The results provide support to decision making on land distribution and sustainable development.

Weerlig is a privately owned commercial farm, which was demarcated in the early 1940s. Olifantputs is situated in the Fransfontein area communal farmland. The village dates to 1954 when the first permanent waterhole was established. Halt is an 'Odendaal farm', which was commercially owned from the early 1940s until the early 1960s. Since then the farmland has been redistributed and resources divided between a few families farming communally. The socio-economic and cultural backgrounds differ between the three farms as do management strategies and opportunities and livelihoods experienced (Hamukwaya 1998; Zeidler 2000).

All three farms are of similar size (+/- 5 000 ha), although they are used by differing numbers of families. The farm Weerlig is owned by one family; some farm workers and their families also live on the premises. Seventeen households are based at the communal farm Olifantputs, whereas Halt, after redistribution, is currently shared among three families. The three farms were chosen for their environmental similarity, including soil and vegetation types, but differing land tenure and management systems. The farms fall into a similar broad rainfall bracket with mean annual rainfall between 150-250 mm (Barnard 1998) and, taking the variability of rainfall into consideration, a rainfall range of 179-587 mm per year (Dealie et al. 1993). Local rainfall variability is significant and may differ greatly even within the boundaries of one farm. Because ecological frame conditions are similar at the three farms, it can be predicted that any differences in current habitat condition are attributable to differences in land and natural resource management strategies and opportunities on site.

Results from a bio-physical assessment of the farms indicate that the ecological resource base is more constrained on the communally owned farms than on the commercially owned farm, particularly so under high land use intensities (Zeidler 2000). The study also revealed that it is not stocking numbers per se that cause degradation of the natural resource base. Therefore other constraining factors were investigated, especially on the communal farm Olifantputs which is the most seriously degraded.

The communal land tenure system per se does not constrain sustainable land management (e.g. Scoones 1995). Often it is 'outside' issues that constrain management. These may include lack of de-stocking because of limited opportunities related to market availability and poor policy frameworks. Individual farmers have a good understanding of the management issues at stake. If we consider land use intensity as mainly imposed through high stocking numbers and poor grazing practices, according to the study at Olifantputs the main issues that cause overstocking are:

- A few farmers keep extremely high numbers of livestock on the farm, ranging up to 200 cattle and 240 goats. These are resident and absentee farmers. The majority of people living at Olifantputs own relatively small numbers of cattle, usually below 40 head or no cattle at all. Goat herds range between 50 and 150 head for an average family, while several families only keep individual animals and make a modest living off their livestock.
- 'Foreign' cattle that use the limited grazing as well as water resources. These animals come from neighbouring villages and cannot be controlled. The residents of Olifantputs call for a fence to improve management of their own grazing and water. However, considering that only 10% of all cattle observed at the waterhole seem to be 'foreign', ownership structures at the village itself appear to contribute to the problem of overstocking, and need to be addressed at village level. One household alone makes up 43% of all cattle drinking at the borehole.
- Lack of incentive to de-stock in poor rainfall years. This is a result of, for example, poor prices fetched on the market for livestock from communal areas, which value an average goat of a communal farmer 30% lower than goats from commercial farms (AGRA auction at Outjo, October 1998; Murorua, personal communication). This situation is compounded during times of prolonged drought when many animals are in poor condition. The loss of animals to predators, on account of theft and disease, threatens the income base of farmers. At Olifantputs, 6% of cattle were lost in the year 1997/98 to these factors, and almost 20% of small stock.

- Lack of communal decision making and support systems, as well as competitive farm management.
- Lack of safe and reliable places to move animals for emergency grazing. Farmers seem reluctant to leave their livestock in emergency grazing areas. There they have little control over their animals, particularly if these areas are far from home, and often these areas have limited water available and the payment of herders is expensive. Although most farms used for emergency grazing in 1998 were at a distance of only 30-50 km from Olifantputs, these areas were often considered unsafe. It seems that farmers at Olifantputs have become settled and are not keen to move with their animals themselves. They prefer to employ herders or caretakers, although it is difficult to oversee livestock management at a distance from Olifantputs.
- The grazing areas are used to the extreme. Emergency grazing areas are made available privately or through the government, often only at a very late stage when on-farm resources are already heavily used. (At Olifantputs vegetative biomass available was less than 12 kg per ha in October 1998, though there were still animals grazing on the farm.) Similarly, animals seem to be moved back to the farm early, either because of concerns connected to the emergency grazing areas or in hopeful anticipation of the onset of the rainy season. Little is known of the condition of the emergency farms themselves. One such farm, known as Halt, is characterised by poor soil condition and poor overall biological integrity.
- Grazing areas cannot be managed, e.g. rested. This is based on a lack of consensus amongst farmers to set grazing areas aside; free grazing by cattle is practised. Also, there are no camps or fences in place that would direct the movement of animals. Water points distributed across the farm could reduce land use intensity at 'peak sites' at the village and could possibly reduce movement costs of animals. However, such an intervention could also reduce management options and lead to an even more pronounced overuse at these additional water points, if not managed carefully. It may help to train herders to recognise habitat condition and become involved in the planning of where to move herds.

These issues have mainly been raised by the farming community itself at Olifantputs and are in line with issues addressed in the book "Living with Uncertainty" (Scoones 1995). Many management aspects crucial to the facilitation of adaptive range management in arid environments are not in place at Olifantputs.

There are also a number of additional issues relating to desertification, or ongoing loss of productivity at Olifantputs. One of the most pressing issues would be the amount of groundwater available at the study farm, and the fact that the Directorate Rural Water Supply (DRWS) budgets consumption at Olifantputs at only two thirds of actual consumption. The village is assumed to consume 13 100 l per day, whereas cross-validated data derived by the Namibian Programme to Combat Desertification (NAPCOD) calculate a daily consumption of up to 20 278 l per day (Zeidler et al. 2000).

It is necessary to assess whether the level of income that can be generated through farming activities in an area as marginal as Olifantputs will be sufficient to fulfil the expectations people have for development and their own livelihood security. This is especially true under extreme situations such as prolonged drought, when safety nets are essential. It seems that farming alone does not provide sufficient income to support families at a level that would be desirable for rural communities in Namibia and be a 'buffer' for disaster situations. Therefore other sources of income need to be developed. Sandford (1995) reckons that, instead of spending government money on rangeland development and land redistribution that might only bring meagre rewards, it might be more economical to spend the resources on re-equipping the expanding pastoral population for non-pastoral occupations. How this can be brought forward in the context of rural development in Namibia is currently being explored by various programmes and needs to be addressed through appropriate policy development.

The number of issues arising under land tenure, illustrated by this case study, suggests that this system alone should not serve as a template for land redistribution and improved livelihoods without consideration of other, apparently more important factors of political, cultural, social and economic significance.

Land redistribution and social considerations

If neither climate nor the land tenure system fully explain constraints to sustainable rural development, nor provide the template upon which land redistribution can be planned, what other elements require consideration? Perhaps more important are the social factors affecting sustainability. These would include addressing questions such as who has or should be given land, who is given land, and the ethnic and gender aspects of land occupation and land redistribution. Consequences of not addressing these issues include exacerbation of economic inequalities and class relations as well as an increase in forced responses to economic and environmental distress such as absenteeism or forced sale of assets (Devereux and Naeraa 1993).

As illustrated in the case study, flexibility of land use and management, as a middle- to long-term strategy, is a major component of long-term sustainability (Devereux and Naeraa 1993; Jacobson et al. 1995). It includes variation of livestock types or of the number of livestock per unit area depending on last year's and this year's rainfall, and on the management response that was applied to past variability. In addition to this, flexibility may include diversification to different types of livestock or different types of land use. Increasingly, it may also imply greater reliance on alternative incomes (NAPCOD 2000).

A flexible response has several major prerequisites. Natural resource users, those involved on a day to day basis, must have access to information, decision-making powers, and the right to act on decisions made. This is only possible when, for example, the owner and the manager of livestock and natural resources are identical or when a good cooperative management association exists. Most frequently, few or none of these conditions are present, even in land redistribution programmes. Instead, unequal power relationships, gender inequalities, inadequate institutional arrangements or simply financial constraints prevent adequately flexible responses to rainfall variability under any land tenure system. These conditions may be inherent in the traditional social system of rural society or may arise from inadequately planned resettlement or land redistribution programmes.

One frequently observed factor in unsustainable conditions in rural Namibia is that the owner of livestock and the main decision maker concerning their management and sale is an absentee farmer earning an income in a distant town (Jacobson et al. 1995). This situation constrains flexibility and contributes to land degradation. On one hand, the absentee farmer is not able to make rapid decisions nor act on current environmental conditions. At the other extreme, the absentee farmer may view livestock not purely as economic goods, but rather as a symbol of status. The increased livestock numbers that are an investment to the town dweller place added pressure on rangelands and on the villagers managing these assets on his behalf. In either approach, the absentee farmer does not normally empower resident farm managers to respond flexibly to environmental or economic opportunities or constraints.

As illustrated in the case study, one farmer in a village may own a disproportionate number of livestock while other residents have few or none. Usually the large herd owner is a male who if present may dominate all decisions taken, for example, concerning grazing management. This may be done indirectly by simply moving his own livestock when and where he wishes, or it may be done in some sort of loose association with other, smaller farmers. This can lead to a number of economic distortions for the village. For example, if, as happens in some cases, every village member pays an equal amount per person for water provision, the richer farmer with more livestock pays the least for water consumed. If a drought develops and a percentage of all livestock dies, the farmer with more animals may face the end of the drought with at least some animals remaining, while smaller farmers could have lost everything. Such developments serve to reinforce social structures and inequalities, be they on a formal or informal basis.

Should the one large farmer in a village not live there permanently, he either uses family members to represent his interests or hires village residents or outsiders. Where family members represent his interests, it is often women or older people and children who are expected to do so. This may place undue burdens on older people who are often looking after grandchildren as well and may effect schooling opportunities for younger family members. In the village hierarchy, the remaining family members may not participate in decision making if it is a male dominated structure.

In western Bushmanland where San people have been given land and resettled, many of the villages have an absentee farmer, in most instances from a different ethnic group (SDP7). In such a situation, a few San men are hired by the absentee livestock owner to manage his assets. The remainder of the village is disadvantaged by the presence of livestock that trample and consume the veld foods that people prefer. In established villages as well as in areas where land redistribution has taken place, flexibility, and hence the sustainable use of natural resources is curtailed.

Rural-urban migration, not just absentee management, is an approach used by some farmers to cope with aridity and climate variability (Devereux and Naeraa 1993; Jacobson et al. 1995). Individuals or entire families may relocate from a rural to an urban household. If an individual relocates, it means less labour available to the remaining rural household and, in some instances, the rural household may continue to provide benefits from natural resources available in the rural area only. Additionally, it may entail either remittances to the rural household, or mean that the urban dweller invests, for example in livestock, and then expects the rural household to take care of this investment (Seely 1999). All of these same responses to unsustainable farming conditions may also take place after land redistribution. Planning and preparation for coping with aridity and climate variability are essential, both by land users and also by authorities involved in redistribution programmes.

Land reform – the policy/ legislation framework

A number of documents formulated since the independence of Namibia directly address land reform and redistribution while others address sustainable development and, implicitly if not explicitly, the concept of land redistribution. These include, inter alia, the SWAPO Manifesto 2000, the draft Communal Land Reform Bill, the Agricultural (Commercial) Land Reform Act (Act No.6 of 1995), the draft Namibia Water Policy 2000 and draft Water Bill, the National Agricultural Policy 1995 and the Wildlife Management, Utilisation and Tourism in Communal Areas Policy 1995, the Ordinance No.4 of 1975 amending Regulation No.304 relating to Nature Conservation, and Nature Conservation Amendment Act No.5 of 1996).

Only some of this policy and legislative framework takes into consideration traditional rural social structures or the aridity and variable climate of Namibia, often assuming instead that existing patterns are conducive to sustainable development. An example is the high priority placed on irrigated agriculture for job creation and growth, wherein new social structures are required and the natural variability of Namibia's arid climate can be partially circumvented (SWAPO's plan of action 1999). Three objectives of SWAPO policy include: to bring small-holder farmers into the mainstream of the Namibian economy; to redress past imbalances in the distribution of land as a resource; and to create employment through full-time farming.

In view of the need for flexibility and quick response time to Namibia's arid and variable climate, at least two of these three objectives run contrary to current developments taking place in the country. While it is extremely important to redress past imbalances in the distribution of land as a resource, it must be remembered that the condition of renewable and non-renewable natural resources is what gives land its value for people. Land itself is not a resource. Moreover, full-time farming is decreasing rather than increasing under any land tenure system.

The Agricultural (Commercial) Land Reform Act (Act 6 of 1995) takes into consideration varying rainfall and quality of farmlands. Indeed, the pattern of the acquisition of commercial farmland by government confirms this recognition. The Act itself, appropriately, does not take the next step of addressing who is to receive redistributed farmland and how it is to be managed. In terms of ensuring the success of any land redistribution, such considerations are essential.

Environmentally sustainable land use is incorporated into the National Land Policy (1998) in both urban and rural contexts. However, other sections, e.g. that on land enclosure, ignore environmental considerations and refer only to spatial planning and consultation with users. This document highlights the attention paid to sustainable development in policy development juxtaposed with the neglect of existing rural social structures or regulations, training, capacity building or all the other aspects of management essential for sustainable development with or without land redistribution.

Similarly, the draft National Resettlement Policy (2000) addresses resettlement that is 'institutionally, socially, economically and environmentally sustainable and which will enable settlers to become self-supporting'. This document also emphasises the concept that land with its associated natural resources alone will address previous imbalances. In the recent past, these expectations have led to mixed results. In some instances inappropriate land use has been promoted, while in others the natural tendency for absentee farming, or farming without associated responsibility for environmental sustainability, has asserted itself. For resettlement and redistribution to be successful, political and social goals must be amalgamated with environmental realities.

The National Agricultural Policy (1995) also supports sustainable development in Namibia. Should this policy be implemented, agricultural development, whether or not it is in conjunction with land redistribution, would be enhanced. Similarly, the National Drought Policy and Strategy (1997) specifically addresses the arid and variable climate of Namibia. It points out that dry times are natural occurrences for which planning and preparation are essential. This includes flexibility, adaptability and rapid response. 'Drought', for which planning and preparation are insufficient and which requires external intervention, is an infrequent occurrence in Namibia. These same policies do not, however, directly take into consideration the traditional rural structures and their effects on the sustainability of land use.

The draft Water Bill provides many tools that, if applied, would support positive results from land redistribution. It reinforces the Constitution wherein it states that all water belongs to the state. Riparian rights (exclusive rights for people living along a watercourse) and allocation of water rights with land rights are both excluded. While these have implications for land redistribution, equally they have implications for existing land owners and residents. Decentralisation (cf. Decentralisation Enabling Bill 2000) is also promoted by the draft Water Bill, and the concept of Basin Management Committees as primary planning and management units is being explored. All of these aspects have implications for land redistribution as well as sustainable development of Namibia but, again, all ignore existing rural social structures.

In summary, environmentally sustainable development and land redistribution coupled with enhanced livelihoods are entirely compatible. Nevertheless, multiplication of current practices will not be sufficient to ensure the desired outcome. Appropriate concepts and approaches are available but capacity, interest and willingness to change are limited. As long as long-term sustainable development, including by definition economic, social and environmental aspects, is seen in opposition to the immediate needs and development of people, land redistribution will not address the objectives sought by all Namibians.

Bibliography

Barnard, P (ed.) 1998. Biological diversity in Namibia – a country study. Namibian National Biodiversity Task Force. Windhoek

Dealie, FF / Hamata, SA / Kambatuku, JR / Molapo, M / Parenzee, LG / Soroses, FW 1993. Rainfall in Namibia. What is normal? Desert Research Foundation of Namibia, Windhoek

Devereux, S / Naeraa, T 1993. Drought and entitlement decline in Namibian agriculture. Multi-Disciplinary Research Centre – Social Sciences Division, University of Namibia, SSD discussion paper no.3. Windhoek

Devereux, S/ Rimmer, M / LeBeau, D / Pendleton, W 1993. The 1992/3 drought in Namibia: an evaluation of its socio-economic impact on affected households. Multi-Disciplinary Research Centre – Social Sciences Division, University of Namibia. Windhoek

Hamukwaya, P 1998. Historical and present land management and land-uses at three selected farms in southern Kunene region. Research report. TOEB project/DRFN, Windhoek

Heyns, P / Montgomery, S / Pallett, J / Seely MK 1997. Namibia's water: a decision makers guide. MAWRD/DRFN. Windhoek

Jacobson, PJ / Jacobson KM / Seely MK 1992. Ephemeral rivers and their catchments: sustaining people and development in western Namibia. DRFN. Windhoek

Kakujaha, O / van der Linden, E / Rudd, T / Shiimi, T / Simon, E 1999. State of the environment report on the socio-economic environment in Namibia. GRN, Ministry of Environment and Tourism, Directorate of Environmental Affairs. Windhoek

NAPCOD 2000. Phase III proposal. DRFN/NEPRU. Windhoek

Sandford, S 1995. Improving the efficiency of opportunism: new directions for pastoral development. In: Scoones, I (ed.) 1995, pp.174-182

Scoones, I (ed.) 1995. Living with uncertainty: new directions in pastoral development in Africa. IIED. London

SDP 7 1999. Development options for resettlement in northeast Otjozondjupa. DRFN. Windhoek

Seely, MK 1999. Desertification in Namibia: rural – urban interactions (paper presented at the UNCCD Conference of Mayors, Bonn)

Seely, MK / Hines, C / Marsh, A 1995. Effects of human activities on the Namibian environment as a factor in drought susceptibility. In: Moorsom, RJB / Franz, J / Mupotola, M (eds.). Coping with aridity. Brandes and Apsel/ NEPRU. Windhoek

Seely, MK / Jacobson, KM 1994. Desertification and Namibia: a perspective. In: Journal of African Zoology 108(1), pp.21-36

UNDP 1998. Namibia human development report: environment and human development in Namibia. United Nations Country Team. Windhoek

Zeidler, J 2000. Establishing indicators of biological integrity in western Namibian rangelands (doctoral dissertation, mimeo, Dept. of Animal, Plant and Environmental Sciences (APES), University of the Witwatersrand. Johannesburg

Zeidler, J / **Seely,** MK / **Rahim,** A / **Bruzak,** G 1999. Indicators and monitoring systems at a community and household level: a case study of the communal farm Olifantputs. Occasional papers series. DRFN. Windhoek

2 SOCIAL INEQUALITIES AND SOCIAL INSTITUTIONS

Religion and its impact on Namibian society
Paul Isaak / Christo Lombard

Difference, domination and 'underdevelopment' – notes on the marginalisation of Namibia's San population
James Suzman

Women's advancement in Namibia – the concept of empowerment revisited
Saskia Wieringa / Immaculate Mogotsi

Understanding the family sociologically in contemporary Namibia
Volker Winterfeldt / Tom Fox

Small town élites in northern Namibia – the complexity of class formation in practice
Mattia Fumanti

Youth in Namibia – social exclusion and poverty
Pempelani Mufune

Two societies in one – institutions and social reality of traditional and general law and order
Manfred O Hinz

RELIGION AND ITS IMPACT ON NAMIBIAN SOCIETY

Paul Isaak / Christo Lombard

This article had its origin in a letter, written by the editors of this book, to two colleagues in UNAM's Department of Religion and Theology. The editors asked their theological counterparts to reflect on five key areas where the impact of religion on Namibian society is obvious and sociologically interesting.

Paul Isaak, Head of Department, agreed to write a response based on his own experience as a Namibian, theologian, academic, and church leader (Part 1). This broadly representative approach of an 'enculturated' Namibian theologian serves as a realistic sounding board for the more diverse assessment given in Part 2.

Christo Lombard, Director of the Ecumenical Institute for Namibia at the University, undertook a discussion of the five key areas with experts from civil society and from different academic disciplines, including Religion, History, Law and Sociology. It was agreed that this group would work with a functional(ist) definition of religion, allowing a more sociological approach to the questions, thereby providing the reader with a rich and even contradictory variety of perspectives in Part 2. This section represents excerpts and quotations from the various discussions and brainstorming sessions. Hopefully the final text, combining Parts 1 and 2 and including a variety of different reactions to the five important issues, will stimulate readers to critically reflect further on these penetrating sociological questions.

Five key areas as formulated by the editors

Dear Professores Isaak and Lombard,
Assuming that you have had an opportunity to peruse our proposal concerning the publication of the Sociology Reader, the editors would like to direct your attention specifically to the draft on 'Religion and its impact on Namibian society', presented here, asking you kindly for your academic expertise and contribution. Of course, there is no end to questions regarding religious matters. With an eye to the Reader, however, we are not thinking of strictly theological, pastoral or philosophical issues here. Nor do we consider the political angle, in the narrower sense, of the stance taken by Namibian religious institutions towards Namibian society. Rather, it is the pervasive presence of religion in social relations which calls for analysis.

To raise but a few issues, tentatively and with no claim for completeness, we have drafted statements and questions on the following five areas. Their respective introductions serve to clarify their sociological setting:

Christianity and Namibian culture
Christianity, as we well know, was an import into Namibia. It arrived in the region with a colonial political administration close on its heels. Some would argue that it was very much part of the colonisation process. Certainly it displaced local religious belief and practices. It was active in promoting its own monopoly of religious ideological belief.

Giving a picture of the impression a Western stranger may form of Namibian society today: As compared with European societies, which in many ways appear more secular-

ised, Namibian society displays a deeply religious character – at least at first sight. The influence of Christian morality seems to create an outlook on life significantly determining everyday actions, and not always in a positive sense: the extent of dependence on authority, for example, is one of those aspects which may strike a visitor, even giving rise to a feeling of uneasiness.

Can you give a sketch of the history of religion(s) in Namibia? Referring mainly to the Rhenish and the Finnish missions, what was their role in breaking up pre-colonial Namibian cultures? On the other hand, what was their contribution to a modern Namibia? Did the South African policy of 'indirect rule', fostering traditional authorities, widen the cultural and moral influence of the protestant churches in the Ovambo and Kavango regions? How deep or intensive is this religiosity really? Has Western religion paved the way for an unquestioning attitude of dependence on authority in social (and political) life? Or has it just deepened such an attitude, already finding it part of Namibian ethnic cultures? How far-reaching is the cultural dominance of Western religion? What significance have local religions today? How is it that indigenous African cultures in Namibia historically allowed foreign cultural dominance to such an extent and in such a relatively short period of not even two centuries? How come that contemporary Namibian Christian culture does not (yet?) reflect the Western trends of secularisation? Concerning this, do you notice a difference between rural and urban society in Namibia? Are there regional/ethnic distinctions?

Religion and sexuality

Recently, South African AIDS activist Rowan Smith advocated education on human sexuality, starting at the age of six or seven in schools, to provide the indispensable cultural counterpart to medicinal strategies. Addressing a Windhoek audience, Smith's call represents one of the rare occasions in Namibia where a representative of the churches publicly established a connection between Christian morals and the epidemic – a connection which politicians have frequently been reluctant to voice.

Sociologically, it is remarkable that sexuality is such a non-issue in Namibia's contemporary society which is deeply moulded by nearly two centuries of Christian ethical influence. An illiberal wall of silence is erected around sexuality as a natural expression of our social existence. On the other hand, it is pervasive in the public in all its negative forms, for the most part connected with male dominance over women and children – rape, abuse, violence and crime; and it is forced on the public in forms officially declared as deviant – homosexuality. Astonishingly, or perhaps not, Namibian AIDS awareness campaigns hush up any association between Christian sexual morals, with their insistence on monogamous relationships, gendered structures of inequality in the family as a social institution, attitudes of male supremacy and female subordination, and the spread of the epidemic.

Can awareness really be created without considering this nexus? Should not the Namibian churches initiate a self-critical debate and reconsider their own responsibility, addressing the faithful and deliberately breaking this wall of silence? After all, they are certainly the most pivotal moral institution, and they form an integral part of Namibian civil society, as limited and immature as this may yet be.

Religion and reconciliation

Forgiveness and reconciliation are more than merely secular guidelines of Namibian post-apartheid policies. They have comprised more than a rational compromise to prevent flight of 'white' capital with the attainment of independence, or a concession to pressures of the

Western Contact Group during the process of transition, to prevent the kind of racially motivated retaliation of which they had been accused in the past.

There is no doubt that forgiveness and reconciliation also reflect a fundamental religiosity which shapes interpersonal relations in this society to an extent perhaps no longer found in more secularised Western societies. On the other hand, as a fundamental value-orientation and attitude towards society, they are diametrically opposed to an orientation recognising and accepting that conflicting social forces and interests shape society. Philosophically, the idea of contradiction as a motivating force of social change represents an alternative. In a way, forgiveness/reconciliation may be seen as a proposition to conceal social antagonisms in terms of economic, racial or gender exploitation.

Given the prominent role of Christian faith, do you think the creators of the moral guidelines of reconciliation were aware of this ideological opposition? Could the extensive significance of religion have simply obscured their views? Or did they make their deliberate choice?

Religion and patriarchy
Patriarchy is a structure as well as an attitude. Culturally, it perfectly amalgamates Christian and African variations. It conciliates dominance and subordination. Cultural socialisation, a lifelong process to which we are inevitably exposed, transmits patriarchal attitudes from generation to generation and perpetuates the structure.

How relevant was the contribution of Namibian cultures; how relevant that of the new religion? How do you judge its impact on gender inequalities in Namibian society? Do you see a difference between urban and rural communities in this respect? Can you detect a trend for change recently; are there obstructive forces of conservation? To what extent has modernisation transformed the gendered picture of Christian ethics, and to what extent have they resisted transformation? Has the colonial reshaping of society also transformed the gendered worlds of customary culture; to what extent has it resisted transformation?

Religion and public discourse
Given the hegemonic cultural role of Christian religion: How would you envisage the future needs of religious education at school level? Do you see a moral responsibility of the churches as well as of the religious individual in matters of human rights, such as economic rights, political freedom, cultural rights, gender equality, and individual rights of self-determination regarding sexual preference? On an even broader level of what might be seen as political interference: should the churches take part in political life, acting as the moral conscience of the government? How would you depict the political role of the Council of Churches in Namibia (CCN)? How would you define a desirable relationship between religion and the state? Should the institutional churches be(come) part of civil society? If civil society is to be understood not just as a political entity, but as a politically acting social entity: where would you see its social structural roots in present-day Namibian society?

We are well aware of the fact that such a wide range of questions could create problems. Even two expert academic contributors might not be in a position to provide insight to all fields, within the restricted timeframe available. Therefore, we suggest that you involve further key persons and colleagues, asking them to intervene and help with their expertise in specified fields.

Formally, this will result in a 'dialogical format', requesting different contributors to share their views based on a sequential exchange of ideas. We think the outcome shouldn't even be too 'streamlined' editorially, so that the article when finally published will reproduce the discussion initiated by you. We hope this might not only solve the unfortunate problem of being pushed for time, but could also facilitate a more creative, deliberative essay-type format, liberating it beyond a classical academic exercise.

Ending on a more personal note: as editors, in the process of planning and drafting the sociological framework for this contribution, we ourselves were surprised at the extent of what we earlier called the 'pervasiveness of religion' in the social relations of Namibian society, even if we have only scratched the surface.

Best regards,

Volker Winterfeldt / Tom Fox (Department of Sociology, UNAM)

Part 1: Theological response

Paul John Isaak:

What will follow to address the five areas, as identified by the editors, is based mainly on my own experience of life: that which I internalised from my infancy and acquired through the culture by my being born and having grown up in such an environment. Such a process is called enculturation; the process through which a human being acquires his/her own culture. This differs from what anthropological science calls acculturation, namely the knowledge that is indirect, abstract and rationalised when the researcher comes into continuous first-hand contact with a certain culture. In short, acculturation is culture-contact which an outsider has. My knowledge and perspectives on the given five areas, on the other hand, is direct. It is based on the learning experience by means of which an individual is initiated and grows into his/her own culture and gains competence or enculturative experience.

History of Christianity in Namibia

Stephen Neill (1966:266) summed up the history of Christianity in Africa "in three words – gold, ivory, and slaves". Africans could not see Christianity as their religion, especially as its missionaries were easily seen as the precursors of the trans-Atlantic slave-traders or, as John Mbiti (1969:231) puts is, "there is no priest and a European – both are the same." Likewise, Christianity in Namibia was introduced during colonial times in an aggressive manner. Christian missionaries regarded African religion as "paganism, heathenism, primitive barbarism and superstition" (Mbambo 2000:115). Christianity had one main task: to christianise Africa and to win souls for God. But what the missionaries did not realise was that they were busy removing the fertile soil from the fields where they intended to sow. The end result was cultural deforestation and spiritual erosion, which produced schizophrenic Christians. No wonder the Africans used to say:

> "The white missionaries gave us the Bible and taught us to pray and while praying they took our land and cattle, now we are left with the Bible, they have the land and everything" (Mbambo 2000:119).

To sum up: this was the period in which Christianity was propagated and promoted as the religion of civilised people. The propagation of Christianity in all its manifestations was so successful that it became a dominant religion in Namibia, a position that it holds to this day. Today it is estimated that 90% of the Namibian population is Christian.

Africans today, as religious and political communities, are caught between two religious traditions. The challenge is to address the relationship between religion and people's cultural heritage and identity. In the words of Kameeta (1995:99-100):

> "We do not need to import any other culture from another continent to worship God in Africa and Namibia in particular. God has created us and He wants us to worship Him as He created us and not as falsified by other people with their cultures and traditions. When we worship Him as we are and with what we have, we enrich and strengthen the unity and fellowship of the church and add to her beauty. To be Christian cannot mean ceasing to be a human being living in Namibia. But neither can to be a Namibian mean ceasing to be Christian. To be a true Christian is not to have a split personality. I am one person with one personality as a Christian who is a Namibian."

Religion, sexuality and HIV/AIDS

It is good to deal with issues that challenge Christians and people of other faiths; to address issues such as sexual morality from religious perspectives. Sometimes, due to the attitudes of religious people and cultural taboos, one is prevented from talking openly about sexual matters. However, in the face of HIV/AIDS we are challenged to talk openly and freely about human sexuality.

At the outset one must state, from a religious and traditional cultural perspective, that the solution regarding HIV/AIDS is not only to be found by referring to condoms. What is needed today is to stress time and again the marketing or proclamation of sound Christian, religious and traditional cultural morals based on abstinence from sex before marriage and faithfulness within any marriage relationship. Today, promiscuity and drug abuse are key avenues for the spread of HIV/AIDS. Our message on abstinence has to focus on regaining a sense for the deeper meaning and purpose of sex as the celebration of a mature love in a committed relationship, which provides a 'nest' for the future generation.

Across the southern quadrant of Africa, the HIV/AIDS nightmare is real. The word not spoken is HIV/AIDS, and here at ground zero of humanity's deadliest cataclysm, the ultimate tragedy is that so many people don't know – or do not want to know – what is happening. The victims do not cry out. Doctors and obituaries do not give the killer its name. Families recoil in shame. Leaders shirk responsibility. The stubborn silence heralds victory for the disease: denial cannot keep the virus at bay.

HIV/AIDS is no longer a problem 'out there', to be ignored by religious communities. Sooner or later we shall be confronted with the reality of this virus. In the social environment where up to a third of the population is infected, it is more than likely that many church members and people from other faiths are infected as well. Taking Paul's picture of the body seriously, we can say that the body of saints (believers) is HIV positive. Put differently, our church has AIDS. It has become our problem; we have to deal with it; we have to become instruments of God's redeeming love.

To become instruments of God we need to revisit the African concept of ubuntu or khoesib: a person remains a person, as long as she/he is embedded in the solidarity of the community, regardless of her/his condition, situation or performance. In other words, the disease affects not only the physical body; it also affects the social body. If the social body, namely the 'cognatus, ergo sum' (I belong through blood relations, therefore I am), is threatened, then the whole existence and survival of the human race is endangered.

The family is often the most important group to which an individual has membership, and in which close relationships exist, so it is here that death will have its greatest impact. The loss of a parent, a sibling, a fellow learner or student, or a spouse disrupts established family patterns and requires a caring community and ministry. The religious, cultural and social implications are that such family members are subjected to great emotional distress as well as a burden of care on family members, often intensifying destitution and disruption of family life, and resulting in children being orphaned.

HIV/AIDS in Africa bears little resemblance to the epidemic in Europe or America, where it is limited to specific high-risk groups and brought under control through intensive education, vigorous political action and expensive drug therapy. Here the disease has bred a Darwinian perversion. Society's fittest, not its frailest, are the ones who die – adults spirited away, leaving the old and the children behind.

Therefore, there is a need to talk openly about human sexuality, safer sex and the use of condoms in the face of the challenges posed by HIV/AIDS. Many religious people think they can talk about morality without talking about condoms, which would be interpreted as advocating sex and promiscuity, so they talk only about morality. What we need is to put the two together. One way of putting the two together is to use the expression, 'rule and exception', as a guideline.

A 'rule' is something that can apply to all people; but besides that rule, there are many perfectly legitimate exceptions. When we speak of an 'exception,' that should on no account be misunderstood in the sense of devaluation. It simply indicates that 'exceptions' cannot be generalised in the same way as can 'rules'. A glance at the history of Christianity provides us with many examples of such exceptions: for example, monastic life or the Protestant orders for women who remain unmarried. None of those who have chosen this way of life would want to make it a general rule for all people. The decisive point is that both types – the rule and the exception alike – are to be measured by the same ethical yardstick, namely that life is served by whatever sustains, develops and preserves human life. In short: Lebensdienlichkeit (whatever serves life).

Today, the religious and cultural message on the prevention of HIV/AIDS must include the application of the 'ABC' principle, namely A is for abstinence; that is, abstain altogether from sex before marriage; B stands for be faithful in marriage or any sexual relationship. This is the way and it guarantees life. And if you find that you cannot follow this teaching, then choose C for condom. As a rule one must not lose sight of the fact that the A and the B come first. All people are required to follow this ethic of rule. Be faithful in whatever sexual relationship you are involved, be it heterosexual, homosexual, monogamous or polygamous (Saayman 1994:175). The church, religious communities, parents and individuals should devote themselves to the difficult principle of promoting sexual discipline among the unmarried. The religious communities and society should say in no uncertain terms that it would not tolerate promiscuity or any kind of behaviour which endangers human well-being. Having said that however, the discussion shouldn't end there.

At present there is no cure for AIDS. As such, one should revisit the guideline for 'rule' that includes 'exception', namely, if you cannot follow the rule, then choose the guideline of exception, namely the option of C (condom).

Reconciliation from religious and moral perspectives

As of 21 March 1990 the new and first authentic government of an independent Republic of Namibia proclaimed the policy of national reconciliation, calling upon all Namibians to reconcile with one another. This policy, which was also supported by the churches, urged Namibians to bury their differences, extend the hand of friendship to one another and be united as one nation. But what is reconciliation?

There are three words in Oshivambo that deal with the concept of reconciliation: ediminafanepo (you forgive someone and he/she in turn forgives you), ehanganifo (someone takes the hand of one person, and then takes the hand of another person, thus bringing them together); and etambulafano (two people accept one another following a quarrel; acceptance takes place on an equal footing). In Khoekhoegowab there are many words for the concept of reconciliation. The focus falls on the prefix re -, which means 'again'. These words convey the sense that something, which has been destroyed, should be rebuilt. Peace which has been destroyed should be re-established, or a relationship should be renewed. The words are //kawa-/haos and //kawa-/hû. The underlying notion is that of beginning anew, unconditionally. In Otjiherero the word okuhangana means 'peace', or 'being together again, being one'. Okuisirisana means 'to forgive one another'. Again, reconciliation points to peace, unity and the re-establishment of a relationship. The Tswana word for reconciliation is kagisano. This means 'to live together in peace after a quarrel or a dispute'. The verb agisanang means 'to reconcile'. After an issue has been settled, the parties should see to it that peace is maintained. Therefore, reconciliation has the sense of living or staying together, maintaining peace, or giving someone a chance. In Afrikaans, the word for reconciliation is versoening. The verb is versoen, from which one draws both the verb and the noun soen ('kiss'). Those who have a relationship close enough for them to be kissing are assumed to have been reconciled.

Thus, in most of our indigenous languages there is the idea of living together in peace, of coming together, of joining hands and having peace, whatever the case may be. The final concept conveyed is that something new should have been established, so as to live together in peace and harmony. The important issue is that the dispute or enmity should be done away with after an intensive discussion and a commitment from both parties to forgive each other. However, what does reconciliation entail?

Reconciliation is a religious, social, economic and emotional issue. The core issue involved is grounded in the reality that people were oppressed, that racism was practised, that there was a sense of being lost, displaced and homeless. The yearning to belong somewhere, to be somebody, to have a home and to be safe, is a deep and moving pursuit. Having lost one's place and yearning to find it are haunting images.

Consequently, reconciliation is not merely a spiritual affair or a case of forgiveness or of avoidance of conflict, but is a religious, moral, social and economic issue; a human right that demands a transformation of the entire human situation in all its aspects; a situation in which the hungry are fed, the sick are healed, and justice is given to the poor.

In Namibian society today, reconciliation must deal with the right to land, the reparation of losses or injuries inflicted through deliberate forms of injustice such as detentions, torture, dehumanisation, underpayment and exploitation; and the denial of the right to a home, to employment, to basic human rights, to a healthy environment and to development. There are three interrelated reasons why the church and religious communities should be part of the reconciliation and healing process.

Firstly, the healing of memories is necessary because people's lives can be greatly hampered by painful experiences from the past, which still live deep inside them. These experiences could be the loss of loved ones through death, or anything else that left people deeply self-doubting, feeling guilty, insecure, or afraid. Today, many Namibians are still traumatised by the fact that during the era of illegal occupation of Namibia and the liberation struggle many Namibians 'disappeared' and their bodies were buried in unmarked – and therefore unknown – graves. Yet it is the basic right of a human being to have a proper funeral, because death is ultimately connected to reconciliation. The dead should be given a proper funeral so that their souls will rest in peace. Otherwise, it will always haunt the society.

Secondly, people struggle to forgive. When they have been deeply hurt, or suffered a serious loss through the malicious action of another person or persons, they find it very hard to put it behind them and reconcile with those that have caused their hurt or loss. Therefore, if it is true that 90% of the Namibian population are Christians, the role of the church is to create platforms to enable those who feel the need to be reconciled to share their pain. Pain must be 'heard' in order to be healed. People must be given opportunities to share their painful memories and to relive them with someone whom they trust. They may need to do this several times, as memories tend to come back little by little rather than all at once.

Thirdly, the role of the church in the ministry of reconciliation is crucial in encouraging people to become integrated within themselves and within society. This integration process begins when people move from the broken-ness of their painful memories to a sense of healing and wholeness. It is important to note that the memories themselves do not change: their meaning does. While people can still remember bad experiences, they learn to see them in a new light. In the light of our faith, we realise with Paul that "for those who love God, all things work together unto good". Thus, the irreconcilable can be reconciled and the unhealable can be healed.

Gender and religion

It is not only racist beliefs that are promoted in the name of religion. Women have also been subordinated through the teachings of the Christian church. There are many means by which this has occurred, one of which being the most commonly accepted image of God the Father. For, as the Asian theologian Song (1982:16) points out:

> "God in traditional theology is masculine from head to toe. Such a God is a personification of male power, authority, and even brutality. In the name of this masculine God, theology has justified the subservient position of women in church and in society; the church has refused to ordain women to the priesthood and perpetuated the hierarchical structures centred in male power."

The power which this religious imagery and its entrenchment in the popular mindset have is similar in some ways to the manner in which religion has been used in racist agendas and belief systems. Just as some see white people as being closer to God than others, so men are seen as having a closer 'tie' to God than women.

Women's societal position as inferior to men has been encouraged not only by the masculine image of God, but through the use of biblical passages including the following:

> "Wives, submit to your husbands as to the Lord. For the husband is the head of the wife as Christ is the head of the church. His body, of which He is the Saviour. Now as the church submits to Christ, so also should wives submit to their husbands in everything" (Ephesians 5:44-24).

Women are placed in a position of submission. There is a great deal within the Bible about cherishing women, about honouring women, about respecting women; but women are still placed in a position of being defined by the men around them. Women should be passive and appreciative, and the most honoured are those who are virginally pure. The Virgin Mary is revered; women who stray from this ideal are sinful, leading men into temptation. Through such teachings, stereotypes about women are fostered. What does it mean to be a good woman? What does it mean to be a bad woman? In patriarchal societies, religious and otherwise, it is the men who provide society's answers to these questions.

In the United States and Europe, while the status of women overall has improved, there are still many issues that need to be addressed. Some of these are the lack of women in positions of power in political, economic and religious institutions; domestic violence; inadequate childcare; and the negative or stereotyped portrayal of women in the media. All of these examples represent the victimisation of women because of the view that the man is dominant.

Women in Africa face many of these same issues, in addition to traditional practices and standards to which they are subjugated. Within the context of their societies, men have found that they can use the Bible to justify women's inequality. However, women have been able to separate such thinking from the actual spirit within the teachings of Christ. The Bible was written within a specific historical context and this must always be acknowledged. Feminist theologians have delved deep into the Scripture and found a great deal that is in fact conducive to the promotion of women's equality.

Such exegeses acknowledge that men are the ones who have been providing the interpretation of Christ's message for too long. Religious teachings in themselves are not exclusive of women's equality: rather, it is the religious teaching provided through male-dominated institutions that have been used to uphold the social dynamic in which women are viewed as less capable than men. Just as some male theologians are questioning the teaching of the church, but not necessarily the messages of Christ, so women can find support within the spirit of the church, if not the particular teachings that they received from male church leaders.

The role of religion in public life
In Namibia today, we seem to be experiencing confusion when it comes to the working relationship between the church and the government. For instance, when should the church retain its autonomy, its right to make its own decisions without government interference; or when must the church maintain its integrity, the necessity for the church to be what it is rather than a channel for carrying out government policy? Furthermore, the church has the freedom to witness, the moral necessity of expressing its inner convictions, even when these run counter to political expediency. We need to debate these issues today, because when it happens that the church becomes a politicised church and our faith becomes a privatised business then the price is too high. Instead, church-state relations should always be that of institutional separation and functional interaction.

With functional interaction and institutional separation we have in mind that churches and government have areas of common interest – usually involving human welfare – in which they can cooperate towards common objectives. Today, with the growing complexity of modern society, both the church and government have an important stake in solving problems that affect the lives of people. But while solving these social issues and problems, the church should remain the church and the government should remain the government. But the question is: why are we experiencing an identity crisis in the church when it comes to its mission in this world?

During the years of colonialism and oppression, the Namibian church essentially said 'No' to any kind of cooperation with the racist South African regime. It was very easy to galvanise people into action, to excite and attract sympathy against the evil of political, economic, racial and gender exploitation. The objective was straightforward. Black people were opposed to apartheid and colonialism in Africa. The task of the church was made relatively easy because there was an identified common enemy. People walked arm-in-arm with Jewish, Christian, and Muslim leaders to oppose apartheid and colonialism.

Namibia gained its independence on 21 March 1990. On that day, the age of saying both 'No' and/or 'Yes' to the government began. The churches however did not know at what moment to say 'No' and at what moment to say 'Yes'. It was not clear that the prophetic 'No' under the new situation must include the prophetic 'Yes' to options for socio-political and economic renewal. In other words, the task of the church in an independent and democratic state is to learn when to say 'No' by remaining vigilant to the dangers of political power, namely its ability to serve its own interests rather than the common good. In short, the prophetic struggle against injustice must continue.

In any situation, the most important task of the church is simply to tell the truth. Many Namibians feel that in the first years of independence, religious communities, member churches of the Council of Churches in Namibia (CCN), and other non-member churches neglected the prophetic role of being the barometer of the conscience of the people. Instead of having candid talks with the government on the ex-detainee issue, gender equality, economic justice, and adequate pensions for senior citizens, or the right to access to the land, the attitude of the leading bishops has been that of neutrality and silence.

From a theological and political point of view, the church is an institution of Christians in society. As an institution it has the right to practice and manifest its functions in society. As an institution in its own right, it makes statements explaining its views on issues that involve its members in many kinds of activities. Some of these activities are promoting human rights and fundamental freedoms, and reconciliation and nation building. The doctrine of the church is always to defend jealously these rights and to insist that its voice be heard on any public issue.

Part 2: Inter-disciplinary perspectives: a report of a dialogue between various experts

Christo Lombard:

As suggested by the editors, I consulted with a group of experts (who discussed the five questions during several sessions) and compiled a short reader of some of the interesting, provocative and in some cases even contradictory answers that came out of these dialogical brain-storming sessions.

The discussion partners included the following academics and civil society leaders: Prof Brian Harlech-Jones (Department of English, UNAM), Dr Christo Botha (Head of the History Department at UNAM), Dr Wolfram Hartmann (History Department, UNAM), Ms Annelie Odendaal (Sociology Department, UNAM), Ms Dianne Hubbard (lawyer, Legal Assistance Centre), Ms Pandu Hailonga (Director, Centre for Global Education), Mrs Marita Kotze (Religious Education specialist, formerly from the National Institute for Educational Development, NIED), Mr Samson Ndeikwila (Director, Forum for the Future), and Ms Pauline Dempers (Executive Committee member of the Breaking the Wall of Silence (BWS) Movement). The questions were also discussed with a group of students from the Centre for Global Education. Where applicable, such as where direct inputs from these individual experts are quoted, their contributions will be presented under their respective names. For the rest, the group entrusted me to act as a scribe to compile the short summary of ideas. As can be imagined, it is quite impossible to do justice to the full range of perspectives that came to the fore during the discussions. We can simply recommend this inter-disciplinary method of dealing with complicated societal issues, and trust that the selections/examples presented here will trigger lively debate amongst students and scholars.

Early in the process of brain-storming, the core group that met regularly identified the need to agree on a few definitions and assumptions about religion. Understandably, these points of departure will still be interpreted and applied differently by different commentators. Due to lack of space only the following considerations, addressing important presuppositions on the meta-level of discourse on which some consensus was reached, will be shared here.

The function vs. the substance of religion

For the purposes of academic and inter-faith debate it is important to avoid exclusivist, essentialist definitions of religion. Such definitions, assuming a specific faith stance on 'the supernatural', tend to undermine social science scrutiny of the social functioning of religion in a specific context (Mann 1983:328). Functional definitions of religion arose principally from Durkheim's rejection of the Tylorian approach that saw religion as primarily involving a belief and institutions directed towards deities or other supernatural beings such as ancestors or nature spirits. Our group decided to follow Durkheim and the sociologists of the functional school, who see the essential character of religion as its promotion of group identity, order and solidarity:

> "Religion, it is argued, achieved this end through embodying in its beliefs the common value system of the community or society, answering the major and ultimate questions faced in that society, and through its practices revitalising commitment to these values and identity in the social group which shared them." (Mann 1983:328)

While respecting substantial definitions of religion, our study group avoided an approach to religion that defines it with reference to specific 'revelations' about the transcendent world. We found it more useful to investigate religion as a *human* phenomenon, as a dynamic human construct, dealing with human meaning, ritual and morality in actual day-to-day activities. For the purposes of answering sociological questions about Christianity and traditional African religion in Namibia, religion is thus defined, with Monk (1994:3) as "any person's reliance on a pivotal value or a group of related values in which that person finds essential wholeness as an individual and as a person-in-community." This definition is in line with the two major functions of religion as underlined by the anthropologist Clifford Geertz (1973:89, 126): providing a comprehensive system of symbols for understanding the nature of reality and providing a system of values that demand complete devotion. It also takes seriously the insight that reality, also religious reality, is a 'social construct' (cf. Berger and Luckmann 1966). We however do agree with Berger (1969:177) that in all functional religious constructs some or other (substantive) idea of a 'sacred cosmos' does come in, which will influence the definition of the pivotal values giving such a construct (e.g. 'Namibian Christianity') its identity.

When religion is studied in concrete historical and sociological detail as part of the human process of ongoing change and adaptation, justice can be done to its positive and negative influences, and the impact it has had on human affairs. In sociological debate it is not particularly useful to repeat idealistic definitions and perceptions about e.g. 'Christianity', 'African traditional religion', 'the church' or 'Christian morality'. Such approaches, working with essentialist, stagnant definitions, ignore the reality that all human phenomena are in constant flux, where interests (personal, social, economic, political and spiritual) determine the way. Thus, although religions tend to 'conserve' their credos, communities and cults (rituals), they do also tend to debate and adapt the level of their codes (rules for behaviour), since these are always in play in everyday decisions and actions. In our analysis of the five questions on religion in the Namibian context, we sense that there is a severe struggle below the surface, a reorganisation of codes, based on new readings of the function of religion and value orientation in Namibian society.

The elusiveness of 'secularisation'
Although the editors base some of their questions on the 'secularisation theory of modern culture' (accepting that the progressive, Western world has relegated the

importance of religion into virtual obscurity, and anticipating that this process will follow in other parts of the global village), our group agrees that religion has shown astonishing resilience against the rumours of its demise, not only in the 'third world', but also in unexpected contexts worldwide. Thomas Luckmann's distinction between 'secularisation from without' and 'secularisation from within' may be instructive in this regard (Berger 1970:3-5). This process of 'secularisation from without' is described as the (typically European) process in which people became 'secularised' from the influence of the outward religious institutions, such as the organised church, while the inherent religious values based on the underlying 'symbol systems' were still treasured. 'Secularisation from within' is depicted as the (typically American) process in which people still outwardly conform to the lifestyle of 'going to church', while their personal definitions of religion have shifted towards more secular understandings, such as 'spirituality for family life' or 'moral instruction for the next generation'. In Africa (Namibia) another 'mix', or type of secularisation, may be in process, as evidenced by the fact that the reference to Namibia as a 'secular state' in the first line of our Constitution, will probably never lead to the typical First Amendment interpretations of the United States of America, where religion is relegated out of the public domain and freedom of religion is personalised.

The point here is the following: Since religion can be defined as a socially constructed and value-oriented phenomenon, it may be premature to speak about secularisation of a society in the sense of the demise of religion in that particular society. The presumed 'demise' may simply be another case of traditional religious symbols and values that are redefined, revitalised, recontextualised, in order to forge a new solidarity or identity in or for that society – in line with the prime function of religion. Of course, the substance of the rhetoric used to depict the 'sacred cosmos' implied in a specific religion will always be in play in these dynamic processes, and will also be subject to change and adaptation (cf. Berger's "Sociological definitions of religion", 1969:175-77).

Questioning the idea of a 'pristine' form of Christianity or African religion

A further implication of this insight into the dynamic nature of culture (including religion) connecting the work of historians and sociologists is the fact that 'Christianity' in Namibia cannot be studied or evaluated as a 'pure' Western phenomenon. Wherever a religion is introduced into any culture, anywhere on the globe, some form of *inculturation* takes place, affecting the nature – the 'ingredients' – of that religion. This was also true when the Gospel was introduced to 'Europe': Christianity became 'westernised' precisely because of this process. Similarly, Christianity was absorbed into African culture in many different ways, and underwent significant changes in the process from the very start. In biblical scholarship it is now accepted that there were several strands of 'Christianity' in the formation of the New Testament traditions, represented by for instance the different gospel writers, Paul, Peter, James and John. Likewise, in spite of some common denominators used in defining African religion, such as the concept of *ubuntu* ('person in community') or the spirits of the ancestors, it would be impossible to find an original, pristine 'African traditional religion' (Shutte 1993:8). In revisiting and reconstructing our history, which clearly bears the marks of clashes of 'culture on culture' and 'religion on religion', we would be well advised to avoid idealising 'pure' forms of either Christianity or African culture.

In Christian missionary circles the approach called inculturation has now become prominent, indicating a deliberate recognition of the fact that religion is always part and parcel of culture. Taking 'the other's culture' seriously is not only important during the unique stage of first contact between the Christian message and a particular, hitherto non-Christian, culture. It is now realised that culture as such is a developing process and that there will always be an ongoing dialogue between faith and culture, even within 'Christianised' cultures (Lombard 1999:353-8). Faith itself does not and cannot exist except in cultural form. However, inculturation transcends mere acculturation, which may lead to a simple "juxtaposition of unassimilated cultural expressions", or to "a form of syncretism, in which illegitimate symbiosis occurs that is harmful to the authentic Christian meaning"; Christian inculturation is a "truly critical symbiosis" where the Christian experience is really integrated within the local culture (Shorter 1988:12).

The historical reality of enculturation (insertion in your own culture) and acculturation (influence of your culture by other cultures), which both take place naturally, serves to warn us against unnatural attempts at internal or external manipulation of indigenous culture. Culture may be manipulated internally (e.g. through rampant Christian, Muslim or other forms of fundamentalism), to preserve at all costs a 'pure' or 'authentic' culture against any 'contamination' from the outside. The threat of external manipulation, through transculturation or cultural imperialism, is just as real (Shorter 1988:7).

A 'common humanity' hypothesis for Humanities and Social Sciences

The Humanities (subjects such as History, Philosophy, Religion) and the Social Sciences (subjects such as Sociology, Psychology) share a keen interest in understanding our human existence. They are, however, frequently divided by methodological presuppositions. Whereas it is quite common for historians, theologians and philosophers to presuppose the possibility of a domain of 'shared human values' (or a 'common humanity'), beyond different religions or philosophies, sociologists tend to focus on differences in respect of human *phenomena* in the actual interplay of everyday life. (For a critical discussion of some of these theoretical issues, cf. Pratt 1978:90-100 and De Beer 1991:24-53). Without providing a solution to this methodological dilemma, we agree with Robert Belah that the arbitrary boundary between the Social Sciences and the Humanities should be opened up by the praxis of the Social Sciences as 'public philosophy':

> "Social science is not a disembodied cognitive exercise. It is a tradition, or a set of traditions, deeply rooted in the philosophical and humanistic (and, to more than a small extent, the religious) history of the West. Social science makes assumptions about the nature of persons, the nature of society, and the relation between persons and society. It also, whether it admits it or not, makes assumptions about good persons and a good society and considers how far these conceptions are embodied in our actual society." (Belah 1985:301)

We also agree with Berger that working *inductively* (from human experience towards conclusions) rather than *deductively* (from abstract principles down to human details) could be worthwhile, especially in the study of a complex phenomenon such as religion. Berger developed the notion of 'inductive faith', or "signals of transcendence within the empirically given human situation" (Berger 1970:52-75). It implies studying religion not via doctrines and ideas about the meta-world (theologically), but via traces of such a world that may be accessible *in* the realities of everyday living.

This can be illustrated by an interesting example: the growing realisation that the world's major faith traditions, in spite of very marked doctrinal differences, do in fact agree on the basic elements of a 'global ethic' (cf. Küng 1990; 1993). In fact, in 1993, at the centennial celebrations of the World Parliament of Religions, participants representing all the major religions of the world agreed on the text of a document called Toward a Global Ethic. Globalisation, not only in economic or political or human rights terms, but also in terms of shared values, has become possible because of the inductive realisation that all people on our planet share a common humanity. Behind the different canons of Judaism, Islam, Christianity, Buddhism, African religion, etc., all share the common human values of respect for others, and the conviction that humanity can only survive if all agree not to murder, lie, steal or covet; to respect parental authority and live in responsible sexual relations. Although some religions claim to have received these 'laws for humanity' through supernatural revelation, these insights have also been discovered and strengthened through 'inductive human experience'. This experience has freed people from a rigid identification of their credos with their moral codes; it has also opened new opportunities for religious tolerance, cooperation and synthesis.

This realisation of shared values has become easier since the collapse of the canons of Western-dominated 'modernism'. The legitimacy of different cultural, religious and personal perspectives presuppose a common humanity and shared values. They are espoused in the new post-modern paradigms of truth and enshrined in progressive constitutions, in which religious and cultural freedoms are guaranteed, worldwide. In the study of religion, therefore, both these aspects are to be respected: the fact of different interpretations and traditions, but also the assumption of the possibility and even necessity of common ground on the values that ensure human conviviality.

A post-modern approach to perspective, subjectivity and objectivity

If one thing is clearly illustrated by the different approaches and answers given to especially the historical questions posed by our editors, it is the acceptance of a new realisation in the social sciences: that there is no final, objective, normative account of events; that 'facts' are always interpreted constructs of events, and that subjectivity (perspective) is the presupposition of objectivity; that there is no neutral, purely objective observation post available in judging human affairs. (Van Peursen 1968; Belah 1985:302-3; Grenz 1996:131). Thus, when contributors such as Wolfram Hartmann and Christo Botha emphasise 'agency' in history against 'victimisation', they do not claim their view on Namibian history to be the final word; they simply try to counter a defeatist ('Africa as the victim of history') interpretation of colonialism with an alternative perspective, that of 'human agency in history'. This does not imply a denial of the very powerful forces of Hegel's dialectic of *Historie* at work in the missionary work during German colonial hegemony. Of course it is possible to study this whole period of change under the heading of a powerful hegemony that crushed a more vulnerable culture: politically, militarily, economically, religiously and socially (cf. Samson Ndeikwila's frank account of the 'dominance of Western religion and culture'). The question is however, whether the big dialectics of history are not accompanied by the human agency of all the players, by what Kierkegaard called *Geschichte*, the personal experience, the internalisation of history (as illustrated by Paul Isaak's personal poem "Caught between two religious traditions" on the effect of colonisation on the minds of his people, Isaak 1997:4).

We are convinced that the post-modern insights into the inter-textual nature of reality provide fruitful tools for understanding the complicated processes involved in the confrontation between cultures, religions and ideologies (cf. Grenz 1996 for a religious assessment of the post-modern accents of inter alia Foucault, Derrida and Rorty). People, cultures, political structures, religions are 'texts' confronting one another (cf. Barthes 1970; 1981:139 on the inter-textual nature of reality; Belah 1985:303 describes any living tradition as a "conversation, an argument about the meaning and value of our common life"). Even though some players in this game may seem to have unfair advantages of power and experience, the 'texts' involved always clash through communication, or communicate via the clashes. Words, phrases and ideas do rub off and become part of new 'syntheses'. A proselytising religion, such as 'Western Christianity', cannot simply be imposed on people 'from the outside'; it does take some 'agency', 'internalisation', 'inculturation' for a new mix of religion or culture to become accepted, unless of course cultural schizophrenia remains the final, cynical word.

In what follows, a selection of statements or quotations from the expert group, dealing with the five questions or aspects thereof (briefly indicated by italicised phrases taken from the editors' letter), will be strung together without any forced effort to smooth the rough edges. However, different as these perspectives may

The impact of Christianity on Namibian culture

Brian Harlech-Jones:

The role of religion in breaking up pre-colonial cultures; foreign cultural dominance
Regarding the history of mission in Namibia, I think that the early period should be viewed in three phases (cf. Nambala 1994:59-142):
- the Rhenish Mission's work amongst the Nama-Oorlams in the central and southern parts of the country;
- the same society's work amongst the Herero people in the central-north areas;
- the Finnish missionaries' work in Ovamboland.

Because of their history and heritage, the Oorlams identified closely with Western values and culture. Nama-Oorlam chiefs eagerly solicited the presence of the Rhenish missionaries, who were valued because they provided formal education, information about the wider world, and knowledge of medicine and other skills. Often, missionaries employed lay people with useful, practical skills in for example carpentry or blacksmithing. Moreover, the presence of a missionary often attracted traders, who were valued because they purveyed a large range of sought-after articles which the local people could not easily acquire on their own.

With regard to the Herero people, it seems that it was only after the catastrophe of the German-Herero war of 1904-1905 that there was significant conversion to Christianity. At that time, the Hereros were so shattered, numerically and spiritually, that they embraced the succour that the missionaries and Christianity provided. Up until that time, over a period of more than fifty years, the missionaries had made little impact on the Hereros, because, until the 1890s at least, the latter were largely self-sufficient, both materially and culturally.

The relationship between the Finnish missionaries and the Ovambo kings and people is less easy to analyse. However, it might provide a significant case study of the interplay between Western/Christian values and indigenous values. The Finnish missionaries were not directly supported by a colonial power; nor were they directly involved in trade. They thought that the presence of German soldiers and civilians could introduce the Ovambo people to some of the less admirable aspects of Western culture. For these reasons, it seems that the relationship between the missionaries and the indigenous people was less confounded by 'extraneous' factors than elsewhere.

There were also other factors that distinguished the Finnish Mission from the Rhenish Mission. For instance, the Finnish mission only used Oshivambo as the medium of instruction in its schools. Also, the Finns recognised the need to hand over control of the church to local interests. This was accomplished by the early 1960s, apparently without rancour, unlike the situation in the Rhenish Mission which was marked by considerable rancour and a number of secessions.

In summary, there are at least three scenarios of adaptation to mission and Christianity in Namibia, in the early period:

- In the south and centre-south, the Nama-Oorlams, who already shared many of the same values and beliefs, eagerly solicited the presence and message of the missionaries.
- In the centre and centre-north, amongst the Hereros, Christianity spread as part of a process of violent, coercive colonial imposition.
- In the central north region, amongst the Ovambo people, indigenous actors probably largely controlled the spread of Christianity and Western culture.

How is it that indigenous African cultures in Namibia historically allowed foreign cultural dominance to such an extent and in such a relatively short period of time?
Firstly, this question reaches far wider than just Namibia or Africa. For instance, how was it that the Anglo-Saxon tribes in England accepted Christianity during a period when conversion seemed to offer few political or economic advantages? Although it is possible that the answer might be found in practical advantages (e.g. the organisational capacity of the church), it is likely that the church also purveyed ideas that provided more powerful explanations about the meaning and purpose of life, as well as about how human beings might better live together.

Secondly, we should resist the assumption that cultures have an unsullied, pristine form, and that any change represents derogation from the ideal form. Achebe (in his two 'early period' novels, Things fall apart and Arrow of God) showed that there were paradoxes and contradictions within Igbo culture for which Christianity, and the Western education that the missionaries provided, seemed to provide 'solutions'. Of course, all cultures and human systems have their paradoxes and contradictions – and most people, everywhere, and at all times, struggle with these issues. Furthermore, all cultures change continually. In the process of change, they resolve some issues, which in turn give rise to new complexities. Also, isolationism is the exception. The vast majority of cultures and societies are in continual contact with other cultures and societies; the interacting parties react to, and influence each other on an ongoing basis.

Samson Ndeikwila:

Missionary role in breaking up pre-colonial Namibian cultures
Both Rhenish and Finnish Lutheran missionaries came to Namibia under the influence of anthropological literature which portrayed black people as inferior creatures. Their Christian background was conservative evangelist; they were

fierce warriors for heaven, preaching that the new converts should count themselves lucky that they were temporarily suffering in this temporal world, as this suffering would soon be exchanged with eternal happiness in heaven. Their understanding was that Christianity was one and the same thing with Western culture, and the way to enter heaven was through Western culture. They sincerely believed that everything African was inferior and evil. An African therefore had to abandon his/her culture and adopt Western culture as a gate to heaven. With good intentions influenced by cheap literature, and driven by a mistaken understanding of Christianity, these missionaries impacted destructively on indigenous Namibian cultures.

Missionaries' positive contribution to modern Namibia
The missionaries were sincere and compassionate but naïve people, committed to the cause of helping 'God's unfortunate creatures'. Often they mediated in local conflicts. They expanded their work widely, and established schools and health centres within the reach of their mission stations. They trained indigenous people in the use of medicine. During the time of South African rule, the churches united entire communities against apartheid. At mission schools indigenous people learned to read and speak foreign languages, which opened their eyes to their sufferings under foreigners. This led ultimately to the indigenous people freeing themselves politically.

How deep or intensive is (Christian) religiosity in Namibia?
There is a difference between religiosity and faith. Religiosity is the outward showing of spiritual belief. Faith is an inner conviction and leads to commitment to a spiritual life. The real question is 'how deeply do Namibian Christians understand the source of their faith, the Bible?' Many Christians understand very little about the Bible. Therefore Christianity in Namibia, and perhaps in Africa, is like a shrub showing leaves but having very shallow roots. Any strong wind can blow it away.

Western religion and the attitude of dependence on authority
Dependence on authority is evidence of a sense of powerlessness and fear imposed on indigenous Namibians over the years. The words of a person in authority were final: in the traditional family set-up a child should not answer back when an older person speaks; at customary courts, the proceedings implied that the accused was presumed guilty and had therefore to prove him/herself innocent. The chief/headman had overall power over his subjects. In the church a pastor/priest/preacher would say whatever he liked without anyone raising an objection, and at missionary schools any critical expression of a different opinion was viewed as evidence of disbelief in God. Among Namibians in exile, expressing a contradictory opinion from the official version was suppressed as evidence of underground activities of the enemy. During the South African era, many Namibians learned to smile outwardly while weeping inside. Today, to oppose anything said by a government representative is labelled unpatriotic. Many Na-

mibians (both black and white), and even foreigners, are afraid to express themselves. Namibians have learned to pretend, to nod in agreement whenever someone with power speaks. People have learned what are the 'right' things to say in public. They have also learned to be part of the crowd, not sticking out their necks. For these reasons it is difficult to know what comes from the heart, and what is false.

Dominance of Western religion and culture within a short period of time
Western religion is intertwined with Western culture. The older generation is outwardly religious/Christian and the youth are under the influence of the Western cultural patterns such as dressing, eating and ways of thinking. Information in the media is Western-oriented. It is said that Namibia is the most westernised country in Africa, though in spite of that, a growing number of Namibians prefer indigenous names to Western names. Learned and adventurous foreigners in the past came to simple-minded Namibians with a new religion hidden in books, medicine in bottles or wrapped in papers, different types of strange foodstuffs, travelling in oxen-drawn wagons and armed with powerful weapons. Everything was strange and superior to what they had, and this they admired in awe.

Contemporary Christian cultures vis-à-vis trends of Western secularisation
Educational levels are low among the majority of Namibians and the pastor/priest/church is still held in high esteem. The majority of the people are under the influence of the radio which they listen to in their mother languages. Except in the urban areas not much influence comes from the TV, which is therefore no competitor to the church, especially in rural areas or among the urban poor.

Rural/urban and regional/ethnic differences?
Due to influences of TV, urban life and everyday contact with foreigners, urban communities are more westernised and secularised than rural folk. Equally, big urban centres such as Windhoek, Swakopmund and Walvis Bay are more westernised. Ethnic-wise, Basters/Coloureds and Damaras/Namas have adopted more from the west than from anywhere else.

Christo Botha:

The impact of Christianity on Africans
This was not a one-sided process by any means. The selective manner in which Christianity was embraced, often resisted, and valued as much for the material advantages it could bring as for its spiritual values, proves the point. The great variety of churches within the African community, from denominations originally derived from Europe (such as Lutheran, Anglican and Methodist) to schismatic and independent African churches, demonstrates a vibrant yet selective response to Christianity. To equate tendencies among Africans (patriarchy, the avoidance of sensitive issues like HIV/AIDS) simply to the influence of Christianity, is to ignore

the way in which Africans continue to display a variety of approaches to religious and secular matters. There is still much ambivalence concerning the relationship between Christianity and African traditional religions, often playing itself out in diverse ways (such as praying before a football match after a *sangoma* was consulted).

Two remarks are worth making in this respect. Africans are increasingly displaying an ability to express themselves on matters that differ from political or religious orthodoxy, even though such tendencies are hamstrung by many obstacles including poverty, lack of formal and higher education, and a functioning civil society built on widespread literacy and exposure to foreign ideas. They also continue to object to ways in which the actions of Westerners are considered incompatible with the ethics of Christianity. There appears to be a continuing ambivalence towards what constitutes the essence of Christianity and African traditional cultural and religious values and how these should be integrated into a corpus of moral and spiritual values.

Marita Kotze:

The impact of Christianity on Africans
The impact of Christianity on Namibian culture is widespread. Christianity was not brought into Namibia by white colonialists only, but also by people such as the Oorlams. It is also clear that it was never completely integrated in its 'pure' form either in Namibia or in the Western countries from which the different strands of Namibian Christianity originates. To compound the difficulty, Christian National Education was a deliberate colonialist attempt at converting Namibia to 'pure' Christianity. This constituted religious abuse of Namibian society and strengthened a negative understanding of missionary work during Afrikaner colonialism. Religion – in Namibia's case, Christianity – can play a tremendous part in structuring societies, very often through its abuse. It also has immense strength in empowering people to overcome abuse. The mission schools, as can be seen in the biographies of many African leaders, were the places where people learnt to overcome the abuses of colonialism.

Wolfram Hartmann:

Christianity, as we all know, was an import into Namibia
Yes, Christianity was an import into Namibia, as it had been an import to Europe one and a half millennia earlier. (What the authors of the question had in mind was probably rather the notion that Christianity was exported from Europe to Namibia?) What needs to be considered, then, is that this import happened with the considerable assistance of local and indigenous people. The first bearers of Christianity were hybridised Oorlam groups trying to evade the worsening social and economic conditions of the Cape colonial nexus, moving in a northerly direction into present-day Namibia. These groups actively requested the presence of

missionaries. Jonker Afrikaner, settling at Windhoek in the late 1830s, invited both Wesleyan and Rhenish missionaries. When the missionaries from these two mission societies decided that confessional differences precluded successful conversion pursuits, the Rhenish missionaries decided to move north into Hereroland, where they established themselves at Otjikango, Okahandja, Otjimbingwe, and Scheppmannsdorf near the coast. This settlement was actively supported by local Otjiherero-speaking rulers.

This so-called import had three different trajectories in Namaland, Herero/Damaraland and Ovamboland (cf. Harlech-Jones). This needs to be taken into account in discussions about 'Christianisation' in Namibia, particularly as the question is whether this religion was primarily exported from Europe or rather imported into Namibia.

It arrived in the region with colonial political administration close on its heels
In the case of Namaland there were roughly seven decades, and in Hereroland roughly four decades between the first arrival of missionaries and the formal establishment of colonial German control; this can hardly be termed 'close on its heels'. In the north, evangelisation was at first viewed with suspicion, even resisted, and only very gradually could it make inroads after the arrival of the Finns in 1870. Catholic and Portuguese influence from the north also needs to be accounted for in this context. It would probably make more sense to discuss the arrival of European religious ideology in terms of European commercial penetration, and the advantages of this sought by local populations and their rulers.

Some would argue that it was very much part of the colonisation process. It was active in promoting its own monopoly of religious ideological belief
This sounds pretty determinist. A question to pose here would be on the existing indigenous belief systems eradicated by Christianity: in other words, was Christianity not a viable alternative to existing ideology and did it not answer specific needs coherently? If we accept that Christianity was an imposition, only passively suffered by local populations, we automatically assume that 'Namibians' did not actively consider their options in the given historical situation, etc. This, by implication, is yet another disempowering and patronising facet in the treatment of social science issues regarding Africa, albeit one that is actively embraced by Africans across the continent in victimising fashion.

Even though the missionary effort was not particularly successful in the beginning in terms of conversions – in Hereroland it took missionary Hahn twenty odd years before he was able to christen his first Herero convert – the missionary presence was actively encouraged by local populations in a situation of large-scale social turmoil and economic upheaval in the wake of Oorlam migratory movements. Put differently, a missionary was generally able to facilitate trade, broker knowledge and provide new skills, which was necessary for the survival of the new situation. This then challenges the notion of a Golden Age, an age in which Namibians were living in peace and ordered along socio-economic lines in different economic and environmental habitats.

Religion and sexuality

Samson Ndeikwila:

Challenging the churches to break the taboo on sex-talk
Traditionally, talking about sexuality has to a large extent been *taboo* in most Namibian communities, and this attitude was reinforced by two centuries of Christian morals. As such, the whole Namibian society, including the churches, has not yet seriously debated sexuality in an informed way. On the one hand, Namibian church representatives have been making uninformed, incoherent, shallow and moralising statements on what they see as negative forms of sexuality. On the other hand, Namibian civil society organisations have not yet jointly challenged the churches as the 'most pivotal moral institution' to convene a self-critical national colloquium to discuss the different aspects of sexuality, including HIV/AIDS in the country.

Annelie Odendaal:

HIV/AIDS, prostitution, homosexuality, rape and abortion as test cases
HIV/AIDS is increasing everywhere in Namibia. It remains a controversy, however, whether prostitution should be legalised to control the spread of HIV/AIDS in Namibia, or whether male prisoners should be given condoms. Ninety percent of Namibia's population is claimed to be Christian, and even though Namibia is a secular state, parliamentary debates relating to aspects of human sexuality, e.g. prostitution, abortion, rape, domestic violence, and homosexuality, frequently reflect the moral impact Christian values have on decision making in Namibian society. The former Deputy Minister of Prisons, Mrs. Michaela Huebschle, for instance, was reported by the media to have unsuccessfully attempted to persuade Parliament to provide condoms for prisoners in several parliamentary debates during her term of service.

Deteriorating socio-economic conditions in contemporary Namibia often promote sex as a commodity, and poverty largely contributes to changes in sexual behaviour and attitudes. In Namibia's male prisons, for instance, hunger, drug addiction and sexual starvation are usually the main reasons for exchanging sexual favours. Witnessing sexual activity in prisons involves getting accustomed to behaviours such as masturbation, prostitution, and same-sex relations, as well as being confronted with sexual violence in the form of male rape. Religion, ironically, is strongly emphasised in prison rehabilitation practices. In a Christian society such as Namibia's, same sex intercourse, especially between men, remains unacceptable for most. Male prisoners who admit to having sex with fellow inmates insist they will not use condoms for the fear of being labelled homosexual, since this could jeopardise their parole conditions or early release from prison.

On the other hand, whereas male sodomy was a criminal offence prior to independence, the existing law on sodomy no longer applies in Namibia. Although the sodomy law still exists on Namibia's law books, it became overruled by the Namibian Constitution. Men engaging in consensual same-sex activities can therefore no longer be charged with a criminal offence. Even though prostitution remains an illegal act in Namibia, male prostitution in Namibian prisons is overlooked and is not interfered with. Male rape in prisons, however, if reported, is severely punished in accordance with the new Namibian Combating of Rape Act that was introduced in May 2000. This act is gender neutral and gives legal recognition to the fact that men can be raped.

In addition to prostitution and homosexuality, abortion remains a major controversy in Namibia to further illustrate the strong influence of Christian values on law-making in the country. On the other hand, abortion, as much as the use of contraception, is still met with fierce resistance by men. Some people attribute the high incidence of babies being dumped or killed after birth to the fact that abortion is illegal in Namibia. The frequency of abortion, including illegal abortion, in Namibia, however, is not known yet.

Although Namibians were promised in 1996 that abortion would be decriminalised, the country's Abortion Bill was rejected in Parliament just before the 1999 major elections. The Minister of Health and Social Services, Dr Libertina Amathila, announced that the bill had been shelved because 99% of Namibians were not interested in the bill. Despite strong statements from activists, she would not be drawn into public debate on the issue. That the bill was rejected on religious grounds, and mainly because the churches were against it, came as little surprise.

Marita Kotze:

African understanding of sexual morality
African sexual culture differs totally from Catholic celibacy. African sexuality has always functioned within the tribal system. As it is today, without the community to authoritatively interpret its own binding traditions, people tend to make their own laws. New views in the field of bio-ethics challenge the churches to think again about different kinds of sexual orientation and expression. An open discussion exposes the heartless control mechanisms of celibacy as well as the oppression of gays and lesbians. Bio-ethics also cast a different light on mental illness and criminal tendencies. This knowledge demystifies aspects of human nature that were formerly relegated to the powers of darkness that could only respond to religious ritual, again attributing undeserved power to religious leaders.

Mathew Jibben, Centre for Global Education student:

African understanding of sexual morality
The church in Namibia has created a wall of silence that surrounds issues of sexuality, relationship ideals, and gender structures. It is certainly something that will paralyse any attempt that the church makes at combating a problem such as AIDS. It seems silly that an issue such as AIDS, one that is clearly linked to sexuality, the act of sexual intercourse, gender roles as played out in society, etc. is dealt with by ignoring all of those issues. It is like trying to balance a budget or get out of debt without acknowledging things like loans and interest rates – it cannot be done. If anything, any solution that the church could come up with while skirting around such issues falls short in effectiveness since the issues it ignores are certainly ones that would come up at a later date and destroy the previous 'solution'. The solution would simply be a Band-Aid over a gaping wound. The lack of addressing the pertinent issues when handling a problem like AIDS only shows an attitude of unwillingness to move forward with the times. In the case of the church, I believe that this is done to retain power. If the church were to give up some of the influence that it has in the areas surrounding AIDS, then it would no longer hold the position that it currently does.

Reconciliation *versus* conflict?

Christo Botha:

Different considerations for reconciliation
The decision to embrace reconciliation may or may not have been influenced by Christian values and beliefs. There are however other considerations: the recognition that a more vindictive approach (winners take all) would have exposed Namibia internally to disruptive inter-ethnic and inter-community conflicts about issues such as 'collaboration'. Also, material considerations played a role, such as the objective analysis of the potential benefits of a policy of reconciliation to the Namibian economy, by avoiding drain of capital and doubt about future investments. Political leaders often stress that reconciliation has an economic side and that black poverty is the biggest threat to peace (T. Mbeki). The attitude is: our patience cannot be maintained indefinitely. The readiness to forgive may be as much an African characteristic as one influenced by Christian values. Afrikaners seem to be markedly reluctant to embrace reconciliation where it entails specific sacrifices, material and spiritual.

Samson Ndeikwila:

Forgive and forget?
Since the days of the churches' support of the independence struggle, Namibian church leaders have been manipulated by political leaders, thus opening the way

for the church to be subordinated by the state after independence. Most of the statements the church leaders have been making were also meant to impress their ecumenical partners. Church leaders have been carried away by the political rhetoric of 'forgive and forget the past'. Some church representatives have even attempted to compare the role of the Namibian government with Christ as mediator between God and humankind. As such, the Namibian model of forgiveness and reconciliation has not healed but concealed deep wounds that continue to fester as time goes on.

Christo Lombard:

Reconciliation – coming to terms with the past
The official SWAPO policy of national reconciliation is, as the editors suggest, more than a rational compromise to prevent the flight of 'white' capital, or the concession to pressures of the Western Contact Group who wanted to ensure peace and stability in the transition to independence and self-rule in Namibia. These concessions were accepted by both South Africa and SWAPO, as the 'constitutional principles' of 1982 which 'refined and strengthened' UN Security Council Resolution 435, the basis of Namibia's peace plan (cf. O'Linn, Lombard et al. 1987:11-13; 104-107). The policy of national reconciliation not only embodied the spirit of the compromise that made the ceasefire and an internationally accepted peace plan possible. It indeed also linked up with the Christian ethos of forgiveness and reconciliation, and was therefore supported by the Christian churches and the community at large.

However, as a number of critical analysts soon pointed out, the way this policy was formulated and implemented, was exposed as also providing a welcome cover-up for atrocities committed by all the camps in the conflict: the South African government, their local agents and the SWAPO movement (Steenkamp 1995:95-114; Leys and Saul 1995:1-8;196-203; Trewhela 1991:67-72). The idea of 'forgive and forget' may have been embraced by some, pragmatically, in order to bury the memories of a bitter past: colonial oppression and genocide, racist apartheid and repression, inhuman economic exploitation, and degrading educational and social policies. It certainly also provided a much-needed smokescreen to conceal enormous human rights abuses and atrocities against humanity, perpetrated on both sides. The Parents' Committee exposed already in the 1980s that church leaders in Namibia and Europe were well informed about the truth of what really happened e.g. in SWAPO detention camps, but preferred to remain silent. Pastor Salatiel Ailonga and pastor Siegfried Groth also pointed to the scandal, in confidential letters to the Namibian bishops, the Lutheran World Federation, the United Evangelical Mission and the World Council of Churches. Groth expressed his concern again in his book, Namibia, the Wall of Silence, 1995. These documents show that the policy of reconciliation has another face: it became a conspiracy of silence on injustices and atrocities (cf. Trewhela 1991; Lombard 1998:174-189).

When, in 1989, a group of ex-detainees decided to speak out and ask for justice (the normal instinct to confront injustice), they were silenced as disturbers of the peace. They returned to Namibia during the period the United Nations Transition Assistance Group (UNTAG) controlled the transition process, just before the first elections, after they had escaped the notorious dungeons of Lubango where they saw many of their comrades die and disappear (cf. the Report to the Namibian People, for details of the inhuman torture and detention.) They in fact gave the church leaders another chance to rectify their short-sighted and timid defence of 'national reconciliation', by replacing it with a truthful vision of real reconciliation. However, the same church leaders who courageously spoke out against the apartheid policy and political oppression of the white South African regime, seemed to remain silent and fearful, powerless, in the face of the new SWAPO government's. SWAPO's manipulation of the content of the (religious) concept of reconciliation and the disappointment with the churches' inertia started the BWS group (cf. BWS 2001:1-10). The concept of reconciliation was in fact allowed to be abused in the name of 'nation-building' and 'peace' (cf. Wink 1998:24-32). In spite of promises of a national conference on reconciliation and active efforts by a few individual church leaders, the pragmatic politics of the leadership of the CCN bitterly disappointed church members (cf. Lombard 1998 for a detailed analysis).

What is the secret of this moral inconsistency, not only from a theological but also form a sociological perspective? Of course, one can argue that the church leaders voice the concerns of the majority, as they were doing in the apartheid era. However, between 'then' and 'now' there are many intricate differences, which can only be interpreted with a sense of irony.

- Then the majority wanted justice, now they perhaps only want stability (but what then about the Christian sense of social justice?).
- Then the majority was oppressed; now it is the minority who are marginalised and want justice (but what about rule number one of liberation theology: that God sides with the oppressed and marginalised?).
- Then the church leaders received credit for their courageous actions, now they also receive credit, but for their cowardly actions (because, if they were consistent they would also be criticised and ostracised by the new rulers of today, as indeed happened to pastor Groth and pastor Nakamhela).
- Then their actions were courageous and prophetic, now their lack of action is pathetic and cloaked in 'priestly' garments (but they do not even fulfil their pastoral duty to the ex-detainees, let alone the prophetic duty to demand truth and retribution for those falsely accused of being spies and traitors, and inhumanely detained and tortured).
- Then their moral high ground was genuine and gave people hope, now their lack of integrity destroys hope (because they are now seen to side with the powerful against the powerless).
- Then they challenged the powers-to-be with conviction and faith, now

they opportunistically collude with those new in power (but seemingly do not realise how they have compromised the Christian message under pressure and manipulation from the political rulers).
- Then they formulated religious and moral arguments against oppression, now they accept, by and large, the hollow arguments for and shallow definitions of reconciliation provided by the political leadership (in the process losing all credibility, not only for themselves, but also for the liberative role of religion in Namibia).
- Then they acted in a patriarchal, authoritarian way on behalf of the people in need in order to bring about a just and democratic system (cf. Steenkamp 1995:101-112), now they enhance the old Namibian authoritarian ethos within the newly founded democracy (ironically becoming a stumbling block for progress on sexual, gender and social justice issues and democratisation).
- Then the white Dutch Reformed Church endorsed racist and anti-communist policies and opposed the prophetic church, now they easily join the ranks of the 'enemy' in the Council of Churches (who, ironically, staged a 'reconciliation ceremony' with smiles and embraces in stead of acts of genuine retribution and contrition). The editors' questions all express an undercurrent of concern about the confluence of 'religion' and 'power'. Their concern is acknowledged and underlined in the above 'devil's advocate' examples the discussion group gives of the inconsistencies of religion, or the political involvement of religious leaders.

Of course, this 'weakness' of religion in the face of secular power, injustice and human rights abuse, is of no consolation to ordinary people who wished they could trust religion to have intrinsic power to empower 'the underdogs' against negative forces at work in history. The disappointment of the SWAPO ex-detainees, who directed their request to the CCN leadership in order for their version of the truth to be heard, only to be shunned, is understandable (cf. The BWS Statements and Clippings from Namibian newspapers between February 1996 and November 1997). Their case is an interesting one. It does not only illustrate that civil society, through organisations such as the National Society for Human Rights, BWS and Forum for the Future, will replace the churches as 'the voice of the voiceless', if the churches do not participate in these justice agendas. Their case also shows how ordinary believers will create a new theology when the 'official' theology does not work for them any more (cf. Cox 1973:16-19).

In South Africa, ordinary church people and theologians such as Archbishop Desmond Tutu were forced by the Truth and Reconciliation Commission to link the concepts of reconciliation, truth and justice. Likewise, those who suffered human rights abuses at the hands of their own Namibian liberators, had to redefine 'reconciliation'. They laid open the human conflicts involved in it, not allowing that they were hidden under the carpet of 'forgiveness' (cf. Wink 1998:34-54). As in similar contexts (e.g. in Latin America, other African countries and the Philippines), reconciliation has received an alternative definition in the BWS movement. It that does not avoid the issues of truth and justice and confrontation. It asks penetrating historical and political questions about what happened in the darker corners of the liberation struggle. Their approach to reconciliation does not follow the route of simply equating reconciliation with forgiveness. Reconciliation becomes a process in which various steps follow one another in order for forgiveness to be meaningful. There are four crucial elements: investigation (establishing the truth of what happened); mediation (where willingness to forgive can play an important role); adjudication (to let justice be done); and settlement (redress, retribution, restoration and reconciliation; cf. Bronkhorst 1995 and the extended bibliography in Wink 1998). This combines 'forgiveness' and 'confrontation'.

Religion, patriarchy and gender inequality

Annelie Odendaal:

Masculinity, male dominance and violence in gender relationships
Patriarchy – the system of male dominance – was one of the few non-racial institutions in pre-independent Namibia. To a certain extent it was reinforced by Western religious practices. It is so firmly rooted in Namibian society today that it is frequently identified with the culture and customs of different communities. Patriarchy in its present form affects a large number of Namibians and has its origin in the social institutions and history of Namibia. The perceptions of narrowly defined gender roles are transmitted through a range of social institutions: the media, family, churches, schools, and cultural groups.

Even today many men in Namibia believe that it is their cultural duty to discipline women by beating them. Some still insist on their marital rights by raping their wives, and attempt to prove their masculinity through criminal acts of physical force. The four cultural factors that are strong predictors of wife abuse in most countries are sexual economic inequality, violence as a means of conflict resolution, male authority and decision-making in the home, and divorce restrictions for women.

To challenge patriarchy and question male privilege and domination in contemporary Namibia is often regarded as an attempt to destroy African tradition(s) and culture(s). The emotional pleas against the Married Persons Equality Bill in the Namibian Parliament in 1995/96 clearly revealed the deep-rooted cultural and religious belief that a man should be the head of the household and have marital power over his wife (cf. Guide to the Married Persons Equality Act 2001:30-33). The late Nathaniel Maxuilili of the National Assembly, for instance, maintained: "We are not allowed to change the status of men and women, not at all. That is what God said. The women must be subjected to their husbands as the head. We must be very careful of women, that women want to take over power. We will never allow it." (Becker 1996:7-8).

In Namibia and southern Africa, however, it was in fact the introduction of colonial systems and urbanisation that led to the transformation of the traditional African family structures and practices. Modern division of labour not only altered the position of men and women within the family and broader society, but also intensified various forms of economic and social inequality. The Western influence in terms of economic practices and urbanisation continues in Namibia today with direct effect on family structure and the position of women. Depending on the region, an estimated 36-49% of households are headed and supported by women. In male-headed households, despite the responsibility they assume for child rearing, financial support and agricultural production, women have been subordinated to men in their communities. Traditional law still excludes them from the right to land and cattle. Inequality and exploitation are ingrained by tradition, socialisation and law, and are often reinforced by established religious practices. independence raised the expectation that inequality would be eliminated through affirmative action. Transforming a gender biased, ethnically fragmented society with extreme imbalances in access to resources remains a challenge, however. Legal change can facilitate changes in the status of women. However, unless accompanied by a reorientation of social attitudes and traditional practices towards gender, legal reform will have little impact.

Both the new Namibian Combating of Rape Act and the proposed Domestic Violence Bill are regarded as revolutionary and progressive in international legal circles. In many countries a woman is still considered a minor who cannot enter into legal contracts without the consent of her father or husband. In the new Namibia, a woman has equal rights and can purchase, dispose of and bequeath property without the supervision of a man. Women with matching experience and qualifications are entitled to equal pay for equal work with her male counterparts. Notwithstanding that, culturally the Namibian society remains a male dominated society. It is one thing for legislators to make laws that promote gender equality, but quite another to implement the meaning of these laws in families and workplaces. Not only is it difficult for men to transcend culturally sanctioned behaviour and practices that harm women, it is also a challenge for women themselves to overcome their own ingrained submissiveness. Therein lies the challenge of contemporary Namibian churches. Religion, as one of the most powerful institutions in transforming social consciousness, can contribute significantly towards changing deeply embedded patriarchal beliefs in Namibian society.

Elizabeth Wells, Centre for Global Education student:

Namibian cultures and Christianity combine in patriarchy
The church has been and still is a patriarchal institution which has contributed greatly to the gender inequalities of today. I think that in Namibia it is a combination of the traditional practices of various ethnic cultures combined with the male dominated Christian mentality that has exacerbated these inequalities. There are still communities where men are allowed to have multiple wives. Christianity itself

condemns this, but in a society that has been built on the need to survive by producing as many offspring as possible, this outweighs the need to follow religious doctrine. Also, because of their dominant gender roles in the running and protection of the community, the position of men is higher in status terms, and so violence against women continues. With the introduction of Christianity, ethnic communities can now use religion as justification for their inert position, especially when it comes to sexual abuse, where the church has always occupied an ambiguous stance.

Religion in public discourse

Christo Botha:

Churches and morality
The church should be the embodiment of a superior morality and provide ethical guidance. This should inform its approach towards government. When government acts in a way that contradicts or undermines Christian values, the church has a duty to respond. The reason why the church is silent in Namibia when government exhibits a selective morality (gay bashing and an apparent condoning/approving of examples of conspicuous consumption and corruption), should be judged against the background of history (colonial domination), African marginalisation (and consequent feelings of inferiority) and the need to avoid social conflict. This is especially relevant when one considers the fragile character of most African states and the high premium that is placed on conformity. One should rather look to possible authoritarian tendencies in traditional African societies, which evidence suggests was often actively reinforced by colonialism, or propagated where it did not exist. This is not to deny that Christianity may have aimed to reinforce certain authoritarian tendencies and helped to perpetuate conservative attitudes, but it again denies African agency and initiative to suggest that they did so as Christian stooges.

Marita Kotze:

How would you envisage the future needs of religious education at school level?
Given the understanding of religion with which the discussion group agreed to work, a tremendous amount is required from the educational system. It requires from 'society,' i.e. parents, teachers and children, that they begin to share this more sophisticated understanding. But the majority does not. On the contrary, they often even regard such an approach as 'evil' or 'from the devil.' Nevertheless, the churches as well as the religious individual should be given informed support in matters of human rights, economic rights, political freedom, cultural rights, gender equality, as well as individual rights of self-determination regarding sexual preferences. The churches should take part in political life, acting as the moral conscience of the government.

Curriculum theory demands that school curricula should, like religion, reflect the current understandings of a society. There seems to be tremendous pressure on the school system to rectify the wrongs of societies worldwide. Education is seen to be the panacea for all the ills of society. An appropriate response from responsible educationalists should then be to address the needs of the school system and society. A curriculum developer has to balance the three major foci in curriculum development: the needs of society, learner needs and subject content.

Curriculum workers make an all-out effort to convince teachers that the successful teaching of Religious and Moral Education does not depend on Christian commitment, and is not a more sophisticated guise for colonialism. It is dependent on finding applicable models for learners to take moral responsibility. Studying religion as phenomenon and not as theology, creates the awareness that today's problem of consciousness not only affects Christianity or African traditional religions, but all religion. Today we have ethical and conceptual problems that could formerly be easily managed from faith perspectives and obedience to religious structures. These societal problems pertain not only to Namibia, but are universal. An attempt to deal with these matters has been consistently made in the Namibian school syllabi since independence. Discussion of problems is encouraged from the religious perspectives of the learners and can lead to new insights.

Namibian Religious Subjects have set examples of working for gay and women's rights. When Population Education was introduced in Namibian schools, the syllabi were made more explicit, but the roots were there from the beginning. Yet, the fact that the questions are asked is an expression of the need to revisit the issues. There is a need for empowerment of all concerned to enter into open discussion with our youth on decision making on sexual issues. Ultimately, individuals are empowered to use the positive aspects of their own traditions. The churches can develop new interpretations of these.

Religious processes imply male-female relationships. Most of them try to protect male dominance, often simultaneously trying to placate women. In our Namibian syllabi, women's empowerment is taken seriously in the context of Population Education. Care is also taken to ensure that both men and women are treated respectfully. The Judaeo-Christian tradition has a strong patriarchal strain, but it also has a corpus of content that favours equality between the sexes.

Concluding remarks

In a study on the invention of 'African religion', Henk van Rinsum illustrates how we have all become "slaves of definition" in respect to Africa (Van Rinsum 2001:39-43;96). Van Rinsum follows Edward Said's analysis of 'Orientalism' as an attempt of the West to define and control the East (Said 1978). He quotes father Placide Tempels, whose *Bantu Philosophy* has had a tremendous influence on the thinking about Africa:

> "We do not claim, of course, that the Bantu are capable of formulating a philosophical treatise, complete with an adequate vocabulary. It is our job to proceed to such systematic development. It is *we* who will be able to tell *them*, in precise terms, what their most inmost concept of being is. They will recognise themselves in our words and will acquiesce, saying, 'You understand us: you know us completely: you know' in the way we know'." (Van Rinsum 1998:2; Tempels 1959:25)

In a compelling argument Van Rinsum exposes the religious and academic arrogance of these well-intended missionaries and their later *nemeses*, the expatriate academics and development experts. Their 'help' to Africa suffered from the objectifying and degrading definition of the African as *unbeliever* and *ignoramus*. He also addresses the double alienation and identity crisis the African faces. He quotes Voltaire:

> "You have made ample use of the time of ignorance, superstition, and infatuation, to strip us from our inheritance and strangle us under your feet, that you might fatten on the substance of the fortunate. But tremble for fear that the day of reason will arrive." (Voltaire, in: Okot p'Bitek 1971:112)

In another ground-breaking study on the use and abuse of 'people's religion', Harvey Cox (1973) analyses the crisis of religion in the modern era. The crisis is determined by what he calls "the seduction of the spirit" (Cox 1973:16). The *story* function of religion is dominated by the *signal* function. The s*tory*, i.e. the expression of 'genuine collective interiority', identity through sharing the same memory, values and ethos, is displaced by the signal, i.e. the institutionalisation, organisation, systematisation and eventually manipulation of people's faith, through clerical religion.

One cannot avoid the suspicion that this is what also happened in the Namibian context: 'people's religion', whether rooted in African stories or in a mix of African and Judeo-Christian stories, have been manipulated by missionaries, sangomas and modern-day church leaders. The living function of religion, to create hope, meaning and liberation, has been stifled by a moralising system, with signals – the "do's" and "don'ts". It is increasingly controlled by religious and political leaders, or a combination of both. However, if we can believe Cox, eventually the real thing will emerge again and again. 'People's religion' actually does not need apologetic defence against those who dismiss it as delusion, superstition or opiate. This optimism is shared by Gerrie ter Haar. In her study of what she calls 'community religions' (religion as practised traditionally, in local communities), she asserts that these religions collectively have more adherents than any of the major world religions or book religions (Ter Haar 2001:16).

Cox may be too idealistic in his expectation that theologians of the future will discover the debunking ('making fun of') task of theology, in what he calls "theology as play":

> "The theologian's job is to be a persistent muckraker of spurious mystiques. He is the 'demythologiser', the exposer of fraudulent meanings and pasted-on values. He is the theologian

as jester or holy fool, the one who pricks the pretences and shouts out for everyone to hear that the king has no clothes... Denying the powerful their mystique destroys the fear they must nurture in the souls of the powerless. Dismantling and deflating auras, halos and nimbuses is part of any theology devoted to human liberation." (Cox 1973:319-320)

Would it not be interesting, also sociologically, to have a few of these 'holy fools' around in the world?

In The Human Search for Meaning (Krüger, Lubbe and Steyn 1996:4-5), the authors identify two main functions of religion. It provides 'roots' to people (security, identity, meaning, integrity, stability), but also 'wings' (to soar beyond the known into the world of wonder, awe, reverence, liberation). Walter Wink has devoted his whole career as a theologian to 'demythologise' an all too comfortable Christianity, based only on the roots function. In his book, When the powers fall (1998), he presents an interpretation of the life of Jesus, as inaugurator of the 'rule of God' in human life, which corresponds closely with the debunking task of theology that Cox advocates.

Jesus' preaching of God's rule ('Kingdom') took place in a specific context: against what Wink calls 'the Domination System' of the world powers and human politics in the time of the Roman Empire. In an absorbing analysis Wink portrays Jesus not as "a minor reformer, but as an egalitarian prophet who repudiates the very premises on which domination is based: the right of some to lord it over others by means of power, wealth, shaming, or titles." In his beatitudes, his healings, his table fellowship with outcasts and sinners, Jesus declares God's special concern for the oppressed. His followers are not to take titles (such as rabbi); they are to maintain relationships free from any aspect domination in a discipleship of equals that includes women. The hierarchical relationship of master and slave, teacher and student, is not to persist. Jesus councils his followers to sell everything and warns the rich that they have no access whatever to the new society coming.

According to this analysis of what Christianity means, in any context (in the West or in Africa), an egalitarian society presupposes non-violence. Violence is the way some are able to deprive others of what is truly theirs. Inequality can only be maintained by violence. The root of violence, moreover, is domination. Jesus' critique is also directed against the law as a system of oppression "which had been subverted by the Domination system and made to serve the powerful, the wealthy and the shrewd. He prophesied the end of the temple" (Wink 1998:10).

The attentive reader will have noted that this concluding perspective goes beyond a mere 'functionalist' definition of religion, and mixes theology with sociology. If we take seriously what religion is ('roots' and 'wings'), what it has become in many instances, unfortunately also in Namibia (signals of control and domination rather than stories of liberation), but also what it could become (a powerful 'people's force' for breaking down all remaining systems of domination), the impact of religion on society can again be good news to the poor, and a social phenomenon to be welcomed and not wished away as redundant in our 'modern world', and with that, a new sociological phenomenon.

Bibliography

Barthes, *R* 1975. The pleasure of the text. New York: Hill and Wang
Barthes, *R* 1981. Textual analysis of Poe's 'Valdemar'. In: Young, R (ed.). Untying the text. A post-structuralist reader, pp.133-161. London: Routledge and Kegan Paul
Belah, *R* / **Madsen**, *R* / **Sullivan**, *WM* / **Swidler**,*A.* /. **Tipton**, *SM (eds.)*1985. Habits of the heart. Individualism and commitment in American life. Berkeley: University of California Press
Becker, *H* 1996. Married Persons Equality Bill: what some of our lawmakers have to say. In: Sister Namibia, vol.8, no.1, March/April 1996
Berger, *PL* / **Luckmann**, *T* 1966. The social construction of reality. Garden City NY: Doubleday
Berger, *PL* 1969. The sacred canopy. Elements of a sociological theory of religion. Garden City NY: Doubleday
Berger, *PL* 1970. A rumor of angels. Modern society and the rediscovery of the supernatural. Garden City NY: Doubleday
Bosch, *DJ* 1993. Transforming mission. Paradigm shifts in theology of mission. Maryknoll NY: Orbis
Breaking the Wall of Silence Movement 1997. A report to the Namibian people. Historical account of the SWAPO spy drama. Windhoek: BWS
Bronkhorst, *D* 1995. Truth and reconciliation. Obstacles and opportunities for human rights. Amsterdam: Amnesty International
BWS 1996/7. Statements and clippings (February 1996 – November 1997). Windhoek: BWS
BWS 2001. Response to the question: "What do you want us to do?" from the Council of Churches in Namibia (CCN). Windhoek: BWS
Cochrane, *R* 1991. Women in South Africa. In: Ackermann, D (ed.) 1991. Women hold up half the sky. Pietermaritzburg: Cluster Publications
Cox, *H* 1973. The seduction of the spirit. The use and misuse of people's religion. New York: Simon and Schuster
De Beer, *C* 1991. Pitfalls in the research process. Pretoria: HSRC
Foucault, *M* 1977. Discipline and punish. The birth of the prison. New York: Vintage Books
Geertz, *C* 1973. The interpretation of culture. New York: Basic Books
Grenz, *SJ* 1996. A primer in postmodernism. Cambridge UK: WB Eerdmans
Groth, *S* 1995. Namibia. The wall of silence. Wuppertal: Peter Hammer
Guide to the Married Persons Equality Act 2001. Windhoek: Legal Assistance Centre
Isaak, *PJ* 1997. Religion and society: a Namibian perspective. Windhoek: Out of Africa Publishers
Isaak, *PJ* 2000 (ed.). The Evangelical Lutheran Church in the Republic of Namibia in the 21st century. Windhoek: Gamsberg Macmillan Publishers
Kameeta, *Z* 1995. Worshipping God as Africans. In: Lombard, C (ed.) 1995. Worshipping God as Africans. Windhoek: EIN Publications
Kathindi, *N* 1991. Women in Namibia. In: Ackermann, D (ed.) 1991. Women hold up half the sky. Pietermaritzburg: Cluster Publications
Krüger, *JS* / **Lubbe**, *GJA* / **Steyn**, *HC* 1996. The human search for meaning. Pretoria: Via Afrika
Küng, *H* 1990. Global responsibility. In search of a new world ethic. London: SCM
Küng, *H* 1993. A global ethic. The declaration of the Parliament of the World's Religions. New York: Continuum
Küng, *H* / **Tracy**, *D* 1989. Paradigm change in theology. Edinburgh: T & T Clark
Leys, *C* / **Saul**, *J (eds.)* 1995. Namibia's liberation struggle. The two-edged sword. London: James Currey
Lombard, *C* 1998. The role of religion in the reconstruction of Namibian society: the churches, the new kairos and visions of despair and hope. In: Lagerwerf, L (ed.). Reconstruction. The WCC Assembly Harare 1998 and the churches in southern Africa, pp.162-197. Zoetermeer: Meinema

Lombard, C 1999. Inculturation and ecumenism. In: Lombaard , C (ed.). Essays and exercises in ecumenism, pp. 353-368. Pietermaritzburg: Cluster publications

Mann, M 1983. The Macmillan Student Encyclopaedia of Sociology. London:Macmillan

Mbambo, S 2000. Religious change in Namibia. In: Journal of Religion and Theology in Namibia, vol.2. Windhoek: EIN Publications

Mbiti, J 1969. African religions and philosophy. London: Heinemann

Meena, R 1992. Gender in southern Africa. Conceptual and theoretical issues. Harare: SAPES Books

Monk, R / **Hofheinz**, WC / **Lawrence**, KT / **Staney**, JD / **Affleck**, B / **Yamamori**, T) 1994. Exploring religious meaning (4th edition). Englewood Cliffs: Prentice Hall

Nambala, S 1994. History of the church in Namibia (ed. OK Olson) St Paul: Lutheran Quarterly

Neill, S 1966. Colonialism and Christian missions. London: Lutherworth

O'Linn, B / **Lombard**, C et al. 1987. The choice! Namibia Peace Plan 435 or Society under siege! Windhoek: Namibia Peace Plan 435

Pratt, V 1978. The philosophy of the social sciences. London: Methuen

Saayman, W 1994. AIDS. In: Villa-Vicencio, C (ed.) 1994. Doing ethics in context: South African perspective. Cape Town: David Philips

Said, E 1978. Orientalism. New York: Pantheon

Shutte, A 1993. Philosophy for Africa. Cape Town: UCT Press

Song, CS 1982. The compassionate God. New York: Orbis Books

Steenkamp, P 1995. The churches. In: Leys, C / Saul, J (eds.) 1995, pp.94-114

Szasz, J 1970. The manufacture of madness. New York: Harper and Row

Talavera, P 2001. Challenging the Namibian perception of sexuality (draft for comments). Windhoek

Ter Haar, G 2001. Between blessing and bane. Religion and human rights today. In: Journal of Religion and Theology in Namibia, vol. 3, pp.1-36

Van Peursen, CA 1965. Feiten, waarden, gebeurtenissen. Amsterdam: J.M. Meulenhoff

Van Rinsum, H 2001. Slaves of definition. In quest of the unbeliever and the ignoramus (doctoral dissertation). Maastricht: Shaker Publishing

Wink, W 1998. When the powers fall. Reconciliation in the healing of nations. Minneapolis

DIFFERENCE, DOMINATION AND 'UNDERDEVELOPMENT' – NOTES ON THE MARGINALISATION OF NAMIBIA'S SAN POPULATION

James Suzman

In a glass cabinet not far from the customs channels at Windhoek's Hosea Kutako International Airport, a life-size model Bushman[1] stands sentinel, under a banner advertisement for one of Windhoek's tackier curio shops. For many visitors to Namibia, the idea of the 'Bushman' (like the Welwitschia, the dunes of the Namib and Etosha Pan) is iconic of the Namibian 'experience'. The hunter's presence in the baggage hall announces to the visitor that he or she has indeed arrived. However, few San in Namibia are aware of their iconic status in the West or of the vast, predominantly romantic mythology associated with them.

While their popular image has persevered, their status as autonomous polities primarily reliant on hunting and gathering has not. The last century has seen Namibia's San population evolve into a largely landless, relatively impoverished underclass dependent on a range of opportunist economic strategies in order to survive. By 1990, the San were considerably worse-off than any other language group in Namibia across a spectrum of human development indices, to the extent that there is a clear link between an individual's identification as 'San' and a marginal social and economic status (Suzman 2001). Notwithstanding a few clear exceptions, San in Namibia are marked by:

- An almost universal lack of de jure land rights or equitable access to natural resources.
- Extreme poverty and dependence on welfare programmes, food aid, piecemeal labour and begging.
- Very low levels of basic literacy and numeracy compounded by poor school attendance and high drop out rates.
- Poor basic health care, squalid living conditions, a high incidence of social (in particular alcohol related) problems and life expectancy considerably lower than national averages.
- Weak representation in political structures or administrative structures and limited capacity to advocate their own interests at national, regional or local level.
- A sense of extreme social and political alienation from the mainstream compounded by social discrimination and prejudice.

So clear is the extent to which class and ethnic identity are bound up in the case of the San that some commentators have argued convincingly that the 'tradi-

---

[1] There is some debate regarding which label best represents those people that have at various times been lumped generally under the labels San, Bushman or Basarwa. For the purposes of this paper I will use the label "San" given its growing currency in Namibia despite its etymologically pejorative connotations (see Guenther 1986).

tional' hunting and gathering lifestyle of the San represents an adaptive response to poverty (e.g.Wilmsen 1989). While in the case of the Kalahari Basin San populations, this argument is not strongly supported by sociolinguistic or historiographic data (see for example Lee and Guenther 1991 and 1995), there is little question that San integration into and growing dependency on the colonial political economy over the last century was very much on terms other than their own. Moreover, it is clear that their participation has been limited by various mechanisms to the very lowest rung (Wilmsen 1989; Motzafi Haller 1986; Suzman 2000c).

This paper details some aspects of the complex history of Namibia's diverse San populations. I argue that their marginal status is not (as is popularly understood) primarily a consequence of their one time spatial, cultural, racial or social isolation from others so much as a history of conceptual and marginalisation by them. I examine the interplay between imagery, social practice and power in relation to land, development and identity, and in so doing discuss how, over the last century, marginalisation has become iconic of the San experience in 20th century Namibia.

The popular image of the San as a hunting and gathering archetype was largely inspired by the main corpus of scholarly work about them, published between the late 1960s and the late 1980s[2]. Much of this work (which has been subsequently labelled 'traditionalist') focuses on the small proportion of the San population who still relied on hunting and gathering as their primary form of subsistence[3]. Informed by a resurgence in evolutionary theory these studies aimed to elaborate on the 'foraging mode of production'. They were premised on the notion that San were stowaways in the spatial and temporal margins of the 20th century, and aimed to offer a glimpse of a way of life that until 10 000 years ago was a human universal. The prominence granted these studies in both the popular and academic domains effectively masked (as it still does) the complex and sometimes tumultuous history of relations that ultimately shaped life for the majority of San in 20th century Namibia. Only in the last decade have scholars sought if not to place relations between San and others at the centre of analysis (e.g. Gordon 1999; Suzman 2000) then to at least afford them some explanatory value (e.g. Sylvian 1999, Widlok 2000).

Imagery and alterity

During the early 20th century both white colonials and the majority of their non-white subjects articulated qualitatively similar mythologies concerning Bushmen. These mythologies positioned San as proximate 'others', and social inferiority in terms of the shifting symbolism by means of social status was appor-

---

[2] Concerning Namibian San populations, see for example the classic ethnographies of Lee 1976, Marshall 1976
[3] The majority of these studies took place in the Nyae-Nyae region of Namibia and the Dobe/CaeCae region of Botswana among the then relatively isolated Ju/'hoansi (see Marshall 1976; Lee 1968 1979 and 1984; Lee and DeVore 1976)

tioned. Over time as the San came to be increasingly dependent on the dominant political economy, these mythologies were mobilised to limit the extent of their engagement in it to its lowest tier.

The mainly Bantu speaking pastoralists and cultivators that settled in Namibia during the 18th and 19th centuries considered San alterity[4] to be manifest in a variety of ways. Apart from (as for instance in the case of some Kalahari Basin San groups) self-evident physiological differences, the San were marked out by their distinctive languages, distinct (but varied) cultural practices and, most importantly, their primary reliance on hunting and gathering. Among peoples for whom social status was expressed partially in terms of livestock capital, San did not fit conveniently into existing social categories. Not only did they rarely own livestock, they invested them with little symbolic value beyond that of their immediate utility. This meant that San were not considered to be merely low status or impoverished Bantu, but to occupy a space altogether beyond this social paradigm. While the sorts of social action this conceptual exclusion justified were mediated locally, it prescribed the level of San participation in local political structures as they became progressively more directly dependent on it.

European mythologies of the San and other 'primitives' have been explored in greater depth than those of their African counterparts (Gordon 1992; Wilmsen 1989; Schrire 1982, etc.). There is little doubt that the majority of Namibia's white immigrants during the 20th century brought with them a well established 'Bushmen'-mythology, the roots of which stretched back beyond the musings of Rousseau (Schrire 1982). The variant of this mythology that Namibia's colonial officials and white frontier farmers brought with them was a potent concoction. It was brewed from the genocidal encounter between Afrikaners and Bushmen in the northern Cape during the 18th and 19th centuries, spiced with European narratives of social Darwinism, and served up in a Calvinist chalice. They considered 'Bushmen' to represent the 'lowest' expression of humanity – a position that generated a distinct set of stereotypes, attitudes and debates. Despite this, the values Europeans attached to the idea of the 'Bushman' varied greatly. Some celebrated their 'noble savagery', 'primitive simplicity' and apparently organic link to 'nature' whereas others decried their 'debased' and 'brutish' ways and declared the noble savage a myth. Whatever the values and meanings people projected onto them, the Bushman provided an icon of alterity against which others could define their own achievements or failings.

Land and power

The extent to which popular mythologies about 'Bushmen' shaped their engagement in the emergent colonial state is well demonstrated by the way in which their rights to land were eroded. During the colonial period many non-white Namibians' lands were appropriated by successive colonial administrations on behalf of white

---

[4] The term *alterity* is derived from the Latin "alter": the other, the diverse.

settler farmers or were declared off-limits for nature conservation. What distinguished the San from others in this process was that, where others were usually relocated to newly established 'Native Reserves', the San were incorporated into the farms where they became an important source of generational labour[5] for white farmers[6]. Moreover, Bushmanland notwithstanding, in areas not zoned as commercial farmland or conservation areas, San territories were also ceded to others displaced by the colonial regime. Thus by 1971, 66% of Namibia's 22 000 San lived within white commercial farming areas and 31% in native reserves under the control of Herero, Kavango and Ovambo traditional authorities (Marais et al. 1984). Only the remaining two percent of Namibia's San population retained partial de jure control over their traditional territories (Suzman 2000c).

As much as hunting and gathering in the Kalahari was not necessarily as affluent a lifestyle as initially celebrated by Lee (1968 and 1984) and Sahlins (1971), traditionalist studies demonstrate that relative to the insecurity of subsistence agriculture in the semi-arid Kalahari, hunting and gathering wasn't too shabby an option[7]. Long before any Harvard researchers ventured into the Kalahari, the notion that San were affluent in their own 'primitive' way had some currency. Thus, for example, in 1953, the SWA's Bushman Commission resolved that "in their environment and leading their own lives, (Bushmen) were on the whole healthy and hardy people" (Schoeman et al. 1953:8)[8]. That San were able to remain "healthy and hardy" depended on their retaining access to sufficient natural resources. Hunting and gathering is a non-intensive form of land use, and while by no means the overt logic of their tenure system, San territories had to be large enough to adequately provide for their owners throughout the year (Barnard 1992). Contingent on ecological constraints and access to water San territories ranged in size from around 8 000ha in the relatively opulent Nyae-Nyae to 50 000 ha in areas such as the Central Kalahari[9].

Studies of historical relations between San and others (e.g. Gordon/ Sholto-Douglas 1999; Suzman 2000a) suggest that the San remained economically and politically autonomous as long as they did so not in spite of their primary reliance on hunting and gathering, but rather because of it. This work suggests that San foraged only opportunistically and episodically on the periphery of the emergent world system as it penetrated deeper into the Kalahari over the last three centuries. Their primary reliance on hunting and gathering meant that as long as they maintained adequate access to natural resources they retained the

---

[5] Generational farm workers (as opposed to migrant workers) typically retained no rights to residence outside of their workplaces. It was often the case that farm working families would work on farms over several generations, hence the term generational.

[6] The only other population group to experience similar levels of disenfranchisement were disaggregated Khoekhoegowab (Damara) speaking groups such as the G/obanin who articulated only superficial ties with the areas that were to become Damaraland.

[7] Van der Sluys

[8] Such views are sometimes reasserted in San oral histories. Hei//om oral historians, for example, have suggested to me that initial contacts between them and Ovambo speaking peoples were initiated by the latter when they trekked south in search of food after poor rains and harvests had led to famine.

[9] See Barnard 1992 for a useful comparison of territoriality among diverse San groups.

capacity to 'drop out' and 'live off the land' as huntergatherers, an ability that Gordon (ibid.) has argued further entrenched others' convictions of San alterity.

It is clear that well into the 20th century a significant proportion of Namibia's San population maintained control over their customary lands. In the western Kalahari, Ju/'hoansi, 'Au//eisi and Nharo speaking San vigorously defended their territories from what they perceived to be the aggressive advances of pastoralists, who in turn developed a healthy respect for the poisons into which San dipped their arrows (Gordon and Sholto Douglas 1999; Suzman 2000; Guenther 1993). In other areas like Mpungu in Kavango, the natural resource base was sufficient to accommodate others without precipitating competition, conflict or colonisation.

It was only by virtue of the events put into play by the German colonisation of Namibia and the subsequent consolidation of this process under South African rule, that most Namibian San groups by turn surrendered control over their traditional lands, and with this their political and economic autonomy. Colonial administrators did not consider the appropriation of San territories to be an act of disenfranchisement. Because they understood San to be 'nomads', they argued that San could not 'own' land. Indeed, because foraging and hunting were essentially non-transformative modes of engaging with the environment, it was widely believed that, like the wild game, San constituted part of the landscape for colonisation. As such, farmers who were allocated farms in areas where San lived rarely tried to drive them away but instead enticed, convinced and, in some instances, forced them into forming the nuclei of their long-term workforces.

Thus, while white colonists constructed their conflicts with Bantu agro-pastoral polities in colonial Namibia to be explicitly (although not exclusively) about land and the control of it, their struggles with Bushmen were framed in a dialectic of civilisation and savagery. Up until the 1960s, debate at government level on the issue of land for any of the Namibian Bushmen groups was framed within a paradigm of 'nature conservation'. If Bushmen were to be granted land, it was not due to considerations concerning any objective 'rights' to have land, but rather whether or not they, along with other elements of their 'habitat' might be preserved from 'extinction' in their 'natural' environment for the purposes of scientific study. If there were, after all, special reserves for elephants and lions, it was reasoned, then why not for the Bushmen (Gordon 1992:161-167)? Significantly though, by this time most San were regarded as too 'sullied' after contact with others to be 'preserved' for science. Thus for example, Hei//om San that were hitherto considered 'part and parcel' of Etosha were expelled from the Game Reserve on the recommendations of the Bushman Commission because they were clearly no longer 'pure' (Schoeman 1953 and Gordon 1992).

The process of land dispossession was accelerated during the late 1960s and 1970s. In line with the recommendations of the Odendaal Commission, the few remaining areas in Namibia where San retained a substantial degree of autonomy were brought directly under the administration's authority. Apart from Bushmanland (which was home to fewer than 1 000 Ju/'hoansi at the time of its formation), all other areas in which significant San populations lived were gazetted variously as 'communal land' under the control of other traditional authorities or conservation areas administered through the Department of Wildlife. This process ensured that San were gradually forced to enter into economic relationships with their new neighbours on whom they became progressively more dependent. It also signified an end to their economic and political autonomy.

Colonial life

White farmers and colonial officers understood 'Bushmen' to be inherently limited in their capacity to be 'civilised' and articulated the increasing integration of San into the colonial political economy as a process of 'domestication'. Individual Bushmen were positioned on a scale of wildness and tameness according to the extent to which they were exposed to and had absorbed 'civilising influences'. Hunting and gathering San in their 'natural' state were considered 'wild' or 'pure' whereas those in the service of whites, or who lived among Bantu speakers were seen to have been partially 'tamed' (Gordon 1992:137-146). It was also widely believed that if left unattended, a 'tame' Bushman would slide precipitously back to his 'wild' state. Indeed, the potential for Bushmen to be 'domesticated' was a theme of episodic debate among Namibia's frontiersmen, anthropologists and government officials, one that came to the fore most aggressively after the small Bushman rebellion north of Gobabis and the dramatic killing of the Magistrate van Rynveld in 1923 (see Suzman 2000 and Gordon 1992)[10].

With no independent rights to residence in commercial farming areas, San tolerated often appalling living and working conditions (see Gebhardt 1978:168, Suzman 1995a). Farmers justified the low wages they paid to San farm workers (if paid at all) by claiming San neither understood nor needed money; they justified providing poor or no housing because 'Bushmen', being 'bush-men' neither required nor desired the material comforts of 'civilisation'; and they justified the frequent beatings to which they subjected their San workers by arguing it was the only way that the 'child-like' San could be made to 'understand' (see Suzman 2000a and Gebhardt 1976).

For San living and working in 'native reserves' like Hereroland, Ovamboland and Kavangoland, conditions were not much better. Subject to similar stereotypes they came to provide a lower tier labour pool for the communal area farmers on whom they depended. As on the white-owned farms, San participation in reserve life was mediated and limited by their perceived alterity – only rarely were they granted the right to own or use land for agricultural purposes or afforded the status of social or 'tribal' equals[11]. In some instances San came to be attached to households where in return for their labour they could claim the household's patronage. In others, survival necessitated the adoption of diverse and opportunist

---

[10] During the 1930s and 1940s it was only farmers whose land bordered on the Hei//um occupied Game Reserve no.2 (now Etosha Pan National Park) that suffered "Bushman depredations" of their stock.

[11] There were some exceptions to this, most notably in areas such as Nganjera in present day Omusati. Gordon and Sholto-Douglas 1999

economic strategies. Depending on the time of year and location, San variously scraped a living by taking on piecemeal or casual labour, hunting and gathering, begging and theft.

Closer physical proximity to San did not detract from the apparent verity of popular mythologies that attested to their difference. Rather it led to the refinement of their popular stereotype and simultaneously granted it the added sophistication and authority borne of first hand 'experience'. Moreover, it allowed for the dominant signifiers of San alterity to be frequently updated in appropriately contemporary terms to the extent that San responses to the manner of their inclusion in the colonial political economy were taken to substantiate the position that they were indeed 'children of nature', ill equipped to cope with the rigours of 'modern' colonial life. Dependent on a political economy in which they retained little access to or control over the various mechanisms of power meant that San in many areas came to be articulate aspects of their social experience in terms of dominant categories, practices and, in some instances, values. Many came to devalue their 'hunting and gathering past' and the contemporary identity and stereotypes this imposed on them. Moreover, some considered seriously the possibility that they were indeed inferior to others in important ways and that their marginal position might reflect some form of natural hierarchy.

Independence and underdevelopment

With independence, the passion of national liberation gave way to triumphal narratives of 'development' and 'nation building' as the formal organs of the colonial state were transformed from instruments of oppression to the engines of national development. Like the majority of 'non-white' Namibians in the run-up to independence, most of Namibia's 28 000 San were buoyed up by the rhetoric of emancipation and warmly embraced the possibility of a 'new Namibia'[12]. Flush with victorious goodwill, the SWAPO government assured San that not only were they aware of their "dire plight" but also that they would "help them find their place in the New Namibia" (GRN 1992).

For many San the rhetoric of national development took on an air of theatricality not long after independence. Proposed policy initiatives to expand San access to land failed to deliver, as did initiatives aimed at improving their economic status. Thus, at the cusp of the third millennium many San were materially worse off than they were before independence (Suzman 2001). Apart from the disappearance of cash wages for the 6 000 San that were economically dependent on the South African military machine, generational farm working San have also found themselves in an increasingly insecure economic position. Since the 1970s there has been a continued decline in employment levels on the commercial farms which

---

[12] The extent of San involvement in the SADF meant that not all San were to keen on independence. Five hundred San soldiers and their dependants accepted the SADF offer of repatriation in Schmidtsdrift in South Africa in 1989. The majority of these immigrants were !Xu and Kxoe that entered Namibia from Angola in 1974.

are now down to pre-1950 levels despite a greater than fourfold increase in the rural population (Suzman 2001).

The extent and form of San marginalisation is such that only extreme measures are likely to effect a substantial change in their collective status. Although government has gone to some lengths to ensure policies are appropriate to addressing San needs, they have proved reluctant or unable to implement these effectively[13]. Indeed, contrary to development planners' hopes and expectations, their designation of the San as a site for 'development' has further entrenched existing social and economic hierarchies and simultaneously provided a novel vocabulary for the reiteration of unequal relations between San and others. Presently, government-led San development in Namibia offers an insight into how policies are 'localised' in practice and reformulated with few apparent contradictions on the basis of existing power relations and the narratives and practices through which these are expressed and enacted. From the point of view of many San, their relationships with their 'developers' are no more than a new spin on an enduring pattern of relations.

Broadly defined, development is controlled or managed 'social change', and in this sense it is explicitly about the exercise of power (Van Ufford 1993; Hobart 1993). It implies the dominance of the developer's worldview over those to be developed, and a lopsided structural relationship between a 'developed', empowered and knowledgeable core and an underdeveloped, ignorant and 'disempowered' periphery. Contemporary, nominally post-modern development practice seeks to subvert this polarity by emphasising local knowledge, participation and capacity building as a path to 'empowerment' (Gardener and Lewis 1996:108-119). As much as this emphasis on 'empowerment' rarely unhinges the structural relationship that makes development necessary (Rahnema 1992), it has proved, in practice, to be comparatively effective. As a result 'participation' and 'empowerment' are key phrases in the contemporary global 'development' lexicon and are, as is the case in Namibia, often enshrined in policy.

Development in action, however, rarely mirrors the virtuous ideals outlined in policy and planning documents. Although clauses and articles concerning empowerment and participation are essential to the ideological legitimacy of development policy, they are often the early casualties in the development process. In some instances this is because other elements of policy are inconsistent with these principles. But, more often than not, it has been because as policy is implemented, it is reconstituted in terms of 'local' knowledge, local practices, prevailing power relations and the representations through which these are mediated. The extent to which San inequality is embedded in normative social practice has apparently overwhelmed any democratising urges to forge a 'genuine' participatory framework. Many of government's dealings with San populations have

---

[13] See Suzman 2000b for a more detailed discussion of government policy vis-à-vis San.

been conspicuously top-down, paternalist and in some cases explicitly disempowering[14].

That this has been possible is partially a result of the fact that since independence the status of Namibia's San has been conceptualised as a problem of 'underdevelopment'. San 'underdevelopment' is understood to be a contemporary manifestation of their 'hunting and gathering culture', which in turn is seen not only as an obstacle to development, but the subject of development. From this point of view economic transformation is cultural transformation, and presently the desired end of the development process is the re-acculturated, self-sufficient, subsistence farming San[15]. These ambitions allow for little emphasis to be placed on 'local knowledge', which, being 'cultural knowledge' is not only ignored, but explicitly devalued since it is perceived to be part of the problem itself. In this sense, San are not simply thought of as 'ignorant', but also to have the 'wrong' sort of knowledge. The low emphasis placed on participatory decision-making, empowerment and capacity building are not seen to contribute to the problem but to constitute an important part of the solution.

In the years immediately following independence government asserted that San development was a priority and tasked the newly formed Ministry of Lands, Resettlement and Rehabilitation (MLRR) to take the lead in this process. Assisted substantially by the Evangelical Lutheran Church in Namibia (ELCIN) and the Lutheran World Federation, the MLRR adopted a strategy that aimed to 'transform' San into self-sufficient agriculturalists over a period of five years. In west Bushmanland and west Caprivi this involved allocating San agricultural plots based on the Ovambo/Kavango model and the provision of agricultural extension services and training. It was assumed that San would gratefully accept these efforts and, under the paternal guidance of their developers, easily achieve anticipated goals within the stipulated timeframe. By 1995, no MLRR San project had come close to achieving its stated aims.

Ignorance is not simply the antithesis of knowledge, it is a value-laden concept that often implies, "if not actual iniquity, at least stupidity, failure and sloth" and the frustrations of government officials charged with San development are often phrased in similar terms (Hobart 1993). While material and other constraints also contribute to the problem, the consistently poor yields of San subsistence agricultural projects for example, are informally spoken of as a consequence of certain

---

[14] The extent to which local practice can subvert ostensibly positive policy is most clearly evidenced in reference to the formal state recognition of San traditional leaders. In Namibia, legal and constitutional provisions exist for the symbolic continuity of "customary" or "traditional" legal and administrative structures through granting traditional authorities a state-recognised role. In line with constitutional stipulations legal provision is made for the recognition of leaders from all "traditional communities" whether or not they may had had formally institutionalised leadership structures in the past. Despite this, when the Government of Namibia announced in 1996 which traditional leaders (and hence traditional communities) would be formally recognised by government not one of the six San traditional authorities that applied were listed. All six San authorities appealed this decision and in the case of two, those of former Bushmanland, their appeal was upheld. In the case of the four remaining traditional authorities, the government deferred its decision.

[15] Thus for example, when the MLRR allocated agricultural and residential plots to San resettled in west Tsumkwe during the early 1990s, these were based largely on Ovambo/Kavango-style residential plots rather than the kin-based residential clusters favoured by the San, as it was felt that it was more appropriate to subsistence farming. Jansen et al. 1994

obstinately unyielding cultural (or racial) traits on the part of the target community, rather than any flaws in project design or mistakes in management or implementation. Indeed, as was the case when San entered sustained relationships with others as clients or labourers during the 18th and 19th centuries, the interaction between San and others within a development framework has led to the greater elaboration and sophistication of their popular stereotype.

At national level, the valorisation of cultural factors as a major impediment to San development has a number of important consequences. Not least, it positions them, yet again, as the authors of their own misfortune. Not only does this justify the continuing 'paternal' guidance of others, it also relegates political process and power relations to a position of secondary explanatory value. This, in turn, allows for matters like land access, rights issues, and empowerment on a national scale to be deferred altogether.

The continued marginalisation of San during the 'development' era is telling of the enduring currency of popular narratives that ascribe their status to their being 'child-like', 'primitive' or as is now the case, 'underdeveloped'. An examination of their recent history reveals the extent to which their contemporary status is bound up in their colonial encounter and the structural relations that emerged from it. Indeed, the history of San in Namibia provides a compelling example of the interplay between structures of power and the dynamic systems of knowledge that constitute them. Based on current trends it seems unlikely that the situation will improve radically in the near future, although the increasing sophistication of San political ambitions and their growing capacity to mobilise development support might effect some positive changes. Certainly, a crucial component of any initiative to change the substance of San marginalisation must inevitably involve the subversion of the dominant stereotypes of alterity to which they remain subject.

Bibliography

Biesele, M / Gordon, R / Lee, R 1986. The past and future of !Kung ethnography: critical reflections and symbolic perspectives, essays in honour of Lorna Marshall. Hamburg: Helmut Buske Verlag
Biesele, M / Schweitzer, P / Hitchcock, R *(eds.)* 2000. Hunters and gatherers in the modern world: conflict, resistance and self-determination. New York: Berghahn Books
Devereux, Stephen / **Katjiuanjo**, Vemunavi / **van Rooy**, Gert 1996. Living and working conditions of farm-workers in Namibia. Multi-Disciplinary Research Centre – Social Sciences Division, University of Namibia; Legal Assistance Centre. Windhoek
Dickens, *C* 1853. Household works, London
Gardener, K / Lewis, D 1996. Anthropology, development and the post-modern challenge. Pluto Press, Milton Keynes
Gebhardt, *F* 1976. The socio-economic status of farm labourers in Namibia. In: South African Legal Bulletin, vol.4 (1 and 2)
Gordon, *R* 1992. The Bushman myth: the making of a Namibian underclass. Oxford: Westview Press
Gordon, R / Sholto-Douglas, R (1999). The Bushman myth: the making of a Namibian underclass: second edition. Oxford: Westview Press
Government of the Republic of Namibia (1991). National Conference on Land Reform and the Land Question. Windhoek: Government Printer

Government of the Republic of Namibia (1992). Regional conference on development programmes for Africa's San Population, organised by the Ministry of Lands, Resettlement and Rehabilitation. Windhoek: Government Printer

Guenther, M 1986. "Bushmen" or "San". In: Biesele / Gordon / Lee (eds.)

Guenther, M 1993. Independent, fearless and rather bold: a historical narrative of the Ghanzi Bushmen of Botswana. In: Journal of the Namibian Scientific Society 44, pp.25-40

Hitchcock, R 1991. Human rights, local institutions and sustainable development among the Kalahari San. Paper presented at ASSA meeting, Nov. 1991

Hitchcock, B 1992. Communities and consensus: an evaluation of the activities of the Nyae Nyae Farmers Co-operative and the Nyae Nyae Development Foundation in northeastern Namibia. Windhoek and New York: Ford Foundation

Hobart, M (ed.) 1993. An anthropological critique of development: the growth of ignorance. London: EIDOS, Routledge

Jansen, R / Pradham, N / Spencer, J 1994. ELCIN Bushman rehabilitation and settlement programme-evaluation (final report). Windhoek: ELCIN

Leacock, E / Lee, R (eds.) 1982. Politics and history in band society. Cambridge University Press

Lee, R 1968. What hunters do for a living, or how to make out on scarce resources. In: Lee R / Devore, I (eds.) 1968

Lee, R 1984. The Dobe !Kung . New York: Holt, Rinehart and Winston

Lee, R 1991. Reflections on primitive communism. In: Ingold / Riches / Woodburn (eds.) 1991

Lee, R 1992. Art, science, or politics? The crisis in huntergatherer studies. In: American Anthropologist no.94

Lee, R 1993. The Dobe Ju/'hoansi. Case studies in cultural anthropology. Orlando, Florida: Harcourt Brace College Publishers

Lee, R / Devore, I (eds.) 1968. Man the hunter. Chicago: Aldine Publishing Co.

Lee, R / Devore, I 1976. Kalahari hunter-gatherers: studies of the !Kung San and their neighbours. Cambridge (Mass.): Harvard University Press

Lee, R / Guenther, M 1991. Oxen or onions: the search for trade (and truth) in the Kalahari. In: Current Anthropology 32(5), pp.592-601

Marais et al. 1984. Ondersoek na die Boesmanbevolkingsgroepe in SWA (The Brand Report: SWAA Development Directorate). Windhoek

Marshall, L 1976. The !Kung of Nyae-Nyae. Harvard University Press: Cambridge (Mass.)

Rahnema, M 1992. Participation. In: Sachs, W. (ed.). The development dictionary: A guide to knowledge as power. Zed Press: London, pp.116-32

Sahlins, M 1972. Stone age economics. London: Routledge

Schrire, C (ed.) 1982. Past and present in hunter-gatherer studies. Orlando, Florida: Academic Press

Schoeman, P 1953. Report on the preservation of the Bushmen

Solway, J / Lee, R 1990. Foragers, genuine or spurious: situating the Kalahari San in history. In: Current Anthropology no.31, pp.109-46

Sundermeier, T et al. 1966. The Mbanderu. Windhoek: MSORP

Suzman, J 2000. Things from the bush: a contemporary history of the Omaheke Bushmen. Basel: P.Schlettwein Publishing

Sylvian, R 1998. Our hands made them rich: gender, politics and labour on commercial farms in the Omaheke region of Namibia. University of Toronto, Medusa Graduate Seminar, Feb. 24 1998

Sylvian, R 1999. "We work to have life": Ju/'hoan women, work and survival in the Omaheke region, Namibia (doctoral dissertation). University of Toronto

Van Ufford, P 1993. Knowledge and ignorance in the practices of development policy. In: Hobart (ed.) 1993

Wilmsen, E 1989. Land filled with flies: a political economy of the Kalahari. University of Chicago Press

WOMEN'S ADVANCEMENT IN NAMIBIA – THE CONCEPT OF EMPOWERMENT RECONSIDERED

Saskia Wieringa / Immaculate Mogotsi

Introduction

Various policies and strategies to improve the position of women in Namibia have been advanced. In the National Gender Plan of Action (1998-2003), subtitled "Effective Partnership Towards Gender Equality" (Department of Women's Affairs (DWA) 1998) the various government initiatives to promote women's advancement are outlined. In the document called "National Gender Policy", published a year earlier by the same Department of Women's Affairs, the "empowerment of women is seen as a prerequisite for achieving conducive and sustainable, political, social, cultural and economic security among all people of Namibia" (DWA 1997:7). Women's empowerment is thus one of the core concepts of national policies to achieve 'gender equality' and indeed to enhance the welfare of all Namibians. However, what is understood by this concept is not always clearly spelled out.

Gender, a contested concept

Women's empowerment is a major issue in women's studies and gender planning. It can only be addressed meaningfully if the concept of gender is used in such a way that the full range of the concerns women are confronted with, are incorporated – from physical to symbolic, religious and legal to political and economic issues. The deployment of the concept of gender as an analytical tool is one of the greatest gains of women's studies. Seeing the categories of 'women' and 'men' not as biological phenomena (sex) but as cultural constructions (gender) and thus essentially unstable, has had major theoretical consequences. Gender allows us to see both femininity and masculinity as being produced by and reproducing themselves in particular discursive patterns. It also allows us to understand the wide variety of gender patterns, including the grafting of more than one gender upon one particular sex. This is the case for instance with the female husbands in various African formations (Tietmeyer 1985).

Neither women nor men are homogeneous social categories; they are divided by class, age, race, ethnicity and sexual preference. Yet there are some systematic similarities that both men and women share, however differently they may be experienced. It is gender analysis that addresses those similarities (Imam 1997). A theory of gender relations should avoid the Scylla of essentialism and the Charybdis of cultural determinism, and analyse both sex and gender, both bodies and cultures, in the ways they interact and mutually shape each other. It is of critical

critical importance to reflect on the mechanisms by which sexual difference is created and naturalised (Blackwood and Wieringa 1999).

Since the introduction of the concept of 'sex/gender system' by Rubin (1975), several theories have elaborated on the concept of gender (Flax 1990; Nicholson 1995). We find the approach of Scott (1989) the most useful for this chapter. She suggests gender is both "a constitutive element of social relationships based on perceived differences between the sexes" and "a primary way of signifying relationships of power" (1989:94). Scott further suggests that gender operates in four interrelated configurations. First, in culturally available symbols that portray both womanhood and manhood. Second, by supplying normative concepts that usually operate in binary ways. Third, Scott notes that struggles over these concepts and symbols are political. The last element Scott distinguishes is that of subjective identity. Historical analysis can shed light on the sociocultural and political processes in which shifting and multiple identities are being formed.

The following illustrates some of the gendered symbols that exist in the Namibian context. In general women are perceived as submissive beings with inferior status; they are seen not only as child bearers but also as 'natural' child rearers. Men are seen as heads of households and providers. In some ethnic groups in the Kavango, men are referred to as cocks, bulls and sometimes male springbok; these concepts carry connotations of strength and endurance and portray men as the protectors of households. Women's symbols mostly refer to their reproductive roles, they are sometimes called grain storage or traditional bags used for collecting wild fruits (Iipinge et al. 2000). The Christian churches play a particularly important role in this respect. They propagate a model of womanhood in which women are supposed to emulate the model of virginity; they have to be pure, chaste and virgin until marriage. Men are seen to be superior to women (Mogotsi 1998).

Since the 1980s, debates on differences among women and the diversity of gender constructions have proven fruitful. Especially post-structuralist writers take difference as the starting ground of their politics and writing. Rather than locating women's 'essential' difference in relation to nature, they focus on the plurality of women's experiences. 'Difference' is thus no longer an essential quality but a location of politics (Flax 1990; Haraway 1991).

Differences among Namibian women are not only based on cultural, economic, religious or ethnic practices; there is also a marked difference between those who left the country during the war for liberation, which lasted for twenty-two years, and those who remained behind. The women who went into exile transcended their traditional female role, as many of them participated in the war for liberation. Some became troop commanders, others were given training in various disciplines (see also SWAPO 1987, Becker 1993 and Hubbard and Solomon 1995). They suffered with their male comrades, as in the South African attack on

SWAPO's refugee camp at Kassinga (Angola)[1]. Some received secondary and tertiary education.

Differences among women, on the basis of class, religion or sexual orientation have often led to fragmentation and bitterness. Fierce struggles arose as to which kind of oppression was primary, sex or class? Or race after all? As though it were possible to define once and for all a fixed hierarchy of oppressions in the face of the multiple levels of oppression and exclusion most women and men face. More recently, especially after the Fourth Women's World Conference held in Beijing in 1995, the richness of women's diverse experiences has been rediscovered as a source of strength that need not lead to dispersion or fragility. Solidarity need no longer be built on homogenising discourses such as nationalism, communism or a global sisterhood but may more fruitfully be built on the basis of shared interests (Dean 1996; Pringle and Watson 1992). Thus present-day feminist organisations, also in Namibia, realise that negotiation for shared priorities and the building of (shifting) coalitions, can be important features of political life.

The multiple oppressions women and men face can only be understood meaningfully in their particular historical and cultural context. There is no fixed formula to analyse them. Neither an additive (sex plus class, etc.) nor a linear multiplying model, as Imam (1997) suggests, can capture the enormous complexities of the ways in which layers of oppressions intersect. For instance in Namibia, deeply divided by inequalities of class and race, these factors impact differently on the gender construction than in more egalitarian communities. As Cock (1980) analyses for southern Africa, maids and madams both face gender discrimination though the ways they live their genders are vastly different. A gender struggle alone will not eliminate poverty nor racial inequality. The political empowerment of the 'madam' will not immediately be of benefit to her maid. But class struggle alone will not end gender discrimination (see for instance Coward 1983).

Gender is primarily a relation of power. We see power not only as operating 'from above' but as permeating all formations (Foucault 1976)[2]. People are not passive beings, but through exercising agency they have the power to address their conditions of life, either resisting or submitting to oppressive relations. They may both produce new (either more egalitarian or more oppressive) relations of power, and/or reproduce existing power structures (McNay 2000). The distinction between compliance, support, resistance or submission depends on the level of consciousness people have about their lives. It also depends on the practical and symbolic strength of the power relations they are faced with, as well as on the interests particular actors have in the current system of power relations.

---

[1] This camp accommodated some 4 000 people, mainly women and children. The casualties were enormous: almost 600 people were killed, and over 1500 people were wounded. Moleah 1983:286

[2] Foucault analysed the way power is diffused through society and has to be understood in a much broader context than only the dominance of the state or the dyadic relationship between oppressor/oppressed (Foucault 1976). Feminist thinkers have reacted in various ways to Foucault's theories. Hartsock 1990 has criticised Foucault for undermining the possibilities of political action while other authors, such as Scott 1989 assert that Foucault's conceptualisation of power stimulate women to think more creatively about central concepts in feminist theories, such as equality and difference.

In this respect it is important to mention that silence may constitute a critical dimension of power. That which is not spoken about also cannot be contested. In Namibia, for instance, sexuality is an area in which a culture of silence reigns. If sexuality does not become a topic for open and serious discussion, gender inequalities will not be addressed. For struggle can only take place where 'needs' are defined (Fraser 1989); that is when they are brought into the discursive realm and ultimately into the political arena.

Feminism

Feminism should be understood as a complex, multilayered transformational set of political practices and ethics, elements of which may be in contradiction with each other, and intersect with other transformational practices, such as the struggles against oppression on the basis of class, race, ethnicity and sexual preference[3]. Feminist processes are located at the intersection of the material and the ideological, of the discursive and the physical. Its long-term objectives are to transform society by feminising and democratising domestic, social and political life; many feminists are also actively involved in socialising the economy and ending racial discrimination. This last point is of course particularly important in a post-apartheid state such as Namibia.

Racial discrimination resulting from the apartheid state has been abolished according to the Namibian constitution. However, we should mention that racial divisions do not simply fade away or decrease with the advent of political democracy. Rather they continue to be reproduced in new forms and given new material weight in socio-economic life, manifesting clearly in the allocation of resources (Braham et al. 1992). What is apparent in the Namibian situation is that the struggle that was historically fought on the basis of race has assumed a new form, in which the class factor has become predominant, but is still combined with race and gender. Black women are to be found in the lower echelons of all the institutions where they are employed, where the pay is lowest, the hours longest, and most frequently involving physical heavy labour (Labour Resource and Research Institute 2000).

Deconstructing sexual difference will also affect other binary constructions, based as it is on a radical rethinking of the use and abuse of binary thinking in general. Dividing social categories into an 'own' and an 'enemy other' goes beyond the recognition of differences. It involves the exaggeration and naturalisation of differences, the homogenisation of both sides of the divide and the creation of a hierarchy between the two poles. Analytically the concept of 'feminism' is not only linked to transformative processes, but to the shifting and unstable concept of 'woman' itself, to identity and consciousness. Feminism is thus not only transformational politics and ethics but also a discursive process, a process of producing

---

[3] There is no consensus on what a transformed world should look like and it may be impossible even to conceive of such consensus. See also Wieringa 1995. Transformation should not be seen as a product or as a fixed goal in a distant future, but rather as a process.

meaning, of subverting representations of gender and of creating new representations of gender, of womanhood, of manhood, of identity and subjectivity and of collective self.

Women's studies, the academic offspring of feminism, often faces criticism; it is said to be a white and middle class phenomenon. But, as Imam (1997) writes, it is actually less Western-dominated than most other social science paradigms, such as modernisation theory or historical materialism. Third world women have for so long criticised white Western feminism that it has incorporated many insights related to the poverty and racial inequality women in Africa and elsewhere face.

Women's interests in Namibia

Women's interests in Namibia are addressed by various groups in the country, such as the Gender Training and Research Programme at the University of Namibia, Sister Namibia, the Ministry of Women Affairs and Child Welfare and by gender planners in development agencies. Gender planning is best seen as a set of situated practices of feminist activity. Practitioners should learn to ask both analytical and ethical questions, based on the explicit concern with the relations of oppression women are faced with, both of gender as well as with the gendered effects of race, class, ethnicity, age and sexual preference (Wieringa 1994).

There are various levels in Namibia where women still experience inequality, though given the scope of this paper only two areas will be highlighted. Discriminatory laws are being replaced with more equitable laws, but one area which still seriously discriminates against women and needs to be addressed is customary law. Since the majority of Africans continue to reside in communal areas, they remain disadvantaged by the inequitable distribution of land[4]. Women are particularly affected, although the impact might not be homogenous across all communities and regions. Even today rural women only gain access to land through their relationship to men. The security of land rights is jeopardised by discriminatory marriage customs and inheritance systems that favour men. Often widows are forced off their land and into the households of relatives. Another area where Namibian women still feel the pinch of inequality is when dealing with commercial institutions such as banks. In theory, no discrimination against women by commercial banks is allowed and all customers are supposed to be treated equally, yet women tend to have more difficulty acquiring loans owing to a lack of collateral and credit record (DWA 1995).

Several reports, such as the first country report on the Convention on the Elimination of All Forms of Discrimination Against Women (CEDAW) (DWA 1995) and the Namibian version of "Beyond Inequalities" (Iipinge and LeBeau 1997) eloquently list Namibian women's major gender interests.

---

[4] For example, about 4 000 commercial farmers, mostly white, control 44 percent of arable land in contrast to about 67 percent of the African population who have access to only 41 percent of agricultural land, much of which is of poor quality. Iipinge / LeBeau 1997

In spite of a progressive constitution (discussed later in this chapter) prohibiting discrimination on the grounds of sex, and Namibia's ratification of CEDAW in 1992, there are still areas in which women's legal equality with men is not assured. A promising development is the passing of the Married Persons Equality Act in 1996, but it still has to be assessed whether this law is fully observed.

Various reports mention male dominance in the area of sexual relations; this is exacerbated by the culture of silence reigning on issues of sexuality. The situation is particularly worrying in the light of the HIV/AIDS pandemic facing Namibia today. There is a prevalence rate of 20% among sexually active adults (UNAIDS/WHO 1998). Male promiscuity is commonly accepted, while female sexuality, especially in the rural areas, is more strictly controlled. Yet in urban areas women also engage in sexual relations with multiple partners. Religion is often used to justify male dominance, e.g. in the areas of family planning and male control within the household. Economically worst off are female-headed households. The rate of female unemployment is higher than that of men; men control the higher echelons of the civil service and business sectors. Sexual violence, such as rape and domestic violence, is on the increase.

The situation of Namibian women can only be understood by taking into account the cruel legacy of German colonialism, of apartheid with its labour migration and pass laws as well as the effects of the long liberation war. To bring about a transformation towards greater equality, changes on all these levels will be needed.

The so-called 'empowerment approach' (Moser 1993, Sen and Grown 1985; Wieringa 1994 and 1998) attempts to address women's central gender interests. Adherents to the empowerment approach draw on certain aspects of feminist thought and recognise that feminism is neither a recent nor a Western phenomenon (Jayawardena 1986). Women's subordination is seen as a holistic process, encompassing all aspects of women's lives. The central focus is a critique of the way power and development are interlinked, seeking ways to 'empower' women and specifically to address the particular construction of sexual differences and their unequal effects. Empowering women does not mean reversing existing power hierarchies, but rather to empower women and/or women's groups to make their own choices, to speak out on their own behalf, to control their own lives and to help change society towards more egalitarian relations of class, race and ethnicity. In the process men will also be empowered to critically assess their way of 'living a masculine life'. Political mobilisation of women and consciousness raising are important elements of the empowerment approach, and women's organisations are seen as vital actors in development processes.[5]

Power relations basically have three dimensions: oppressive/coercive, challenging/critical and creative. The process of empowerment of both women and men is related to all three dimensions: exposing the oppressive power of the

---

[5] This is one of the central concerns of DAWN group (Sen / Grown 1985). See also Wieringa 1988 and 1995

existing gender relations, critically challenging them and creatively trying to shape different social relations.

There is no consensus among those who advocate the empowerment of women as a central element in development processes. It is therefore better to speak of empowerment approaches. Unfortunately the central concerns of gender planners have not always centred upon women's empowerment and the transformation of gender relations. Development planners are searching for easy schedules, quantifiable targets and for simplicity, while addressing enormously complex situations. The empowerment approach is often seen as 'too difficult'. Planners want to fix problems which took ages to evolve, in projects of a few years' duration (see also Anderson 1992). They are often impatient with feminist theory building, which they see as too complicated and as not directly relevant to their daily work.

Feminism and nationalism

As McClintock writes, "all nationalisms are gendered, all are invented and all are dangerous (...) in the sense that they represent relations to political power and to the technologies of violence" (1995:352). This is also relevant to the Namibian situation, which only became independent in 1990, after a bitter struggle for liberation against the apartheid colonial state. Women reproduce nations not only biologically, but also culturally and symbolically. In the process of constructing a nationalist state, not only the state itself is created, but also the symbolic apparatus which holds the state together. It signifies the context in which its citizens operate and in which they negotiate their own identities as women and men. And this is a political, and often a violent process, as recent Namibian history can witness.

Namibia's recent history knows three different constructions of womanhood in relation to state processes: the pre-colonial, the colonial and apartheid states and the post independence constructs. The colonial state introduced the emphasis on motherhood and domesticity of women that was characteristic of the Victorian, European societies (Comaroff 1991 ; Walker 1990). Both women and colonised people in general were seen as childlike, emotional, unreasonable and instinctive, and in general as closer to nature. This association of women and people in the colonially-dominated countries with nature was used as a justification for white male European superiority. This arrogance was bolstered by depicting Asian and African societies as backward, stagnant, chaotic and primitive (de Groot 1991). At the same time 'native' women were sexualised and exoticised (Gouda 1995; Stoler 1995).

The 'mission' of white men thus was to bring 'culture' where nature reigned and especially to improve women's degraded status. Paradoxically, appeals to a 'natural' Victorian morality and a desire for 'social reforms', which in some instances may have benefited women, in other cases eroding their political, economic and sexual rights (Comaroff 1991; Walker 1990).

As in other post-colonial states, Namibian women and men have to negotiate their identities in the shifting and multiple constructions of nationalism, gender and sexuality. During the liberation struggle, the notions picturing men as protectors and providers and women as homemakers were challenged, for very practical reasons. The process of change had already set in, due to the migrant labour system under colonial rule. Women had to take on tasks that were traditionally considered male tasks such as working the land and herding cattle. Similarly, during the war many women underwent military training and fought alongside men. For many women this meant personal emancipation from traditional roles (SWAPO 1987; 289).

However after the attainment of independence women were excluded from decision-making positions and the labour market, and were systematically driven back into traditional female roles (Ministry of Labour 1998). The only two female portfolios cover health, social services and women and children. They reflect SWAPO's view of women whose primary responsibility is in care-taking and their role as mothers of the nation. However, the divide is not always between men and women. During the formulation of the Women's Manifesto by Sister Collective in 1999, in preparation for the national elections, disagreements occurred among women's organisations where issues were raised that were at odds with the views expressed by SWAPO[6].

The political empowerment of women is an important aspect of the overall process of women's empowerment. Women's political rights are guaranteed in the Namibian constitution. Article 10 states that "all persons are equal before the law and no person may be discriminated against on the grounds of sex". Article 23 makes provision for affirmative action for women, while Article 95 names the enactment of legislation to ensure equality of opportunity for women as one of the "principles of state policy". The National Gender Policy and the National Plan of Action, which have been approved by Cabinet and Parliament, back these up. The implementing responsibility falls under the Ministry of Women Affairs and Child Welfare.

While the Namibian government and the National Assembly have committed themselves to supporting women's rights, the National Council, consisting of representatives from the various districts, have voiced opposition. One of their major concerns is support of the rights of traditional communities. This implies the upholding of patriarchal structures of leadership and male sexual domination (Cooper 1997). Namibian women's struggles for equal rights are thus far from over, in spite of the progressive laws outlined above.

The presence of women in decision-making positions in government has improved greatly since independence. Yet women are still seriously under-represented in senior and management positions. Women are not well represented in the parastatals, for example only one Namibian woman was found

---

[6] The major concerns raised were related to the human rights for lesbians and homosexuals and the call for the withdrawal of Namibian troops from the Democratic Republic of Congo. The Namibian 9.10.1999; Windhoek Observer 16.10.1999

to be a Chief Executive Officer (CEO) out of twelve major parastatals. Women's representation in the Namibian Army and the Police Force is very low, especially in decision-making positions. Although the Namibian constitution makes provision for affirmative action, it is not implemented thoroughly (Mogotsi and Muthile 2000).

Conclusion

Namibia is a young nation, struggling with a legacy of many forms of oppression. It is important that all its citizens benefit from the fruits of the process of development and empowerment that the nation is determined to chart. However, as we have made clear in this chapter, women are still lagging behind and women's voices are hardly heard in the major decision making arenas. It is imperative that gender concerns and women's empowerment are given the political and analytical attention they should have, although, as we have made clear, gender struggle alone will not end poverty and racial inequalities.

Bibliography

Anderson, Jeanine 1992. Intereses i justicia – a donde va la discusion sobre la mujer y el desarollo? Lima: Entre Mujeres
Braham, Peter / **Rattansi,** Ali / **Skellington,** Richard (eds.) 1992. Racism and antiracism, inequalities, opportunities and policies. The Open University. SAGE publication
Becker, Heike 1993. From anti-colonial resistance to reconstruction. Namibia women's movement from 1980-1992 (doctoral dissertation). University of Bremen
Cock, Jacklyn 1980. Maids & madams – a study in the politics of exploitation. Johannesburg: Raven Press
Comaroff, John / **Comaroff,** Jean 1991. Of revelation and revolution – Christianity, colonialism and consciousness in South Africa. Chicago: University of Chicago Press
Cooper, Allan P 1997. State sponsorship of women's rights and implications for patriarchalism in Namibia. In: Journal of Modern African Studies, no.35.3, pp.469-483
Coward, Rosalind 1983. Patriarchal precedents – sexuality and social relations. London: Routledge and Kegan Paul
Dean, Jodi 1996. Solidarity of strangers – feminism after identity politics. Berkeley: University of California Press
Government of the Republic of Namibia 1995. Convention on the elimination of all forms of discrimination against women (CEDAW) – first country report. Department of Woman's Affairs (DWA). Windhoek: Office of the President
Government of the Republic of Namibia 1997. National gender policy. Department of Women's Affairs (DWA). Windhoek: Office of the President
Government of the Republic of Namibia 1998. National gender policy and national plan of action on gender. Department of Women's Affairs (DWA). Windhoek: Office of the President
Government of the Republic of Namibia 1998. Namibia labour force survey 1997: an interim report of analysis. Ministry of Labour. Windhoek
Flax, Jane 1990. Postmodernism and gender relations in feminist theory. In: Linda J. Nicholson (ed.). Feminism/postmodernism, pp.19-39. New York and London: Routledge
Foucault, Michel 1976. Power/knowledge (ed. by C. Gordon). New York: Pantheon
Fraser, Nancy 1989. Unruly practices – power, discourse and gender in contemporary social theory. Cambridge: Polity Press
Groot, Joanna de 1991. Conceptions and misconceptions: the historical and cultural context of discussion on women and development. In: Afshar, Haleh (ed.). Women, development and survival, pp.107-35. London: Longman

Gouda, Francis 1995. Dutch culture overseas – colonial practice in the Netherlands Indies 1900-1943. Amsterdam University Press

Haraway, Donna J 1991. Simians, cyborgs and women, the reinvention of nature. London: Free Association Books

Hartsock, Nancy 1990. Foucault on power: a theory for women? In: Nicholson, Linda (ed.). Feminism/postmodernism, pp.157-75. London: Routledge

Hubbard, Dianne / Solomon, Colette 1995. The many faces of feminism in Namibia. In: Amrita Basu (ed.). The challenge of local feminisms – women's movements in global perspective, pp.163-186. San Francisco & Oxford: Westview Press

Iipinge, Eunice / Phiri, Fashion / Ndjabili, Agnes (eds.) 2000. National gender study, vols.I and II. Windhoek: University of Namibia.

Iipinge, Eunice / LeBeau, Debie 1997. Beyond inequalities – women in Namibia. Windhoek/Harare: UNAM / SARDC (WIDSAA)

Imam, Ayesha M 1997. Engendering African social sciences: an introductory essay. In: Iman, Ayesha M / Mama, Amina / Sow, Fatou (eds.). Engendering African social sciences, pp 1-31. Dakar: Codesria Book Series

Jayawardena, Kumari 1986. Feminism and nationalism in the Third World. London: Zed Books

Labour Resource and Research Institute (LaRRI) 2000. Export processing zones in Namibia: taking a closer look. Windhoek: Friedrich Ebert Stiftung

McClintock, Anne 1995. Imperial leather – race, gender and sexuality in the colonial context. New York and London: Routledge

McNay, Lois 2000. Gender and agency – reconfiguring the subject in feminism and social theory. Cambridge: Polity Press

Mogotsi, Immaculate 1998. Formal education and pregnancy among learners in Namibia (MA thesis). The Hague: Institute of Social Studies

Mogotsi, Immaculate / Muthile, Bernadette 2000. Namibian women in decision making positions (mimeo). Windhoek: UNAM

Moser, Caroline ON 1993. Gender planning and development – theory, practice and training. London, New York: Routledge

Nicholson, Linda 1995. Interpreting gender. In: Nicholson, Linda / Seidman, Steven (eds.). Social postmodernism – beyond identity politics. Cambridge: University Press

Pringle, Rosemary / Watson, Sophie 1992. Women's interests and the post-structuralist state. In: Barrett, Michelle / Phillips, Anne (eds.). Destabilizing theory, contemporary feminist debates, pp.53-73. Cambridge: Polity Press

Rubin, Gayle 1975. The traffic in women. Notes on the political economy of sex. In: Reiter, Rayna (ed.). Towards an anthropology of women, pp.157-211. New York and London: Monthly Review Press

Scott, Joan W 1989. Gender: a useful category of historical analysis. In: Weed, Elizabeth (ed.). Coming to terms – feminismt, theory, politics. New York: Routledge

Sen, Gita / Grown, Caren 1985. DAWN – development, crisis and alternative visions – Third World women's perspective. Stavanger: Verbum

Stoler, Ann 1995. Race and the education of desire – Foucault's history of sexuality and the colonial order of things. Durham and London: Duke University Press

SWAPO Department of Information and Publicity 1987. To be born a nation – the liberation struggle for Namibia. London: Zed Press

Tietmeyer, Elisabeth 1985. Frauen heiraten Frauen – Studien zur Gynaegamie in Afrika. Hohenschöftlern: Renner

UNAIDS/WHO 1998. Report on the global HIV/Aids epidemic

Walker, Cherryl (ed.) 1990. Women and gender in Southern Africa to 1945. Claremont: David Phillip

Wieringa, Saskia E (ed.) 1988. Women's struggles and strategies. Aldershot: Gower Press

Wieringa, Saskia E 1994. Women's interests and empowerment: gender planning reconsidered. In: Development and Change, vol.25, pp.829-850

Wieringa, Saskia E (ed.) 1995. Sub-versive women – women's movements in Africa, Asia, Latin America and the Caribbean. London: Zed Books

Wieringa, Saskia E 1998. Rethinking gender planning. A critical discussion on the concept of gender. In: Journal for Gender, Technology and Development, pp. 21-37. AIT, Thailand

UNDERSTANDING THE FAMILY SOCIOLOGICALLY IN CONTEMPORARY NAMIBIA

Volker Winterfeldt / Tom Fox

Introduction: the Namibian Background

There is a dearth of sociological studies of the family in Namibia. One of the primary reasons for this is the historical predominance of anthropological studies in the country, a subject area that was favoured in the colonial era. In general, studies generating exploitable information on social structure issues seem not to have been encouraged. If there were any, their databases were "not only limited, but (...) also meticulously dis-aggregated along ethnic lines"[1]. Since independence, sociology in Namibia has not yet been able to redress the balance. Thus, on the issue of 'family', two main directions of research are found:

- firstly, anthropology concerned itself with the more 'exotic' aspects of family life such as ritual and rites of passage studies and the function of the family within these social factors. On the whole, the reference point was an emphasis on ethnic differentiation and on the 'traditional';
- secondly, empirical quantitative research has chosen rather loose explanatory variables which are often inadequate. They focus on the term 'household' as an operationalisation imperative and, as such, as a very restricted alternative to the term 'family'.

In summary, the overall problem is threefold: the predominance of anthropology reflecting the paucity of sociological paradigms on family life; a lack of conceptually accurate empirical research; and a weakness or absence of innovations and exposure to the developments experienced in sociological family studies from other parts of the world.

This paper will report on the results of a preliminary literature research and review the limited number of available sociological reports and monographs on the Namibian family. Its aim is to define the nature of the current problem and to suggest a way forward for a study of structural changes of family life in Namibia.

The legal framework

The Namibian Constitution (Art.14) defines the family as "the natural and funda-

---

[1] Tapscott 1993:30

mental group unit of society"[2], limiting its legal background to the age of majority (for marriage: 18 years). It implicitly links family with marriage[3].

In relation to marriage, both civil and customary laws continue to operate. Civil and customary laws are – normatively speaking – modelled on patriarchal relationships, giving women (and children) an inferior status. The Married Persons Equality Act of 1996 for the first time legally redresses marital power and gender discrimination within the family[4]. However in practice, obviously, it has first to overcome the normative influence of the deep-rooted tradition formed by Roman-Dutch common law as well as by the ethnic varieties of customary marriage, not to speak of the legacy of missionary Protestantism.

The economic setting

Even after a decade of independence, the former colonial system of ethnically-based indigenous reserves and "homeland" systems shapes the lines along which the structural transformation of Namibian family patterns takes place. Historically dispossessed of land, confined to regions of questionable agricultural suitability either overpopulated or severely underpopulated and lacking appropriate infrastructure and services; having moreover to cope with the hardships of arid climate, the rural majority in search of economic security experiences the typical encroachments of underdevelopment. As a characteristic feature of the densely populated subsistence agriculture areas of the north, the compulsion to migrate fundamentally moulds Namibian family patterns. The mining industry, urban job opportunities and commercial farming attract potential wage labourers of both sexes, who leave their original family environment looking for a cash income. Labour migration thus reshapes the structures left behind as well as setting up new social structures of reproduction.

Urbanisation has become a major trend in past decades[5] which any Namibian approach to the sociology of the family has to take into account. Except for the almost exclusively white-owned commercial farming businesses, agriculture does not guarantee the material basis for security of the majority. Subsistence economy is the basis for agricultural activity of most ethnic communities of Namibia, indeed the vast majority of households. But these only partly manage to live on the food it provides. The remaining food stocks and any additional non-food items have to be obtained through market channels. Thus, commercialisation and monetarisation of the labour force as well as of household resources become a major agent of change in urban and rural surroundings. Urbanisation contributes to the transfor-

---

[2] Government Gazette 21.3.1990:11
[3] "Men and women of full age (...) shall have the right to marry and to found a family. They shall be entitled to equal rights as to marriage, during their marriage and its dissolution." Government Gazette 21.3.1990:10
[4] Hubbard gives an account of the legal situation at independence. Hubbard 1991:6-8 (civil marriage):9-10 (customary marriage):12 (rights of single mothers)
[5] National population growth rate: 3,1%; urban population growth: 4,5%; Windhoek population growth: 5,4% per annum between 1991 and 1995. In the last decade, 68% of the migration to the Windhoek area has been to Katutura. Pendleton 1997:1, 6

mation of gender relations, and transforms the generational and numerical composition of rural households; it also contributes to the growing number of urban households. In its wake, a range of distinct structural variations have come into existence.

This trend, once established, develops dynamics of its own. The cultural attraction of urban life itself furthers migration – the promise of better services in health and education, the spread of consumer attitudes and desires. Both push and pull factors are at work. On the other hand, cultural uprooting and socio-economic disillusionment also reverse the trend, thereby making migration a two-way process.

Transformations of this kind not only reflect economically or politically forced trends of mobility. The conceptualisation of social change within the dichotomies of 'traditional-modern' or 'rural-urban' (common dualities in Namibian social sciences) fails to identify the class-specific background of social change. Socio-economic transformations since independence have fostered class and class-cultural differentiations of the family as a social entity. Though the nuclear family model is commonly classified as the typical 'urban' type, it rather reveals the emergence of strong class characteristics in the rising petty bourgeois and bourgeois non-white élites of the new Namibia[6].

With its material and cultural aspirations and achievements emulating Western capitalist standards and values, the nuclear family also serves as a focus and a profile for social success and status for new social groups. Looking at family patterns, we see that migration and immersion in urban life are initiating a process of class conversion. Urbanisation reshapes the interrelation between family and class. The increasing dependence on wage labour subjects the work force originating from family-based subsistence agriculture to a rationale of existential decisions which is increasingly shifting from use-value orientations to the normative world of exchange-value determination. The cultural connotations of the family which migrants bring to town begin to weaken and come under the influence of market rules of efficient economy of family reproduction. The family forfeits its existence as a productive unit, becoming almost exclusively a reproductive entity.

Concomitant structural changes are inevitable. It must be emphasised, however, that under current Namibian conditions this is not by any means an exclusive process and, moreover, it is a reversible one. Due to the peripheral, underdeveloped character of economy and society, lack of stability is currently the distinguishing feature of any social structure and its future social course. Presumably, it is this background which can explain not only the spread of family types, but also their existence as distinct from nuclear or extended family models. The peripheral society being in a constant state of flux indicates a constantly shifting character, displaying a social reality all of its own. This flux currently takes on a seemingly permanent character, particularly in the face of major migratory

---

[6] As well as in the different ethnic groups of the bourgeois class of (former or present) European origin, obviously.

movements that impose pressure and complexity on Namibian family structures. The resulting formations – as in the case of the family – cannot simply be interpreted either as manifestations of the disintegration or of the survival of the 'traditional' extended family, or as a (sometimes imperfect) emerging 'modern' nuclear family type. Something more complex and diverse than this is taking place. Modern Namibian family studies have fallen short of either empirically or theoretically articulating this situation.

Conceptual considerations

A critical revision of some of the recent contributions to the southern African debate on the sociology of the family reveals three major research standpoints which in our opinion are of importance for the conceptualisation of Namibian research:
- equating family structures with household membership;
- conceiving structural transformation as disintegration (or survival) of traditional family patterns;
- modelling social change along the lines of ethnocentric assumptions.

We concentrate in the following on Thabo Fako's important but contradictory valuation of social change. Reflected in the empirical trends of emerging household patterns in post-independence Botswana, it is interpreted in terms of a dissolution of the pre-capitalist extended family type. We also highlight Margo Russell's critique of Anna Steyn's ethnocentric description of an assumed trend regarding the establishment of nuclear family patterns among contemporary black South African families. This critique, directive and valuable as it is, by tending to describe change merely in terms of a temporary alteration of traditional structures, in some of its aspects exposes itself to the very same criticism of ethnocentrism and teleological explanation that it raises.

Disintegration revisited: Thabo Fako

Separation of family members, scattered multiple residence, male absenteeism: these are some of the main elements Thabo Fako lists in analysing contemporary Tswana family life[7]. These elements describe social processes that are characteristic of other sub-Saharan societies. Resulting from colonial and post-colonial socio-economic factors of change, they lead to the "emergence of new, traditionally unorthodox, family forms"[8]. Identifying Fako's concept, the extended family model represents its point of departure, historically as well as logically. The traditionally "complicated multiple residence pattern"[9] puts Tswana extended families structurally under considerable pressure today, since economic migration comprehensively undermines the principle of common residence.

---

[7] Fako 1996:1
[8] Fako 1996:2
[9] Fako 1996:3

It is this principle of threat to traditional Tswana family life which induces Fako to distinguish between the household as the real economic, cohabitative collectivity and the family as the purely symbolic 'core unit'[10]. With respect to empirical research, he also defines the family as a 'methodological construct', 'meaningless' as a sampling unit and 'of no practical value'[11]. For this reason, he proposes that for research purposes, for example in terms of national development planning, only the 'household' should be deemed a valid research instrument and, therefore, introduced as the basic sampling unit. Fako's suggestion is – in our view, and looking at it from a conceptual point of view – questionable. Without doubt it reflects current practice (also Namibian practice), based on pragmatic decisions connected with empirical research needs. On the other hand, it encumbers exactly this empirical research with a theoretical burden, determining the conclusions beforehand.

This is both procedurally and theoretically subject to criticism. Fako analyses the process of social change, the emergence of new structural variations, in the light of what he calls the plague of family disintegration[12]. This leads to his particular concern for the retention of the traditional family and traditional family values[13]. Consequently, the approach runs the risk of classifying contemporary family forms as incomplete or deficient variations of a desired original. Inadvertently, reminiscence of the pessimistic bias and concerns of classical family debates in Western sociology rears its head[14]. However, in contrast to Margo Russell, Fako gives

---

[10] Fako 1996:10.

[11] Fako 1996:4. Unfortunately, Fako's distinctions in the article in question are somewhat blurred. The definition of the household as an "essentially social-psychological unit" (p.3) contradicts the subsequent one which characterises the household primarily as an economic unit (p.4). In fact, this contradiction effaces the borderline between household and family, by attributing the household a number of functions and elements which the sociology of the family usually reserves for the notion of family. Also in another respect the distinction fails to shed an accurate light on the empirical circumstances, that is, where the article differentiates between minor and extended units of the family. "Tswana families lived as households", including relatives "which formed a loosely defined extended family (p.3) (...) Several closely related households with primary dwellings in the same part of the village, make up the loosely-coupled extended family group (...) many ..functions necessary to the maintenance of the household may be carried out by family members living in other dwellings (p.4)". But, since the distinction between household and family is introduced as of practical necessity for research, it should be unequivocal. Throughout the article's "Conclusion"-chapter the term 'household' does not any longer appear, whereas it dwells largely on the family, that notion which previously had been attributed only little practical value.

[12] Fako 1996:8. The southern African debate shows other examples of a ideologically affected concern for the family. Anna Steyn introduces her report on a survey on the moral and ethical aspects of marriage and family life with a very firework of prejudices: "The escalating family disorganisation as reflected in an increasing divorce rate, nonmarital cohabitation, single-headed households, increasing family violence and a decrease in family size has lead to a great deal of concern in regarding the family as an institution." Steyn 1996:1. In this report, Steyn reveals a very contradictory position. On the one hand she makes a distinction between objective elements of change of the contemporary family in South Africa and their subjective processing in terms of the cognitive realisation of values. The latter suggest that the family still "is a vigorous and adaptable institution" (op.cit:9). On the other hand, her own, subjective interpretation of what she depicts as objective elements of change (see the above citation) centres on the characterisation of the process of change as disintegration.

[13] The "requisites in the evolving definition of family (cohabitation, sharing of food, joint finances, shared household work, intention to remain together, self-perception as family, distribution of costs and benefits) are substantially facilitated by effective common residence which further helps to bond members of the core family unit through intimacy, interdependence, and concern for one another. Inability to establish and sustain effective common residence weakens the institution of the family and its role as an agent of socialization that is relevant for family life education." Fako 1996:10

[14] The European and American debate, also on the background of an alleged disintegration, deplored the historical loss of functions of the Western family on its way to modernity. A notion introduced in 1946 by René Koenig, the disintegration of the family included: loosening of kinship ties, negative effects of female professional activities, disorganisation of the family in terms of a dysfunctional destabilization of internal relationships and of disappearing order potentials within the family, as well as its diminishing social prestige. Loss of functions, this meant: crucial family functions, such

social change its right, in the sense that he avoids assessing structural variations in the family as a temporary aberration, even though the form of change is for him undesirable.

Ethnocentrism revisited: Margo Russell's critique of Anna Steyn

Russell (1994) in her appraisal of Steyn's 1993 empirical study advocates the necessity of checking for the co-residence of relatives in black households. A balanced portrayal of current family patterns requires an illumination of kinship relations within the household[15]. She holds that in order to avoid ethnocentric viewpoints based on the concept of the nuclear family, a clear distinction has to be made between "a man's kin and those of his wife, between a son's offspring and those of a daughter"[16]. Such a distinction "is the underlying structuring principle of co-residence in unilineal descent systems." Therefore "its maintenance (or neglect) in contemporary black households would be a useful index of the survival or disintegration of this descent system"[17].

Russell suggests that in viewing multigenerational (black) family households, current structures of generational representation should not be misinterpreted as tendencies of social change of family structures[18]. Research, from her point of view, must not assume that structural changes in family biographies represent the emergence of separate types[19]. They may be fortuitous changes in generational representation "in response to the vicissitudes of death and migration"[20].

This statement has to be taken very seriously and – in the case of Namibia – at the same time to be assessed with caution. Without doubt, any ethnocentric model of an alleged transition from extended to nuclear family types in the course of societal modernisation during the last decades should be questioned. But equally, the opposite position of interpreting actual change a priori as temporary variations of persisting extended family structures has to be rejected as similarly ethnocentric[21].

---

as productive, educational and welfare functions, transferred to newly created social institutions. All these processes beginning with the rise of bourgeois society were seen responsible not only for establishing the nuclear family, but also for confining the family to the private sphere of social life.

[15] Russell 1994:58

[16] Ibid., the reason being that black African children "grow up using quite different words for father's, as distinct from mother's brothers: the former are all their 'fathers', intimate elders of their lineage. The latter are merely 'uncles'." (p.58)

[17] Ibid.

[18] Russell 1994:60

[19] Russell 1994:59

[20] Russell 1994:60. Thus, as a rule, what "matters is not the form in which the household presents at any one moment, but the rules about co-residence which determines the range of relations likely to be found within a household over time."

[21] Actually, the correspondent Western concept is in itself highly questionable. On the one hand, it generalized the existence of the extended family all over Europe (cf. Le Play, Riehl, Otto Brunner) and all over society, thus not differentiating between regional peculiarities and between class specific formations of the family (cf. Laslett's critique, as well as Mitterauer's). In fact, the family patterns of the affluent strata of the landed peasantry and of the artisan guilds (according to Otto Brunner's concept of the medieval 'ganze Haus' (the 'whole house') were indicated as common ones. Moreover the concept in its assertions statistically exaggerated the size of the extended family (cf. the critique of Schuhmacher and Vollmer 1982). Last, but not least, the extended family was pictured as an isle of autonomy and self-sufficiency within the subsistence mode of production, without any market integration. This romantic portrait also did not bear close scrutiny (cf. critique of Irmintraut Richarz 1991). On the other hand, it even more generalized the historically subsequent nuclear family model, attributing it not only a universal character, detectable in every single

It is only through research that the question can be answered as to whether a difference in the family types considered here should be judged either as a temporary shift or a lasting structural change due to evolving conditions of the socio-economic environment since independence (and not simply to biographical coincidences within the family). To formulate a sociological hypothesis: a high empirical incidence of one or more specific variations in the generational composition of inter- and intra generational co-residence within the family points to a new social reality; or as Durkheim would say: an authoritative reality sui generis. If it is nevertheless interpreted as the temporary variation Russell deems it to be, the reasons for this temporary character should duly be stated and not merely implicitly presupposed.

According to Russell's central hypothesis, "blacks in both urban and rural areas have a distinctive system of household formation, quite unlike that operating amongst whites"[22]. Notwithstanding the necessity for some of the family members to migrate in order to obtain a cash income, this phenomenon is to be attributed to the fact that the rural extended family remains the core unit – a permanent social grouping – while every other kind of household structure (especially the urban one) is seen only as temporary. This assertion has the character of a paradigm in Russell's line of thought; it is stated but not clearly conceptualised.

Turning to another aspect of Russell's conceptual background: as do Fako and Steyn, she defines families/households exclusively by membership. Households are, sociologically, allotted either to the multigenerational or to the nuclear type, subject to their personnel i.e. depending on the number, gender and generation of their members. The very attributes of structural description – 'extended' and 'nuclear' – stress this governing factor of number. Aspects of change i.e. functional change – in the character of the household are not reflected, although they represent the whole range of structural variations between the two analytical extremes of the supposed developmental model.

But one and the same personnel – for example, of a household consisting of a "single father living with his children plus (...) his sister, or his mother", to cite

---

culture all over the world, but also universality all over time (Murdock 1949). Once the generalized existence of both the extended and the nuclear family had thus been theoretically established, these served as historical points of departure and of destination for constructing an evolutionary model. In this exceptionally ethnocentric manner, an odd sociological course of progress from the family model of medieval middle European landed peasantry to the family model of American urban middle classes of the 1940s of this century was consecrated. That is to say, any accusation of ethnocentrism, in addition, has to point out the fact, that the very concept, as by the sociology of the family applied to European and American societies, proves empirically wrong and historically incorrect.

[22] Russell 1994:62. She underlines her argument by showing the results of the 1991 South African census, according to which the differences in size between rural and urban black households are not significant ones. It has to be remarked, in our understanding, that Russell's statement is questionable, if one looks at the figures (p.62). The assertion of a "similarity in the pattern of urban and rural blacks, and the difference between this pattern and that displayed by whites, who likewise show very little variation from rural to urban areas" (p.63) is contradicted by the aggregated representation of the figures. Up to a household size of three members, white rural (59,12% of all households) and urban (57,84%) households show no significant difference. In the same category black rural (27,71%) and urban (36,34%) households do statistically differ. In comparison with that, the bulk of black rural households is to be found in the category of household sizes including 4 to 6 members (54,99%), whereas in that category the number of black urban households is notably smaller (44,35%).To sum up, it can be said, that white households concentrate on sizes of smaller number, black households in urban areas show a more equal distribution between the different household sizes, in that differing notably from black rural households whose bulk is to be found in the more populated households; thus, there is definitely a difference in the pattern of urban and rural blacks, contrary to what Russell advocates.

Russell[23] – may form a 'traditional' multigenerational family, in accordance with traditional subsistence patterns of division of labour. It may, on the other hand, constitute a new and different urban, though still multigenerational family which is founded on the dependence of several of its members on wage labour rather than domestic subsistence activities characterising a rural economy. Whereas some of the traditional cultural features of patriarchal authority may persist, its basic lines of gender division of labour may already have changed[24].

Obviously, this does not mean that this specific family unit is no longer based on a gender division of labour, but its underlying character has changed. To mention only a few aspects: on the economic side, dependence on the (vicissitudes of the) labour market, on salaries, on a monetarised supply with basic goods through a capitalist consumer market; commercialisation of leisure time. On the cultural side, subjection to a new concept of time, both in work and everyday life; subjection to the authority of economic agents, (partly) replacing kinship-shaped authorities and the obligations of its normative world; clashes of different cultural experiences between and within the generations of the family. All this implies a subsequent structural change of family pattern in the long run, or at least the possibility. Its whole functional determination has undergone a transformation owing to the different functional requirements of its new socio-economic environment. In short: it is about to develop a different class character.

Summarising our arguments concerning Russell's contribution, with a view to the Namibian situation:

- her critique of the poorly reflected ethnocentric models of change from multigenerational to nuclear family patterns is justified and valid;
- her comment on the persistence of multigenerational patterns of family life is valuable;
- her critique of an interpretation of the process of social change relating to family patterns as 'disintegration' is of theoretical importance;
- on the other hand, from a sociological point of view, a limitation to defining persistent or changing family patterns only through its personnel should be avoided;
- there is no sociologically valid explanation for the statement that new empirical structures of the family should be interpreted only as 'frozen parts' of the patrilineal extended family system[25]; this underestimates actual moments of change;
- the personnel, the members of a household/family, act within a distinct socio-economic and cultural environment which reflects a particular class cast. It is this class specific stamp which not only defines functions and activities of the family in a new and different way, but which also may, in

---

[23] Russell 1994:61
[24] E.g., the male household head earning a living as wage labourer, no longer as communal subsistence farmer; children going to public schools; sister combining household work (now mainly based on market supplies) with an informal job as housemaid for a few hours a week.
[25] Russell 1994:61

the long run, 'restructure' family patterns in Namibian society;
- despite all this, figures for the Namibian situation show a remarkable difference in the size of households of rural and urban areas. This without doubt illustrates changes in their multigenerational composition – the decreasing personnel affects every generational level. It is not, as Russell correctly criticises of Steyn's concept, to be interpreted as a shrinking at the expense only of the grandparents' generation; therefore, this process is not necessarily to be seen as the family historically turning to nuclear patterns. Instead of this, changes reflect contemporary forms of development (not progress) between two (conceptual) extremes: the extended, multigenerational, unilineal family and the nuclear, two-generational, bi-lineal family model.
- If research shows that such structures become a dominant feature of the family 'landscape' in Namibia, the sociological conceptualisation of family structures has to acknowledge this as a phenomenon of change, and should not to limit itself to interpret it as a momentary aberration from traditional, integral structures.

Empirical research: a review of Namibian studies of family and family-related issues

A preliminary literature research, first of all, reveals the dearth of sociological studies of the family in Namibia. The relevant reports and monographs are quite restricted in number. Under the heading of 'household' the majority of them shows a somewhat pragmatic approach to family issues; a minority though expressly deals with specific aspects of family life, but does so with poor conceptual frameworks. However, raising questions regarding the literature allows us in this review to clarify the empirical basis of the contemporary Namibian family and family studies in the region.

Looking for statistical data on households, the Central Statistical Office's *Housing and population census of 1991* and its *Namibia labour force survey of 1997* offer the most valuable sources.

The 1991 Census provides overall figures on household sizes and on their distribution by rural and urban areas. It also attempts to differentiate between household types (e.g.: single parent, couple, extended family).

Dwelling on the household size:
- households of 1 to 4 persons amount to 130 000 (51%)
- households of 5 and more persons amount to 125 500 (49%)

of a total of 255 000 households constituting a household population of 1,32 million. The average household size is 5,2 persons. Differentiating between urban and rural areas, the distribution of households basically follows that of the population – 70% rural households as compared to 30% urban households. The latter are generally smaller. In the category of up to 4 persons per household, the percentage of rural households is lower; the percentage of households of 5 or more persons is notably higher in rural areas. The average household sizes amount to 4,7 persons and 5,4 persons in urban and rural areas respectively.

The Census attempts to differentiate between household types. Households of single parents or couples (living alone, or with one or more than one child, that is to say, two-generational households) are distinguished from single parents or couples living in multigenerational households. The latter make up for a third of all households. It is interesting to note, that whereas two-generational households are termed households, the Census associates multigenerational households with 'family', i.e. extended family – without giving any reasons other than the existence of at least one additional generation.

The distribution of 'extended family' households by urban and rural areas differs when comparing single parents with couples. The percentage of single parents' multigenerational households in rural areas exceeds that in urban areas by more than 50% (20,5% urban to 31%. rural; all figures pp.37-38). On the other hand, the percentage of couples living in multigenerational households does not show significant differences. That is to say: multigenerational households are common in both rural and urban areas. In town, households seem to reproduce traditional patterns of cohabitation quite successfully; while the villages experience the effects of migration, showing a greater number of single parents living in multigenerational households.

In a regional comparison the Census shows that the largest households (6 persons on average) are found in the north of Namibia, namely in the Oshana, Oshikoto, Ohangwena and Kavango regions, with an ethnic majority of Oshivambo speaking people.

The 1997 Survey, as well as the actual labour report, also deals with some scattered statistical evidence on household characteristics, mainly reproducing the analytical patterns of the 1991 Census.

As far as the household size is concerned:
- households of 1 to 4 persons amount to 136 000 (50,0%)
- households of 5 or more persons amount to 136 000 (50%)

of a total of nearly 272 000 households amounting to a household population of 1,4 million. There are 16 000 more households than in the '91 Census. Since the distribution of the population by size did not change significantly (households up to 4 persons: 1991 51%, 1997 50%; households of 5 or more persons: 1991 49%, 1997 50%), it seems that the first half decade of independence did not bring about much change in household size patterns. The average size figure confirms this, as in 1991 it was 5,2 persons.

There is a slight difference in the distribution of the population by urban and rural areas. Compared with 1991, when 27% lived in urban and 73% in rural areas, in 1997, 32,4% lived in urban and 67,6% in rural areas. This change reflects a certain trend of urbanisation (all figures: tables 3.1. and 3.2.)

Another trend of interest for the family issue is reflected in the Labour Force Survey. Namibia's population is very young. 40,4% are aged below 15, and the majority of these young age classes lives in rural areas – nearly ¾ of them (420 000 = 74,1%). Looking at the dependency ratio – the relation of population portions of non-working age (0-14 and over 65 years) and of working age (15-64 years) – by rural and urban areas, the concentration of non-working portions in the rural areas becomes obvious. ¾ of the non-working age population lives in rural surroundings, but only 60% of the working age population lives there. Combining the trend towards urbanisation and age distribution of the population by areas, the figures suggest that there is a migrational trend to the urban areas of Namibia which mainly involves the economically active population aged 15 - 64.

There are a number of conclusions to be drawn and of questions arising from the combination of these findings. Summarising the results of the survey:
- although there is an urbanisation trend, household structures have not notably changed in terms of size distribution;

- on the other hand, children and the elderly do not participate in the trend of urbanisation to the same extent as the economically active population.

Thus we pose the question: the size distribution of households remaining stable and the young majority of the population being concentrated in rural areas, what is the composition of urban households? The trends could suggest that they would mainly be composed of an adult workforce of both sexes. In fact, the Survey shows a nearly equal distribution by sex in more or less all age groups of the urban population, whereas the distribution by sex in rural areas is unequal, the female population (53,4%) exceeding the male population (46,6%). Moreover, in the age classes up to 20 years males form the majority of the rural population, while in the age classes from 20 - 49 they are in the minority – confirming a statistical trend of rural-urban migration of male workers (all figures tables 3.3 and 3.4.). On the other hand, the trends could simply explain the fact that owing to the smaller number of children, the average urban household is notably smaller in size (4,4 persons as compared to 5,6 persons in rural households). The number of urban households in every single category up to five members is higher, as compared to rural households, while households of six or more persons are more numerous in rural areas.

Looking at possible developments since 1991: there are only minimal changes in the national distribution of households by size, looking at the single categories. Differentiating between urban and rural, contrary trends are detected. Urban households up to a number of five slightly increased in percentage, while those of six and more slightly decreased. There is an opposite trend in rural areas: households up to a number of seven slightly decreased in percentage of the total number of rural households of all sizes. Households of two persons constitute the only exception, increasing by 0,5%. Rural households of eight and more persons in 1997 formed a greater proportion of the total.

The 1997 Survey provides some interesting data concerning sources of income of Namibian households (tables 3.8 and 3.9). This information could be of interest when correlating it with the size distribution of households. The questions to be answered, checking a plausible assumption, are these: is there any statistical relationship between subsistence farming as the main source of income of rural households and their bigger size? Is there any correlation between the prevalence of wages and salaries as main sources of income of urban households and their relatively smaller size?

- First to the figures on the all-Namibia distributions: 27,5% of households indicate subsistence farming as their primary source of income. The figures rise as high as 72% in the former Ovamboland region. 45,2% of households indicate wages and salaries as main source.
- Comparing urban and rural areas: subsistence reproduction plays practically no role in urban areas (1,0%), whereas 75,0% or all urban households mainly live on wages and salaries. Subsistence farming, however, does play a major role in rural households.

On the basis of the data supplied by the Survey, there is no possibility of correlating distributions by sources of incomes with household size distribution. Nevertheless, the question remains to be answered, as part of an empirical research based on a broader concept of the family. Do variations in household sizes and composition depend on the sources of income, or, to be more precise, on the way in which income (in cash or kind) is generated; do they depend on the underlying modes of production?

In 1993 a programmatic monograph on *Social science research priorities for Namibia* was edited by K.K. Prah, at that time a senior researcher at the Multi-Disciplinary Research Centre, Social Science Division at the University of Namibia. It sees Namibian research as a utility of political planning for a more equitable society. Following this context of social rationalisation, research on household and family is deemed necessary for providing "knowledge of settlement patterns and the basic demography of the country"[26] and as such is advocated as one of the objects of prioritisation. One of the early researchers of NISER[27], Chris Tapscott, detailed the elements of empirical research calling attention to the social structure of rural households, their sources of income, the functioning of the extended family system, the social and economic linkages between rural and urban areas[28]. These patterns were to become the family-related section of a number of socio-economic surveys carried out by the Social Science Division (SSD) at the University of Namibia in the following years. Though Tapscott's suggestions basically leave scope for a wider interpretation of family research in terms of enquiring after the mode of production on which family structures are founded, these patterns actually introduced a model which confined the family to its basic physical framework and economic character.

The first of these surveys, in collaboration with the Directorate of Rural Development of the Namibian Ministry of Agriculture, investigated the *Southern communal areas*. It reports in general on the living conditions of non-white ethnic groups in the survey area, namely Namas and Bondelswarts. Family issues are touched upon as statistics of household structure and composition, as well as of some economic indicators. A specific conceptualisation of the family is missing owing to a purely statistical orientation.

The second of these surveys, published in 1994, concentrates on the *Eastern communal areas* and its Herero population majority of the former South West African reserves, Hereroland East and West. Similar to its predecessor, this report addresses family issues purely in terms of general household statistics.

The third report of the year 1996, looking into the *Living and working conditions of farm workers in Namibia*, is conceived as an investigation into the material conditions of life of a specific occupational group, combining different regional study areas. Taking the possible effects of the 1992 Labour Act into account, it focuses on commodity and cash sources of income of the surveyed households, on assets and budgets. Unfortunately, it does not give any information on size, composition or other details of farm workers' households, thus missing the opportunity to provide empirical evidence for the conceptualisation of the class-specific aspects of the notion of the family.

Yaron et al., studying *Rural development in the Okavango region of Namibia*, report on a project completed in 1992 in the north-eastern Ovamboland region on the border with Angola. The area, which contributes to the regional and national streams of urban migration, is analysed – as far as the family is concerned – only in terms of structural and compositional household details. However, the study contains a theoretically remarkable attempt to re-define household income sources by distinguishing in detail between subsistence and market related in-

---

[26] Tapscott, in: Prah:31
[27] Namibian Institute of Social and Economic Research, later transformed into the Social Sciences Division of the Multi-Disciplinary Research Centre (SSD-MRC) attached to UNAM, the University of Namibia
[28] Tapscott:31 lists the single aspects of this research in detail: "the present social structure of rural households; – the functioning of the extended family system and the extended linkages between rural and urban areas; – the sources of rural income, and household survival strategies: – the extent of migrancy, levels of remittances to the rural economy".

comes. This attempt implicitly sheds light on the conceptual necessity of looking at the empirical articulation of the subsistence mode of production, under the auspices of the dominance of capitalist money and market relations. If family structures are not to be envisaged within the classical extended/nuclear dichotomy, their analysis indeed has to be based on a correlation of production relations and their social expression.

Van Rooy et al. in 1994 presented a report on *Household subsistence levels in Namibia* based on a project comparing survey areas in three different regions. As its central topic, the household is pictured by means of statistical evidence on some indicators of structure, composition and economic basis, with a particular emphasis on gender differences.

This gender aspect guides the study of Iken et al. of *Socio-economic conditions of female-headed households and single mothers in the southern communal areas of Namibia*, published in 1994. It gives a detailed analysis of the high incidence of 'non-conventional' families, i.e. families where the household head is living without a spouse. The report focuses on the particular economic vulnerability of female-headed households. It highlights the difference between 'non-conventional' and single-person households, as well as the high incidence of smaller household sizes in younger age groups.

> In relation to the family, an interesting inference be drawn from the report: non-conventional households are not generally single-person or one-generation households[29]. So, conventional families cannot be set apart from the relatively new phenomenon of non-conventional families by simply assuming that they differ in the number of members. This underscores the fact that, sociologically, it is not sufficient to define family merely along variations in size. The distinction between 'nuclear' and 'extended' family pattern is but a first, descriptive step in a sociological definition.
>
> Non-conventional families vary in size and present varied patterns of co-habitation and division of labour. The spouse missing (whether male or female), the household head resorts to combining with other people in forming a household. For research purposes, it is indispensable to get further information relating to the additional members[30]. Nevertheless, some typical patterns do emerge, looking at households by size and age of household head. Non-conventional households, as a rule, are young households, headed by people of the age groups of 15-19 and 20-24 years. These are generally households of the size category of 1 to 3 members. In all the other age groups of household heads, households are more evenly distributed by size categories[31].

The *Namibia poverty profile*, drawn up by Devereux et al. in 1995, contains no specific data on correlation between household structures and poverty indicators, apart from a rough all Namibia classification of households according to their level of food consumption.

---

[29] "This suggests that (...) there are usually other people who reside with the head. This has obvious implications for the division of labour, specifically child rearing, within the household." Iken et al. 1994:15

[30] Kin or not kin (are additional members relatives or are they not?); if kin: kinship patterns (are they of the same generation – sister, brother, cousin; of the older generation – aunt; of the younger generation – own / other children?); if not kin: which relationship?

[31] Though with one clear limitation: irrespective of their age, female heads tend to live in households of not more than five members

UNDP's *Namibia human development country report 1998* on Namibia (focusing both on poverty and environmental issues) only revisits older data of the Central Statistical Office's National Household Income and Expenditure Survey when turning to family-related issues. It emphasises the differences in incomes and income sources between rural and urban households as elements of typical poverty patterns.

Two Namibian studies deal with urbanisation as an effect of migration. Frayne's *Urbanisation in post-independence Windhoek* looks mainly at the physical and infrastructural dimensions of its dynamic. The social aspects are omitted, surprisingly, given the topic. This gives Frayne's study a somewhat technocratic character. Pendletons's *Katutura in the 1990s* reports on two surveys conducted in 1991 and 1996 in Katutura, the northern township of the capital Windhoek, where the non-white majority of the population was confined to[32]. It provides detailed material on urban households. In particular the regional provenance of migrants and the geo-ethnic patterns of urban settlement are highlighted here. The report discusses the material and motivational background of urban migration, also providing data on age structure and changes in the gender aspects of households, income and housing patterns.

A number of studies focuses on the social situation of children. UNICEF and NISER in 1991 published a *Situation analysis of children and women in Namibia*. It is interesting to note that throughout the document, the contemporary family is of no analytical importance as a structural backdrop to the social conditions of Namibian women and children[33]. The same applies to the *National programme of action for the children of Namibia*, formulated by an Inter-ministerial Standing Committee of the Namibian National Planning Commission in 1993. Nowhere in the otherwise extremely detailed topical introductions and operational objectives is the eminent role of the family in guaranteeing sound social surroundings for children taken into account, analytically or practically[34]. A similarly critical judgement has to be applied to the report of Botaala's *The family in transition*. This study of child rearing practices among the Nama of the Karas and Hardap regions of Namibia was presented in 1995 to UNICEF. Its sociological framework on the family remains vague, professedly due to the empirical emphases[35], and it displays no real analytical content. Family structures as such are mentioned but in passing[36].

---

[32] Katutura was established in the 1960s after the ejection of the black population from the Old Location and other districts of Windhoek implementing the policy of segregation of the South African Odendaal Plan.

[33] Though addressing their priority needs as "part of the process of joint programming at country level between UNICEF and the Government of Namibia" (Preface), that is, at highest political level

[34] This is incomprehensible, since the Programme of Action deals with legal and administrative provisions for all those facets of children's' well being, which centre on the family: health care, nutrition and household food security, water and sanitation, socialization, education and literacy; or even with the advancement of women. Only when referring to the malnutrition of mothers and children, does the Household Food Security Programme at least address households as primary targets for economic improvement.

[35] "There are various definitions of the family: it could consist of the father, the mother and children. It could be a nuclear family; grandparent led; extended family; mother led; or a number of mothers living communally, sharing their children. Because of our interest in childrearing and early childhood it should contain at least one child and one adult." Botaala 1995:2

[36] "The majority of the families were of the extended type". Botaala 1995:vii

In comparison, *Children in Namibia*, a report presented by SSD, UNICEF and the Legal Assistance Centre (LAC) in 1995, is conceptually far more sophisticated. It presents a comprehensive account of the constitutional, legal and social environment of the precarious situation of children. Referring to the family, it highlights the cultural variety of family concepts in Namibia. It is this range of definitions of the family, produced by ethnic traditions as well as by the socio-economic conditions of Namibian society, that induces the authors to suggest its substitution with the notion of 'household'[37]. In its statistical elements, the report touches on labour migration as a major driving force of change in family patterns, on the urbanisation trend and on the persisting rural links of households. In analysing the household composition, it attempts an integration of the whole range of structures existing beyond the dichotomy of extended and nuclear households.

> Gender-based income inequalities of households; the impact of patriarchal structures; higher dependency ratios of rural and of female-headed households; polygyny as an ethnic characteristic of households of the north-eastern regions and correspondent 'second house'-relationships; three-generation female-headed households and missing-generation female-headed households – all these facets add up to an iridescent picture of the contemporary Namibian family.

Summarising this review of the existing Namibian research: first of all, there is no specific field of study that truly focuses on the sociological analysis of Namibian family structures in transition. Secondly, empirical research only provides scattered data on various elements of the topic, but not exhaustive relevant information. Thirdly, except for a few unsystematic attempts, what is missing is a conceptual framework considering the structural peculiarities of the Namibian family, against the background of the international debate on the sociology of the family.

Conclusions: directions for Namibian family studies

In order to facilitate a critical assessment of our arguments and line of thought, we firstly draft our definition of the terms 'family' and 'household'. It is – as far as 'family' is concerned – deliberately arguing on a general level of sociological theory, the core assumption of our contribution being precisely the necessity of first revising the conceptual background of the sociology of the family in Namibia. The peculiarities of sub-Saharan societies and cultures with respect to the shaping of their past and present family types can be assessed against this background. As far as the suggestion to analyse the 'household' rather than the 'family' is concerned, thus enhancing the practicability of field research, we do not see an adequate sociological reason for such an a priori definitory rejection of the term 'family'. From a conceptual point of view the two notions are interchangeable, as long as they share the same integral subject. They simply look at the

---

[37] SSD/LAC/UNICEF 1995:27

same issue from different angles, 'household' essentially relating to economic functions[38]. However from an empirical point of view, since quantitative research on family issues *has* created a conceptual difference between the two notions, that difference has to be specified.

Following this definitory draft, we hypothesise the necessity of combining the sociological fields of development and family theory in order to provide an appropriate framework.

'Family' and 'household' – a definitory approach

Referring to its Latin linguistic roots, the term family[39] indicates its patriarchal origins, pointing to a social unit of blood relatives, dependents and slaves, placed under the supervision and the legal authority of the male dominus, father and (land)lord. The members of the family form an economic unit of production and reproduction headed by the pater familiae.

These historical origins emphasise the economic ties of the social group, which form the basis of its hierarchical structure grounded on power. The aspect of blood relationship plays a role, but is not the only focus. Stress is also put on co-habitation, on the house as a unit of production and of individual and social reproduction. This original notion of 'family', so obviously and closely linked to European history and culture, has undergone considerable historical change[40]. Where capitalist industrialisation restructured societies along the lines of a bourgeois class dominance, it has become the elementary social unit of reproduction. It has shrunk in size[41] and generally lost its original productive functions. Depending on cash income provided by wage labour, it now draws its material inputs mainly from the commodity market although certain subsistence patterns may remain relevant. It is shaped by the immediate blood relationship of the parent-children generation forming the familiar nucleus of cohabitation.

Admittedly, a closer look shows that a considerable number of modifications form an integral part of the picture. Firstly, the above model, in the strict sense, mainly describes the bourgeois class-type model of the modern nuclear family. On the other hand, in concomitance with the advance of wage, market and money relations throughout capitalist economy, this nuclear type increasingly becomes the dominant family model, within all classes of society[42], particularly within the

---

[38] For example, the German debate of the 1980s on class theory advocates this interchangeability. It conceives the household as an income-pooling unit and, as such, as the basic analytical unit of class analysis in highly industrialised societies of the post-war period. Economic, social, and cultural elements of class determination centre on that unit, which – combining the said elements – is identified with the modern family in welfare societies. Cf. Bischoff et al. 1982, Hirsch / Roth 1986.

[39] 'Familia', which is derived from 'famulus' (servant)

[40] The social history of the family follows a path of multilinearity. Taking the Roman family type as a notional point of departure does not reflect an ethnocentric bias; this choice simply has etymological reasons.

[41] Though the size statistically varies along class lines.

[42] All the more, as the 19th century sees a cultural crusade in Europe directed at the establishment of the bourgeois family model and its intrinsic values all over society. In the name of moral progress, the 'lower classes' are forced into a life-long education, which aims at their cultural 'uplifting', in order to prevent them from both moral decay and revolutionary diversions. Pedagogy as a science is born. It is in this century that compulsory public education -for all classes – divests the family of one of its important functions. Obviously, this has also structural effects on the family in all classes.

petty-bourgeois strata. Moreover, in peripheral as well as in metropolitan societies, the historical heritage of pre-capitalist family formations structured a variety of family types. They were (and are) as dissimilar to the nuclear model as some of its more recent patterns of the fordist era of capitalist development.

Evidently, such a structural variety of class-related family forms is even more significant in peripheral, developing societies. Where structural heterogeneity (in terms of the hierarchical intertwining of modes of production and of the articulation of relations of social classes, originating from different historical formations) dominates the scenario, the historical-traditional element plays a central role in retarding the process of nuclearisation of the family. The adaptation of such traditional patterns of cohabitation and reproduction accompanies the establishment of family forms directly linked to the metropolitan spheres of peripheral societies.

Looking at the *structural aspects* of the concept of 'family':
- based on the fundamental mother-child dyad[43], its structure is given by the number, provenance and generational status of its members; all are defined culturally, meaning that individual cultures or a complex of cultures define the structure of the family, and not universal patterns;
- family forms part of a larger social system, and as such is determined by the basic economic and class configurations of the latter;
- the family is a partial social system, interrelated with other social systems;
- it is a structured social system, showing a power structure historically based on patriarchal authority, male dominance; thus historically defined, it structures inequalities of gender;
- it forms a minor unit of the predominant social order, defining role distribution and arrangements of authority culturally along the lines of generation, gender and economic dependence; defining partnership, parenthood and relationship between brother and sister;
- the taboo of incest and rules of kinship serve as a normative basis for the retention of structures in all cultures;
- all this points to the fact that the family is a social institution, a publicly acknowledged and constitutionally protected institution;
- sociology regards it as the most important primary group for human beings.

Looking at its *functional* aspects:
- family is a functional unit;
- its functional definition is subject to historical change; regardless of change throughout time, family serves as an association for sexual reproduction and as a basic unit for social reproduction; as a household

---

[43] Eickelpasch 1974

unit;
- also, regardless of historical change, it is the central place of socialisation and enculturation, the basic unit of psychical reproduction in the sense of the 'reproduction of human characters' (Horkheimer); education and socialisation produce what sociology calls the sociocultural personality or, rather emphasising the class/cultural aspects of social behaviour, 'habitus' (Bourdieu);
- it is a moral unit;
- it is a legal unit[44]; its internal as well as external relations with other societal spheres are defined by law;
- it is an instrument for allocating social status.

Looking at its *actional* aspects:
- it is a unit of action;
- though the family represents a system of power relations, it is also built on internal solidarity; it is a unit of interaction, based on gender division of labour as well as on co-operation;
- self-perception as family is the prerequisite for its acting as a unit; this includes the intention to remain together, be it involuntary, forced on the individual by realising existing relations of dependence, or voluntary;
- it is a unit of intimacy and privacy[45].

The definition of the term 'family' includes the sphere of sociocultural interaction. Thus combining aspects of structure, function and action, the family appears as a unit of structuration.

In contrast with this, the constraints of operationalisation burdened empirical research with a conceptual restriction. This is true at least of Namibian research. As a result, many crucial defining aspects of the modern Namibian family are disregarded; only its (even narrowly defined) economic description as a household unit is highlighted. For the purposes of conducting empirical research, the term 'household' then becomes a notion mainly focusing on the bare physical aspects of family structure: on its personnel, and on some economic determinations. In connection with these, cohabitation and gender are also observed.

In principle, there are no serious objections to be made against such restrictions if the purpose is primarily a pragmatic one – if it were not for the tacit reintroduction of all the remaining attributes of the family concept into research – by the back door as it were. When deciding on the content of empirical research in detail (selection of existing statistical material, of topics for questionnaire or inter-

---

[44] In those societies which have developed an institutionalised legal system. Based on the mother-child-dyad (Eickelpasch 1974), throughout history patterns deviating from the prevailing legal norm complemented the predominant feature.

[45] As such it is specially protected by law, at least in those societies which have adopted legal systems founded on Western legal traditions.

views), the prevalent notions inevitably play an important part. Undoubtedly, they prejudice the findings.

Sociology of development and sociology of the family
Conceiving the family as a unit of structuration, i.e. explicitly introducing and combining its different aspects of structure, function, and action, could help to solve the conceptual problem. This means:
- not equating family structures simply with household membership;
- not conceiving structural transformation as disintegration (or survival) of traditional family patterns;
- not modelling social change along the lines of ethnocentric assumptions.

The diversity of conceptual conclusions, as seen with Fako and Russell, shows the need for an appropriate framework for the interpretation of structural transformation in Sub-Saharan Africa. The dubious assumption of dualism generally underlying the study of socio-economic change is drawn from the intellectual world of modernisation theory. Notwithstanding more than three decades of endless debate and radical criticism, it still exerts its formative influence on those simplistic dualistic concepts which continue to determine research on the sociology of the family. Sociologically unable to cope with the complex requirements of social reality, they still suggest a notion of change travelling on a 'unilineal trajectory'[46] as from simple to complex, from traditional to modern, from 'primitive' to 'Western', from agricultural to industrial; or, as in our case, from extended to nuclear reproductive units.

Referring to 'traditional' social organisations in structural transformation such as the family, it has to be emphasised that their sociological definition calls for the inclusion of the whole range of productive and reproductive, of economic and cultural elements of such a social entity – where the term 'traditional' refers to the fact that they originate from pre-capitalist social formations, and survive (in colonial and post-colonial formations) by adaptation to the new mode of production and its functional requirements without completely losing their definition according to their pre-capitalist roots; that is to say, where the term 'traditional' actually reveals that they are a product of changing structural conditions, and as such are not at all 'traditional' in the common sense of the word. Contrary to the practice of mainstream empirical sociological research, as has already been said, the family cannot be reduced to its personnel, to its statistical appearance.

As in South Africa, labour migration in Namibia mainly follows economic needs and constraints (and, in part, cultural aspirations). It forms the backbone of the structural transformation of the family as a social institution. However, in some respects the scenario is different and quite complex. The structure of the Namibian economy has been historically deformed along the lines of its forced integration into the colonial South African capital and commodities' markets, bear-

---

[46] Logan 1995:3

ing now the basic marks of peripheral capitalism⁴⁷. The juxtaposition of subsistence and capitalist, of formal and informal sectors, of wage labour, unemployment and subsistence labour, of marginalised and integrated sections of the population, of ethnic cultural influences and Western, globalised elements of culture – this juxtaposition has for quite some time become a persistent structural characteristic of (under) development.

This implies beyond doubt that the process of labour migration is a multidirectional one[48], not merely limited to the flow of labour force into the urban areas in search of cash income. It should not simply be seen as restricted to the classical aspects of urbanisation connected with the establishment of capitalist social relations. This in turn implies the juxtaposition of different types of family, their discrete and continued existence in contemporary Namibian society. They neither represent passing realities of a unilineal process of historical elimination of pre-capitalist social structures, nor merely the survival of the latter. In our understanding, changing family patterns in Namibia should not be interpreted within such a conceptual framework of disintegration of traditional forms (as Fako does with relation to Botswana); or of their cultural persistence or revival (as Russell does in criticising Steyn's model of the nuclearisation of contemporary black families of urban South Africa); or of their mere shrinking in size in the course of modernisation and urbanisation (as the bulk of Namibian empirical research implicitly does).

We suggest that they should be interpreted within a conceptual framework of adaptation of structures of different origins and aspects to current individual needs and structural conditions of socio-economic nature. Certainly not dualism arising from the discredited tradition of modernisation theory, but rather concepts such as that of Logan's continuum should determine the sociological imperative. With Logan[49], we envisage the continuum as a typological variety, a side-by-side of structural appearances which systematically recognises the diversity of the family in developmental contexts.

In contrast with Logan, though, we emphasise the long-term prevalence of capitalist market factors over use-value or traditional market orientations in the normative determination of social action connected with the formation of a family. This is to say, the process of social change – though multidirectional in its short-

---

[47] Its extreme dependence on primary sector exports and consumer goods' imports perpetuates an imbalance which prevents the establishment of sound patterns of self-sufficiency. The economy is dominated by a primary sector where mining plays the major role and commercial agriculture is not designed to satisfy domestic needs. Its chronically weak secondary sector still shows classical colonial birthmarks, even a decade after independence, balanced, self-sustained industrialisation having been prevented. The hypertrophied tertiary sector mainly depends on external incentives. Fluctuations of regional and international demand on the domestic primary sector which influence the volume of tertiary sector activities, cannot be compensated by a tourism industry suffering the restrictions of an ecologically highly susceptible environment.

[48] As Logan argues, it needs to be emphasised (...) that (...) resources, including labour and capital, can and do move back and forth from subsystem to subsystem, in response to personal, household, and community responses to economic, social and political imperatives. This is not to suggest that the process is chaotic. It is far more complex than a one-factor flow between discrete sectors: the process is multidirectional (...) and, within the constraints of economic, political, and social conditions, actors make deliberate, proactive choices regarding the mix of traditional and market principles to maximize their goals." Logan 1995:15

[49] Logan's continuum approach identifies change structurally as a series of subsystems which display a different mix of behavioural patterns. At its one end, the continuum is predominantly (not purely) traditional, and at the other, it is predominantly (not purely) modern market." Logan 1995:3

and medium-term aspects – is dictated by a distorted integration of Namibian society into global settings, be it regional or more extended metropolitan markets. This is suggested by the available Namibian data of the last one or two decades, as far as the structural transformation of the Namibian family is concerned.

In closing, a final remark stressing the importance of the notion of the family for general sociological theory: the family as the income-pooling unit of cohabitation (household) and as the basic unit of cultural structuration of the individual habitus, represents the basic analytical unit of class analysis, of stratification theory, and not the individual. Therefore, comprehensive knowledge of the structural transformations of the Namibian family forms a basic prerequisite of attempts to investigate the social structure of post-independent Namibia, another blind spot of Namibian sociology.

Bibliography

Bischoff, Joachim 1988. Dienstleistungsgesellschaft – Ende des Industriezeitalters? In: Sozialismus, no.9
Botaala, Zimba RF 1996. The family in transition. A study of child rearing practices and beliefs among the Nama of the Karas and Hardap regions of Namibia – report for UNICEF and UNAM. Windhoek
Devereux, Stephen / *Katjiuanjo*, Vemunavi / *van Rooy*, Gert 1995. The living and working conditions of farm workers in Namibia. Multidisciplinary Research Centre – Social Sciences Division University of Namibia. Windhoek
Devereux, Stephen / *Fuller*, Ben / *Moorsom*, Richard JB / *Solomon*, Colette / *Tapscott*, Chris 1995. Namibia poverty profile (SSD Research Report no.21). University of Namibia, Windhoek
Eickelpasch, Rolf 1974 . Ist die Kernfamilie universal? In: Zeitschrift für Soziologie
Fako, Thabo 1996. The definition and functions of the family: towards a rationale for teaching family values through schools in Botswana. In: South African Journal of Sociology, Feb. 1996, vol.27, issue 1 (here: Internet Version, 13 pp.)
Frayne, Bruce 1992. Urbanization in post-independence Windhoek. Windhoek
Government of the Republic of Namibia 1991. Housing and Population Census 1991. Central Statistical Office. Windhoek
Government of the Ruplic of Namibia 1992. Socio-economic survey: southern communal areas. Ministry of Agriculture, Water and Rural Development, Directorate of Extension and Engineering Services. Windhoek
Government of the Republic of Namibia 1993. The National Programme of Action for Children- annual report 1993. National Planning Committee, Inter-Ministerial Standing Committee. Windhoek
Government of the Republic of Namibia 1994. Socio-economic survey: Eastern communal areas. Ministry of Agriculture, Water and Rural Development, Directorate of Extension and Engineering Services; Multidisciplinary Research Centre – Social Sciences Division, University of Namibia. Windhoek
Government of the Republic of Namibia 1998. The Namibia labour force survey 1997: interim report. Ministry of Labour and Central Bureau of Statistics of the National Planning Commission. Windhoek
Hirsch, Joachim / *Roth*, Roland 1986. Das neue Gesicht des Kapitalismus. Vom Fordismus zum Post-Fordismus. Hamburg
Hubbard, Dianne 1991. Women and children in Namibia: the legal context .Namibian Institute for Social and Economic Research, NISER Discussion paper no.3. University of Namibia, Windhoek
Iken, Adelheid / *Maasdorp*, Melinda / *Solomon*, Colette 1994. Socio-economic conditions of female-headed households and single mothers in the southern communal areas of Namibia. Multidisciplinary Research Centre – Social Sciences Division, University of Namibia. SSD Research report no.17. Windhoek
Logan, B. Ikubolajeh 1995. The traditional system and structural transformation in subsaharan Africa. In: Growth and Change, fall 1995, vol.26, issue 4, p.495 (here: Internet Version, 21 pp.)

Pendleton, *Wade* 1997. Katutura in the 1990s (SSD Research report no.28). UNAM, Windhoek
Richarz, *Irmintraut* 1991. Das ökonomisch autarke 'Ganze Haus' – eine Legende? In: Ehlert, Trude (ed.). Haushalt und Familie in Mittelalter und früher Neuzeit, pp.269–279. Sigmaringen
Russell, *Margo* 1994. Do blacks live in nuclear family households? An appraisal of Steyn's work on urban family structure in South Africa. In: South African Sociological Review, vol.6, no.2, April 1994, pp.56-67. Cape Town
Steyn, *Anna F* 1996 . Values that support quality marital and family life. In: South African Journal of Sociology, Nov. 96, vol.27, issue 4, p.143 (here: Internet version: ebscohost)
Tapscott, *Chris* 1993. Research priorities in the social sciences and appropriate structures in Namibia. In: Prah, KK (ed.), pp.29-35
UNDP 1998. Namibia human development report 1998. United Nations Country Team) Windhoek
UNICEF / NISER 1991. A situation analysis of children and women in Namibia. Windhoek
University of Namibia, SSD / LAC / UNICEF 1995. Children in Namibia. Reaching towards the rights of every child. Windhoek
van Rooy, *Gert /* **!Naruseb**, *Gottlieb /* **Maasdorp**, *Melinda /* **Eele**, *Graham /* **Hoddinott**, *John /* **Stone**, *Simon* 1994. Household subsistence levels in Namibia: three selected communities. NISER. Windhoek
Yaron, *Gil /* **Janssen**, *Gertie /* **Maamberua**, *Usutuaije* 1992. Rural development in the Okavango region of Namibia. NISER. Windhoek

SMALL TOWN ÉLITES IN NORTHERN NAMIBIA – THE COMPLEXITY OF CLASS FORMATION IN PRACTICE

Mattia Fumanti

Introduction – theoretical framework

> "The result of the Gondo enquiry suggests the need to recognize the dualistic nature of an élite, in the corporate body of which is encapsulated the community in continuity and change." (Vincent 1971:254)

Contemporary studies of African politics generally tend to produce simplistic theories stressing the nature of the post-colonial state as solely dominated by corruption and authoritarianism (Mamdani 1996). According to this model, subjects in post-colonial states are simply subjugated by the local and national élites who act as though governing a Persian satrapy. More recently, John Saul (2000) in analysing the situation in South Africa – the closest to Namibia for its apartheid legacy – leaves no space for alternative approaches to his class analysis. Nonetheless, various scholars have highlighted that a useful approach to the nature of the post-colonial state does not allow for its classical reading in terms of the dichotomies hegemony/counter hegemony or resistance/accommodation (Werbner 1996; Mbembe 1992; Bayart 1993).

Following this train of thought, I will convey a complex and less essentialised image. I draw from field research conducted in Rundu, the capital of the Kavango region, over eighteen months. Post-apartheid Namibia, like a number of other post-colonial countries, inherited from the colonial regime a system of racial and social inequalities in which the élites play a central role (Tapscott 1993). The term 'élite' in this article indicates the local post-independence black élite composed of a heterogeneous group of civil servants, high-ranking officials, church and traditional leaders. De facto next to this black élite and sometimes intertwined with it, a Portuguese and South African white élite dominates the economy with its business activities, for example: retail shops, supermarkets and tourist lodges[1].

An analysis of statistical data on the level of education and income and a certain degree of self-image would suggest the presence of a bourgeois class detached from the rest of the population. However, I will argue that at this stage, the élite in Rundu does not possess a clear class-consciousness comparable to European bourgeois classes. Although we observe a process of social stratification in its infancy, the current situation highlights a model in continuity and change. In fact, access to a recognised position of privilege within the community depends on the ability of the individual member of the élite to compete for the

---

[1] Although the racial divide between these two élites seems to highlight unsettled issues inherited from the colonial past, I recognise how the complexities and intricacies of the relationship between political and economical power need a further analysis to be carried out at a later stage of my fieldwork.

traditional title of 'Esimbi' (Big-man)[2], redefining and remodelling it. In this process, such individuals make use of strategies involving negotiation, compromise and adaptation to meet the values and expectations attached to this title, but adapt them to a modern and westernised context. To draw a distinction between the traditional and the new masimbi, I will call the latter quasi-masimbi, borrowing the expression from Kampungu (1967).

In Rundu, a high degree of flexibility and adaptation is the main characteristic of power relations. The strong ties built around client networks rule the political arena. To maintain their legitimacy, the leaders are under obligation to redistribute resources to their supporters, a system similar to Sahlins' (1963) big-men. In my view the élites are not a ruling class, but rather redistributors and patrons deeply rooted in a system of reciprocity.

In this respect, the idea of the circulation of élites theorised by Pareto (1900) and, consequently, the Gramscian notion of the reciprocal assimilation of the élites (1983) becomes in my view useful tools for the understanding of complex élite strategies, such as 'manoeuvre' (De Boeck 1998) or 'straddling' (Medard 1992). In Pareto's view, élites are tactical and strategic actors, but in their tactics and strategies they are not detached from the values and sentiments they bring to bear. In fact, the quasi-masimbi of Rundu, exposed prima facie to a Western model, face many dilemmas and predicaments. Looking at the recent events affecting the region, I will emphasise through the perspective of middle-range studies in Africa, the centrality of local and regional élites as mediators and brokers which is a theme so central in Vincent's (1971) seminal work. In this sense, the élites as intermediaries between the state and the rest of the population create and confirm interpretations of life.

The core of this theme calls for research beyond the limits of locality. The élites as mediators are co-opted into political ranks beyond the local level, and at the same time operate within multiple networks, contributing actively to the political life of post-colonial Rundu.

Rundu élites: a socio-economic analysis

Rundu, a medium-sized town on the Namibia-Angola border in the northern region of Kavango, was only founded in 1936 with the establishment of the Commissioner of Native Affairs for the South African Union[3]. Along with its administrative function, the settlement originally served as a recruitment centre for migrant labourers sent to the farms and mines in the southern regions of the country. In the past thirty years Rundu's population has reached today's peak of 44 000 inhabitants (Urban Dynamics Africa 2000)[4].

---

[2] Esimbi / Masimbi are Rukwangali terms, the language spoken by the Kwangalis, the largest ethnic group in Kavango, and the lingua franca of the region.
[3] SWAA File 519/1 Source: National Archives of Namibia
[4] My acknowledgment goes to Mr.Ted Rudd of Urban Dynamics Africa for his permission to utilise these statistical data.

There are several reasons for Rundu's growth, such as the influx from Angola and the rural areas, the decentralisation process and the illusory improvement of the economic environment. The term 'illusory improvement' is used here to indicate that the economy of the region de facto retains a subsistence character. People from the rural areas move to town, with its business opportunities, with the expectation of getting a job and improving their lives. They are attracted by the 'illusory welfare' created by retail trade and the consequent circulation of cash. However, such economic activity has not brought real growth. Instead, it is at the root of a process of rapid urbanisation and social problems, namely high unemployment and alcoholism.

With its urban character and as an administrative centre, Rundu emerges as a mediating locus between rural Kavango and the economic core regions of Namibia. It is characterised by ethnic, religious and administrative heterogeneity. The presence of different ethnic groups, a variety of major religious denominations and new religious movements, and the administrative pluralism give vent to competing arenas of power.

In this setting, élites become mediators, although extremely diverse in their nature. Categorising the black élites and their clientele according to level of education, income, level of mobility, and involvement in community life, we can identify an initial set of distinctions. 2,6% of Rundu's population has a tertiary education diploma. 2,8% has an income ranging between N$6 000 and N$8 000 per month[5]. In addition to a university degree and a high income, the privileges of the local élites extend to positions in the local associations for the promotion of community life, and they are senior church members and SWAPO officials.

This situation results mainly from the apartheid system and the marginal position of the region in the politics of post-independence Namibia. First of all, the Bantu Education politics adopted by the South African administration excluded large strata of the population from tertiary education. As a result, a great number of teachers, approximately 50%, are still underqualified. The ratio of school failures at all levels is still high, with only 8,6% reaching grade 12. Nevertheless, the teaching profession entitles its members to material and social benefits. Secondly, the struggle for independence has largely shaped the political landscape of post-independence Namibia, favouring certain ethnic groups based on their level of involvement in the liberation struggle. As a consequence, the scarce resources allocated to the region privilege a limited number of persons mainly affiliated to the SWAPO party, widening the gap between educated and uneducated people.

Analysing the biographical trajectories of these individuals, we can identify a common pattern. Many of them were formerly teachers, school principals and junior civil servants in the pre-independence Kavango administration. They gained

---

[5] According to recent statistics (Urban Dynamics Africa 1999-Ministry of Basic Education, Sport and Culture 1999) the region counts 12,1% illiterates and 8,6% with a senior secondary school certificate (grade 12). The number of graduates and postgraduates is a mere 0,3% and 0,2% respectively. Concerning the income distribution in Rundu town, the figures show 10% of households with a monthly income below N$200 and an average monthly income ranging between N$400and N$600.

access to diplomas and university degrees through kinship ties and the church, in particular the Catholic church and ELCIN[6]. After independence they were appointed to senior posts by virtue of their knowledge, education and involvement in the liberation struggle.

The emergence of the quasi-masimbi

In the Kavango social structure a prominent figure is indicated as esimbi (big-man). Traditionally, this is a title reserved for males. Regardless of principles of descent, the masimbi (big-men) rise to positions of prestige on the basis of their ability to accumulate wealth – that is, cattle, support for their relatives and the possession of intellectual usimbi, namely knowledge of traditional values and high moral qualities[7]. These values become the condition sine qua non for nomination to a public position. It is the prerogative of the hompa (chief), after consultation with other masimbi and members of the community, to nominate an esimbi. Once nominated, the masimbi become political figures occupying posts within the traditional courts (nonmpanguro), mediating between the traditional leaders and the commoners[8], and later on between them and the state authorities. This position of prestige is therefore filled with expectations both by the chiefs and the population[9].

The emergence of an 'educated' élite and the impact of a cash economy brought apparent changes to the traditional system of power. Access to the status of big-man in an urban context is no longer a prerogative of males since a number of women are recognised as 'big-persons'[10], or individuals belonging to the higher ranks of the traditional social structure. The parameters of wealth have shifted from the accumulation of cattle to the accumulation of cash. Also, Western status symbols have come into play. Thus, the reproduction and adaptation of the intellectual values, the usimbi, attached to the traditional title of esimbi, have increasingly become the gateway to this prominent position. Nevertheless, in today's Rundu, any individual willing to reach the status of big-man has to maintain the most important features of the traditional model, though he adapts them to a modern and westernised context, namely accumulation and redistribution of wealth, support for his kin, mediation with the authorities and possession of knowledge and formal education.

---

[6] Evangelical Lutheran Church in Namibia; the role of the churches has been and still is fundamental in the history of Namibia. The churches played a big role in the liberation struggle of the country (Katjiavivi 1989) contributing especially education to the shaping of the first generation of formally educated individuals. As one of my informants pointed out to me: "To have a church leader in your family was very important at that time (...) these pastors who had studied abroad (...) when they came back they made sure their children would receive a proper education".

[7] According to Kampungu 1967:6 the Masimbi had to possess the following moral qualities: nondunge (wisdom or knowledge), unongo (goodness), nomukaro do nongwa (good behaviour), efumano (fame, good name), kapi si murudipagi govhantu (no murderer), kapi si murodi (no sorcerer).

[8] "Since the masimbi were the mouthpiece of their respective areas they usually presented the views of the people (...) in this sense the advisory function exercised by the masimbi can be said to be representative of the people." Kampungu 1967:13

[9] As Kampungu pointed out: " Someone is esimbi by reason of his kinship group who look up to him, because of his wealth, and therefore considers him as much". Kampungu 1967:9

[10] Asked what she thought to be the reason for that one of the interviewees answered: "Well, I think it has to do with education, but mostly with the position that you are holding and your income". Interview with 012 07/01/01

Borrowing the expression from Kampungu, I will call him and his like quasi-masimbi, to convey both the new trends and the strong continuity defining this élite, although their communities actually address them as masimbi. The quasi-masimbi represent a first generation of educated urbanites maintaining strong ties with their villages of origin and their ekoro (extended family). They travel to their villages on a regular basis to visit their families, providing assistance in various forms, such as money, goods and medicines. Based on their authority, they settle family disputes. Often, in their urban homes they host relatives working or studying in Rundu[11]. Likewise, the attendance at and contribution to private celebrations such as weddings and funerals is instrumental in reinforcing their status vis-à-vis the expectations of their affiliates. Moreover, in the era of the HIV/AIDS pandemic, in view of the low quality of urban health services, and considering the mediocre standards of living in the region, the role of the quasi-masimbi becomes fundamental in providing funeral services[12].

Similar to the case of Gondo, Uganda, illustrated by Vincent (1971), an argument which echoed Nadel's work (1956), we observe a 'strategic élite' which mediates between the internal structure, very often of conservative orientation, and the external relations, with their innovative pressures. The élites in Rundu, therefore, appear to be at the cutting edge of societal change within the community, managing key tasks of contact and relations with the state, but maintaining at the same time the values of society.

The predicaments of the élites – straddling and circulation

The quasi-masimbi move with the times, mediating between traditional and Western values/expectations. In the main, in being 'innovative', to borrow Nadel's expression (1956), they tend to assimilate Western consumer aspirations. This can be observed in Rundu in access to certain commodities, services and status symbols – mobile phones, satellite TV, housing in the former white residential areas, education for their children in the former white-only colleges. However the enduring importance of local values creates a real predicament, well illustrated by Pareto (1900). I would like to call it a typical 'élite dilemma'. Referring to the extended family, one esimbi told me: "Our relatives always come and ask for money (...) we give it to them, because it is so, but sometimes we cannot (...) they don't understand (...) it is not like in the past (...) now everything costs money..."[13]. Élites, caught in this moral predicament, tend to compromise. They navigate between the two systems of values, between the Western, individualistic, cash-oriented one and the traditional, redistributive, community-oriented culture.

---

[11] Generally the host would be the maternal uncle/aunt bringing to the fore a set of responsibilities deeply embedded in the Kavango matrilineal kinship system.

[12] As one interviewee explained to me: "I didn't have time to rest during the past few weekends (...) I have been running up and down the whole region (...) We had to bury so many people (...) every Saturday we had a funeral (...) now it is becoming worse".

[13] Interview with 001 28/01/2000

The quasi-masimbi profit from their mobility and their position of power in gaining access to the national arena where they build local and trans-local networks of relationships. Frequent trips to the capital to attend workshops and conferences on various matters facilitate the establishment of preferential links of power. Also, some of the most eminent members of the local élites are based in the capital promoting the process of network building on the spot.

According to Chabal/Daloz (1999) and Medard (1992), these networks take the shape of a patron-client relationship. Contrary to the understanding of several scholars (Mamdani1996; Saul 2000; Bayart 1999), these are not solely the loci for corruption, authoritarianism and nepotism. On the contrary, given their character of mutuality and reciprocity, hegemony and domination play a distinctly secondary role. We cannot conceptualise African political systems merely in terms of a straightforward division between the rulers and the ruled, between dominators and dominated[14].

The redistributive and dynamic nature of these power relations is well illustrated by the public roles of the quasi-masimbi and their involvement in community life. At the local level they act as members of different committees and associations, holding key posts in religious institutions, in cultural and traditional societies, in health care, sports and gender associations.

Medard's (1992) concept of 'straddling' illustrates this system. Straddling, or chevauchement, means the ability to occupy at the same time quite different and seemingly incompatible positions. This must not be confused with a cumulus. It rather resembles a cursus, in other words the ability to use an old position to get a new one, while at the same time reinforces the previous one, perhaps even leaving it to a loyal affiliate, thereby maintaining the system. In Rundu, the appointment of someone loyal is perceived as a seminal aspect of ascendance to the élite. With reference to someone who was appointed to an higher post leaving a job he occupied for many years, people expressed a common view: "The guy is having the chance of appointing someone (...) he should just do it (...) he should not miss the chance".

At this point of my analysis, the introduction of the concept of 'circulation of élites' is imperative. In Medard's view, positional change assumes the form of circulation. It is regarded as a means of guaranteeing continuity in power for the big-men. It does not necessarily imply any rise and fall of élites. In the case of Rundu, the circulation can be observed mainly within the context of the countless associations and committees to whom the élites are affiliated. Extremely heterogeneous in its composition, each committee attracts influential persons from different fields and areas of specialisation. The quasi-masimbi circulate within this complex and volatile scenario reinforcing their status. At the same time, they often find themselves caught on the horns of a dilemma of conflicting interests.

---

[14] "Patrons suffer considerable constraints. The maintenance of their status is entirely dependent on their ability to meet the expectations of their clients, who in turn must placate their own clients." Chabal / Daloz 1999:28

Contrary to the classical approach to Pareto's work, in my view the circulation of élites can only be understood in the 'longue-duree'. It is a system of strategies and moral commitments, and a process of adaptation by those involved on both sides of the system of power. Once again, this illustrates the nature of the dilemma that the élites face when caught between contradictory systems of values. Pareto's work paves the way for the concepts of political hybridity and of reciprocal assimilation of the élites. These concepts advanced through Gramsci's work and have contributed to the understanding of politics in post-colonial society, especially in the arguments of Bayart (1993) and De Boeck (1996). According to these scholars, the fusion of élites through a process of reciprocal assimilation gives shape to the politics of the post-colonial societies. In particular, the multiplication of state occasions contributes to the formation of alliances between the members of the élites (Bayart 1993; De Boeck 1996).

As a consequence of the unstable situation in the Kavango region in recent times and the dramatic effect the spilling over of the Angolan war had on the population, local élites emerged vis-à-vis national politics. The frequent official functions, highlighted by the frequent visits of the President and various SWAPO dignitaries to Rundu, shed light on the complex scenario wherein the local élites meet with the national élites. Religious as well as traditional leaders and high-ranking government officials raise the demands of their communities, they co-opt each other at different levels of power, assimilating their competitors' demands and forming all sorts of ad hoc alliances in order to have their own requests represented.

Conclusion

The situation in Rundu reflects the contradictions and complexities of post-apartheid Namibia.

The impact of the cash economy and the adoption of neo-liberalism contribute to the reinforcement of the gap within the population. In a region such as the Kavango, still heavily dependent on a subsistence economy, the access of a few to privileged positions of power has pushed forward the process of social stratification. The birth of a modern black élite composed mainly of high-ranking officials illustrates this process. If we merely take into account the statistical data and the assimilation of Western values by this local élite, we may be tempted to assume we are already witnessing a bourgeois-capitalist class. In this respect the strategies of the Rundu élites emphasising visibility and respectability, typical of European bourgeoisie, would appear as indications of class-consciousness.

To such an interpretation grounded in a Marxist approach (Saul 2000) I have tried to oppose a more de-essentialised image. I aimed to show the limits of the classical approach on post-colonial Africa based on the dichotomies hegemony/counter hegemony or resistance/accommodation. My idea is that behind the redistribution of wealth and power there is a complex system of moral values, negotiated by the élite to meet their affiliates' demands.

This very same élite is exposed prima facie to modern values but is still tied to traditional orientations. Thus, it appears to be facing real dilemmas. The strong ties with the ekoro (extended family) and the villages of origin, and the obligations connected with these social institutions, all influence the élites' politics. The concepts of 'straddling' and of 'the circulation of élites' illustrate the emergence of the élites as brokers between different value systems more generally as mediators between the centre and the periphery of the country. The élites strategically work their way towards a privileged position without detaching from their affiliates' values and expectations. In the marginal context of Rundu, the élites compete over the conferment of traditional titles. The acquisition of the title of esimbi, although reworked in the contemporary urban context and therefore characterised in this article as quasi-masimbi, is the sign of the ability to negotiate, compromise, assimilate and mediate between different centrifugal forces at work and of enduring the rule of traditional values. The patron-client relationship emerging within this context illustrates the multiple predicaments and moral commitments.

Bibliography

Bayart, *JF* 1993. The state in Africa: the politics of the belly. London: Longman

Bayart, *JF / Ellis, S / Hibou, B (eds.)* 1999. The criminalization of the state in Africa. Oxford: James Currey

Chabal, *P / Daloz, JP (eds.)* 1999. Africa works: disorder as political instrument. Oxford: James Currey

De Boeck, *P* 1996. Postcolonialism, power and identity: local and global perspectives from Zaire. In: Ranger, T / Werbner R P. Postcolonial identities in Africa. London : Zed Books

Fisiy *C / Goheen, M.*1998. Power and the quest for recognition: neo-traditional titles and the new élite in NSO Cameroon. In: Africa (special issue) vol 68 (3)

Government of the Republic of Namibia 1999. Annual report for the year 1999. Ministry of Basic Education, Sports and Culture. Windhoek

Gramsci, *A 1983.* Cahiers de prison vol.II. Paris: Gallimard

Kampungu, *R* 1967. Developments in Okavango. In: KGO(K) N1/12/2 – Source: National Archives, South Africa

Mamdani, *Mahmoud* 1996. Citizen and subject. Postcolonial Africa and the legacy of colonialism. London: James Currey.

Mbembe *A* 1992. Provisional notes on the postcolony. In: Africa vol. 62 (1), pp.3-37

Medard *JF* 1992. Le big man en Afrique: esquisse d'analyse du politicien entrepreneur. In: L'annee Sociologique vol.42, pp.167-192

Nadel, *S* 1956. The concept of social élites. In: International Social Science Bulletin vol.8, pp.413-424

Pareto, *Vilfredo* 1901. Un applicazione di teorie sociologiche. In: Rivista italiana di sociologia: 402-456

Pareto, *Vilfredo* 1981. L'equilibrio sociale. In: Trattato di sociologia generale, vol.5. Milano- Edizioni di Comunita'

Sahlins, *M* 1963. Poor man, rich man, big-man, chief: political types in Melanesia and Polynesia. In: Comparative Studies in Society and History, vol.5, pp.285-303

Saul, *J* 2000. South-Africa's tragic leap to the right. In: The Namibian: 6-8 Friday July 14 2000

Tapscott, *C* 1993. National reconciliation, social equities and class formation in independent Namibia. In: Namibia: Africa's youngest nation. Journal of Southern African Studies (special issue), vol.19 (1)

Urban Dynamics Africa 1999. Household survey report. Prepared for Lux-Development in co-operation with Ministry of Regional and Local Government and Housing and Rundu Town Council
Vincent, J 1971. African élite: the big-men of a small town. New York, London: Columbia University Press.
Werbner, RP 1996. Introduction: multiple identities, plural arenas. In: Ranger T / Werbner RP (ed.). Postcolonial identities in Africa. London: Zed Books

YOUTH IN NAMIBIA – SOCIAL EXCLUSION AND POVERTY

Pempelani Mufune

Introduction

The majority of Namibians are young and fit into the category 'youth'. According to SIDA\CSO (1995) estimates, 61,8% of all females are 24 years or younger, and 63,8% of males are 24 years or younger. This fact is related to Namibia's high dependency ratio. Moreover, Namibian youth is the cohort that experiences and embodies the social changes resulting from the transition from colonialism to post-colonialism. They can be seen as agents of this transition from authoritarianism to democracy and from a racially divided society to a more integrated nation. This cohort undoubtedly serves as the barometer of transformation of Namibian society. Presenting recent and representative information on young people, this chapter reflects on Namibia's achievements – or lack thereof – in the reduction of social exclusion and poverty.

Defining youth

Youth is an elastic concept. Young people are described variously as young adults, teenagers, adolescents or juveniles, and they all qualify under the rubric youth. This is indicative of the problems of definition. In general, the interval between childhood and adulthood is called youth. But what this period actually comprises changes from one society to another, depending on the variety of roles, attendant circumstances, social change and the complexity of the society under scrutiny. For instance, in the 20th century many countries passed laws mandating compulsory education until the age of 16, though many adolescents remain in school beyond that age. Also, sexual maturity and adult economic responsibility do not occur simultaneously. This extends the period of youth, as do increased demands for a highly skilled labour force.

Therefore, experts suggest that a consistent definition of youth should not fix age limits (Hurrelman 1989). It is a phase of life, characterised by particular experiences reflecting societal culture and the context for personal growth. We add, with regard to this article, that it must be made clear from the outset that we refer to youth as a categorical group, with individuals belonging to different class, ethnic, gender and other groups.

Namibia's legislation has pragmatically opted for an age-based definition of youth, in order to implement its programmes related to income generation and vocational training. Namibian youth are defined as those between 15 and 30 years of age. They are considered important by politicians and the general public. The country spends the biggest share of its budget on educating the young; multipurpose youth centres have been established regionally. The fight against HIV/AIDS – a disease that is consuming the country – is focused on the youth. The future of the country is seen as predicated on how successfully parents and authorities socialise and control young people. Thus youth is both a *signifier* and an *embodiment* of significant social change (Pearson 1994).

Social transformation occurring in the country becomes discernible through the situation of young people, and the youth in turn give actual expression to changes. When social conditions harden, young people are usually among the first to manifest this. Unemployment, dropping out from school, addiction – these are some of the 'key defining features' outwardly manifested. Conversely when living conditions improve, young people will react, showing educational enrolments in greater numbers, declining unemployment and propensity to follow fashion trends. The analysis of the social situation of the youth today therefore should reveal the extent to which Namibia's development policies in the past decade have been able to tackle issues of poverty and social exclusion that were at the forefront of the fight for independence. Development, in this context, is seen in terms of increasing productivity and standards of living. It implies longer life expectancy, more adequate diets, better services, better housing and more consumer goods.

Poverty and social exclusion as social problems

Like inequality and order, poverty is one of the major concepts of social science required to understand and explain society (Townsend 1993). Similarly, Hardiman and Midgley (1989) argue that poverty is the central problem of development studies. It is for this reason that such studies focus on the third world. Issues of poverty are intertwined with those of inequality although the two concepts may be analytically separate[1]. Poverty is not just an aspect of inequality, though it is an unacceptable extreme of inequality. In this sense poverty is the end result of inequality. This makes poverty not only an academic issue but also a moral and political one (Alcock 1997). Where inequality is greatest, poverty is likely to be great. Yet not all inequality necessarily results in poverty. Chambers (1994) maintains that poverty is in some cases a situation of changed lifestyles and circumstances as people find they are deprived and are rendered powerless by social change. However, issues of poverty also touch on broader ones of social structure and are linked to class domination. Poverty cannot be seen entirely as a matter of subjective factors, as the social structure in which the poor are embedded plays a crucial role. Chambers (1994) may be right in insisting that contrary to popular belief, the poor are not necessarily indolent, improvident or fatalistic. Many of them want to exist autonomously and with self-respect.

---

[1] "The most important distinction between the two is that whereas poverty ... is a prescriptive concept, inequality is a descriptive concept. Inequality is simply a state of affairs – probably an inescapable if not even a desirable one". Alcock 1997: 6

Conceptions of poverty

As a state of affairs, poverty is a seen as a condition afflicting a given number of people. It is thus an absolute or a relative condition. Some definitions involve poverty datum lines and hence aim at finding a mechanism with which to assess the size of the problem (Kabeer 1991). They are mainly concerned with the extent of deprivation rather than the social structure of poverty. As a result the poor are presented as a group without highlighting their separate identities or the reasons why they happen to be poor. In other words the social structures producing poverty and/or in which poverty is enmeshed are of little concern.

Absolute poverty is the inability to attain a minimum standard of living (Bernstein 1992). People are in poverty if they are continuously struggling to preserve themselves and their dependants from physical want. Some may find themselves in a situation in which they have temporarily or permanently failed in the struggle and therefore have fallen into physical want. These are the very poor or the destitute (Illife 1987:2), living in absolute poverty. As Townsend (1993) noted, this conception of poverty rests on the idea of subsistence and/or basic needs. Theoretically we can conceive of a yardstick applicable to any society, involving a fixed level. Below such a poverty line, poverty begins, above it poverty ends (Haralambos et al. 1985). This yardstick invariably involves judgements of human needs; usually it is defined in terms of the resources necessary to maintain a healthy physical efficiency. Illife's physical want is thus reduced to its bare minimum of food, clothing and shelter.

The notion of subsistence in defining poverty has come under criticism. It elevates physical needs at the expense of social needs. People are not simply biological organisms requiring replenishments of energy, they do not simply consume goods; they produce them, and in so doing they establish relations involving others (Townsend 1993). Everywhere, people use facilities and utilities that are public goods. Taking this into account, notions of subsistence have to be transcended by introducing the idea of basic cultural needs, as Haralambos et al. (1985) noted. The concept of absolute poverty dubiously assumes that there are minimum basic needs for all people regardless of the occupational structure and the distribution of leisure pursuits in a given society. Furthermore there is no consensus on the minimum resources required for survival. Where the conceptual framework agrees on some minimum requirement, the calculation of costing is extremely complex and controversial. Moreover, in third world countries the minimum requirements as listed by the ILO usually go beyond the capacity of these countries to afford them (Ramprakash 1991).

The concept of *relative poverty* is a reaction to criticisms voiced against the definition of poverty in absolute terms. In particular the idea of standards relative to time and place has been advanced in place of absolute ones. Poverty is considered relative in terms of "judgements by members of a particular society of what is considered a reasonable and acceptable standard of living and style of life according to the conventions of the day" (Haralambos 1985:142). The notion of relative poverty thus relates to "inequality, distributive justice and power relations"

(Ramprakash 1991:49). It is usually measured as a particular fractile of income. Thus the poor may for example be said to be the bottom 19% of people in the income distribution of a country. The figure of 19% would be constant regardless of changes in the economic growth of the country. This 19% would remain so even if the individuals in it were not suffering from physical want.

This concept of poverty is also inadequate. In a world of rapid social change, a definition of poverty based on relative standards is fluid and must constantly change to keep up with changing expectations (Haralambos et al. 1985). Furthermore, it is dubious to assume that society-wide standards exist upon which to base the relative poverty concept. Standards have to vary according to class, ethnicity, religion, region, etc. (Haralambos et al. 1985). In the last analysis, both the relative and the absolute concept of poverty use measures which are arbitrary and subjective (Ramprakash 1991).

Poverty has also been conceived from a process perspective, as some course of change characterised by a series of different conditions over time that people pass through. Sen's (1991) view of poverty as a matter of *entitlements* emphasises the social relations by which individuals and groups of people gain command (entitlement) over resources[2]. Entitlements are about who ought to get what under what circumstances (Devereux 1993). They constitute social rights, indicating the totality of things an individual can have by virtue of his or her rights (Sen 1981). Entitlements can be established through endowments (e.g. property and wages) or any other assets, through personal capacity or through social institutions (Kabeer 1991). Entitlements therefore depend on a person's position in society (their occupation and/or class, what they produce, where they live, how much land they own or have access to, what skills they possess, etc.) and on rules which make their claims over resources legitimate. Such rules may be legal or moral.

Poverty from such a perspective reflects inadequate entitlements (de Waal 1990). The problem does not so much result from shortfalls in the resources of a given society, so much as in the loss of entitlements to those resources on the part of the poor. This may be due to market failure, unemployment, administrative collapse, etc. (Fitzgerald 1991). Sen (1981) identified four main types of entitlements – trade based ones (centring on exchanges of ownership); production based ones (centring on the right to appropriate what one creates or is created for him); those based on one's own labour (combining the previous two); and those based on inheritance or transfer (referring to such things as gifts and bequests).

The entitlement approach has encountered several criticisms. Sen's view (1981) was accused of depicting the victims of poverty as essentially passive (Fitzgerald 1991). Evidence indicates that poor people are not necessarily victims

---

[2] "The process of poverty relates to reproduction or change in the distribution of resources which make up the capacity of the poor to meet basic needs" (Kabeer 1991, p 244). Entitlements are formally conceptualised as "Sets of alternative commodity bundles that a person can command in a society using the totality of rights and opportunities that he or she faces" (Sen 1984, p 497). Thus it is the resources one can acquire through use of various legal channels of acquirement open to someone in his or her position (de Waal 1990).

of forces beyond their control as they resist impoverishment. The entitlement approach may also be too economic-focused. It concentrates on command of resources through production and exchange. Forgotten are contributing events such as migration, disease and social disruption. For example, HIV/AIDS and the breakdown it produces may erode entitlements. Concentrating on entitlements also leaves corresponding obligations on the part of other individuals in wider society out of the picture that must respect the rights and claims being put forward (Fitzgerald 1991). Furthermore, the poor may be quite prepared to trade off resources for family dignity, security and self-respect. Some who have these intangibles may not consider themselves truly poor.

Social exclusion

Sen's concept of poverty is related to the concept of social exclusion. It stems from the idea of failure to fully take part in society's affairs resulting from lack of capabilities and entitlements, and not simply material possessions. Social exclusion can be defined as "the process through which individuals or groups are wholly or partially excluded from full participation in the society in which they live" (quoted in De Haan 1998:2). Like poverty, it is a prescriptive concept, suggesting an unacceptable state of affairs (Alcock 1997:6). It stresses the process by which people become poor or excluded and marginalised. The focus is on the mechanisms and institutions that make people different i.e. poor or excluded. The concept emphasises the causes of the phenomenon of deprivation. Social exclusion is a multidimensional concept emphasising that disadvantage and deprivation have many facets, such as low income, lack of dignity, poor nutrition, vulnerability, etc. They may result in an inability to fully participate in societal affairs.

The foregoing conceptualisation of social exclusion and its relationship to poverty have been critically explored from various perspectives. Poverty may be defined as an element of social exclusion, but social exclusion may also be identified as the underlying, real cause of poverty. Moreover, poverty and social exclusion may be treated as alternative concepts (De Haan 1998)[3]. Above all, social exclusion has its origin in Western countries, and imposing it on the analysis of third world countries may pose serious conceptual problems. More specifically, it has been argued that the majority of people in Africa suffer from social exclusion, as they are forced by adverse circumstances to exist outside the formal economy. In political terms African states are patrimonial states. They have little regard for the rational legal authority associated with a means of administration in which the planning and integration of activities imply universal standards in providing for citizens. It is a situation where many groups strive not to be included so as to escape taxes and other unequal obligations of citizenship.

---

[3] Thus Alcock 1997:6 argues that although social exclusion refers to circumstances of deprivation and disadvantage extending beyond material resources, people may be excluded even if they are not materially poor.

Dimensions of poverty and social exclusion among youth in Namibia

How do the above ideas on poverty, social exclusion and deprivation relate to young people in Namibia? In the Namibian context (and probably the African context) exclusion from labour that is remunerated (employment) or confinement to poorly remunerated unskilled labour are likely to associate individuals with poverty and deprivation. To have a job is crucial for the individual's position in the economies of African countries, and formal education is intimately linked to occupational attainment and élite formation in the African social context (and indeed in all other countries with lower levels of industrialisation) (see Buchman and Hannum 2001). Exclusion from education is thus a serious deprivation that has repercussions for an individual's life chances. Investment in education can produce other resources (e.g. in the form of increased income). In Pierre Bourdieu's sense it may be considered a form of capital, allowing people to create wealth.

Exclusion from labour-based entitlements

The absence of entitlements other than that based on unskilled labour may result in absolute poverty; for example, young people having dropped out of school can only sell unskilled labour. In addition, the youth have few ways of disposing of their labour for income, as they lack work experience. The value of unskilled labour is low and diminishing in the face of mechanisation. Consequently, when competing on the labour market, entitlements to remunerated work are shrinking. Although the age groups between 15 and 30 years are the most able-bodied to do unskilled labour, the opportunities are lessening. In relation to older people, youth have little entitlement to semi-skilled or more skilled work. Age is an important factor in conceptualising labour-based entitlements because it differentiates the conditions under which people sell their labour power. On average, adults have a number of ways in which to sell labour and dispose of it such that it brings income. In comparison, most youth's labour (as well as that of women) is confined to the home. Where it is remunerated at all, the returns are low.

Unemployment

The importance of paid employment for the individual to escape social exclusion and poverty cannot be overestimated, since unemployment also affects a person's social status (Bessis 1995) and his/her sense of personal dignity. Some authors claim that the informal sector presents a viable alternative to regular, salaried employment. This alternative is quite unsatisfactory, in that it offers only a very unstable, low productivity subsistence activity.

In Namibia, increasing unemployment has led to a heterogeneous labour market with plenty of irregular and poorly paid jobs, accounting for rising social exclusion. As in the rest of the world, in the Namibian context employment remains the most reliable insurance. It allows the individual to access an income that meets his individual and family needs (including school fees, medical fees, adequate nutrition and shelter) and some additional wants (e.g. consumer goods and better services). Furthermore, employment (like school) for youths provides a structured, regular opportunity to use their skills, talents and knowledge to contribute to society. In this sense it provides them with an aim in society. They feel that they are doing something useful, thereby promoting their sense of self-esteem and identity. The social contacts that they make at the work place serve to validate their inclusion in the mainstream of society.

Formal sector unemployment is not equally distributed across social groups, being much higher among the youth. Some argue that the penalties for high unemployment among the youth include anti-social behaviour, alienation, lost output, frustration, etc. (Hodson and Sullivan 1995).

The Ministry of Labour's Namibian Labour Force Survey of 1997 indicates that joblessness excessively affects the young[4]. Around 62% of youths aged between 15 and 19 years are without jobs, 55% of the 20–24 years old are unemployed, and 41% of the 25–29 year olds (GRN 1998). These unemployment rates by far exceed those of adults. Fewer than 20% of those above 50 years of age are unemployed, and the unemployment rate of all non-youth averages fewer than 30%.

Gender reveals an important factor in unemployment. Female youth are more likely to be jobless than any other group in Namibia. Compared with a 57% unemployment rate among male youth between 15 and 19 years, of the respective female age group, 66% are jobless. Similarly, in comparison to the 61% of females between age 20 and 24, only 47% of males are unemployed. It must be pointed out that women in Namibia have less access to employment in general. An average of 65% of female youth is unemployed. On top of this, most of the employed women are in very low paid jobs. In Namibia lower wages are paid to women generally, and particularly to younger women with disrupted education. Most single mothers have less education than their peers and have very few skills to enable them to get into jobs that can pay a decent wage.

Rural youth are less disadvantaged than urban youth with regard to unemployment. 72% of the youth between the ages of 15 and 19 years old in urban areas are unemployed, as against 57% of their rural counterparts (GRN 1998). Rural-urban differences may however reflect the definition utilised in measuring unemployment. Fewer rural people are likely to be looking for work, as work opportunities do not exist. It is probable that the duration of unemployment for younger people is also much longer than for older people.

Many of the jobless youth have relatively poor education (i.e. secondary education or less). The Labour Force Survey indicates that 13% of the unemployed have no formal education at all. Surprisingly, this is exceeded by the unemployment rate of those with primary and secondary school education. This is explained by the fact that those without formal education are more likely to accept anything that presents itself – even the most menial of jobs. Moreover many of them have

---

[4] Its definition of unemployment is any person that has been looking for paid work in the last two weeks but unable to get it. GRN 1998

little hope of obtaining jobs and are thus not looking for them. However, most of the unemployed have primary or secondary education (41% primary school education, 44% some secondary education). Only a tiny 1% of the unemployed have post-secondary education[5].

Street-work as a special case of labour-based exclusion

Failing to find employment, many of Namibia's young people end up joining that part of the informal sector called "working the streets"[6]. In sociological parlance, street-work is classified as a part of hustling work. More formally:

> The most basic feature of workers who hustle for a living is that they do not have full time conventional jobs; rather they seek their living in other ways. Sometimes they may work at low paying jobs, temporary jobs, but at other times they may do any number of things to earn an income (...) They must be alert at all times to opportunities for making a living (as) found in their environments. As a result, their histories reflect frequent job changes, and outsiders often describe them as unstable (Miller 1981, pp.134-35).

The above description of street work does not differ much from a description of many activities in the informal sector. Of course, hustling work is informal sector work. Normatively, however, hustling work is usually relegated to 'non-work' in official definitions, as many consider it immoral and undesirable. But moral evaluations only hide the fact that what people are doing comes up to work (Miller 1981). Street youth engage in all sorts of acceptable and non-acceptable activities. What they do is not counted in official statistics. Nonetheless, street-work provides something of value to those who pay for it, and it is considered work by the participants. On the other hand, it is marginal work because it departs, in very significant manner, from the dominant employment norms. Its content is generally seen as illegal, it is institutionally irregular, it is unstable and it fails to provide adequate wages to enable an individual to make a living.

Institutional irregularity: The work in which street youth engage is almost always informal. It does not conform to the Namibian government's regulations covering child labour, fair wages and working hours. Furthermore there is no institutional reporting of income earned, no monitoring of health, safety or working conditions. Street youth act out of mere necessity. Most of them come from female-headed households. Their backgrounds are characterised by poverty and larger family sizes (with an average of 10 members) whose make-up put them more at risk to the vagaries of the economy than regular 'nuclear' families (Tacon 1991). For them to survive requires that all members above tender age have to work. In other words, being on the street is one coping strategy that such families use to deal with their marginality and vulnerability.

---

[5] According to the Labour Force Survey "unemployment rates for those with educational qualifications beyond secondary education are very low, almost an order of magnitude lower than for those with less formal or no formal education". GRN 1998:34

[6] Work, in this context, should be seen as "any activity or effort of an individual that is undertaken for the purpose of providing goods and services of value to others and that is considered by the individual to be work". Hall 1994:5

Instability of street-work: by definition street youth do not have readily available addresses. They are always on the move as they are afraid of authority figures such as the police. The activities that they engage in involve very temporary relationships with members of the public that employs them. Few are sure of where their next money will come from.

Illegality of street-work: In Namibia street work is seen as illegal. Firstly, it is activity that is informal, and by virtue of the fact that it escapes government tax it is illegal. Street-work requires taking opportunities and some degree of evasion and deceit. This is necessary to persuade members of the public to part with some of their money. Evasiveness is also necessary to deal with adults who are for the most part antagonistic. The main engagements of street youths, for instance, include guarding cars in parking bays, begging, pushing trolleys for consumers, washing cars and selling bottles (Rose-Junius 1993). Although these activities are to some extent tolerated as legal by those requiring them, the public in Namibia is very suspicious of the intentions of those who do that type of work. Street-work contravenes the norms and values of larger society.

There are reports that street youth inhale glue, petrol and other substances in order to escape the harsh realities of being on the street. These suspicions are enhanced by the fact that not all of their activities are legal. Thus selling sex, stealing from individuals and stealing from parked cars are not uncommon (Rose-Junius 1993). According to Tacon (1991) two out of five street boys have been, at some time, arrested in Namibia, although 80% were released. This situation further attests to the perception that street-work is illegal.

Street-work wages (and the impossibility of making a living): Most of the youths on the street in Namibia are simply trying to earn a living. Tacon (1991) found that the youths earned between N$1 and N$9 per day. The average earning per day for Rundu was N$1, for Keetmanshoop N$3 and for Windhoek N$5. Most of the money was spent on food for themselves and the family. Rose-Junius (1993) confirms Tacon's findings, indicating earnings ranging from N$2 to N$20 per day. Many street youth share their earnings with siblings and parents. Although part of their activities are paid monetarily, some income is received in kind.

Part of the reason why street-work is so poorly remunerated is because street youth are either poorly educated or have no education. A small number of street youth in Tacon's sample (i.e. 6,3%) had never been to school. 48% had dropped out and 45,6% of the sample was still attending school. Of those who had dropped out, 52% failed to pass grade 2 and thus were functionally illiterate. 88% of those who had attended school had failed to go beyond grade 7[7]. Their educational performance seems to have been passed on from the respondent's parents[8]. The combination of low social economic background and low education has worked to expose youth frequenting Namibian urban streets to vulnerability.

---

[7] Rose-Junius' (1993) study also concluded that many of these young people have not gone far in the education system. The majority of the respondents i.e. 66% were not in school and most did not contemplate returning to school unless their guardian's inability to provide food and the requisite school materials were addressed.

[8] Thus Tacon 1991 found that 44% of the respondents fathers and 34% of the mothers had never gone to school.

In the Namibian context they are generally defined as lacking employable skills. Lack of skills to sell makes it difficult for these young people to get even irregular jobs. Many of them are not seen as strong enough to tackle the usual manual demands associated with unskilled work because they are too young.

Exclusion from capital based entitlements

Capital is any resource that is used to produce other resources that take the shape of commodities. The three most important tangible forms of capital in Namibia are land, capital goods and financial capital. Land remains the most important asset in the rural economy. For many rural Namibians without a bank account or property, land remains the only tangible wealth that they know. It enhances a household's productive base (in terms of crop and livestock production), and hence its capacity to meet its longer-term consumption requirements as well as offering the possibility of meeting more immediate needs (Kabeer 1991:254). Capital goods that include physical objects such as trucks, machines and buildings are important, especially in urban settings. For instance a person with a house may rent it out for an income or for money to invest in other ventures. Cattle might be considered an important rural capital asset in the Namibian context. One can sell milk and meat from cattle on one hand while the cattle's manure and power can be used for farming. Financial capital includes creditworthiness as well as investments, for instance in unit trusts. These are important in urban settings where there exist the facilities and infrastructure that make them possible.

Few young people independently have access to land, capital goods and financial capital in Namibia. Young people's access to property is mainly through kinship as in marriage and inheritance. Young people inherit much less than older ones; young women inherit even less in Namibia. In rural areas young people may have access to some communal land but since they do not have title deeds they cannot use it as collateral for loans. Land (especially in rural areas) in any case cannot easily be converted into cash. Collateral is important for an individual to secure credit. It is important because if the loan is not repaid then the lender may sell the capital assets – the collateral – to recoup the losses. It may be argued that this situation equally affects communal peasants regardless of age because there is no private title on land to serve as security for financial institutions. While this is true, the situation is worse for young people because their rights of use to communal land may not be secure. Many young people and their mothers have been thrown off the communal land once their male guardians died. Young people do not have the net-worthiness (i.e. the value of the collateral minus outstanding indebtedness) to attract credit since few of them have access to land, livestock or machinery. According to the 1991 Population and Housing Census most young people in Namibia between ages 10 and 29 live in rural areas. There are no banking facilities in most of these areas, and they thus cannot have access to loans and financial capital. Few young people independently have cattle. This means that they have less access to what livestock can provide: food, income from the sale of animals, meat products and milk products (ILO 1996). They also have less access to dung for fertiliser, draught power and even social and cultural status. Young women and female-headed households in Namibia are in an even worse position in this regard (ILO 1996). In the case of widowhood, young women are not guaranteed their spouse's property, as male relatives of the spouse often grab it.

Exclusion from normative entitlements

Normative entitlements relate to claims and rights to resources embedded in and derived from social institutions and relations, involving kin. The entitlements of women and youth are mostly normative, as opposed to men's which are material. For many Namibian women to stake a successful claim to resources such as land, cattle, house, money, etc. they must make the successful transition from daughter to wife to mother. Each status step gives them greater claims to the property controlled by the male guardian. When something goes wrong in this chain of events, problems arise for the woman concerned. For example, if the husband dies, the woman's widowhood might abruptly descend into poverty, especially if she has no adult sons to stand up for her in terms of support and protection. Divorce may result in essentially the same thing. Failure to get married may exclude a woman to certain entitlements. The principal protection women have against loss of status lies in the normative obligation men have towards women (wives).

In Namibia, we increasingly witness a distressing phenomenon: babies having babies. Namibia's teenage mothers are among the most vulnerable groups in society. The rate of teenage pregnancy is high. According to the Demographic and Health Survey of 1993, by age 19, approximately 45% of all girls have already started child bearing. In the rural north-east the figure is as high as 75%. Countrywide, 22% of the girls in the age group 15–19 are mothers (MoHSS 1993). What does this mean in terms of poverty and social exclusion? Poverty is high among single mothers (families) for several reasons, including high unemployment levels and employment in very low-paid jobs. Most single mothers have very little education or skills that are required in jobs that pay a living wage.

Many single mothers do not receive child support from the procreators[9]. Maintenance is not paid for a variety of reasons. Many of the young fathers do not care, have disappeared or even deny fatherhood. In any case, since they are not employed, or find jobs on a piecemeal basis they are not in a position to help their children. Where child support was being given, it was terminated once the father entered a new relationship or married. Young women, especially if they had little formal education, did not have enough knowledge to claim maintenance (Iken et al. 1994).

---

[9] According to Iken et al. 1994, in the southern communal areas in only 3 out of 33 cases did the father of the child contribute regularly to the child's expenses. Even in these cases the amount was quite low. They found (p 39) that in the cases where the father had a permanent job and regularly paid maintenance, the amount paid was around N$100 per month, "which must be regarded as very little considering the cost of clothing, hostel fees, food and other necessities".

Over the years, marriage has become a less secure social status for women due to the forces of social change (Kabeer 1991). Economic pressures erode male normative commitments as dictated by traditional culture(s). Many men walk out of their wives' lives, and by so doing abdicate their financial and other responsibilities. Female-headed households, a regular aspect of rural southern Africa, are among the poorest in rural areas. Their very existence reflects erosion of male normative commitments. Marriage on the part of young women with children does not necessarily change the situation, as husbands are not keen on supporting children fathered by other men (Iken et al. 1994).

Education and social exclusion

Education is one of the most important factors affecting the development of youth. It addresses the transmission of knowledge through formal or informal channels, and is a powerful instrument of social inclusion. In many cases the term education is reserved for schooling (i.e. formal education). The main function of formal schooling is to pass knowledge from generation to generation. Education can be a means for social exclusion or social inclusion.

The inclusionary nature of education is recognised in Article 28 of UNICEF's convention of children's right (of which Namibia is a signatory). It recognises the right of the child to education on the basis of equal opportunity. It urges compulsory free primary education and the accessibility of secondary education to all children, the introduction of free education and the offering of financial assistance to support the schooling of the needy. It urges governments to encourage regular school attendance and to prevent dropping out. By making it a right, the convention recognises that education not only incorporates an important and valuable potential but also represents an important participatory process for youth (Klasen 1999). As a matter of fact the "early calls for mass education in the 18th and 19th centuries viewed the inclusionary nature of the education process and the fostering of citizenship through education as more important than the skills one may acquire through education" (Klasen 1999:11).

In Namibia, achieving education (especially up to secondary school graduation and beyond) not only opens doors to the world of formal employment, it also gives and improves the capacity to speak English – the official language – necessary to ensure meaningful participation in post-independence society. Access to quality education has great intrinsic worth as the fight for independence centred on equal access to educational opportunities, denied by the very inferior Bantu education.

Education however, can also be a source of exclusion. Some education is so inferior that it fails to develop an individual's talents, abilities and potential. The grossly inferior Bantu education was a case in point, right up to independence. Education can also be exclusionary where access to schools is restricted through social mechanisms, e.g. to pupils living in urban areas rather than to rural dwellers, to children from one ethnic group only, males rather than females, the wealthy rather than the poor. It is exclusionary where cultural mechanisms hamper equal participation in instruction, e.g. cultural prejudices and expectations, gender socialisation, poor training in English due to poor performance of teachers. Furthermore, some educational policies may fail to stem (in some cases even instrumentally promote) social exclusion as young people become adults.

Table 1: School enrolment by sex in Namibia, 1999 (in %)

Namibia	Females			Males		
Age	Attending	Population	Enrolment	Attending	Population	Enrolment
6	483	868	55,6	423	787	53,7
7	548	636	86,2	550	651	84,5
8	578	626	92,3	531	603	88,1
9	542	576	94,1	489	545	89,7
10	637	670	95,1	567	615	92,2
11	591	628	94,1	570	613	93,0
12	604	632	95,6	541	587	92,2
13	624	651	95,9	573	613	93,5
14	516	547	94,3	520	564	92,2
15	514	570	90,2	493	550	89,6
16	554	644	86,0	466	557	83,7
17	410	530	77,4	404	503	80,3
18	393	582	67,5	352	513	68,6
19	257	513	50,1	282	472	59,7
20	222	541	41,1	214	478	44,8
21	137	479	28,6	175	444	39,4
22	103	453	22,7	126	371	34,0
23	88	474	18,6	99	384	25,8
24	72	477	15,1	47	331	14,2
Total	7873	11097	70,9	7422	10181	72,9

Source: CSO 1999. Mid-decade survey of children

To what extent does education support or hinder social exclusion in Namibia? Since independence Namibia has done well in raising the enrolment ratio[10]. The Namibian government commits about 21% of its budget to education.

The relevant age categories for school enrolments are those from 6–24 years. About 55% of Namibian children 6 years of age are presently enrolled in school. According to the Ministry of Basic Education and Culture (MBEC), fewer than expected 6 year olds are in school because many children only start school at a later age (MBEC 1998). Females have a very slight advantage in enrolments[11]. Enrolment is greatest between the age of 7 and 16 years, with more than 80% of

---

[10] Net enrolment ratio is the enrolment for the age group that corresponds to the official school age of people at a certain stage of education.
[11] Whereas 56% of females aged 6 years are enrolled in school, 54% of the males are.

those eligible attending school (females: more than 90%)[12]. An interesting pattern must be noted: females continue to hold a slight advantage until age 17 years, but after 17 years male enrolment is significantly higher than females'. This conforms to cultural expectations. Males are expected to go on to higher education. Many females find themselves out of school by this age for various reasons including motherhood. Most of those who graduate from secondary school do so between the ages 18 and 23.

As shown in the above table, these are precisely the age groups with low enrolment rates. Few youths graduate from secondary school.

Drop out and failing (repetition) rates give an indication of these problems, measuring the performance of the school system. Youth that drop out are automatically excluded from the intrinsic and instrumental benefits that come with successful graduation from the school system. Table 2 shows the dropout rates at various points in the Namibian school system.

Table 2: Drop out rates (%) in Namibian schools, grades 1-12, 1993-1997

Year	Drop out rates					
Grade	1	2	3	4	5	
1993	9,6	5,4	3,2	5,4	7,2	
1994	7,2	3,0	2,3	6,9	6,3	
1995	7,1	3,3	3,5	5,6	6,7	
1996	3,1	2,4	2,4	4,6	5,2	
1997	3,9	0,1	2,9	4,6	6,1	
Grade	6	7	8	9	10	11
1993	5,7	9,4	11,0	9,5	21,5	7,3
1994	6,8	8,9	10,2	8,6	22,5	4,7
1995	7,1	8,8	9,0	7,5	30,9	5,2
1996	6,4	8,1	9,9	8,2	29,2	5,6
1997	5,8	8,3	9,7	8,7	45,8	4,9

Source MBEC. 1998 Educational statistics. Windhoek 1999

In Namibia there is no qualifying examination in the transition from primary to secondary school. The dropout rate from grade 7 to 8, therefore, does not differ from the other grades. Students must pass from junior secondary school in order to enter senior secondary school. They sit for the examination in grade 10. Table 3 reveals the high attrition rate at this level.

---

[12] For males more than 90% of the eligible are enrolled in the ages 10 to 14 years.

Table 3: Area of residence and educational exclusion in Namibia

Educational region	Indicator of exclusion					
	Money spent on learner '95 (N$)	'98 Teacher-learner ratio	'98 dropouts in grade 10	'98 female-male dropouts in grade 10*	% learners in private schools	Grade10 learners passing (%)
Katima	1348	21,4	26,5	24,1 (28,8)	735 (2,3%)	38,5
Rundu	1102	27,8	58,2	49,7 (67,9)	348 (0,7%)	37,4
Ondangwa East	808	37,0	65,8	60,8 (69,4)	1400 (1,1%)	36,1
Ondangwa West	925	32,6	51,8	50,8 (59,1)	392 (0,3%)	37,8
Khorixas	2540	26,0	28,9	28,1 (29,6)	2285 (6,1%)	52,7
Windhoek	2420	25,4	22,6	19,0 (25,9)	9321 (11,0%)	67,1
Keetmanshoop	2376	24,3	35,7	32,7 (38,3)	6256 (18,0%)	67,1

Source MBEC (1999) 1998 Educational Statistics Windhoek
Female figures are in parenthesis

There are many variations in school enrolment based on regional differences. Rural areas inordinately suffer from poverty[13]. UNDP (1999) estimates that more than 80% of the poor live in rural areas. As a result, most students in rural areas are from low-income families. Many have low educational achievements. Their educational disadvantage is not only associated with poverty but also with mastering the English language. Rural students have comparatively low educational aspirations, as their circumstances are such that advanced education is not perceived as necessary or desirable for people who are preparing to be subsistence farmers.

Things are quite different in the case of urban schools. For one, these are the areas where formerly white schools are located. In the colonial era, some black schools had pupil-teacher ratios of 60 or 70 pupils while white schools were below 15:1 (Tabachnik 1998). Unlike those in white schools, teachers in black schools were minimally prepared. Buildings without electricity, scarcity of books and writing materials in black schools compare badly with well equipped modern white schools (Tabachnik 1998:10). Most of all, financial discrimination hit the black schools[14]. At independence, the government formed a single unified system from the 11 racially and ethnically based systems in existence. It adopted a policy of

---

[13] UNO 1999 estimates the Human Poverty Index in the urban districts as follows: Windhoek 17; Khorixas 12; Keetmashoop 17,5. Rural educational districts have higher poverty levels. Thus Katima Mulilo with 25, Rundu with 27, Ondangwa East with 28,5, and Ondangwa West with 24.5 are poorer.

[14] According to Coombe 1993, the previous government spent relatively more on these schools than on historically black schools. Thus in 1986/87 average per student expenditure in white schools (17 000 students) was R3 213, in Ovambo schools (181 000) students R329 and in the whole country (312 523 students) it was R797. This expenditure translated into educational advantages for those that were in formerly white schools. In 1989 white students accounted for about 36% of the 31 883 subject entries for final year secondary school examinations although they constituted only 5% of the population. Similarly about 47% of all candidates for mathematics in 1989 (13 541) were white. The figure for physics was similar.

education for all (see Amukugo, this volume) that emphasised access, equity, quality and democracy. Although things have changed there is still a long way to go.

Rural–urban disparities are also reflected in the allocation of resources. More money is spent on individual learners in regions that encompass urban areas. These include Windhoek (Otjozondjupa, Omaheke and Khomas); Khorixas (Kunene and Erongo); Keetmanshoop (Hardap and Karas). Urban educational districts also have lower teacher–learner ratios. Rural educational districts are disadvantaged. Thus Katima Mulilo (Caprivi), Rundu (Kavango), Ondangwa East (Ohangwena and Oshikoto), Ondangwa West (Omusati and Oshana) has much smaller budgetary allocations per student. The exception is for Katima Mulilo whose student–teacher ratio is 22,4 : 1[15]. The provision of teachers' housing and electricity and telephone supply at school also show considerable rural–urban differences[16].

Conclusion

Poverty and social exclusion are serious problems for Namibians in general and Namibian youth in particular. We identified exclusion from labour-based entitlements as significant. Namibian youth are the last to be hired and the first to be fired in employment when they do not have the requisite skills. Some sections of youth do have an advantage in the unskilled labour market, but with mechanisation and competition for jobs, opportunities in this sector are shrinking. In terms of capital based entitlements, few youths in Namibia have independent access to land, capital goods and finance. Their access to capital is through family inheritance, yet they inherit far less than older people. Female youth are not even assured of inheritance, especially the uneducated in rural areas.

Female youth get access to material possessions mostly through normative entitlements. High rates of teenage pregnancy, single motherhood, lack of child support from fathers and the erosion of male normative commitments due to sociocultural change have all combined to intensify the social exclusion and poverty of some categories of female youth. Since independence, the state's commitment to education is gradually providing the youth with skills to prevent extreme poverty and lack of opportunity. However unequal access to resources has yet to be overcome and the task is far from complete.

The Namibian educational system still generates exclusion among youth, barring many rural youth (and those from lower economic classes) from the opportunities opened up by formal education. As adults, through the nexus of educational outcomes and unemployment and the shanty housing dynamics, they

---

[15] Teacher-learner ratios are very high in some schools. About 42% of all schools in the rural Ondangwa East have 40 or more learners to a teacher. Similarly, in Ondangwa West about 1% of the schools have 60 learners per teacher while 14% of the schools have 40 learners to a teacher.

[16] For example, electricity distribution is as follows for urban districts: Windhoek (88,7%); Khorixas (66%); Keetmanshoop (100%). Rural areas show the following distribution: Katima Mulilo (32%), Rundu (25%), Ondangwa East (18%), Ondangwa West (17%). Certainly, rural students are disadvantaged in terms of facilities.

are again prey to social exclusion from developmental achievements. Poverty and exclusion among youth must be addressed in earnest as it has the potential to generate discontent and social dislocation. Government-supported poverty reduction schemes must include young people. They must be of a quality sufficient to seriously attract the youth.

Bibliography

Bernstein, H 1992. Poverty and the poor. In Bernstein, H / Crow, B / Johnson, H (eds.). Rural Livelihoods. Oxford University Press
Bessis, S 1995. From social exclusion to social cohesion: a policy agenda. UNESCO MOST papers no.2. Paris
Buchman, C / Hannum, E 2001. Education and stratification in developing countries: a review of theories and research. In: Annual Review of Sociology vol.27, pp.77-102
Chambers, R 1994. Rural development. New York: Longmans
Devereux, S 1993. Theories of famine. London: Harvester/Wheatsheaf
Devereux, S/ Fuller, Ben Jnr / Moorsom, Richard JB / Solomon, C / Tapscott, Chris 1996. Namibia poverty profile. Multidisciplinary Research Centre – Social Sciences Division, University of Namibia
Devitt, P 1977. Notes on poverty-oriented rural development, extension planning and the poor. London: ODI
de Waal, A 1990. A reassessment of entitlement theory in the light of recent famines in Africa. In: Development and Change vol.21 no.3, pp.469-490
Fitzgerald, E 1991. Economic reform and citizen entitlements in eastern Europe. UNRISD Discussion paper no.27
Giddens, A 1990. Sociology. London: Polity Press
Haralambos, M / Holborn, M 1985. Sociology: themes and perspectives. Causeway Books: London
Haralambos, M (ed.) 1985. Sociology: new directions. Causeway Books: London
Illife, J 1987. The African poor – a history. Cambridge University Press
Kabeer, N 1991. Gender dimensions of rural poverty: analysis from Bangladesh. Journal of Peasant Studies, vol.18 no.2
Klasen, S 1999. Social exclusion, children and education: conceptual and measurement issues. Background paper for the OECD. http//:WWW1.oecd.org/els/pdfs/EDSCERIIEDOCA004.pdf
Lewis, O 1966. The culture of poverty. In: Scientific American vol.214, pp.19-25
McPherson, S / Midgley, J 1987. Comparative social policy and the Third World. St Martin's Press: New York
Ramprakash, D 1991. Crushing rural poverty. Food Production and Rural Development Division, Commonwealth Secretariat
Sen, A 1981. Poverty and famines: an essay on entitlement and deprivation. Oxford: Clarendon Press
Slattery, M 1985. Urbanization. In: Haralambos, M (ed.)
Stark, R 2001. Sociology. Wadsworth: New York
Townsend, P 1979. Poverty in the United Kingdom: a survey of household resources and living standards. London: Penguin Books
Townsend, P 1993. International analysis of poverty. London: Harvester
van Rooy, Gert / !Naruseb, Gottlieb / Maasdorp, Melinda / Eele, Graham / Hoddinott, John / Stone, Simon 1994. Household subsistence levels in Namibia: three selected communities. NISER: Windhoek
UNICEF 1995. Children in Namibia. UNICEF Office Windhoek
UNO 1999. Common country assessment of Namibia. UNO Windhoek
UNDP 1999. Namibia human development report. Windhoek

TWO SOCIETIES IN ONE – INSTITUTIONS AND SOCIAL REALITY OF TRADITIONAL AND GENERAL LAW AND ORDER[1]

Manfred O Hinz

Discontent with the 'white man's law'

In one of the first consultations with traditional leaders and members of traditional communities[2] about the future of traditional law and traditional courts after independence[3], the participants expressed their concern about magistrates' courts and the law applied by these courts. Magistrates' courts were called *courts of the white man* and the law administered by these courts *white man's law*. Most participants of the Okahao meeting (like those consulted and interviewed subsequently in other parts of Namibia)[4] favoured traditional courts over state courts. The reasons given were that traditional courts were locally available. Traditional courts were more accessible because people could speak their own languages in them. They were also less costly than state courts. Traditional judges were in a better position to assess cases brought before them because they were familiar with the local environment. Traditional courts applied the law known to the people.

The reluctance in accepting state courts was undoubtedly also caused by the low numbers of magistrates and magistrates' courts operating at the time of independence. In 1990, only 18 magistrates held court at 12 places. In the whole of the far north there was only one resident magistrate, namely in Katima Mulilo for Caprivi. Magistrates residing elsewhere served the former Ovamboland and Kavango[5]. The only place where periodical courts took place in Ovambo was Ondangwa. This picture changed drastically in the first years of the 1990s[6]. At the end of 1994, the number of magistrates was increased to 43, holding court at 23 places. Three magistrates' courts with a total of six magistrates were established in the Ovambo regions at Oshakati, Ondangwa and Uutapi and one court with two

---

[1] The following relies on some of the author's previous publications: part two is based on Hinz / Katjaerua 1998:5f, 86ff; part three on Hinz 2001c.
[2] The terms traditional and traditional community are terms of the Traditional Authorities Acts No.17 of 1995, and No.25 of 2000. See part 4 of this article where I will come back to the anthropological debate about the validity of the terms and the validity of the dichotomy of traditional and modern.
[3] At Okahao (Onganjera), September 1991
[4] The last consultations/ interviews were conducted in June 1994. They were part of a survey undertaken by the author and S Joas for the Ministry of Justice and resulted in Hinz 2001a.
[5] The area known as Ovamboland was divided into four regions when the new regions were established as stipulated by the Constitution: Omusati, Oshana, Ohangwena and Oshikoto. The borders of Oshikoto reach beyond the former Ovamboland and include Tsumeb. The Kavango region comprises of the pre-independence Kavango with parts of West Caprivi added.
[6] See Truter 1994; Hinz 2001b:81

magistrates in Rundu. In addition to this, court offices for periodical courts were built outside the mentioned places of residence.

The view on the workload of the courts complements the picture[7]. In 1990, 364 criminal cases were recorded at the Ondangwa court, which was the only court office for Ovamboland, served from Tsumeb at the time. The Oshakati and Ondangwa Magistrates' Courts recorded a combined total of 5 881 cases in 1992 with a substantially increased number of civil cases. Generally, magistrates' courts spent 25 times more time on civil matters in 1994 than in 1990. This figure basically remained at this level in 1993 and 1994.

Assessing the workload of traditional courts in comparison to state courts is difficult. The consultations for the above mentioned survey revealed that traditional courts were more active in the northern parts of the country than in the south, i.e. the Nama-speaking areas. In most of the northern areas, courts were normally held at the three levels of traditional authority: the level of traditional councillor, the level of senior traditional councillor[8] and the level of the supreme traditional leader, the chief, the king or the king's council. The hundreds of headmen in some communities are responsible for their wards, in which they also adjudicate cases brought before them. As yet no figures are available on the number of cases dealt with at the lowest level. What could be established is that courts at the level of senior councillor may hear five to seven cases per week. Given the number of again five to seven senior councillors in each of the fifteen communities of Ovambo, Kavango and Caprivi[9] the estimated number of cases handled traditionally may be an amount which would bring the state courts close to collapse if these cases were to be handled by them.

Social acceptance of traditional authority after independence

A more systematic approach to establishing the role and function of traditional law and order was undertaken after the enactment of the Traditional Authorities Act No.17 of 1995, the first after-independence legislation on traditional rule[10]. Up to then, traditional authorities had exercised their duties and functions, at least from

---

[7] See Truter / Hinz:ibid.

[8] Senior traditional councillor replaced senior headman as traditional councillor replaced headman. It is important to note that sec 4(1)(b) of Traditional Authorities Act 17 of 1995, limited the functions and duties of traditional councillors "to advise the chief and the senior councillors in the performance of their duties". However, headmen have always been the leaders of traditional wards, referred to as omwene gwomukunda in Oshiwambo (Oshindonga). This explains why in some cases (Ondonga, Oukwanyama) hundreds of persons were gazetted as traditional councillors (cf. GN No.64 of 1998). This is a clear indication that the Traditional Authorities Act of 1995 did not change the authority and powers of headmen; they remained the prime administrators in and of communal land in their areas of jurisdiction under customary law. The Traditional Authorities Act No.25 of 2000, recognised this reality by adding to the description of the duties and functions of traditional councillors words, which could already be found in the respective description for senior councillors in the 1995 act. According to the 2000 Act, traditional councillors shall also "exercise or perform such other powers, duties and functions as may be delegated or assigned to any of them by" the chief or head of the community (see sec 10(1)(b) of Act No.2000; and cf. sec 4(1)(a) of Act 1995).

[9] See the seven recognised Ovambo communities, the five communities in Kavango and the three in Caprivi, GN No.64 of 1998.

[10] As amended by Act No.8 of 1997 and now replaced with Act No.25 of 2000. Mistakenly called Act No.2001 in sec 21(1)). Act 25 of 2000 came into operation on 17 May 2001 (GN No.93 of 2001) and repealed Acts No.17 of 1995 and No.8 of 1997.

a formal legal point of view, as stipulated in various pieces of inherited legislation, some dating back to 1922, the year in which the South African Administration enacted the Native Administration Proclamation No.11 of 1922.

In accordance with Article 102 of the Constitution of Namibia, the government of Namibia provided for the establishment of elected sub-central structures with the adoption of the Local Authorities and the Regional Councils Act[11], as early as 1992. The re-structuring of the traditional structures had to wait until 1995 – in actual fact until 1997 after the responsible ministry for traditional authorities, the Minister of Regional, Local Government and Housing, decided to amend the 1995 Act and to suspend its implementation until the proposed amendments were approved by Parliament. This happened with the Traditional Authorities Amendment Act No.8 of 1997, which eventually led to the process of recognising and registering traditional authorities[12]

Traditional authorities were the sole agents of government in pre-colonial times. They continued to perform (local) governmental functions under colonial rule. Colonial governments understood the importance of traditional authorities, and used them for colonial interests. Traditional authorities responded to this in various ways: They resisted, they accepted, they accepted and developed their own agenda at the same time.

Is there still a role to play for traditional authorities after the democratic order was introduced when Namibia achieved its independence? To what extent do traditional authorities still command the respect of their people? How is it perceived by the people that there are now two authority structures in place: the structures of traditional authorities and the structures of 'modern' authorities, in particular the formally elected local and regional representatives?

These questions formed the background of research projects conducted by the University of Namibia: The project *Political and Economic Sustainability of Traditional Authorities* (PESTA) was initiated by the Centre for Applied Social Studies (CASS) at the Faculty of Law of the University of Namibia. The idea of PESTA coincided with a similar move undertaken in the Department of Political and Administrative Studies of the University of Namibia. The latter concentrated on traditional communities in southern Namibia, while the PESTA project looked at the north[13].

When the research framework of the projects was discussed, there was an assumption that the results of the projects would differ in that the research of the northern communities would show a much stronger support of traditional leader-

---

[11] Local Authorities Act No.23 of 1992; Regional Councils Act No.22 of 1992. The Local Authorities Act and the Regional Councils Act were substantially amended by the Local Authorities Amendment Act No.24 of 2000 (in force since 15 February 2001, see GN No.29 of 2001) and the Regional Councils Amendment Act No.30 of 2000 (in force since 5 March 2001, see GN No.35 of 2001) respectively.

[12] See GN No.65 of 1998; GN No.98 of 1998; GN No.99 of 1998; GN No.307 of 1998; GN No.113 of 1999; and GN No.61 of 2001.

[13] The results of the southern Namibia project are contained in Keulder 1997; the PESTA results in Hinz / Katjaerua 1998; cf. also Keulder 1998.

ship than the research conducted in the south. Another assumption was that the support for traditional rule would differ with respect to age, gender and education.

The outcome of the projects did not prove these assumptions; the result was a very unanimous and broad support for traditional rule[14].

Traditional authority enjoys recognition and acceptance in an exceptional manner. There is no significant difference as to the degree of recognition and acceptance between the communities in Ovambo, Kavango, Caprivi and the researched communities in southern Namibia. Parameters such as exposure to the war, party affiliation and distance to the centre of the country appear not to be significant in terms of the amount of recognition and acceptance. Recognition and acceptance of traditional authority is also not significantly a function of age, gender, or education. People are not likely to distinguish between legitimate and illegitimate traditional leaders. The 'puppet issue' – i.e. leaders being put into their positions of leadership by the colonial administration – is obviously not of importance. The reason for this may be seen in the respect people have for traditional authority as an institution, which is being distinguished from the respect for the incumbent leader.

Modern authority appears in elected structures and is expected to secure 'modern' goods, such as electricity, water and sanitation. Elected office bearers are seen as the intermediaries between the traditional communities and the structures of the state. Elected structures are perceived as the *technical* side of government. They are more the agents and spokespersons of the substantial government, which vest in traditional leaders, than what they are constitutionally expected to be, the representatives of those who elected them.

Traditional authorities are expected to secure an orderly life in the environment of the community. Traditional authority represents the substantial side of government. This perception is supported by the closeness of traditional authority to the community and local knowledge, but also by the *'traditional'* in the traditional authority. The traditional conceptualisation of legitimacy sees traditional authority grounded in the blessing that traditional authority receives from the ancestors as the creators and guarantors of the community[15].

The framing of regional councillors as governmental *technicians* may also explain why many people maintained a relatively negative picture of the councillors[16]. Many people exhibited a strong tendency to separate party politics from the performance of traditional authority. Support to traditional authority is not supporting tribalism. Community membership is not restricted to belonging to the same ethnic group. There are (as there always have been) mechanisms to take note and care of *foreigners* and to integrate them into the community.

Traditional authority has a future: it needs to be strengthened in general; traditional courts need strengthening in particular. Traditional leaders are capable

---

[14] The following is primarily based on the PESTA project.
[15] Cf. also Hinz 1998
[16] The general feeling was that the councillors did not deliver. It would be interesting to test this feeling again after the second regional and local government elections and the improvement of regional infrastructures.

agents of change. It will, however, still take some time to achieve gender balance. There is some willingness to address the issue of women in traditional authority. Educational exercises may contribute a lot to enhance developments in the right directions.

Dual structure and unitary state

Questions about the relationship between traditional authorities and (other) sub-central governmental structures have more than academic relevance. The debated location of traditional authorities in the overall societal and state structure is, in theoretical and practical terms, a permanent challenge to the ongoing process of, in particular, translating the constitutional orders as they emerged within the framework of what has become known as the *new constitutionalism* in Africa, and for which the constitutions of Namibia and South Africa are prominent examples, into respected and working legal orders[17].

The Namibian Constitution recognises customary law as part of the law of Namibia and determines it as having the same status as common law (Art. 66). As customary law provides for the existence, roles and functions of traditional authorities (supreme traditional leaders, leaders' councils, senior traditional councillors and traditional councillors), the recognition of customary law encompasses recognition of traditional authorities as they have developed in the various traditional communities over the years. Otherwise, the Constitution does not pay explicit attention to the role and function of traditional authorities and their relationship with (other) governmental structures.

However, Article 102 of the Constitution deserves noting as this article provides for the establishment of the Council of Traditional Leaders. The function of this Council is limited "to advise the President on the control and utilisation of communal land and on all such matters as may be referred to it by the President for advice" (Art. 102(5))[18]. Art. 102 of the Constitution is the first article in Chapter 12 which deals with *Regional and Local Government* and is entitled *Structures of Regional and Local Government*. Although no explicit link between the otherwise very detailed system of regional and local government and traditional authorities can be found in Art. 102 (and the subsequent articles), the fact that the Council of Traditional Leader has been made part of the *Structures of Regional and Local Government* is an indication of the constitutional intention to view traditional au-

---

[17] One dispute between state organs and traditional authorities has become a matter of contest before a court of law since the adoption of the Namibian Constitution and the enactment of the Traditional Authorities Act No.17 of 1995: the case of the Herero communities under Paramount Chief Riruako. The case of the Khwe in the western part of the Caprivi strip fell dormant after the late Chief of the community fled to Bostwana during the Caprivi crisis, but may be revived in view of the reluctance of the government to recognise the community in terms of the Traditional Authorities Act.

[18] The Traditional Authorities Amendment Act No.8 of 1997, introduced an additional duty of the Council by providing for the President to refer certain applications for approval of designations of traditional leaders to the Council for "consideration and recommendation" (see sec 5 of the amended 1995 Act). A recent interview with a prominent traditional leader in northern Namibia indicated dissatisfaction with the limited role of the Council and expressed hope for an extended mandate. Such an extension would not necessitate an amendment to the Constitution, but could be achieved by merely using the empowering clause in Art. 102(5).

thority within the broader context of regional and local government. This indication is further supported by Art. 102(1), which sets the general basis for *regional and local units,* but leaves the determination and definition of these units to parliament. In other words, the constitutional framework did not provide for a countrywide (or as it's said in South Africa: "wall-to-wall"[19]) system of local authorities in the narrow sense of the concept of local authority. By not providing such a wall-to-wall system, the Constitution implicitly accepted the situation on the ground in that traditional authorities have been performing the functions of local authorities.

The enactment of the Local Authorities Act, the Regional Councils Act, and the Traditional Authorities Acts, concretised the situation to some extent:

The modifications by the Local Authorities Act No.23 of 1992, as amended, resulted in a fundamental shift in authority from traditional leaders to the relevant bodies established under the Local Authorities Act. The shift in detail has to be identified by way of interpretation of the act and the practice employed on both sides – that of local and that of traditional authority – as the act did not explicitly repeal any relevant provision of customary law as provided for in Art. 66 of the Constitution. Not even the issue of customary land rights was made part of the legislative considerations, resulting in uncertainty in some of the areas proclaimed as municipal areas so far occupied and utilised in accordance with customary law and under the administration of traditional leaders. Resistance to orders to move eventually resulted in administrative schemes of compensation for the expropriation of rights under customary law[20]. No systematic evaluation has been undertaken to investigate the presence of traditional authorities in proclaimed local authorities' areas[21], the functions performed and the relationship between the two authorities[22].

The original Regional Councils Act, i.e. Act No.22 of 1992 is easier to assess from a legal point of view, though difficult from a practical political one. The legal assessment is relatively easy because regional councils, unlike local authority councils, had, with the exception of the authority in settlement areas[23], as yet no executive authority over the residents of the region[24]. The assessment of the political weight of regional councils is not easily done. It is obvious that regional offices in areas which used to be remote from any type of administrative centre have become focal points for governmental and non-governmental activities, and in particular sub-centres for development. The enactment of the Decentralisation Enabling Act 33 of 2000 will change the position of regional councils. The Decen-

---

[19] Cf. Department of Provincial and Local Government (2000)
[20] Cf. Bruhns Hinz (1997):29
[21] Being either municipalities, towns or villages, see sec 2 of the Local Authorities Act
[22] Research on traditional courts in the Kavango region revealed that the Sambyu Traditional Authority continues its judicial functions in that part of Rundu that forms part of the Sambyu traditional territory. The Uukwambi Traditional Authority established even a new office in Oshakati.
[23] See secs 31 and 32 of the Regional Councils Act of 1992 and its amendment of 2000.
[24] See sec 28 of the Regional Councils Act of 1992 and its amendment of 2000, and in particular sec 28(1)(b) and sec 29.

tralisation Enabling Act sets the framework for the transfer of authority from the administration through ministries to regional councils[25].

Before the Traditional Authorities Act, 17 of 1995, was drafted and enacted, a presidential *Commission of Inquiry into matters relating to Chiefs, Headmen and other Traditional or Tribal Leaders* was targeted to investigate the situation of traditional leadership in Namibia. The first paragraph of the findings of the Commission categorically stated: "The retention of the traditional system at this stage of socio-economic development in Namibia is necessary"[26]. The findings further emphasised that many persons to whom the commission could speak underscored the need for enabling traditional leaders to perform administrative as well as judicial functions as representatives "of their group and protectors of their group rights"[27].

The Traditional Authorities Acts of 1995 and of 2000 essentially confirm the role and function of traditional authorities as they developed within the framework of the customary laws observed by the various traditional communities. Section 10 of Act 1995 and sections 3 and 7 of Act 2000 contain long lists of tasks, which basically centre on the observation and application of customary law. Assistance to the police and other law enforcement agencies are special functions. *Promoting peace and welfare in the community* is the overall function of traditional authority for which all explicitly listed functions are examples. In other words, what the Traditional Authorities Acts expect from traditional authorities is the performance of judicial and executive duties that have direct impact on the members of the community.

On the crucial question of the requirements for a traditional leader to assume power, the Traditional Authorities Acts accepted a two-step approach: The first option is to allow for customary law to govern the designation of traditional leaders. (Sec 5(1) of Act 1995 and Act 2000) The second is the option of election by majority vote, which will be employed in cases wherein no customary law for the designation of the new leader exists or the customary law is uncertain or disputed amongst the member of the community. (Sec 5(9) of Act 1995 and Act 2000).

Sec 16 of the Traditional Authorities Act 2000, describes the relationship between traditional authorities and organs of government by stating:

> A traditional authority shall in the exercise of its powers and the performance of its duties and functions under customary law or as specified in this Act give support to the policies of the government, regional councils and local authority councils and refrain from any act which undermines the authority of those institutions.

---

[25] The Decentralisation Enabling Act No.33 of 2000 is in force since 5 March 2001 (GN No.34 of 2001). See also sec 44A of the Regional Councils Amendment Act No.30 of 2000, which empowered regional councils to enact regulations in the field of trade, business, occupation and other activities for gain outside local authority areas.
[26] Republic of Namibia 1991:66
[27] Ibid:67

It is worthwhile noting that this section, which is the only slightly changed repetition of sec 12(1) of the 1995 Act, had an additional second sub-section. Sec 12(2) of the 1995 Act stipulated that

> where the powers of a traditional authority or traditional leader conflict with the powers of the government, regional councils or local authorities councils, the powers of the government, regional council or local authority council, as the case may be, shall prevail.

A clear-cut provision that seemingly would have allowed the organs of the state very easy ways of handling conflicts! However, I do not know of any case where sec 12(2) of the 1995 Act was offensively applied.

Sec 16 of the 2000 Act appears less strict than the repealed sec 12. Whether or not it truly reflects a conceptual change has yet to be seen. Looking at the remaining language of sec 16, the following can be said: When traditional rulers and agents of the (modern) government differ, there is, indeed, no automatic *prevailing* of the governmental view. The governmental position could, nevertheless, be that the traditional view would qualify to be set aside as *an act of undermining* the authority of the government[28] In this sense, almost everything could be called *undermining* what is not in line with the view of the government. Therefore, the change from sec 12 in the old Act to sec 16 of the new could eventually be no more than a cosmetic change, as the new Act would still result in requiring traditional authorities to accept the views of government, just as any other sub-central agent of government has to follow the words of his or her superior.

Could a regional council, for instance, overrule the decision of a headman who declined the request of the council to allocate a piece of land that the council identified as most suitable for a school or a clinic with reference to sec 16, because objections to the decision would be *undermining* the authority of the council and, therefore be invalid? What would be the legal situation if the overruled headman decided to appeal to a court of law against the council decision?

In arguing the case, the council could place emphasis on the traditional authority being a sub-central organ of state, thereby having no right on its own against another, higher organ. Art. 1(1) of the Namibian Constitution could be referred to in support of the argument that the constitutional decision for the state to be a *unitary state,* required vesting the right of conclusive decisions in the organs of the state. The traditional leader could oppose this argument by referring to rights vested in him/ her under customary law[29] and, in particular, could recall his/ her different, i.e. traditional legitimacy that determined his/ her special status. However, would such a special status place him/ her outside the command structure of the administrative hierarchy?

---

[28] The jurisprudential alternative could be to interpret undermining in a restrictive manner, an exercise, which would require legal creativity and would most probably only happen when a dispute would be brought before a court of law.

[29] Including land use rights according to customary law, which could even qualify for claims for compensation under Art. 16 of the Constitution

Tradition and modernity

These are questions for which not only jurisprudential answers, but also political anthropological reflections will be needed. The jurisprudential answers must re-examine the role and function of constitutional principles and requirements in a situation of political and legal pluralism[30], an exercise which is certainly beyond the scope of this article. Political anthropological reflections will suffer from the relatively (in terms of empirical and theoretical research) unexplored relationship between traditional and modern structures. However, the evidence available allows at least some hypothetical remarks, which will conclude this article.

The concluding remarks will have to go back to the beginning of this article where the concepts of *tradition* vis-à-vis *modernity* were introduced with particular reference to the language of the law.

The Traditional Authorities Acts (of 1995 as well as of 2000) not only use the term *traditional*, but even define it in the context of *traditional community*. The definition employs outdated concepts which may have had a meaning for traditional communities in the past when the degree of external influence was minimal[31]. The definition employs concepts such as *endogamous* or *exogamous clans*, which have no meaning to the people anymore[32]. Does this mean that the dichotomy *traditional* versus *modern* is nothing but a legal fiction? What does this imply regarding the assumption that there is more than one society within the overall national society?

It would indeed be misleading if the use of the dichotomy and the inherent assumption of the existence of more than one society within the national society were to be perceived as though there were clearly separated and geographically distinguishable worlds, the world of modernity here (i.e. in Windhoek, Swakopmund, Otjiwarongo, etc.) and the world of tradition there (e.g. in Namaland, Kaokoveld, remote areas of Ovamboland, etc.). *Traditional* and *modern* have become ways of describing social patterns and features of life, *ideal types* in the sense of the sociology of Max Weber. There is a concept of *tradition*, and there is a concept of *modernity*. Both concepts, or elements of them, may be employed by the same person, depending on the situation and the merits of the case. Legal anthropologists refer to certain behaviours of people as *forum shopping* in order to describe what happens when people choose between traditional and modern courts not because of their belonging to the traditional or, respectively, modern system, but because of benefits which they calculate they could receive from the court chosen.

Elected regional leaders, such as governors of regions, may behave in a given situation as if they were traditional leaders. High officials from the central govern-

---

[30] Cf. Griffiths 1986 and Hinz 2001d
[31] See sec 1 of the Act (Act No.17 of 1995 and Act No.25 of 2000) which says: "'traditional community' means an indigenous homogeneous, endogamous social grouping of persons comprising of families deriving from exogamous clans which share a common ancestry, language, cultural heritage, customs and traditions".
[32] Cf. here Shamena 1998 and Hinz 2001d

ment may leave their governmental authority behind when they pay respect to the king of the community where they come from. Traditional leaders may demonstrate their traditional superiority over regional councillors by deliberately placing councillors of their areas into a traditionally defined status understood by everybody to be below the authority of the traditional ruler.

There is more than mere forum shopping, forum swapping and power play, and this is the growing awareness that there are indeed different sources from which modern authority on the one side and traditional authority on the other derive their legitimacy. This awareness has led to what I would term *constitutional compromises*; compromises which recognise political and legal plurality.

Two recent examples: The first example concerns rights over communal land. There were long debates before the Communal Land Bill eventually accepted the sovereignty of traditional leaders over communal land[33]. The Communal Land Bill indeed abandoned the simple and sometimes politically convenient position that there was only one sovereign of communal land, the Government of Namibia[34]. The second example is taken from the Traditional Authorities Act of 2000. Sec 3(3)(c) of this added to the duties and functions of traditional authorities the authority of *making* customary laws. Although the authority to legislate has been claimed by traditional authorities as an inherited authority since *time immemorial*, the debate about this authority had difficulty in accommodating it, in view of the constitutional assumption of the elected parliament being the only legitimate lawmaker. Jurisprudence opposing the jurisprudential relevance of political and legal pluralism may offer constructions of mandated authority to traditional rulers by Parliament[35] and maintain the fiction of political and legal centralism. Such a fiction is virtually useless from a practical and anthropological point of view, when one considers that the authority of making customary law is not subject to approval by any organ of the state, thus being comparable to the lawmaking by Parliament. In other words, the acceptance of the traditional power of lawmaking by the Traditional Authorities Act of 2000 reflects the acceptance of the plurality of societies within the national society.

These acts of recognition of political and legal plurality are constitutional compromises as they compromise the inherited and widely dominant constitutional concept of the state as the monopoly of authority and power. However, they do not compromise the overall binding and guiding nature of the constitution and, in particular, the binding force of human rights enshrined in it. Compromises of this kind contribute to peace in the society, as the recognition of societal forces strengthens the challenge to exercise the accepted authority in a responsible

---

[33] Cf. secs 2(4), 3(a) and in particular sec 20 of the Bill (Bill 10 of 1999) which says: "Subject to the provisions of this Act, the primary power to allocate or cancel any customary land right in respect of any portion of land in the communal area of a traditional community, vests – (a) in the Chief of that traditional community; or (b) where the Chief so determines, in the Traditional Authority of that traditional community."

[34] Cf. Bruhns / Hinz 1997

[35] Cf. D' Engelbronner-Kolff 1998, who gives an account of the relevant arguments. However, d'Engelbronner-Kolff (1998:75) holds that lawmaking of traditional authorities is power vested in the communities by virtue of their customary law status.

manner. The compromises also generate new platforms for significant political discourse. This discourse will establish the future directions for the development of state and nationhood and, with it, the capacity to accommodate more than two societies within one.

Bibliography

Bruhns, *P /* ***Hinz,*** *MO* (eds.) 1997. The role of traditional authority in a changing Namibia. Proceedings of the First National Traditional Authority Conference. CASS paper no.37. Windhoek:

D'Engelbronner-Kolff, *FM* 1998. The people as lawmakers: the juridical foundation of the legislative power of Namibian traditional communities. In: D'Engelbronner-Kolff, FM / Hinz, MO / Sindano, JL (eds.), pp.62-82

D'Engelbronner-Kolff, *FM /* ***Hinz,*** *MO /* ***Sindano,*** *JL* (eds.) 1998. Traditional authority and democracy in southern Africa, Windhoek: New Namibia Books

Department of Provincial and Local Government 2000. A draft document towards a white paper on traditional leadership and institutions. Pretoria

Government of the Republic of Namibia 1991. Report – Commission of Enquiry into matters relating to chiefs, headmen, and other traditional leaders. Windhoek

Griffiths, *J* 1986. What is legal pluralism? In: Journal of Legal Pluralism and Unofficial Law, pp.1-55

Hinz, *MO* 1998. The 'traditional' of traditional government. Traditional versus democracy-based legitimacy. In: FM D'Engelbronner-Kolff / MO Hinz / JL Sindano (eds.), pp.1-13

Hinz, *MO* (assisted by ***Joas,*** *S)* 2001a. Customary law in Namibia: development and perspective, 6th ed., CASS Paper no.47. Windhoek:

Hinz, *MO* 2001b. To achieve freedom and equality: Namibia's new legal order. In: Diener, I / Gräfe, W (eds.). Contemporary Namibia. The first landmarks of a post-apartheid society, pp.75-91. Windhoek: Gamsberg Macmillan

Hinz, *MO* 2001c. Traditional authorities – sub-central governmental agents? In: Amoo, SK / Hinz, MO / van Wyk, D. Ten years of Namibian nationhood Pretoria (forthcoming)

Hinz, *MO* 2001d. Das Projekt Tradition. Dilemma des neuen afrikanischen Konstitutionalismus. Paper presented at the Carl von Siemens Foundation, 31 January 2001. Munich

Keulder, *C* 1997. Traditional authorities and regional councils in Southern Namibia. Windhoek: FES

Keulder, *C* 1998. Traditional leaders and local government in Africa – lessons for South Africa. Pretoria: HSRC

Shamena, *NE* 1998. The concept of 'traditional community'. In: D'Engelbronner-Kolff, FM / Hinz, MO / Sindano, JL (eds.), pp.323-327

Truter, *FH* 1994. Division Lower Courts: report on the first five years (mimeo). Ministry of Justice. Windhoek

© John Liebenberg, Collection National Union of Namibian Workers

Rights

© Julika Komnik, Collection National Union of Namibian Workers

School

© Estelle Coetzee, Collection Sister Namibia

Habitat 1953

© University of Kiel, Collection Katesa Schlosser

Habitat 1999

© Collection Namibia Housing Action Group

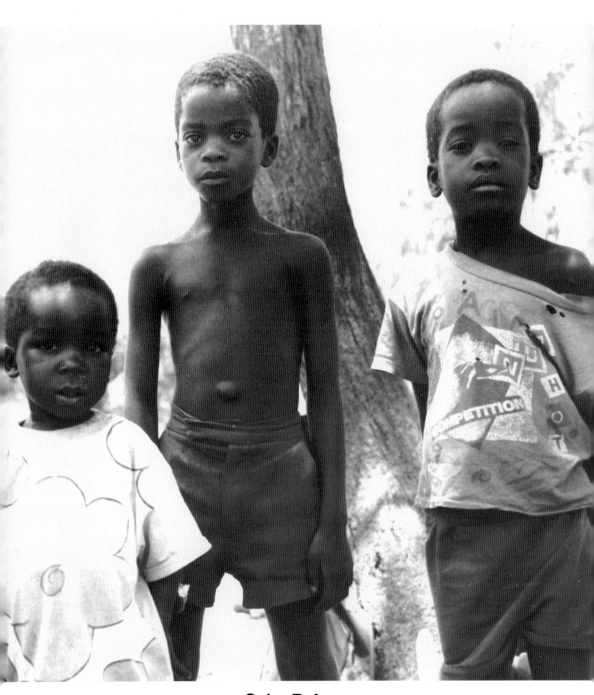

Osire Refugees

© André du Pisani

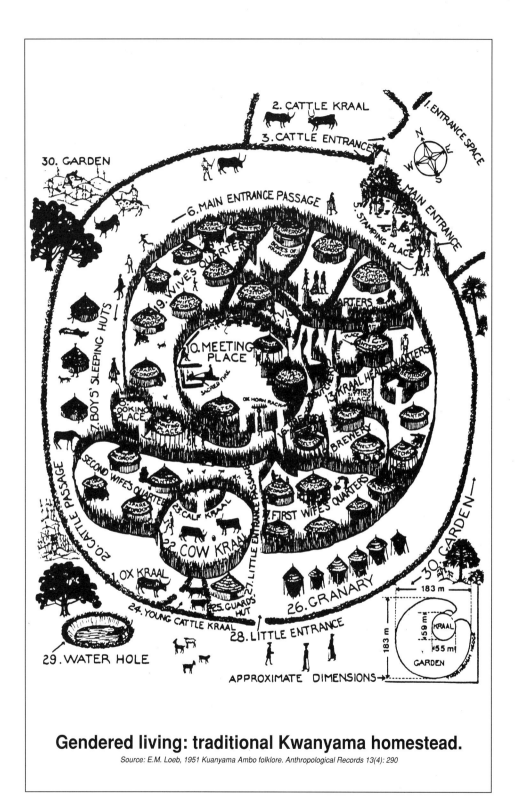

Gendered living: traditional Kwanyama homestead.

Source: E.M. Loeb, 1951 Kuanyama Ambo folklore. Anthropological Records 13(4): 290

Living past
© Shane !Noarises, Collection Sister Namibia

Friendship
© Tandeus Emvula, Collection Sister Namibia

Always waiting for rain

© Tom Fox

Migrant labour
© A. Schmerenbeck, Collection Namibia Scientific Society

Not their land
© Collection National Union of Namibian Workers

Survival

© A. Schmerenbeck, Collection Namibia Scientific Society

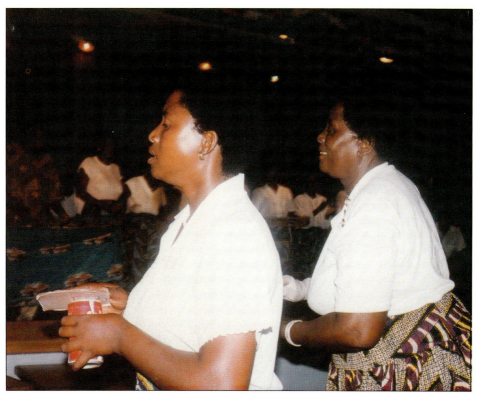

Appropriation

© Danie Botha, Collection Ecumenical Institute of Namibia

Youth and Death
© Tom Fox

Herbal Pharmacy
© Debie LeBeau

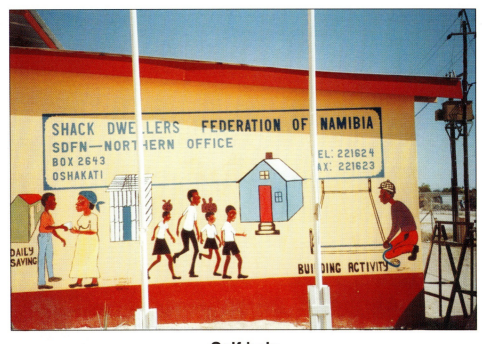

Self help
© Collection Namibia Housing Action Group

Social status
© Tom Fox

OTJIWARONGO SURVEY RESULTS

Total shacks surveyed	750
Number of people in shacks	3607
Number of people per shack	4.8
Percentage Females	51,9%
Percentage Males	48,1%
Male headed households	51%
Female headed households	49%

OCCUPATION

Percentage people with income	24%
Percentage adults without income	33,6%
Percentage children + student	42,4%

Percentage with income doing:

• Domestic work	41,6%
• Formal work	40,5%
• Self employment	0,06%
• Unemployed	
• Pension	11,3%

INCOME

Average Income	N$ 516—43
No income reported	26%
N$ 1·00 — N$ 600-00	55,7%
N$ 601-00 — N$ 1200-00	12,9%
N$ 1200-00 — Plus	5,4%
Average years in house	7,5
Average years in Otjiwarongo	18,6
Affordability for house and land	N$ 65—70

Fieldwork
© Collection Namibia Housing Action Group

Mass

© Danie Botha, Collection Ecumenical Institute of Namibia

Banking

© Tom Fox

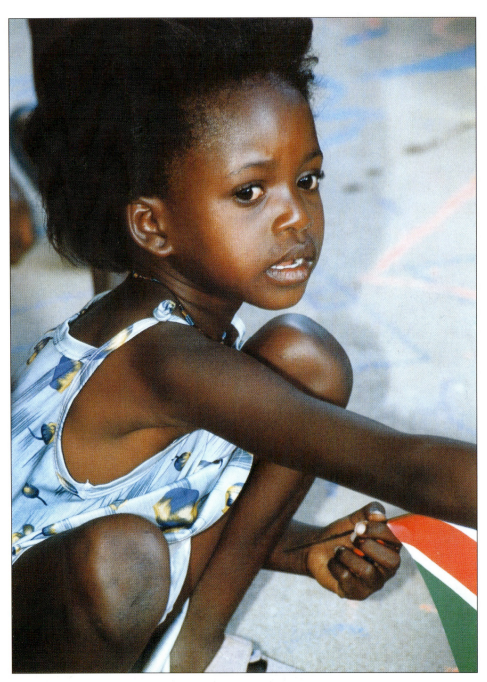

Future

© André du Pisani

© Jeanette Cross, Collection Sister Namibia

Drinking

3 TRADITIONALISM, CULTURE AND ART

Traditionalism – social reality of a myth
Volker Winterfeldt

'Education for all' in independent Namibia – reality or political ideal?
Elisabeth Magano Amukugo

Constructing cultural identities in contemporary musical traditions – strategies of survival and change
Minette Mans

(Con)fronting the mask – some (con)texts of protest in Namibian drama
Terence Zeeman

Entertainment through violence? The social impact of the visual media in Namibia
Tom Fox

Namibian society in fiction – the Namibian novel
Chrisna Beuke-Muir / Helen Vale / Marianne Zappen-Thomson

TRADITIONALISM – SOCIAL REALITY OF A MYTH

Volker Winterfeldt

The conceptual frame

When relating today to traditional culture and traditional ways of living, Namibians frequently fall back on their personal experiences of a pre-modern, non-urban way of life. They refer to their rural origins. Such an approach is a (biographical) matter of course for a society in transition, whose written tradition, moreover, is quite recent.

A critical look at this frame of reference reveals their common denominator. Reference is made to the colonial past rather than to the more 'genuinely' African, that is pre-colonial social formations. Contrasting 'tradition' and 'modernity' in such a way involves the risk of denying the indigenous societies a history of their own, since they are identified mainly with their colonial distortions. Is it not an irony of history when a newly independent society – unconsciously and unwillingly – equates its colonial uprooting with its sociocultural roots?

To put a certain stress on this conceptual critique is not merely following an academic exercise. To explain the reasons: Namibian scholars are often – one is inclined to say – trapped in this distorted view of the historical transformation of society. The colonial past is associated with tradition, whereas colonial transformation is interpreted in terms of modernisation, in the end creating those patches of modernity in everyday life which are ascribed to metropolitan culture. Rural vs. urban, tradition vs. modernity, often overlapping with African vs. Western and even female vs. male – these are the conceptual oppositions typical of the common understanding of the historical transition from the plurality of South West African social formations to the one and integrated Namibian society. Even the advocacy of an 'African Renaissance' is not free from this bias.

A piece of evidence

Douglas Taylor presents an expressive and colourful report on a visit to the Ju/'hoan -'Bushmen' living in the north-east of Namibia[1]. They are often described, in tourist terms, as the "most primitive of peoples". Some of the Ju/'hoansi live in Nhoma village, north of Tsumkwe. Visiting the Nyae-Nyae Conservancy, Taylor observes some increasing contradictions characteristic of the transformation of the lifestyle of this community of seemingly 'traditional' hunters and gatherers. In Nhoma, they have also "turned their hands to untraditional pursuits such as agriculture"[2]. Conflicts with neighbouring communities result from this, as cattle

---

[1] Published in the "Namibian Weekender" edition of March 24 2000
[2] Italics: VW

breeding threatens the 'Bushmen's' farming, habitat and game hunting. Taylor paints a vivid picture of the change affecting the community:

> "Utility rules at Nhoma. Man-made containers of plastic or metal have largely replaced traditional gourds, ostrich eggs or tortoise shells. Steel for arrowheads and knives is more readily available than before and plastic and canvas chairs are among the few luxuries they can afford. Mosquito nets hang inside the grass huts – a necessary protection against malaria". Many of them, Taylor continues, are "garbed in a colourful mixture of Western clothing (...) and traditional jewellery".

On the other hand, his following description of a spring hare hunt and a 'veldkos' gathering as well as of their fire-making skills shows the liveliness of the Ju/'hoan culture in terms of their technological traditions. Taylor concludes by emphasising the economic constraints leading to the commodification of labour and to the monetarisation of everyday life:

> "I would like to be able to relate the idyllic images of self-sufficiency that 'Bushman' culture has always conjured in my mind, but their new reality stands in contrast with these. The women outnumber the men to almost two-to-one in Nhoma village, an indication that many of the men are living and working in Tsumkwe to bring in the hard currency the Ju/'hoansi are increasingly dependent upon (...) My impression is that the huntergatherer subsistence of the Ju/'hoan people has been disturbed, but not yet obliterated."

Taylor's piece of evidence proves how improbable it is today in Namibia's modern nation state that a community could actually survive in a state of candid innocence, managing to preserve its ancient mode of production handed down from generation to generation. Not even a social group like the Ju/'hoansi – which in the understanding of the public still stands for the extreme traditionality of their way of life based on an almost complete dependence on nature – seems to be void of the influences of the expanding market economy affecting their labour force, their mode of subsistence, their lifestyle and culture. But, as matters stand, this should not come as any surprise to the sociological observer. If we accept that nowadays we have to envisage the nation state as seriously endangered in its integrity and transformed by an all-pervasive globalisation, we have all the more reason to take note of the fact that such a transformation will not stop at internal structures either. Islands of unspoilt tradition in the midst of a sea of transition are a myth.

The material background of recalling tradition

All the same, the myth lives. The existence of such a deep-rooted consciousness of tradition cannot simply be dismissed. It does represent an essential pattern of contemporary Namibian culture. However, such traditionalism, this recurring reference to the cultural past and its normative prescriptions, is not just an individual appearance. It does not only reflect common patterns of biographical experience in a young post-apartheid society wherein the majority of its urban residents lived their infancy and youth in rural society. It is the setting of a postcolonial class system under construction that forms the wider material background, if we look at it from a general sociological perspective. The evident contrast between contemporary rural and urban Namibian society is tangibly and continually fed by mechanisms beyond the individual sphere.

Two of these social mechanisms are to be discussed: the continued cultural effect of the multigenerational, extended family system, and the cultural impact of the incorporation of traditional authorities into the modern Namibian state apparatus.

Two centuries of European cultural influence may have brought significant alterations to the set of Namibian kinship and lineage structures, but they did not completely replace the customary extended family. It is and remains characteristic of the agricultural subsistence economy, and its persistence makes this large unit still a major image of both rural and urban Namibian society. Whatever its ethnic variations, economically it is shaped by the redistribution of goods/wealth within the household and between families. Redistribution follows the principle of reciprocity, that is, a pattern dictated as much by cultural tradition as by the economic prerogative connected with the control of the means of production. Kinship bonds and generational (inter)dependence render purely economic exchange superfluous, as Meillassoux (1960) explained in his analyses of African lineage systems[3].

This web of mutual social obligations, which regulates the flow of prestations and goods, builds on generational and gender authority. The family order opposes the male elder to women and young men. The authority and dominance of the patriarch is anchored in the prestige the lineage attributes to social knowledge – a knowledge well acquainted with the past and focusing on it: customs, genealogy, community history[4]. The elder appears as the guardian of tradition; his authority emanates from this guardianship. From this perspective the vitality of tradition is still embodied in the extended family system. As long as this 'traditional' family dominates the picture of everyday life, it will nurture traditionalism.

The other social mechanism mentioned is the cultural impact of the reorganisation of the administrative framework of the independent Namibian state. It also provides for a strong social efficacy of traditionalism. To illustrate the hypothesis: just a few years ago, the Traditional Authorities Act No 17 of 1995 restructured the rural bodies exercising jurisdictional and administrative authority over their communities. It followed the directions formulated in the Namibian constitution whose Article 66 (1) addresses common and customary law as equal, parallel elements of the existing legal body, provided their compatibility with the statutory rulings[5]. Thus, the Act again institutionalised the concept of 'tradition' not only verbally, but also legally as well as politically, as had been done before in colonial times. In particular, it contributed to the formation of a cultural reality on

---

[3] Until wage labour, money and commodities begin to shape relationships within the household, evidently

[4] Cf. Coquery-Vidrovitch 1976:94-95. Through the institution of the dowry, the elders control marriage, reproduction and progeny. Thus, generational and gender hierarchy is institutionalised permanently through alliances between the elders of neighbouring clans.

[5] Government Gazette of the Republic of Namibia no.2 – Constitution of Namibia; Windhoek, 21 March 1990:38

particular, it contributed to the formation of a cultural reality on the matter. As a side effect, the Act re-defined the relationship between customary and general law by stating the exact terms of their division of responsibilities. It laid down the jurisdiction and restrictions of traditional authorities, eventually subordinating 'traditional' law to the 'modern' legal body of the independent state and its commitment to fundamental human rights [6].

Hinz, in his study of the legal framework and the social reality of customary law in Namibia, lists some 40 distinct paramount units of traditional authorities all over the Namibian territory. Some of them preside over a structure of up to several hundred sub-units (senior headmen, village headmen)[7]. As it is, only a minority of them were taken over from pre-colonial structures, but all of them were (re)shaped in the colonial era by statutory determination and changing times.

Tradition on the matter has its history of unequivocal colonial character. Peltola states that 'tribal' identities, in several cases, result from early colonial efforts to institute and stabilise the structures necessary for indirect rule. 'Tribes' and 'tribal' identities – the very basis of 'traditions'- were created by and under colonial circumstances; they were not of indigenous, autochthonous origins[8].

This 'history of tradition' which is highlighted here in order to emphasise the dissimilarities between pre-colonial and colonial 'traditions', in the South African era sees its first important landmark in the South African Native Administration Proclamation, Act No.11 of 1922, which applied to the mandated territory of South West Africa. It provided for the institution of reserves and for the confinement of the indigenous population to these areas, executed on the basis of their preceding territorial expropriation[9]. The mere fact, and even more the extent of the displacement of the population (obviously including the previous German measures), prove that it might not be appropriate to assume an unbroken line of indigenous administrative tradition which is, to a great extent, bound up with the rural élite's customary control over access to land. To a certain extent, the Ovambo and Kavango regions present an exception to this rule, as far as their retarded historical inclusion into the colonial regime exempted them from the process of displacement. But this does not mean that their pre-colonial administrative structures were preserved throughout the era of colonial governance, thus presenting a continuity of tradition.

---

[6] We find this prevalence of Roman-Dutch law, based on the statutory rulings of the colonial regimes, throughout South West African history. Hinz, [4]1998:9 points to the "repugnancy clause" ruling "that customary law repugnant to public policy and natural justice should not be applied".

[7] Hinz, [4]1998:29-34

[8] Peltola 1995:230 mentions the case of the "Ovambo" communities: "In former times, there never was an identity of a tribe calling themselves Ovambo: there were Kwanyamas, Ndongas, Ongandjeras, etc.". He adds, pointing to the Damara speaking population groups: "Neither did a Damara identity exist (...) Dealing with separate and small groups was not considered effective. Therefore, they were grouped into 'tribes'. If such a tribe did not have a leader, the Germans nominated one. This is how, in 1902, Cornelius Goreseb was nominated by the Germans to govern eleven Damara-speaking groups. He was given a salary and some other 'means of government', such as a few guns." Peltola also refers to the Lozi-speaking people in the Eastern Caprivi. In the course of German colonial policies they were divided from the Barotse kingdom they politically belonged to, and treated as distinct and independent 'tribes'.

[9] By Crown Land Disposal Proclamation No.13 of 1920, which declared land "previously (...) inhabited and/or used by 'aboriginal natives' (...) to be crown land, i.e. land owned by the state". Hinz [4]1998:225

In actual fact, South African policy until the implementation of the Odendaal Plan mainly confirmed the existing external boundaries of spatial segregation established by German authorities. The internal structure, and the functions of a 'native' administration to be instituted, were then determined by Native Reserve Regulations, Government Notice 68 of 1924[10]. Formal enactment specifically for South West Africa followed, with Native Administration Proclamation No.15 of 1928. It was with this statutory decision that in principle the role of 'traditional' leaders was recognised. It was later detailed by the Regulations Prescribing the Duties, Powers, and Privileges of Chiefs and Headmen, GN 60 of 1930, which gave the particulars of the administrative authority of chiefs and headmen. It is of importance to note that ward headmen, expressly[11], were to be appointed by the South African Administrator[12]. Such headmen were not the same as the local village representatives previously appointed by the indigenous paramount chiefs[13].

Furthermore, the Native Reserve Regulations of 1924 had empowered the district's magistrate and the superintendents to take control of land allotments and residential matters, and to direct the headmen. With that, it laid the foundations for effectively curbing one of the most vital rights of 'traditional' authorities[14] by creating a competing prerogative on the side of the colonial officers and their African representatives at the said ward level. Thus this bottom layer in particular of the personnel of 'traditional' authorities proves to be a creation of colonial rule. Similar intrusions into the land rights of the indigenous élites were made possible by the Bantu Areas Land Regulations, R 188 of 1969. It vested the colonial administration with the right to grant permission to occupy 'reserved' land for public use (schools, churches) or in the public interest (to widows' families). However, and this also has to be stressed, all these measures did not replace the duties and privileges of the customary administrative and social élites. Rather, they were subjected to colonial control and dominance by being integrated into the hierarchical system of foreign rule.

The policies of 'separate development' for African and white communities, first cast into statutory language with the Development of Self Government for Native Nations in South West Africa Act No.54 of 1968, re-designed 'traditional' authorities[15]. Between 1968 and 1977, Ovambo, Kavango, Eastern Caprivi, Damara, Nama, and Rehoboth communities were recognised as 'self-governing', traditional units by a number of specific regulations. This enactment of apartheid policies was repealed by Representative Authorities Proclamation, AG 8 of 1980. Apart from the abolition of that fake apparition of self-governance though, the groundwork of local, 'traditional' administration remained the same.

---

[10] With the exception of the Ovambo and Kavango regions
[11] See section 2 of GN 60 of 1930
[12] Through magistrates and superintendents, respectively
[13] Cf. Hinz [4]1998:51-59 for details concerning the historical development of the administration of 'native' affairs.
[14] Hinz [4]1998:238-239
[15] A subsequent Proclamation recognised the existing seven tribal and communal authorities in Ovamboland. Tötemeyer 1978:56

It is interesting to note, however, that the efforts of South African policies to stabilise colonial dominance by indirect rule, by (re)creating 'traditional' authorities, also had the very opposite effect. Accusing traditional authorities and traditionalism of complicity with the colonial masters, 'modernising' indigenous élites in Ovamboland emerged. They expressed their opposition to the apartheid system by propagating and living a 'modern', westernised value, often being involved in 'modern' professions. Gerhard Tötemeyer, currently Deputy Minister of Local Government, within the scope of his research for his doctoral thesis pointed to the process of differentiation of 'modern' and 'traditional' élites as well as of rural and urban cultural worlds. Amongst teachers, religious leaders, officials, clerks, traders, nurses, and traditional leaders, the extent to which the individual felt bound to his ethnic group and the need to preserve his cultural roots varied substantially. Serious questioning of 'tribal' allegiance went hand in hand with the decreasing identification with the customary ways of life and spiritual quality. Similarly expressive were the highly critical attitude towards upholding the customary communal system of land tenure and the widespread demand for the introduction of permanent private land ownership. The reservations against the customary system of inheritance and the increasing esteem for money and professional occupations can also be taken as signs of crisis within the customary system of values[16].

Only the Constitution of independent Namibia repealed the legal body of ethnic representation and administration[17]. But, again, this seems to have been a somewhat prophylactic measure, assuring the independent state of the option of a future reformulation of its relation with the 'traditional' layer of administrative structures. As mentioned above, the Traditional Authorities Act of 1995 once again stresses the independent role of the 'traditional' section of the administration, as defined in colonial times, while at the same time it subjects it to the dominance of the 'modern', general law and the 'modern', superior organs of the state apparatus.

With that, it also guaranteed the continuity of 'tradition' in post-colonial Namibia. Today, the influence of 'traditional' governance on the management of everyday life is considerable. Executing customary law, its administrative fields include issues of marriage, divorce, inheritance, land tenure, residence, property, and (in part, differing from region to region and from community to community) of corporeal integrity[18]. It is also empowered to perform minor police duties, as well

---

[16] Even if its conceptual framework uncritically opposing the paradigms of 'tradition' and 'modernity' is questionable, Tötemeyer's research is highly interesting and productive, from a sociological point of view. The analysis consistently addresses issues of social change in colonial times. The PhD thesis gives an insight into the differentiation of the indigenous social structure, even before the New Dispensation policies began to transform Namibian society radically. Tötemeyer interviewed some 220 representatives of different Ovambo élites at the beginning of the 1970s in the Ovambo regions and in Katutura. Tötemeyer 1978:58, 77, 146-148

[17] As listed in Schedule 8 of the Constitution. See Government Gazette of the Republic of Namibia – Constitution of Namibia:80, Windhoek 21 March 1990.

[18] Hinz [4]1998:9, 121-127

as other executive functions; it has been conferred an important conservative cultural mission[19].

Keulder (1997) criticises the unspoken line of thinking permeating the Traditional Authorities Act. It opposes the two realms of the 'traditional' and the 'modern', an opposition which is clearly following the Weberian paradigm of rationalisation[20]. But reality differs from that. As a matter of fact, what is commonly termed 'traditional', in the case of several of the communities of southern Namibia, proves a 19th century phenomenon[21]. In this context, Keulder speaks of invented traditions, recurring to Eric Hobsbawm's hypothesis. He ascribes the 'invention of tradition' the intention of creating a basis for a social group's identification with the terms of reference imposed on it by its own élites.

There is no doubt that tradition in Namibia, 'invented' as it is, forms part of social reality. But such an 'invented' reference to the past should definitely not be confused with the pre-colonial state of affairs. Keulder makes it plain that the historical communities of southern Namibia and those 'traditional communities' to which the wording of the Act appeals are not congruent[22]. Williams goes a step further. In her monograph on the history of the Ovambo kingdoms she emphasises the dynamic character even of pre-colonial traditions. Analysing the oral traditions of Ovambo clans, she shows that not even this genuinely indigenous set of customs, norms and values remained static throughout the centuries[23].

Hybridity in transition – re-invented traditions

The concept of 'invented tradition' – which Keulder eventually paraphrases as a culture of hybridity[24] – is perhaps better conceived as re-invented tradition. It corresponds to an internal cultural revival, directed at identification as the basis of social cohesion. Identification combines both the creation of an identity and the assimilation to the normative and values of a social group. Thus, in addition to its original expression, we have to take into consideration the subsequent stages of

---

[19] See section 10 on 'Functions, duties and powers of traditional authorities'. Government Gazette of the Republic of Namibia No.1158 – Traditional Authorities Act No.17 of 1995:8-9, Windhoek 26 September 1995

[20] Keulder 1997:2. The Act addresses rural communities – unintentionally – as remnants of tribal social life, as Keulder (p.56) maintains: "'Traditional community' is here little more than a euphemism for tribe. Although the ideology of tribalism no longer forms the basis of governance and dominance, new divisions of power and dominance have emerged: that of rural vs. urban, and ,traditional' vs. ,modern'. In many ways the subordinates have remained the same despite the changes in ideology."

[21] The communities in question, mostly being descended from 19th century Oorlam groups from the Cape Colony migrating to the north, acted as agents of modernisation themselves, already in pre-colonial times. "These forces, each in its own unique and peculiar way shaped, influenced, changed and redirected not only the social, economic and cultural aspects of the Nama communities, but had a substantial influence on their leadership structures and practices." Keulder 1997:2

[22] In his introductory remarks, Keulder (p.4) maintains "that the Nama speakers (...) under the influence of Christian missionaries, colonial administrators, a variety of cultural brokers and their own inventions, have either lost or never possessed the qualities that according to the Traditional Authorities Act constitute a ,traditional community' or a 'tribe'."

[23] "Nevertheless, one has to accept the fact that Ovambo tradition has not been static (...) First, we have to look into the impact of neighbouring kingdoms such as those of the Ovimbundus (...) Second, there was the impact of the Imbangala expansion, which resulted in a change of the balance of power in the region (...) Third, resulting from the expansion of Christianity in the19th century, foreign cultural values were assimilated." (p.12-13)

[24] Relating to the blending of Proto-Nama and Oorlam components (p.5)

active re-formulation of tradition as well. In colonial South West Africa, and again in post-colonial Namibia, political administration was reorganised along the lines of an integrative opposition of the 'traditional' and the 'modern' political institutions. This continually renews the cultural impact of the contradiction between past and future, and keeps it effectively alive. Paradoxically, tradition always seems to be in a state of flux. As a historical expression of changing culture, it should be seen for what it is – a process; and under no circumstances can it be referred to as a static quality.

Why re-invent tradition? When dealing critically with the current trend of traditionalism, this question demands an answer. Its complexity very quickly points to another question: who re-invents tradition?

Pre-colonial societies, this has already been proposed, constructed their traditions culturally as a means of enhancing social integration in an environment of internal social conflicts and of contradictions with external opponents, encountered in the process of migration to or within the south-western territory. The South African colonial regime re-invented tradition a second time. It also institutionalised a new bottom level of the state apparatus. In so doing, the colonial regime in its turn depended on the traditional structure of hierarchy, to a certain extent, which it had chosen as its collaborative basis. This reference to the tradition of structured inequality and hierarchy, as a rule, suited the elitist elements within the local community, notwithstanding all its racial and political contradictions. Therefore, re-invented tradition, even if based on a clear, one-sided structure of dominance, likewise shows an element of mutual dependence, of concurrence in governance, by means of institutionalising cultural contradictions. As far as independent Namibia is concerned, the process of nation building under new class signs plays a role. Integrational aspects of social cohesion as well as hierarchical aspects of economic, cultural, political and social dominance have to be considered, whereas the racial aspect is eliminated.

Again: why re-invent tradition? The concept of peasant 'traditional' social life is, in its inherent logic, always opposed to 'modern', bourgeois social reality. It displays a distinct character of artificial being. What we detect is a cultural invention, related to the identification and self-identification of social groups. It presupposes the clash of different social formations as well as their internal contradictory structuration. The interaction of these unequal partners – on the basis of conflict – is guided by the artificial distinction between 'tradition' and 'modernity', introduced with the intention of social dominance and political power[25].

The current use of the concept reflects three subsequent stages of such an identificatory invention, amalgamating them into its current substance:
- The self-identification of a community in pre-colonial times, its 'original' ethnic invention in terms of characteristics and superiority, divulges its internal hierarchy of status and power. Here, identification is needed to

---

[25] "All traditions (...) are invented traditions (...) Moreover, traditions always incorporates power, whether it is constructed in a deliberate way or not." Giddens 1999:3

- legitimise and minimise hierarchical conflicts, with an eye on the realisation of tasks and goals. Thus it contains an instrumental element.
- The re-invention of a sociocultural identity in a colonial environment, redefines 'tradition' on a racial basis of inferiority. Its inferior status is not only a cultural one, but a social one as well, displaying the inferior status of the 'traditional' identity within the scope of 'modern' bourgeois society. This serves as a means of positioning (and self-positioning) indigenous social groups within the frame of the colonial structure of dominance and legitimation.
- The second re-invention occurs in a post-colonial environment. It displays all the characters of the colonial identity which is grounded on the blending of Western, Christian, capitalist elements of culture and society. However it refers to that identity as the genuine, originally indigenous one; it denies its character of cultural hibridity. It confines the community in question again to inferiority by defining it as 'traditional', implying backwardness as opposed to progress or development. However, at the same time this confinement also becomes an element of appraisal, a change of character which reflects efforts to build a common, post-colonial national identity of anti-colonial character based on indigenous, non-Western values. But both aspects claim the superiority of the enlightened, modernised and westernised black-African urban society, as well as its efforts to disentangle from their inferior identity which colonialism imposed on it. The conflictual identity of post-colonial society becomes evident, the need (functional as well as political) to integrate elements differing in culture ethnically and divided by class interests; the need to maintain, at the same time, a hierarchical structure of status and power. This can be seen as a typical contradiction of a restructuring class society shifting from colonial to indigenous political and (prospectively) social structures of dominance.

Dwelling on the latter, and adapting Robert Gordon's central theme of the construction of an identity of 'otherness', one may hypothesise: reference to 'tradition' in contemporary Namibia also reflects the cultural efforts of the African urban middle classes to construct its identity by contrasting it with its own peasant class, rural origins. Class formation then appears as accompanied by the ex-post construction of the 'other' society. Becoming aware of the new capitalist social environment, the new metropolitan strata re-define their origins. Thus, traditionalism, being attributed to the 'other', unconsciously becomes part of one's own class identity. The cord is not yet cut – class identity still makes reference to one's own former 'otherness'.

In terms of *cultural reality*, this corresponds to what has been termed a 'culture of hybridity', blending different ethnic elements into a hierarchical system.

In terms of *social structural reality*, this reflects the subordination of the peasant strata to the dominant social system as a whole and its dominant class élites in particular, by (partly) co-opting the local élites and privileging them, as against their communities.

In terms of *political reality*, this reflects the creation of an administration of hybrid character (since it combines – against all sacred rules of bourgeois separation of power – jurisdictional and executive powers). It functions as a semi-independent bottom layer of a state apparatus in developmental transition which does not yet have the means of building an exclusively bourgeois-type structure made in one 'modern' casting.

In terms of *developmental reality*, this represents a transitional structure of change, not a static traditional element within a modernising structure. Thus transition should be understood as a structural state of affairs – addressed in its quality of hybridity – and not as a merely temporary occurrence on its way to a (teleologically defined) modernity.

Conclusions

The cultural oppositions observed above – rural/urban, tradition/modernity, African/Western, female/male – deserve a thorough revision in the light of socio-economic and cultural facts. Historical evidence shows that what is usually addressed as being typically rural, as originally African, as the quintessence of traditional social life and culture, in fact derives from the colonial transformation of peasant society (and is not seen as preceding it). Most of the features of what is understood as customary life display clear traits of the influence of Western culture, of military, political, economic and social domination by foreign rule.

Giving some examples to make such a hypothesis more evident:
- today's well-known patterns of gender division of labour in rural economy are taken as 'traditional'. But the extent to which male labour vacates the countryside has considerably enlarged women's tasks in quantity and quality;
- most of the areas of residence of the different ethnic groups of Namibian society are not at all traditional; expropriation, displacement and geopolitical segregation speak a clear language; moreover, south of the Red Line, even the seemingly most traditional habitat is of purely colonial 'tradition';
- the political patterns of 'tribal' and communal self-administration were instituted and controlled by the colonial regime, subjected to their needs; the eminent role of the ward headman is a function of colonial rule instituting an intermediary between chieftaincy/nobility and villagers as a means of control; it does not in all cases correspond to the structures of the pre-colonial indigenous polity, which is rather based on the subordination of the lineage's self-administration (along the lines of generational and gender hierarchy) to the chief; the figure of the dominating ward headman is an additional administrative layer introduced by South African rulers;

- the ethical basis of indigenous cultures has been radically altered by the evangelical efforts of the Christian churches; the partial transition from polygamy to monogamy is but one example for this process; nevertheless, it is this already deeply transformed culture which is referred to as the 'traditional' one.

It is not pre-colonial culture to which one refers; in reality, it is the ancestors' culture, as it is known to the individual by oral tradition, by his/her experience of rural life or by the relation with kin. Who really knows about the pre-colonial culture of the ethnic group he/she belongs to? Oral tradition, as just mentioned, bases itself on the experience of colonial cultures as transmitted by the older generations. And: written tradition, that is the other side of the coin, has been developed by colonial or Western historians and anthropologists.

Again, these deliberations are not an academic digression. Looking at the effects of a given phenomenon implies addressing social change, analysing transformation. Logically, this presupposes the notion of a transition from – to, from a former to a new state of affairs. As it seems, commonly such a transition is wrongly interpreted as effecting change from 'tradition' to 'modernity.' Although this view is widespread, and as such it undoubtedly represents social reality, it has in sociological terms to be criticised and revised. If we should at all think along the lines of a contrast between the 'traditional' and the 'modern', this should be based on the comparison of pre-colonial social formations and colonial society.

Connecting the above to the issue of social development may make the argument clearer: it is not by dismissing tradition or traditional attitudes and resorting to modern paradigms in economic planning and activity, in social and cultural life, that development can be achieved. This is simply accepting the Western path of development as a value – and the blame for the existing lack of development. At the same time, if the idea of African Renaissance is to be more than an ideology of 'modern' African political élites of bourgeois class stamp, it has to pick up the thread of pre-colonial culture and social life, and not of its colonial distortions. It is by analysing the historical process of transformation that we learn that colonialism has created a society which actually is trapped in the contradiction between tradition and modernity. This trap is a product of colonial exploitation and transformation. The colonial impact has called a halt to autonomous development. It has imposed new class structures. It has created a specific contradictory economic structure which is subject to external, imperialist needs, be it of the colonial master's economy or the global market. It actually prevents us from overcoming all that is associated with tradition: the persistence of a subsistence economy, the extreme reliance on agriculture and natural resources, the inability to set up an industry processing the available natural and human power resources, the restricted commodification of production and labour, and at the same time the dominance of the capitalist sector of the economy based on the exploitation of the labour force, and cultural attitudes binding individuals to class and gender structures of subordination.

Social development, we conclude, is not achieved by overcoming tradition and by modernising, but by dealing with the social contradictions brought by colonialism. Class structures based on the exploitation of labour do not disappear with independence. They shape economic and social policies of inequality which counteract efforts for social development.

Bibliography

Coquery-Vidrovitch, *Catherine* 1976. The political economy of the African peasantry and modes of production. In: Gutkind, Peter CW / Wallerstein, Immanuel (eds.). The political economy of contemporary Africa, pp.90-111. Beverly Hills / London

Giddens, *Anthony* 1999. Tradition (lecture no.3 of the BBC-Reith Lecture Series. Website: http://www.lse.ac.uk/Giddens/reith_99/week3/week3.htm

Hinz, *Manfred O* [4] 1998. Customary law in Namibia – development and perspective. CASS paper no.41. Windhoek

Keulder, Christiaan 1997. Traditional authorities and regional councils in Southern Namibia. Windhoek

Meillassoux, *Claude* 1960. Essai d'interprétation du phénomène économique dans les sociétés traditionelles d'autosubsistence. In: Cahiers d'Etudes Africaines, no.4, pp.38-67

Meillassoux, *Claude* 1981. Maidens, meal, and money – capitalism and the domestic community. Cambridge / New York

Peltola, *Pekka* 1995. The lost May Day – Namibian workers struggle for independence. Jyväskylä

Tötemeyer, Gerhard 1978. Namibia old and new – traditional and modern leaders in Ovamboland. London

Williams, *Frieda-Nela* 1991. Precolonial communities of southwestern Africa – a history of Ovambo kingdoms 1600-1920. Windhoek

'EDUCATION FOR ALL' IN INDEPENDENT NAMIBIA – REALITY OR POLITICAL IDEAL?

Elizabeth Magano Amukugo

Introduction

In all countries of the world, governments undertake periodic reviews to change, revamp, adopt and revitalise educational programmes so that they are able to achieve their intended goals effectively.

Education in Namibia has undergone reform during various historical epochs from colonial times to the post-colonial period. These educational development phases were, as Amukugo (1995:1) observed, "accompanied by a general pattern of political and socio-economic changes in the Namibian society; each phase in the development of education therefore seems to have corresponded to a new political and socio-economic reality".

During the pre-apartheid period until 1962, education reform programmes were partially intended to bring missionary education curricula in line with the colonial policy of divide and rule and to create a cheap labour pool for settlers and colonialists. In apartheid[1] Namibia (1962-1976), education served not only the purpose of reproducing cheap African labour power; it also served to legitimise the colonial social order as natural and given, through a conscious distortion of historical facts. During what Amukugo (1995:72) called the "false de-colonisation period" (1977-1987), educational reform programmes served to conceal the 'reproduction'[2] function of education. In addition, the system helped to create an African middle class to serve as intermediaries between the colonial state and the African working class. In independent Namibia (1990 – present), educational reforms were aimed at addressing disparities within the educational system that resulted from decades of colonial rule. The new government hence adopted a policy of 'Education for All', which outlines four major goals: access, equity, quality and democracy.

Namibia's educational reform programme is seen by many as having yielded good results in the post-independence era. Six years after independence, more than 90% of school age children were enrolled in school. Moreover, grade 12 enrolment quadrupled between 1990 and 1996 (UNDP 1997:4). These figures, it is claimed, testify to the fact that government efforts towards implementing the policy of 'Education for All' have been successful, and that equity within the edu-

---

[1] In the literal sense, apartheid means separate development for the black and Coloured ethnic groups and the white minority. In our view, however, apartheid served as a colonial state ideology that aimed at justifying the socio-economic inequalities created by the colonial capitalist mode of production.

[2] Reproduction in education as per 'reproduction theory' (Amukugo 1995), suggests that education fulfils a definite function in the reproduction of society through reproducing labour power.

cational sphere is being achieved. In this study, the validity of this argument will be questioned.

The policy of 'Education for All' in Namibia[3], while recognising the continental and global context of the concept, attempts to bring it in line with the Namibian reality. The aim is to provide equitable access to schooling, to improve efficiency and quality, and to facilitate the democratic participation of civil society in the educational policy making process (ibid.:32-44).

It is furthermore meant to provide a broad framework for educational reform in Namibia. The policy document is widely used by educational policy makers, school administrators and educationalists.

It is our submission that there are many social factors which militate against the realisation of these educational goals. What goes on within the educational sphere cannot be treated in isolation from the socio-economic reality of any given society. Interpreting equity in terms of school enrolment rates can be misleading. It can, in fact, obscure inequalities within the educational system, as enrolling in school does not guarantee staying beyond four years (literacy cut-off point) or completing the basic (grades 1-10).

Earlier research (Amukugo 1995:214-216) has suggested that it will take years and perhaps generations before substantive changes in terms of improved public schooling can take place. Government educational reform policy, it is held, could lead to the perpetuation of inequalities and class differences in an independent Namibia. The question is: has the situation changed since the implementation of 'Education for All' during the first ten years of independence?

Colonial Namibia's economic set up was essentially capitalist. The capitalist mode of production was hegemonic and gave its overall characteristic to the economy. It is this economic structure that the current Namibian government inherited at independence in 1990. Ironically, the new government, whilst critical of the fact that the ownership of productive assets is in the hands of a small minority as a result of apartheid policy (National Planning Commission, NDP1 1996:24), chose to retain the same capitalist economic system after independence. It is not by chance that Namibia ranks among the most unequal societies in the world. Hence, the richest 10% of the society receives 65% of the income while the rest (90%) share the remaining 35% amongst themselves (UNDP 1999:25).

Democracy and education: a theoretical framework

Perspectives on democracy
The concept of democracy, which dominated African academic and political debates during the 1960s and 1970s, is not easily defined. In fact there does not appear to be a consensus on what democracy entails (Sachikonye 1995; Oyugi & Gitonga 1995).

---

[3] Toward Education for All – a development brief for education, culture and training. Namibia, Ministry of Education and Culture 1993

Conceptually, African theoretical debate on democracy has centred around three major perspectives: the static, the liberal and the popular or progressive perspective (Sjivji 1991; Sachikonye 1995).

The basic characteristic of liberal democracy has been summarised by Amukugo (1998) as follows:

> It subscribes to political pluralism. In accordance with this attribute, all members of society have an equal right to choose political parties and leaders of their choice, to represent their interests at the political, legislative (parliament) and government (executive) levels. Both the participation in politics and the selection of office bearers is to be done in accordance with rules set by the constitution. The judiciary is to adhere to the rules set by the legislators. The ultimate goal in this liberal/constitutional democracy, is to achieve and uphold an equilibrium (i.e. peace and harmony within society) without necessarily achieving equality within the economic sphere, since it is a democratic right to be rich or poor". In: SAPEM 1998, vol.11, no.6, p.11)

Liberal democracy can also be described as a conception of democracy, which results from, as well as reflects, the political requirements of a market economy. It serves to legitimise socio-economic and political order in a capitalist society. According to the Progressive Democracy school of thought, democracy can be regarded as an important scale through which the socio-economic well-being of a given society can be measured. This understanding of democracy pre-supposes that social inequalities are radically reduced through a fair redistribution of power and resources within society. In the African context, this radical conception of democracy is seen by many as providing an alternative to the Western inspired liberal democratic view.

In general, therefore, progressive democracy suggests a radical move from democracy in name and appearance only to a substantive form of democracy.

Democracy and education

Education does not function outside the socio-economic, political and ideological structures of society. In the post-colonial Namibian context, 'democracy' as an educational goal aims to teach learners how democratic societies operate and the obligations and rights of citizens." It suggests further the need for learners to understand that democracy means more than voting, and that poverty (malnutrition, economic inequality and illiteracy) can be an obstacle to democracy (Ministry of Education and Culture 1993, Toward Education for All, pp.41-42).

The philosophy behind goals of democracy, access, equity and quality in Namibian education expresses a radical metaphysical viewpoint. If implemented, it could bear a healthy relationship between democracy and education. In view of the interface between education and social reality, however, only an analysis of concrete educational practice can reveal the true meaning behind an educational ideal. In other words, the democratic nature of Namibia's education will be determined, in part, by its educational practice.

'Education For All' in Namibia

Namibia gained its independence 42 years after the Universal Declaration of Human Rights in 1948, which emphasised the right of everyone to education. The concept of 'Education for All' was therefore already on the global agenda. In 1990, a World Declaration on Education for All was adopted by the World Conference on Education for All, in Jomtien 1990.

The right of all citizens to education became part of independent Namibia's constitution. The policy of 'Education for All' was therefore partially meant to meet the constitutional requirement of providing free and compulsory schooling for primary school learners. In concrete terms, government set out, first and foremost, to establish a unified educational system by merging eleven ethnic/racially based administration authorities (Bantustan governments)[4] into one single Ministry of Education and Culture. The relevant policy document, 'Toward Education for All' was based on four major goals: access, equity, quality and democracy.

By access is meant that government would commit itself to providing universal basic education, and to ensure that the majority of Namibians would have acquired primary education (grades 1-7) by the year 2000. Through equity, government is to reduce inequalities of the colonial era by means of affirmative action; constructing an equitable educational system through providing enough schools and classroom; minimising differences in school facilities and equipment and in teacher's level of preparation; and by providing a more equitable allocation of resources. Quality in education is to be achieved through providing good schools; ensuring that teachers are sufficiently prepared for their tasks; moving from examination-centred education to developing skilled learners, as well as developing an integrated curriculum. Democracy is to be achieved by developing a democratic education.

A closer look at the four major goals of education as elucidated in 'Toward Education for All', is clearly biased towards primary and secondary education. Whilst teacher education is mentioned in passing and/or as a necessary component for primary and secondary education, higher education is conspicuously absent.

Since Namibia came from the philosophical tradition of 'apartheid' education, it would have been necessary to define the goals of education broadly so as to include higher education. Its absence is indicative of the place it occupies (or not) on the priority list of the Namibian government.

Implementing 'Education for All': some empirical evidence

A comparative analysis of the present educational situation in six out of thirteen

---

[4] The apartheid colonial government has restricted Africans to Bantu homelands. In 1977, a second tier government consisting of 11 Bantustan governments was established in order to administer African Affairs. Within this framework, each Bantustan government became responsible for the provision and financing of education for its ethnic/racial group within the Bantu homeland boundaries. The education of the whites and that of urban Africans (minority blacks), was administered and financed by the central government. But, lack of resources in the Bantustan homelands had a negative impact on the provision and quality of education for Africans (Amukugo 1995).

regions could help us in assessing the success or failure of 'Education for All' in independent Namibia. This analysis, along with the level of literacy would serve as an indicator of inequalities within the educational system and by consequence, within society.

Literacy levels of a people normally give an indication of the extent of their poverty. It is worth mentioning that the illiteracy level of Kunene, Ohangwena and Kavango (disadvantaged regions) is 55%, 48% and 44% respectively. In comparison with Khomas, Erongo and Karas (advantaged regions), theirs is only 12%, 19% and 17% respectively. The national average illiteracy rate for Namibia is 32% (UNDP 1997:12). This means that the poorest regions in Namibia have an illiteracy rate far higher than the national level.

A look at the repetition and dropout rates and the formal qualifications of teachers in the above-mentioned regions indicates the quality of education offered to the different regions. It also reveals the extent of inequalities with regard to education provision across the country. Evidence from statistical data for the years 1992-1998 published by the Ministry of Basic Education and Culture suggest that some progress has been made towards reducing the gap between less and more affluent regions. However, the three 'disadvantaged' regions have done worse than the 'advantaged' ones, with the former having repetition rates above the national figure and the latter below the national level.

A reduction in repetition rate would normally mean an improvement in the educational system. In the Namibian context, however, the dramatic reduction in repetition rates after 1995 could be attributed to the introduction of the automatic promotion policy. It allows pupils to move on to the next grade irrespective of examination results. The reduction has been more dramatic in disadvantaged regions, indicating a previously higher repetition rate in these regions owing to poor socio-economic conditions. Reducing the repetition rates through automatic promotion does not really improve the education situation in disadvantaged regions. It merely pushes the problem under the carpet, rather than resolving it.

The dropout rates during the period 1992-1997 indicate that far more students in disadvantaged regions leave school (in grade 1-10), than their counterparts in advantaged regions. The grade 10 dropout rates for Ohangwena and Kavango increased and reached the alarming levels of 60% and 44% respectively in 1997, as compared to 28% and 17% respectively in 1992. The corresponding figures for Erongo and Khomas in 1997 are 21% and 10% respectively, as compared to 22% and 15% in 1992. On the whole, the dropout rate for all grades in disadvantaged regions was consistently above the national level during the entire period. It can be attributed to the poor socio-economic conditions. Rural pupils in grade 10 are considered old enough to join the labour market. Consequently, many leave school in search for work and in order to contribute to their families' subsistence. In this respect, government's intention with regard to making basic education (up to grade 10) more accessible and equitable comes into conflict with the socio-economic reality.

Statistical data from the Ministry also suggest that by 1997, 65% of teachers in Kavango did not have grade 12 education, as compared to 88% in 1992. This gives us a 23% improvement during a five-year period. Ohangwena improved from 77% to 33%, a 44% improvement during the same period. Teachers with more than two years of tertiary education remained at the disgraceful levels of 2% and 1% for Ohangwena and Kavango respectively. In comparison, teachers with grade 12 qualifications have been persistently below 40% in Erongo between 1992/1997. In Khomas, figures have dwindled from 55% in 1992 to only 19,4% in 1997. In terms of teachers with more than two years of tertiary education, Erongo and Khomas can boast of 20% and 39% respectively as compared to 2,3% and 1,3% for Ohangwena and Kavango respectively.

It is evident that the quality of primary and secondary school education depends on the quality of its teachers. The fact that there are few qualified teachers in disadvantaged regions has, by consequence, a negative effect on the quality of education. On the whole, the evidence suggests that advantaged regions have a greater number of better-qualified teachers, and lower dropout and repetition rates at all levels. These disparities indicate that regional equity within the educational system has not been substantive. It also shows a tendency towards unequal distribution of resources, both material and human, which is undemocratic.

The findings of "A situational analysis of education in the Kunene region" conducted by Amukugo in 1998 reflect an educational reality in the Kunene region. Seven secondary schools visited had no electricity; books were insufficient; schools lacked science laboratories despite science subjects being taught. Most teachers were not adequately prepared to implement the International General Certificate of Secondary Education (IGCSE). Other disadvantaged regions are not any different in this respect.

The empirical evidence lays bare the limits of educational reform. Problems in education cannot be effectively resolved in isolation from the broader socio-economic issues.

Higher education and democratisation

Students who enrol in higher education are a product of secondary education. Therefore, a review of primary and secondary education alone would give an incomplete picture of the state of education in the country. A look at the state of tertiary education is hence called for. Higher education does not only create new knowledge through research and produce graduates, but also provides a practical service to the school system, the wider community, and plays an active role in policy development. This view is in line with the University's Mission Statement (University of Namibia, Annual Report 1999:4)

At independence in 1990, Namibia did not have a university. Instead, a sub-standard institution of higher learning, the *Academy for Tertiary Education*, established in 1980, served the purpose of a university. The Academy comprised of a university component, a technicon and an out of school learning section.

Like other sectors of education, the development of higher education in Namibia was negatively affected by the colonial past and needed urgent attention in terms of both institutional and content reform. The Presidential Commission on Higher Education in 1991 recommended that the Academy be abolished and replaced by two legally autonomous institutions: the national University of Namibia and the Polytechnic of Namibia (Namibia, Report of a Presidential Commission 1991:229). The Commission, whilst acknowledging that both the University and the Polytechnic are senior institutions of higher learning (ibid.:165), recommended that, in the interim, the University become "the senior institution in the higher education, the only one empowered to award degrees". The Polytechnic was to play a major role in the advancement of sub-professional education and training for the whole country" (ibid.:5) by offering diplomas. Holders of these diplomas could then apply for admission to part 2 of a 'BTech' degree at the University of Namibia (ibid.:166).

In line with the Commission proposal, the University of Namibia was founded in 1992, in terms of the University Act No.18 of 1992. The Polytechnic of Namibia was established in 1994, in terms of the National Vocational Training Act of 1994.

We shall next attempt to review the role of higher education in effecting the Education for All Agenda.

The University of Namibia
According to the University of Namibia's first Five-year Development Plan (1995-1999:3), the Academy's enrolment figures of 1989 (a year before independence) concealed "gross imbalances with respect to geographical origin, ethnic groups, and in some fields, also (gender imbalances)". This required change.

The type of education offered by the University is reflected by the kind of Faculties of which the institution is comprised. The University's Academic wing currently has seven Faculties, as opposed to five during the Academy days, and two major centres. The University has retained five of the original Faculties (Economics and Management Science, Education, Humanities and Social Science, Nursing and Health Science and the Faculty of Science). It has, however, added on two Faculties and one Centre (Agriculture and Natural Science, Law, and the Multidisciplinary Research Centre), that are crucial to the socio-economic development of Namibia. All of the curricula indicate an attempt to meet the human resource needs of the country. While the University retained similar faculties as the Academy, its curriculum content was revised in an attempt to bring the educational content in line with changing socio-economic development.

It is possible to assess whether the university education has contributed to implementing the goals of access and equity in education, by studying the enrolment figures. Statistical data (University of Namibia, Office of the Registrar 2001), indicate that the total enrolment has changed very little over the years. That is, from 3 794 (in 1992) to only 4 269 (in 1999). This gives an increase of only 475 (11%) in eight years. For a country that gained its independence only ten years ago, the enrolment figures are far from meeting the required human resources needed for socio-economic development.

There could be several factors contributing to the stagnating enrolment rates at the University.

- Higher admission requirements (which is justifiable) mean that most grade 12 leavers from disadvantaged regions cannot gain entry to the University. As such, admission requirements – perhaps unconsciously – serve as a sorting instrument: a real dilemma.
- Automatic promotion in Namibian schools leads to students proceeding to senior secondary level without being truly prepared. Consequently, few learners from disadvantaged regions would qualify to enter higher education institutions. In other words, the secondary education system does not adequately feed the next level – higher education.
- The University does not receive adequate funding from government and/or the private sector, as observed in the Mawditt Report (2000). In fact, the student financial assistance from government decreased between 1993 and 1999. Thus, while 44% of full-time students at UNAM received bursaries in 1993, only 38% received bursaries in 1999. The corresponding figure for the first year students was 24% in 1993 and a mere 14% in 1997 (University of Namibia, Office of the Registrar 2001). The decrease in student financial assistance from government means that fewer students gain access to higher education.

It is equally interesting to see what areas of study UNAM students choose. According to the Office of the Registrar (2001), 2 868 full-time students were registered at UNAM during 1999. Of these, 26,5% were in Economics and Management Sciences, 23,7% in Education, 14,6% in Humanities and Social Sciences, 13,4% in Medical and Health, 12,9% in Science, 4,9% in Agriculture and Natural Resources and 3,7% in Law. These figures suggest that the majority of students choose Economics and Management Sciences followed by Education. Science, which the Namibian government sees as one of its top priorities, takes just a fifth place on the students' priority list. The number of students studying science has, however, more than tripled from only 105 in 1992 to 371 in 1999.

It can be concluded that the university is failing on both equity and access criteria as a result of both internal and external factors. Moreover, stagnating enrolment figures reflects the socio-economic inequities within society.

The Polytechnic of Namibia

The Technicon section of the Academy offered courses at both National Certificate (grade 10) entry level and National Diploma (grade 12) entry level. The Technicon was generally equipped with good facilities and a professional staff. Access to formal apprenticeship, however, was generally reserved for the white youth, who also had the opportunity to study at South African technicons (Presidential Commission on Higher Education:142, 147). The Academy's (Technicon's)

course content included: management and administration (business, personnel and public), commerce, cost accounting and secretarial, as well as nature conservation (ibid.:147), since these areas of study corresponded to the areas of employment traditionally reserved for whites in colonial Namibia.
- The Polytechnic only has four schools (Faculties), namely:
- School of Business and Management;
- School of Communication, Legal and Secretarial Studies;
- School of Engineering and Information Technology; and
- School of Natural Resources and Tourism (Polytechnic of Namibia, Annual Report 1999:6).

The new institution offers a much broader variety of courses, which are relevant to Namibia's labour market. There is also a clear shift in emphasis, as far as course content is concerned. The Polytechnic's Annual Report of 1999 shows that most students take commerce and management courses (73,4%). A mere 9% takes engineering and related subjects. The number of students studying the natural science fields at the Polytechnic shows a trend similar to that at the University. The student's low participation in the natural sciences studies may be a reflection of poor performance in mathematics, chemistry and physics in secondary schools countrywide, as reflected in hitherto annual IGCSE and (H)IGCSE) results. It indicates a failure to do away with colonial legacy, when the majority was denied access to these subject areas.

Financing higher education
The Mission statements of both UNAM and the Polytechnic envisage their terms of reference within the scope of Namibia's socio-economic development. In addition to adequately trained human resources, this requires sufficient financial resources. UNAM's Annual Report (1999:43) reflected an alarming deficit of N$26,6 million in 1999 as compared to a deficit of N$7,2 million two years earlier, in 1997. In contrast with UNAM's 1999 huge budget deficit, the Polytechnic boasts a N$1,3 million surplus. It is encouraging to see the Ministry taking more interest in higher education finances of late, as expressed in the commissioning of a feasibility study. The consultant (i.e. Mawditt) was specifically tasked to look into the resource allocation for higher education. Mawditt's conclusion suggests that the University of Namibia has been underfunded in relation to its role and place within the Namibian society.

The same report also concluded that the Polytechnic is in its infancy (but) has made a marked entry into the higher education arena". It needs technical support at all levels" (ibid.:52). For the two institutions to implement their missions therefore, output-based funding is necessary. Government's overemphasis on basic education to the detriment of higher education has led to the current inadequate funding of (especially) the University, and needs to be reviewed.

Gender and education in independent Namibia

Simone de Beauvoir (1988:9) once observed that:

> "since patriarchal times women have in general been forced to occupy a secondary place in the world in relation to men (...) and further that this secondary standing is not imposed of necessity by natural 'feminine' characteristics but rather by strong environmental forces of educational and social tradition under the purposeful control of men".

De Beauvoir points to multiple factors that lead to gender inequalities within society. Apart from education, cultural, social and economic factors are all causal. Namibia, as part of the global village, is not exempted from this complex process.

Namibia's total population is 1,8 million, the number of women slightly exceeding that of men. However, women in Namibia have historically been and still are more exposed to poorer socio-economic conditions than men. A question can be asked as to why this is the case.

Our point of departure is an understanding that women in Namibia are by no means a homogenous group with similar or identical problems, having historically been divided along class, racial, gender and ethnic lines which results in these various factors contributing, collectively or individually, to the oppression of women" (Amukugo 1993. Advancement of women in Namibia – a critique).

Education and gender division of labour in the Namibian society

A gender-biased division of labour is a reflection of gender inequalities within society. Education plays a role in this process by providing skills necessary for the labour market, as well as by inculcating sociocultural norms. Formal education, as one of society's agents of socialisation[5] is a process through which a human being learns to understand his/her environment (the world around him/her). It helps develop the individual's spontaneous consciousness as well as awaken or develop her/his critical consciousness. It is through the socialisation process that gender roles and stereotypes are transmitted from one generation to another. These stereotypes and a gender role-based division of labour are mainly responsible for the persistence of gender inequalities within a society.

Referring to the situation of gender division of labour in southern Africa, Meena (1992:12) clearly observed:

> "There is substantial evidence documenting the existing unequal division of labour between sexes in (the southern African region). Women constitute a majority of the agricultural labour force, while occupying the lowest positions in the formal sector as either semi-skilled or unskilled employees. At household level, they perform most of the domestic or what is known

---

[5] Socialisation is the transmission of the ongoing meanings of various subcultures that makes up an entire society (Levitas 1974). Thus, an individual or social classes acquire culture (consciousness, values, intentions, as well as the capacity to choose between good and bad), through a life-long process of socialisation. Education, as one of society's agent of socialisation, is a process through which a human being learns to understand his/her environment (the world around him/her). It helps develop the individual's spontaneous consciousness as well as awaken or develop his/her critical consciousness. It is through the process of socialisation that gender roles and stereotypes are transmitted from one generation to another.

as reproductive tasks (...) studies also indicate that while women carry a heavier load in production, they do not enjoy similar rights in terms of access to resources, which include land, credit, and they do not enjoy similar rights in decision-making".

Mbilinyi 1990 (in: Meena 1992:15) links education and unequal division of labour. These views have been confirmed by a more recent publication (SARDC 2000), which speaks volumes about discrimination against women in southern Africa, based on practices and prejudices about the 'place of women' in society, and about the absence of women in major – decision-making roles in the economic, political and public life in general.

Namibia's social reality testifies to the role that the educational system plays in the creation of a gender-segregated labour force. Education does not always determine women's access to position of influence. Thus, although statistical evidence (Amukugo 2000) shows that compared with men more Namibian women and girls enrol at all levels of education, from primary to higher education, through adult and literacy programmes, it is also evident that the high participation of women in education has so far not been commensurate with the positions offered to women within the Namibian labour market. Employment, training and promotion of women (by men who dominate the decision-making processes) do not always take into account the abilities of women and their potential contribution (Amukugo 1993). Women are often employed far below their level of competence, many a time under the supervision of men who ought to be their juniors. Statistical evidence from the Office of the Prime Minister[6] suggests that decision-making positions in political, legislative, and business administrations as well as in the economy are dominated by men.

Conclusion: can 'Education for All' help to eradicate inequalities within society?

The policy of 'Education for All' is confronted with the educational problems and practices inherent of Namibian society within which the education system functions.

In our view, the basic aim of education is first and foremost to develop the human being's capacity to gain a correct reflection of reality in thought, and to use that realisation in improving his/her environment. This conception of education emphasises the important connection that exists between ideas and concrete objective reality, and runs counter to the idealist notion of education, with its one-sided emphasis on the human being's mental capacity. The current educational concept is based on the idealist metaphysical viewpoint of liberal democracy, however, which stresses the importance of ideas above the objective world around us.

Secondly, educational issues are treated in isolation from the socio-economic context. Moreover, facts about educational issues are presented in a fragmented

---

[6] GRN Department of Women Affairs 1999:63

manner rather than being part of the whole. By so doing, reality is obscured and a false image created in the minds of the people. As an example, all children in Namibia are free to attend a school of their choice. In reality, however, parents' financial position determine that choice.

Thirdly, the idea of 'Education for All' serves as an ideological tool of the state, by means of which basic liberal democratic principles of individual freedom, equity, equal opportunity and democracy are put across in the most abstract sense, without relating those to concrete reality. The aim is to create and uphold peace and harmony within society, without concrete commitment to the socio-economic realisation of those ideals.

Our analysis suggests that our educational policy fails to bring about substantial changes. Regional equality with regard to reducing the repetition rates, dropout rates and in terms of a fair distribution of qualified teachers across regions, is far from being achieved – at least, the achievements so far are not commensurate with the resources and time committed to the education sector. From the point of view of equity, disadvantaged regions are still struggling with the problems of inadequate facilities and educational equipment. In terms of quality they have to make do with a large number of ill-prepared and unqualified teachers, which militates against the successful implementation of a student-centred approach to teaching and learning. With regard to access, we can hardly talk about a just provision of basic education given high repetition and dropout rates in disadvantaged rural regions where the majority of the population lives.

Access to higher education is equally a problem. The poor socio-economic conditions under which the majority of the people lives, and the unequal distribution of material and human resources in schools nationally, have led to the incapacity of secondary education system to feed higher education with adequately prepared learners. In 2000, for example, only 3 000 out of 11 000 secondary school leavers qualified to enter the University and the Polytechnic. There is also an urgent need to draw a clear line of demarcation between the distinct roles and place of both the University and the Polytechnic. Given Namibia's shortage of resources it makes sense for the University to retain its status as the country's only University, offering degrees and carrying out research. For the time being, the Polytechnic should concentrate on being a technical- and career-oriented institution, offering diploma courses and reaching out to all technical institutions countrywide.

It can also be concluded that the education of women matters a great deal not only in terms of preparing them for future employment, but more importantly, in terms of developing their critical consciousness of themselves, their environment and their society. Despite women's high level of participation in education, however, the education system's role in creating a gender-segregated labour force and its function in reproducing a gender-biased ideology in society, contributes to channelling women into service-oriented positions and low-paid jobs within the labour market. Moreover, and more importantly, it does not substantially improve the circumstances of the majority of women surviving outside the formal labour market, in subsistence economy.

It goes without saying therefore that as long as liberal democracy continues to be the basis upon which 'Education for All' rests, and as long as the economic base remains unchanged, real access, equity, quality and democracy within the educational sphere will not be achieved. 'Education for All' will then remain a political ideal in conflict with the socio-economic reality.

Bibliography

Amukugo, EM 1993., Advancement of women in Namibia – a critique. Paper presented at a Seminar on Women and democracy in Namibia. Namibia Institute for Democracy. Windhoek

Amukugo, EM 1995. Education and politics in Namibia. Past trends and future prospects. Windhoek: Gamsberg Macmillan

Amukugo, EM 1998. Can liberal democracy deliver equity in education? In: Southern African Political and Economic Monthly (SAPEM), vol.11 no.6, pp.11-14. Harare

Amukugo, EM 1998. A situation analysis of education in the Kunene Region. Report prepared for the UNAM Epupa Project Research Team. University of Namibia. Windhoek

Amukugo, EM 2000. Women and education in independent Namibia. In: Journal of Practice in Education for Development, vol.5 no.2, pp.51-58.

De Beauvoir, S 1988. The second sex. London: Pan Books

Lakin, E 1996. The eternal agenda. In: UNESCO. Education for All 2000 – six years of Education for All, July – September 1996, no.24. Paris

Mawditt, R 2000. Resource allocation for higher education institutions from the funds of the Republic of Namibia: the feasibility of a formula based process ("Mawditt Report"). Ministry of Higher Education and Employment Creation: Windhoek

Meena, R 1982. Gender in southern Africa: concepts and theoretical issues. Harare: SAPES

Government of the Republic of Namibia 2000. Education in perspective – Namibia's first decade. Ministry of Higher Education, Vocational Training, Science and Technology. Windhoek

Government of the Republic of Namibia 1993. Toward Education for All: a development brief for education, culture, and training. Ministry of Basic Education and Culture. Windhoek: Gamsberg Macmillan

Government of the Republic of Namibia 1992, 1993, 1994, 1995, 1996, 1997, 1998. Education statistics. Ministry of Basic Education and Culture. Windhoek

Government of Namibia 1996. First national development plan, vols. 1 and 2. National Planning Commission: Windhoek

Oyugi, WO / Gitonga, A (eds.) 1995. Democratic theory and practice. Nairobi: East African Educational Publishers

Polytechnic of Namibia 1998. Annual report. Windhoek

Sachikonye, L (ed.) 1995. Democracy, civil society and the state. Southern African Political and Economic Series (SAPES Trust). Harare

SARDC 2001. Beyond Inequalities – women in southern Africa. Harare

Shivji, I (ed.) 1991. State and constitutionalism: an African debate on democracy. Southern African Political Economy Series (SAPES Trust) Harare

University of Namibia 1991, 1999. Annual report. Windhoek

University of Namibia 1995. First five year development plan 1995-1999. Windhoek

University of Namibia 2001. Statistical data (unpublished). Office of the UNAM Registrar. Windhoek

UNDP 1997, 1999. Namibia human development report. Windhoek

CONSTRUCTING CULTURAL IDENTITIES IN CONTEMPORARY MUSICAL TRADITIONS – STRATEGIES OF SURVIVAL AND CHANGE

Minette Mans

Discourse on the vitality of Namibian societies as cultures is scarce[1]. Terms such as 'society' and 'culture' are so loaded with preconceived ideas that initiating discourse is difficult. Nevertheless, this chapter attempts to describe culture, society, tradition and identity from the author's point of reference, and then constructs several generalised deductions regarding cultural strategies in Namibia[2]. The ways in which people deal with changes in their environment (whether within or beyond their control) are under discussion. This implies that social and cultural forms are generated and sustained through the strategies of individuals and individual groups. I will not go into detailed discussion but will restrict myself to general cross-cultural comparison within Namibia.

Background

According to archaeological and historical evidence, the Namibian region has witnessed several migrations of groups of people moving from one area to another over the past few centuries. Groups interacted with others peacefully or through conflict, through integration or separation. These interactions resulted in cultural changes even in the distant past. During the 19th century colonial adventurers, missionaries and settlers arrived, and in the 20th century the apartheid system brought its own peculiar demographic changes and social systems. Presently we experience the profound effects of the worldwide media and the travel industry on economic, political and cultural practices within the region.

Namibia is striving towards economic and social development as a nation-state. While it would appear obvious that the aim of development is to help people, there is a tendency to see human or social development as 'soft-core', implying that social ills will be eradicated automatically through economic and technological development. The neglect of cultural development issues could have a negative impact. It is "the cultural perspective (that) gives hope of humanising development policies to go beyond mere economic growth towards a more equitable, sustainable development of *societies*" (my italics, Arizpe in Kirdar 1992:117). Development programmes that fail to take cultural values into consideration could result in unpredictable changes to social structures and cultural production systems (e.g. agriculture). The effects of uninformed development plans will only become apparent in time. In most social and political arenas cul-

---

[1] By discourse I refer to "all forms of spoken interaction, formal and informal, and written texts of all kinds" (Potter and Wetherell 1992:7).
[2] The data rely on the author's ongoing research and several field trips between 1993 and 2000.

tural insight is of great importance. Often the success of national and international interactions amongst groups of people is dependent on cultural perceptions, preconceptions and misconceptions. Within the context of understanding social movements the use of music, as one cultural form, is only beginning to receive attention. I approach this matter beginning with my use of the terms culture, tradition and cultural identity.

Culture and society

As this chapter will look specifically at culture and the social milieu in which Namibians operate, it is important to note that culture and society, while inextricably linked, are not identical. Society refers to an aggregate of individuals; culture refers to their common attributes. Society may contain many cultures, yet culture can reach across more than one society. One can say that culture develops out of a group's ways of surviving in their particular time, environment and circumstances. Cultural practices therefore grow in a very basic way out of having to deal with the demands of an environment and work, developing social behaviours and spiritual beliefs to guide them. As constantly changing systems of production, values and beliefs, cultures are determined by many factors including history, systems of meaning, structures of power, politics and economics, but also by individual and group choices. Within societies, the cultural processes, categories, knowledge and feelings have over time become organised into systems that include ideological (beliefs), attitudinal (attitudes towards sex, for example, or fear of spiders), sociological (rules, laws, values, customs, institutions) and technological (material, production, protection) components. In Namibia, the institutions and laws of the dominant (ruling) culture have been used to subjugate other cultures in subtle and not so subtle ways. Apart from constructing cultural 'otherness' between cultural groups, one also finds that culture can therefore be used as an instrument of domination within a group, shaping social relationships in terms of class, generation or gender.

Culture is an abstract system constructed by a group of people, and it undergoes changes and adjustments. Seen within the broad perspective of social, economic and political relations, culture is a dimension that comprises the underlying codes of behaviour, values, and systems of knowledge of societies. The culture of a society motivates certain forms of behaviour; it provides criteria for evaluation; it forms a basis for social stratification in terms of class, rank, and status; it functions as a system of production and consumption, and an important mode of communication.

Because culture is an abstract entity it only becomes observable through its traditions of music and dance, art and artefacts, dress, language, daily functions, production systems, and the articulation of mythology, belief and value systems. Culture is therefore embedded in the ways in which phenomena such as religion, ritual and tradition (all of which encompass arts, language, mythology, beliefs, and values) are produced. Performance (music, dance, stories, ritual) is both "a web of meaning to be read from its surrounding context and (...) a form of communicative praxis in which meaning is always emergent, relational" (Erlmann 1996:16). These phenomena are layered through periods of time, thus reflecting aspects of history in the present day.

Tradition

The term tradition is often used in relation to culture and requires close scrutiny. Traditions reflect a measure of stability through time, creating group identities, also in music. However, traditions do undergo the changes that are inherent in all societies. Tradition is "a concept that combines the stable nature of a culture's way of life with the implication that by its very existence over long periods of time this way of life is subject to change" (Falck and Rice 1982:3). Because the term 'tradition' is sometimes interpreted as inflexible and unchanging, Coplan (1994:19) suggests that the term 'custom' has more value as a label for "organic, situationally flexible cultural practices". The term tradition cannot always be understood in terms of 'older', or relating to cultural roots. Moreover, certain aspects of what is claimed as tradition may have been deliberately invented in the service of political interests. There are numerous cases of 'traditional' dances or ceremonies that on closer inspection turn out to have been created consciously at a specific time or place for political reasons, for example certain forms of oudano that developed to express political resistance during the 1970s and 1980s. Certain forms of this play emanate from older rituals such as olufuko, but have been undergoing constant change for recreational as well as political reasons. Hence 'inventions' may eventually come to be seen as tradition through customary use.

While some traditions are seen as rituals having outlived their original use (such as initiation rituals), others may be so significant as to be almost sacred and to embody the identity of a community (such as n/om tzisi, the healing ritual of the Ju/'hoan people)[3]. It is in these significant forms that music and dance traditions become a way of life, a means by which a community knows itself, and recognises and expresses its relations to the most fundamental things, such as its origins, its language, its neighbours, and so on (Lees 1994:2, 3). In this way traditions link people (intellectually and emotionally) to their cultural roots and practices through the passage of time, conveying a sense of cultural history and identity.

Cultural identity

Cultural systems provide a basis for personal and group identity so that people 'belonging' to a particular cultural group tend to share aspects of cultural identity. Culture unifies and separates people within a group and between different groups by providing ways of identifying themselves and those who are 'others'. Within the

---

[3] See Olivier 1994, for more complete descriptions

setting of a group, the members' unification and separation follows hierarchical lines of gender, generational and social authority suggested by their specific culture. Members internalise norms, consciously or unconsciously, that relate to social hierarchies of power and inequality. Hence identity formation rests upon the drawing of boundaries between 'us' and 'them' in terms of various units such as association with family, gender, place of residence, economic position, employment, and ethnicity. This is replicated in many musical practices.

It is important to note that cultural identity structures how one experiences life. It determines how norms and values are taken up and how people behave as a result. But when one group interacts (through trade for example) with another group who differs culturally, certain individuals may identify with and assimilate certain 'other' practices into their own cultural identity, in this way changing their culture and that of the group. Thom (1996) describes cultural identity as something that "defines who we are, and how we are viewed by other people". In addition, cultural identity is a construction of how we define ourselves.

Unlike personal identity, cultural identity refers to the unit with which a person identifies. It is conceived in terms of a group and the feeling of belonging to a group or various groups. The term cultural identity may denote ethnic stereotypes to some, but the notion is that it signifies the ways in which people perceive and experience their own culture and those of others – forming and adapting their own cultural identities through selective assimilation or repudiation of aspects in the cultures of others. This implies an element of personal choice in the construction of an individual's cultural identity – identifying with something. An identity is based on the conscious and subconscious decision to identify with significant cultural components like hierarchic structures and values, and phenomena such as hairstyle, linguistic expressions and music. Similar to the reactions of certain groups of Ghanaian artists (Svašek 1997), individuals may consciously repudiate aspects of a specific, stereotyped cultural identity, for example certain Namibian musicians reject 'traditional African music' as their culture. By claiming freedom of expression and access to international markets and styles, they create their own cultural identities. Identities are therefore not an indication of timeless and static qualities but are rooted in complex histories, discourse and interpretations of inter-group relations. They are also influenced by access to education, employment, and other opportunities (Cooper 1998).

The means through which cultural identities are formed include immersion (enculturation), oral and written procedures, exposure to the media, and not least, educational and other institutions. Music and dance are ways in which these factors are concretised and made visible to others.

Different cultural Identities?

From the above we can deduce two statements important for this chapter:
- culture contains an element of stability that we often refer to as tradition or custom, and

- culture is always changing, having a dynamic quality that seeks new experiences and adapts to new situations.

In real life both static and dynamic qualities, to use Pirsig's (1991) terms, blend to create the peculiarities of a culture in a particular time and place. The question is, why and how do changes take place?

According to transactional theorists, "through the realisation of goals in the performance of specific behaviour (...) the ideas, and the manipulations of ideas, upon which the goals and behaviour are based, are reinforced and revalidated" (Riches 1979:8). Seen in the perspective of cultural change, certain events in societies lead to the realisation that new goals (or benefits) need to be planned and negotiated. An example of a new goal may be integration into another society, or a settlement in which two parties agree to differ but cooperate. In order to identify and meet such a goal, the society in question may employ strategies that ultimately change the cultural identity of those involved. I am going to discuss a few such strategies, but first, music as a very important index of culture needs closer inspection.

Music in society

Music is something people do and it is always informed by the social context or culture from which a person or group emerges[4]. Insofar as music making represents and is social action, we realise that music is a potent form of social expression. It is a medium through which history, ideology, religion, emotion, education, social class and expectations are expressed. It is both a personal and social system of knowledge and meaning and involves the reciprocal influence of the individual and his/her social context. Hence the individual is influenced by the social context in which he or she lives, experiencing and socially evaluating certain kinds of music. But individuals also exert influence on the society through the music that is produced and 'consumed'[5]. This affects the kinds and frequency of music that is produced. Music is thus a form of social collaboration, and is based on a cognitive construction of 'musical world' that contributes to "how people make sense of other people and themselves" (Fiske and Taylor 1991:14).

The construction of a 'musical world' takes place over a period of time and is embedded in the culture's cosmology, thus reflecting its values and beliefs. But people also actively construct and change their own values, beliefs and thereby their cultures. Their musical world and musical cognition include all their music (songs and their structures, categories and repertoires of music, instrumental pieces, instruments used, dances and their structures, categories and repertoires of dance), as well as all the rules (play frame) guiding the practice and circumstances for the performance of the music. The practice categorises music for

---

[4] Within the broader African context, music-making includes dance or play, using the body and instruments.
[5] By *consume* I am referring to the notion of buying music as a commodity for sale at shops (tapes, CDs, DVDs, etc.) at theatres and clubs, and even at private functions.

everyday and for special occasions, music for children, adults, males, females, commoners, specialists and royalty. There are also exclusions indicating who may not perform certain things. Thus cultural groups have constructed musical worlds according to their ways of life, systems of production, values and beliefs – they have enculturated their social system. Being part of a musical culture involves identification with both the process (praxis) and the environment of music making.

Process
In musical terms the process refers to sounds, patterns, structures and contexts that form the internalised mental templates. Templates or models (Arom 1991:xxi) are specific to cultures or sub-cultures. They are stored in the memory of a people and include knowledge of all the sounds and movements that belong together, the patterns involved, and the context for use that cultural insiders have developed. Such a template includes all the elements that identify the particular piece of music or song, and that guide the user in terms of its performance. Hence, the process with which a group identifies includes the knowledge of appropriate songs, embellishments to songs, and the ability to create appropriate variations. Based on this aspect of musical identity, members of a group are able to recognise qualities within a musical performance and transmit this recognition of 'correct' and 'good' sounds and movements to one another. Over time, given that performance by different communities of the same culture may involve different variations, templates can and do, change.

Environment
A musical environment includes all the expectations and understandings referring to the when, where and why of the musical event and is based on culturally organised rules or expectations. Environment includes contextualisation of time, location, functions, history, beliefs and values, as well as the economic framework for performance (for example commercial, or recreational). It also provides reference to whether a performance is private or public, whether it has restricted or open attendance, whether it is urban or rural, and whether it is a power (ritual) performance or recreational.

Social functions of music in Namibia

Broadly speaking, probably the most important function of communal music making is socialisation. Socialisation refers to the processes during which certain behaviours, morals and values considered to be healthy and useful in and to that society, are taught and learnt. Socialisation occurs in diverse ways and contexts. Processes and methods may include reward and punishment, reinforcement, group consensus, compliance or rebellion, social interactions, models and various incentives. Simply put, music creates a context or framework through which people may relate to one another in different ways. This social interaction takes place within the framework of social function and context. Social functions are woven into individual, familial and collective existence, while the social context includes all the details of a particular situation, circumstance, time and place.

Socialisation through music

Musical performance, dance, stories, narratives, games and ritual are situations where knowledge, life skills and social values can be transmitted. Music and dance have certain explicit, observable functions relating to occupation or celebrations, but there are implicit meanings underlying performance. Certain actions and sound patterns carry meanings that cultural insiders can interpret. These meanings may relate to the importance of seasonal actions in an agricultural environment, or to inner-city terminology and rhythms of 'gangsta-rap' loaded with meaning for members of that sub-culture. Music and dance link with the philosophical and moral systems that lie at the root of social structures, and can be seen as a metaphor of life[6].

Music communicates important messages in terms of social structure – the relationship order between different generations, genders, occupations and lineages. Mazrui points out that in many indigenous societies there are no non-relatives, both in Africa and elsewhere (1990:148). The result is that societal roles and activities relate to broad definitions of kinship, for example the ways that Ovahimba structure their society (and even their cattle herds) around their matrilineal and patrilineal clans (Jacobsohn 1990), and among Herero people these structures are declaimed in chants and songs (Ohly 1990, Kavari 2000). Similarly, Vakwangali, Hambukushu and Aawambo history, lineage and totems are communicated orally in praises and chants[7]. Williams quotes informants saying:

> Yes, we remember the past of our people, although we did not have a tradition of writing it down (...) Our children know our past because we told them, and we know because our parents and elders told us; this is how we remember our history (ondjokonona) (Williams 1994:12).

In the past, social positions were customarily defined by the importance of the musical instruments people were allowed to play and the roles they were allowed to take in the form of masks, spiritual healers, vocal leaders, or initiators of the dance. This is still observable in certain forms of play where the order in which people take turns indicates their status within that particular group. Thus, the play may begin with the smallest children, working up to the most experienced, or conversely, the wife of the king may begin, followed by relatives and then the rest of the crowd. This order establishes and sustains certain cultural inequalities within and between groups.

Traditionally, men and women's work functions define the genres of performance. Gender roles are reinforced by means of separate genres of musical

---

[6] A term used by Dagan 1997

[7] In addition to Williams 1994, see Gibson / Larson / McGurk 1981: The Kavango peoples, for discussion on clans and kinship among people in the Kavango region. Research in the Omusati region by Mans (1999-2001) has resulted in several recordings of such music.

performance, such as omupembe, outjina or omuhiva. Women's song categories often include lullabies (although men are not excluded), birthing songs, maize stamping, hoelng and threshing songs, and songs relating to girls' transformation ceremonies. Men's song traditions in Namibia typically include boys' transformation songs, herding, praising, healing, hunting and drinking songs as well as the lonely songs of migrant workers. Women were rarely allowed to play important instruments such as drums, although the contract labour system contributed to changes in this regard (see later).

There is often teamwork with neighbours helping one another, and there are specific categories of song for this task, for example oviimbo vyo kulima in Oluzimba, ondjambi or iikungungu in Oshindonga. There are songs which act as preparation for a role, one example being the songs of Ju/'hoan people that teach about the character and habits of animals and birds – important knowledge for a future hunter.

Music and dance sustain certain social practices that in turn sustain and support vital creative processes. For example, Small (1984:177, 178) points out that improvisation only really flourishes in communal performances where musicians and their listeners know one another well. When groups sing/play/dance together for any length of time, they develop a robust group style, and an empathy which controls but also allows greater freedom to explore new dimensions of sound and movement. The self-confidence that is nurtured in communal performance, where individuals explore, express and create within the secure boundaries of custom and a supportive atmosphere, is seldom seen elsewhere.

Music provides a medium for inter-generational and intra-generational socialising. Children and young people are often welcome in recreational musical events such as oudano, omutjopa, Namastap, etc. While there are many categories of performance for children alone (iiyimbo yaanona, outetera, omukwenga, and so on) there is also musical play for parents and children, for example the Khoekhoe game of abate (mothers and small children). Since the demographic changes caused by obligatory school attendance has had an impact upon the traditions of learning music orally from elders, many of the musical categories in which children were involved now become their own responsibility or that of the education system.

Music is a powerful political tool. Musical performance plays a role in the construction, expression, and legitimisation of power relationships in the modern world. In many countries governments may align themselves with or against particular 'cultural troupes', and may even exert influence that may reshape dances "to suit its (a government's) own national or regional interests" (Ottenburg 1997:14). Stokes (1994:8) argues that because music is so intensely involved in the propagation of dominant classifications, it plays an important role in the hands of government in the development of new states, or the reinvention of states. In Namibia music and dance have long been utilised in praise of leaders. In earlier times, Valozi chiefs used to retain personal musicians and travelled accompanied by a silimba player[8]. In other regions there is similar evidence of special music and dance performances relating to political structures. Examples are the royal music of Sambyu and Gciriku people where the status of those in power was defined and confirmed by these performances. During the struggle for political independence music was an important way of instructing the youth in terms of ideology and for developing and maintaining patriotism. Music wields this significant ideological and political power because it can touch us in ways and places that nothing else can (Bowman 1994:20).

Rituals are a means of perpetuating prevailing values, powers, and the meaning of life – an aspect of the static side of culture. Existing Namibian rituals include healing ceremonies, the casting out of (evil) spirits, religious rites, initiation rites, wedding rituals, inaugurations and funeral rites among others. In the past the ritualisation of rites of passage informed and prepared the younger generation in terms of social expectations and community ethos. Examples include efundula, olufuko and ohango in northern Namibia, ethuko, etanda and ouwhame in the Kaoko, simbayoka in the Caprivi, !khae-oms in the south and Ju/'hoan tcòqmá in the east. In all of these the music plays a cardinal role. There were in the past also ceremonies for raising energy and power that may or may not have been related to healings. Olundongo in the Kunene region is a case in point, having been a way for men to raise the spirit to fight or raid, but ol(r)undongo can also be used in traditional healing practices. Music and dance are vital to the creation of an atmosphere of power and of energy in healings. Among Ju/'hoansi in the Nyae Nyae area songs for spiritual healings (*n/om tzisi*) are sung frequently and "the goal of the healing ritual is to repel any illness and death which is threatening the equilibrium and cohesion of the group" (Olivier 1994:3). The mental-spiritual state achieved by means of this ritual is believed to contribute to the social well-being and stability of the community. In a Valozi healing ceremony (*nyakasanga, liyala and kayowe*)[9] music is necessitated by the need for energy and power that is freed through singing, drumming and dance, allowing spirits to be identified and possibly dismissed. Similarly in the healing (*arub*) practised by Damara people in the northwest. In light of the fact that these rituals are today being replaced by institutionalised church rituals and medical practices, different meanings and values are transmitted and absorbed.

A final, very important function – music and dance are used to maintain happiness and vitality in social worlds, because this is an inherent affect of musical performance. Communal performance (the predominant form of indigenous practice in rural Namibia) creates social cohesion that smoothes the way for interpersonal communications. This inclusiveness of participation results from a fundamental philosophy based on sharing[10] (Asante 1987:168) and is demog-

---

[8] The last known Valozi chief's musician playing the 'old music' in Namibia is Mr Sikwalunga Mului, from Bukalo in eastern Caprivi.

[9] Described in more detail in Mans 1997

[10] According to Asante, Afrocentric discourse hinges on human relations to one another, to the supernatural and to their own being.

raphically influenced by our low population, demanding everybody's participation for a performance to be successful. The encouragement, criticism and support achieved through communal participation in Ovahimba ondjongo for example, is a case in point. Individual performers are encouraged to create song texts and dance movements within the general constraints of style. The group responds in turn by rewarding the performance through enthusiastic response and commentary. Thus personal enjoyment, the energy to continue, and social integration are reinforced.

Cultural strategies for survival and change

Having explained some general concepts, let us look at some of the causes that contributed to the diversification of Namibian cultural traditions and the cultural strategies that people are employing today. We know that the sociocultural interactions of colonialism, resistance politics and mission outreaches had great impact upon cultural development in Namibia. To ensure the continuation of the cultural practices deemed important by members, actions were taken to discard, maintain, restore, revive, create, merge or synchronise these practices within changing cultural environments. In Namibia several different strategies are observed and below a few are selected for discussion.

Missionary influence and relinquishing of rituals

During the 19th and early 20th centuries, colonial adventurers, traders, settlers and missionaries moved ever deeper into the territories occupied at that time by diverse groups of agro-pastoralists. Increasing numbers of mission stations and missionary activities across the country created a cultural environment where on the one hand 'foreign' religious music was introduced – even imposed – and on the other hand many indigenous musical practices were frowned upon and branded pagan. It was especially the transformation (initiation) ceremonies and healing rituals that were targeted by missionaries, as these practices came into direct conflict with the Christian church paradigms. Many dances and the use of drums were discouraged or even abolished. Because cultural practices involve the totality of a people's existence, the effects were multitudinous. Some music went 'underground', others were forgotten, and others were unaffected. Even today, for example, people in some areas practice the Damara healing ceremony arub surreptitiously due to church censure. Other ceremonies, such as the Mbalantu girls' traditional marriage olufuko and a Valozi girl's coming-of-age (simbayoka), have ceased to be practised. Mbalantu women who underwent olufuko about fifty years ago and who wore the age group hairstyles of aafuko ('brides'), namely eefipa, eembuvi and the final omhatela, were told to cut these elaborate styles and were encouraged to adopt European-style dress[11]. Thus, the omhatela headdress that previously carried high social status, signifying among

---

[11] According to M. Mbwada, Outapi 1999

other things that a girl was not pregnant before olufuko, became something to hide. As a result of these actions, many of the 'unwanted' rituals and ceremonies have ceased to be performed and their music is rapidly being forgotten. Amongst young Namibians nowadays, the traditional healing and initiation ceremonies are stigmatised and people have generally discarded these practices. Most Aawambo girls today would strongly resist undergoing olufuko or efundula[12]. The strategy employed in this case involves the relinquishing of 'undesirable practices', a detachment of cultural ties with those rituals that are perceived as having outlived their function and value. In the place thereof, new music is adopted.

Thus missionaries contributed to rapid change in musical practices through the teaching and performing of church hymns as the means of creating a religious social body during services. This contributed to the assimilation of a new (foreign) homorhythmic and homophonic musical style based on Western Baroque chorales. Traditional Aawambo, Kavango and other tonal systems were adapted to absorb the new sounds. These adaptations are evident throughout the country, and one of the direct results has been the establishment of many choirs (a musical construction borrowed from Europe as far back as the late 19th century) and brass church bands. It is a feature of colonial occupation around the world that colonisers promote their own culture as superior. Hence, not only churches but most institutionalised music-making (for example schools) in Namibia promoted European music as innately superior, thus creating an sense of cultural inferiority amongst indigenous people regarding their own musical practices. Music from elsewhere is often considered 'better'. This contributed to the pressure towards rapid assimilation of Western musical characteristics. Thus, in the music of people who had regular interaction with English, German and Afrikaner settlers (through labour, intermarriage and formal education) there is further evidence of the adoption of melodic, harmonic and rhythmic structures that strongly resemble European music. I refer here to the resemblance of langarm dances to German waltzes, while the accordion and guitar accompaniment is reminiscent in musical structure to Boeremusiek (which itself is a syncretised form of German folk music). It must be said, however, that although subtle variations and the emphasis on enticing dance meter places the adapted music firmly within the African aesthetic. The strategy employed here involves syncretising, that is adopting and absorbing the 'new' music, but with slight changes and adaptations lending it a new 'flavour' that becomes the typical cultural sound of the group. People therefore took the foreign music they encountered, remoulded and reinterpreted it by incorporating the foreign elements. In some cases the indigenous language and music underwent major changes to do this. By adopting the guitar and keyboard as traditional instrument, adjustments had to be made to traditional melodies. In the case of Khoekhoe-speakers such as Damaras, these adjustments influenced the meaning of words that were sung (because the Khoekhoe languages are tonal) and re-

---

[12] According to Lukileni / Namupala / Gabriel / Angombe, Windhoek 1999 / 2000, who believe they speak for most young women today

sulted in adapted melodies. The adoption of a different ('foreign') tonal structure therefore had far-reaching effects on the music. Syncretisation continues at great speed in urban areas (see below).

Contract labour and creative change

The contracted labour system of the past, which established recruiting organisations (including certain missionaries) in northern Namibia, began in 1926. Men were taken into labour in mines, factories, farms and construction sites for periods of two years and longer, and were able to visit their families only on completion of a contract. In most cases they then signed a new contract and left home once more. The effect of the men's terms of absence on the northern societies such as the Aawambo people is felt even today. Women were compelled to take stronger roles in the day to day running of affairs and became more involved in local governance and economic self-management than among other populations in Namibia. In turn, the men who worked in towns often consorted with women and men of other cultures. Their own cultural profiles thus underwent diverse changes. When they returned home periodically, they effected changes in the form of new material goods, including objects such as radios, record players and records (later cassette tapes). Hence new and different forms of music were introduced into the family and the local community. As there was status attached to returning home with cash money and new objects, the new music was imbued with added status, being more 'now', and more fashionable. From discussions, it appears as though there may have been resistance to some of these changes from the women who remained behind and coped with household and land. It is therefore not surprising that feminine forms of music and play are far more commonly performed nowadays in northern Namibia than men's play (c.f. uudhano versus omupembe). Conversely, men's traditional music in the Omusati and Oshana regions includes not only working songs such as ousita (cattle herding chants) and iiyimbo yokekango yomongwa (songs for collecting salt) but also categories called oushwe (songs for walking and carrying loads) and oupongo (loneliness songs). These categories of song appear to have existed prior to contract labour, but along with gender roles within those cultures, the performance modalities and possibly even the musical structures were adapted to function in the relative absence of members of the opposite sex. Hence uudhano songs have only female vocal parts sung by a leader and chorus. Men's songs like oupongo and oushwe can be sung alone or as a group. The texts in both cases reflect the environment and circumstances of the performers. This helps to explain why relatively little music (except church songs) has been found in the central north of Namibia that is sung by men and women together. Although we do not know what the situation was a hundred years or more ago, it seems probable that strategies employed for cultural survival in the last fifty years involve the development, adaptation and extension of existing musical categories to reflect the changes to the social environments of both genders. Both structural and process adaptations were employed over time to make these musical categories viable.

Apartheid and cultural isolation

Another strategy found in Namibia is closure and restriction. During the apartheid regime from the 1940s, cultural differences were used as a divisive strategy, with 'retribalisation' being implemented in Namibia after 1948 (Silvester 1998:140). By emphasising the 'otherness' of people with different cultural practices, the (South African) rulers of the time were able to create suspicion and mistrust, thereby strengthening the patriarchal role of the government as decision-maker and 'provider', and eliminating democratic process. Separateness was emphasised and people of different languages and cultures were settled in 'homelands' and educated in the Afrikaans language and their own language(s), but they were not encouraged to integrate with members of different language or ethnic groups. Separation, in some cases, led to forms of cultural isolation, where people retained what was already in existence with little assimilation of anything from outside, with the ironic result that these groups developed and retained many musical qualities unique to their culture. This occurs in varying degrees, from almost complete stasis and closure to partial restriction. Thus a visitor to the north-western Kunene region will find that the vocal tones and phonic structures used by Ovahimba as well as Damara people are unique in Namibia and show little evidence of musical interaction with others. When recordings made over eighteen years ago by Haacke and Namiseb in 1983[13] were compared with those made by Mans in 2000 hardly any change was perceived – evidence of stasis. Through isolation both the process and environment of music making within a cultural group becomes more bound by custom. The qualities and patterns making up the musical templates of these groups appear to have turned inwards, looking towards that which was peculiar to that society. Variations and changes were made and continue to be made, but within strict customary boundaries defined by history and practice. The cultural strategy employed in isolation therefore has been to delve deeper into that which 'belongs' and to reject aspects of new, different or 'other' identities. This does not imply that music has necessarily stagnated, merely that people explore and change mainly within the culturally accepted framework of 'our identity'. However, even apartheid was not able to keep musical sounds completely isolated and in the older musical traditions of that area many of the rhythmic patterns employed in play and ritual resonate among other cultural groups within Namibia and across the borders.

Resistance and rejuvenation

From the 1960s onwards, during the period of active political resistance against the South African occupation, many people who left the country to join the struggle settled periodically in camps of the People's Liberation Army of Namibia (PLAN) across the border, mostly in Angola and Zambia. In these camps Namibians of different cultures and language groups were thrown together in a situation that bonded them through a common goal. Music was not absent from their lives,

---

[13] Field video recording in Sesfontein, W. Haacke 1982

and Sabine Zinke, for example, recorded several hundred different songs, mostly in Oshivambo dialects but also in Khoekhoe, Rukwangali, Otjiherero, Silozi, Setswana and others. In order to meet the demands of this new society, with its different class and gender structures, there had to be adaptation. Furthermore, musical performances during this period were often subjugated to the aims of the cause, with the expression of patriotic fervour, hope for political freedom and hatred of the enemy being uppermost. As well as expressing feelings of social cohesion (and homesickness), certain forms of musical play became important means of recreation, education and political expression. Not only did uudhano (oudano) of Aawambo people flourish; the interaction with activists from South Africa, Zimbabwe and Botswana had a great impact on other forms of music. Chorale singing of resistance songs in four-part harmonies based on the European primary chords that have become such a prevalent form of music making in other parts of southern Africa, did not pass Namibians by. Zinke's recordings show that an impressive number of songs sung in Oshikwanyama, among whom the diatonic, homophonic structure was not customary, had taken on this character. But it was not only homophonic music that was assimilated. Many forms of uudhano illustrate cultural interaction with the music of Congo and West Africa (e.g. ndombolo), even while retaining the resistance texts that date from the 1970s and 1980s, deriding the South African leaders Verwoerd, Vorster and Botha and praising Namibian resistance leaders Nujoma, Toivo, Ithana and others. This can be seen in children's play such as 'osamangela'. Two forms of assimilation were used: one involving the assimilation of new tonal structures and musical performance modes into existing musical repertoires, and the other involving the adoption of new (foreign) movements styles and complete songs, but utilising existing texts or creating new ones in Namibian languages. From this it can be seen that change and assimilation can be creative, leading to changes in existing forms and the creation of new forms.

Independence and cultural revivalism
Since independence in 1990, the need for social reconstruction has contributed to the understanding that new emphasis must be placed on cultural pride, on identifying characteristics of 'Namibian-ness'. This has led to the institution of cultural festivals and competitions all over the country. Similarly, the pressure from tourists wishing to see 'authentic' Namibian cultural performances has resulted in the establishment of numerous 'cultural groups', meaning bands of like-minded people who have an interest in preserving qualities of their customs and who have an interest and ability in performance. These new performance systems require new aesthetics. Whereas communal performances traditionally involve the freedom for "anyone who knows how" to perform and improvise, and where all onlookers are active participants, the new performance system involves rehearsed and choreographed performances for a non-participant but critical audience. Performers delve into their cultural histories, and from the past create 'new' performances. Town groups compete against rural groups whom they regard as having more

knowledge and skill in cultural matters. The town groups often draw members from cultures other than that being performed. Although this happens across the nation, the groups from the Kavango, of mixed Kwangali, Mbukushu, Sambyu and Gciriku members, have made great impact in this genre. The Uukumwe Culture Group is a case in point. Firmly rooted in older traditions, their music now combines traditions of these different groups into one seamless performance. They base their performance on shared traditions, but in each section emphasise that which is peculiar to the specific performance category and language group, for example litembu, kambamba or nondere. In the above case it appears that the present cultural strategy of confluence and adaptation is currently employed by a few key actors. It involves a creative merging and flowing together of shared qualities for new and different situations. In this way they are vivifying their music "through the effective uses of music and dance that are congruent with their distinctive world views and historical anomalies" (Kealiinohomoku 1997:141).

Urbanisation and global trends – adopt, detach, become a star

It is particularly in urban areas of Namibia that the global trends take root most rapidly. Although demographic changes mean that the rural-urban dichotomy is fast becoming redundant, I refer to it in terms of urban cultural changes. Towns are usually multicultural.

Music and dance in urban areas are more institutionalised than in the distant rural areas. In towns the youth seek formal music and ballet lessons for certification. The implication of this trend is mainly financial: tuition involves acquiring expensive musical instruments, classes and transport, and concerts, clubs and recordings similarly require funds. The cost of these instruments and the expense of tuition and transport place formal music tuition beyond the reach of most Namibians, ensuring that in most cases it remains the prerogative of the élite. Although efforts have been made to alleviate such expenses through subsidised rentals and tuition fees, costs remain prohibitive for the majority. Strangely, the result appears to contribute to the perceived value of such lessons, and townspeople in the lower income groups make many sacrifices to give their children this opportunity. More fundamental are changes to the urban performance aesthetic. Where egalitarian participation is the norm in rural traditions, the notion of 'special talent' and 'artist' have taken firm root in the global music world and industry. Young performers aim for a profession either as concert or commercial musician or published composer. Audiences observe (though don't participate) and buy recordings, but set fairly rigid standards of performance. Because few individuals believe that they can perform at the level required by consumers, they come to believe that they lack the ability – "I can't sing". The incidence of people singing, playing and dancing for their own pleasure is decreasing and thus the socialising role of music and dance is being minimised. Having now become 'artists', commercial musicians demonstrate widely disparate cultural profiles, yet the influences of 'world-beat' and Afro-beat, gospel trends and American hip-hop and rap are prevalent. Each of these reflects and constructs different value systems and contains its own meanings. Within urban society therefore, local artists gather followers who are members of a sub-culture who subscribe to those particular systems. Examples include Rastafarian supporters of reggae, 'home-boy' supporters of hip-hop, and so on. In coping with ever-changing urban environments, some cultures appear to have discarded some of their music, without really adapting or changing that music. Such appears to be the case with Afrikaans people, who in early days practised a syncretised dance-play (volkspele) that was an adaptation of early German folk music. Previously small bands with accordions and guitars were common at social occasions, playing mainly Boeremusiek. Nowadays volkspele has all but disappeared as people have loosened their ties to the Voortrekker image. Other classical and popular Western music (especially American Country and Western) has all but taken its place, often sung in English by Afrikaans speakers. However, there are still bands that perform music reminiscent of Boeremusiek in the central, eastern and southern areas, where the preferred social dance form is langarm. From this it appears that while certain aspects of musical culture have been discarded, other, not dissimilar but foreign forms have found new life and reinterpretation. The strategy here too involves the apparent discarding of traditional music and the adoption, as is, of new music. From early observations it appears as though the local trends (individual strategies) vary and include: adoption of non-indigenous music without change; new songs in various languages created in a revival of an older style like in the songs of Jackson Kaujeua; syncretisation like in the reggae of Ras Sheehama; and in a few cases confluence where Afrikaner, African and American jazz influences combine like in the music of Reho Combo.

Concluding remarks

Although the above discussion is by no means exhaustive, it emphasises the important role of music in society, and ways in which music and dance are involved in the construction and maintenance of societal systems. The essay introduces the variety of strategies that cultures may employ in choosing who they want to be and how they will manage it. While the results of present trends in urban societies will only become apparent in the future, it is clear that Namibian cultures are vibrant, ever-changing constructions of systems. People themselves are instrumental in bringing about cultural change in reaction to their changing environments. Because we are able to observe the effects of development and change through musical practice, development agencies should be informed by the need to preserve the cognitive base "that enables peoples to adopt, evaluate and create their own development options for the future" (Arizpe in Kirdar 1992:119). Effectively, this statement means paying attention to the cultural needs and expressions of the people, wherever and whomever they are.

Bibliography

Arom, *S* 1991. African polyphony and polyrhythm. Musical structure and methodology. Cambridge University Press

Asante, *MK* 1987. The afrocentric idea. Philadelphia: Temple University Press

Bowman, *WD* 1994. Sound, society and music 'proper'. In: Philosophy of Music Education Review 2, no.1 (Spring), pp.14-24

Coplan, *D* 1994. In the time of cannibals. The world of music of South Africa's Basotho migrants. University of Chicago Press

Dagan, *E* (ed.) 1997. The spirit's dance in Africa. Evolution, transformation and continuity in Sub-Sahara. Montreal: Galerie Amrad African Art Publications

Erlmann, *V* 1996. Nightsong. Performance, power, and practice in South Africa. University of Chicago Press

Falck, *R* / **Rice,** *T* (eds.) 1982. Cross-cultural perspectives on music. University of Toronto Press

Fiske, *ST* / **Taylor,** *SE* 1991. Social cognition (2nd edition). New York: McGraw-Hill

Hargreaves, *DJ* / **North,** *AC* (eds.) 1997. The social psychology of music. Oxford University Press

Hartmann, *W* / **Silvester,** *J* / **Hayes,** *P* (eds.) 1998. The colonising camera. Photographs in the making of Namibian history. University of Cape Town Press

Heywood, *A* / **Lau,** *B* / **Ohly,** *R* (eds.) 1992. Warriors, leaders, sages and outcasts in the Namibian past – narratives collected from Herero sources for the Michael Scott Oral Records Project 1985-1986. Windhoek: MSORP

Jacobsohn, *M* 1990. Himba, nomads of Namibia. Cape Town: Struik

Kavari, *JU* 2000. The form and meaning of Otjiherero praises (doctoral dissertation). School of Oriental and African Studies, University of London

Kealiinohomoku, *JW* 1995. Holistic cultural indices. Cross-cultural dance resources. Workshop at the Conference on Confluences – first South African music and dance conference, incorporating the 15th symposium on ethnomusicology, 16-19 July 1997. Cape Town

Kirdar, *Üner (ed.)* 1992. Change: threat or opportunity for human progress? Vol.IV: Changes in the human dimension of development, ethics and values. New York: United Nations

Kinahan, *J* 1991. Pastoral nomads of the central Namib desert. The people history forgot. Windhoek: Archeological Trust, New Namibia Books

Lees, *H* 1994. 'Something rich and strange': Musical fundamentals and the tradition of change. In: Musical connections: tradition and change. Proceedings of the 21st World conference of the International Society for Music Education, Tampa, Florida, USA, pp.1-7. Auckland: ISME

Miescher, *G* / **Henrichsen,** *D* (eds.) 2000. New notes on Kaoko. Basler Afrika Bibliographien. Basel

Mans, *ME* 1997a. Dances Namibia should not forget. In: Dagan, E (ed.). The spirit's dance in Africa. Evolution, transformation and continuity in Sub-Sahara. Montreal: Galerie Amrad African Art Publications

Mans, *ME* 1997b. Namibian music and dance as Ngoma in arts education (doctoral dissertation). Music Department, University of Natal. Durban

Mans, *ME* 1997c. Ongoma! Notes on Namibian musical instruments. Windhoek: Gamsberg Macmillan

Mans, *ME* 2000. Epera and oudano: creating a sense of holism in the classroom with Namibian music and dance. In: de Quadros, A (ed.). Many seeds, different flowers. The music education legacy of Carl Orff. Perth: CIRCME

Mans, *ME* 2000. Unlocking play in Namibian musical identity. Paper presented at the Conference on Playing with identity in contemporary African music. Nordiska Afrikainstitutet Turku, Finland (forthcoming)

Mans, *ME* 2001. Playing the music – comparing performance of children's song and dance in traditional and contemporary Namibian education. In: Thompson, CM / Bresler, L (eds.). Music as a species-specific adaptation. Chicago: Kluwer (forthcoming)

Mans, ME / **Olivier**, E / **Riviére**, H 1998-2001. Field research for the project "The living musics and dance of Namibia: exploration, education and publication. Project supported collaboratively by the French Mission for Cooperation and Cultural Affairs in Namibia, and the University of Namibia

Mazrui, AA 1990. Cultural forces in world politics. London: James Currey

Mudimbe, VY 1988. The invention of Africa. Gnosis, philosophy, and the order of knowledge. Bloomington and Indianapolis: Indiana University Press

Olivier, E 1994. Musical repertoire of the Ju/'Hoansi: identification and classification. Proceedings of the Meeting on Khoisan studies: multidisciplinary perspectives. Köln: Rüdiger Köppe Verlag

Ottenburg, S 1997. Some issues and questions on African dance. Introduction to: Dagan, E (ed.). The spirit's dance in Africa. Evolution, transformation and continuity in Sub-Sahara. Montreal: Galerie Amrad African Art Publications

Pirsig, RM 1991. Lila. An inquiry into morals. UK: Corgi

Potter, J / **Wetherell**, M 1992. Discourse and social psychology. Beyond attitudes and behaviour. London: Sage

Riche, D (ed.) 1979. The conceptualisation and explanation of processes of social change. The Queen's University Papers in Social Anthropology, vol.3. Belfast: Queen's University

Small, C 1984. Music. Society. Education. London: John Calder

Stokes, M (ed.) 1994. Ethnicity, identity and music. The musical construction of place. Berg Ethnic Identity Series. Oxford/Providence: Berg

Svašek, M 1997. Identity and style in Ghanaian artistic discourse. In: MacClancy, J (ed.). Contesting art. Art, politics and identity in the modern world. Oxford: Berg

Williams, F-N 1994. Precolonial communities of Southwestern Africa. A history of Ovambo kingdoms 1600-1920, (2nd ed.). Archeia no.16. Windhoek

Zinke, S 1992. Neue Gesänge der Ovambo. Musikethnologische Analysen zu namibischen Liedern (doctoral dissertation). Fachbereich Kultur- und Kunstwissenschaften, Humboldt-Universität zu Berlin

(CON)FRONTING THE MASK – SOME (CON)TEXTS OF PROTEST IN NAMIBIAN DRAMA

Terence Zeeman

Introduction[1]

This chapter is concerned with two inter-linked commentaries: the first involves an examination of our conventional expectations of the actor in a role, and the second explores the emergence of protesting performers featured alongside their characters in contemporary Namibian resistance or protest drama and poetry[2]. In particular, I will be looking at Vickson Hangula's *The Show Isn't Over Until...* that contests the perceived neglect and continuing marginalisation of the Namibian performing artist in state-sponsored, post-independence reconstruction and development. While the content of this dissatisfaction is easily read in the narratives of the play, I hope to show here that by unsettling and upsetting 'conventional' modes of theatre production and reception, Namibian performing artists lever their drama from its conventionally covert forms in order to achieve a staging of alternative and more aggressive stances.

Fronting the mask

Those of us who worked at the National Theatre of Namibia in the early 1990s suspected that the Windhoek Theatre was home to ghosts[3]. The then stage manager, who was often required to work very late at night, was particularly convinced. After midnight, when no one else was in the building, lights would switch on, toilets would flush and the tinkle of the piano upstairs in the rehearsal room could be heard. We may never know whether the Windhoek Theatre was in fact visited by ghosts, but it is the case that many theatres in the world are considered haunted by the ghosts of 'characters' that actors had once brought to 'life' on stage and later abandoned in the theatre after the play had closed. It is said that the disembodied 'characters' remain in the charged atmosphere of the dark theatre, reduced to the substance of memories waiting for the next performer's body to reincarnate them. For what is a character but an entity created by an actor – a 'something' that 'appears' to be like a person in action and seemingly repre-

---

[1] This article draws on some material first presented in the preface to New Namibian Plays vol.1, edited by Terence Zeeman, published by Gamsberg Macmillan, Namibia. 2000. THE SHOW ISN'T OVER UNTIL ... is included in this volume.

[2] By contemporary Namibian resistance or protest drama I refer to the post-independence drama that has moved beyond the challenge of destroying an apartheid regime (which preoccupied the 'resistance' drama of circa 1990 that included plays such as Freddie Philander's The Curse / Katutura '59 and King of the Rubbish Dump, Kubbe Rispel's Die Droom and Die Stoel, the work of the Bricks Theatre Collective and the independence dramas by George Weidemann and Dorian Haarhoff produced by Aldo Behrens of the then School of the Arts of the Windhoek Academy and later the University of Namibia).

[3] The author was executive director of the NTN from 1991-1993.

sentative of 'us'? An ephemeron? Yet, so compelling is the 'presence' of character that we can speak of characters as if they are human, and as such we can be tempted to discuss and analyse 'their' conflicts and 'their' circumstances as if they were a product of a 'real' society.

This is arguably, even certainly, an oversimplification, but I would suspect that most regular theatre-goers would, if asked, agree that an actor at work on stage in a play is not actually (really) the character being portrayed. Conversely, most audiences would admit that their enjoyment of 'conventional' drama is enhanced if they (the audience) are able to regard the actor as the character – that their pleasure in going to the theatre involves a certain degree of 'let's pretend'. This may be especially true of television soap opera where we follow the doings of the character (in what we call the plot or the story) with little thought for the craft of the actor or medium through which the character is produced. In fact, if we did go to the theatre and saw self-conscious actors confusing their dialogue or laughing when they were supposed to be crying or forgetting their lines, we would not be satisfied and we would agree with Shakespeare that such 'an unperfect actor (...) is put beside his part'.[4] In such a 'conventional' theatre, the audience expects the actor to keep up the mask of character and not let it slip. Only after the play is done, can the actor remove the mask of character and become 'himself' again.

In the convention of the theatre, 'we' (that temporary society assembled as audience) participate in an entertaining and pleasurable deception: an agreement to view the events of the stage as if they were, plausibly and reliably, the products of actual lives lived – as if the characters portrayed were representative (standing in the place of) of society in general or a society in particular. I use the term 'convention' here (aware that the theatre accommodates an enormous range of conventions and genres) in an attempt to coin what is perhaps a 'typical' or layman's expectation of the actor's work in the theatre and the drama: that is, to offer a pretence (a mimesis) that is 'lifelike' and 'real' and to construct a persona/mask of character that eclipses the actor's own self in performance. It is perhaps still commonly believed that a 'good' actor is one who convinces his audience that, for the duration of the play at least, he is the person he is playing[5]. And so, it is not uncommon for television soap opera actors to be recognised more easily as the characters they play and to be addressed by their characters' names or even, if their 'characters' are particularly nasty or evil, to receive hate mail from viewers who have confused actor with role.

If this sort of drama can be regarded for the moment to be usual or 'conventional' then we might agree that most of the scripted and published drama presented in Namibia today follows the convention described above – that of requiring the skilful actor to 'pretend' to be someone else – to put on the mask of character in the performance – to represent and to re-present the character 'truth-

---

[4] Shakespeare, Sonnet 23
[5] I refer to those audiences whose expectation, experience and enjoyment of the theatre and the drama it presents falls loosely or exclusively within the bounds of 'plausibility' – whether presented as realism or as a departure from it.

fully', because the story (and the characters within the story) portrayed by the actors is more important than an observation of the actor's own production of it.

And for good reason. If the situation and story of the drama concerns itself with pressing and serious social concerns (as the protest or 'issues-based' play does), all the more reason for the actor to make sure the play is not marred by a performance that draws attention away from the illusion of reality and appearance of truth that the play proposes. For this to be effective, convention requires the mask of 'character' to remain in place.

The published protest or 'issues based' drama of Namibia offers many such conventional roles: The 'old location' woman (Handjievol) and her struggle against the white brute of a policeman (Lombaard) in Freddie Philander's *The Curse;* Kubbe Rispel's crazy president (the Leader) who is obsessed with the cleanliness of his throne in *Die Stoel;* the tribal chief (Chief Lewanika) who faces resistance from his wives protesting against a tribal polygamous patriarchy in *God of Women* by Sifso Nyathi and the Ancestral Roots Travellers; Norman Job's *Mai Jekketti*, which explores issues of inheritance; Hendrik Dollar and Jan van Rand (personifications of the Namibian ten dollar note and the South African ten rand note) working through the challenges to reconciliation and economic integration in Petrus Haakskeen's *Finders Keepers, Losers Weepers;* the Mother's bloody revenge against the Father's abuse of their child in Laurinda Olivier-Sampson's *A Moment in our Lives;* and the sad tale of the Luderitz fisherman (Newton) caught up in illegal diamond smuggling in *Onele yo Kawe* by Kay Cowley and Tanya Terblanche[6].

All the plays listed (and they may be considered a representative selection of the script-based drama of post-independent Namibia) require of the actor a conventional task: to work in such a way that the audience constructs the illusion of lives lived in a 'society' that is recognisably resonant with their own. Persuaded by the events on stage, the audience might be moved to protest or, at least, moved to greater sensitivity to the issues presented. The actor's work is part of this process, encouraging the illusion by remaining 'hidden' behind the mask and in subjugation to the role – what I have referred to in the title as Fronting the Mask. In such a system:

"The artist shall remain a puzzle
Not the Who, but the Why"[7]

The willingness of audiences to participate in the 'as if' (let's pretend) premise of the theatre (its almost magical tricking of the audience's collective 'mind' into viewing fictional events as if they were real), invites, even tempts, the empiricist (and sociologist?) to regard the theatre as capable of rendering, in microcosm, the

---

[6] I have listed only published scripts in the interests of providing the student reader with accessible references.
[7] Christi Werner 2000:54, Battered Paintings for Sale. In: Poetically Speaking, compiled by Siballi E I Kgobetsi, published by Gamsberg Macmillan, Namibia

dramas of 'real' life. The many metaphors and analogies linking theatre with actual human experience further encourage the association:

> Give me a poem that can
> Lift the eyelid and open the ear-curtain
> A poem i can engrave on stone
> Act out on stage
> ...
> Madame Poet in me
> Select and arrange
> Words of my range
> Words that move my mind
> Closer to scenes seen or unseen[8]

Shakespeare's *Macbeth* has this well-known analogy:

> Life's but a walking shadow, a poor player,
> That struts and frets his hour upon the stage,
> And then is heard no more[9].

Likewise, the ephemeral qualities of the theatre (here today, gone tomorrow) are often evoked as analogous to the human situation. Jacques' line in Shakespeare's *As You Like It* is perhaps the most obvious:

> All the world's a stage
> And all the men and women merely players (actors):
> They have their exits and their entrances;
> And one man in his time plays many parts...[10]

and Antonio's quip in *The Merchant of Venice* is even clearer:

> I hold the world but as the world, Gratiano;
> A stage where every man must play a part...[11]

Contemporary comparisons between life and the theatre are commonplace. Former British Prime Minister, John Major, resigning after his election defeat said: When the final curtain comes down, it's time to get off the stage[12]. In everyday conversation, we refer to events happening behind the scenes, or longing for a change of scene, or the need to set the scene. If the world (the collective bustle of human traffic we call 'our world' or 'our society') is likened to the ephemera of the theatrical performance (re-presenting the conflict of the human will that is the engine of drama), so too the theatrical performance and the drama it produces

---

[8] Siballi E I Kgobetsi 2000:13. Give me a poem. In: Poetically Speaking, compiled by Siballi E I Kgobetsi, published by Gamsberg Macmillan, Namibia
[9] Shakespeare, Macbeth, Act 5, Scene 5
[10] Shakespeare, As You Like It, Act 2, Scene 7
[11] Shakespeare, The Merchant of Venice, Act 1, Scene 1
[12] The Guardian 3 May 1997

can be easily confused with (substituted for) its twin or its mirror, 'life'. It might be then that the theatre is seen as a useful laboratory for the sociologist tempted to investigate the conflicts presented by 'characters' as if they were representative (accurate and real).

I say 'tempted', for a performance is more than the character's journey. The 'ephemerons' which produce drama are actors, not characters and it is here that the sociological 'pulse' of the theatre can be taken by examining more closely what the artists say about themselves than what their characters say in the dramas they produce.

Let's go to Parliament urges playwright and poet Keamogetsi J Molapong in a remarkable call to artists:

Let's invade Parliament
Exhibit our interests
Perform our hunger to them
Let's sing to them of our thirst
And do the poverty dance
...
Let's screen for them the movies
Depicting our (the artists') honest suffering
With detailed pain and curse
...
Let's recite poetry of a failure
To appreciate visual art
Understanding performing art
Let's colonise Parliament
...
Let's persist with our art
Speak through our poems
Draw with our sweat
On the canvasses of our skin[13]

Confronting the mask

A decade after independence, Namibian playwrights continue to script their protest and disappointment that the mechanisms used to articulate cultural activity remain hidden and bound in the bureaucracy of the state.

Almost ten years to the day after Namibia's liberation from apartheid South Africa, Namibia's artists called for a protest march through the capital city – to 'agitate for a better deal'[14]. 'If we do not make noise, who will make noise for us?' asked Vickson Hangula, a very popular Windhoek playwright. Prominent choreographer, musician and activist, Banana Shekupe called for more government support: "Arts played a big role in our liberation struggle. It opened the eyes of the international community to the plight of Namibians. President Nujoma was always

---

[13] Joseph Molapong, Let's go to Parliament. In: Poetically Speaking, compiled by Siballi E I Kgobetsi 2000:56, published by Gamsberg Macmillan, Namibia
[14] The Namibian March 31 2000

at the forefront of the arts then, and it was hoped that he would support the arts industry in an independent Namibia".[15] The administrative secretary of the Namibia Arts Union quoted from the petition:

"For a long time, (those engaged in) the arts industry and arts in Namibia have not been regarded as serious entrepreneurs whose industry needs the kind of incentives accorded to other professions".[16]

I list a brief record of similar discontent:

"Most of those in charge of government arts and culture institutions are out of touch with the real cultural needs of Namibians. Our (the artists') efforts are hardly ever acknowledged."[17]

"In Namibia, culture and politics are inseparably part of our existence. Proof of this is the fact that some artists working for the government get paid to shut up and toe the line, a very unhealthy situation."[18]

"The non-payment of (arts) workers in the Ministry of Basic Education's Arts Extension programme is to my mind the worst case of bureaucratic harassment against people who play a pivotal role in the human resource development of the Namibian nation (...) Among those artists negatively affected are respected people who have contributed considerably to the cultural emancipation of the Namibian people in the dark days of the liberation struggle and should be respected as such."[19]

"...self-taught artists with practical skills should be allowed to be working as full time teachers in schools; courses and the format of lecturing at the College of the Arts should also be changed to suit the needs to aspiring artists and academic qualifications should not be the sole criteria for artists to develop their skills at government institutions."[20]

Vickson Hangula's play *The Show Isn't Over Until...* enjoyed a wave of popularity – playing to packed houses in Windhoek in October 1997. The next year the play won the National Theatre of Namibia's Golden Pen Awards and the play was sent by the Namibian government to Botswana as part of a southern African festival. The Namibian High Commissioner, who saw the play in Botswana, wrote to the Namibian President expressing concern about the content and the artists' conduct. The play was later refused funding to participate in the Market Theatre Laboratory Community Theatre Festival (Johannesburg) in May 1999 on the grounds that it contained "anti-Swapo and anti-government propaganda"[21]. This action resulted in national media coverage and an extended debate on artistic freedom in Namibia.

Vickson Hangula's *The Show Isn't Over Until...* is unusual in that is not really what we would normally expect a play to be (a coherent, cohesive story presented by actors pretending to be the characters). Rather *The Show Isn't Over Until...* is

---

[15] The Namibian March 31 2000
[16] The Namibian March 31 2000
[17] Bureaucracy Frustrates Arts Efforts. Vickson Hangula, quoted in The Namibian May 19 2001
[18] Bureaucracy Frustrates Arts Efforts. Yellow Solo, quoted in The Namibian May 19 2001
[19] Freddie Philander, Personally Speaking, The Namibian February 9 2001
[20] Youth Speak out on Arts and Culture Development. Snobia Kaputu, as reported in The Namibian May 5 2000
[21] The Namibian 21st May 1999.

about four actors and their director who are rehearsing 'a play'. As the initial stage directions note:

> "A group of actors have the most brilliant play that they are putting on. They are all seasoned actors and have travelled this road many times before, but will their professional differences allow them to 'live it up' in the play? Especially when they know that it is going to be a rather controversial play."

We see bits of the 'play-in-rehearsal' as the actors and their director choose to deal with last-minute problems, but more importantly we see the actors engaged in the process of dealing with the problems that the content of the 'play' they are rehearsing presents. So we, the audience, move between layers of (re)presentation: on the one hand, the conflicts of the 'play-in-rehearsal' which deal provocatively with corruption in government circles and the conflicts of the actors themselves as they prepare the "rather controversial play" that will be presented "tomorrow night". Indeed, when the production opened, some members of the audience enquired of the playwright when all of the 'actual play' was to be produced, disappointed that they only attended a 'rehearsal.' But that is the gimmick, if you will, of *The Show Isn't Over Until...* – that the (real) play is actually the rehearsal of the 'play-within-a-play'.

The subject of the rehearsal (the play-within-a play) is not the primary focus of our discussion here. Suffice it to say that the scenes rehearsed include a brutal and satirical attack on nepotism and tribalism in determining government contracts and the assimilation of former freedom fighters into a modern economy. The actors stop the rehearsal in fear, and for fear that the fictions they fabricate will reflect on their own selves, and that the more successfully they deliver the 'truth' of their performance, the greater the risk of verisimilitude (appearance of truth) progressing to the verity of their (the performers') utterances. They try to change the script. The director says 'No'.

The rehearsal (which is what the actual play concerns itself with) does not proceed smoothly. It is the day before 'opening night' and tensions are running high. Steve, an actor, stumbles on the delivery of a particularly difficult line for him to say – it is a contentious anti-government retort – a warning from a character that civil war is imminent if the government does not start employing former combatants. Steve breaks from the rehearsal to ask the director "Should I really say that?" The director explains: "Say the bloody lines. It is not you saying that, it is the character you are playing. Say it, loud. Action!" Karin, also one of the actors assembled for rehearsal, likewise cannot get 'into character'. She too has a problem with the subject matter and is clearly intimidated by the vituperative outbursts she is to deliver – her character accuses the "bloody SWAPO government" of employing "illiterate memes" and abandoning the "poor AK-47 wielding fools (...) now so poor and hungry in their liberated motherland". It seems the dialogue is too overtly critical of the government. She is afraid that "if Peter Tshirumbu's Men-in-Black (intelligence agency operatives) are in the audience, they will not differentiate between the character and me. That bunch of assholes will soon start following me wherever I go." She adds: "People will think that I (the actor playing the character) am really an anti-government racist." To which the director from hell thunders in rely: "What is this? Where is your professionalism? You are an ACTOR!!"

Karin's dilemma is acute. For an actor, the job of play making (conventionally) involves tricking the audience into an experience of virtually constructing (from the actor's mimesis) that fiction called 'character'. The director wishes the performer's protesting self to be subjugated to such a degree that the self-deceiving audience sees the character's action only (as opposed to the actor's attitude towards this action). As Karin, the actor, achieves the blurring of the boundaries between her self and the 'fake' self she constructs as character, she fulfils the Director's requirements of her: "Put yourself into your character", says the Director to Steve. "Put yourself deeper into your character (...) you are supposed to be the character, not yourself", says the Director to Judy (as well). After all, she is 'only' an actor, but somehow she fears her own complicity. And, confronted with the readiness of the agents of the state to clamp down on resistance (particularly given the play's first performance before a crucial election) she, like Karin, is acutely aware that even the actor's success in fabricating fictions that masquerade as truth (playing the part convincingly) could potentially remove the protection of the conventions theatre employs – that the aesthetic distance between her production of the character and the force and effect of her character's utterances might narrow and fuse, so exposing the actor's 'self' as the source of political agitation, and therefore grounds for complicity in subversion. The actors disrupt the rehearsal, seeking reassurances that the conventions governing the artist's right to "interpret life as artistically as we can" is still intact. The actors cannot be convinced and, as Steve says: "If people attack me for the character I played, I will always refer them to the Director". Karin likewise, after being congratulated by the Director for her performance, says: "You must be prepared to be my bodyguard once Siirumbu's (sic) Men-in-Black start following me around". The Director replies: "Don't worry. I will personally write a letter in Oshivambo to State House explaining that we are only doing a play."

A similar set of concerns is recorded in Shakespeare's *A Midsummer Night's Dream*. The Duke has instructed a group of artisans to perform for the State (on the occasion of the Royal Wedding). As the actors begin to rehearse their comedy they are afraid that their characters' actions might affront the royal audience. In one sequence, Bottom, an artisan actor, is worried about a bit of action he is to play as the character Pyramus. In the play that they are putting on, Pyramus is to draw a sword to kill himself. Bottom is so sensitive to the potential consequences if the Royal audience thinks he (Bottom, the actor) has actually drawn a real sword, that he suggests that prior to his performance, he will stop the show and tell the audience that "I, Pyramus am not Pyramus, but Bottom, the weaver." Another actor is to play a Lion, and again the acting troupe fear the consequences if the fictional Lion were to frighten the Royals. So, once again, the troupe decides to have the actor tell the audience: "If you think I come hither as a lion, it were pity on my life. No! I am no such thing; I am a man as other men are." And if this were not a secure enough disclaimer, the actors decide to cut a hole in the Lion's costume so that the actor's head can poke through, making doubly sure that the audience does not confuse actor and character. So, as the actors attempt to unravel the contradictions between representation and being – the problem of 'acting for' the state while under the cover of character – forces the actor to both front and confront the mask of character. To question, to unsettle and destabilise the authority of the 'conventional mask' exposes the actor as 'imperfect' and 'out of character', therefore debilitating the cogency of authentic voices of protest that appear outside the fictional world of the play masquerading (and accepted by the audience) as 'truth.'

Actors, in 'conventional' systems, produce 'societies' that are fictions – are ephemeral – and do not really 'exist' at any time – even in the play's performance. If they seem to exist, they do so as mere false memories engraved on the audience's imagination. The 'world of the play' then only exists, as Shakespeare reminded his audiences, as 'a dream of passion' and 'a fiction', and the producers of these impressions, the actors are 'shadows' or 'ciphers'. Within this context (or should I say (con)text?), the world of conflict observed and re-presented by the playwright can be dismissed as literally immaterial to the material facts of a (real) society's contradictions, and so the 'truth' however well-presented on the stage, cannot be equated with the 'facts' of real life. Therefore, being ephemeral, 'shadows', 'dreams of passion' or 'fictions', the claim can be made that plays and players ought to present no 'real' threat to the State – hence the Director's letter of explanation to the President.

The Director's assertion that we are only doing a play (rather than something tangibly overt and 'real') and his assumption that this particular form of non-threatening activity would need to be explained to State House might on the one hand be a facetious dismissal of a government so unsophisticated that the conventions of theatre would need some explanation in order to avoid confusion between character and actor. But, given the anxiety that the actors' workings and utterances are under state scrutiny and surveillance, this explanation is perhaps more necessary. The gist of the explanation is then an address to the State: we are only doing a play – we (the performers) are not 'really' agitating for change – just simply narrating, at a remove, the fiction of that agitation which is actually only play-acting and idle.

But it is precisely this problem that the actors in *The Show Isn't Over Until...*want to overcome when telling their own stories. They want to be seen, to be noted, to be taken seriously – not just for the characters they present as artists, but as artists that have their own tale to tell. They would like very much not to be dismissed as ephemera and shadows. For to the actor, playing is work. They complain from the stage, and from within the (con)text of their drama, that "everybody is taking us for granted. Look, now we have to eat brown bread and chips everyday. We have been on the same diet ever since the community theatre days before independence." They point out that performing arts funding from the private sector is spent on shows that "appeal mostly to white, rich audiences" and that "black artists are really marginalised. Actors, Directors, Visual Artists, and the lot". And, as they become more strident: "Most African governments don't think theatre is as important as any other sorts of development (...) we as local artists have a right to be part of this society. And we expect the same support that they give elsewhere in society. Like to soccer, hockey and athletics".

To refer briefly to another play: Keamogetse Joseph Molapong's *The Horizon Is Calling* presents four persons in its cast list, though the names Boetietjie Kavandje, Anna Louw, Donovan Isaacks and Karl Pietersen are not the names of characters – they are the names of the actors themselves, appearing as themselves and as characters. From the stage, Anna and Karl offer affidavits of their own experiences, then interweave these monologues with scenes in which they appear as themselves and as other characters.

Here, the most essential medium of the theatre (the actor's own body on stage) is used by performers as a means of protesting the eclipsing of the artist in national reconstruction.

When the actor (in a play or on the world's stage) is engaged to politicise, the theatre rediscovers the reasons why societies invented/needed the mimetic arts in the first place – that is, the need to test the effects of action. A decade after independence it should not be surprising that plots are more complex. Namibian playwrights are less inclined now to stage, in caricature, the apartheid drama (the black and white 'us' and 'them'). The struggle has moved on. Nevertheless, anxieties remain – albeit perhaps more intricately encoded in the texts represented. As the artists begin to rehearse their protest, they begin to script themselves (their own selves) into the dramatis personae of their theatre pieces, so exposing the performer as a legitimate agent, agitator and 'actor'. The performers do this by projecting their own protesting selves in experiments with theatrical form as opposed to puppeting this protest through the produced 'character' of conventional drama.

> Let's persist with our art
> Speak through our poems
> Draw with our sweat
> On the canvasses of our skin
> Let's not give up yet
> ...
> Let's move the Parliament
> To new grounds, space, time
> Cultured foundations of strength
> Influenced by innovative art[22]

---

[22] Joseph Molapong, Let's go to Parliament. In: Poetically Speaking, compiled by Siballi E I Kgobetsi 2000:56, published by Gamsberg Macmillan, Namibia

ENTERTAINMENT THROUGH VIOLENCE? THE SOCIAL IMPACT OF THE VISUAL MEDIA IN NAMIBIA

Tom Fox

Introduction

When societies experience rising levels of violent crime, public discussion invariably attempts to discover the individual propensities behind this, as well as the institutional causes of aggressive social behaviour. To what extent do cultural influences, arising out of today's immensely popular and ubiquitous mass visual entertainment industry, contribute to the spread of violence in Namibia and other modern societies?

There is currently concern in many countries regarding the negative influence of television and cinema on growing degrees of crime and aggression. The expansion of the global mass media today has a considerable impact on our lives, and very few societies are untouched by it. This article will consider this powerful new phenomenon and discuss the role of media such as films, television, video and music in popular culture as an impacting factor in Namibia. Specifically, it will analyse their role as a stimulator of violence in the context of gender.

Television in Namibia

How influential are the mass media in Namibia? What is the likelihood that they contribute to societal violence? To answer this complex question, the growth of particularly the visual media in the country and their increasing influence should be briefly outlined.

Namibia is a young nation where the impact of mass media such as television and cinema has only relatively recently begun to make its mark. To a large extent, the visual and electronic media are still enjoyed by a comparatively small sector of the population, although access is rapidly growing. In terms of television, Namibia, as with South Africa which controlled the country until 1989, saw the arrival of television very late in its history. As Nixon (1994) shows, the South African apartheid government, dominated by the National Party, did not allow its introduction in South Africa until 1976. This was well after many other nations, including African ones. South Africa was effectively the last industrial economy to utilise the medium.

The ban on television in Namibia and South Africa was essentially ideological. It involved a fear of 'Americanisation' (due to the USA being a dominant production and export centre for programmes), and a perception that political control might be lost as threatening liberal ideas flowed in from abroad. Even after 1976, television remained closely censored to exclude 'undesirable' political and moral material. In Namibia itself, the advent of television came even later. The programmes of the South African Broadcasting Corporation (SABC) only reached a tiny minority of Namibians in the early 1980s as transmission ranges were extended to the country, and a television station was established in Windhoek. In 1990, the SABC was replaced by the Namibia Broadcasting Corporation (NBC) and for the first time the country had its own national programming. However, the lack of competitive national production centres meant that it still depended on imported entertainment. Today, only about a third of the NBC's content involves Namibian-produced material, the majority still being imported. A large proportion of programming originates from the USA – a fact that is of relevance for our discussion on the impact of violent entertainment.

In the 1990s, Namibian television was increasingly reaching a greater proportion of the population. While in 1993 23% of households had access to television, by 1996 this had risen to 30% (Namibia Human Development Report 1999, p.91). In 1998, the Director-General of NBC Ben Mulongeni stated that television probably reaches up to 48% of Namibians (Workshop on National Information and Communication Infrastructure for Namibia 11-13 May 1998, Windhoek). While this seems a rather high figure in relation to what other statistics maintain, we should not ignore the fact that Namibians tend to view communally. As in many other developing societies, this happens either in the home of friends or through sets in public places such as clubs and bars. Access also extends to video cassette recorders (VCRs) through which modern popular films may be collectively watched. Of course, there are virtually no statistics available that have attempted to measure collective viewing. It is likely that over 40% today has television access. The fact remains, however, that television viewing is overwhelmingly an urban pastime, involving up to 60% of households in towns and cities. Less than 10% of rural homes tend to have direct access (Namibia Human Development Report 1999, p.20). Statistics reveal a similar pattern in Zimbabwe where rural–urban television access is 10% and 50% respectively (Waldahl 1998).

In addition to NBC, MultiChoice Namibia provides private sector satellite broadcasting on the Digital Satellite Television (DSTV) system. It extensively links the country and the southern African region with global popular media culture, though a much smaller sector of the Namibian public has access to DSTV. Set-up costs for a dish and decoder, in addition to a monthly fee, are certainly expensive in relation to the income levels of most consumers. MultiChoice estimates that approximately 10% of households had DSTV access nationally in 2000, and probably 25% access in the capital Windhoek, making available a broad range of entertainment. Again, English-speaking programming and movies from the United States and Europe tend to dominate the available channels, although various foreign stations are on-hand according to preference. DSTV is a recent, but increasingly popular competitor to NBC. However, the typical Namibian is more likely to watch state television at present, although this is based on ability to receive rather than on free choice.

Cinema in Namibia

While cinema theatres have been offering popular entertainment for longer than television in Namibia, outlets for the public viewing of films have been few. Windhoek saw two of its original cinemas close in the early 1990s. Currently, there is one modern three-screen complex (to be expanded to five screens in 2002). Run by the South African company Ster Kinekor, it chiefly shows popular (often populist) Hollywood mainstream films. Ondangwa's Cinema Paradiso opened in 2001, and probably has the largest black cinema-going public in the country, given its location. Only two other theatres exist in Namibia: at Swakopmund and Walvis Bay. Thus, there are four theatres in the whole country. A new locally-run cinema is planned for Windhoek's Katutura district in 2002/03. As with television, cinema-going is mainly an urban phenomenon. It tends to be particularly popular at weekends, when theatres can be full. No statistics are available on annual cinema visits. While a large majority never visits a cinema, it does not follow that movies are not generally seen. Recent films tend to be experienced on video by large numbers of people. Video-hire shops are common throughout the country and reflect that video cassette recorder ownership or access comes close to that of television.

Films are classified according to their suitability for different age groups. Classification is intended to protect children from violent content, sex or bad language. Classifications are as follows:
- **All:** films suitable for the family and all ages;
- **PG**: parental guidance: access for young children is possible but parents must accompany the child;
- **PG13:** no child younger than 13 years will be admitted, but parental guidance is required;
- **16:** no child under 16 years to be admitted.

The '16' category denotes that the film has high levels of unsuitable material such as sex and/or violence. Other categories include 'X' which usually may be seen only in private restricted clubs, or 'XX'. The latter effectively bans films that the censor considers unsuitable for public viewing. These categories derive from the South African classification system, as Namibia has no board of its own for the censorship and regulation of films. Cinema theatres are required to restrict access of persons who do not qualify under these categories, although it is unclear whether Namibian theatres have a legal obligation to do so, given the absence of legislation.

Young people and the visual media in Namibia

In 1990, a small-scale survey was undertaken amongst the student population of the University of Namibia. The questionnaire aimed at obtaining an indication of how typical young people of both genders between the ages of 18–25 in higher education were experiencing the modern visual mass media in the country. Exposure to television proved to be greater than that to cinema, with 99% of the sample population watching television at least once per week. Only 1% said they had never viewed television. 70% of students claimed they watched television everyday. Most watched NBC, although 28% had access to the private Multi-Choice satellite network. The latter preferred the television programmes of SABC and MNet rather than NBC. When asked to judge if television in Namibia showed high levels of violence, most thought not (66%), while 30% believed it did. The rest of the sample (4%) did not know. Interestingly, some of those in the 'yes' category cited certain local and other African programmes, as well as the usual Anglo-American products, as worrying in portrayal of violence. The most popular programmes indicated by the student respondents were the so-called soaps "Maria de Los Angeles" and "Generations" followed by the comedy "The Wayne Brothers" and the crime-action series "Eighteen Wheels of Justice".

The survey questions on cinema showed that 56% had never been to a movie theatre. While 44% had visited at some stage in the last year, only 7% of this group went regularly on a weekly basis, and 20% monthly. The most popular types of films indicated by respondents were crime and action, followed by comedies. Although the historical epic "Titanic" was the most regularly cited general favourite, major action productions dominated individual preference overall. They comprised movies such as "Enemy of the State", "The Matrix", "Gone in 60 Seconds" and "Mission Impossible 2" being the most commonly preferred. Surprisingly, male and female respondents tended to like similar films and television programmes, even those with higher levels of violence. This indicates high degrees of uniformity in consumer tastes in gender terms. When asked to express an opinion on violence in the cinema, a high proportion of those who had been to a movie theatre, nearly 85%, thought that films shown were too violent – something of a contradiction, as most of their preferred films were significantly violent in content. Another surprising survey result came in response to the question "do you think that violent media material influences any of the violence in Namibian society"? Over 68% expressed the opinion that it did. However, the nature of the survey was not able to determine exactly why the respondents believed this, although some indicated that killings, assaults and use of guns was being copied by young people or was influencing the upbringing of young children adversely (Fox:1998; 2001).

Some interesting conclusions arise from the survey and from semi-structured discussions with the UNAM students. There is a growing interest and fascination with the visual media in the country. Students, along with the public at large, are experiencing access to new forms of popular entertainment that they find exciting and interesting. There are signs that this is fast taking a central place in the culture of their everyday life. There is some awareness of the media's negative side, but this is experienced as an uncomfortable contradiction alongside their enthusiasm and liking for many of the products of popular culture. This is a central finding of the research. Finally, their other concern is that while enjoyable, films and television largely portray societies and cultures other than their own, given the production origins of much of what they watch.

There was particular interest in the NBC television's "African Movie" initiative in this respect, which began in 2000 by showing mainly 'films' from around the continent. However it was accompanied by criticism of quality, and the fact that many were low-budget video products rather than actual films. Some of these were not above using crime and action formats that showed degrees of simulated violence, rape and use of guns. This detail indicates that, contrary to arguments in a recent report of the Namibian Legal Assistance Centre, local or regional production may not automatically create low-violence material.

Does violence in media entertainment influence social behaviour?

Can communication media adversely influence our behaviours so as to make us aggressive, threatening or even murderous? The question is a controversial one. In recent years, Africa has seen radio used for this purpose, for example in Rwanda and Burundi, to transmit hate speeches and calls to engage in genocide. This contributed to massive loss of life and the destabilisation of an entire society. In this particular case, underlying ethnic tensions and historical events rather than the media itself were behind the violence. Less directly, films or television material have been thought to present simulated violence that adults and children have imitated, or through which they have been influenced in ways that contribute to rising social aggression and even crime. To what extent is this the case?

Media studies in Namibia barely exist, resulting in a lack of evidence and information on the impact of the media in the country. Most work on the media concentrates on issues surrounding the freedom and independence of the press (a task carried out and monitored by the Media Institute of Southern Africa, for example) rather than on issues of the mass media's psychological and social influence. Only one specific study has been undertaken concentrating on the issue of the effect of violent entertainment. In 1998, the Legal Assistance Centre (LAC) in Windhoek carried out a survey on violent content in television programming by the NBC in October of that year. While the research was reported in the press, it remains currently unpublished. Standard coding or content analysis was used to count the number of violent acts, including murder, that were either "portrayed or described". (The Namibian, 17 March 2000). The report estimated that 224 such acts were shown to the public in that month. Between the hours of 2.00 p.m. and 8.00 p.m. weekdays and all day at the weekends, 24 murders, 30 violent assaults and five sexual assaults were portrayed. Some 49 incidents were perpetrated on females, 46 on males and 46 on children. The report estimated that on average, a child would be exposed to 288 murders and 2 600 acts of general violence annually, and that adults would experience a higher figure.

A central rationale of the report was to raise concerns regarding the dangers of exposure of young children and teenagers to violent television entertainment. Children are watching television in Namibia more often and for longer periods as access expands, often unsupervised by adults. Global trends show that children now watch television for relatively long periods compared to the past. In the United States, various studies show the figure to be on average 24–28 hours each week. Therefore, the potential for television to negatively influence the delicate socialisation process of the child and of young teenagers is high. Reliable statistics on how regularly adults and children watch programmes in Namibia do not exist, though the rising access to public and private broadcasting of this nature strongly suggests an already-established and expanding culture of viewing for many homes. The LAC report also cites a number of studies from the United States that claim a positive correlation between television violence and real violence in society. The American Medical Association (AMC), for example, showed that 22–34% of young males convicted for violent acts claimed to have been directly influenced by what they had watched on television. Measures to counter such influence must, the LAC report states, be based on more public responsibility on the part of programme-makers and broadcasters. Families also need to monitor carefully what their children watch. The report also addresses consumers, calling on them to complain more about television content and to actively shape programming policy.

One significant drawback of the LAC report seems to be its weakness in examining in detail the actual context of the violence it measured and quantified. Contextualisation is not apparent in the (admittedly incomplete) press account of the report. This, by the way, is a common outcome of much content-analysis methodology. A distinction needs to be made between programmes that gratuitously show aggression and deadly actions for their own sake, and violence that is intended to be part of the logic of an intelligent or educative plot. The LAC newspaper article does in one instance state that in a certain programme, part of the violence shown was incorporated into a critical portrayal of domestic violence. Nevertheless, a detailed examination beyond quantitative measurement does not appear to have been undertaken. As Sayers (1992, pp.60-61) has argued, meaning is always context-dependent. In-depth explanation requires us, in this case, to study the framework around violence in television, including the motivations and the intentions of the makers rather than simply taking a raw act and judging it without any other forms of social reference. The LAC report, however, does provide a valuable basis for further Namibian research.

Social unease about violent visual entertainment began well before these Namibian concerns. The United States, where the first mass market in television emerged following its introduction in 1939, began a long-running debate over violence in the visual media from the 1950s onward. Internationally, the 1972 United States Surgeon General's Report on Television and Social Behaviour represents a landmark document. It formulates the first major official response to media violence on this theme. It comprehensively articulates the possibility of links between rising violent crime and the negative impact of television violence on the behaviour of children and young adults. This report itself stimulated a plethora of sociological and psychological studies on violence and the media both in the United States and outside.

The effects of exposure to high and regular levels of violence on U.S. television were studied by Belson (1978), based on large-scale interviewing of male 12–17 year-olds. They were questioned on what they watched, the degree of exposure, their cultural and class backgrounds, and the types of play and social activities they engaged in. Their statements were cross-checked with their friend's accounts. Belson generally concluded that high exposure groups (who tended to watch a lot of violent programmes as preference) were more likely to be involved in violent acts such as fighting, assault or crime, a likeliness 49% higher than the low exposure groups. Persistent watching of television violence, whether real, simulated or even in cartoon format, increased the degree to which boys engaged in violence. Belson also pointed to the dangers of 'de-sensitisation' arising from regular exposure to imaginary violence in which one loses the ability to be shocked, or even capable of forming a proper social evaluation of aggressive acts.

In relation to de-sensitisation issues, Winston and Woolf studied a month of children's programming in the United States in December 1996. They concluded that so-called 'unsafe behaviours' were depicted in 47% of such broadcasting'. Children were not being socialised sufficiently regarding the real consequences of violent actions or unsafe behaviours, which were being presented as 'without consequences'. Cartoons (such as Tom and Jerry or Power Rangers) tended to present the highest number of these (60,3%), suggesting that this genre has been understudied in terms of possible harmful effects on the young (Winston and Woolf 2000).

Contrary evidence suggests that this research underestimates the early age-ability of children to distinguish reality from fiction. Studies have indicated that between the ages 6 and 11, the formulation of appropriate judgements about what is real and imaginary in televised images increases. For example, children know when actors are playing parts in programmes with relatively simple story lines, and do not see them and their actions as real. Also, news reports were recognised as factual and not fantasy by young children (Jaglom and Gardner 1981). Hodge and Tripp (1986) in another study emphasise that children's responses to watching television involves 'reading' or interpreting what they view. Watching is not a passive exercise but cognitive. Children learn to rationalise when something is real or imaginary. It is not acts of television violence alone that can affect their behaviour, but the general framework of attitudes in which violence is presented.

These contextual and cognitive aspects aside, there remains the issue in the debate on media violence of children or youths simply imitating actions or events in visual media productions and using them as models for real-life aggression. In a study of convicted violent juveniles in the United Kingdom, biographical inter-

---

[1] Unsafe behaviour was defined as involving actions and incidents that would normally lead to injury or death in everyday life, but did not result in such outcomes in the programmes themselves.

views revealed that much aggressive behaviour had been copied from films or television series. In one case, a 17 year-old boy murdered his father in the manner of a similar homicide he had seen on television (Eysenck and Nias 1980:98).

Recent concerns on violent entertainment in the United States

Violence in American films and television is an issue of global concern rather than merely a national one involving only Americans. We have already indicated how Namibians view high levels of media material from this region. America is the major media production centre, and its media industries dominate global entertainment. Time Warner and Disney alone totalled US$46 billion in media sales in 1997. Seven out of nine of the top media giants are American. A high proportion of their sales are now increasingly generated outside of the United States as nations worldwide buy and show their visual and written material (McChesney 1997). Their products are viewed or read in every country, including Namibia and throughout Africa. Indeed, most films shown publicly in Namibia, as well as substantial video rental, involve watching United States production-based entertainment. The state-run NBC television shows considerable American content. On the other hand, violent media material is certainly not exclusive to American production. A recent European Union report condemned the high number of murders and assaults in European productions (Committee on Social Policy, EU 1995).

Concerns regarding violence in the popular media have currently re-surfaced in the United States following a spate of mass killings by youths in various high-profile incidents. The most serious was certainly the massacre of twelve pupils and a teacher by two young, armed students in Denver Colorado in April 1999. As was reported, the killers, who also died, were heavily influenced by the collections of violent movies and video games subsequently found in their homes. Two major reports were written in response to the tragedies. The first one, "Children, Violence and the Media", was compiled by the U.S. Senate Committee on the Judiciary, published September 14 1999. It argues that media violence is a primary cause of rising youth violence in American society. It cites the 2,8 million juvenile arrests in 1997 involving 2 500 murders and 121 000 other violent crimes. This was up 49% on 1988 statistics. By the age of 18, the American child will have seen 16 000 simulated murders and 200 000 acts of violence from various media forms.

The report states bluntly that the media which today dominates the life of the child is 'exceedingly violent'. The Committee points to the fact that violence in prime-time television has increased: in 1973, five violent acts per hour on average were shown, while by 1994 this had risen to 15. Much of the simulated bloodshed is even glamorised, said the Committee. A great deal of television and movie material was directed at teenagers and the report particularly scrutinised high levels of violence in such products, but also in the aggressive lyrics and sounds of popular music. Video games came in for particular criticism as a majority of the themes revolve around combat and conflict, with scoring usually being around a 'kill' tally. These were also regarded as graphically and visually 'real' so as to confuse and de-sensitise young children. The report asks that video games be taken as seriously as other media forms in terms of the damage they inflict on a teenager and child's socialisation.

One important feature raised by the Committee was its concern over portrayals of violence against women, particularly where films and music indulged in sex-role stereotyping, combined with attacks against females. Many movies showed male-on-female violence, not always intending audiences to view this in negative or disapproving terms. Frequently, music lyrics, on the other hand, explicitly portrayed rape and sexual assault favourably in the music of bands and singers such as Nine Inch Nails and Marilyn Manson. In addition, the fact that teenagers seemed to be the target audience was a central concern of the report.

President Clinton commissioned a further key report from the Federal Trade Commission (FTC), a body concerned with consumer protection in all its forms. The FTC published its findings, "Marketing Violent Entertainment to Children", on 12 September 2000. They expressed the same fears as the previous report on the impact that unregulated television, cinema and video content may be having on children and youth. Its approach was quite different in that it specifically tested how the American voluntary rating system of industry self-regulation was working in practice for films, music and video games. Despite product-ratings and labelling aimed at banning adolescents from consumption, children were able to gain access to inadvisable material, and the marketing and advertising arms of the large media industries were explicitly targeting the under 17s to induce them to consume such products.

Consistently, the FTC found that the marketing of all media routinely targeted young children products with parental warnings and age restrictions. Around 80% of R-rated films (restricted, showing violence or other material not suitable for children) selected by the Commission showed marketing and advertising strategies that were specifically aimed at the 12-18 age groups. Of the music with explicit and aggressive lyrical content, 27% directly identified these ages in industry documents, but the other 73% also did this indirectly. Of the 118 video games examined by the FTC and labelled for 'mature' consumers only, 70% were targeted at under-17s, some as low as age six. As well, restricted violent video games were advertised during children's television programmes at early times.

Such reports are deeply relevant to consumers throughout the world. Modern popular culture is consumed globally, and its influence is extensive. Assessing its impact on contemporary childhood, Murray says: "The current media ecology of childhood includes computers and video games, video cassette recorders and laser discs, and ever-changing audio systems with computer interfaces that could enhance the integrity of both education and entertainment in a multimedia society. However, that integration has not yet occurred (...) (but the media) have dramatically altered the nature of childhood and the development of the child" (p.9). He adds that there is considerable discussion as well as disagreement as to how childhood has been affected by media forms, and that a cautious and measured assessment is required (Murray: in Berry / Asament 1993).

Finally, we should not ignore the fact that the mass media may influence adults as well as children. It is interesting to note that few studies look at the impact of the media on mature populations. Also, in societies that are only now beginning to experience and be integrated into the processes of modern (often violent) global entertainment, the social impact may be of a different and unforeseeable nature and form to Western societies with a longer tradition of familiarity.

Gender, violence and the media

Much of the violence against women that takes place in Namibia and elsewhere is based on fairly rigid cultural perceptions regarding gender roles. They define how women and men should behave. This involves ideologies of what is considered 'masculine' as opposed to what 'femininity' constitutes. The modern mass media itself both reflects and reinforces such stereotyping. As Thompson has argued, the degree to which we draw practically upon the modern media for our worldview today should not be ignored or underestimated. They provide us with news, ideas, symbols and models in addition to general entertainment. They are a key element in both our national and global social outlook, as well as being an intrinsic part of the globalisation process itself (Thompson 1995).

The visual media both reflects and shapes our social structure. It provides us with models of negative or positive personality and behaviours. Gender roles are often narrowly and inflexibly presented in terms of 'acceptable behaviours'. The same applies to other media such as books that also tend to engage in gender divisions. A study of children's literature revealed very strict divisions, with domestic themes for girls and active, even violent themes for boys. Interestingly, there has been considerable resistance on the part of parents to allow their children access to other types of storybooks that reversed or countered such gendered preconceptions (Statham 1986). Signorielli shows that gender stereotyping in TV programmes and advertising is widespread. Strong links are made between attractiveness, domesticity and women. Women remain very under-represented in action and crime series, or if present are largely pictured as decorative, sensual and passive. Men or even boys are more likely to appear as controlling or leading characters, tending to dominate women in relationships. Their portrayal is likely to be independent, aggressive, or on the wrong side of the law. Women, on the other hand, are invariably presented as law-abiding. Soaps (particularly popular in Namibian television) tend to be even more conservative in gender presentation, as are music videos (Signorielli, in Berry and Asamen 1993).

The Namibian media reveal similarly strict forms of gender stereotyping. Vickson Hangula's recent Namibian film "Kauna's Way" is an example on the matter. While attempting to examine how young women at school may be open to sexual abuse by males in authority, the plot was not able to transcend the conventional portrayal of female characters as vulnerable, sensual victims. Revenge against the sexually abusive head-teacher in the film is perpetrated not by the actions of the abused girl herself, but by a gang of vengeful males – a scenario that would not be out of place in a standard Hollywood action movie.

In Namibian society where women are beginning to challenge rigid gender attitudes and stereotypes, men may regard it as legitimate and even 'traditional' to use violence to restore the status quo. In such a climate of culturally-contradictory outlooks, media images of women inappropriately stereotyped, combined with excessive presentation of masculinity, may be misread and taken as legitimising 'control' of women, even condoning violence. Films and television may become responsible for reinforcing the male view that women do not have rights in the 'male domain'. Therefore media policy has to develop instruments to promote responsibility in presenting images of everyday interpersonal relations.

Media regulation and violence in Namibia

In South Africa, the IBA Code of Practice specifically forbids gratuitous portrayals of women as victims of violence, unless there are logical or moral reasons for it. In Namibia, NBC television loosely operates a policy not to show violent or sexually explicit content before 9.00 p.m. when teens or young children may be watching. It is also the prescribed duty of an NBC Selection Committee (which includes individuals from outside the NBC) to consider such content, as well as other broadcasting matters. On a practical level though, the Committee does not have sufficient time to review all or even very much programming prior to broadcast. Thus, control is left to the discretion of station producers, sometimes resulting in unreviewed material being broadcast. Warnings are occasionally made before a transmission where known content is thought to be unsuitable for certain people. The LAC report questioned this framework, stating that it did not provide an effective regulation against violent material (Namibian, 17 March 2000). For example, the official 9.00 p.m. watershed is not applied consistently. While violent material is seldom shown before 9.00 p.m. on weekdays, the weekends can be a different matter, with Friday and Saturday slots showing a diet of action and crime series.

In the past year, U.S. programmes such as "To Catch a Thief", "Homicide: Life On the Streets", "Due South" and "RoboCop" (a spin-off from a popular if much criticised violent trilogy of Hollywood movies) and "Eighteen Wheels of Justice" have all been transmitted before 8.30 p.m. While "Homicide" is an intelligent and well-written police drama, often dealing with complex social issues such as juvenile delinquency, domestic violence (including strong gender concerns) and the relationship between crime and low-income groups, most of the other series cited above opt for simplistic good-versus-evil story lines with violence as the key factor in conflict resolution. All of the series here tend to have a high number of explicit murders and assaults in their plots, reaching their audience early in the evening.

If we accept the view that simulated violent imagery may be harmful to young people, there is evidence and reason for concern. In September 2000, for example, an episode of "Eighteen Wheels of Justice" showed the 'hero' beat up a small-time crook; the explanation offered for this violence was purely based on the rationale that the victim was a 'low-life', who under duress could provide information to solve a crime. A similar assault by the series' hero followed, this time utilising a high-powered water-hose. Justification was presented in simplistic moral terms, as is usual in such basic examples of the crime genre. In a later episode, a woman was sexually assaulted, providing gratuitous justification for the several revenge deaths that followed. While violence in "Homicide" was similarly shown in graphic and realistic detail, though with more dramatic and intelligent motivation, even here the rationale was chiefly for a mature adult audience rather than children. As these examples prove, the watershed time is clearly non-operational.

MultiChoice channels such as the South African MNet station show a wide range of popular films and series from English-speaking production centres. MNet operates a strict policy not to show excessive violence or sexual content or air bad language during children's programmes or early in the evening. This excludes even cartoons that are deemed violent. Both MNet and the SABC are strictly bound by the Independent Broadcasting Authority (IBA) Act of 1993, ensuring that broadcasters adhere to a strict code of conduct. This is reinforced by the independent Broadcasting Complaints Commission of South Africa (BCCSA) that acts on public concerns regarding television or radio content. Clause 2 (b) of the IBA Code of Conduct (revised in 1998) states: "Broadcasting licensees shall not, without due care and sensitivity, present material which depicts or relates to brutality, violence, atrocities, drug abuse and obscenity." Violence that is glamorised or serves no indispensable role in plot development is discouraged. The IBA Code also explicitly condemns films or programmes that promote violence against women.

Violence, however, that is documentary or news-based is not affected. Most complaints to the BCCSA concern sexual, religious or political content rather than violence (BCCSA 1999). Theatrical films, on the other hand, are regulated under the Films and Publication Act 1996 along with printed content. The South African Films and Publication Board (SAFPB) is the statutory reviewer under this Act. Since its establishment, it has intervened on several occasions to actively cut or ban films. The US movie "Kids" (1996) showing scenes of drug abuse, HIV, rape and delinquency was rated 'XX' and therefore banned (South African Mail and Guardian, 13 September 1996). As many films shown in Namibia are channelled through the South African distribution networks and reviewed by the SAFPB, and stations such as MNet are directly monitored by the IBA, some aspects of the Namibian media are essentially externally overseen and censored.

Namibia itself currently has no such independent instruments or extensive legal monitoring of television films and video. Overall, there is very limited regulation. The Broadcasting Act of 1991 provides the main legal framework in which broadcasters must work, but there is no implementing structure equivalent to the South African IBA. Codes of broadcasting conduct are chiefly internal to the NBC. Concerning the regulation of video and cinema films, since independence there has not been a body to view and assess these. In May 2002, the first Namibian media ombudsman Fanuel Tjingaete (also retaining the role of Auditor General) was appointed. His duties involve dealing with public complaints on media issues generally, but the initial emphasis seems geared towards overseeing press issues rather than visual media content. It remains to be seen whether or not his office also has the capacity – or the inclination – to tackle issues of violence in visual media.

Concern over violent media content in Namibia is currently low-key. The public appears to be poorly informed of the media debates in other countries, and film and television material rarely arouses controversy. Most complaints relate to perceived political bias, or to perceived sexually-explicit programmes on NBC, rather than to television and film violence. A parliamentary debate in May 2000 saw Members of Parliament bemoaning too much sex on television, but not discussing matters of violent visual content (Namibian, May 8 2000). There appears to be a tendency to regard violent media entertainment as 'normal' within the general public.

There are relatively few research bodies. The launch of the full report on television violence by the Legal Assistance Centre in the near future may encourage broad discussion by providing relevant information and opinions for the general public.

Conclusion

Violence against women and other forms of interpersonal violence are only just becoming an issue of public concern in Namibia today (UNDP:2001). The international debate on media violence reveals that it is problematic to conclusively establish an unequivocal link between violence in society and its depiction in cinema and television. Yet, even if the levels of media responsibility are difficult to assess, there is sufficient unease in other countries for the issue to be taken seriously and to assume a possible link. What is certain is that the socialisation processes of children and young people are today exposed to a mass entertainment medium that is historically unique, and its impact little understood: populations prior to the mid-20th century knew no large-scale equivalent.

The consumption of media products is an intensely cultural activity. 'Reading' and interpreting media content is an active part of contemporary culture and consumption. Audiences in nations where the visual media were put in place thirty or even fifty years ago have meanwhile been socialised into 'reading' signs and cues encoded within popular visual entertainment. This allows them to better distinguish fact and fiction and to better interpret degrees of subtlety, irony and humour, and to decode violence where it is portrayed for reasons that are gratuitous rather than for critical statement. Such audience 'reading', in order to interpret and comprehend, has developed with the evolution of the mass media itself. It is clearly a luxury to which many developing societies do not yet have access. Here, the consumption of media and the cognitive dissemination of cultural decoding systems are clearly out of balance. Consumers now confront an influential, complex set of communication institutions that they may lack the critical tools to interpret effectively.

The danger may be that Namibian audiences who are new to mass visual entertainment misread images or messages of violence and gender stereotyping, resulting in the reinforcement of socially negative role-models – all the more since Namibia's colonial history of social and political violence has had a lasting effect on post-independence society. Violent, confusing and ambiguous mass entertainment may feed into this background at a crucial and delicate time in the rebuilding of Namibian society and identity, complicating pre-existing sociocultural patterns of aggression and violence. This is why a sober assessment of the mass media in Namibia is necessary.

Bibliography

Belson, W 1978. Television, violence and the adolescent boy. New York: Harper Row
Berry, G / **Asamen,** J 1993. Children and television: children in a changing sociocultural world. London: Sage Publications
Broadcasting Complaints Commission of South Africa 1999. Second quarter rulings, 1999. BCCSA website: www.sabc.co.za/pressindx0799
Buckingham, D (ed.) 1993. Reading audiences: young people and the media. Manchester University Press
Commission on Social Policy, Council of Europe 1995. Television and children. Document number cdps Cp/95. Brussels
Eysenck, H / **Nias,** N 1981. Sex, violence the media. London: Paladin Press
Ferguson, M (ed.) 1998. New communication technologies and the public interest. London: Sage Publications
Fox, T 2000. Survey on youth attitudes to popular entertainment in Namibia. Unpublished discussion paper, University of Namibia. Windhoek
Hodge, R / **Tripp,** D 1986. Children and television: a semiotic approach. Cambridge: Polity Press
Hubbard, Dianne 2000. Violence on TV: murder and assault in our homes dayly. In: The Namibian 17 March
Kelly, H / **Gardner,** H (eds.) 1981. Viewing children through television. San Francisco: Jossey-Bass
Larsen, O (ed.) 1968. Violence and the media. London: Harper Row
McChesney, RW 1997. The global media giants. Website: Media Review: fair.org/extra/9711/gmg
Nixon, R 1994. Homelands, Harlem and Hollywood. New York: Routledge
Sayers, A 1992. Methods in social science: a realist approach. New York: Routledge
Sparks, R 1992. Television and the drama of crime. UK: Open University Press
Statham, J 1986. Daughters and sons: experiences of non-sexist childrearing. Oxford: Blackwell
Thompson, JB 1995. The media and modernity: a social theory of the media. Cambridge: Polity Press
UNDP 2000, 2001. Namibia human development report 1999. Windhoek, Namibia
United States Federal Trade Commission 2000. Marketing violent entertainment to children. United States Government, 12 September
United States Senate Committee on the Judiciary 1999. Children, violence and the media: a report for parents and policy makers. United States Government, 14 September
Waldahl, R (ed.) 1998. Perspectives on media, culture and democracy in Zimbabwe. Dept. of Media and Communication, University of Oslo
Winston, FK / **Woolf,** K et al. 2000. Actions without consequences: injury-related messages in children's programming. In: The Journal of the American Medical Association vol.154, no.4, April

NAMIBIAN SOCIETY IN FICTION – THE NAMIBIAN NOVEL

Chrisna Beuke-Muir / Helen Vale / Marianne Zappen-Thomson

Introduction: literature and sociology

Twenty years ago, reflecting on recent trends in the development of African literature, Eldred Jones stated that no other literary branch was growing at a faster rate than the novel[1]. To a much larger extent than drama or poetry, the novel seems to reflect the experiences of the African peoples from pre-colonial times to post-independence life. Throughout the continent, many writers are engaged in the task of hammering out new values and pointing the way towards the social and cultural reconstruction of their societies.

With regard to Namibia, it is an open question as to whether the novel has left other literary genres trailing. In any event, we have witnessed the publication of a number of prose works since independence. Owing to the country's unique history, the Namibian novel is comparatively young – in fact some of the writings have not yet made the transition from fictionalised autobiographical account or short novella to the novel as carefully composed, comprehensive narrative genre.

Jones's statement contains another element, one that is decisive for a sociological approach to the analysis of literature. He establishes the connection between literary production – incorporating both process and outcome, both act and actor – and the social and historical environment producing it. Thus, both elements come into play, the individual literary achievement embodying the author's unique, creative act and the societal framework within which it comes into being. On the one hand, literary analysis concentrates on philology, poetics, stylistics, literary history and aesthetics; it focuses on the systematic treatment of literary concepts, on methods and theories, that is on the ensemble of 'internal' prerequisites of literary production. Probably the most influential approach centring on these internal aspects is to be found in the hermeneutic school, that interpretive science devoting itself to the 're-construction of the original intention of the author' (Schleiermacher). On the other hand, literary analysis goes beyond the act of textual production, envisaging the literary process in its entirety, comprising also the processes of distribution, reception, impact and assessment of literature.

The intellectual product and its producer, and the societal – i.e. cultural, socio-economic, social structural, political – framework are thus both contributing to the sociology of literature. The creative act results from its social determinants – in fact it is a social act in itself[2]. Literary analysis has to take account of this simple but fundamental fact. Fiction (and with it, the novel) represents a document of social content. Its analysis discovers different social worlds – the world fiction

---

[1] Jones 1983:vii
[2] Obviously, the creative act impacts on the social determinants, in its turn.

aesthetically condenses; the world of the characters set in action by the author (the artistic creation); the world of the author her/himself, as reflected in and through fiction; the economic and technological world of all those involved in aesthetic production (the entrepreneur-publisher, the author, the channels of distribution, etc.); and the world of the consumers (readers) of aesthetic products (texts as commodities). Moreover, the sociological approach to literature demands the disclosure of the hidden symbols of social structure, in a semiotic-structuralist tradition[3], bringing to light the cultural encodings of society.

Namibian prose

Namibian fictional prose comprises nearly all languages spoken in the country. Probably the bulk of it is written in one of the languages of European origin, either German or Afrikaans, the two former colonial languages of Namibia, or English, the lingua franca of independence. Also, there is a considerable amount of prose composed and published in the various indigenous languages spoken in Namibia. Interestingly, much of the latter is not distributed through the typical channels of commercialised book industry. Instead, its dissemination makes use of the existing textbook distribution channels set up after independence[4] and is closely linked with the bureaucratic structures of public administration of basic education. It is obviously directed at a different readership. Serving particularly educational purposes, it is conceived for the Namibian youth.

To some extent, such restrictions in marketability make it rather questionable to assign the vernacular prose in question to the national cultural industry, however small it may be yet. Thus, it may lack the characteristic of a literary commodity which is a typical trait, from a sociological point of view, of the modern novel. Historically, this genre was produced for a relatively solvent readership that is integrated into the cultural world(s) created by the all-embracing commodification of the economy and society and knowledgeable of its cultural decoding systems. A sociological perspective on the novel, in this regard, draws on the holistic picture of a sociocultural ensemble combining social actors and social structures involved in the production, distribution, consumption and reception of a literary work of art. In that respect, the vernacular prose could rather be seen as reflecting the dualisms of an economy which is far from being exclusively centred on capitalist relations of production[5].

---

[3] Cf. Foucault, Barthes, Bourdieu

[4] According to Peter Reiner of Gamsberg Macmillan Publishers, Windhoek, the major publishers of Namibian prose in the vernacular.

[5] Moreover, not all of this prose should be assessed as matching the technical characteristics of the literary genre of the novel, such as (amongst others) a minimum size allowing for the development of a complex plot unfolding through the complicated interaction of complex characters. Several of the prose works in vernacular published by Gamsberg Macmillan are small brochures, written in bigger font, of some 50 to 80 pages. Certainly, reference to length is but an indication, not a crucial argument. This is neither to define the novel by setting a minimum of pages, nor to state that there is not yet a vernacular Namibian novel. On the contrary, it is a major gap in this paper that it lacks any detailed consideration of the many works published in indigenous languages since independence. This is an area which warrants much more research by scholars well versed in those languages. English, Afrikaans and German are only three of the thirteen languages spoken in Namibia and by concentrating on these three only, the authors appreciate that their comments could reflect a eurocentric approach to the subject.

Both Western and African novelists in Namibia, choosing to write in German, Afrikaans or English and producing a comparatively expensive commodity, mainly address an educated, affluent middle class public of Western or African origin. Most of their subject matters centre upon the social and political history of the past two or three decades of the struggle against an oppressive racial and socio-economic system of foreign domination in Namibia. However, the authors differ widely in approach and stance. Recently, the contradictory signs of post-independence society have also come into focus. Tangibly, the need for self-assertion and defining one's own position motivate the authors. Their works, intentionally as well as unintentionally, reflect some of the class structural and ethnic heritage of apartheid. On the other hand, in their variety the new novels reproduce the very different social and ethnic settings found in Namibian society.

Analysing the Namibian novel from a sociological angle, the relationship between the literary genre and Namibian society comes into play. How does such a genre (which in its own cultural history has always been closely linked with the modern, bourgeois setting of classes of Western societies as its substratum) match with a reality still heavily determined by a 'traditional' set of social structural relationships? What are the main social issues reflected in the plot and themes of the Namibian novel? How does it reflect social change? In what way are the authors' ethnic and class origins reflected? Considering its very recent origins, how do the authors handle the literary techniques required by the genre? Do they create a complex web of complex actors and characters within a complex plot from which the 'story' (in fact: the protagonist's social history) emanates naturally and obviously – the fundamental sine qua non of the genre? Do authors remain historians, or do they progress towards becoming exciting, well-versed storytellers?

The literary genre of the novel

The novel was so called because of the perceived 'newness' of the genre in the literary world of late medieval Europe. Novels can be broadly characterised as long narratives in prose dealing chiefly with contemporary life. All these features together distinguished it from the main literary genres (types or categories within literature) recognised previously, namely drama and poetry[6]. Its formal 'newness' consisted largely in its openness and flexibility. It is exceptional in that it disregards the constraints that govern other literary forms, acknowledging no obligatory structure, style or subject matter. Certainly, it has become the most important genre of the modern age[7]. It tends to describe a recognisable, secular social world and is expected to have at least one character, preferably several, shown in their (social) relationships and in processes of structural change; in addition a plot, or some arrangement of interrelated events, is another requirement[8].

---

[6] Pope 1998:209
[7] Baldick 1991:151
[8] Baldick 1991:152

Socially, the emergence of the novel was tied to the rapid rise of a new class: both readers and authors in 17th and 18th century Europe largely originate from the bourgeoisie. The new genre historically reflects the rise and spread of modern individualism; in its turn, individualism reveals the occurrence of an element new in social relations: the autonomous individual. It is culturally portrayed as a unique entity, capable of (or, at least, engaged in) mastering his fate, in a social world becoming increasingly estranged from its aristocratic-feudal traditions and more and more embedded in the developing capitalist environment. *Economically*, the new genre was dependent on the rise of a new range of capitalist enterprises, of publishing houses geared towards the profitability or their investments, as well as on the formation of a fairly solvent social group of buyers. *Technologically*, it was dependent upon the development of a print culture. *Culturally*, it relied on the formation of a readership recruited from the ranks of the rising educated bourgeois and petty bourgeois classes, as well as on the formation of national cultures – in many cases, requiring the development of a national language as a prerequisite.

Historically, the novel developed in different shapes in different cultures. Some ancient prose narratives could be called novels (such as Apulejus' *Metamorphoses*, Petronius' *Satyricon*, or Longos' *Daphnis and Chloë*) However, it is the publication of *Don Quixote de la Mancha* in Spain by Miguel de Cervantes Saavedra between 1605 and 1615 that is most widely accepted as announcing the arrival of the new genre. It became the classical model for many of the baroque picaresque novels, now written in popular Romance vernaculars instead of Latin (this explains the German denomination 'Roman', indicating the novel). As a literary category, the term 'novel' seems to have been coined by the Italian humanist Boccaccio already during the second half of the 14th century, referring to a condensed narrative of a new, unprecedented occurrence.

The novel as a strictly bourgeois genre emerged in the 18th century. In England, Daniel Defoe is regarded as the founder of the English novel with his *Robinson Crusoe* (1719) and *Moll Flanders* (1722) along with Richardson, Fielding and Sterne. In France, Jean-Jacques Rousseau contributed the Nouvelle Heloïse (1761) and Emile (1762) as examples of the educational novel. In Germany, the novels of Wieland, Goethe, Jean Paul and especially the romantic novel (Tieck, Brentano, Novalis, Schlegel, E.T.A. Hoffmann, Eichendorff) established a new national literature. The novel achieved its predominance in the 19th century in England when Dickens and other writers found a huge audience through serial publication. They consolidated the convention of 'realism'. Often put on a level with 'naturalism', this paradigm of the art of narrative postulates the identity of image and empirical world, of fictional representation and actual societal model. Novelistic realism represented a fundamental alternative to normative aesthetics as well as to idealistic literary currents. It introduced the critical representation of contemporary social reality as an aesthetic maxim, a literary tool in the artist's conflict with unjust social conditions, thus creating the genres of the critical social novel and of the historical novel. In 19th century France, realism in literature is associated with Balzac, Stendhal and Flaubert; in Russia with Dostoevsky, Tolstoy and Goncharov; in Germany with Fontane, Keller, Storm, and Raabe; in the emerging Italian national literature with Alessandro Manzoni, the romantic author of the *Promessi sposi*.

The African novel

The modern African novel developed during the second half of the 20th century – the date 1958 is often given, since it marked the publication of Chinua Achebe's first novel *Things fall apart*. Some critics regard Olaudah Equiano's autobiography *The interesting narrative of the life of Olaudah Equiano, or Gustavus Vassa, the African* (1789) as the ancestor of the modern African novel. The new type of narrative has come about with the emergence of a new class – the African intelligentsia, at a time of violent social change characterised by the agitation for national autonomy[9]. Starting with Ghana in 1957, many African states acquired independence in the 1960s. This decade was a time of lively artistic creativity as well as intense political activity. African fiction reflects these processes of change. Gakwandi refers to the African novel as 'the creative interpretation of history, beginning at the time of the colonial occupation of the continent'[10].

Most African countries seem to have passed through the following five stages: pre-colonial (the indigenous societies before the colonial impact); pre-annexation (colonial influence via missionaries, traders, etc.); colonial rule (the establishment and maintenance of colonial government); the period of de-colonisation (marked by liberation struggles and the eventual withdrawal of the colonial power); and post independence[11]. The South African writer, Nadine Gordimer, argues that most African novels reflect this historical experience and therefore deal with five main themes:

- The 'countryman comes to town' theme pictures the problems of adjustment to the city where a rural man seeks employment.
- The 'return of the been to' theme takes up the conflictual integration of the privileged Africans returning from their studies in Europe.
- The ancestors versus the missionaries theme considers the conflict between two religious systems, the one backed by a powerful colonial regime.
- The way it was back home theme portrays pristine pre-colonial life and culture.
- The let my people go theme describes the involvement of Africans with the liberation struggle[12].

---

[9] Ngara 1985:30
[10] Gakwandi 1977:10
[11] Haarhoff 1991:141-142
[12] Gordimer 1973:8

One can add a sixth theme to this list. It is found in the novels written since independence, namely disillusionment and critique of indigenous corruption and of neo-colonialism.

Namibian novel in English

The novel is still a relatively recent development in Namibian literature in English with poetry, drama and autobiography playing a more dominant role. In Afrikaans, the novel is on its way to becoming an established form whilst drama and poetry are relatively neglected; however, in many respects, Afrikaans fiction still finds it hard to free itself from the aesthetic restrictions of fictionalised autobiography. In German all three major genres have shown little significant development since 1990. Prior to independence there was only a limited prose in the colonial languages, apart from the range of oral literature in indigenous languages. It reflects mainly the viewpoints of writers constructing a colonially restricted reality. Lombard and Strauss in their "*Impressions of independence*", a collection of Namibian short stories in English edited 1991, link the lack of a prose writing tradition with the constraints imposed by illiteracy[13].

Ndeutala Hishongwa wrote the first novel in English by a black woman. *Marrying apartheid* was published in 1986 in Australia. Through the physical trials and gradual awakening of the heroine, Hishongwa portrays traditional patriarchy compounded and corrupted by the violence of colonialism and apartheid[14].

All in all, very few books in English by black Namibians were published prior to independence. There are two noteworthy exceptions in the field of autobiography and fictionalised biography with John Ya-Otto's *Battlefront Namibia* (1982) and Helmuth Angula's *The two thousand days of Haimbodi ya Haufiku* (1990). This paucity has now changed. Five novels in particular come to mind, all written in the last twelve years since independence. They are: *Troubled waters* (1992) by Josef Diescho, *Meekulu's children* (2000) by Kaleni Hiyalwa, *The purple violet of Oshaantu* (2001) by Neshani Andreas, *A small space* (1998) and *To dream again* (2002) by Brian Harlech-Jones.

Troubled Waters is Diescho's second novel. Diescho, an academic and writer, studied overseas for several years before returning after independence. The novel is set mostly in Rundu in the Kavango in the mid 1970s at a time when South African soldiers were stationed on the Angolan/South West African border. Both main characters, Andries and Lucia, are culturally, socially and racially alienated from their own societies. In defying apartheid in their personal relationship and reaching out to each other, they are seeking to understand the other's viewpoint and tradition. As the author once explained in a talk to the German Namibian Foundation, 'he turns to her as a barometer of culture while she turns to him as an

---

[13] "There is at present no Namibian short story and novel-writing tradition. One of the reasons for this shortcoming is that a viable local market does not exist. The total Namibian population numbers fewer than 2 million people, of whom between 60% and 70% are illiterate." Lombard / Strauss 1991:iii

[14] Orford 1988

interpreter of white ideas'[15]. Reconciliation is shown by the deepening relationship. The baby to be born out of this interracial love at the end of the novel symbolises new hope for the future, a dismantling of old apartheid structures and the birth of the new nation – Namibia. 'And that is what Namibia is – a baby of unknown parents: we need to take responsibility to bring up that child' (at same talk).

Diescho's technique is unusual in that he has ambitiously chosen to use as his main narrative voice that of the white soldier, a focus that is possible intellectually but not lived and experienced. He admits that this immersion into the Afrikaner psyche was very difficult – a catharsis. With his symbolism of reconciliation, Diescho approaches the genre of the novel within an overarching religious framework of love and reconciliation. To some extent, this reflects the class stance of an African torn between contradicting cultures, or more generally, of an academic, internationally-orientated faction of the new Namibian intelligentsia.

Meekulu's Children is set in a small village in Ovamboland. Hiyalwa portrays the life of those Namibians who stayed in the country, perhaps in (unconscious) reaction to the high sociocultural value attributed in post-independence to exile. With compassion, the story follows a young girl, Ketya. She is orphaned when the South African army murders her parents; her brother and sister disappear. Ketya and her grandmother Meekulu suffer years of violence, hardship and poverty, but are sustained by their loving relationship. Ketya is finally reunited with her siblings after repatriation in 1989, but only after Meekulu has died. The conclusion of the novel marks a 'coming home' in both a literal and metaphorical sense, since the matrilineal home gives the potential for healing and reconstitution of the family headed by a woman[16].

Hiyalwa's work could be viewed as an example of an (auto)biographic plot not yet completely condensed into a novel. The characters remain vague, their personalities emanate from the historical events and not the historical events from their individuality and agency. This would certainly be one of the vital characteristics of the convincing mastery of the novel. Despite the somewhat wooden identities of the protagonists, Meekulu's Children presents a step further in the literary development of plot and the command of the technique of the genre, compared for example with Ellen Namhila's *The price of freedom*, Jackson Kaujeua's *Tears over the deserts* or Kapache Victor's *On the run*.

The Purple Violet of Oshaantu is a first novel, remarkably published in Heinemann's renowned African Writer Series. Andreas looks at a number of gender-related issues: the traditional position of women in Namibia, domestic violence, women's inheritance and property rights, and the nature of inequalities in traditional marriage. Her novel focuses on the close friendship between two rural uneducated women. Mee Ali, the narrator, and Kauna live in a village in northern Namibia in post-independence times. Andreas contrasts the more conventional and balanced Mee Ali to Kauna. The latter, victim of her husband's frequent

---

[15] Diescho, personal note Vale 1993
[16] Orford and Becker 1999:17

abuse, is taught by her sad experience to withstand the all-pervasive patriarchal supervision and domination in her homestead and village. To emphasise the (op)positions, Andreas also contrasts the characters of their respective husbands, Michael and Shange. The plot moves the history of the friendship between the two women into centre stage, once the villagers and in-laws react to the sudden death of Kauna's husband, Shange. Kauna's refusal to mourn her husband according to traditional cultural expectations draws all sorts of reprimands and persecution, including accusations of involvement in her husband's death. Kauna learns to question a traditional society that expects (married) women to accept their individual and social definition exclusively through their husbands. Rural life is presented without nostalgia or idealisation and the tone is occasionally humorous. The author's depiction of the two main characters with their strengths and weaknesses is sound on the whole, as is her portrayal of the nature of relationship between them[17].

Much of the novel is written in dialogue form which is mostly natural, and the author makes use of Oshivambo terms (explained in a glossary) which adds authenticity. The purple violet of the title runs as a motif through the novel and refers to both women, since Mee Ali refers to her friend Kauna as such. Michael, the narrator's loving, responsible husband, also describes his wife as this wild flower. Andreas' novel is ambitious with regard to themes, characterisation and description; though it has weaknesses of structure, plot and language use, in the sophisticated terms of the genre.

There are occasional digressions, such as the vivid description of the market scene which Kauna attends with her aunt Mee Fennie, which add nothing to the narrative and could in fact stand alone as a short story. The author uses flashbacks to the extent that the reader can sometimes wonder where the narrative is placed in chronological terms. Occasionally there can be lack of clarity over the meaning of a sentence where the reader needs to read the passage twice to clarify an ambiguity. Some of the characters are not always totally convincing, in that they seem to represent typical cultural (gender) stances: the good husband, the bad husband, the emancipating women, the traditional one, the dominating woman, the urban women, the bitch who steals the husband, etc. The story or plot, therefore, lives out of these 'masks' of traditional village life, rather than the psyche, moods and contradictions of the protagonists.

A small space is set in Namibia's recent history, covering the very last months of the ailing colonial regime and the immediate transition to independence. Brian Harlech-Jones' protagonists take up several causes: the armed liberation struggle and its betrayal, exile, treatment of detainees, repatriation, reconciliation, the prospect of a non-racial future, the vision of social justice, disappointment at the

---

[17] There are interesting parallels between this novel and So long a letter, by the Senegalese writer, Mariama Ba. Both are first novels, both are written by women and both deal with a close friendship between two women in a male dominated society. So long a letter is in epistolary form. It concerns the lives of two middle-aged women who are subjected to the humiliation of their husbands taking much younger second wives suddenly and without their consent. The two women, who are great friends, handle their similar situations differently. Cooper 1992:57

impossibility of a clean start at independence unburdened by the contradictions of the past, the first indications of an internal political and social differentiation within the new Namibian society once the returnees take over, the suffocation of human rights, gender issues, homosexuality, interethnic love relationship, and cultural confrontation.

The plot is complex, interweaving two different sets of time and space: the time of Jan Jonker Afrikaner in the 1860s and the space of Herero-/ Damaraland, the time of transition in 1989 and the space of Windhoek, the capital city, a space of Coloureds, whites and, soon, Ovambo people. Julienne serves as a catalyst for three generations of Coloured women. Living in Windhoek where the political processes of transition converge, she connects with her ancestor Cornelia, kin to the Oorlam leader Jan Jonker, living in Otjimbingwe. Julienne's (day)dreaming not only allows her to draw on Cornelia's generational wisdom in order to master her own apartheid-ridden life; it also allows Harlech-Jones to picture the difficult but not hopeless relationship between Europeans and Africans in a colonial society. The gap of time between the 1860s and the late 1980s is filled by the third woman, Aunt Margrieta, a child of the first half of the 20th century. With regard to space, living in Otjimbingwe, she embodies Julienne's real connection with the past in which Cornelia lived. She personifies a real, intermediate time and space within Harlech-Jones' literary construction, linking Cornelia (who is to be interpreted as a fictional element within fiction) to Julienne (who is the real element within fiction). To Harlech-Jones, Margrieta presents the literary pretext to introduce new, intermediate historical elements relating to the early history of South African domination and to the history of the Nama.

The author disposes with mastery of the different levels of time and space he creates as a technical tool. Falling back on Julienne's family history, Harlech-Jones manages unobtrusively to sketch the complex socio-historical relations between Namas, Hereros, white missionaries offering religion and hunting for souls, and white traders hunting for profits, bringing a new economy by endangering the traditional one. Later, the intricate net of relations between representatives of different ethnic groups of progressive players in the game for independence comes into focus. This enables the author to depict a differentiated reality of contributions to the liberation struggle, as well as the betrayal of its noble goals. For once it is not narrowed down to the conventional mainstream of PLAN's and SWAPO's opposition against the South African military occupation.

A small space is a technically complex work with its blend of the personal and historical, the past and the present. Through detailed research and the inclusion of archival material, this novel weaves a fascinating tapestry of historical and recent events that give an insight into the making of contemporary Namibian society. The personal element is presented sensitively in the two relationships, both interracial; the one between the British, James Neave, and the Nama woman, Cornelia, in the 1860s, and the second between the white Namibian, Simon, a descendant of Neave, and the young Coloured woman, Julienne, in 1989. Reconciliation, symbolised by the love between James and Cornelia, fails in its first attempt; Cornelia is killed when an army of white traders and Hereros raids the Nama settlement /Ae//gams (later to become the colonial Klein Windhoek). But things look different 120 years later, at the imminent end of colonial society. When Julienne and Simon leave the Windhoek stadium after the celebration and proclamation of independence on 21 March 1990, it is "time for them to go home" together. It is with these words that the novel ends – there is hope that their 'parallel' spaces become reconciled.

It is Harlech-Jones's characters that make history; it is their history that exemplifies Namibian history, not coarse-grained representations of Namibian history that are forced upon the characters. Most of all, the novel is readable, gripping; this is a decisive quality, being the first of the author's novels to be published. It is to be hoped that the novel will soon be available as a book; so far, *A small space* is available on the Internet only, its exclusively electronic distribution perhaps limiting its publicity.

On the debit side, Harlech-Jones occasionally indulges in a display of technical versatility, infatuated with the tool 'space'. Also, the reader is confronted with an overabundance of causes the author advocates – emancipation, rejection of abuse, tolerance, to add but a few to the abovementioned. This creates the impression that this first opus is meant to contain at once all of the concerns on which the author has set his heart. Perhaps this points to a contradiction in the conceptual apparatus of the novel. Humanistic rationality is the novel's central thread, the measure of all things, whereas the plot is of highly political character – but rationality and politics can hardly be reconciled. Whereas the plot must follow the emotional involvements of the protagonists, the author interferes, directing them to rational goals. Perhaps, this expresses Harlech-Jones' aesthetic contradiction as well; from a sociological point of view, does it stand to assume that this is a contradiction typical of the author's (unconscious) class stance as a liberal academic?

Harlech-Jones' *To dream again* has only recently been published (May 2002). It may be assessed as the most accomplished Namibian novel to date. However fictitious the settings in Harlech-Jones' new fiction may be, it is a work of social realism. The author manages to retain the interest of the reader throughout with the story of Kerem; even more than in *A small space*, readability becomes the novel's trademark.

Kerem is a black child growing up in Keretani, a fictional southern African country, in the decades before independence. The novel traces the path of the protagonist from rural village to primary school and thence to prestigious high school on scholarship in the capital, Fort Marnay. We follow Kerem's ongoing friendship with Father Arbuthnoir, the white priest; his close relationship to his parents and their death in a landmine explosion; his growing conscientisation and involvement in the liberation struggle as a student; his years of exile in London after suffering detention at the hands of the KNF (Keretani National Front, the liberation movement and subsequent ruling party); his relationships with Rita (the white British girlfriend) and with Sanomi (his childhood sweetheart), his eventual return to the independent Keretani. Kerem's story is skillfully interwoven and contrasted with that of Nozam, his age-mate and class-mate who comes from the same rural highlands village of Totudi.

The author's primary concern is not so much with the social landscape as with the reaction of his two main characters, Kerem and Nozam, to that landscape and how and why they develop in such different ways (informal interview with Vale, 30 May 2002). The novel is strong on plot, the characters are rounded, the tone is often satirical, the imagery vivid and the dialogue convincing. Jones has managed to achieve both simplicity and fluency in this novel which deals with social and political change in themes very familiar to the African novel – struggle, exile, liberation, return, disillusionment and corruption – as well as the more general concerns of childhood, friendship, education and integrity.

At one level the novel can be seen as a Bildungsroman (in that it deals with the individual development and education of the main character); but at another level it offers a perceptive insight into and indictment of liberation movements, post-colonial government in Africa (with their machinations, internal power struggles and self-seeking politicians), the role of the church before and after independence and the processes of social differentiation of the indigenous society. Kerem's history incorporates both individual and social development. The small peasant boy advances to become a newspaper editor; he himself experiences social ascent. But his independent views will make him a dissident in his own country, once he returns from exile. He practises critical journalism, revealing plots laid by the former freedom fighters in conjunction with the internal collaborators. His dissidence provides Harlech-Jones – unconsciously – with a mirror in which the social structural concomitants of many a liberation struggle or social revolution are reflected. Kerem exposes the machinations of the new black élite, of the new 'fat cats'. What on an individual level shows as their personal greed, lust for power or simple opportunism, on a societal level appears as an element of social transformation – and Kerem is there to point to the fact that the formation of an indigenous affluent class follows the customary colonial model: it is based on the exploitation of one's fellow citizen. "Something is rotten in the state of Denmark" – but Harlech-Jones' disillusionment does not go so far as not to allow him anymore to dream again the dream of a just liberation.

The novel's title is a quotation from Shakespeare's The Tempest and relates to Kerem's dream or anticipation of independence for his country. The author uses the first person narrator to good effect with Kerem telling his story chronologically from childhood, though it is interspersed with comments from the adult Kerem reflecting on his earlier experiences. Herein, perhaps, lies a weakness of the narrative. The author, a white southern African academic, has undertaken to put himself into the mind of his young black African protagonist in order to write in the first person – just as Diescho in Troubled Waters portraying his Afrikaner protagonist. The adult Kerem is a consistent character, since he is portrayed first in London's Western, metropolitan social world and then, back in Fort Marnay, in a modern, westernised professional environment. But the youthful Kerem and his social environment remain rather colourless in Harlech-Jones' narrative. Although brought up in a peasant southern or central African homestead, his family is described as a nuclear family; he is devoid of a boy's duties, mainly presented as a pupil. Moreover, as reflected in the father's highly intellectual relationship to Father Arbuthnoir, the white, liberal, humanistic priest, he looks ageless, not childlike. Even the parents' loving relationship seems somewhat ideal in terms of equity and gender. All this may contribute to a certain difficulty in consistently motivating Kerem's turn to the liberation movement. Kerem, once at high school, is attracted by oppositional stances within a very short period of time, not really allowing him to assume a far-reaching transformation. A possible motivation could be found in his character stamp through the long contact with Father Arbuthnoir's humanism. But then, this is to motivate participation in the political struggle by pointing exclusively to Western values. Again, as in the previous novel, the main characters' political attitudes seem to tell their own story about the author himself.

Harlech-Jones (writing as H. Jones for this novel) has lived in Namibia for the past 22 years and through political upheavals similar to those described in the novel, playing an active role during the transition period. It is significant that he has first hand knowledge of the peace process as his historical non-fiction work, A New Thing? The Namibian Independence Process, 1989-1990 (1998) shows, which documents South West Africa's transition from South African rule to independence as Namibia in March 1990.

The new Namibian novel in German; does it exist?

According to the census of 1991, Namibia has a population of about 1,4 million, of which 12 827, that is 0,92%, are German speaking[18]. German is one of Namibia's national languages and still influences the everyday life of many Namibians. This includes the German daily newspaper (Allgemeine Zeitung), as well as the German Radio Service on NBC. Last but not least, German culture also materialises in the variety of typical German commodities, imported as well as locally produced, and German cuisine and its many restaurants.

German literature written since the arrival of the German settlers in 1884 has mainly been in the form of accounts of early settler life (Margarethe von Eckenbrecher *Was Afrika mir gab und nahm* – Africa: what it gave and took from me). The social Darwinist idea of survival of the fittest became another dominant theme. Hand in hand with it goes the idea of justifying the move to the colonies because of restricted space for expansion in the motherland (Gustav Frenssen *Peter Moors Fahrt nach Südwest* – Peter Moor's journey to South West); Hans Grimm *Volk ohne Raum* – Nation without space).

Short stories about hunting expeditions, about nature and life on the farms were quite popular, written by both male and female writers (Bernhardt Voigt *Die Farm am Seeis-Rivier* – The farm on the Seeis River; Lydia Höker *Um Scholle*

---

[18] National Planning Commission 1993:459

und Leben – For clod and life). The authors saw themselves as amateurs; writing for them was a way of remembering the events in their new 'Heimat', or new home country. Then and now biographies and autobiographies played a very significant role for very much the same reason. What individuals experienced in South West Africa and still experience in Namibia seems to differ from the average European lifestyle to such an extent that many deem it necessary to write it down. The most outstanding book in this category is *Sheltering Desert* by Henno Martin. It recounts the harsh experience of two German geologists hiding and surviving in the Kuiseb valley at the beginning of World War Two, in order to escape internment by the South African army. The book has been re-published recently.

The two most well-known pre-independence German novels about Namibia were written by Uwe Timm (*Morenga* 1981) and Jürgen Leskien (*Einsam in Südwest* 1991 – Lonely in South West), both non-Namibians.

Literature in German since independence

The only Namibian novelist in post-independence Namibia writing in German is Giselher W. Hoffmann, who to date has published seven books. Kathrin Thölken presented the only anthology, *Blutkuppe*. Journals like the "Afrikanischer Heimatkalender" at times publish individual poems. No German plays have been produced in independent Namibia.

There seems to be a dearth of German novel production in Namibia. The reason why German Namibian literature in general does not develop significantly may be twofold. Firstly, the few bookshops existing in Namibia sell the latest books imported from Germany. The German speaking reader in Namibia does not experience a vacuum and therefore may not feel the need to become an author him/herself. Though the German speaking community is concerned about the fact that not enough children's and youth literature is available, that does not give rise to a German Namibian production. Secondly, there could be a language problem, since the country's language policy after 1990 promoted English to lingua franca.

Giselher W. Hoffmann is a Namibian by birth, living in Swakopmund. Writing, at present, seems to be his profession. He belongs to the white German speaking community. His novels are read mainly by German-speaking Namibians with whom he shares a cultural and class background. His narrative is characterised by the very gripping description of hunting experiences in Namibia (*Im Bund der Dritte* – Three in a bond), the description of the very particular environmental characteristics of Namibia (*Land der wasserlosen Flüsse* – Country of dry rivers) and the evocation of historical events (*Die verlorenen Jahre* – Lost years).

His fictional characters come from various cultural and ethnic backgrounds. However, there seems to be little scope for change to a modern urbanised Namibian society. Social transformation is occasionally depicted, but Hoffmann's narrative mainly focuses on the disintegration of traditional communities (the Ovahimba in *Schattenjäger* – (Shadow hunters, 1998); the Herero in *Die schweigenden Feuer* (1999, Silent fires), his latest production. Urban life does not really figure in his plots, with the exception of *Schattenjäger*, where the difficult relationship between the Afrikaner and the German community is interwoven with a picture of the labour migrants' fate, a plot mainly set in the struggle for independence. Hoffmann tends to typify characters according to the stereotypes of ethnic alterity. This includes the description of 'the' Boer as much as of 'the' Herero and 'the' Himba (Schattenjäger, Die schweigenden Feuer). His protagonists do not embody the transformation to a new society centring round the new black political and commercial élite. Considering the lack of any other German novels though, Hoffmann should be given credit for taking up Namibian themes. It is through endeavours like these that the German speaking community is forced to take a closer look at itself and its position in Namibian society.

The new Namibian novel in Afrikaans

Afrikaans literature has a long and noteworthy history in Namibia, starting considerably before independence. M. E. Hubregtse (pseudonym, Eva Walters) published her first novel *Eensaamheid* (Loneliness) in 1925[19]. In the period that followed, many more works of prose were produced: juvenile literature, border literature, pro-Afrikaner literature, historical novels, travel accounts, country literature, autobiographies, and after the 1970s, liberation and transitional literature. Although in smaller numbers, several volumes of poetry were also published, as well as two plays. During the ten years since independence, about twenty Afrikaans works of fiction have been published, of which only one, *Rookkringe* (Circles of smoke, 2000), a first novel from Elsa van der Merwe, was published locally.

Of the works with a Namibian theme, those of the authors Piet van Rooyen and George Weideman are the most prominent. Not only did they produce prize-winning literature, their narrative also reached a broader general public. Van Rooyen's books have an explicit Namibian theme, while Weideman's latest novel, *Draaijakkals* (The jester, 1999) deals only partly with the Namibian situation. Weideman (author of eight books since 1990), a lecturer at the University of Namibia during the 1980s, is now living in South Africa.

Van Rooyen, also a lecturer at the University of Namibia, is a born Namibian. Three of his books, *Die spoorsnyer* (The tracker, 1994), *Agter 'n eland aan* (Following the eland, 1995) and *Die olifantjagters* (The elephant hunters, 1997) received major awards, Spoorsnyer the CNA–prize and the Sanlam/De Kat-prize, while Olifantjagters won the MNET-prize.

The novels of Van Rooyen

Die spoorsnyer narrates the story of three men tracking down four Bushmen who had stolen livestock from a farmer. Three men get together on the trail; Paul, the main figure, is the Bushman tracker, then the sergeant and the journalist. The

---

[19] Meyer 1994:15

journalist is on an exploratory mission, observing intensely the art of tracking and of survival in the veld. He intends to record Paul's talents minutely, mythical as they are to him in their nearness to nature, a more and more extinct art. The thieves are eventually tracked down, but Paul is shot in the process. The reader is left with the possibility that the journalist and the sergeant would die, since Paul's death leaves them without a guide capable of leading them back safely through the arid desert to civilization.

Agter 'n eland aan autobiographically relates Piet's and his family's farewell from Stellenbosch (South Africa), his wife's birthplace. They give up a secure living and move to Namibia where they have to start all over again, as the author dreams of his own farm.

In *Die olifantjagters* the white narrator, accompanied by a white professional hunter, Huger, and three Bushmen, sets off to kill the mighty elephant bull, Max-amesi, that had been wounded by one of Huger's clients. The narrator works for the Bushman Foundation, and enters into business relations with Huger, hunting elephants for ivory. The profits go to the Foundation in order to help the Bushmen to extend their cattle farming. During the hunt, two of the Bushmen die, the woman //Uce of malaria while Slinger is charged by the elephant. The narrator falls in love with /Asa, Huger's Bushman wife. Discovering her unfaithfulness, Huger kills himself. Finally, /Asa saves the narrator's life and leads him back to civilization.

Autobiographical aspects

In all three works of prose of Van Rooyen, strong autobiographical elements are present. Especially *Agter 'n eland aan* could be defined rather as a fictionalised autobiography than a novel. The theme is woven around the main character, Piet, who longs for Namibia, his native land where he left behind his soul. By not returning, not only would he break a promise made to himself, but also go against his own nature. The material is presented as a travel account-with-memoirs, and deals with the author's experiences after returning to his country of birth during the independence process.

In *Die spoorsnyer* the journalist-author character, and in *Die olifantjagters* the narrator's connection with the Bushman Foundation can be related to Van Rooyen himself. Through these autobiographical aspects, the reader is confronted with the author's struggle to come to terms with the constantly changing situation in his country during the first decade after independence.

Modern man in search of a new identity

Susan Faludi, an American journalist, discusses the problems that American men experienced after the Second World War in her book, *Stiffed. The betrayal of the modern man* (1999). The rise of feminist movements during the last few decades replaces the traditional dominant male role, making man an inactive onlooker. As a white male in independent Namibia, Van Rooyen experiences the dilemma of belonging to a group forced to adapt to the new role of spectator. This brings to the fore the sociological issue of the male having to redefine masculinity for himself, and for his community.

The representation of the Bushman

Van Rooyen, in all three novels, goes after the eland, the eland being the metaphor for the good, the sacred, to try to find his primordial roots. He believes that what he has lost along the way can be found in the age-old existence of the Bushmen. The Bushman is very much part of the cultural history of Namibia. In more than 60 Afrikaans works of fiction before 1990, the main characters were Bushmen. In all three books mentioned above, Van Rooyen writes about the Bushmen. There are three aspects in the lives of Bushmen that he really admires, aspects that modern man has lost, truths that are covered only deep in the unconscious mind as reminders of man's aboriginal existence. They are the ability to understand the language of the nature and animal (the art of tracking), the ability to lose the Self through trance, and the ability to become fully part of the Other through means of the dance[20].

Through the act of tracking, the hunter becomes one with his prey; man and animal are connected through the track. When in trance, man is connected to the spiritual, the dead, God and the animals, and through dance people of the small community connect with one another. In Van Rooyen representation, the Bushmen live close to nature in a desert area where life is hard. People who live in this way, connected with nature, are stripped to the very essence of the Self. In *Die olifantjagters*, Huger, the professional hunter married to a San wife, says: "As jy die Boesman ken, dan weet jy waaroor dit gaan. Jy kan mooi agter hom sien (...) ("When you know the Bushman, then you know what it is all about. You can see clearly what is going on behind him":32).

Van Rooyen's Bushman characters act as the white characters' saviours. Though conceived along the conventional anthropological lines of the Bushman's pristine nature, the cultural construct of *otherness* is turned upside down. In *Die spoorsnyer* the journalist and the sergeant are totally dependant on Paul to survive. In *Die olifantjagters* the Bushman woman, /Asa, not only saves the narrator's life, but also his soul.

Van Rooyen is by no means blind to the problems the San people face in their struggle for individual and ethnic survival. He describes them in a tarnished manner. In *Agter 'n eland aan* they are represented as drunkards who do not care about the cattle the Foundation gave them in order to help them to adapt from their hunting lifestyles. But he does it against the background of the expansion of the dominant white society imposing such changes on the Bushmen.

For Van Rooyen, the Bushmen's way of life points out the answer to existential questions worrying the uprooted modern man. The narrator in *Die olifantjagters* therefore says: "(E)k (...) glo dat die primitiewe rasse soos die Boesmans iets uit ons onskuldige pasgeskape natuur oorhou waarna ons kan teruggryp as die

---
[20] Van Rooyen 1999:5

ontgogeling te dringend raak. Hulle is die primitiewe spoorsnyers wat ons moet leer om die vae spore van ons verlore self te sny" ("I believe that the primitive nations like the Bushmen still possess something of our innocent, new born nature, something we need to fall back on when the disillusionment becomes too pressing", p.43). Through the Bushmen, Van Rooyen seems to find the answer in the search of his lost self.

Conclusion

The definition of the borders separating novel and autobiography need further refinement. How do writers manage to bridge the gap between the two genres representing two different literary techniques, two different tools for condensing and processing individual and social reality? However, as pressing as these questions may be, space does not allow us to consider them in this chapter.

It is important to state that a sociological perspective is but one of several ways in which to approach the novel form. There are some standard ways of differentiating a novel from other forms of narrative prose, such as those based on a perceptual, structural, mythic, philosophical or subjective analysis[21].

We would argue that treating fiction as a sociological document only rather than as an artistic creation, may be a risk. Such an approach might evaluate literature more on cultural and ideological criteria rather than aesthetic ones.On the other hand, there is also a corresponding danger of treating fiction as an artistic creation only. This understanding disregards that any literary creation inevitably reflects a context of social relations and structures. Every work of art embodies the social conditions of artistic production, its social environment and the social world that made it.

A vital aspect of the novel as a new literary genre lies in its aspiration to create/shape acting characters. This is closely linked with the rise of bourgeois individualism permeating modern culture, and it is through the nature of the characters that realism shines through and that history is demonstrated. Sociology of literature, in conceiving the individual first and foremost as a social being reveals to what extent the assertion of individuality is produced in and by a specific society, our modern society. The emphasis on individuality stands for the bourgeois genre of the novel.

In a society like the Namibian which is not typically bourgeois, culturally and socially, but rather based on the development of typical dichotomies of rural/urban, traditional/modern, communal/bourgeois, the novel most probably reflects the conflicts in which individual characters find themselves involved. These characters originated from a 'traditional' world where they never were 'individuals' in the bourgeois sense of the word. They develop and experience their individuality, imposed on them by the historical circumstances. Individual development and the development of individuality create a conflict within the

---

[21] Stewick 1967:3

individual which is uprooted from her/his origins. The circumstances forming the individual character inevitably shine through – indigenous society and culture, inter-ethnic conflicts, European occupation and colonisation, the devastating impact of Western culture and Christian evangelisation; colonial wars, exile, migration, political activism, the aspiration of the new black élites.

In Namibia the novel in English has been in nature essentially socially realistic, reporting on history and the social and moral world and reflecting the historical and social circumstances outlined above (see in particular *Meekulu's children*, *A small space* and *To dream again*). Those Namibians who turn to creative writing seem to be not only of reflecting their own social reality but also coming to terms with a traumatic past.

Whilst the Namibian government has adopted the politically expedient policy of national reconciliation as the major cornerstone of its philosophy, we would argue that it is not yet possible to speak of the Namibian novel as an integrated, cohesive, reconciled entity but would rather speak of a fragmentation of novels in embryonic form, deriving from different histories and traditions and revealing very different ethnic and class cultural experience.

Bibliography

Andreas, *Neshani* 2001. The purple violet of Oshaantu. Oxford: Heinemann
Angula, *Helmut Pau* 1990. The two thousand days of Haimbodi Ya Haufiku. Windhoek: Gamsberg Macmillan
Ba, *M* 1981. So long a letter, Oxford: Heinemann
Baldick, *C* 1991. The concise Oxford dictionary of literary terms. Oxford University Press
Cooper, *B* 1992. Debates, dilemmas and dreams. Johannesburg: Heinemann-Centaur
Diescho, *Joseph* 1992. Troubled waters. Windhoek: New Namibia Books
Equiano, *Olaudah* 1789. The interesting narrative of the life of Olaudah Equiano, or Gustavus Vassa, the African (ed. by Edwards, P 1988. Harlow: Longman
Faludi, *Susan* 1999. Stiffed. The betrayal of modern man. London: Chatto & Windus
Gakwandi, *SA* 1977. The novel and contemporary experience in Africa. New York: Africana Publishing
Gordimer, *Nadine* 1973. The black Interpreters. Johannesburg: Sprocas and Raven Press
Haarhoff, *Dorian* 1991. Study guide for English 1. Windhoek: University of Namibia
Harlech-Jones, *Brian* 1998. A New Thing? The Namibian Independence Process, 1989-1990. Windhoek: Ecumenical Institute of Namibia
Harlech-Jones, *Brian* 1999. A small space. Website www.online.original.com
Hishongwa, *Ndeutala* 1986. Marrying apartheid. Australia
Hiyalwa, *Kaleni* 2000. Meekulu's children. Windhoek: New Namibia Books.
Hoffmann, *Giselher W* 1991. Die verlorenen Jahre. Swakopmund: Hoffmann Twins
Hoffmann, *Giselher W* 1983. Im Bund der Dritte. Swakopmund: Hoffmann Twins
Hoffmann, *Giselher W* 1989. Land der wasserlosen Flüsse. Swakopmund: Hoffmann Twins
Hoffmann, *Giselher W* 1998. Schattenjäger. Swakopmund: Hoffmann Twins
Hoffmann, *Giselher W* 1999. Die schweigenden Feuer. Swakopmund: Hoffmann Twins
Jones, *BH (i.e. **Harlech-Jones**, Brian)* 2002. To dream again. Cape Town: Kwela Books
Jones, *E* 1983. Recent trends in the novel. African literature today, vol.13. London: James Currey
Kaujeua, *Jackson* 1994. Tears over the deserts. Windhoek: New Namibia Books
Lombard, *J / **Strauss**, J* 1991. Impressions of independence – six Namibian stories. Windhoek: Gamsberg Macmillan

Meyer, *AC* 1994. Namibies-Afrikaanse Literatuur (doctoral dissertation). University of South-Africa
Namhila, *Ellen* 1997. The price of freedom. Windhoek: New Namibia Books
Ngara, *E 1985*. Art and ideology in the African novel. London: Heinemann
Orford, *M* 1988. Namibian women's writing marginalised. In: Africa News Service. Durham: African Virtual Gateway
Orford, *M / Becker*, *H* 1999. Home and exile: Ovambo women's literature. Paper presented at Zimbabwe Book Fair / Women Writers' Conference. Harare
Pope, *R* 1998. The English studies handbook. London: Routledge
Stewick, *P* (ed.) 1967. Theory of the novel. New York: Free Press
Timm, *Uwe* 1981. Morenga. Reinbeck bei Hamburg: Rowohlt
Van der Merwe, *Elsa* 2000. Rookkringe. Windhoek: Out of Africa Publishers
Van Rooyen, *Piet* 1995. Agter n eland aan. Cape Town, Pretoria: Queillerie
Van Rooyen, *Piet* 1994. Die spoorsnyer. Cape Town: Tafelberg
Van Rooyen, *Piet* 1999. Bemoeienis met die ander: Boerskrywer en Boesman. Langenhoven lecture presented at the University of Port Elizabeth
Van Rooyen, *Piet* 1997. Die olifantjagters. Cape Town: Tafelberg
Victor, *Kapache* 1994. On the run. Windhoek: New Namibia Books
Walters, *Eva* 1925. Eensaamheid. Pretoria: Van Schaik
Weideman, *George* 1999. Draaijakkals. Cape Town: Tafelberg
Wozniak, *Janina* 1985. Deutsch-Südwestafrika in der Kolonialliteratur. Ein Überblick. In: Interessengemeinschaft deutschsprachiger Südwester, pp.212-214
Ya-Ndokomani, *L* 1998. Interview with I. Mbise and H. Vale on drama in Namibia, July 1998
Ya-Otto, *John* (1982) Battlefront Namibia. London: Heinemann

4 SEXUALITY AND HEALTH

The culture(s) of AIDS – cultural analysis and new policy approaches for Namibia
Tom Fox

Sexual cultures in transition in the northern Kunene – is there a need for a sexual revolution in Namibia?
Philippe Talavera

How to make sense of lover relationships – Kwanyama culture and reproductive health
Britt Pinkowsky Tersbøl

Traditional and Western medical knowledge systems in Namibia – is collaboration in diversity possible?
Debie LeBeau

THE CULTURE(S) OF AIDS – CULTURAL ANALYSIS AND NEW POLICY APPROACHES FOR NAMIBIA

Tom Fox

Introduction

Since the first cases were diagnosed in the mid-1980s, the HIV/AIDS pandemic has undeniably had a devastating impact on Namibian society. But then, why is it a pandemic, the sociologist may naïvely ask? What precisely are the underlying social processes feeding into and accelerating the disease? The epidemiology of the virus is linked to distinct sociocultural settings; and these settings represent a unique environment and cause of the appalling success of HIV/AIDS over the last decade.

Cultural explanations for the spread of HIV/AIDS are not new. However they have only recently begun to be utilised in Namibia as a practical and valid research approach in relation to the disease. They have yet to be taken seriously by state, non-governmental organisations and HIV campaigns officially charged with ameliorating the pandemic. Various international studies in the 1990s have indicated the usefulness of a cultural perspective (for example: Ford 1991; 1994), though limited work utilising such a cultural framework has been undertaken in Namibia to date. Amongst the Namibian studies, Tersbøl (this volume), and LeBeau and Fox et. al. (2000) have looked at sexuality and culture. They focus mainly on northern Namibia, specifically on Oshivambo and Oshikwanyama linguistic communities. Also, Talavera is currently engaged in research amongst Himba groups in Kunene (this volume). All have dealt with aspects of sexuality, culture and HIV/AIDS linkages.

The integration of cultural analysis into the study of HIV/AIDS is necessary, along with related policy measures to combat the pandemic. Surprisingly, culture as a conditioning frame for human behaviour remains a neglected factor in the fight against the disease. While HIV/AIDS awareness campaigns partially recognise cultural aspects, they do not do so systematically or in depth. The culture behind HIV/AIDS, or the cultures of HIV/AIDS, remain a marginalised phenomenon. While other variables are undoubtedly also important -a plurality of influences holds sway for all forms of explanation – the neglect of cultural systems has the serious practical effect of weakening both the understanding of the social processes generating HIV/AIDS, and the effectiveness of the health campaigns directed at breaking the destructive hold of the pandemic.

What is cultural analysis?

How can culture be applied to the study of HIV/AIDS? What is cultural analysis? Basically, it represents a field of study grounded in the disciplines of sociology and anthropology. It regards human action and behaviour as regulated (in certain structuralist accounts as 'determined') by specific norms and institutionalised values. All people tend to act in relation to regularised norms; and while degrees of choice are clearly available to them, much of their actual behaviour is carried out within the limits of these formalised social parameters. Socialisation processes convey to them the fixed and changing ways of life, the cultural norms of society: in early life through the institution of the family, through education systems, via the day-to-day interactions with the immediate community in which we reside. After childhood, other institutions and social members constantly reinforce these. Globally, the mass media and the world of commercialised consumption have in recent years become a powerful new socialising influence. They impact on our way of life, and even on the structures of sexuality.

Societies encapsulate different traditions of sexuality: cultures based on monogamous sexual relationships will expect men and women to have one long-term partner at a time, to the exclusion of others[1]. In polygamous societies the norm differs, with men having several sexual partners at the same time. Usually, such patriarchally-shaped culture denies the same variety to women. Gay sex relationships tend today to be more tolerated in Western societies than in other parts of the world. The very existence of these types of behaviours arises from the cultural systems of specific societies, and not directly from unfettered individual choices. Both Durkheimian sociology and Foucault's work express this quite well.

Durkheim argues that a collective consciousness envelopes the individual as a reference point for his/her behaviour. Thus, we stand in the middle of a cultural matrix of reason and emotion that profoundly influences us. For sexual practices, sanctions and taboos are set up to ensure compliance with the community sentiment of what is permissible. Punitive and restitutive law is brought into force when the person crosses the line between the acceptable and the profane in sexual matters (Durkheim:1896; 1980). Similarly, for Foucault there are historically-constructed 'social regimes' (in different forms in different societies) that have a significant bearing on the mentality, subsequent actions, and daily decision-making processes of individuals and groups. The French sociologist speaks specifically about power in this respect. Power relations of an impersonal nature run in and through social institutions and individuals, as well as across the macro- and micro-practices (actions) of subjects (Foucault:1970).

Foucault argues that norms and values around sexuality themselves encapsulate power relations of particular epochs, which cannot be reduced to class or individual power: power is everywhere, but often invisible, except in its socio-legal forms as law. Modern societies tend to shift power more and more into an individual, internalised acceptance of power structures, embodying a characteristic feature of the modern, individualised social being. Power is the force (neither benign nor oppressive) that shapes our behaviour. Sexual culture and its norms of

---

[1] Although the practice of 'serial monogamy' – staying with one sexual partner for a limited period of time before moving on into other limited monogamous relationships (as practised in the United States and European countries) may also be culturally prevalent.

licit and illicit, permitted and forbidden, are its expression (Foucault 1978:83). On the other hand, power (including its sexual forms) is always contested: "where sex and pleasure are concerned, power can 'do' nothing but say no to them (...) its effects take the form of limit and lack" (Foucault 1978:84).

In the case of Namibian society, we will see how relevant this statement is to contemporary conditions. People either challenge 'traditional' practices, or they seek to reinforce old sexual norms against challenge. Foucault is correct to tell us that of all the areas of social life, sexual practice and identity are the most difficult for power relations and authorities to control and contain. It therefore produces the most contradictory, and most resistant, forms of response. Women's rights, gay rights, the call for more open discussions of sex: all represent the struggle to redefine sexual parameters against 'regime' prohibition.

Cultural analysis can be used to locate and analyse underlying social mechanisms and norms that generate the types of sexual behaviour favourable to the spread of HIV. So far, health campaigns have generally failed to evoke a decisive public shift away from high-risk sexual behaviours, despite providing information and warnings about the disease. A cultural approach goes a long way toward explaining why these campaigns have met with minimal success. A cultural analysis of HIV/AIDS within an anthropological and sociological framework represents one important (if neglected) element necessary both in understanding the social, norm-based generators of the disease, as well as explaining current weaknesses in programmes to combat HIV/AIDS[2].

Rational choice and HIV/AIDS campaigns

Namibia, as with southern African societies generally, stands at the epicentre of the current HIV/AIDS pandemic. Africa contains 90% of the total global infection rates that affect over 40 million people worldwide. Internationally, some 26 million people to date have died (UNAIDS 2002). Why is Namibia amongst the seven nations worst affected in world terms? According to a recent report by the Social Impact Assessment and Policy Analysis Corporation (SIAPAC), by the end of 2001, 219 000 people from all social levels were living with the HIV virus in Namibia (The Namibian, May 21, 2002). Following years of positive improvements, life expectancy dramatically decreased by 5,7 years between 1995 and 1998, and impacted on the economy by shaving off nearly 2,5% in gross domestic product (UNAIDS, June and December 2000). The SIAPAC report more pessimistically sees longevity rates as falling to below 40 years over the coming decade, reaching levels of fifty years ago. Why are Namibian rates so high? Why have the extensive, apparently well-organised health campaigns in the country (and in other African states) had only partial or no impact on the spread of HIV/AIDS and

---

[2] A recent southern African regional report recognised that policy measures to alleviate HIV had made little headway, and that a better understanding of the underlying processes was now necessary (SADC 2000:147).

on attempts to curb life-threatening sexual behaviours of the population (SADC 2000)?

The problem, we argue, lies substantially with the initial methodological philosophy and construction employed in health campaigns – in particular, their operating concepts. There is a tendency for health campaigns to adopt individualistic categories in the formative stages of planning, and to the neglect the sociocultural context that holds the key to why diseases such as HIV/AIDS spread. The social processes and structures behind the movement of HIV are largely unstudied in Namibia.

The practical orthodoxy of health campaign philosophy is to attempt to ameliorate a specific disease-based health problem by encouraging hygiene practices and/or a shift in behaviour. Usually, a particular population group perceived to be suffering in health terms is targeted, or more commonly a national community. In the case of HIV/AIDS, large-scale national populations are the end-recipients of information and warnings. These warnings, usually instigated by ministries of health and non-governmental agencies in the country, are designed to create a 'positive' response inducing a qualitative change in people's behaviour. Results are measurable, in success terms, if infection rates begin to fall. But – and this is a big 'but' – while communities are the target of the organised health messages, in reality these campaigns tend to see the individual as the primary object of influence, an abstractly-conceptualised individual. The broader structural context of community, society and (importantly) culture, are at best token concepts in orthodox campaigns, that rarely examine sociocultural variables meaningfully.

Is this individualistic approach useful? To push our argument ahead: the main (but not sole) cause of HIV infections is through exchange of body fluids during sexual intercourse with a person living with the disease. It automatically follows that sexual activities and behaviours are heavily implicated in epidemiology and transmission. Still, health campaigns conceptualise sexual activity as an 'individual' matter. Sexual behaviour and sexuality generally are socially constructed and regulated. Their specific character or regime will differ from one society to another, or indigenously from community to community. An understanding of this sociocultural framework is therefore important for assessing the socio-structural influences on not only sexual behaviour, but all forms of human behaviour.

Individuals, while capable of choice, are rarely the free independent agents that health campaigners assume; they make minor and major life decisions bound up within the limits of institutionalised social networks. As Anthony Giddens' theory of structuration tells us, people are social agents who operate within contexts of complex written and unwritten social structural rules that are both enabling and constraining. Some are universal, others peculiar to certain cultures. We make our decisions on how we behave or act in accordance with shared social frameworks that involve sets of rules, resources and norms (Giddens:1984). We are therefore constituted beings, according to our local and national settings. To leave these frameworks mute and unexamined when attempting to understand sexual behaviour, is untenable in ameliorative policy terms.

Rational choice and health campaigning

The assumptions about expected individual responses to Namibian HIV/AIDS campaigns information and directives (to the 'Say No To Sex' programme of the mid-1990s, for example), as in other countries, tend to be based on the recent vogue for 'rational choice' models, either coincidentally or by design. They are derived from the works of Bates and North, and were first used in neo-liberal political economy in the 1980s[3].

The 'rational choice' approach has since become paradigmatic for a certain school in the social sciences. It uses a simplified set of assumptions about human motivation that takes the individual as its reference point. Individuals supposedly act to maximise their interests through the calculation of personal costs and benefits. All behaviour reflects a rational calculation of gains and losses ('how can I succeed? What are the risks?'). The approach, in its turn, draws heavily on the classical paradigm of economic rationality as developed by the theory of marginal utility in the 1910s, and applied by Max Weber in formulating his concept of social action. The 'rational choice' approach is thought to be the key to understanding most types of human actions and behaviours, including sexual (T.Philipson and R.Posner 1995:839).

Health campaigns assume that if adequate information is provided, the person will then rationally assess facts and argument and apply it to their own situation. They will calculate what the benefits are to him/her in responding; and what the risks and losses of not reacting are. The assumed, and indeed planned, campaign outcome in the case of health matters such as HIV/AIDS is that people will (or should) automatically choose to change their behaviour rather than continue to indulge in risky life-threatening sex. In other words, they have a rational choice to make.

There are serious flaws in such an approach when confronted with cultural theory. Much individual behaviour arises out of cultural systems and structures. Is it conceivably useful that systems of norms, values and prescriptive sociocultural rules be left out of the picture? As Leys has pointed out, there is often a conflict between individual and collective preference that cannot be accommodated within the assumptions of rational choice theory (C. Leys 1996:96). Collective culture-based influences entail group norms and 'ways of life' of a population. They have a tendency in certain respects either to set limits on, or to rule out, 'rational' individual decision-making. This is true for anywhere, and is not peculiar to Africa or Namibia. Social life is never entirely an individual matter, despite being one of the unsustainable myths of neo-liberalism and its rational choice offspring. It is difficult to change medically-threatening human behavioural practices while neglecting the sociocultural norms underpinning that behaviour.

---

[3] This was first applied to development issues: in Bates' case, to the problems of agricultural efficiency and productivity in Africa (discussed in Leys 1996:80). Later, the approach was taken up in other areas of the social sciences, and in practical public policy, eventually being applied to health programmes.

Another critic of this approach has argued that the rational choice philosophy "only works if all types of behaviour are taken as rational or maximising interests". Yet people may act on the basis of other factors, such as habit or custom, impulse or emotion (Mufune 2000). Mufune points out that there is a marked non-rational character to many of our actions, echoing the Weberian distinction between rational and affective or emotional human action. More specifically, in the cultural context, the collective values of our society and community may act as a profound counterforce to individual rational choice assessment.

Culture and HIV/AIDS: Namibia

In 1998, qualitative research on HIV and sexual behaviours was undertaken in four regions of northern Namibia. Oshivambo linguistic communities were exclusively chosen to ensure a relatively stable and consistent cultural target group. The research showed a range of significant cultural influences on health risk-taking behaviour in relation to HIV/AIDS, and sexually transmitted infections in general (LeBeau, Fox et al. 2000). It is such cultural influences that have to be identified and interpreted in relation to the structures of contemporary sexuality. They represent precisely those cultural variables that cultural analysis highlights, and that need to be addressed in HIV/AIDS health campaigns in Namibia.

Namibian cultural traditions can be seen as an important source of the transmission of the pandemic. Namibia has a complex multicultural character, not unusual in southern Africa, producing distinct identities within and across different ethnic groups. At the same time, Namibian cultures are today beginning to substantially share national values and norms, beyond their unique value systems. Nation-building is slowly bridging the former ethnic exclusivity, and dissolving it[4]. At the same instant, local and national culture is increasingly influenced by new exogenous values transmitted by the ubiquitous global mass media. However, so-called traditional or ethnically specific values continue to exert authority, but entwined in complex ways with emerging sociocultural norms of a cosmopolitan character.

Due to this complexity, contemporary Namibian culture is neither immediately 'recognisable' nor particularly easy to construct as a system or structure that can be readily applied to the question: how does culture contribute to the spread of HIV/AIDS? Cultural analysis has to avoid falling into the trap of ignoring a century of external interference and cultural transformations. Displacement and exogenous socio-economic values brought by colonialism, contact with other peoples and places via the migratory character of the contract labour system, as well as rapid globalisation since the 1980s, have made the very idea of coherent exclusive identity highly problematic for all Namibian ethnicities. Also, this makes the concept of what is and what is not 'traditional' extremely problematic – 'tradition'

---

[4] Talavera discusses this process in this volume.

being a process of constant renewal where previous values are disembedded and replaced in complex manner.

Cultural regulation of sexuality in North Namibia

The research undertaken by the present author and team from the University of Namibia in 1998 shows that amongst the Oshivambo linguistic communities of Eenhana, Outapi, Tsumeb and Oshakati, there prevailed a synthesis of old and new ideas about sex and sexuality. Respondents over 35 years had more 'old-fashioned' perceptions on matters of sexual behaviour. The attitudes of young people under 21 years often reflect stronger modern influences in sexual matters; but combined with the assertion of older cultural norms. Marked differences of views in gender terms also became apparent.

As in the past, young people are formally restricted by rules governing sexual relations and behaviours. Sexual boundaries, as in all societies, are carefully drawn and defended according to collective norms.

> Young men in Tsumeb under 20 years were aware of cultural regulations that forbade both sex and girlfriends until a specific age: "According to our tradition a boy of our age was not allowed to have a girlfriend. If you stay in your father's house, you are not allowed to have a girlfriend or have sex. The father tells you when it is the right time to have a girlfriend. The right time is when you are over 20," one male youth said. Usually, this regulation is still operative after the youth has left home. The father is responsible for finding land for his son's homestead suitable for crops; but the son has no sexual freedom until marriage: "you are being given a key, but it is not a guarantee that you are free. If your father hears that you are going out with girlfriends, he may still come and question you about it. And if you respect your parents, then you have to do what he says" (men 15-19, Tsumeb). Similar views were expressed in other research sites, and parental approval of marriage partners was vital. The age when females were allowed to engage in sex was perceived to be 18 years; less than for men. Marriage was a precondition for sexual relations; but before marriage, the efundula ceremony had to have been undertaken, where girls pass into womanhood. This has largely (but not entirely) fallen into disuse in recent times, although thought to have been replaced by less formal family gatherings fulfilling a similar social function.

In theory, this type of social environment (despite its paternalistic-authoritarian leanings) provides the conditions for holding HIV/AIDS epidemics at bay. Reality is different. The research provides sufficient evidence revealing the complexity and contradictory character of sociocultural structures. Elements described so far are based on a culture of monogamy. They probably reflect Christian-religious influences introduced by European missions more than a century ago. Yet, potentially pre-colonial variables of a polygamous culture also appear in the respondents' views. Community members frequently referred to the existence of polygamous-style practices in Ovambo cultures both before and after formal marriage. These we examine below.

Poly-partnerships and HIV: males

The issue of multi-partner sexual relations is obviously relevant for the cultural analysis of the HIV/AIDS pandemic.

> "According to the culture, it is allowed for a man to have more than one wife. For example, (a man may have) five wives in the house, and others outside" (women 30-49, Tsumeb). Both younger and older respondents were widely and distinctly aware of such a norm conflicting with Christian monogamy. An informant of nearly fifty years of age said that his grandfather had ten wives. He thought there were still enough people with four wives in parts of Eenhana in 1998, although one wife due to Christian influence was now chiefly the norm. Moreover, males and also women tended to have sexual partners outside of single-partner marriages as in the old days. This may be a reflection of such past practice. The only restriction was that a man could not have sex with another man's wife without being fined in cattle or other property; or being forced to leave the district in the event of being propertyless and unable to pay.
>
> An elderly Eenhana headman in his seventies stated that multiple sex partners were "part of tradition"; and to have a relationship with just one female has always had negative connotations, suggesting poverty, low status and "weak manhood". An ability to materially support many women implies wealth and sexual prowess: one was "a big man". Many male informants suggested that such thinking has survived the constraining power of over a century of European Christian ideology pertaining to one man, one woman partnerships. Several older female community members maintained that men in the area had always had children outside marriage with other women: "Some men continue this practice even today. But now it is risky with STDs (sexually transmitted diseases; TF) and AIDS. Men don't take account of this." (women 30-49, Eenhana). The abovementioned elderly Eenhana headman made an interesting and relevant statement on sexually transmitted diseases: "a long time ago, a man who did not suffer from (what we now call) gonorrhoea or syphilis was not a real man." As it seems, sexual diseases, both before as well as after marriage, interestingly symbolised status in matters of love and sexual success over women. No men interviewed during the research appeared to value STDs in this way today, most being relieved that there were effective clinics provided by government to deal with STDs. Having many lovers was not however the norm for women, according to men: "It is alright for a man to have several women, but not for women to have more than one man, because even in the Bible we read that Solomon had 20 wives (...) the Bible does not say that a woman may have more than one sexual partner" (men 30-49, Tsumeb).
>
> An Eenhana pastor stated that in the past, unmarried men would have lots of girlfriends, even though they were not meant to have sex with them before marriage; and married men would take up to four wives. In reality, people privately had sex before marriage and outside of it, despite being forbidden. Aspects of the 'traditional' culture still seem to prevail in this respect, in conflict with church morality: "I think people want to follow their traditional culture (...) and men have many partners. But to promote tradition now is very dangerous in the time of AIDS". He thought people were now more promiscuous than in the past.

The anecdotal evidence and public opinion on polygamous relationships shows the weight of cultural factors that possibly originate before Christianity. Surprisingly, there is a clear awareness of polygamous relationship amongst young people below the age of nineteen, who ironically are quite prepared to utilise this 'traditional' knowledge as a justification strategy (either open or secret) for breaking with the wishes of parents' more conservative Christianised cultural norms. We see Foucault's 'contestment' concept in operation here. Cultural values become a role model for action and cultural justification, impacting on the construction of personal and group sexuality. In the same instance, it becomes obvious that such polygamous values (in the colonial past and at present) exist in uneasy contradiction with Christian culture, and have done so for a long time. The need for a conceptualisation of 'cultural contradiction' emerges in order to capture the inconsistencies prevailing in social institutions and structures.

Poly-partnerships and HIV: females

There may, however, be a growing female variant of multi-partner relationships emerging in modern Namibia: a different form of contestment arising from the re-negotiation of gender norms, and tied to economic strategies – albeit receptive to HIV transmission. The role of women is changing in the country despite deep-seated conservative values. Winterfeldt has shown that a larger proportion of women now engage in internal migration, breaking what was in the past a distinctly male phenomenon. In 1995, nearly half of the arrivals in Katutura (Northern Windhoek) were women; a significant rise from the low levels of the apartheid era (Winterfeldt: this volume). Today they seek the economic opportunities of employment and income that were previously the preserve of men.

In the face of poor formal prospects, aspirations toward improved lifestyles for women also results in alternative strategies to obtain money and gifts. Boyfriends or sexual partners capable of supplying income and goods are deliberately sought.

> In Eenhana, men between the ages of 15 and 29 years talked of local girls having sex chiefly for money or gifts, usually with recent in-migrants such as the military, local government personnel or businessmen: "Girls have a tendency to fall for men who have come from other areas such as Windhoek because they have money. But once those men have no money, they just drop them and look for others who have it." Wage-earning individuals are financially attractive to local people, particularly those with relatively well paid state employment. Poor girls seemed to be prepared to risk health problems. Sexual attitudes of this kind should not be mistaken for formal prostitution and be interpreted in purely economic terms. They rather reflect a typical example of that kind of 'regulated' behaviour cultural analysis centres on. There did not generally appear to be widespread formal prostitution, although it probably existed more in urban than rural locations.
> Young women and single mothers were most likely to engage in sex with affluent individuals, with money or gifts as the primary goal; but this is an informal transaction, or part of a temporary relationship rather than formal prostitution. It is difficult to put this risk-taking behaviour purely down to poverty. It might be the case for single mothers with little or no income; but for teenage girls this appeared to be a strategy to overcome limited material lifestyles, rather than seeking a route out of absolute deprivation.
> The public often referred to the men providing such gifts in exchange for sex as 'sugar daddies'. The term has passed into common usage, indicating men usually into their thirties or older. An Oshakati AIDS counsellor saw them, rather than the girls, as the problem in terms of spreading HIV/AIDS: these old people, these sugar daddies, are a big problem because they think of culture, because they say even our forefathers were having many wives. They do not think about today's situation, they don't want to (consider) that because they think it was being done in their old society. They just follow their old style." The respondent interest-

ingly again raises the theme of patriarchal 'tradition' as a cultural force (or excuse) over behaviour.

Women's involvement with multiple sex partners for material gain or other reasons, may be less of an attempt to 'capture' a previously male-exclusive institution, than a by-product (even an unintended consequence) of new gender freedoms encouraging new cultural norms in a transforming Namibian national culture[5]. As women slowly break – or are forced to break – the ancient grip of patriarchal control, they gain civil and sexual self-determination. However, these still limited advances in the lives particularly of young women today arise within the context of the HIV/AIDS pandemic in a nation that is the seventh worse hit in the world. Certainly, gender equality needs to be reconciled with strategies to defeat the HIV/AIDS threat. To emphasise this again: this is a culture-based problem with which health campaigns must grapple.

Patriarchy, masculinity and HIV

Aspects of an enduring patriarchal culture run through all levels of Namibian institutions and structures. This is certainly not unique to Ovambo citizens within Namibian society. Government policies since independence have attempted to modify the more repressive facets of this entrenched patriarchy through civil and criminal legislation; efforts that reach into domestic sexual relations themselves. Curtailing rape and extending sexual rights is gradually being enforced; new identities, roles and responsibilities for women are being carved out, but in the face of resistance. Sexuality has become a highly contested terrain in Namibia. The ensuing struggle may well be behind rising levels of domestic violence, and possibly rape.

Patriarchal cultural norms were, not surprisingly, apparent at all four research locations of the 1998 study. The issue of whether or not a woman can deny a male partner sex, and for what reason, revealed itself as directly impacting on the epidemiology of HIV/AIDS. In this respect, patriarchal 'norms' distinctly showed the relevance of the power of cultural systems in assisting deadly transmission processes. Culturally, HIV transmission may be closely linked to the aspect of sexual self-determination: When can a woman refuse sex in Ovambo societies?

> According to older Outapi male community members there were certain strict taboos: "A woman can refuse sex when she is pregnant, or finds out that you are having sex with another woman. Also when a woman is menstruating." On this statement regarding refusal for infidelity, females largely disagreed, saying that men would not accept this as an excuse; although a failure to financially provide for a wife or regular girlfriend was a good reason for refusal.
>
> A common male attitude tended to be that, at all times, the man would decide when he required sex, not the female partner. A large proportion of young and older men in the 15-29

---

[5] Conservative reactions to this change are inevitable, an elderly woman in Eenhana saying, "Girls are starting to do what boys do. They are really losing their cultural values."

> age cohorts expressed similar view to the following: "A woman has no right to refuse if she is not pregnant or menstruating. In our culture women are not allowed to refuse. Men can overpower her or chase her from the house for refusing. It is only with recent laws and developments that women have the right to refuse." (men 15-19 and men 20-29, Outapi). In marriages, women certainly were not allowed a voice. Oshakati males stated that a wife has no right to refuse sex with her husband. Refusal without good reason could result in beating and forced sex.
> In pre-marital relationships, similar attitudes were revealed. Young females expressed the view that even at an early age, a girl who says 'no' to her boyfriend provoked physical violence: "whatever you say (to avoid pressures for sex) ... boy gets angry and he will even beat you" (women 15-19, Oshakati). Young Oshakati males openly admitted that pressure for sex could involve force, implying that it was occasionally necessary whenever women prevaricated or resisted. During laughter from the other interviewees at the idea of a female refusing sex, one said: "Most girls when you meet them first time, she won't say straight that it's yes (to sex). Only later if you force her will she (agree). We use force because we have to." (men 15-19, Oshakati). On the other hand, according to Tuupainen (1970), rape among the Ovambo people has always been considered a serious crime, therefore it is unclear if such views are ancient or recent.

Situations of forced sex give women little opportunity to protect themselves from HIV infection. Even where sex might initially be consensual, the male may not then wish to use a condom and not accept the female partner's reasoning as a reason for ceasing to continue. This presents serious doubts as to the cultural appropriateness of rational choice-oriented awareness campaigns.

> Both in and outside marriage, there was not only an anti-condom attitude on the part of males, but a violent reaction to female requests for condom use. The Eenhana researchers came across a woman awaiting treatment at the Eenhana State hospital for severe facial wounds inflicted by her husband. She explained that, being afraid that he was sleeping with other women, she had asked him to use a condom in fear of catching HIV/AIDS when he demanded sex. He then beat her badly, so that she had to flee their home. Another female informant said: "In some situations the rights of women are violated by men: There was one woman whose husband was working in Oranjemund and his wife heard that he had girlfriends in Oranjemund. When the husband returned home, his wife asked him to use a condom when having sex and the husband then beat his wife to the point where she had to go to hospital. When the husband was asked there (at the hospital) why he had beaten his wife, he said it was because she had asked him to use a condom and she had no right to do so ."(woman 35).

The above examples directly reveal the tensions that arise from situations where women try to protect their sexual health in relation to males who jealously guard their patriarchal authority. The construction and maintenance of sexuality is an interactional process which is patterned within and across gender lines – that is, in day-to-day relationships between men and women, women and women, and men and men. It is also closely entwined with authority structures that are embedded, as Foucault has made clear, within cultures. When women, either out of personal choice or in a defensive response to the perceived risks of HIV/AIDS, attempt to alter well defined and deeply embedded culturo-sexual patterns, they meet with culturally based power structures. Changing or reconstructing culturo-sexual patterns for reasons of personal survival, even when public health may require it, is a difficult negotiative process particularly when one partner regards his entrenched authority as threatened. Men tend to use violence under the assumption that it is perfectly legitimate to reinforce the status quo, while seemingly disregarding the health catastrophe of HIV/AIDS that surrounds them. Supposed cultural norms in this form consequently present serious health repercussions. Health campaigns need to address the specifics of these directly, by challenging patriarchal norms in this form. All the same, one gets little sense of the highly contested nature of male-female relations, and of (the necessity of) a transforming sexuality, in current HIV campaigns.

Conservative culture and the spread of HIV: not talking about sex

An important factor regarding the cultural environment of HIV/AIDS is the evident aversion in Ovambo culture to any public discussion of sexual issues. Talking about sex is severely sanctioned. In this context, the idea of stigma comes to mind in which both HIV and sexual intercourse are stigmatically linked in the culture as forms of impurity, resulting in cases of AIDS sufferers being blamed and spurned for catching the disease (Goffman 1990). While modern opinions on sex seem to be modifying 'tradition' in this respect, particularly amongst the young, the continued resistance and repression about free and open discussion is a factor that HIV/AIDS campaigns surely must directly confront: the public may well be rejecting campaign information simply because it breeches the 'permissible'. Even openness in family settings was regarded by respondents as unacceptable.

> As an Eenhana senior teacher said: "Sex in this culture, and talking about sex, is considered a taboo. As a youth, I wasn't told anything about sex by my father. I just had to experience it (...) At the school here, learners are becoming pregnant simply because they were not informed (by their parents)."
> This was also true for females, as Eenhana women in their twenties told us: "In the past, girls only got to know about sex the day they got married. Nobody told you anything about sex (...) But these days things have changed (due to AIDS) and we must now teach them (young people) at an early age before they make mistakes." As well, discussing sexual matters with children is frowned on. A headman, deeply critical of both sex education in schools and (in his view) explicit HIV/AIDS campaigns, said: "Kids are not allowed to talk about sex, only adults. If you tell a kid about sex, you are telling them what adults are doing. So you can only tell adults." Community members under thirty years of age generally insisted that it was time to break the taboo against talking about sex, both for children and adults.
> Condom-use remains a culturally contested subject amongst conservative and religious respondents. Some individuals complained that schools and government officials, particularly from the Ministry of Health, were promoting 'immoral' condom use amongst young people. Christian morals sometimes challenge sex education. An Eenhana ELCIN pastor thought that: "if we tell people about condoms then we are (going) against the Bible. We just tell them (instead) to behave themselves, like in the old days." Rather, as a Tsumeb pastor added, the church's anti-AIDS education had to be built on the grounds of morality, and encourage chastity. In a general respondent survey of Eenhana, Outapi, Tsumeb and Oshakati, 22% thought condoms were against God, and a similar number of people disapproved for other reasons.

Christianised aspects of Ovambo culture are directly impacting on the Namibian state's own health campaign policies regarding condom protection. Overt resistance on the part of several Protestant church leaders and their congregations was pronounced and negative. An atmosphere of repression over sexual matters, rebounding on discussion of key aspects of HIV, is in evidence.

Concluding remarks: cultural contradictions and HIV

What arises out of the above that can be constructive for combating HIV/AIDS and reducing its impact? We have already referred to the need for the main campaigns to engage with the specific cultural variables that contribute to the pandemic, and to rely less on rational choice-based strategies that target individuals. Underlying community cultural processes and structures must be examined as a chief source of explanation for the spread of AIDS. We would add that other processes generating AIDS, from within the underlying levels of the development process, also need attention.

Yet, this in itself is no easy task for either sociologists or health campaigns. Social structures and their cultural systems are rarely the streamlined, logical-rational forms we assume they are. Mann has said, "societies are much messier than our theories of them" (1986:4). Above responses and reactions to sexual matters reveal this to be true. The value of postmodernist cultural theory is to show that we have in the classical and recent past overemphasised this logical character. We have sought to explain away inconsistencies and contradictions as mere aberrations. We note from the Namibian case examples that cultural processes specifically relating to the construction of sexuality reveal marked divisions, conflict and (to use Foucault's term) contestment. Even regarding so-called 'traditional' cultural values, conservatives today seem unable to agree on core norms; and as we saw, young males even usurped 'traditional' institutions of polygamy, to pit them against religious conservative values stressing monogamy and sexual abstinence. These are expressions of what we call cultural contradiction. Cultural contradictions are here defined as "conflictual elements or behaviours within a cultural system or systems that compromise key values normally relied upon by institutional authority to regulate or condition the actions of members within that culture". All societies exhibit sociocultural contradictions, nowhere more so than in the field of social sexuality.

The idea of 'contradiction' is grounded in philosophy as the 'unity of opposites' as Hegel, and later Marx, referred to it. The interaction of incompatible ideas and interests, tied up in the same holistic unity, shapes and moves human society in creative (sometimes destructive) directions. Human social life is a dialectical process in this philosophy; as are contradictory ideas and behaviours. In all societies, cultural contradictions and contradictory values are always present. No society exhibits pure structural consistency in terms of norms and regulations, nor uniformly consistent behaviour, particularly as regards culturally generated behaviours and processes. Sexual culture is the most difficult area of social life for power and authority systems to control and regulate; while centralised monopolistic sexual norms remain the most problematic to ideologically maintain and defend. This is precisely because the rationality of human actors is here exceptionally counterbalanced by powerful forces of desire and pleasure (Foucault 1978). The result: enforcement followed by immediate resistance.

Sexuality is a highly contested social landscape. There are 'traditions' that society's members follow but also break; people breach rules, either secretly or overtly depending on the repressiveness of the politico-legal setting. Social and cultural norms are both followed and broken at an individual level: either openly as a sexual-political act of defiance (for example, the gay or women's movements) or, more commonly, in the private sphere away from the gaze of society. We often 'know' what our culture wants from us in terms of behaviour. However, our individual needs or interests may compel us consciously to go against social norms, resulting in behaviour contradictory to assertive general value-norms. This is typical rather than aberrational. Such behaviours should not be seen as abnormal, 'rogue' or deviant. They are simply contradictory: no more and no less.

It is this fact in itself that requires both recognition and incorporation into our analysis. Just as theories and studies of society would find it fruitful to recognise and utilise contradictory forces as part of their methodological landscape, so too would health campaigns. An understanding of why people break norms, how cultural systems encourage this from 'traditional' or from modern frameworks, and how this feeds into disease patterns, is our key to understanding the current pandemic.

Health campaigners and public bodies are frequently frustrated and confused by the disappointing impact of their HIV programmes. They promote condom use, but against ingrained (and unchallenged) conservative institutions and culture. They demand public sexual abstinence (the 'say no to sex' campaign) in the face of both the rise of a new and more sexually liberated youth culture, and 'traditional' assertions by males of multi-partner sexual-cultural practices. In these respects, there is a (presumably unintended) contradiction in the campaigns themselves, in which conservative values are both enforced and challenged at the same time. The messages received by the public are, therefore, potentially confusing where abstinence and condom use are promoted simultaneously.

It would be incorrect to state that HIV campaigns completely ignore cultural variables: there is a growing awareness of how gender inequality exposes women to HIV, as the issue of male refusal to consider condom use showed in our empirical evidence. Campaigns are beginning to reflect this important insight. Here, campaigns tentatively nod toward the need for confronting and transforming the more negative elements of masculinity. Yet, the overall importance of a thorough analysis of cultural contexts of AIDS – the culture(s) of AIDS – has yet to be properly appreciated, quite apart from incorporated into campaign planning and implementation. This includes cultural contradictions as part of this schema, for the complexity of the sociocultural terrain must be grasped.

Lastly, campaigns need to recognise their own conservative-religious prejudices – their members are, after all, a product of their society. The plethora of HIV workshops across Namibia so frequently produces presentations and views, from campaign officials and others, that the breakdown of 'morality' is the source of the pandemic; enforcement of traditional ethical values being then proposed, to the detriment of realistic and more deeply analytical solutions. Campaigns for open discussion of sexuality and recognising the importance of cultural systems has borne fruit in societies as far apart as Thailand and Uganda. Perhaps it is time for Namibia to follow suit. For the sake of objective assessment and policy effectiveness, culture must be taken seriously and be seen to matter as a key methodological tool.

Bibliography

Durkheim, E 1896/1980. The division of labour in society. UK: Routledge
Ford, NJ 1994. Cultural and developmental factors underlying the global patterns of transmission of HIV/AIDS. In: Phillips, D / Verhasselt, Y (eds.). Health and development. London: Routledge
Ford, NJ / Koetsawang, S 1991. The sociocultural context of the transmission of HIV/AIDS in Thailand. In: Social Science and Medicine 33 (4)
Foucault, M 1970. The order of things. London: Tavistock
Foucault, M 1979. The history of sexuality, vol.1, London: Allen Lane
Giddens, A 1984. The constitution of society. London: Polity Press
Goffman, E 1990. Stigma. London: Penguin
LeBeau, D / Fox, T et al. 2000.Taking risks, taking responsibility: an anthropological assessment of health-risk behaviour in northern Namibia. Windhoek: French Cooperation/Ministry of Health
Leys, C 1996. The rise and fall of development theory. London: James Currey
Mann, M 1986. The sources of social power, vol.1. Cambridge University Press
Mufune, P 2001. Social scientific explanations of AIDS patterns and policies in southern Africa: some critical notes. In: Hope, KR (ed.). AIDS and development in Africa.
Mufune, P / Fox, T et al. 2001. Changing patterns of sexuality in northern Namibia: implications for the transmission of HIV/AIDS. In: Society in Transition: 3 (2)
Philipson, T / Posner, R 1995. On the micro-economics of AIDS in Africa. In: Population and Development Review, no.21(4)
SADC 2000. Regional human development report000
UNAIDS 2000. Report on the global HIV/AIDS epidemic. Geneva
UNAIDS 2002. AIDS epidemic update. Geneva
UNDP 1998. Namibia human development report. Windhoek: UNDP

SEXUAL CULTURES IN TRANSITION IN THE NORTHERN KUNENE – IS THERE A NEED FOR A SEXUAL REVOLUTION IN NAMIBIA?

Philippe Talavera

Introduction

Large-scale behavioural change has taken place in Namibia over the last few decades. Starting in the 1980s with the struggle for independence, it gained momentum with the New Dispensation and finally with the emergence of the newly formed republic. This first wave of change provided many new opportunities for travelling and interacting to people who had previously been confined to certain areas. This has been accompanied by development measures, particularly for the regions north of the Veterinary Cordon Fence (the so-called Red Line).

According to G. Rotello (1997:5): "in fact, HIV is extremely selective and only produces epidemics when a population's behaviour provides it with a niche. Without favourable conditions, HIV cannot spread in a given population." He further emphasises that "large-scale changes in human behaviour provided HIV with radically new opportunities to spread." Therefore, only large-scale changes in human behaviour will be able to stop the spread of the epidemic and eradicate this disease.

The first large-scale behavioural change has offered a perfect ecological niche for HIV to spread among the Namibian population. People being more mobile, sexual encounters have become easier. Furthermore, laws prohibiting sexual relations and ultimately marriage between ethnic groups have been abolished. This has resulted in the possibility for most Namibians to experience sexual contact with members of other cultural groups, and has therefore favoured the circulation of the virus in all strata of the society. A second large-scale change in human behaviour, to stop the spread of the epidemic, has yet to occur.

The present paper will discuss the need for a sexual revolution – a revolution in sexual attitudes – as an alternative to the current spread of the HIV epidemic, based on evidence from Kunene North. A short historical background will be given in order to understand the set-up under which the traditional sexual culture developed and established itself as an institution. Then, the first wave of changes brought by independence will be analysed, and its effect on the HIV/AIDS epidemic demonstrated. In order to fight against the epidemic, the need for a second large-scale change under the form of a sexual revolution will be discussed.

Historical perspective

It is important to remember with Mort (1987:41) that "the construction of the sexual was grounded in particular historical conditions and social relations (...) We are dealing with specific sexual practices, religion, medicine and sanitary science, whose organisation was an active force in the production of the sexual meanings in play." The current situation can therefore only be understood from a historical perspective.

It was the rationale of apartheid policies to divide countries into ethnically defined zones, keeping populations under strict spatial control, limiting exchange and contact. Kunene North, at the time called Kaokoland, was no exception to the rule.

In 1920, by Proclamation No.40, the boundaries of the Outjo District were defined as including the whole of Kaokoland. However, the Native Commissioner of Ovamboland usually controlled the northern parts of the area. The Administrator General of South West Africa asked white farmers to move out of Kaokoland (Bollig 1996). In 1922, Kaokoland was proclaimed a reserve (Bollig 1996) and in 1923 it was divided into three reserves, with Vita Tom or Oorlog as Chief of the Ovaherero, Muhona Katiti as Chief of the Ovahimbas and Kahewa-Nao as Chief of the Ovatjimbas. (Van Warmelo, 1951; Malan et al., 1974; Bollig 1996).

In 1925 all people between Otjokavare and Ombombo were ordered to move north of the line Ombombo-Otjondeka, creating a buffer zone of more than 100 km in width between commercial farms and communal ranching areas. Another buffer zone was created between Kaokoland and Ovamboland, though it was smaller (Bollig 1996).

From the 1930s onward, trade with Angola was prohibited, exchange with markets to the South virtually impossible, and bartering with Ovambos hampered due to the regulations on livestock movements (Bollig 1996 in: GRN 2000).

In 1946, after an outbreak of foot-and-mouth disease in Ombalantu, Kaokoland was declared a quarantine area and all trading between Ovamboland and Kaokoland was forbidden. Trading across the Kunene became illegal and trading with Ovambo communities was strangled and for decades completely prohibited. Kaokoland was surrounded by buffer zones that were forcibly cleared of their inhabitants. A number of Boer farmers and hunters were expelled from the area and a monetary market severely inhibited (Talavera et al. 2000:11).

The conflict between SWAPO and the South African Defence Force in the 1970s and 1980s did not permit much contact between Kaokoland and the rest of the country. It is only after 1992, once the Kunene region was created by promulgation of the Regional Council Act of 1992, that exchanges were resumed.

It can therefore be considered that from the beginning of the century to 1992 inhabitants from the Kunene North sub-region, mainly Ovahimba and Ovaherero, lived virtually among themselves, within the enclosed framework of their culture, including sexual culture.

The traditional sexual culture among Ovahimba and Ovaherero

Before independence, living mainly among themselves, the Ovahimba and Ovaherero had developed a unique model of sexuality. Defining with A. I. Davidson (1990:308) "the sexual object as the person from whom sexual proceeds and the sexual aim the act towards which the instinct tends", it can be said that:

- The Ovahimba and Ovaherero societies are fundamentally heterosexual societies, the usual sexual object in their cultures being of the opposite sex.
- The sexual act aims at:
  - reproduction, women being firstly mothers and children potential heirs;
  - sexual pleasure for both sexes.

A patriarchal heterosexual polygamous society

The Ovahimba and Ovaherero society is primarily polygamous, each man aiming to marry two to three times. The reason for polygamy is intimately linked to the semi-nomadic lifestyle of the population. Long ago, theft or confiscation of cattle was common. The presence of a large family was a strategy to improve the security of the herd. Men started to marry more women and raise more children. This phenomenon gradually came to be associated with wealth in general and social status. A man who does not possess several wives is nowadays considered as disabled, as best explained by a 75 years old Ovahimba man, "culturally, one wife means one eye, which means that you are disabled or abnormal" (Talavera 2001: 50).

Furthermore, the marital trade is intimately linked to the wealth of cattle. The groom has to pay to his family-in-law a bride price, usually several cattle. Perceived as the 'purchase' of a wife from the side of the groom, it is a trade for the family-in-law, the chance to acquire more cattle, and therefore to renew the genetic material of the herd.

Being 'purchased', the wife belongs to her husband. Therefore, she is expected to act as he expects her to act. It is fundamentally a patriarchal model of sexuality as defined by M. Jackson, who assumes "the biological necessity and inevitability of male dominance and female submission." Most men will primarily choose to marry a woman who knows about cattle, cares for them and treats them well. Only in the second place do they look for a good mother.

The cultural refinement of sexuality in the Ovahimba and Ovaherero society has not been the sublimation of love, but the combination between a rational strategy to best exploit the environment and possessive private relations within the framework of possessive societal relations.

A sexual model shaped by the acephalous organisation of the society

According to Nye, "there is a sense in which sexuality has always been a public phenomenon; public authorities have attempted, aso far as possible, to regulate sexual and reproductive behaviours in the general interest. Such efforts continue to this day." The Ovahimba and Ovaherero traditional society is no exception to the rule. Power is organised on a horizontal level and shifts in power are frequent, according to the domain in question. Some areas of social life are governed by women and some by men; some by traditional authorities and some by individual households. An individual exists in the context of a group and often group interests override individual objectives (Talavera et al. 2000: 72).

It is the community, represented by those attending the meeting, that takes decisions of importance. The individual may not initiate something without the approval of his group. Within these groups forming the community, the voices of the headmen or 'osoromana', councillors or 'orata' and the elders are heard first and carry most weight (Talavera 2000: 72).

Under such a system, any individual expression of sexuality takes place within carefully-defined boundaries. It can be best illustrated by the rules regulating extramarital relations. Officially, sex is permitted only between married individuals. In this case, the couple invariably makes love at the homestead of the man (generally in the hut selected by the woman, as she is the one making the beds). However, especially at time of transhumance, the couple will remain separated for several weeks or months. Extramarital relations are therefore likely to develop. Such relations are tolerated as long as the rest of the community does not know about them. In this case, sex will always take place at the homestead of the woman. She will sing specific tunes at night to call her lover, letting him know that it is safe to come. The lover in turn will leave before sunrise, in order not to be seen around that particular homestead.

If the relationship is discovered, then the husband is allowed to beat his wife (in order to reaffirm his position) and ask the lover to pay a jealousy fine, usually six to eight cattle (linking sex to cattle and economy once more). Furthermore, such extramarital relations are tolerated between married individuals. They are much more controversial between a single man and a married woman. A single man is perceived as a lower social actor and a lower sexual object. Such a man cannot easily seduce a woman, and if she refuses him sex, he can hardly force her into the relationship.

Therefore, the relations between individuals, including sexual relations, are highly controlled by the traditional set-up.

The influence of Christianity on the sexual model

As already stated, the area of the former Kaokoland was isolated for decades from the rest of the country. However, one notable exception to this was the presence of missionaries. Mainly concentrated in Opuwo, missionaries contributed towards development, creating among others clinics and schools.

In their interactions with the local communities, preachers tried to influence traditions and cultural beliefs. However, only a few changes actually occurred. The most notable differences are:

- Both the God of the Africa tradition (idolised and addressed through the

ancestors at the holy fire) and the Christian God are referred to as 'Mukuru',
- The notion of sin, and especially of sexual sin, appears in the culture (such notion was absent in pre-Christian culture, according to elder Ovahimba and Ovaherero). Nowadays, sex is considered sinful because it can bring diseases (reference is made to gonorrhoea and syphilis). Interestingly enough, sexual pleasure is not considered a sin, but a concomitant sexual intercourse.

Therefore, the socio-economic transformation brought by Christianity upon the traditional sexual model can be considered negligible.

Is the sexual model more influenced by culture or by the household economy?

Culturally speaking, the social status of the male in the community is a function of:
- Wealth, reflected in the number of cattle and, to a lesser extent, of small-stock possessed by males. A poor farmer with few possessions represents a lower-status social figure than a successful farmer.
- The number of wives and children he can afford and feed. A single man ranks low in the social hierarchy in comparison with a married man. A monogamous man has a lower status than a polygamous man.

The normative pressure experienced by the individual to marry several time and to keep large herds is at the root of the patriarchal polygamous sexual model typical for the Ovahimba and Ovaherero cultures.

However, given the agro-ecological environment, characterised by an average annual rainfall of below 250 mm, it is a highly risky venture to maintain large herds in the limited space of the communal areas. Drought or disease can kill a large number of animals in a short period of time. To overcome this situation, Ovahimba and Ovaherero farmers have developed a rational strategy: they divide the large herd into smaller units. Each unit is kept in a different area. If drought or disease occur, it is likely that only the unit affected will suffer. In order to look after all units, there is a need for numerous herd-keepers. However, a common traditional belief in the region is that herds should be looked after only by family members (and not by employees). The need to have numerous children arises out of this socio-economic pattern. Consequently, it is in the nature of such normative cultural and economic orientations that reproduction is the main sexual motive.

Polygamy is therefore an economic strategy. As a result, a man will not select his wife according to physical or emotional factors but according to her potential economic value – is she good at herding animals? Will she be able to breed many children? Wives are not preferred sexual objects, but the most efficient economical tools. On the contrary, casual sexual encounters are usually selected according to physical attributes and are based on emotions such as desire and attraction.

Furthermore, formal sexual relations (marital relations) are deeply linked to the economy of the household, the patriarchal model being based on a subsistence oriented livestock economy; for example:
- The groom is expected to pay a bride price for his future wife (girls are of economic value to their parents. They are perceived as a means of circulation needed to ensure the increase in the number of the family's own animal stock)
- In case an extramarital relation is discovered, the lover has to pay a jealousy fine to the husband.

Formal sexual relations are also deeply linked to the position a person occupies in the society. This is best supported by the following two traditions:
- The 'Oupanga' tradition, 'oupanga' being a generic term meaning friendship in Otjiherero, employed here in the sense of 'valued friendship'. When an important person or a valued friend comes for a visit, the head of the homestead, in order to honour the visitor, will lend him his wife for a defined period of time. Usually this is not associated with any other transaction. In this case, the wife is a tool used to establish or maintain valued social linkages.
- When visitors arrive at a homestead, if the wife notices that her husband is sexually attracted to one of the invitees, it is her duty to ask her husband to sleep with the invitee (hence giving him the authorisation to have sex in the homestead with another woman). In this case, sexual activities are relocated to the broader concept of attractiveness and sexual pleasure, unconsciously probably, as well to the concept of polygamy.

Both traditions are based on the fact that sex is pleasurable and held in high esteem, even outside its economic rationale. Finally, the cultural set-up does not favour individualism. As stated, the collective group interests override individual interests and objectives. As such, individual differences are often rejected or denied. A person in particular who expresses a different sexual orientation would very likely be rejected by the community. If not excommunicated, the person would not acquire high social status. For instance, even if homosexuality were acknowledged as existing, there are no 'official' homosexual couples in the area and it is impossible to find a homestead headed by two men.

Culture and economy being intimately linked, with most of the cultural traditions being related to the herd, it is difficult to conclude whether sexuality is more heavily influenced by the one or the other. Therefore, it seems appropriate to conclude that the determinant of sexual structures in the Ovahimba and Ovaherero environment is cultural, influenced by its economic components through the over-riding importance of the herd. Culturally, the patriarchal pattern of power ensures the continuity of a normative structure of male dominance and gender inequity. Economically, it contributes towards prosperous and preferred farming practices.

The sexual cultural model developed by the Ovahimba and Ovaherero inhabitants in Kunene North is therefore:
A patriarchal heterosexual and polygamous model;
- Heavily controlled by traditional normative social values in which the only expression of female self permitted is one of a submissive and consenting woman, always ready to please the husband who 'purchased' her, and a polygamous man multiplying his sexual objects;
- Intimately linked to the wealth of the herd, object-subject of the household economy.

Under such circumstances, it is a model whereby mutual consent is not a prerequisite to sexual intercourse (even though both partners acknowledge that sex is more pleasurable when both partners want it) and the concept of rape does not exist. Violent sex is acknowledged to exist only if extreme – sexual violence against pregnant women, for example, may lead to severe punishment. Finally, the individual does not live in isolation from his society. Motivations, including sexual motivations, are heavily influenced by cultural systems of values.

The first large-scale change: an incomplete process

Early in the 1990s with the promulgation of the Kunene region and the end of the former regime, the region finally began its process of re-integration with the rest of the country. It was initially a very slow process. Until the early 1990s, the population had had very little contact with the rest of the country, except through the previous incursions or occupation of South African Army Defence Force. Remote and difficult to access with chiefly gravel roads and generally poor communications, development progressed slowly in the region. A direct phone line system was only installed in Opuwo in late 1998.

In 1999 Opuwo was selected as the headquarters of the Regional Council and many administrative functions were transferred from Khorixas to Opuwo. This was accompanied by major public works, such as the construction of buildings (offices mainly) and houses. Private entrepreneurs came to the area to open many small businesses. A project to tar the road between Kamanjab and Opuwo has recently been approved. Such development has benefited the economy of the region, as sub-centres such as Okangwati and Kaoko-Otavi have also developed.

The main outcome of this growing change has been an increase in migration from rural to urban areas. Predominantly at first amongst the Ovaherero, this phenomenon is becoming less rare amongst the Ovahimba as well. It is very unusual nowadays to meet people in the region who have never been to Opuwo. Among the male population, one seldom meets someone who has never been to Windhoek or Oshakati. As transport links are improved, people are more mobile and expose themselves to new forms of behaviour, including sexual behaviour. Furthermore, access to television and other forms of media has risen markedly in

Opuwo, bringing modern westernised values and culture into the area for the first time.

Some culturo-sexual changes

Despite an opening up to the larger Namibian community and beyond, traditions have remained very strong in rural areas. Grooms still pay a bride-price and consider wives as their property. Polygamy is still common and the multiplication of sexual partners still deeply embedded. If the lending of wives for the sexual use of honoured guests appears increasingly rare, rape and violence are still prevalent.

Yet, urbanisation has brought about change. In urban areas, so-called sugar daddies (a name given to adult men with a good economic position, including a car and cell-phone) have emerged. They engage in sexual relationships with young girls, usually still of school age, in exchange for gifts. Such girls are extremely vulnerable, as they often come from economically poor backgrounds. They lack opportunities, but know about fashion through TV, radio, and friends at school. As a remedy against poverty and desiring a living standard they feel has been denied them since birth, the girls use sex as a means of achieving and satisfying personal material expectations. Their attitude to sexuality therefore now becomes a tool to access power, money and fashion. Sometimes it also becomes a tool to access education, as the men will pay the school fees or cover university costs. Furthermore, the possibility of migration and travel has increased the chances to meet new sexual partners, multiplying potential sexual objects.

Therefore, such a large-scale change has contributed towards the creation of a favourable ecological niche for HIV/AIDS. This is best illustrated by the results of the past sentinel surveys organised by the Ministry of Health and Social Services.

Table 4: Evolution of HIV prevalence in Opuwo from 1992 to 2000

Year	1992	1994	1996	1998	2 000
Prevalence	3%	1%	4%	6%	7%

Up to 1996, the region was relatively isolated, contacts were not numerous and the spread of HIV very limited. Since 1996, but particularly since 1999, with rapidly-increasing in-migration to Opuwo, sexual encounters with new populations has increased. Because this recent, massive opening towards the rest of the country (and to a certain extent, the world, through growing tourist contacts in the area), the prevalence of the disease is still relatively low – Opuwo has the lowest HIV/AIDS prevalence of all Namibian towns, according to the results of the last sentinel survey.

Keeping in mind that the population is traditionally polygamous and unfaithful (in the sense of non-exclusive sexual links to a single partner), men especially expose themselves to high risk behaviours. Women, consequently, are exposed to the epidemic in the process of sexual intercourse with their husbands or lovers.

The epidemic is now accelerating, with one death a week due to HIV-related conditions reported at the State Hospital in Opuwo (personal data, Linden).

Consequences: an incomplete process

Owing to economic forces such as labour migration, and to cultural motives such as the attractions of urban, capitalist life, the customary mode of subsistence production and the customary way of living are disintegrating in northern Kunene. Therefore, a new model of sexuality arises that contains elements of sexual commercialisation (including the phenomenon of sugar daddies). However the new economic as well as cultural elements do not replace the customary ones; they stand with them on a conflictual basis. Both the forces shaping cultural and sexual attitudes are therefore effective in the process of integrating the Ovahimba and Ovaherero communities into the new Namibia. The rural subsistence economy does not disappear. On the contrary, urban centres like Opuwo become relevant, as do factors such as labour migration. Therefore, people going from rural areas to Opuwo are confronted with this dual custom/new economic situation. This is frequently linked to frustration with the scarce job opportunities in Opuwo for an uneducated rural person.

Another example of the incompleteness of the process is linked to women's rights:

- On the one hand, the status of women has not changed. In rural areas, women are still regarded as 'purchased' goods with no rights. In urban areas, the situation is no better as women face a patriarchal society that is violent and poverty-stricken.
- On the other hand, laws and regulations are changing, promoting equal rights for both women and men. Structures such as the Ministry for Women Affairs and Child Welfare, the Woman and Child Protection Unit, and Women Action Development have been developed and operate in Opuwo.

Therefore the traditional values still deeply embedded in the daily lives of each individual are constantly challenged by new values imported from the 'outside'. Hence a certain loss of identity, or a reconstitution of identity, is especially perceptible with the new generation. The first large-scale change is therefore probably still in process, but as yet incomplete, and has now to face the reality of the HIV/AIDS epidemic. The shift from the former traditional structures (including sexual structures) to a modern format has not been completed, and most individuals now live between the two environments.

A failure to address the problem efficiently

The current national campaigns to create awareness about HIV/AIDS in Namibia focus on the promotion of Abstinence, Faithfulness and Condom use. Abstinence is a rather theoretical and naive concept in the context of the Ovahimba and Ovaherero culture (as in fact in most parts in the world), where children are engaging in sexual intercourse at a very early age. Faithfulness in a polygamous society is also theoretical and, as best explained by Watney (1987:128), "counselling monogamy as an end in itself in such a context is simply putting the cart before the horse, since monogamous sex is no safer that any other kind (as the person is still) at risk of contracting the virus from anyone who has had sex in the last seven years." Finally, the promotion of condoms is extremely difficult in terms of availability, distribution and cultural acceptance (it is culturally not acceptable to see the sperm. The sperm should not be ejaculated outside the woman's vagina. Hence, a cultural taboo to use condoms, as the sperm is then removed from the vagina). The adoption of one of the offered alternatives to unsafe sexual intercourse would require a second major cultural change of sexual attitudes, but none of the campaigns so far have encouraged such a 'revolution'.

The need for a sexual revolution as a second large-scale change?

As explained by Watney (1987:129), "changes in sexual behaviours cannot be forced. They can only be achieved through consent, consent which incorporates changes into the very structure of sexual fantasy. Hence, the urgent, the desperate need to eroticise information about safe sex, if tens of thousands or more lives are not to be cruelly sacrificed on the ... altars of prudery."

However, if the need for stronger, more eroticised sexual information in the HIV/AIDS awareness campaigns is necessary, then the ways of achieving it are far less obvious.

The necessity to break taboos

We can state with Byne (1994:65) that the choices in this respect "lie not within the biology of human brains but rather in the cultures those brains have created", a statement particularly appropriate both for the Namibian context as a whole and for the Ovahimba and Ovaherero cultures in particular.

Recent public statements by high officials, including the President of the Republic of Namibia, have condemned most sexual practices, with the exception of monogamous heterosexual practices in a marital context. For instance,
- sodomy is condemned by law and homosexual relationships have been heavily demonised, with the result that a part of the population feels marginalised;.
- marriage or sexual relationships between black Namibians and white foreigners have been discouraged;
- Sexual activities such as oral sex and masturbation are regarded as degenerate and not to be discussed publicly.

As a result, most awareness campaigns shun discussions of the risks associated with anal and oral sex (with the notable exception of leaflets developed by the 'Take Control' campaign, promoting the use of condoms for all penetrative sexual activities). However, why target individual behaviours and sexual preferences only to deny whole populations full and accurate information of the real risks associated with certain sexual practices? Furthermore, prostitution and commercial sex (including sugar daddies) have also been neglected by campaigns and public discussion.

There is therefore an urgent need to break taboos and openly discuss the real situation, based on whatever form of sex people practice. Sexuality is a complex topic, ultimately unique to each individual, that does not necessarily follow any logic or rule. Sexuality is heavily influenced by impulses and emotion. It is thus of the utmost importance to accept and to relocate sexuality in the context of individual preference and actual practices.

The need to promote sex education in schools

As stated by Grossmann (1995:29), "the pressure of everyday life, the disruptive power of habit can only be overcome through experience, erotic experience, and where would young people get this? (...) Nowhere are they given an inkling of how serious a matter eroticism is."

The youth, especially young girls, are extremely vulnerable. It is therefore important to fully inform them properly at an early stage and to educate them on sex related matters. Talking (or campaigning) about sex and sexual preferences should by no means reinforce existing taboos or attack individual sexual preferences. Sex is natural. It is a pleasurable activity in which all individuals engage. It is natural for a young boy or a young girl to want to engage in and discover sex, and it should be considered normal for the rest of the cultural groups. Sex education should therefore start from the position of Connell (1997): "sexuality involves bodily arousal and pleasure, bodily processes such as pregnancy and childbirth, bodies as object of desire. Sexual practice, then, is body-reflective practice, even in its most refined cultural forms."

It is important for young people, especially when schooled and exposed to more westernised type of societies, to understand how their own sexuality has been constructed and influenced by their society and cultural practices. Sexuality is a taboo subject in Kunene. Parents do not talk about it with children. As a result, children explore it between themselves (the most notable example being the 'ouruwo' game, a game in which children imitate their environment, including the way animals in the herd sexually interact, and during which they often get involved in penetrative sexual activities).

Young people in Kunene do not necessarily understand the processes shaping their own sexuality. It would therefore appear to be important to reverse the process and through proper education give them tools to enable them to understand the forces in place, possibly to deconstruct their existing sexuality and ultimately reconstruct it in new forms. Sexual education in schools should therefore not only comprise biological information but also sociological and psychological tools to help learners to understand how sexuality is constructed.

The remedy: modernisation of traditional culture

As expressed by Godelier (1981), "it is not sexuality which haunts society, but society which haunts the body's sexuality". It is high time to reverse this process. Society needs such a large-scale change. Education can bring changes, changes that should not be feared, as they will not only contribute to the fight against HIV/AIDS but also contribute towards gender equity, freedom of expression and the possibility for the individual to take responsibility for his/her own identity. As best explained by Marcuse (1955:180), "in contrast, the free development of transformed libido within transformed institutions, while eroticising previously tabooed ones, time and relations, would minimise the manifestation of mere sexuality by integrating them into a far larger order, including the order of work. In this context, sexuality tends to its own sublimation."

In the Namibian context, this would mean social acceptance of individual choice. Furthermore, promoting eroticisation, multiplying experiences and sexual preference may in turn result in a decrease in the number of sexual partners. If partners can find different forms of pleasure, then they are less likely to look for satisfaction elsewhere. In the long run, this may contribute to monogamy, therefore decreasing the spread of the epidemic. This is of course highly speculative, but most sexologists agree that when diversity cannot be found in one sexual act, it is then found in the multiplication of the number of sexual partners.

The challenge then is to find a balance between traditional morals and sexual values on the one hand, and modern protective perspectives in the age of HIV. Concluding from the Ovahimba and Ovaherero evidence, it appears that their present sexual culture is incapable of protecting the individual against HIV/AIDS. On the contrary, this culture, appropriate in an HIV-free traditional social context, supports the epidemic by providing the virus with a perfect ecological niche. In the whole of the country, in less than ten years, the disease has spread from a 4,2% prevalence in 1992 to a 19,3% prevalence in 2000, proving that the ecological niche is highly favourable (Ministry of Health and Social Services).

When cultural practices endanger the individual, culture must evolve. If it does not adapt itself to a new situation, then the individual and the whole society is likely to be destroyed. On the other hand, individuals may lose their reference points when culture (the benchmark that shapes their whole behaviour) changes too quickly. This is also detrimental. The individual needs his/her reference points to articulate his/her own life and ultimately his/her sexuality. Change must be acceptable to the individual's self. Therefore, it can only come from the inside, from the customary culture itself. The traditional society must feel the danger to which it is exposing its individuals in order to start reacting, to break taboos, to educate its people into a new sexual behaviour. Such societal change is nothing less than a revolution, in this case a sexual revolution.

However, promoting new forms of sexual behaviour as an end in itself may not be effective. As already stated, cultural practices are the main determinant of sexual structures. The sexual structures being endangered by the HIV/AIDS epidemic have to be changed. However, such change will disrupt the normative structure of male dominance and gender inequity. As a result, the household economy will suffer. How can a change of behaviour take place unless the whole traditional economy is forced to evolve? Ultimately, should the cattle economy be abandoned? If not, how can the new structure offer a proper strategy taking into consideration the agro-ecological environment of the area? If yes, what would be the new basis for household economy? How will gender relations be reorganised? Finally, could the new sexual structures be protective of the individual if the socio-economic transformation and subsequent changes in gender relations have been disruptive?

The first wave of change has been incomplete, bringing in new social elements, diluting some elements of the customary culture but not replacing the traditional structures. Such changes have benefited the individual in many aspects (access to better health and education, for instance) but have not been protective of the individual, as they have contributed towards the creation of an ecological niche for the Human Immunodeficiency Virus. The behavioural change should now be redirected in order to terminate the disease process, but this time should ensure protection to the individuals. As the second change will have to touch directly on some of the traditional structures, a model of adaptation rather than a model of contradiction should be promoted. This change will have to be supported by outside programmes (giving individuals tools to enable them to deconstruct their model of sexuality in order to reconstruct it more comprehensively in a HIV context) but ultimately it has to develop consensually from within the cultural group itself, using references understandable by the targeted population.

Only a second large-scale change can eradicate the pandemic. Coming from inside, it will have to complete the transformations initiated by the first wave and better educate all segments of society. As opportunities have been multiplied, taboos must now be broken. All forms of sexuality should be openly discussed, informing people properly about them and the risks associated to each act.

Without such a massive cultural change, without the elimination of the ecological niche, it is unlikely that campaigns to create awareness about HIV/AIDS will succeed. Without a sexual revolution, succeeding against HIV/AIDS will be impossible. Therefore, the different cultural groups should not only learn about the disease, but should appreciate its effect over its people in order ultimately to react and promote a cultural change. Even if it may sound at first sight contradictory, only an inner-led cultural change will ultimately be able to both preserve core elements of customary culture, and at the same time save its people from the prevailing disease inflicting them.

Bibliography

Bollig, M 1996. Power and trade in pre-colonial and early colonial times in northern Kaokoland. In: Hayes, P / Sylvester, J / Wallace, M / Hartmann, W / Fuller, B Jn (eds.). Trees never meet. Mobility and containment in Namibia, 1915-1946. Windhoek

Byne, W 1994. The biological evidence challenges. Scientific American, May 1994, pp.50-55

Connell, RW 1997. Sexual revolution. Lynne Segal Edition. New York Univ. Press, pp.64-65

Davidson, Al 1990. Closing up the corpses: diseases of sexuality and the emergence of the psychiatric style of reasoning. In: Boolos, G (ed.). Meaning and method: essay in honour of Hilary Putnam. Cambridge University Press

Godelier, M 1981. The origins of male domination. New Left Review, vol.127

Government of the Republic of Namibia 2000. Livestock marketing in the northern communal areas of Namibia. NOLIDEP, Ministry of Agriculture, Water and Rural Development, Windhoek

Grossmann, A 1995. Reforming sex: the German movement for birth control and abortion reform, 1920-1950. Oxford University Press

Jackson, M 1994. The real facts of life: feminism and the politics of sexuality 1850-1940. London: Taylor and Francis

Malan, JS / Owen-Smith, GL 1974. The ethnobotany of Kaokoland. Cimbebasia, vol.2, p.151-178

Marcuse, H 1955. Eros and civilisation: a philosophical inquiry into Freud. New York: Vintage Books

Mort, F 1987. Dangerous sexualities: medico-moral politics in England since 1830. London: Routledge and Kegan Paul

Nye, RA 1999. Sexuality. Oxford University Press

Rotello, G 1997. Sexual ecology: AIDS and the destiny of gay men. Harmondsworth, USA: Dutton

Talavera, P / Katjimune, J / Mbinga, A / Vermeulen, C / Mouton, G 2000. Farming systems in Kunene North: a resource book. Farming System Research and Extension Unit, Ministry of Agriculture, Water and Rural Development. Opuwo, Namibia

Talavera, P 2001. Challenging the Namibian perception of sexuality – the case study of the Ovahimba and Ovaherero culturo-sexual models in a HIV/AIDS context. Kunene Regional Council, Ministry of Regional and Local Government and Housing. Opuwo, Namibia

Talavera, P 2000. Socio-economic analysis. Paper presented at the Meeting on Future of the Kunene North FSR-E Unit , Otjiwarongo, June 2000. Ministry of Agriculture, Water and Rural Development

Van Warmelo, NJ 1951. Notes on the Kaokoveld (South West Africa and its people). Ethnological publication no. 26. Department of Bantu Administration, Republic of South Africa. Pretoria

Watney, S 1987. Policing desire: pornography, AIDS and the media. University of Minnesota Press, Minneapolis, USA

HOW TO MAKE SENSE OF LOVER RELATIONSHIPS – KWANYAMA CULTURE AND REPRODUCTIVE HEALTH

Britt Pinkowsky Tersbøl

Introduction

Within medical anthropology and social medicine, researchers have been attempting to understand why the knowledge that people possess about HIV/AIDS is often not applied to their sexual practices. The aim of this article[1] is to identify factors that influence people to engage in unprotected sex in spite of a relatively high awareness of HIV/AIDS.

Girlfriend-boyfriend relationships, henceforward referred to as lover relationships, will be examined closely in order to understand how their dynamics encourage women and men to engage in risky sexual behaviour. In reaching a better understanding of lover relationships, and women and men's different situations, the chapter will focus on the construction of gender identity among the Kwanyama people in Namibia. The construction of gender identity is thus utilised as the main analytical frame. Gender identities are shaped and altered in interaction with sociocultural factors. Therefore, the investigation into gender, relationship patterns and sexuality should be also entrenched within the study of the sociocultural realities within which people interpret and negotiate their lives and their sexuality (Ray 1996).

It is particularly striking that few Kwanyama of the age group 15–35 are married, in comparison with other African societies. Instead, they are more often involved in lover relationships. The dynamics of these relationships have a profound negative influence on their lives and well-being: the relationships often impact negatively on both their social and economic situation as well as their reproductive health status. From a moral and religious standpoint, these relationships are looked down upon by elderly community members. Moreover, to take a broader view, lover relationships appear to have a negative impact on overall social and economic development in the medium to long term.

Why do people involve themselves in relationships that seem to create many more problems than they solve? In interviews, women would report that their lovers at first declare their eternal love and promise to marry them, but eventually the women are abandoned with yet another unsupported child. Why do women continue to get involved in new relationships with the same sad outcome? Men may approach several women asking them to be their girlfriend. In doing so, men bring upon themselves the commitment to support these women, often failing to

---

[1] This article is based on the author's PhD study on "Sexual relationships and their sociocultural context in north-western Namibia", financed by Danida's Council for Development Research, and the Committee of the North-South Research Initiative of the University of Copenhagen, Denmark. Fieldwork for this study was carried out in rural Ohangwena region in 1998, and in urban Walvis Bay / Kuisebmund in 2000; it comprised close to 100 interviews with men and women.

live up to their commitments in the long term. In the process, they father children that they likewise abandon. Furthermore, women and men engage in unprotected sex, though aware of the risks involved.

This situation appears to be a massive breakdown of 'order', a fall from good 'traditional' virtues and values. Is this scenario caused by women and men's desperate responses to poverty, societal change and the confusion it brings? Or are lover relationships, quite to the contrary, attempts to establish 'order' by maintaining norms and values that are central to the definition of male and female identity in this particular society?

I suggest the latter: I will argue that in lover relationships, women and men attempt to create acceptable conditions of life under the given circumstances. They struggle for social and cultural recognition and acceptability with the means that are at hand. In this process, components of female and male gender identity are the building blocks used both in the attempt to create acceptability, and to create an acceptable life. In trying to acquire an acceptable life and to become acceptable, choices are made that are in reality detrimental to their reproductive health and to their life situations in general.

Types of relationships between women and men

The nature of relationships and conjugal unions has changed over the past century. In Ohangwena, the most common pre-colonial conjugal union is referred to by the Kwanyamas themselves as the 'Kwanyama marriage'. Prior to entering it, the woman had typically passed through the Efundula ceremony, initiating her into womanhood. In connection with the Efundula – or at a later stage – an agreement could have been made between her parents and the man who was to become her husband. After passing through the Efundula, it was acceptable for a woman to conceive and have children irrespective of whether she had a husband or not. Prior to participating in the Efundula ceremony, young women were allowed to have boyfriends who could visit at night. However, only non-penetrative sex and 'sleeping in arms' was allowed. German missionary Tönjes (1996) reported that if a girl became pregnant before passing through the Efundula, she and the man believed to have fathered the child would be burnt alive. The Kwanyama marriage could be polygamous, depending on the wealth of the man. The number of wives would be proportionate to his wealth, the number of cattle that he owned, and the size of his fields. The husband and his wives would live in the same homestead, but each wife would have her own huts and kitchen. Monogamy was primarily found among the poor.

The Christian churches drastically influenced central features of Ovambo culture (Mckittrick 1998:246). This is particularly true of pre-colonial relations between women and men. The churches were opposed to pre-marital sex, and attempted to abolish the Efundula ceremony. Today, Christian marriages are perceived to be the most ideal and prestigious marriage. The celebration of a church wedding is costly, and requires considerable preparation and the involvement of relatives of both the bride and groom.

Weddings performed in the Magistrate's Court are inexpensive, and require no consent or involvement of relatives. Marriages will typically be entered into at the Magistrates Court if the couples need the marriage certificate for any administrative purposes, such as applying for municipality accommodation, or a housing loan (Pendleton 1994:89). This type of marriage could also be chosen by couples who do not have the consent of their families or who can't afford a church wedding. Informal marriages in which couples live together without observing any ceremony are the least prestigious kind of union. Informants, especially elderly informants, were quick to deny the existence of this kind of relationship. Some informants stated that it is shameful to be in such a union. Informal marriages are primarily an urban phenomenon but may also be found in the village setting. Informal marriages could often occur when a person is married but separated from a spouse, and moves in with another partner.

Lover relationships are prominent in the age group 15–35. Particularly people with lower levels of education, low incomes, and people who are unemployed are unmarried. People with close ties to the church are more often married. Lover relationships seem to occur among all ethnic groups of Namibia. Apart from the types of relationships sketched out above, there are other relationships of more casual and short-lived nature. A growing number of women move to semi-urban or urban locations and participate in the nightlife which unfolds around bars and discos. In this context, relationships may be formed that last a few days to weeks, and the exchange of sex for money occurs regularly. This could be categorised as a type of opportunistic prostitution. Many girls who have left school and high school girls who need money for school fees and for modern commodities such as clothes, shoes, and 'hair-dos' would choose to be involved in opportunistic prostitution for a period of time. An increasing number of women operate as full-time prostitutes, charging men for sex directly.

Marriages and lover relationships compared

Lovers do not live together. In formal and informal marriages, couples either live together, or, if one partner has migrated to find employment, the couple at least refer to the same house as home. As with married couples in which the husband very often has migrated to mines and industries in the south, lovers also maintain relationships over great distances. Women living in rural villages in Ohangwena may have lovers in an urban setting 800 km or even 1 600 km away. They will meet a few times a year when the male partner is on vacation. Other lovers reside in the same village or town and see each other once or more times a week.

Formal marriages are entered into as alliances between two kinship groups (Tuupainen 1970). Both kinship groups have duties and privileges in relation to the union (Richards 1950). The alliance would be formed and maintained on the basis of an exchange between the two kinship groups. The husband gains access to and control over his wife's sexuality and her services in terms of labour. In lover relationships, there is no involvement of kin. Here the parents and relatives may not even know the partner, nor his/her kin. The parents may not even be aware that their children are in a relationship of any duration. A crisis in a marriage is also a crisis in the alliance between two clans, the two kin groups intervening to solve the problems. In lover relationships, clan members are not involved. As a consequence, lover relationships are relatively isolated in relation to the social fabric of communities. Instead of relating to affinity in a vertical line towards elders and figures of authority within the clans, lovers relate horizontally, towards peers, friends and in some cases siblings, cousins, etc.

Exchange does occur between the partners themselves, constituting a central aspect of the relationship. Men do not pay the parents of their girlfriends, but are expected to assist them financially by bringing money or commodities. If they have children together, the man is required to contribute to the children's upkeep as well. As within marriage, the male partner gains access to his girlfriend's sexuality through these 'gifts'. He also gains access to her services/labour to some extent. Not living together, it is only when a boyfriend comes to see his partner that she will cook for him and occasionally also wash his clothes, and do other domestic chores on his behalf. Women will benefit from their partners' assistance and they may also gain access to their partner's network in terms of friends and contacts. Men, more often than women, have useful contacts, access to resources, and access to other men's networks. Women may be able to tap into these resources on specific occasions. If, for example, a woman in Kuisebmund needs to build a new shack, she may be able to solicit support from the boyfriend and his network in finding building material, and to access a vehicle for transport, etc.

Having a partner provides both women and men with social status. For women, a relationship brings about the possibility or the aspiration to formal marriage, and a formal marriage is prestigious. Only through having a relationship can women hope to become married eventually. Women who have migrated and moved away from their clan and their village to urban or semi-urban areas may easily be suspected of being prostitutes. This is especially the case if she lives alone rather than with relatives. A longer term partner will help to remove or diminish that suspicion (Campbell 2000). For men, relationships with women also bring status. It is very important for men's status among other men to prove that they can approach women and successfully propose a relationship.

Finally, some lover relationships, as well as some marriages also constitute a platform against the world; within this the partners may find love and understanding. This needs to be emphasised to avoid giving the impression that relationships only revolve around sex and control in exchange for financial aid, with unfortunate consequences for reproductive health and social development. Within lover relationships (and marriages) partners may also find emotional support, friendship and other qualities that will sustain the relationship longer term.

Dynamics of lover relationships

Two aspects of lover relationships, namely the financial support rendered by male partners to their girlfriends and the issue of fertility within lover relationships, are explored here in detail because they play a key role in relation to unsafe sexual practices and potential high levels of transmission of HIV.

The expectation of men to provide support for their female partners is a phenomenon that has been described and analysed by various other researchers in an African context (Haram 1995, Abu 1983). This support can be in the form of money, clothes, food items or general commodities (soap, washing powder, corn flour, etc.). The degree to which a man complies with this expectation is perceived as a reflection of his commitment to the relationship. The degree of support expected will also depend upon whether he is employed, his income level, whether the female partner is employed herself, and whether the couple has children together. Furthermore, it will depend upon whether he has obligations towards a wife, other partners, or other children. A 35 year-old woman with four children from three different boyfriends said:

> "Now I also have a problem with my boyfriend. He has another partner, and still comes to me. I am afraid that he will bring a disease and I cannot share his money with another woman. The other girlfriend is also demanding. I need food for the baby and soap to wash the baby's nappies. But he cannot afford it, because he has two girlfriends."

Support may also depend upon what obligations the man may have towards members of his clan or other households that he is affiliated to (Townsend 1997). Support from a man to his partner is a very important aspect of lover relationships. If, however, the boyfriend does not supply adequate funding, clothing and other necessities, his partner will be dissatisfied and will assume he is losing interest. Women who have jobs, or who can solicit support from their parents or move in with them, are less dependent on support from lovers. If women have other means of supporting themselves and the their children, they may choose to terminate the relationship. The following quote is from an interview with a 30 year-old female informant. She and her three children lived with her parents in a rural village while her boyfriend was working in the capital Windhoek:

> "One day I went to Oushimba[2] to visit him. On the way to come home, he gave me only N$100. I was angry with him because N$100 is too little for me and the children. I went to my house and kept quiet with my children, and I said I don't want him anymore because he doesn't give me anything anymore. You only get help from your parents."

When women find themselves in competition for their partner's income, they can either fight for their position, terminate the relationship, or seek patronage from new partners. A 35 year-old woman said:

---

[2] Oushimba means the South, or the Hereros' country. It encompasses the parts of Namibia which are south of the area generally referred to as Ovamboland.

"I went to Windhoek to my first two children's father. I was there for 8 months, then I went home. I found that my boyfriend and I did no longer agree. He was drinking, and beating me, and he had other women as well. I left him because he started to have other relationships. In the beginning, he supported the children, but when he started seeing other women, he stopped supporting them, and I left him. I went to Ovamboland."

As the above two quotes illustrate, women decide on the future of their relationships in relation to other factors, such as the level of support the partner can render, and his attitude and treatment of them in general. Though women often find themselves in difficult situations financially and socially, they should not be perceived only as passive victims of circumstances. Women are active agents in their own lives, with their own strategies and plans for coping with their situations. Women who have their own income are more likely to terminate a relationship that they are unhappy with than women who have no other means or sources of support. Some women choose to add a second boyfriend to the one they have, in order to improve their financial situation.

Liv Haram (1995) has highlighted the transactional aspect of women's sexuality among the Meru of Tanzania, and illustrates how women barter their sexuality for access to resources and opportunities. Whereas in the old days, access to a woman's sexuality and fertility could only be gained through the transfer of goods from the groom to the bride's kin, female sexuality has now become free-flowing, exchangeable for money or goods provided to the woman directly (1995:32). Haram shows how "the realm of sexuality has its own complex internal politics" (ibid.: 46). In this process, younger women become particularly vulnerable because of their desire for fashionable outfits, creams, and cosmetics, etc. These luxury objects are again seen as prerequisites for 'catching' a marriage partner.

The scenario that Haram presents is in many respects similar to the Namibian context. This dependency that many Kwanyama women eventually find themselves in is basically due to the fact that most women start childbearing relatively early in life. Most become sexually active in their mid-teens. By the time they are nineteen years old, 70% of women are either pregnant or have one or more children. The fathers of these children may still be in school, and unable to render any support. The young mothers would typically stay at home with their parents for as long as the child is breast fed. Later, they may choose to find boyfriends to provide them with support or they may decide to migrate to find employment themselves, leaving the children in the care of their mothers or relatives in the village. Finding employment is difficult as they have no formal qualifications, and jobs are scarce. Some women find domestic work, others work in the fish factories, but as most jobs are in 'male dominated' industries, women have considerable difficulties in finding wage employment. Many choose to try their luck as street hawkers selling fruit, cooked meat, or 'vetkoeks' (fat cakes).

Many of the women who choose to migrate to urban areas find boyfriends there, and therefore manage to get some degree of support from them. Some choose to become pregnant, hoping that the pregnancy will encourage their boyfriends to marry them, or at least to support them longer term. However, many women are pressurised by their male partners to become pregnant. As one woman said:

> "If you don't have children by your boyfriend, he will say 'why should I support you, I am only paying for another man's child'." A 34 year-old female informant said, "Men don't want to use condoms because they want to have babies. A man doesn't want to waste time with me if I won't give him a baby. If you sleep with him with a condom, it is like you didn't have sex, so why should he support you."
>
> A 31 year-old female informant said, "It is difficult if you have a baby. The man will say that you are like husband and wife, so you cannot use a condom. If I had a job, I would not depend on a man to bring money and food on the table. I could just tell him to go if he does not want to use a condom. But now, if I tell him to use a condom, he will just leave and not support me, or bring food. When he comes, he gives you a baby. Afterwards, he looks at you like you are a dustbin. He will not look at you anymore."

As the above statements clearly illustrate, men appear keen to father children by their girlfriends. There is a close relationship between the support that men are willing to provide, and women's ability and willingness to conceive. To secure support from their partners and to try and prevent them from leaving, women will agree to have sex without using condoms. However, the women interviewed had very mixed feelings about this situation, as the above quotes also indicate. Women are aware of the fact that their financial dependency on men causes them to put their health and their lives on the line. But concerns over sexual risk-taking come secondary to immediate needs.

Some men do acknowledge that male conduct often constitutes a problem. A 30-year man said:

> "Black people don't like contraceptives. If the wife says 'let us only have two babies', he does not like that. Every time the men have sex, they want to make a baby. The husband may fear that another man is having sex with her (his wife), so he makes sure that she is always pregnant."

Consequences of lover relationships on reproductive health

The manner in which the relationship between financial dependency, support and fertility are negotiated has dire consequences for the reproductive health status of both women and men. Men choose to have multiple partners that they are expected to support. Women may also choose to have several partners to secure adequate support for themselves and their children. Men appear very keen to father children. Many women are also keen to reproduce.

Condoms are unpopular for a number of reasons, in particular among men. Informants complain that condoms diminish the pleasure of sexual intercourse, that condoms tend to break during intercourse, and that the condoms may disappear inside the women during intercourse. Most problematic is the fact that condoms obstruct fertility, as also reported by Bledsoe (1990), Campbell et al. (1999) and MacPhail et al. (2001). With multiple and changing partners, and the high level of fertility within these relationships, momentum is created for high levels of transmission of sexually transmitted infections, including HIV.

From a reproductive health point of view, it is problematic that lover relationships are fragile and often shorter lived than marriages. With break up of relationships, both women and men change partners more often, increasing the risk of HIV transmission. Lover relationships increase the number of teenage pregnancies and unwanted pregnancies. Evidently, not all pregnancies occurring in lover relationships are unwanted. However, many of the children conceived are left behind with elderly relatives or grandparents who lack the material and emotional means to support them adequately.

In the broader context, they impact negatively on overall social and economic development as well. Teenage pregnancies are part of the reason why young women in particular do not get to fully develop their potential. Women are economically marginalised due to teenage pregnancies and births. They are continuously making themselves more and more dependent on men's support. Men who choose to commit themselves to several girlfriends, fail to support any of them or the children adequately. Children are therefore left in rural areas in difficult circumstances without financial, material or emotional support, leading to further deprivation of future generations. Finally, and obviously, the AIDS epidemic that is in part fuelled by lover relationships further impoverishes the nation, socially and economically.

Gender identity

Beyond the mere dynamics, an analysis of lover relationships requires a basic understanding of what sets them in motion. Thus, gender identities in Kwanyama society come to the focus. What constitutes the essence of masculine and feminine existence in this culture? Gender identity has significance not only for the situation and choices of individuals, but – as structuring principles (Greenhalgh 1995:24) – for society as a whole. Female and male gender identities and their implications for individuals and society will, in the following, represent the main analytical frame. Gender identities are not static categories in any society, but are constructions that are negotiated on the basis of the cultural norms and values of the past and the present. These constructed identities are continuously altered, redefined and adapted in relation to society as it undergoes change (Ali 1996: 98). Different notions of femininity and masculinity may exist simultaneously in one society (Connell 1987). This happens through the individuals' more or less conscious selection of alternative subject positions (or components) available to them. This selection happens through 'practice', in daily life[3] (Moore 1994: 60).

---

[3] When outlining gender roles and identities as they are constructed among the Kwanyamas, it is only too easy to present an exaggerated, generalised picture and leave out much of the variation that naturally exists. It should therefore be kept in mind that the following is a broad overview of tendencies. Men and women are different. The circumstances of their lives are different and how they deal with problems and situations vary. However, it is possible on the basis of the in-depth semi-structured interviews to summarise some of the main components of female and male gender roles and identities.

To be considered a good woman in the Kwanyama society, a woman has to be able to work very hard, and be capable of handling the work of both the rural household and the fields. Women have to be respectful to their partners and to other people as well. A good woman is attentive, and has to have the ability to care for others, especially for children. Apart from working in the household and in the fields, women should also be achievers at school. The promotion of girls' education is desirable for parents with a view to the support their daughter may be able to provide them once she gets a job. One mother with four daughters said:

> "Now there is job equality. Girls can do any job they want (...) the girl is more responsible. If a daughter and a son are both working, the daughter is supporting the parents more."

A woman will only be fully recognised as an adult once she is married and has children. In a rural context, a married woman will then, and only then, get her own 'kitchen' which is basically a fireplace allocated to her for cooking. It is an essential place, constituting her identity and conferring status upon her. She can now send unmarried girls and women to do chores for her, such as fetching water, firewood, and pounding millet – all strenuous and time consuming tasks. In a matrilineal society such as the Kwanyama, the duty of a woman to produce children for her clan is also emphasised (Richards 1950). As part of exchange relations between households (and seen as an obligation to elderly members of the clan), her children can also be 'sent' as a gift from the parents to either her mother's or father's clan or to friends.

Children are also needed to secure the welfare of parents in their old age. As one interviewee said: "A boy or a girl is needed to look after me, buy me a blanket". Because of the desire and obligation to 'send' children, some women are very determined about the number of children they need to have and what sex the children must be. Other women wish to conceive as many children as they will be 'given', as a 24 year-old woman put it in one of the interviews. It is evidently very prestigious for a woman to be in a position to give children away. Not only does the gift of a child relieve the receiver of work in the household, but the gift itself also serves to build close links between the household of the giver and that of the receiver.

In the sphere of sexuality, women are therefore supposed to maintain a disinterested, passive, and innocent attitude. In the sexual act, women must appear aloof and passive as well. Women who take on an active role during sex are perceived to be promiscuous, and obsessed with sex. Sexuality is clearly men's domain and women are not supposed to articulate wishes or needs, but maintain innocence and ignorance. Because of this obligation, it is very difficult for women to voice their concerns about sexually transmitted infections, or to suggest safe sexual practices. As one young woman said:

> "If I show a man that I like having sex with him, when he leaves he will go and tell other people that I am oshikumbu and I like sex."

In terms of male gender construction, specific expectations and norms are imposed on Kwanyama men. Some of them are contradictory and in part mutually exclusive. One very central component of male gender identity is that men, as providers for their families and clan members, must successfully bridge the opposition between rural and urban spheres, coping with the tasks and norms of both rural and the urban environments. In the rural sphere, men are expected to be good at handling cattle and to own cattle themselves. They must also be skilled in building houses and maintaining the homestead. In an urban environment, they must be capable of finding employment and/or starting up a private business, of creating alliances and building networks that can assist them in the towns or cities where their own kin groups may not be present.

Some rural boys are sent off to cattle posts to acquire herding skills and experience with cattle. Others are allowed to pursue schooling as far as their determination, talent and financial support for school fees can bring them. Both groups face a problem. The former may find it difficult to pursue formal education. The latter face the problem that they fail to prove their ability to handle cattle, and thereby miss an opportunity to prove their masculinity. The ideal situation is to successfully encompass components from both a rural and urban context. If a man is only able to accommodate one of the spheres, he is likely to be ridiculed by other men. There are a number of derogatory terms for such men. A person who is not able to cope with cattle, or doesn't like handling cattle is accused of not being a 'house-builder' (omutungeumbo). Such a person is without roots, and is unable to cope in his own house. He may be relatively successful in the urban sphere, but does not hold his rural background in sufficient regards to contribute to a rural household, nor does he go to visit there whenever he can. Other derogatory terms apply to men who concern themselves only with cattle and appear not to have any idea about how to manage in an urban 'modern' environment.

As is the case with women, men are acknowledged as full adult male members of society when they have married, have settled in a house of their own in a rural village, and have fathered children. Tönjes writes:

> "the woman he marries first, i.e. the woman who actually makes him a true man, an omukulunhu, (is the head wife). Every unmarried man is an omumati, a youth even if he is already over forty years of age" (1996:126).

Having children proves men's virility, and masculinity. Having many children by several women proves that the man is not shy to approach women."

One final but very central component of male gender identity is in the sphere of sexuality. Contrary to women, men have to prove themselves knowledgeable, experienced and active, and it is crucial for men to prove that they are virile, fertile, and in command in the sexual sphere. Many men are resentful towards women who are sexually assertive, or appear to enjoy sex. The following statement from a 49 year-old informant provides a very telling summary of the expected roles of men and women in this regard: "For a man to have so many sexual partners is because we believe that if you don't have many girlfriends, you will be laughed at by the other guys. I want to have even 100 children, so that when I die, my history will remain and I won't be forgotten. My wife cannot ask me to have sex with her because she knows the culture that only the man can propose the woman. That is the same. Only the man can ask for sex."

The various expectations and demands pointing towards Kwanyama men are often contradictory or mutually exclusive. Deteriorating conditions in the rural areas caused by population pressure, drought and lack of arable land have made circumstances very difficult for people in subsistence agriculture. The same factors make it difficult for men to settle in rural areas and thereby build up their credibility as 'house-builders'. A man needs cash or cattle to pay a headman to allocate him a piece of land where he can build a homestead and organise his fields. Overall economic regression in Namibian society has forced many factories and mining companies to scale down. At the same time, population growth and high unemployment rates increase competition for jobs. Therefore, finding wage employment is difficult. Without resources, without a job, and without a house, a man cannot marry. This situation leaves men in a social and cultural limbo. The basic building stones of male identity and masculinity are unavailable to men.

How, then, do we make sense of lover relationships in these gendered sociocultural settings? What do lover relationships provide women and men with? Obviously, in the first instance they represent love and romance, the feeling of being desired and wanted by someone special. However, there are the other aspects, analysed above, pointing to material support, livelihood, social status, social positioning within generational hierarchies and gender worlds, and cultural acceptance.

Courtenay (2000) argues that when men are denied access to the social power and resources necessary for constructing hegemonic masculinities, they must seek other resources for constructing gender that validate their masculinity:

> "Disadvantages resulting from such factors as ethnicity, economic status, educational level and sexual orientation marginalise certain men and augment the relevance of enacting other forms of masculinity" (2000:1391).

Boys and men adopt unhealthy beliefs and behaviours to demonstrate manliness. I would venture to argue that there is a clear parallel between the American scenario that Courtenay depicts, and the situation of Kwanyama men in Namibia. Central components for the construction of male gender identity are unavailable to men, so other components are incorporated or even exaggerated. Thus, some men may be compensating for their loss of male pride and status by indulging in promiscuity, and at the same time dismissing health advice and safe sexual practices.

Conclusion: gender, reproductive health and intervention

Both women and men face problems of poverty, lack of education and skills development. Both are confronted with unemployment and financial hardship. Nevertheless their lives and options are very different. Because of gender differences, these problems affect their lives differently, and their gender also prescribes different sets of coping strategies and solutions to these problems. As I have argued above, in the context of lover relationships, women and men are in different ways caught in situations that make it difficult for them to improve their life situations, and to manifest their identity and respectability as adults in their communities.

Economic and social problems are culturally 'translated' into different coping strategies. Men and women make use of lover relationships to short circuit formal structural constraints and thereby attempt to get gender identities to work in their favour. In other words, to be enabling for them. Their intentions, however, may not be exactly the same. Women attempt to improve their present and future material security and social status, and to secure support for their children. By validating their masculinity, man attempt to gain status and authority in a patriarchal world. In this process, the components of gender identities are important tools. In spite of their fear of contracting HIV, women's health concerns become secondary. As part of men's attempts to confirm their masculinity, some men emphasise their sexual capacity without taking precautions to prevent HIV transmission. The construction of male and female gender identities, and the interaction of these identities in the dynamics of the lover relationships, have unfortunate consequences for the reproductive health status of women and men.

What do we need these kinds of considerations for? It is necessary to know the details of how gender identities are composed and how they are expressed in women's and men's relationships. They play a major role in relation to reproductive health problems, particularly in the context of HIV/AIDS. At the same time, gender identities often manifest themselves as obstacles to health intervention and prevention programmes. Identifying underlying dynamics that promote sexual risk-taking is one step taken towards preventing risk taking. If policy makers and planners within AIDS prevention and control do not fully understand the dynamics that influence people's sexual lives, they do not stand much of a chance of halting the epidemic. Understanding gender identities, how they are constructed, and how they influence women and men's lives, including their sexual lives and relationships, is of paramount importance. When designing reproductive health intervention and prevention programmes, the construction of gender identities in any particular context becomes the logical point of departure for the design process. Currently this qualitative sociological context is not adequately considered. Only through analysis of the social contexts of women and men's lives can we have any hope of changing the dynamics and practices that represent a threat to the reproductive health of men and women in Namibia and sub-Saharan Africa.

Bibliography

Abu, Katharine 1983. The separateness of spouses: conjugal resources in an Ashanti town. In: Oppong, C. (ed.). Male and female in West Africa, pp.156-168. London: George Allen and Unwin

Ali, KA 1996. Notes on rethinking masculinities: an Egyptian case. In: Zeidenstein, S (ed.). Learning about sexuality. A practical beginning. The Population Council/International Women's Health Coalition. New York

Bledsoe, C 1990. The politics of AIDS, condoms, and heterosexual relations in Africa: recent evidence from the local print media. In: Handwerker, WP (ed.). Births and power, social change and the politics of reproduction. London: Westview Press

Campbell, C / **Williams,** B 1999. Beyond the biomedical and behavioural: towards an integrated approach to HIV prevention in the southern African mining industry. In: Social Sciences and Medicine 48, pp.1625-1639. London: Pergamon Press

Campbell, C 2000. Selling sex in the times of AIDS: the psycho-social context of condom use by sex workers on a southern African mine. In: Social Science and Medicine 50, pp.479-494. London: Pergamon Press

Connell, RW 1987. Gender and power. Cambridge: Blackwell Publishers

Courtenay, WH 2000. Constructions of masculinity and their influence on men's well-being: a theory of gender and health. In: Social Science and Medicine 50, pp.1385-1401. London: Pergamon Press

Greenhalgh, Susan 1995. Situating fertility: anthropological and demographical inquiry. Cambridge University Press

Haram, Liv 1995. Negotiating sexuality in times of economic want: the young and modern Meru women. In: Klepp / Biswalo / Talle (eds.). Young people at risk: fighting AIDS in northern Tanzania. Oslo: Scandinavian University Press

MacPhail, C / **Campbell,** C 2001. 'I think condoms are good but I hate those things': condom use among adolescents and young people in a southern African township. In: Social Science and Medicine 52, pp.1613-1627. London: Pergamon Press

McKittrick, M 1998. Generational struggle and social mobility in western Ovambo communities, 1915-54. In: Hartmann, W / Hayes, P / Silvester, Jeremy (eds.). Namibia under South African rule – mobility and containment. Oxford: James Currey

Moore, HL 1994. A passion for difference: essays in anthropology and gender. Cambridge: Polity Press / Blackwell Publishers

Pendleton, WC 1994. Katutura, a place where we stay. Windhoek: Gamsberg Macmillian Publishers

Ray, S 1996. Local voices: what some Harare men say about preparation for sex. In: Reproductive Health Matters, no.7

Richards, AI 1950. Some types of family structure amongst the central Bantu: characteristics of matrilineal kinship organisations in central Africa. In: Radcliffe-Brown (ed.). African systems of kinship and marriage. Oxford University Press

Townsend, NW 1997. Men, migration, and households in Botswana: an exploration of connections over time and space. In: Journal of Southern African Studies, vol.23, no.3, pp.405-420: City Publishers

Tuupainen, M 1970. Marriage in a matrilineal African tribe: a social anthropological study of marriage in the Ondonga tribe in Ovamboland. Helsinki: Transaction of the Westermarck Society, vol.XVII

Tönjes, H 1996. Ovamboland, country people mission, with particular reference to the largest tribe, the Kwanyamas. Windhoek: Namibia Scientific Society

TRADITIONAL AND WESTERN MEDICAL KNOWLEDGE SYSTEMS IN NAMIBIA – IS COLLABORATION IN DIVERSITY POSSIBLE?

Debie LeBeau[1]

The colonial context

The colonial era in Africa saw the introduction of Western ('modern') methods of medicine and curing. Little or no effort was made to determine the effectiveness of traditional healing knowledge. Colonial governments attempted to discourage the use of traditional medicine, seeing it as ineffective in the treatment of illness. Its use was assessed as simple ignorance and superstition (Chavunduka 1994:5-6). In many countries traditional healers were illegal under colonial rule because they were thought to encourage the 'belief' in witchcraft (Neumann and Lauro 1982:1820). Most countries in southern Africa had Witchcraft Suppression Acts, which outlawed the practices of divination, spirit possession and witchcraft accusation. Such countries included Botswana (Staugard 1986:64), South Africa (Last 1986:15,19), Zambia (Dillon-Malone 1988:1160) and Zimbabwe (Chavunduka 1994:7).

In Namibia, South Africa's Witchcraft Suppression Proclamation of 1933, supplemented by the Witchcraft Suppression Act of 1957 and amended in 1967 and 1970, applied and regulated the practice of 'witchdoctors' (Administration of South West Africa 1933:138-140; Republic of South Africa 1957:601-603 and 1970:605)[2]. Prejudice against traditional medical knowledge permeates all these laws. The 1933 Act, in its section 1.f, makes it a criminal offence to "pretend to use supernatural powers for the purposes of gain"; similarly, the Amendment Act of 1970 states that it is designed, "so as to make it an offence for a person who pretends to exercise supernatural powers" (RSA 1970:605). The many value laden phrases in these acts include "so-called witchcraft", "pretend to practice witchcraft", "pretend knowledge", and "pretend to exercise" (ibid.). The almost total denial and suppression of traditional medicine prior to independence was due to the historical background and social context within the country. Traditional healers in Namibia were at best ignored, and at worst illegalised (LeBeau 2000).

The post-colonial context

A search of Burman's Guide to SWA/Namibia Laws reveals that none of the above acts and amendments have been repealed or superseded (Burman's

---

[1] I would like to thank all the traditional healers who helped me to understand their traditional knowledge systems, as well as the Western medical practitioners who contributed to the research for this paper.
[2] Although the extent to which the laws were applied is debatable, the important issue is the attempt by the colonial government to label these practices as evil.

1994:w3). Thus the acts of 1933, 1957 and 1970 are still in force as statutes in independent Namibia, though not utilised. Not until 1993 with the passing of the Allied Health Services Professions Act (GRN 1993a:54) were traditional healers recognised (in spirit but not in word) under Namibian law. In part II, section 2(b) this Act indicates that it applies to, "any other profession, after consultation with the Council, which, in the opinion of the Minister, is related to the treatment, prevention or relief of physical or mental defects, illnesses or deficiencies in any person" (ibid.:7).

In addition, the Council for Health and Social Services Professions Act of 1993 provides for the formation and stipulates the functions of a Council for Health and Social Services Professionals (GRN 1993b). In neither of the aforementioned acts of 1993 are traditional healers specifically mentioned. It has been assumed by traditional healers and the MoHSS that their practice falls under the domain of these acts. However, by the end of 2001 there was no governmental act which specifically recognised traditional healers and regulated their practice in Namibia. Most other southern African countries, such as Zimbabwe, have Traditional Health Practitioners Acts which officially recognise traditional medicine[3]. Currently, Namibian laws pertaining to traditional healers do not specifically regulate their practice, though strict adherence to them could in fact mean that most traditional medical practices are against the law in Namibia.

In actual social practice, in Namibia today two medical systems coexist and frequently compete: the traditional and the Western medical system[4]. The lack of formal recognition of traditional medicine, or of greater collaborative efforts between the two systems, arises from a history of colonial dominance as well as from competing world views. The cultural influence of colonisation on Namibia cannot be overlooked when analysing manifestations of its post-colonial medical systems.

Basic premises of post-colonial theory

A post-colonial approach can now be applied to Namibia. It is useful to:
- examine the coexistence and utilisation of diverse medical systems within

---

[3] A Traditional Healers Bill has been drafted in consultation with traditional healers from around Namibia, as well as the WHO and MoHSS. A workshop on the draft bill was held in November 1998. However, as of 2001 this Bill has not been tabled before Parliament.

[4] Although necessary for analytical purposes, post-modern thinkers will take exception to the binary division of medicine into a Western/traditional dichotomy and I will surely be accused of doing violence to the subject. I can only say that I agree with Duncker that, "Writing is, in itself, an act of violence perpetrated against reality" (1996:124). In fact, many healers are not 'traditional' in that they practice faith healing. It is acknowledged that the concept of 'tradition' is problematic in that it can be misunderstood to mean a static, pre-colonial set of attitudes and practices (Barfield 1997:470). However, the word 'traditional' refers to those attitudes and practices which are handed down from generation to generation, embedded in cultural beliefs and derived from the history of the ethnic group (ibid.). In Namibia, many of these attitudes and practices have been influenced by colonialism and apartheid while others remain relatively unchanged from pre-colonial times. However, the important point is that these traditional attitudes and practices have the force of culture behind them, what Barfield calls a social imperative (op.cit.:470-471). Therefore, tradition in this paper is meant to describe a paradigm of beliefs and practices based on culture (Becker 1993).

the same unified social system (macro-level analysis)[5];
- explain attributes of post-colonial society, including cultural beliefs that influence health seeking behaviour (micro-level analysis)[6].

Post-colonial theory is a set of premises in the post-modern school based mainly on Foucault's 'archaeology of knowledge' utilising his triplet of discourse, power and knowledge (McHoul and Grace 1995:22; Wallace 1997:23; Goss 1996:239-251). Post-colonial theory postulates that the imposition of Western social structures onto African social structures created a stratum of power between the colonised and the colonisers.

Central to post-colonial theory is the rejection of the dichotomy of science versus non-science as an axiom of truth. This dichotomy was created by the west as a discourse to legitimate the imposition of power. There is no clear point at which the distinction between science and non-science can be drawn (Seidman 1996:699-720). The dichotomy has allowed for the binary 'knowledge' (scientific) versus 'belief' (non-scientific) paradigm to be used as a tool for subjugating alternative systems of thought. Seidman explains that "science is a boundary creator" and he links "the scientification of social knowledge with the suppression of non-scientific knowledge" (ibid.). Good points out that this paradigm has been used extensively by anthropologists such as Evans-Pritchard, who dichotomised traditional epistemology as 'beliefs' and Western epistemology as 'knowledge' (1996:10-14)[7]. It is the dichotomisation of Western knowledge and traditional beliefs in discourse which forms the basis for propositions of Western superiority.

The introduction of Western knowledge as a source of social power created a "narrative relating a tale of science superseding myth (...) the myth of the modern" (Seidman 1996:699-720). This myth of science and of the rationality of the west has been used to suppress multi-cultural traditions and conceal Western cultural colonisation (ibid.). Thus, from the post-modern perspective, colonialism is viewed as having silenced the voices of the periphery in favour of the dominant voice of the centre (Goss 1996:239-251). In turn, colonialism through its dominant voice, representing the dominant knowledge by virtue of its public legitimacy imposes specific colonial social practices (including medical practices) on the subordinated people (Seidman 1996:699-720). The post-colonial state itself is a creation of the colonial, in that the colonisers "created the discursive space" as a representation

---

[5] A medical system is defined as "the pattern of social institutions and cultural traditions that evolves from deliberate behaviour to enhance health, whether or not the outcome of particular items of behaviour is ill health" (Dunn 1976:135 as quoted in Yoder 1982:8). A medical system is considered a sub-system of the larger cultural system.

[6] For a comprehensive discussion of the influence of culture on health and illness, see LeBeau 2000. In this paper the term 'illness' reflects the patient's experience of non well-being. Illness takes into account cultural beliefs and symptoms which are universally recognised as well as manifestations which are exclusive to a particular culture (McElroy / Townsend 1989:49; Koppe 1995:1).

[7] Good gives a rather convincing discussion of how anthropologists such as Evans-Pritchard have made extensive use of this distinction in their discourse on non-Western social systems (1996:7-21). Evans-Pritchard, writing about Azande medical understanding, states that "Azande believe that some people are witches (...) [but] (...) Azande *know* diseases by their major symptoms" (Evans-Pritchard 1937:21, 482, as quoted in Good 1996:12).

of statehood, by having defined political borders now recognised as post-colonial states (Goss 1996:237-251).

Colonial rule was not simply the imposition of European political and military structures onto the African populations in Namibia. It included religious and medical colonisation as well. While religious colonisation aimed to transform African traditional belief systems, the colonial regime "introduced biomedical practices and institutions as an integral part of its colonising project (...) (which) constituted a justification of colonial rule" (Wallace 1997:16). Throughout the colonial project, medicine was used as a form of social control through the attempted destruction of traditional systems of health and knowledge, and replaced with the Western medical paradigm (ibid.:19). Colonial medical discourse was used in the construction of otherness between systems of medical knowledge, thus supporting the allegations of the superior colonial power (Macleod 1988:1-18; Vaughan 1991:8). Viewed in this way, post-colonial theory postulates that Western medicine is part of a system of colonial knowledge linked to the imposition of power (Seidman 1996:699-720).

Inadequacies in colonial medicine

- Facilities are too far away or inaccessible for much of the rural population. In some areas the average travel time to a hospital or clinic is well over an hour.
- People frequently do not have access to trained staff and proper technical equipment.
- The staff, especially in the rural areas, are poorly trained and unmotivated.
- Doctors tend to go to cities and not to rural areas.
- There are inadequate technical services leading to poor quality care.
- The treatment costs too much, even for state run hospitals and clinics.
- Governments spend a large proportion of their gross national product on Western health care.
- Treatment is divorced from the patient's culture, family and community.
  (adapted from Lashari 1984:175-177; Ojanuga 1981:407-410; Yangni-Angate 1981:240-244).

Table 5: Defects of the western medical system in Africa

Post-colonial discourse brings the colonial shortcomings of Western medicine to light. First of all, the introduction of Western medicine was "mainly directed at the white population and health policies aimed at Africans tended to be repressive" (Wallace 1997:16). Health care provided to Africans was inferior in quality (see Table 1), and moreover, it was inconsistent with the cultural worlds of the African populations of Namibia. It lacked relevant cultural explanations of health and illness, thereby not addressing the culturally defined medical needs of the population (Wallace 1997:16). The Western paradigm, by not recognising and treating illnesses with social/spiritual aetiologies, left a gap which traditional medicine has continued to fill. In the long run, the colonial discourse of knowledge and power was not able to extinguish traditional medicine in Namibia.

Since independence, the post-colonial government has been attempting to address previous imbalances in health care provision through the redistribution of health care services. However, government officials still work within the colonial paradigm by upholding the Western medical system as the only publicly legitimate approach. Due to the fact that post-colonial Namibia still upholds the colonial medical discourse, the failures of Western medicine under colonialism are being reproduced[8].

The discussion on post-colonial medicine involves a critical evaluation of the impact of colonialism on the form of post-colonial society, the type of social institutions which are state-sanctioned, and the implications for the non-state-sanctioned status of alternative forms of medicine. Given the form that Western medicine has taken in Namibia, it has not consistently functioned as a successful tool for curing illness. Social reality reveals that many patients utilise traditional medicine because it can cure universally recognised symptoms as well as exclusively African illnesses[9]. Unsuccessful Western medicine together with residual inequalities in access, as well as a lack of culturally appropriate explanations for illness, are still significant reasons why people turn to traditional medicine to fulfil their health care needs.

Case study: Namibia's two medical knowledge systems

The health care situation in Namibia exemplifies the colonial discourse on the dominance of the Western 'scientific' knowledge system, showing how it has overlooked the voice of the periphery – and its practitioners. The following case study will examine the possibilities and problems associated with any type of collaborative effort between such diverse medical knowledge systems[10].

The Western medical system in Namibia consists of hospitals, community clinics, pharmacies, nurses, doctors, private doctors and a number of other clinical staff. Only medical practitioners within the Western system are recognised by Namibian law. They enjoy special status and more clearly defined rights than other types of healers (Gilbert et al. 1996:50). Health insurance only pays for medical treatment provided by Western practitioners, and only Western practitioners are allowed to treat patients at hospitals and clinics.

---

[8] Seidman hopes that in the future, post-colonial societies will aim to " press beyond the science/non-science binary (...) [toward] a culture organised around epistemological pluralism (...) one that acknowledges multiple knowledges [sic! DL] and is based less on a strong notion of truth as the arbiter of belief than on pragmatics" (1996:699-720). Goss supports this position and adds that dominant knowledge will need to be more rigorously defended, and marginalised knowledge given a chance to defend its position (1996:239-251).

[9] In this paper, the term 'universally recognised symptoms' refers to illness manifestations that are recognised by both traditional healers and Western medical personnel, while exclusively African symptoms are those which have no Western defined equivalent and are, therefore, not recognised by Western medical personnel. Most people in the study population talk in terms of "African/black people's illnesses" and "Western/white people's illnesses". Therefore, this categorisation of illnesses will be used due to the categories used by the people.

[10] Collaboration between the two systems mean keeping the two systems separate but forging linkages and strategies for cooperation between the two independent systems; while integration of the two systems means the merging (in some form or another) of the two systems into one system. This single medical system would function as a whole and have the two previously separate systems as diverse but interrelated units. Integration of the two systems would be a much more dramatic step than simple collaboration.

However, as the example of Katutura[11] shows, the traditional medical system is a strong and lively alternative. It consists of a wide range of traditional healers such as herbalists, spirit mediums, traditional birth attendants, bone setters, faith healers and several combinations of these types of healers. The healers of Katutura offer a variety of healing methods, most of which involve the use of herbs and divination. Although some healers have a high status within their own culture and the African community, they are not recognised within the wider society.

Namibia's two medical knowledge systems differ in many respects. On the other hand, there are areas of overlap which could be starting points for collaborative efforts. Many advantages and disadvantages, as well as problems and possibilities, are associated with collaboration between these two systems, which has been the topic of heated debate in Africa for well over 30 years. The debate for many African countries has centred upon the issue of whether to collaborate, integrate or disregard traditional medicine. Given that the ultimate goal of practitioners from both medical systems is the health of the patient, it would seem that some form of cooperative effort between them would be the most effective means of health care promotion.

The Western medical personnel represent a considerable obstacle to any such effort. Maintaining the colonial discourse on the superiority of their knowledge system, they refuse to effectively examine complementary health care alternatives. Fears and suspicions between traditional healers and Western medical personnel hinder collaborative efforts due to this contested knowledge/power domain, irrespective of the fact that Namibia is fortunate because it can draw on the experience of other African countries.

Traditional healers and the MoHSS

When discussing the Zimbabwean experience, Chavunduka points out that government support was one of the most important events that led to the legitimisation of traditional medicine. He further states that governments must speak in support of traditional healers:

> Attitudes (of the medical community) will not change if there is no voice for traditional healers. In most African countries where traditional medicine is considered a viable complement to Western medicine, there has been an act of government to set the legal status of traditional medicine (Chavunduka 1995).

In Namibia, interaction between the MoHSS and traditional healers has been sporadic and has often not included any form of economic or technical support for traditional healers. For example, there is no office space set aside for the Traditional Healers' Board and meetings are alternately held in members' homes.

---

[11] Katutura is Windhoek's old African township' created by apartheid policies in the late 1950s. Since the liberalization of apartheid within the system of Internal Settlement after 1977 the population is allowed to move where they want and can afford. Although the term 'African urban area' is preferred because it more accurately reflects the living situation of the residents, most readers will rather recognise the term 'township'.

Currently there is no money allocated to the Board, nor is there a mechanism in place for raising funds. Board members must take time out of their busy patient treatment schedules to meet without any form of remuneration. Western medical personnel receive salaries, but traditional healers are expected to leave their work and conduct Board business for free. This lack of infrastructural and economic support further marginalises traditional medicine to a peripheral social position and sends a message to the population that traditional medical knowledge is not a state-recognised system.

The role of traditional medicine in health care provision (especially Primary Health Care (PHC)) has been a main point of departure for workshops, conferences and meetings between the MoHSS and traditional healers (NETHA 1996:2; Omambia 1996). Part of the MoHSS's emphasis on PHC has included the skills upgrading of Traditional Birth Attendants (TBAs) and the utilisation of traditional healers in PHC education and provision (Omambia 1996). However, interaction takes the form of MoHSS personnel attempting to transform traditional healers' beliefs and practices towards a more Western knowledge paradigm, again, thereby implying that traditional medical knowledge is inferior to Western medical knowledge.

Although the level of interaction and cooperation between the MoHSS and traditional healers continues to increase, there is still a divergence between MoHSS personnel and traditional healers' expectations with regard to the question: which form future institutionalised collaboration between the two groups will take. There are some mutual areas of interest (for example an expressed desire to understand each other's practices). But there are also areas where interests diverge, such as healers' expectation that they will be invited to practice in hospitals and clinics, while health personnel emphasise changes of technologies for traditional healers. Again, this discourse indicates divergent paradigms. Western medical practitioners suggest that a change in traditional knowledge systems is necessary, while traditional healers emphasise the need for using traditional knowledge within the Western medical system.

Traditional healers and Western medical personnel

Beyond the existing interaction between the MoHSS and traditional healers, there has been little practical interaction between Western medical personnel and traditional healers. Most Western medical personnel still view traditional healers as 'charlatans' and 'crooks'; while traditional healers steer their patients away from Western medicine for fear of losing the patient or having their 'secrets' stolen. However, on the whole traditional healers in Namibia frequently express their desire to work with Western medical personnel and sometimes utilise Western facilities when it means better patient care. It is not uncommon, especially with urban traditional healers, to hear a healer send a patient to the hospital for a test (such as HIV testing) or ask the patient for their 'health passport'[12]. However, it is rarely the case that a Western doctor refers a patient to a traditional healer.

The following case is an example of how one Western doctor reacted to a traditional healer's request for special permission to see one of her patients in the hospital (see Figure 2). Although it is not intended to exemplify how all Western doctors react to traditional healers, this particular incident is not a unique experience which traditional healers have with Western medical personnel. Tara, the traditional healer in this case, had been informed that it was in the best interest of the mother and the baby to be taken to the hospital. Tara did what she thought was right and best for the patient by taking her to have the baby at the hospital. In return, she was treated badly and humiliated in front of others by the Western medical personnel. When healers experience such treatment, they are likely to

---

A Nama speaking woman, Janet, who was eight months pregnant and having problems with the pregnancy presented herself for treatment at a traditional healer's house. Janet complained that she had been experiencing pain in her abdomen (*"pains with the baby"*) and having unusual discharge. She said she had been to the hospital several times, had sonogrammes and other tests but was told they could find nothing wrong with her. Janet had come to Tara (a traditional healer), *"as the hospital could not help me any more"*. After divination, Tara said there was something else in Janet's stomach along with the baby. Tara said she was going to give Janet herbs to *"clean her out (...) herbs that would clean the womb (...) and something to strengthen Janet to finish the pregnancy"*. This was Janet's third child and Janet had experienced no problems during the other two pregnancies and deliveries. Tara stated that Janet had been bewitched by someone who was jealous of her ability to have beautiful babies, thus Janet was going to have to stay with Tara so that Tara could also cleanse and protect Janet from further witchcraft attacks.

About one month later Janet went into labour and Tara sent her to the hospital to give birth to her baby. Tara indicated that the delivery was very easy and the baby was born with 'nothing wrong'. The following day Tara wanted to see the baby girl and Janet to, *"see that everything was alright"*. When she arrived at the ward Tara told the sisters that she was Janet's, *"Traditional Birth Attendant or Traditional Doctor"* and that she had brought Janet in to deliver the baby. Tara said she would like to see Janet to see how she was doing and *"just have a look at my (meaning Tara's) new baby"*. The nurses were very rude to Tara and said only the father was allowed to see her. There was a Dr Coetzee, a medical doctor who had delivered the baby. Tara then asked him if she could see the baby. Tara said she only wanted to see the mother and baby and would not even touch them due to infection. After Tara had argued with the doctor, he said to the researcher, *"Why should she see her, she's not a doctor"*.

Table 6: Not really a doctor

---

reduce even further their attempts at interaction.

---

[12] Due to the fact that many patients do not go to the same Western health facility each time they seek treatment or that patients are frequently referred from clinics to hospitals, Western health care practitioners use 'health passports'. Health passports are booklets that contain basic demographic data as well as an accounting of Western health interventions. Each time a patient goes to a Western practitioner he or she brings the health passport in which the practitioner writes details of the encounter such as symptoms, tests conducted, diagnosis and medications prescribed.

Advantages and disadvantages to traditional medicine

Namibia's health care system can gain many advantages from using traditional healers in public health initiatives. People have faith in traditional healers. Well respected in their communities, they are part of the patient's culture. They allow the family, and possibly the entire community to be part of the healing process. They treat the spiritual as well as the physical cause of an illness; they are accessible to everyone, even in the most remote villages. They do not require expensive or sophisticated technical equipment; and it is economically viable to use traditional healers since no initial funding is necessary because traditional healers are already in place within the communities (Lashari 1984:175-177; Ojanuga 1981:407-410; Yangni-Angate 1981:240-244).

Due to the divergence of medical practices and opinions, there are several areas of disagreement between traditional healers and Western medical personnel:

- both medical doctors and traditional healers are frequently not willing to refer patients to each other;
- Western medical personnel do not know, therefore they do not trust, the herbs given by traditional healers;
- many traditional healers have little experience with Western medical techniques;
- both traditional healers and Western medical personnel feel that their healing techniques are the best;
- there is debate as to whether and how much remuneration traditional healers should receive for their services;
- there is general disagreement as to where traditional healers should practice, be it in hospitals, in separate wards or in private practice (Lashari 1984:175-177; Ojanuga 1981:407-410; Yangni-Angate 1981:240-244);
- Often medical personnel would like to silence or even extinguish the voice of traditional healers, whom they see as a threat to their state sanctioned monopoly over medical knowledge.

Areas of collaboration

Several African countries have experimented with collaborative efforts between traditional healers and Western medical personnel, showing promising results in some areas. Their experience presents a model for collaborative efforts in Namibia. The areas include mental health care, diarrhoeal disease control, promoting childhood immunisation, utilisation of Traditional Birth Attendants (TBAs) in midwifery, STDs and risky sexual behaviour control and AIDS patient care (Lashari 1984:175-177; Ojanuga 1981:407-410; Yangni-Angate 1981:240-244).

AIDS patient care is particularly important given the serious nature of the AIDS pandemic particularly in southern Africa. Currently, traditional healers are among the principal health care providers for AIDS patients. Historically, traditional healers have proven their proficiency in the treatment of vomiting, diarrhoea and skin disorders, which are some of the primary symptoms of AIDS patients. Traditional healers can be used in an AIDS Home Based Care programme. In addition, traditional healers have played an important role in counselling AIDS patients and their families, as well as providing traditional purification ceremonies which allow the patient to be re-integrated and accepted by their society. It should be emphasised here that traditional healers must be trained about mechanisms of AIDS transmission and the biological basis for the disease so that they do not contribute to the spread of the disease. However, sanctioning their participation in the fight against AIDS would take some of the health care burden off of Western medical facilities.

Collaboration, cooperation, integration

Before there can be successful attempts at collaboration and/or integration of traditional and Western medicine, there needs to be some basic rules of cooperation. Some of these are:

- *recognition* – both Western and traditional healers need to be instructed about each others' healing techniques, becoming sensitive to the social status and position of each other within the society. Healers should learn basic biomedical techniques (such as hygiene and oral rehydration) while Western medical personnel should learn aspects of culture that influence health and illness. Traditional healers should be encouraged to refer notifiable diseases to Western personnel while Western personnel should be trained to refer certain illnesses to traditional healers (such as AIDS patients or cultural illnesses);
- *respect* – Western medical personnel and traditional healers should learn to treat each other with mutual respect and dignity. Traditional healers should be trained to recognise harmful practices while Western personnel should come to respect the magico-religious side of cross-cultural healing;
- *reward* – both Western medical personnel and traditional healers should receive remuneration for their training time. There should be a pay scale which recognises the services provided by traditional healers and they should be remunerated accordingly. Traditional healers should also receive certain basic materials and equipment (such as oral rehydration solutions and condoms), as well as recognised certification (adopted from Bastien 1994:133-137).

One crucial obstacle to collaborative efforts still remains: the attitude of Western medical personnel. Questioning the traditional healers' professional skills and qualifications, they exclusively perpetuate the dominant position of Western medical knowledge. They tend to dismiss traditional knowledge without attempting to understand it. Many Western medical professionals fear that collaboration could send a message to communities that traditional healers are equally skilled.

Due to the reservations of both Western medical personnel and traditional healers, integration of the two systems is currently not desired by either party, nor would such a system be likely to succeed in Namibia at present. Nevertheless, collaboration has been the only successful alternative in other African countries. Given the sociocultural framework of post-colonial Namibia, it represents the more likely alternative to the exclusivity and dominance of the Western medical system in Namibia.

Conclusion

Namibia, as a post-colonial society, is experiencing rapid social change and social disequilibrium. Its colonial social structures are being dismantled and new structures defined. Social change has been brought about by recent restructuration of the political dispensation, as well as by urbanisation and modernisation[13]. Unfortunately, with regard to the medical system, the new political dispensation still has an irresolute stance towards colonial structures, giving preference to Western colonial-style medicine, thereby perpetuating mistakes made in the provision of Western medicine to the African population.

As the aforementioned case study shows, neither of Namibia's medical knowledge systems alone can provide for the physical as well as social/spiritual health care needs of the population. There are advantages and disadvantages to both systems as well as problems associated with collaborative efforts. However, several areas of cooperation have enjoyed varying degrees of success in other countries, thus presenting a potential template for collaborative efforts in Namibia.

State-sanctioned formal recognition of the traditional knowledge system has to be the first step in creating a uniquely Namibian health care system which does not continue to silence the periphery in favour of the dominant science/knowledge/power paradigm of the Western medical system. In its turn, the Western medical paradigm – itself having for a long time marginalised indigenous medical knowledge in the very societies it originates from – ought to follow the more pragmatic course it has been forced to adopt when opening up to alternative homeopathic or holistic approaches.

Bibliography

Administration of South West Africa 1933. Witchcraft Suppression Proclamation, Proclamation No.27 of 1933. In: The laws of South West Africa. Windhoek
Barfield, Thomas (ed.) *1997*. The dictionary of anthropology. Blackwell: Oxford

---

[13] Although modernisation and globalisation are undeniably impacting Namibians at both the social and individual level, these facts post-date colonialism due partly to world sanctions against apartheid which led to Namibian isolation. It must be emphasised that of importance here is the deliberate attempts of the post-colonial government to dismantle the racist colonial structures existing at independence.

Bastien, Joseph 1994. Collaboration of doctors and nurses with ethnomedical practitioners. In: World Health Forum, vol.3, no.1, pp.8-13
Becker, Heike 1993. Namibian women's movement 1988 to 1992. ISSA Wissenschaftliche Reihe
Burman, S 1994. Burman's guide to SWA/Namibia laws. Windhoek: GRN
Chavunduka, GL 1994. Traditional medicine in modern Zimbabwe. University of Zimbabwe: Harare
Chavunduka, GL 1995. Personal communication to the author, 7 July. Harare
Dillon-Malone, Clive 1988. Mutumwa Nchimi healers and wizardry beliefs in Zambia. Social Science and Medicine, vol.26, no.11, pp.1159-1172
Duncker, Patricia 1996. Hallucinating Foucault. London: Picador
Gilbert, Leah / **Selikow,** Terry Ann / **Walker,** Liz (eds.) 1996. Health in the social context. SA: Ravan Press:
Good, Byron 1996. Medicine, rationality, and experience: an anthropological perspective. New York: Cambridge University Press
Goss, Jasper 1996. Postcolonialism: subverting whose empire? Third World Quarterly, vol.17, no.2, pp.239-251
Government of the Republic of Namibia 1993a. Allied Health Service Professions Act No.20 of 1993. In: Government Gazette no.710, 2 September
Government of the Republic of Namibia 1993b. Council for Health and Social Services Professions Act No.29 of 1993. In: Government Gazette no.763, 17 December
Koppe, Ineke 1995. Yitondo Ya Nyambi (The medicine of god): Research on illness and healing in a north-Namibian village (MA thesis, mimeo). University of Utrecht
Lashari, Mohammad Saleh 1984. Traditional and modern medicine – is a marriage possible? World Health Forum, vol.5, pp.175-177
Last, Murray 1986. The professionalisation of African medicine: ambiguities and definitions in the professionalisation of African medicine. In: Last / Murray / Chavunduka (eds.). Manchester University Press
LeBeau, Debie 2000. Seeking health: the hierarchy of resort in utilisation patterns of traditional and Western medicine in multi-cultural Katutura, Namibia (doctoral dissertation, mimeo). Rhodes University. Grahamstown, SA
MacLeod, Roy 1988. Introduction. In: MacLeod, R / Lewis, M (eds.). Medicine and empire: perspectives on Western medicine and the experience of European expansion. London
McElroy, Ann / **Townsend,** Patricia K 1989. Medical anthropology in ecological perspective. Colorado: Westview Press
McHoul, Alec / **Grace,** Wendy 1995. A Foucault primer: discourse, power and the subject. London:University College
Namibia Eagle Traditional Healers Association (NETHA) 1996. The role of traditional medicine today: healing. Paper presented to Sociology nursing class, 26 April, mimeo
Neumann, AK / **Lauro** P 1982. Ethnomedicine and biomedicine linking. Social Science and Medicine, vol.16, pp.1817-1824
Ojanuga, Durrenda Nash 1981. What doctors think of traditional healers – and vice versa. World Health Forum, vol.2, no.3, pp.407-410
Omambia, David 1996. Information from the MoHSS position on traditional healers in Namibia. Interview, 6 March 1996 and lecture to Sociology nursing class on 29 March
Republic of South Africa 1957. Witchcraft Suppression Act No.3 of 1957. In: Statutes of the Republic of South Africa, Criminal Law and Procedure
Republic of South Africa 1970. Witchcraft Suppression Amendment Act No.50 of 1970. In: Statutes of the Republic of South Africa, Criminal Law and Procedure
Seidman, Steven 1996. The political unconscious of the human sciences. Rationality and society, vol.37, no.4, pp.699-720
Staugard, Frants 1986. Traditional health care in Botswana. In: Last / Murray / Chavunduka (eds.). The professionalisation of African medicine. Manchester University Press
Vaughan, Megan 1991. Curing their ills: colonial power and African illness. New York: Cambridge University Press
Wallace, Marion E 1997. Health and society in Windhoek, Namibia, 1915-1945 (doctoral dissertation, draft). University of London
Yangni-Angate, Antoine 1981. Understanding traditional medicine. World Health Forum, vol.2 no.2, pp.240-244
Yoder, Stanley P 1982. Issues in the study of ethnomedical systems in Africa. In: Yoder, Stanley P (ed.). African health and healing systems: Proceedings of a symposium. Los Angeles: Crossroads Press

EPILOGUE

SOCIOLOGICAL PERSPECTIVES?

Volker Winterfeldt / Tom Fox

How many times have we – the editors – been asked this question: what is this ominous 'sociological perspective' you demand of us, the authors?

Many of the academics and professionals we approached to write for this book have many years of experience and reputation in their respective fields of expertise. But only some have a sociological background. This "but" – indicating the accidental fact of not being linked to the social sciences academically, professionally or epistemologically – is meant in anything but a derogatory sense. It simply reflects the situation in which our discipline finds itself in Namibia. When we first proposed the publication of a Reader focusing on Namibian sociology to our prospective authors in July 2000, we had to state that Namibian sociology was (as it is today) just "'under construction', effectively overcoming the limitations imposed on the discipline during the colonial era in which it was practically banned from the academic ranks"[1]. Namibian sociological literature is sparse. Few titles exist in print as a resource for sociologists, students, or for the broader public. On the other hand, the rapid development of post-colonial Namibian society confronts sociology in the country – and especially we, the academic staff, at the Department of Sociology at UNAM – with an overwhelming variety of new topical needs. It was in the light of such a rationale of providing knowledge "closely related to the developmental needs of the country" (ibid..) that we turned to the authors in this collection, asking for their expertise in fields as diverse as economics, environment, governance, culture and arts, health and sexuality, gender.

A sociological perspective? In a first outline of this project, we detailed our understanding of the topics we had requested. Understandably, our authors persisted in probing. What more could we offer? In a second response, the editors drew up a more general theoretical picture of what could be seen as a sociological approach. To conceive of the respective topics sociologically, we suggested the following procedure, in good old Durkheimian methodological tradition: "*social issues should be explained by means of their social causes*"[2].

We wrote: "This implies two things: methodologically speaking, sociology always attempts a causal explanation; and such an explanation investigates (hu)manmade actions and structures. Looking, for example, at the fields of race, gender or the environment, sociology does not enquire as to (their) 'nature', but their social valuation. Their 'nature' is socially constructed. As social constructs

---

[1] Fox / Mufune / Winterfeldt 2001. Proposal for publication of a Reader in Namibian Sociology
[2] Fox / Mufune / Winterfeldt 2001. A sociological approach. 21.9.2001

they reflect societal/social contradictions, at a structural as well as at an actional level.

As with most academic disciplines, in sociology there are differing perspectives, ranging from the radical (e.g. Marx's and marxist sociology) to the conservative (e.g. functionalism). On yet another level, perspectives again differ in their analyses, ranging from positions that emphasise *structure* as the key to understanding societies and their issues, to positions which are grounded firmly in *action of individuals and the underlying meaning* as a basis for social knowledge. Such a juxtaposition of structure and action, on the other hand, is rather artificial; it ignores the fact that action always comes to pass within structure, influenced by structure and, at the same time, creating structure. Therefore, sociology should reflexively combine both, and in many ways all sociology studies the interaction of individuals and groups within their larger social settings. It studies interactive links or, in other words, causality. Social causalities emanate from contradictions inherent in the structure of society, from its historically constructed social class frame. The reflection on the notion of contradiction is crucial to sociology. The term indicates the general conditions within which social action takes place, conditions shaped by the positional inequality of individuals and groups and their clashes of interest. Thus, sociology would rarely ignore the macro-social environment.

This is also true of social issues and social problems: poverty, for example, cannot be studied in isolation, as an issue in itself. Both the individual and group dynamics, but also the structural factors influencing poverty from the broader society, would be systematically considered (e.g. state and state policies, economic influences and conflicts of interest, the impact of cultural traditions and customs, power distribution in the society and élite dominance, education factors, etc.).

Nor would those operating in a sociological perspective be satisfied with being purely descriptive or simply presenting so-called 'hard facts'. Description and fact need explanation – causal explanation. They do not provide this in themselves. Consequently, their very 'status', as facts, is established theoretically, not empirically. Again, the example of poverty: in a community, poverty can be 'measured' and described. But from society to society the very definition of poverty varies – beyond the 'hard data' – depending on its social environment. Its sociological analysis requires the explanation why that group experiences the degrees of poverty that it does – as a group, as opposed to affluent groups, who do not. This will require reference to structural and institutional factors, to the contradictory frame of action that constitutes this group as a group.

In summary: sociology is empirical and also theoretical. A sociological approach will also have a critical dimension. It will make hard, critical points about an issue or problem by laying the blame for the causes of a social contradiction firmly where it belongs, no matter where research leads it. Obviously, in this, sociology does not differ from other disciplines."[3]

---

[3] Fox / Mufune / Winterfeldt 2001. A sociological approach. 21.9.2001

After the first stage of the planning of this book we suggested a twofold improvement, reconsidering the original format of the project. We proposed that the editors enter into an ongoing discussion of abstracts and drafts, at all stages of the contributors' creative work, placing the editors in a better position to offer advice on a sociological approach. In this way, two years of intense interaction began. For the editors, themselves, subject to the sometimes narrow specialisation of their discipline, this marked a period of 'initiation' into topical ranges previously not in their field of vision – a time of learning.

Certainly, the essays in this book do not offer the final word on the sociological issues raised. They invite further development and discussion. After all, if it is true that sociology deals with the patterns of human interaction, then all sociological analysis is processual analysis. Consequently, its subject matter is never complete.

Against this background, in this epilogue, we take up some of the central themes of sociology. Some key themes run through the contributions in one way or another, sometimes explicitly discussed, sometimes missing. In coming back to some of the analyses by commenting, debating, even contesting, we aim to point to the necessity of further debate: sociology *is* debate. Also, this allows us to reflect further on the sociological perspective. Of course, we are well aware that there are several, often contradictory sociological approximations: sociological perspectives, as a plurality. Even if, at first sight, this may appear inconsistent, does this not teach us that the best sociological perspective lies in interdisciplinary debate? This is what the editors have come to conclude here.

Subject matter and methodology

With the benefit of hindsight, the editors feel that they confronted Paul Isaak and Christo Lombard and their other authors with an almost impossible task. The scope of questions posed to them on the sociology of religion would require much more than the two dozen pages (and the limited time frame) accorded. However, the format chosen by the group highlights the sociological perspective, even if partly through its exclusion. It amalgamates two contrary approaches:

- dealing with society (social issues) from a religious/theological perspective;
- dealing with religion (religious issues) from a societal/sociological perspective.

It is not the subject matter that constitutes the sociological perspective. It is its conceptualisation, and causal analysis with reference to structure, action and their mediating cognitive elements, that make it sociological. The emphasis on communicative (inter)action embedded in time and space, the focus on the construction of social relations, the analysis of causal correlations – these may be stated as some of the constitutive elements of a sociological perspective.

To underline this by referring to an innocent example: who would ever think of (road) traffic as a sociological issue? And yet, how deeply 'social' is its activity. It is based on role-specific interaction of all sorts (pedestrian, driver, passenger, policeman); it takes place within physical structures (rural gravel roads, tarred roads, urban streets, highways, tunnels); it has its own economy (it costs money and its earns money; it links external and internal markets; it is based on production, distribution, finance, services); it has its own culture (it is based on communication – verbal, and non-verbal by gestures, by symbols such as traffic lights, zebra crossings, road signs; it is based on strict norms: legal norms, such as traffic laws, regulations and conventions; customary norms; it is gendered (clearly based on all sorts of reservations concerning the admission of women to interaction, or even their exclusion; driving attitudes themselves are seen as gendered: gendered prejudices qualify (good) male drivers and (bad) female drivers); it is based on power (institutionalised power, appropriated power, patriarchal power); to a high degree, it symbolises social status (the old derelict rust bucket vs the latest posh model, the sporty racer for the successful urban youth, the inaccessible Wabenzi world, sugar-daddy's tool for womanising).

Common denominators or dividing line?

In its introduction, Part Two of the essay on "Religion" raises a crucial epistemological issue. Do 'Humanities' and 'Social Sciences' differ epistemologically in assuming the existence of 'shared human values'? Do sociologists "rather tend to focus on the differences in respect of human phenomena" in interaction? The discussion group proposes an interesting approach. The theoretical opposition between the Humanities and the Social Sciences implies that subjects such as History and Religion are not to be classified as Social Sciences, whereas Sociology and Psychology are not to be categorised as Humanities. It also implies that the Humanities deal with the human being as such (human constant factors), whereas the Social Sciences focus on interaction as such (social variables).

The juxtaposition of the 'human' and the 'social' tends to logically rule out the *exclusiveness of the social existence of the human being* that is central to a sociological perspective. But we would maintain that any theological perspective enquiring into 'human nature' must also take this into account. The 'social' cannot be assigned to the realm of interaction, exclusively, distinct from the 'human'. Interaction points to our social existence. Co-existence is the crucial context of human existence. Human *praxis*, based on interaction and structured in terms of division of labour, generates culture (religion!), production and reproduction of human life – in short, human existence in all its interdependent aspects.

The 'human constant factor' is itself socially constructed. The mere fact that in communicating we refer to 'common humanity' by symbols (language) points to its *social* reality. Sociology subsumes religion in "cultural universals" (Giddens). In this respect it differs from a strictly theological explanation of religion as originally non-historical and coming upon humanity "through supernatural revelation". However, by defining religion as a cultural characteristic of all human societies throughout history, it offers an alternative, common conceptual ground. Religion becomes a social (and therefore, sociological) phenomenon, "discovered and strengthened through inductive human experience". However sensible the separation of Humanities and Social Sciences may be in practical respects, academically and with regard to the generation of knowledge, we should not throw the baby out with the bathwater: they both share an identical foundation in the (scientific/philosophical) image of man. In that respect, sociology belongs as much to the Humanities, as theology belongs to the Social Sciences. The existence of a "common humanity as working hypothesis" acts as a common denominator.

Inductive or deductive method?
Can one, then, assume that there remains a dividing line between Humanities and Social Sciences owing to their different methodological traditions? The discussion group on "Religion" maintains – with the sociologist Berger – that reference to the inductive method presents the better option in the process of the intellectual assimilation of facts. Reading from facts rather than reading into facts: Berger's 'construction of reality' favours a non-ideological methodological ideal by following the philosophical traditions of empirism. However engaging any reference to a non-dogmatic methodology seems – after all, who wants to be accused of a pre-established bias of subjectivity in the pursuit of knowledge? – the history of controversial epistemological debates shows that inductionism does not really sit on the fence, despite its claim of objectivity. As a methodological principle, it traces the traditions of critical rationalism, as put forward against positions of the Frankfurt School's critical theory, in the famous *controversy over positivism* in the social sciences in the 1960s. By then already, Popper's advocacy for an unprejudiced, analytical, empirical method (induction) based on the principle of experimental falsification so dear to the natural sciences was contrasted with the assertion of a heavily biased speculative-ideological approach on the side of the (Marxist) sociohistorical sciences. Inductionism not only reflects, to some extent, the epistemological stance of positivism, its limitation, in principle, of the validity of human cognitive perception to experience (the positive: esse est percipi). Also, it adopts the classical Weberian stance of value freedom, influential in the historical and social sciences since the early 1900s, when Weber began his lifelong struggle against the spectre of the 'grand social theory' of Marx's Historical Materialism.

As the above example of the – artificial – opposition of the 'human' and the 'social' shows, to "work inductively" in itself may entail a deductive stance by constructing two incompatible poles. Without doubt, its alleged neutrality towards facts, historical or social, remains to be questioned – the same facts, by the way, that Berger addresses as constituting a socially *constructed* reality. From a purely methodological point of view, Durkheim's suggestion of reverting to an intersubjectively verifiable causal method (in his The Rules of the Sociological Method, 1896) seems to offer a more appropriate way out of the dead-end of mutual allegations of determinism/subjectivism.

Cognition and social structure

Talavera's contribution on sexual culture emphasises the link between *behaviour* and *behavioural changes* and the spread and containment of HIV/AIDS, in this notably differing from the conventional rationale of southern African awareness campaign policies. Sociologically, Talavera's distinction works from the fundamental difference between *knowledge, attitude and practice*. He argues that a set of political, economic and cultural changes, beginning in the late 1980s in Namibia, set in train large-scale changes in individual attitude. They affected the customary normative framework of social control of sexual behaviour. Thus, the increasing 'promiscuity' created an ecological niche for the spread of HIV/AIDS. Analysing the specific sociocultural setting in the Kunene North region, Talavera maintains that only a second large-scale revolution in attitude can bring about the behavioural conditions suitable for the containment of the epidemic. Such an revolution is understood in terms of an ultimate liberalisation of sexual morals, or in terms of the liberation of the individual from the present restrictive sexual morals. The latter no longer reflect the traditional patriarchal societal rules and norms; on the other hand, they do not yet compare with modern models of sexuality centring on the self-determined individual. The transformation of attitude, he argues, has to develop from within customary culture.

In its *analytical* sections, the line of argument follows a consistent sociological pattern:
- in general, embedding traditional sexual models of behaviour in the pre-capitalist economic, political and cultural structures of the Ovahimba and Ovaherero societies;
- in particular, linking changes in sexual attitudes with the transformation of the material basis of social life after independence, especially referring to increased spatial mobility of populations.

However, in its *concluding* sections, the article changes its perspective. When pleading for a second large-scale sexual revolution as a prerequisite for a successful behavioural offensive against the epidemic, the article's line of argument advances cultural instruments only. The author concentrates on the necessity for breaking taboos, promoting sexual education in schools and evolving new morals on a societal scale. All of this implies accepting a new, individualised sexuality. Cognitive changes are no longer described as a consequence of socio-economic transformations and the subsequent shifts in gender patterns of power. They are a must for society, indispensable for countering the threat of the pandemic.

From a sociological perspective, this raises a certain paradigmatic doubt. Talavera himself realises the contradiction when advocating the modernisation of traditional culture 'from within', favouring a model of adaptation and not of contradiction. The question remains, to what extent, in principle, can cognitive changes on a societal scale be expected to occur independently of a more general social structural transformation? Would not the shift require exogenous pressures, in that 'tradition' by itself is hardly capable of a revolution in attitudes?

Process and structure

Processes of social change transform social structures. But how are processes to be understood in terms of structure? How are they 'translated' into structure? Talavera's (implicit) notion of the relation between transformation and structural state exemplifies the issue. The uniqueness of the models of sexuality (the traditional as well as the post-independence model) is consistently considered against the backdrop of changing socio-economic structures. Emanating from social structures and social practices, cultures undergo transformation. Implicitly, transformational structures are described as sequences of structural states. One state of affairs, as it seems, is replaced by the subsequent one. Owing to economic forces, such as labour migration, and also to cultural motives, such as the attractions of urban capitalist life, the customary mode of subsistence production and ways of life in the northern Kunene are affected. Therefore, a new model of sexuality arises that contains elements of commercialisation of the body.

But further clarification is required regarding the structure of such transformations. Looking at the present state of affairs, not at the processes, the new economic as well as cultural elements do not, in reality, replace the customary ones. They come to complement them, co-exist with them, on a very conflictual basis. Both the forces shaping cultural and sexual attitudes are effective in the process of integrating the Ovahimba and Ovaherero communities into contemporary Namibian society. The rural subsistence economy does not disappear all at once. It is rather that the attraction of urban centres like Opuwo additionally come into the picture. Labour migration also arises as a new element. The present pattern is actually characterised by the integration of conflicting economic and cultural structures.

From a sociological perspective, the protraction and deviation resulting from such a structurally heterogeneous pattern must be taken into consideration, particularly as Talavera's proposed alternative model of sexuality moves the individual onto centre stage; an individual whose traits appear typical rather of contemporary Western, highly industrialised, capitalist societies. Does such an idealised individual really have a material (structural) basis for existence in the present northern Kunene? Can it be created 'from within' customary cultures? And in the absence of a corresponding material basis, can the current contradictory subject be reshaped by means of education and cultural socialization? Within Talavera's scenario there are conflicting social structures and cultures, accompanied by conflicting models of sexuality. But neither of them corresponds to the model of a self-centred, self-determined, autonomous individualism.

Social stratification: individual and class

Based on 18 months of intensive field research in Rundu, Fumanti's report on the emergence of local élites vividly portrays the process of social stratification on a micro-level of analysis. His empirical findings trace the constitution of a public sphere, the space where the process of social restructuration materialises. The quasi-masimbi advance to the ranks of the élite by investing in economic, educational and political opportunities. Élite formation is depicted in terms of selection, cooptation, and access to positions of political influence/power – those very positions that constitute the public sphere.

The empirical picture necessitates a more detailed consideration of the relation between élite formation and class formation. Re-interpreting it from the perspective of social stratification, a question arises: where does the means of investment come from that the quasi-masimbi are provided with? The study does not enquire into their sources of wealth, it only logically presupposes them. Fumanti's approach implies two things: first, élite formation is realised by political means; and second, it requires the availability of a degree of economic wealth. Thus, the study tacitly assumes that the prospective 'big-men' already are in possession of means of investment.

The processes analysed in relation to the concept of élites call for a necessary integration of class theory. Constitution and circulation of élites also represents the genesis of class formation. Fumanti shows élite groups originating from the subsistence economy but integrated into the modern capitalist market economy, accumulating modest wealth over time. They invest their resources to gain power and prestige in order to further their upward mobility. On the other hand, the close links they retain with the milieu they originate from, as well as their cultural identification with it, prompt them to continue acting within the sociocultural settings of their origins. Social advancement is not conceived mainly or exclusively by adapting to Western/capitalist consumer attitudes and its corresponding social status. In their restricted customary regional or local context, a clear-cut bourgeois future is not yet readily available. Owing to their cultural stamp, such a choice might not even be conceivable, and is anyway still mainly identified with a 'white' *Lebenswelt* (world or way of living). All these elements force the quasi-masimbi to opt for an individual path deeply embedded in their customary society.

This setting recalls the sociocultural attitudes of the emerging bourgeois social groups in 17th and 18th century northern and central Europe. Owing their initially modest economic status to their intellectual (academic) or professional (public service, liberal professions) achievements, they strove for the consolidation of their new social status by acquiring feudal estates, to be conferred with the aristocratic title and prestige attached to feudal property. The purely economic rationale of social ascent typical of the industrial society to come, did not yet determine their actions. Thus these new social figures still held the values of the aristocratic feudal society they could not yet transcend.

The conceptualisation of social restructuration with reference to élites is helpful at a micro-level, describing processes typical of a society in transition. However, in a wider-ranging sociological perspective, it should not fall short of clarifying its relationship with the categorical apparatus of social structuration in terms of class. Divesting the concept of élite of its wider social structural implications restricts it to a descriptive tool of research, and strips it of its analytical potential.

Determinism or disregarding the social reality of power?

In its historical discourse, Part Two of the essay on "Religion" exemplifies the epistemological critique of the social sciences. Criticising sociological 'determinism', it stresses the role of the Oorlam Nama groups as the "first bearers of Christianity". The discussion group emphasises the indigenous 'agency' or active adaptation of Africans to the process of evangelisation. Historically, Jonker Afrikaner is identified as such an agent, inviting the services of the Rhenish Mission, in the 1840s.

The plea for the inductive method formulated by the discussion group lends additional weight to this digestion of historical facts. However, three objections may be raised.

- The fact that the Oorlam Namas had been in close contact with a christianised settler society in the Cape Colony, does not, per se, imply that they were the 'bearers of Christianity' when they expanded across southern central Namibia in the 18th and 19th centuries. This remains to be proven (particularly as the statement of 'agency' is methodologically under the self-imposed obligation to read from the facts rather than into facts).
- With reference to the 'invention of tradition', Keulder[4] suggests that Oorlam society during the period of migration apparently revived and strengthened its cultural autonomy (tradition) as a means of social integration of their community, to overcome internal social contradictions. This process of cultural self-assertion served to mitigate conflict between leadership and community members, itself arising from the need to militarise the community. This would streamline the intrusion and settlement in a hostile environment. It served as an instrument of internal domination. It has to be carefully examined within the overall picture of Oorlam culture, whether or not such a re-traditionalisation historically combined with the process of internal evangelisation.
- The early history of conflicts between the London Missionary Society (LMS) under the direction of Abraham and Christian Albrecht and the Oorlams under Jager and Titus Afrikaner, quite at variance with the emphasis on indigenous agency, is omitted. The first mission station, established in Warmbad in 1806, was destroyed in 1811. Johann Hein-

---

[4] Keulder, Christiaan 1997. Traditional authorities and regional councils in Southern Namibia, Windhoek: FES

Heinrich Schmelen's new mission station, established in 1814, had to be given up in 1822. In 1819, Robert Moffat had to throw in the towel after only one year of missionary work among the Oorlams. In 1822, James Archbell, representative of the Wesleyan Missionary Society, relinquished his activity, again after only one year. His Wesleyan colleague, Barnabas Shaw, held out for six years (1820-1825) before returning to Cape Town. Dierks[5] also points to the violent death of missionary William Threlfall in 1825, which prompted Europeans to "shun Great Namaqualand until the mid-1830s". All missionary societies experienced the severe dissatisfaction of the Oorlam Namas. Though Jager Afrikaner himself accepted baptism in 1815, the Oorlams put considerable pressure on the London and Wesleyan Missionary Societies until the 1830s, forcing them to discontinue their work amongst the Kai//khaun (the Khauas Nama or Red Nation). Only when both Nama factions formed an alliance in the 1830s, did this pressure weaken. Moreover, it was only in the 1840s that Jonker Afrikaner built his famous /Ae//Gams (Klein Windhoek) church and requested that the missionaries of the Rhenish Missionary Society settle in Windhoek – only after the LMS had first entrusted the Wesleyans with their activities and had then transferred their missionary work to the Rhenish Mission[6]. The pre-Rhenish period of conflictual relationships is missing in the historical discourse of the essay.

There is no doubt of the necessity to synthesise 'imposition' (from outside) and 'agency' (from inside) in the process of cultural domination, as stated in Christo Lombard's introductory paragraphs. On the other hand, the empirical picture given by the discussion group somewhat one-sidedly reflects the famous Weberian paradigm, according to which sociocultural entities (ethnic groups, societies) living in cultural contradiction with 'mainstream' society tend to be more open to modern, Western cultural influences. Adapting them and adapting to them, they often become modernising agents, in cultural as well as in economic respects. Weber's paradigm, embedded in the broader conceptual context of cultural rationalisation, in emphasising agency, certainly underestimates power.

Agency and imposition still remain two distinct elements of one process: agency is a possible consequence only where imposition takes the lead. Following the essay, however, it is only through the acceptance of the "viability" and greater "coherence" of Christianity that the "eradication of indigenous belief systems" becomes historically possible. The statement, implicitly builds on the questionable allegation of a cultural superiority of Christianity – an inductive method? Eradication indicates the action to which acceptance is the reaction. It is in this sense that the editors refer to the 'imposition' of Christianity. (Besides, every imposition implies acceptance, even if acceptance is forced upon the victim

---

[5] Dierks, Klaus 1999:8. Chronology of Namibian history – from pre-historical times to independent Namibia. Windhoek
[6] Dierks op.cit.:7-11

– a sociological truism. In the long term, no acceptance can rest on mere passive suffering.) In this context, imposition does not allude to a process of violent, forced evangelisation – the combination of bible and gun. Rather, it points to the creation of a constraining societal structure where offering an alternative belief system (albeit through power of persuasion) is coupled with the Western missions' attitude of cultural 'superiority' over African 'primitivism' (as Ndeikwila points out).

But, more important: imposition points to the effect of power differentials. It is the scanty reference to such power differentials that makes the insistence that Christianity in Namibia arose as a matter of indigenous agency as somewhat questionable. All the more so, since the essay's differentiation between the export of Christianity from Europe and its import into Namibia rests on two assumptions: that exporting and importing agents differ – European exporters and Nama importers; and that europeanised Christianity had already undergone a process of africanisation when it reached Namibia. But this is historically contestable for the initial Namibian period until 1840, as we have seen. In addition, what warrants the assumption that a common interest between missionary societies and indigenous agents cannot be assessed as an imposition of a new belief system? Does imposition only occur in the case of an external – 'foreign' – intrusion? Is influencing control exercised by indigenous élites 'agency' void of power aspects, therefore not to be classified as 'imposition'? Do power relations never exist within and between indigenous societies?

Is, by implication, the mention of those power differentials inherent in colonialism's impact on indigenous societies per se "yet another disempowering and patronising facet in the treatment of social science issues regarding Africa"? Power is indeed a leading theme of the questions we presented to the discussion group – deliberately. Implicitly and explicitly, we pointed to the link between culture (religion) and domination as reflected in social relations. This was done in view of ethnic and racial relations, colonial political relations, but also of integrative normative authority, gender relations, generational relations, interpersonal relations. But wherever this was underlying a question referring to the historical context of the clashes of cultures, the tenor of the discussion group's answers tended to interpret this as a negative approach, as simplification and determinism, as not taking account of 'agency', or as discriminating against indigenous cultures – in short, as typically 'sociological'. However, the evangelisation of South West Africa has not been spared coercive elements. After all, it was not an autochthonous element of indigenous nature. Yes, it is necessarily a typical feature of a sociological perspective to analyse power relations in social interaction.

The power of definition – alterity

In his paper on the San, James Suzman applies an interesting anthropological concept: alterity. Its usefulness in a sociological context can now be considered. Although Suzman does not specifically define it, its primary meaning becomes clear within his textual framework. Its literal Latin meaning is 'otherness', suggesting a state beyond or outside (life, society), also implying 'division of the self'. On a sociological level, this indicates separating or making marginal in the context of change or, more specifically, structural transformation. It might be applied to a group within a society, or to an entire social formation. Yet, more than just 'change' is implied in alterity, certainly for Suzman. Change is not a neutral process, but is steeped in interactional social relations involving 'power'. As British sociologist Michael Mann has argued, social change and power are causally connected.

To the previous association with change we can now add: identity – both as we collectively see ourselves, and as others would want us to be collectively seen, to be 'identified'. Alterity, in Suzman's ethnic framework, reads as the ability to (negatively) shape the identity of others in a way that impacts on their social position in terms of resource-access, class and status. Alterity shapes the identity of certain social groups such as the San as a marginalising process – thus the reference to otherness, i.e. to be pushed to the social edge, beyond the mainstream. This is part of a process of historical construction dominated by powerful groups. These confer 'ethnic' personality.

Alterity, then, is intimately tied up with power and the imposition of identity. It is a socio-historical construction, dominated by the powerful, casting a shadow also over the present. In the case of the San, their identity has been 'made' for them under past circumstances, a colonial ethnic identity still held in a post-colonial world. The San's exoticism and low status continues to be unquestioningly accepted by contemporary post-independence authority (political and academic) as strongly as in the past, and by general society, becoming a prop to their social neglect and poverty, in that it confers 'ethnic' characteristics that either romanticise or stigmatise, or both. This is the central tragedy that Suzman presents us; imposed identities that ultimately undermine and destroy.

Alterity is conceptually useful also in its flexibility: beyond its ethnic context, we can see it as being applicable to shaping class, gender, even political identities. It indicates that social and cultural identity contains both self-determination and determination from outside, definitely reflecting societal power differentials. Transcending its anthropological content, sociology can appropriate it, in and for the Namibian context.

As yet another facet of the power of definition, the issue of tradition raises itself here. The essay on "Traditionalism" in this book carefully contrasts approaches that pose tradition unproblematically and in idealistic manner, ignoring its past and present constructions. We can say that tradition is in part 'imagined', in part real. What we envisage as traditional, as an exclusively endogenous structure of values and lifestyles, will usually have undergone compromise and incorporation with external elements. This is particularly true in a colonial capitalist social formation. Contemporary Namibians may well wish to imagine what a traditional past might have been, but for the purposes of restoration in modern circumstances, they may not neglect the reality of its re-shaping under the pressures of European religion(s), culture(s) and economy. What looks like 'tradition' turns out to be a dynamic rather than a static term – constantly open to external interventions. Even before European colonialism, it was probably thus.

Associating tradition with alterity, may be fruitful. San alterity involved exotic identity that was/is imposed for general public consumption, local and international, without the participation or voice of the 'identified' group – a rather extreme application of both the cultural power of definition and the political power of exclusion. In another respect, in the case of present 'political traditionalists' in Namibia, alterity may be a positive nationalist strategy for re-asserting a tradition-based *modern* national identity; a tool for nation building, or to gain personal/group power advantage. This entails an attempt to impose new identities on the community (e.g. 'what was or was not normal in our culture') with the aim of legitimising political claims.

In summary: first, in the case of the San, we have the severe marginalisation of the 'identified' and 'traditionalised' group – literally expected to live tradition that is both defined for them and imposed on them; second, we have alterity as a political strategy (we do not suggest that it is automatically a cynical one). Tradition in the former is burdensome; in the latter, revivalist, idealist, linked into an imagined pristine past. Both traditionalist-alterist strategies seek different results. The former, control, the latter a new legitimacy and cultural assertion, itself only understandable (in Namibia at least) in a post-colonial context. We may see 'traditional' communities as engaged in such alterity strategies, as well as 'modern' church authorities – shaping new (secular or religious) identities that exclude, contradict or weaken their past close identifications with colonial authority, including apartheid; in this case, the church as eternally 'humanist' and universal, the political tool of no-one.

Tradition and alterity are complementary to the same process. To mark or stigmatise (in Goffman's sense); to identify and separate as strategies of control or marginalisation; to empower or legitimise by re-moulding or replacing pre-existing (negative) identities. Traditionalising (if we may add yet another term) encapsulates both. There are clearly some interesting possibilities presented in both the articles on 'Traditionalism' and the 'Marginalisation of the San' for addressing each other in a fruitful sociological manner along the lines of their respective approaches – interrogating 'tradition' both for the purpose of demystifying and understanding it.

Social rationalisation

Seely's and Zeidler's essay on environmental management minimises the tension inherent in its *system theory* approach by discussing the weight of social over natural factors. Natural factors such as aridity and climate variability are not regarded as an adequate template for designing a sustainable policy of land redistribution, no more than existing variations in land tenure in Namibia. The authors underline the necessity for taking into consideration the traditional social system of rural society, unequal power relationships, gender inequalities, and inadequate institutional arrangements. However, the "need for flexibility and quick response time to Namibia's arid and variable climate" remains the ultimate rationale for policy development and legislation. Within this conceptual design, social conditions are seen as variables influencing environmental management. Where social constraints are addressed, it is assumed that through education/information (i.e. by *cultural* means) and through empowerment (i.e. by *political* means) change directed to a more sustainable future of land management could be achieved.

Nature, society, economy, culture, the individual: all sub-systems respond to structural-functional necessities dictated by sustainability, the ultimate condition of overall systemic preservation. In the light of ineluctable constraints – typical of the design of system theory – *faith in rationality* becomes the decisive paradigm. The dissemination of a rational culture of management of the environment (and its adoption by all parties involved) is seen as a condition for sustainability and a sustainable land redistribution policy. But it is more than just a condition: rationality is the last resort in view of the threat posed by irreparable environmental damage such as desertification and soil erosion.

Interestingly, the belief in the social feasibility of both individual and systemic rationality appears as a motive running right through Seely's and Zeidler's essay. Fox's contribution on the "Culture(s) of AIDS" in this book has indicated that a similar rationale – in the shape of rational choice theory – tends to dominate AIDS awareness campaigns regardless of its frequent cultural inadequacy. But such scientific faith in reason goes further. On a more general level, the sociological debate in the Western welfare societies of the 1990s has led to the formulation of the notion of *social rationalisation*. Drawing inspiration from different traditions of the discipline, it combines streams as disparate as Weber's concepts of cultural rationalisation and bureaucratisation and Daniel Bell's theorem of the preponderance of knowledge in post-industrial society. It shows elements of structural-functionalist system theory and Giddens' belief in the new self-reflexivity of modern industrial societies. It reflects chaos theories, and – last but not least – Ulrich Beck's gloomy picture of risk society. The idea of social rationalisation gives a new interpretation of the concept of cultural rationalisation. It assumes its fundamental applicability not only (in retrospect) to the interpretation of the cultural process in terms of modernisation, but to the present societal body in its entirety. Threatened by (nuclear, environmental, political) crises of their own making, even by self-destruction, modern affluent societies develop a degree of reflexivity allowing them to overcome even their basic inner contradictions that result from uncontrolled modernisation. Thus reaching the age of maturity, until then unimaginable, modern society becomes theoretically capable of self-reflexive automatic control. With reference to the conceptual antitheses in the social sciences at the turn of the new millennium, one could summarise: 'social rationalisation' finally beats 'contradiction'. Rationality, forced upon society by adverse circumstances, allows us – for the first time in social history – to overcome social antagonisms not by means of power, but by reason. Power itself – possibly that is what one has to infer – is defeated by reason?

At this point, our (generally sceptical) sociological training suggests a number of questions. Seely's and Zeidler's essay has here merely served as a starting point, allowing us to exemplify (questionable) intellectual developments in the sociological field. Yet, its approach to agriculture as a systemically defined management task, to some extent, reflects certain undercurrents typical also of environmental sociology. With regard to the practical aspects of land redistribution discussed in the essay, we allow free rein to scepticism: are there not structural restrictions/barriers to such a rational culture? Is not the 'traditional' rural world in many respects far from adopting such a rational cultural attitude? Does it not follow a different cultural rationality based on 'traditional' social structures? If so, can one assume that awareness, educational campaigns and professional training alone could secure the dissemination of a modern (capitalist) rationality? Socio-economic relations rest on cultures, cultures stem from social structures, social structures stem from socio-economic relations. Is not a radical re-formulation of these relations an indispensable condition for creating an appropriate cultural (as well as political and organisational) framework for sustainability?

Agriculture is a system socially regulated and ruled by different cultures displaying different rationalities. Subsistence economy and market orientation in Namibia, as elsewhere, follow conflicting rationales. Can policies simply 'transplant' the rationale followed in commercial agriculture into communal agriculture, in order to "facilitate adaptive range management in an arid environment"? Besides, where do we have to identify the future of Namibian agriculture; as lying in the capitalist market or in subsistence production? Moreover, does agriculture altogether guarantee a future to its populations? Does sustainability possibly imply the absorption of parts of rural society into non-agricultural sectors? However, is this compatible with the well-known political rhetoric of the 'land question' in southern Africa? On closer view, the 'land question' dissolves in a variety of 'land questions', in turn resulting in a variety of social questions, all related to social equity. Sustainability, in environmental terms, has to be translated into equity within sociological frames of reference.

Secularisation and individualisation

The editors' focus on secularisation, in relation to "Religion", takes a comparative view of religiosity by superficially contrasting Namibian and Western European contemporary cultures. We would neither maintain (projecting Weber's theorem of rationalisation into present time) that secularisation has, in European societies, "relegated the importance of religion almost into obscurity"; nor would we classify the Western world as "progressive", thus implying both a cultural and social backlog of the non-Western world, as argued by most of the modernisation theories.

Yet, implicitly the question presented to the discussants betrays a specific picture of Western European societies. There, secularisation reflects the historical (not evolutionary) process of the diminishing impact of religion on public life and institutions, while at the same time religion and religiosity gain ground in the private sphere of the individual. In this sense, secularisation would indicate a distinct social process: the *individualisation* of religious matters. This is not at all a process testifying to the "importance" of religion or its "demise", and it is not assessed as 'progressive', or the reverse. Our view does not differ fundamentally from Luckmann's perception of a 'secularisation from without', except for the fact that, in addition, we would assign the two components – public religion and individual value-orientation – to two distinct socio-historical phases. The one process started in the Napoleonic era and gradually advanced throughout Europe over the past two centuries, progressing faster in the central European protestant environment than in the mediterranean catholic world. The other one is recent. It depicts developments after World War Two typical of affluent welfare societies in which public welfare institutions replaced religious institutions in providing services to the individual (education, culture, health, alms, etc.), without accounting for the individual's spiritual needs.

With regard to a future (urbanised) Namibia, therefore, in a sociological perspective the question seems of importance whether 'competing' or alternative secular moralities will come to complement Christian morality, in such a way reflecting the social process of the individualisation and pluralisation of ethic orientation.

Conclusion

Sociology is debate. We hope that this collection of contributions to the analysis of Namibian society and sociology has made this clear, in all its ambiguity: sociology lives off debating its findings; therefore, its findings are debatable.

In this concluding chapter, we have basically touched on aspects that either call for more decisive sociological interrogation, or which suggest further fruitful possibilities toward a more social-minded insight into Namibian society. Our aim has, at all times, been primarily to lay the groundwork for a timely application of sociology to Namibia and its regions. Others, we hope, will now take up this critical discourse. If commentary and sociological research were to be left just to us, then our aim of expanding a sociological perspective in the country would remain isolated and unrealised. Building knowledge and understanding Namibian social structures and institutions – in an epistemological as well as an ontological sense – is a task that we hope will not remain just with us. Critical responses to this volume will hopefully be followed up by demonstration of further work: we modestly hope for 'better' sociology from others.

Lastly, it is hoped that the current text will help to realise one of our other key goals: informing public policy. Sociology has, since its birth nearly two hundred years ago, had a strong policy-orientated character. Using sophisticated social theory and empirical methods, it has provided practical solutions to complex social issues, utilisable by government and other agencies. Since the early days when industrial society came into being, sociology grew with it; it analysed, criticised and suggested ways for industrial civilisation to overcome its central weaknesses, its injustices and dysfunctions. The tools and methods of sociology have historically been primed by experience and praxis to make sense of the problems caused by growth and uneven development – not dissimilar conditions to those that Namibia itself faces today. The constitution of a *Namibian* sociology is intended to serve the same practical end. The intransigent social problems of the country (some of which are addressed in this volume) may themselves benefit from a specifically sociological interrogation in the failure of other approaches. At the very least, a multi-disciplinary strategy to ameliorate some of the more serious issues must contain a sociological strategy and dimension.

Sociology, however, is not automatically the policy tool of governmental power, a knowledge agency strictly in state service. While sociology can fruitfully inform policy, it is also ready to challenge it, along with authority and power groupings in and outside of the state. Thus, it is a discipline of 'negative antagonism', as Adorno once called it. Taking Habermas' notion of the 'public sphere' (Öffentlichkeit) as a starting point, we would see sociology's societal function as essentially stimulating the development of an informed 'counter public sphere'. Namibia, as with everywhere else, has its public sphere. Sociology can provide critical knowledge and debate to enhance its character – not as a technocratic, policy-orientated 'official' authority, but as another actor in a public arena of critical debate.

A self-reflexive closing remark: any sociological perspective betrays the sociologist him/herself. His analytical stance locates him/her within the contradictory picture of a specific social structure, culturally, socially, politically. This implies two things: sociological findings are socially biased, inevitably, and they are of a transitory nature, reflecting the dynamic character of present society. As sociology, therefore, attempts to comprehend and articulate society, it does not forget that it is firmly structured into society as both agency and expression of its conflictual structures.

ABOUT THE AUTHORS

Amukugo, Elizabeth Magano Member of Parliament (Congress of Democrats) National Assembly; previously Head of Department and Senior Lecturer at the Department of Educational Foundations and Management, University of Namibia. Bachelor of Science, Master of Social Sciences, PhD in Education, all degrees from Lund University, Sweden. SWAPO member from 1974 to 1999, forced into exile 1974, via Angola to Zambia, leaving for Sweden in 1979. Book: *Education and politics in Namibia – past trends and future prospects*, Windhoek ²1995.

Beuke-Muir, Chrisna Lecturer, Section Afrikaans of the Department of Germanic and Romance Languages, University of Namibia; MA University of Stellenbosch; currently working on a PhD in Afrikaans literature focussing on the prose of the Namibian author Piet van Rooyen. Contributing to Afrikaans poetry programmes for the theatre; involved in theatre production in Belgium; recent publication: *Die kwesbaarheid van die moderne man en die manifestasie daarvan in die prosa van Piet van Rooyen* (Stilet (13)2, June 2001).

de Waal, Johan Member of Parliament (Democratic Turnhalle Alliance), Chairperson DTA/UDF Coalition, Parliament of Namibia, responsible for Finance, Trade and Industry; Chairperson DTA of Namibia; Chairperson of the Standing Committee on Public Accounts of the National Assembly. B.Comm. (econ), University of Pretoria, trained in Organisation and Method Study; cattle farmer; businessman.

Fox, Tom Lecturer, Department of Sociology, University of Namibia, previously holding lectureships in the UK at Coventry University and at Birkbeck College, University of London. He has written and taught in the areas of development, medical sociology, social theory, and the mass media. Currently, he is engaged in research into contemporary mass communications and their role in the construction of social and personal identity. Working with the United Nations Development Programme (UNDP) and French Cooperation as a research consultant, and with the British Council on cultural matters relating to contemporary cinema. Publications: *Taking risks, taking responsibility: an anthropological assessment of health risk behaviour in north-west Namibia* (Windhoek, 1999, co-author); *Beyond Afro-Pessimism* (South African Sociological Association Selected Papers – Conference 1997).

Fumanti, Mattia PhD candidate, University of Manchester (UK); BA Humanities and Social Sciences, University of Rome 'La Sapienza' (Italy); research scholarship from University of Manchester for fieldwork in Rundu, Namibia 1999-2001, focusing on *Youthful élites subjectivities in Rundu*.

Graf, Roland Co-owner of typoprint (Pty) Ltd, Windhoek. Since 1975 in the graphic and printing trade in Namibia. Sculpturing and painting, for many years active in monoprint-art, etching and wood cutting. Contributing several works to group exhibitions in Namibia. Took part in several workshops for graphic art. Cover etching and design for Namibia•Society•Sociology.

Hinz, Manfred Dean and Professor of Law, Faculty of Law at the University of Namibia, Executive Director of the Centre for Applied Social Sciences (CASS, affiliated to UNAM). Doctorate and higher doctorate (Habilitation) in Law, University of Mainz (Germany). In 1971, he was appointed full professor at the University of Bremen where he founded the Centre for African Studies in 1975, from which he started cooperating first with SWAPO and later with the United Nations Institute for Namibia, Lusaka. In 1989, he went to Namibia where after independence, he assisted the Ministry of Justice. He was later seconded to the now UNAM Vice Chancellor's office to help build up the Faculty of Law, joining the Faculty with its inception. CASS succeeded the Bremen based Centre for African Studies. CASS is affiliated to the UNAM. Hinz has published widely in his areas of specialisation, in particular in the field of legal and political anthropology, constitutional and international law.

Isaak, *John Paul*   Chairperson of the Synod of ELCRN, the Evangelical Lutheran Church in the Republic of Namibia, the second largest ecclesiastical institution in Namibia. Associate Professor and Head of Department of Religion and Theology at the University of Namibia. Master of Religion, Berkeley, California (USA); MTh and PhD Chicago University (USA). Recent publications: *Religion and society: a Namibian perspective*, Windhoek 1997: *The Evangelical Lutheran Church in the Republic of Namibia in the 21 century*, Windhoek 2000.

Jauch, *Herbert*   Director of the Labour Resource and Research Institute (LaRRI) in Katutura, Windhoek. Associated with the Namibian labour movement for the past 12 years; national secretary of the Namibia National Teachers Union (NANTU) (1990-1993); member of the economic policy subcommittee of the NUNW (1993-1995). His fields of research for the trade unions in Namibia and the SADC region include the analysis of export processing zones (EPZs), labour hire companies, structural adjustment programmes, and a recent study on the impact of globalisation on Namibia's economy that received considerable public attention (*Playing the globalisation game. The implications of economic liberalisation for Namibia*: Windhoek 2001). His work also entails designing trade union education courses and materials. He holds two teaching degrees, and MA, Political Studies, University of the Western Cape, South Africa.

LeBeau, *Debie*   Senior Lecturer, Department of Sociology, University of Namibia. American by birth, in Namibia since 1990. Her main area of interest is medical anthropology, also involved in researching social issues that affect women and children. PhD Rhodes University (SA), thesis on *Seeking health: the hierarchy of resort in utilisation patterns of traditional and Western medicine in multi-cultural Katutura, Namibia* (mimeo, publication forthcoming).

Lombard, *Christo*   Professor of Religion and Theology (MTh; DTh) and Director of the Ecumenical Institute for Namibia, at the University of Namibia; previously Head of the Department of Religion and Theology and Dean of the Faculty of Humanities and Social Sciences at UNAM. Studied at the universities of Stellenbosch, Western Cape, Basel and Utrecht. Fulbright Senior Africa Research Fellow at the Graduate Theological Union, Berkeley, California (1998/9) and UNESCO Chair for Africa at Utrecht University (1999). Chairperson of the Curriculum Committee for Religious Subjects, that changed the school system in Namibia into a multi-faith, learner-centred approach (1990-1993). Involved in ecumenical and multi-faith initiatives in Namibia (such as the Jubilee 2000 debt forgiveness campaign, inter-faith discussions and "Worshipping God as Africans"), and civil society action (such as the Breaking the Wall of Silence movement). Published widely in the field of religion and society (editor or co-editor of 19 books and the *Journal for Religion and Theology in Namibia*).

Mans, *Minette*   Associate Professor, Department of Performing Arts, University of Namibia; PhD University of Natal (SA), doctoral studies in music education and ethnomusicology. Active in various international committees and commissions, Mans currently serves on the International Commission on Music in Schools and Teacher Education. In Namibia, she is a National Examiner for Integrated Performing Arts. For several years she was involved in Namibia's educational reform as Chair of the Curriculum Panel for the Arts (NIED). Her research has included a four year collaboration with the Centre National de Recherche Scientifique (CNRS), Paris, France. More recently, she was awarded a grant as Guest African Researcher at the Nordic Africa Institute in Uppsala, Sweden. Her current research involves a thorough mapping of Namibian music-dance practices. She has published widely in international journals and the Internet, one of her online articles being nominated for the SIG AERA Best Article Award in 2001. Publications also include the book *Ongoma! Notes on Namibian Musical Instruments* and chapters in several other books.

Melber, *Henning*   Research Director at the Nordic Africa Institute in Uppsala/Sweden, formerly Director of the Namibian Economic Policy Research Unit (NEPRU) in Windhoek (1992-2000). Melber came to Namibia in 1967 as the son of immigrants. Joining SWAPO in 1974, he was exiled between 1975 and 1989. PhD Political Science (1980); Higher Doctorate (habilitation and venia legendi in Development Studies) Sociology, University of Bremen (Germany), 1993. His numerous publications include: *Namibia – A Decade of independence, 1990-2000* (Windhoek: NEPRU 2000, (editor and co-author); *Namibia 1990-2000. Eine analytische Chronologie* (Windhoek: Namibia Scientific Society 2002).

Mogotsi, *Immaculate*   PhD candidate, Institute of Social Studies, The Hague (Netherlands), doctoral thesis on *Women's strategies to prevent HIV/AIDS*. Previously teaching Sociology of Gender at the University of Namibia. Writings: *Policy on Teenage Pregnancy and the School Systems* (MA thesis); contributions to the Namibian National Gender Study (2000), and the Social Cultural Research Project (UNFPA): *Male Involvement in Reproductive Health (in print) (1999)*.

Mufune, *Pempelani*   Associate Professor and Head of Department of Sociology at the University of Namibia; PhD Michigan State University, USA; lecturing in sociology at the University of Zambia, Lusaka, and the University of Botswana, Gaborone. Member of the editorial board of *International Sociology*, journal of the International Sociological Association. His writings on youth include *Street youth in southern Africa* (International Journal of Social Sciences vol.52 issue no.164, June 2000); *Youth and development in southern Africa* (Development Southern Africa vol.16 no.2, 1999); *Youth policy and programmes in the SADC countries of Botswana, Swaziland and Zambia: a comparative assessment* (co-author, International Social Work 1994).

Pinkowsky-Tersbøl, *Britt*   PhD candidate University of Copenhagen (Denmark), Institute of Public Health, Department of Women and Gender in Development. Her research interest includes gender, reproductive health, incl. HIV-AIDS, and general sociocultural issues. MA in Anthropology, University of Copenhagen, Denmark. Working for UNFPA in Namibia prior to commencing her PhD, primarily concerned with youth, gender and reproductive health, especially male involvement in reproductive health.

Seely, *Mary*   Executive Director of the Desert Research Foundation of Namibia (DRFN). PhD, University of California; Honorary Doctorate, University of Natal, Durban; honorary staff member of the Universities of California and the Witwatersrand. Recent teaching focuses on developing training materials for rural communities and university level extra-curricular short courses in the management of natural resources and control of desertification. Recent publications range from books supporting popularisation of natural resource management to contributions to journals on desertification and biodiversity.

Steytler, *John*   Currently principal economist in the Bank of Namibia, responsible for Statistics and Publication. Master Degree Philipp University in Marburg (Germany), 1996: MSc Financial Economics, University of London (UK), 2001. PhD candidate University of Natal, Durban (SA). Area of research: inter-relationships between financial sector development and economic growth, property rights and integration.

Suzman, *James*   Currently Smuts fellow in African Studies at the University of Cambridge, UK. He has worked extensively among the San communities of southern Africa. Most recently, coordinator for the European Union's Regional Assessment of the status of the San in southern Africa. Publications: *Things from the bush* (PhD thesis, Schlettwein Publishers, Basel 2000); *An assessment of the status of the San in Namibia*, Windhoek, April 2001 (Legal Assistance Centre).

Talavera, *Philippe*   Currently in charge of "Ombetja Yehinga, The Red Ribbon" (Kunene Regional Council), a programme to create awareness about HIV/AIDS. Working for various development agencies in northern Namibia since 1997; operating in the Kunene since January 1999, PhD in Veterinary Science, College of Veterinary Sciences of Lyon (France); Certificate in Biochemistry, option Endocrinology, University of Medical Sciences of Lyon (France). Recent publications: *Farming systems in Kunene North, a resource book* (co-author), published by the Ministry of Agriculture, Water and Rural Development, Namibia, Windhoek 2000; *Challenging the Namibian perception of* *sexuality – the case study of the Ovahimba and Ovaherero culturo-sexual models in northern Kunene in an HIV/AIDS context* (forthcoming).

Vale, Helen   Senior Lecturer at the English Department, University of Namibia, since 1992; previously teaching literature at the University of Swaziland. Holding a law degree, London School of Economics, UK; MA in African Studies, London School of Oriental and African Studies, UK; Dip.Ed., University of Surrey. Currently working on her doctorate. Her research interests are both educational and literary with a particular focus on southern African literature. Publications: *Overview of Namibian literature in English since independence* (co-author); several study guide books for the Centre of External Studies, University of Namibia (*Principles of Literature* (co-author, 1991); *Practical Criticism and Poetry* (co-author, undated).

Wieringa, Saskia   Associate professor in Women's Studies, Institute of Social Studies, The Hague (Netherlands); Senior Research Fellow, University of Amsterdam (Netherlands). PhD in Cultural Anthropology, University of Amsterdam. Responsible for setting up women's studies programmes at UNAM and other universities on behalf of the Dutch Ministry for Development Cooperation. She has widely researched and published on women's movements and organisations, gender planning and sexual politics. Her latest book is *Sexual Politics in Indonesia* (Palgrave-MacMillan, 2002).

Winterfeldt, Volker   Lecturer, Department of Sociology, University of Namibia; previously teaching Sociology at the University of Tübingen (Germany), 1984-1996. MA in Sociology and German Language and Literature, PhD in Sociology, University of Tübingen. Fields of research: general sociological theory including political economy, class theory, gender, theories of structural transition. Joining UNAM in 1998. Publications: *Die Konstitution des bürgerlichen Staats in Indien. Zum Verhältnis von Formbesonderung und Klassencharakter* (The constitution of the bourgeois state in colonial India; Berlin 1987); *Klasse? Sozialstrukturkategorie in der Kritik* (Class? A critical analysis of a category of social structure; forthcoming, 2003).

Zappen-Thomson, Marianne   Senior Lecturer, Department of Germanic and Romance Languages, University of Namibia; Doctor of Literature (DLitt) University of Stellenbosch, SA. Having gained extensive teaching experience at various universities in South Africa, she returned to her native Namibia, teaching German at UNAM. Her emphasis on Foreign Language Teaching in 2002 resulted in the introduction of the Postgraduate Diploma Translation project at UNAM, in co-operation with the Bonn University (Germany), funded by the German Academic Exchange Administration (DAAD), where Zappen-Thomson is a project coordinator. Her interest in intercultural communication is reflected in her recent publications: *Interkulturelle Kommunikation oder Lernen in einer Begegnungsschule. Dokumentation 1999*; *Interkulturelles Lernen und Lehren in einer multikulturellen Gesellschaft – Deutsch als Fremdsprache in Namibia* (Windhoek 2000).

Zeeman, Terence   Lecturer in Theatre Studies, University of Ulster (Northern Ireland). Bachelor of Fine Arts in Directing, Baylor University, Texas (USA); Master of Fine Arts in Professional Training, University of Alabama (USA). In the early 1990s, Zeeman was Executive Director of the National Theatre of Namibia and also Head of Drama, the University of Namibia. Frequently travelling to Namibia to continue research and publication in Namibian drama. Publication: *New Namibian plays vol.I*, Windhoek 2000.

Zeidler, Juliane   Managing Director of Integrated Environmental Consultants Namibia (IECN), currently appointed to implement the United Nations' *Dry and sub-humid lands programme* of the Convention on Biological Diversity (CBD) at the CBD's head office of the UN in Montreal, Canada. 1991-2001 Desert Research Foundation of Namibia (DRFN), concerned with the implementation of Namibia's Programme to Combat Desertification (Napcod). PhD in Ecology and Natural Resources Management, University of the Witwatersrand, Johannesburg (SA), MSc in Resource Conservation and Biology, University of Witwatersrand, MSc Goethe University, Frankfurt (Germany).

E-mail addresses

Amukugo	e.amukugo@parliament.gov.na
Beuke-Muir	chrisna@mweb.com.na
de Waal	jcdw@iway.na
Fox	tfox@unam.na
Fumanti	mattia.fumanti@stud.man.ac.uk
Hinz	lawfac@unam.na
Isaak	pisaak@unam.na
Jauch	larri@mweb.com.na
LeBeau	lebeau@mweb.com.na
Lombard	clombard@unam.na
Mans	mmans@unam.na
Melber	henning.melber@nai.uu.se
Mogotsi	Mogotsi@iss.nl
Mufune	pmufune@unam.na
Pinkowsky Tersbøl	b.tersbol@socmed.ku.dk
Seely	mseely@drfn.org.na
Steytler	john.steytler@bon.com.na
Suzman	jsuzman@cs.com
Talavera	talavera@iafrica.com.na
Vale	hvale@unam.na
Wieringa	wieringa@iss.nl
Winterfeldt	vwinterfeldt@unam.na
Zappen-Thomson	mzappen@unam.na
Zeeman	TS.Zeeman@ulst.ac.uk
Zeidler	julianez@iafrica.com.na

INDEX OF TABLES

Table 1: School enrolment by sex in Namibia, 1999 (in %)
Table 2: Dropout rates (%) in Namibian schools, grades 1-12, 1993-1997
Table 3: Area of residence and educational exclusion in Namibia
Table 4: Evolution of HIV prevalence in Opuwo from 1992 to 2000

Table 5: Defects of the Western medical system in Africa
Table 6: Not really a doctor